W9-AHK-044

CHAPTERS IN THE FORMATIVE HISTORY OF JUDAISM

Current Questions and Enduring Answers

Jacob Neusner

Studies in Judaism

University Press of America,® Inc.
Lanham · Boulder · New York · Toronto · Oxford

Copyright © 2006 by
University Press of America,® Inc.
4501 Forbes Boulevard
Suite 200
Lanham, Maryland 20706
UPA Acquisitions Department (301) 459-3366

PO Box 317
Oxford
OX2 9RU, UK

All rights reserved
Printed in the United States of America
British Library Cataloging in Publication Information Available

Library of Congress Control Number: 2005935826
ISBN 0-7618-3385-4 (paperback : alk. ppr.)

⊖™The paper used in this publication meets the minimum
requirements of American National Standard for Information
Sciences—Permanence of Paper for Printed Library Materials,
ANSI Z39.48—1984

Studies in Judaism

EDITOR

Jacob Neusner
Bard College

EDITORIAL BOARD

Alan J. Avery-Peck
College of the Holy Cross

Herbert Basser
Queens University

Bruce D. Chilton
Bard College

José Faur
Bar Ilan University

William Scott Green
University of Rochester

Mayer Gruber
Ben-Gurion University of the Negev

Günter Stemberger
University of Vienna

James F. Strange
University of South Florida

CONTENTS

Law, Language, Dialectics

Book Reviews

Preface

The documentary reading of the Rabbinic canon continues to turn up engaging questions and interesting problems for study. The first eight chapters represent examples of historical and history-of-religions questions precipitated by the documentary perspective. The next four focus on literary problems within the same framework: the treatment of 56, 70, and 132-135 in successive canonical compilations, the comparison and contrast of Rabbinic and Christian writings on the same topics, the comparison and contrast of Halakhic and Aggadic documents on the same topic (Chapters Ten and Eleven), the theological description of a Rabbinic document (Chapter Twelve), and some historical problems dealt with in Chapters Thirteen and Fourteen. The history of law defines the topics of Chapters Fifteen and Sixteen, for tractates Besah and Tohorot, respectively. Some free-standing essays and half a dozen book reviews complete the account.

This collection of eighteen essays and six book reviews represents about two years of work, from late-2003 through mid-2005. These have been particularly productive years, as my research professorship at Bard College from 2000 has been in general. The stimulation of colleagues, particularly Professor Bruce D. Chilton, and the cordial relationships of learning and collegiality with many others at Bard account for that exceptional productivity. I continue to benefit from conversations, in person and in writing, also with colleagues scattered hither and yon. Some of the essays in this collection depend heavily on the learning and critical thought of others in cognate fields, Tanakh and Dead Sea scrolls for example, to whom I am much indebted.

The reason I periodically collect and publish essays and reviews is to give them a second life, after they have served as lectures or as summaries of monographs or as free-standing articles. This serves a readership to whom the initial presentation in lectures or specialized journals is inaccessible. Some of the essays furthermore provide a précis, for colleagues in kindred fields, of fully worked out monographs, particularly the first, second, third, and eleventh: *The Vitality of Rabbinic Imagination: The Mishnah against the Bible and Qumran.* Lanham, 2005: University Press of America, *Is Scripture the Origin of the Halakhah?* Lanham, 2005: University Press of America, *How Important Was the Destruction of the Second Temple in the Formation of Rabbinic Judaism?* Lanham, 2005: University Press of America, and *Praxis and Parable: The Divergent Discourses of Rabbinic Judaism. How Halakhic and Aggadic Documents Treat the Bestiary Common to Them Both.* Lanham, 2005: University Press of America.

As to academic lectures: the fourth, "How pivotal," was an address at the University of Hartford in 2004. The eighth, on altruism in Judaism, began as a conference paper at a study conference on altruism in world religions held at Bard College in 2004. It will appear in *Altruism in World Religions* (Washington, 2005: Georgetown University Press), which I edited with colleagues. The seventh, on theological foundations of tolerance in classical Judaism, was prepared for a study conference at Bard College, at the University of Bologna, and at the American University of Cairo, in meetings to be held in 2006-2007. The ninth chapter was a lecture for faculty at the Jewish Theological Seminary of America in 2004; the paper on the exaggerated importance assigned to the destruction of the Second Temple served on that same visit also as the Bokser Memorial Lecture at the Jewish Theological Seminary of America and also as a paper at the Karl-Johan Illman memorial conference at Åbo Akademi University in 2004, 2005 respectively. The twelfth chapter is revised from my *The Implicit Norms of Rabbinic Judaism. The Bedrock of a Classical Religion.* Lanham, 2005: University Press of America.

I complete this collection on the eve of my seventy-third birthday. I plan now to turn to a literary problem, once more asking, what of the Bavli? I wish to find out whether modes of normative *analysis* governed, and these transcend the rules of dialectical argument commonly adduced[1] in evidence of the way in which the Bavli governed right thinking. Further work beckons on the character of formative Judaism.

Jacob Neusner

Research Professor of Theology
Senior Fellow, Institute of Advanced Theology
Bard College
Annandale-on-Hudson, New York 12504-5000 USA
Neusner@webjogger.net

ENDNOTES

[1] See for example my *Jerusalem and Athens: The Congruity of Talmudic and Classical Philosophy.* Leiden, 1997: E. J. Brill. *Supplements to the Journal for the Study of Judaism.*

1

The Vitality of Rabbinic Imagination

THE MISHNAH VERSUS THE BIBLE AND QUMRAN
TWO COMPARISONS

Assessed against comparable documents of Scripture and the Qumran library, the Mishnah shows itself as a triumph of imagination. It exhibits remarkable capacity to think in new and astonishing ways about familiar things. In these pages I compare the Mishnah to a biblical codes and a codes found among the Dead Sea Scrolls. The comparison affords perspective upon the uniqueness of the Mishnah in its Israelite context of Scripture and tradition.

Looking forward, everyone recognizes that the Mishnah forms the starting point for the entire Halakhic tradition of normative Judaism — Tosefta, baraita-corpus, Yerushalmi, Bavli, and beyond. But the true distinction of the Mishnah emerges only when we look backward from the Mishnah to models of how rules were collected ("law codes"). The models supplied by Scripture in the Covenant Code, the Priestly Code, the Holiness Code, and the Deuteronomic Code, or formed by other heirs of Scripture, those represented by the Damascus Covenant (CD) and the Manual of Discipline (1QS) of prior centuries define the context of comparison. I have chosen only two cases. But the outcome for all of them is simply stated: there is no comparison.

What is at stake in the outcome? Though tempted by embedded personal bias, I do not argue that the Mishnah is superior to all prior codes, except by its own criterion. But I do maintain that the Mishnah by any objective criterion is different from them all. And I explain the difference by appeal to the Mishnah's authors' intellectual vitality to imagine paths to truth none had trod before.

The governing category-formation of this study — law codes and how they compare — demands attention at the outset. A law code, a collection of norms or rules, is measured by three criteria: by [1] its comprehensiveness in coverage of its topics, by [2] its cogency, and by [3] its capacity for extension to cases and circumstances not explicitly addressed by the code itself. A collection of laws that covers a topic in a comprehensive way is different from one that covers that same topic in a superficial or episodic way. One that is cogent (by any criterion of cogency, whether philosophical or literary or mythic) in its topical expositions is different from one that is incoherent. One that can set forth generative principles subject to generalization is different from one that supplies ad hoc, case-by-case inert information. A comprehensive, cogent, encompassing code serves the purposes of the society that is conceived to require the code — the provision of regulations for the social order — in a way different from one that is occasional, incoherent, and particular to its miscellaneous cases.

Linked to Scripture and in dialogue with Scripture,[1] the Mishnah struck out in new paths altogether from those set forth by Scripture's codes and those that imitated them. The capacity to think in fresh ways about Scripture's own imperatives and their implications attests to the validity of Rabbinic imagination that reaches concrete expression in the Mishnah, a triumph of reconstruction and creative recapitulation. But in so stating, I have gotten ahead of my story. Let me start from the beginning.

I have too long postponed defining my terms. *A mishnah,* defined generically, is a recapitulation, in an exact sense a re-collection, of Israelite laws. In the categories of the Pentateuch as titled in the English-speaking West, Genesis, Exodus, Leviticus, Numbers, Deuteronomy, the last-named taking the form of a survey of laws already set forth, then, *a mishnah* is *a deuteronomy.* The biblical and Qumran codes all fall into the category of a *mishneh-torah,* a recapitulation of the law of the Torah.

A single trait suffices to answer the question, What makes *the* Mishnah different from *a* mishnah — any other, prior re-collection, or deuteronomy, of Israelite laws? The comparison sets forth a simple answer. Some of the prior codes compete in comprehensiveness, some in cogency, but none in capacity for extension and amplification, in syllogistic character, as I shall explain. And that is where I identify the marks of imaginative vitality. Those that compete in cogency do not attempt a comprehensive topical exposition, and those that undertake a comprehensive presentation do not exhibit an obvious principle of cogency.

The Mishnah is distinctive in one aspect and unique in another. It is singular, first, in combining cogency and comprehensiveness. But it is absolutely unique, second, in undertaking syllogistic discourse to turn facts into examples, cases into facts illustrative of comprehensive principles affecting a variety of types of circumstances or transactions. That is how the Mishnah attests to massive intellectual energy, which completely redefined the modes of thought and inquiry characteristic of all prior exercises of collection and organization of the norms of the Israelite social order.

What is not at stake? The issue addressed here does not concern influence of earlier on later authorities or continuities from one document to another, other than Scripture. People make much of continuities of detail, which they maintain prove the unity of Jewish law and the normative standing, through all time, of a particular Judaic system (ordinarily: the Rabbinic one). The standing of the Mishnah and its law does not come to definition in the appearance, in the Mishnah, of details that surface also in law codes of other communities of Judaism. The Mishnah is autonomous by reason of its system, its generative logic, its intellectual capacities. I do not for one minute conceive that the first and second century Rabbinic sages consulted or even knew about the law codes of the Qumran library or conceived of Scripture's codes as free-standing models for their enterprise. They ignored the prior models they had in hand from Scripture.

Scripture supplied no model for the framers of the Mishnah, for the several collections of laws of Scripture were embedded in narratives, and the Mishnah invokes no narrative of origins and authority. The Mishnah's definitive conception — a law code standing on its own and systematically expounding the law in a topical program, lacking narrative and bearing no theological implications — followed no precedent or parallel in Scripture. Nor does the Qumran library supply a comparable exercise of analytical presentation.

But the framers of the Mishnah, for all their originality, took up the task carried out by the authorities represented in the Manual of Discipline or the Damascus Covenant or the Temple Scroll, and they recapitulated the work of those who produced Scripture's Priestly Code (among the biblical codes) and certainly responded to that work. They undertook the same work as occupied the legislators of Qumran, and so they contemplated the result of the legislators of Deuteronomy — not a historical judgment of continuity, but a phenomenological judgment based on an imagined synchrony of the codes. "The Mishnah against the Bible and Qumran" therefore means to say, the outcome of viewing all present on the same stage in a sudden magic moment of illumination.

If therefore we can imagine that the framers of the Mishnah met one day to plan their document in light of the decisions made by others past and present who had undertaken the same task, to define its indicative traits, using our minds we may reconstruct from what they did or did not do their judgment choices made by others. That is, they chose ways of constructing their code markedly different from those chosen by others. I repeat: I do not claim they knew the prior codes as free-standing composites or as independent documents. But as to the approaches and methods of the prior codes, the Rabbinic sages can have carried matters out in the ways taken by others earlier. Then, by comparing and contrasting the Mishnah's traits with those of the earlier compilations, we gain perspective, from what others did, upon what the Mishnah's authorship did do: their intellectual vitality.

By what criteria of intellectual activity? The opening paragraphs have already signaled the answer. Three pertain: [1] cogency, [2] comprehensiveness, and [3] capacity for extension and amplification. Thus we assess whether facts are inert or generative, self-contained or outward facing. The laws in an excellent mishnah will prove coherent, not merely random bits of information treated as free-standing episodes but syllogistic in their consequence. The laws of *an* excellent mishnah will cover a broad range of important topics pertinent to the Israelite social order. The topics that it covers will be systematically expounded. The framers of the Mishnah took up the topics of the Scriptural codes and in one way or another addressed every one of them. But they did not regard themselves as limited to Scripture's topics, introducing their own as well, and they did not set forth a tractate to cover every topic of Scripture, imposing their own sense of proportion on the biblical program of laws. They made their own decisions on matters of coverage. That independence of thought characterizes imagination and energy of intellect.

Above all, the imaginative code will present rules in patterns susceptible to development and so yield further analytical propositions and secondary syllogisms. It will impose patterns upon bits and pieces of data (cogency). It will address the widest program of topics (comprehensiveness). It will construct a syllogistic discourse, signaling problems of a theoretical character that invite further analysis (capacity for extension), moving from "two apples and two applies equal four apples" to "two and two are four" (anythings).

THE BOOK OF THE COVENANT (EX. 20:22-23:33) AND MISHNAH-TRACTATE BABA QAMMA

The sole comparison of Scripture's law codes to those of the Mishnah involves the book of the Covenant and its topical correspondent, Mishnah-tractate Baba Qamma. It is anachronistic to speak of "the Book of the Covenant," as though the Rabbinic sages recognized in Ex. 20:22-23:33, a free-standing law-code, a model for their own work. We have no reason to impute to the framers of the Mishnah the recognition that the biblical codes stood each on its own. We have every reason to affirm the opposite: they deemed the Pentateuch a unitary text addressing a singular historical circumstance: Moses' transmission of God's will expressed at Sinai to Israel fresh out of Egypt. But the Rabbinic sages did recognize those traits that distinguish one Scriptural composition or composite from another, the integrity of the Priestly Torah, Torat Kohanim, for example. Their critical acumen is demonstrated in every line of the late antique Midrash-compilations. Not only so, but when the Rabbinic sages composed Mishnah-tractates, at some points they did refer to scriptural codes and systematically responded. Sifra is a fine example of that fact. What concerns us then is not how the Rabbinic sages anticipated the results of scholarship many centuries later. Rather, for purposes of comparison and contrast, it is how the Rabbinic sages treated topics addressed in common by Scripture's codes and by corresponding Mishnah's tractates.

Had they articulated their judgment of the diverse presentation of topics in common, what do we imagine the Rabbinic sages would have told us? First, they did not propose to recapitulate the traits of Moses's Torah in their mishnah-deuteronomy. The Mishnah does not submit to the formal or topical program of

Scripture but organizes matters in its own way. Accordingly, what is clear from what the Mishnah's compilers produced is that they did form an independent judgment. That emerges from the fact that while they reverently recorded and expounded Scripture's laws, they did not simply recapitulate in their own wording the statements of Scripture.

Nor, second, did they commonly follow the topical order and program of Scripture, though some tractates, e.g., Mishnah-tractate Yoma/Leviticus 16, do exactly that. In general what the Rabbinic sages did was to reorganize in their own framework, by their own hermeneutics to extend and amplify Scripture's topics and to place them into the sages' own systematic context as this chapter and Chapters Three through Five make clear.

And still more important, third, the Rabbinic sages brought to the exposition of topics shared with Scripture an analytical method and program unimagined by Scripture. It is there that we shall identify the qualities of the Mishnah that mark the code as unique by the criteria set forth in the Preface to all prior codes produced by communities of Judaism.

If then the Rabbinic sages stood in judgment upon what we now recognize as the Book of the Covenant, Ex. 20:22-23:33, of what did that judgment consist? We find the answer at the points of topical intersection of the Mishnah-tractate that covers some of the same ground, Mishnah-tractate Baba Qamma. With what outcome? The Rabbinic sages can have recognized the topical cogency of parts of the Book of the Covenant, but the miscellaneous character, by the same criteria, of other parts. They are likely to have found missing some of the important components of the comprehensive legal system they found in Scripture and brought to full articulation. But that is a happenstance, we have no definitive topical catalogue to consult in evaluating any of the ancient codes.

From their treatment of topics shared in common with the received codes, we may intuit what they thought of prior presentations of the same topics. And as I shall now show, they will have deemed shallow and superficial the syllogistic work of Scripture on the very topics that they shared with the Book of the Covenant. They will have had compelling reason to point to their work in the Mishnah as the model of how to present data to form important propositions, capable of extension beyond the topical limits of the laws that embodied and realized those propositions. On that basis, for the case at hand, the Mishnah will emerge as unprecedented.

I. COGENCY, COMPREHENSIVENESS

Cogent by what criterion? A universally-applicable criterion for cogency evades definition. What coheres in one context — successive, intersecting topics — appears episodic in another. Hence while the exquisite topical arrangement of the Mishnah in its six divisions, and the cogency of the topical expositions in the Mishnah's sixty tractates cannot fail to impress us, that is because we to begin with find the cogency of uniform topics logical. That represents a judgment of self-evidence of certain principles of natural philosophy. Category-formation viewed in the abstract responds to more than a single principle. But subjective judgment case by case need not suffice. For we can form an objective judgment of whether the governing principle of cogent category-formation has been *consistently* applied. That will impart cogency of an entirely formal character.

Comprehensive in what context? The Mishnah sets the standard of comprehensiveness, with its sixty principal topical category-formations. No prior Israelite code, not the ones presented by Scripture, not the ones surviving in the caves of Qumran, competes, though the Deuteronomic code of Dt. 12-26 comes close. When it comes to comprehensiveness, a simple criterion serves. The Mishnah covers six principal topics, all of them defined by internal evidence. And these six principal topics break down into at least sixty systematic topical expositions. That sets the standard, by which all prior codes are found wanting.

A précis of the Book of the Covenant will allow us to form an objective judgment on that matter of cogency and comprehensiveness. How does the program of the Book of the Covenant compare? The topical program of Ex. 20:22-23:33, rules and admonitions of the covenant, follows the following plan, so Moshe Greenberg:

> These consist of cultic regulations, civil and criminal laws, and socio-moral exhortations, arranged as follows: (a) rules concerning access to God in worship (20:22-26), (b) the emancipation of Hebrew slaves (21:1-11); (c) homicide and assault (21:12-27); (d) the homicidal ox (21:28-32); (e) injury to property, i.e., to animals (including theft) (21:33-22:3); and to crops (22:4-5); the responsibility of bailees and borrowers (22:6-14); seduction (22:15-16) from the vantage point of the father's interest, i.e., the bride price; (f) a miscellany of religio-moral admonitions and commandments (22:17-23:13); (g) a cultic calendar (23:14-19).[2]

Greenberg comments, "A fairly clear principle of association and gradation is discernible from (c) through (e); the precedence given to (b) is conditioned by the situation — limitation of slavery among Hebrews being the chief boon that their liberator conferred upon them...." Frank Cruesemann sees a range of topics: "Along with the actual judicial pronouncements, there are cultic and religious, ethical and social demands together with their theological and historical foundations. The entire composition is dominated by the first and second commandments"...[3] (That is a matter taken up in detail by Professor Kaufman's appendix.)

Noth sees the composition as originally an independent book of law: [4] "...we have in Ex. 20:22-23:33 a collection of judgments of differing form and differing content which...are customarily described as the 'Book of the Covenant.' It is probable that this collection once formed an independent book of law which has been inserted into the Pentateuchal narrative as an already self-contained entity...." The composition covers these topics as identified by Noth, with his outline indicated IN SMALL CAPS:

21:1-11 THE LAW FOR SLAVES

21:2 When you buy a Hebrew slave
21:7 When a man sells his daughter as a slave...

21:12-17 OFFENCES PUNISHABLE BY DEATH

21:12 Whoever strikes a man so that he dies shall be put to death
21:15 Whoever strikes his father or mother shall be put to death
21:16 Whoever steals a man shall be put to death
21:17 Whoever curses his father or his mother shall be put to death

21:18-36 BODILY INJURY, CASES THAT DO OR DO NO RESULT IN DEATH

21:18 When men quarrel and one strikes the other with a stone or his fast...
21:20 When a man strikes his slave
21:22 When men strive together and hurt a woman with child
21:26 When a man strikes the eye of his slave
21:28 When an ox gores a man or a woman to death, the ox shall be put to death.
21:33 When a man leaves a pit open
21:35 When one man's ox hurts another's so that it dies

22:1-17 DAMAGE TO PROPERTY

22:1 If a man steals an ox or a sheep
22:2 If a thief is found breaking in
22:5 When a man causes a field to be grazed over
22:6 When fire breaks out and catches in thorns
22:7 If a man delivers to his neighbor money or goods to keep
22:9 For every breach of trust...
22:10 If a man delivers to his neighbor an ass or an ox or a sheep or any beast to keep and it dies...
22:14 If a man borrows anything of his neighbor and it is hurt or dies...
22:16 If a man seduces a virgin who is not betrothed and lies with her, he shall give the marriage present for her and make her his wife.

22:18-31: a long sequence of Apodictic laws (Noth, p. 185)

22:18: You shall not permit a sorceress to live.
22:19: Whoever lies with a beast shall be put to death
22:20: Whoever sacrifices to any god save to the Lord
22:21: You shall not wrong a stranger or oppress him...

22:25: If you lend money to any of my people who you who is poor, you shall no
be to him as a creditor

22:28: You shall not revile God

22:29: You shall not delay to offer from the fullness of your harvest

22:31: You shall be men consecrated to me; therefore you shall not eat any flesh
that is torn by beasts in the field

23:1-9 Apodictic regulations for the conduct of cases at law[5]

23:1: You shall not utter a false report

23:4 If you meet your enemy's ox or his ass going astray, you shall bring it back
to him

23:6: You shall not pervert justice due to your poor in his suit

23:9: You shall not oppress a stranger

23:10-13 SABBATH YEAR AND SABBATH DAY

23:10 For six years you shall sow your land and gather in its yield, but the
seventh year you shall let it rest

23:12 Six days you shall do your work, but on the seventh day you shall rest

23:14-19 SPECIAL CULTIC REGULATIONS

23:14: Three times a year you shall keep a feast to me

23:18: You shall not offer the blood of my sacrifice with leavened bread or let
the fat of my feast remain until the morning

23:19: The first fruits of your ground you shall bring into the house of the Lord
your God

The sequence, 21:12-17, 21:18-36, and 22:1-17, cohere in the exposition
of the laws of torts and damages, inclusive of the death penalty, but by the same
criterion that classifies those passages as a systematic exposition, 21:18-23:9 form
a miscellany:

21:1-11 The law for slaves
21:12-17 offences punishable by death
21:18-36 Bodily injury, cases that do or do no result in death
22:1-17 damage to property
22:18-31: A LONG SEQUENCE OF APODICTIC LAWS (NOTH, P. 185)
23:1-9 apodictic regulations for the conduct of cases at law
23:10-13 Sabbath Year and Sabbath Day

We may judge the Book of the Covenant as cogent in some, though not
all, of the parts, if surely not as a whole. That is because topical coherence
characterizes some of the divisions but not others, e.g., 22:18-31, a "sequence" that
is hardly sequential in any but a formal sense. If topical cogency inures in 21:1-

22:17, then by that criterion 22:18-31, 23:1-9 are scattered and incoherent.

What about comprehensiveness by the criterion supplied by the Mishnah? Following Noth's outline, then, we find coverage that forms a counterpart to the following topics of the Mishnah:

ZERA'IM: 22:25 (Shebi'it); 23:10-13 Sabbath Year (Shebi'it); 23:14-19 Special cultic regulations (23:19: Bikkurim)

Mo'ED: 23:10-13 Sabbath Year and Sabbath Day (Shebi'it, Shabbat); 23:14-19 Special cultic regulations (23:14: Hagigah)

NASHIM: 21:1-11 (21:2: Qiddushin)

NEZIQIN: 21:12-17 offences punishable by death (Sanhedrin); 21:18-36 Bodily injury, cases that do or do no result in death (Baba Qamma); 22:1-17 damage to property (Baba Qamma); 22:18-31: a long sequence of apodictic laws (22:18-20: Sanhedrin); 23:1-9 apodictic regulations for the conduct of cases at law (23:1: Sanhedrin' 23:4:: Sanhedrin)

QODOSHIM: 22:31 (Hullin); 23:14-19 Special cultic regulations (Zebahim)

TOHOROT: —

The Mishnah more consistently applies its principle of cogency to its exposition of topics than does the Book of the Covenant, with its one comparably-coherent topical composite, Ex. 21:12-22:17 (following Greenberg) showing what might have been done. But then the long conglomerates of apodictic law by the same criterion prove to be topically incoherent. The Sabbath as a theme forms an exception and takes a paramount position in the counterpart to Zera'im and Mo'ed. But by contrast to a paltry handful of verses in the Book of the Covenant, the Mishnah treats the Sabbath in two distinct divisions, each with its indicative marking, the Sabbath in the context of the agricultural rules of sanctification, the Sabbath in the context of Appointed times. The upshot is, only Sanhedrin and Baba Qamma intersect with the Book of the Covenant and present the sole possibility for comparison as to cogency. It follows that the Mishnah is consistently cogent in its topical compositions, and it is incomparably more comprehensive than the Book of the Covenant.

II. SYLLOGISTIC CHARACTER: COMPARING THE BOOK OF THE COVENANT AND MISHNAH-TRACTATE BABA QAMMA

The difference between a syllogistic presentation of the law and making a collection of episodic, inert rules emerges clearly in the comparison between the Book of the Covenant and Mishnah-tractate's presentations of the same specific rules. The former cannot conceive a context beyond the data, and the latter exercises its gifts of generalization and analysis to open possibilities of extension and amplification. The Book of the Covenant presents information, the Mishnah constructs information into patterns subject to analysis. It not only seeks and transmits knowledge, it tests knowledge. Above all, the Mishnah in treating the topic systematizes and organizes the data, inviting an analytical program of comparison and contrast that is unthinkable, indeed contextually incomprehensible, in Scripture.

I refer to an exemplary passage, Ex. 21-22, where we may succinctly compare the presentation of the matter in the Book of the Covenant with Mishnah-tractate Baba Qamma Chapter One. We begin with the pertinent statements of the Book of the Covenant, for reasons that quickly become self-evident:

Ox: "When one man's ox hurts another's, so that it dies, then they shall sell the live ox and divide the price of it; and the dead beast also they shall divide. Or if it is known that the ox has been accustomed to gore in the past, and its owner has not kept it in, he shall pay ox for ox, and the dead beast shall be his" (Ex. 21:35-6)

PIT: "When a man leaves a pit open or when a man digs up a pit and does not cover it, and an ox or an ass falls into it, the owner of the pit shall make it good; he shall give money to its owner and the dead beast shall be his" (Ex. 21:33)

CROP-DESTROYING BEAST: "When a man causes a field or vineyard to be grazed over or lets his beast loose and it feeds in another man's field, he shall make restitution from the beast in his own field and in his own vineyard" (Ex. 22:5)

FIRE: "When fire breaks out and catches in thorns so that the stacked grain or the standing grain or the field is consumed, he that kindled the fire shall make full restitution" (Ex. 22:6)

Ex. 21:35-6 yields two rules. First, in the case of an ox that gores, the surviving ox is sold and the proceeds divided; but that is where the owner of the goring ox could not have foreseen the possibility of goring; if the ox's history of goring shows that he should have made provision, the foreseeable incident has been caused by his negligence, with the stated outcome. Second, negligence involves inanimate as well as animate causes. The same principle is operative for the third and the fourth rules. That sum and substance is the lesson of the four causes of damages to property: compensation gauged by culpability: the possibility of foreseeing damages and preventing them.

Now let us see how the Mishnah presents the same four matters in its opening statement on torts and damages. We shall observe how the four items of Scripture form into a single coherent statement, yielding a generalization rich in implications for further cases:

M. 1:1 [There are] four generative causes of damages: (1) ox [Ex. 21:35-36], (2) pit [Ex. 21:33], (3) crop-destroying beast [Ex. 22:4], and (4) conflagration [Ex. 22:5]. What they have in common is that they customarily do damage and taking care of them is your responsibility. And when one [of them] has caused damage, the [owner] of that which causes the damage is liable to pay compensation for damage out of the best of his land [Ex. 22:4].

M. 1:2 In the case of anything of which I am liable to take care, I am deemed to render possible whatever damage it may do. [If] I am deemed to have rendered possible part of the damage it may do, I am liable for compensation as if [I have] made possible all of the damage it may do.

What M. Baba Qamma 1:1 contributes is a systematic analysis of the category-formation, generative cases of damages. The data of Scripture are drawn together into a common genus, and in due course will be speciated. M. 1:2 introduces the issue of responsibility and its gradations. If one is responsible, one is liable. If one is responsible in part, one is liable for the entire body of damages. These principles extend to an unlimited number of cases, the details of Scripture being reworked into an encompassing set of generalizing principles.

The Mishnah has treated the cases of Scripture as species of a genus and has articulated the rule of the genus, capable of extension to an unlimited range of other species. It has spelled out the full range of responsibility ("In the case of anything of which I am liable to take care, I am deemed to render possible whatever damage it may do. If I am deemed to have rendered possible part of the damage it may do, I am liable for compensation as if I have made possible all of the damage it may do"). It has defined the specifics required for applying Scripture's general rules ("a tooth is deemed an attested danger in regard to eating what is suitable for eating"). In the manner of geometry, they showed how, within a given set of postulates, a range of problems was to be solved to yield a proof of a set of theorems.

Let us turn to the comparison of Ex. 21:33, the pit, and Ex. 22:4, the crop-destroying beast, with the Mishnah's counterparts.

When a man leaves a pit open or when a man digs up a pit and does not cover it, and an ox or an ass falls into it, the owner of the pit shall make it good; he shall give money to its owner and the dead beast shall be his" (Ex. 21:33)

Scripture's message is, one is responsible for leaving a pit without making provision for the damage it may do. Now how does the Mishnah-exposition proceed?

Damages done by the pit

M. Baba Qamma 5:5: He who digs a pit in private domain and opens it into public domain, or in public domain and opens it into private domain, or in private domain and opens it into private domain belonging to someone else, is liable [for damage done by the pit]. He who digs a pit in public domain, and an ox or an ass fell into it and died, is liable. It is all the same whether one digs a pit, a trench, cavern, ditches, or channels: he is liable.

Scripture ignores the context of the pit, not distinguishing public domain, where one has no right to dig a pit, from private domain, where he does. It further extends the case of the pit to cover trenches, caverns, ditches, or channels. The former point is the more important, the latter merely clarifies the obvious: pit represents what fits into its classification.

M. Baba Qamma 5:6 A pit belonging to two partners — one of them passed by it and did not cover it, and the second one also did not cover it, the second one is liable.

[If] the first one covered it up, and the second one came along and found it uncovered and did not cover it up. the second one is liable. [If] he covered it up in a proper way, and an ox or an ass fell into it and died, he is exempt. [If] he did not cover it up in the proper way and an ox or an ass fell into it and died, he is liable. [If] it fell forward [not into the pit] because of the sound of the digging, [the owner of the pit] is liable. [If] it fell backward [not into the pit] because of the sound of the digging, [the owner of the pit] is exempt. [If] an ox carrying its trappings fell into it and they were broken, an ass and its trappings and they were split, [the owner of the pit] is liable for the beast but exempt for the trappings. [If] an ox belonging to a deaf-mute, an idiot, or a minor fell into it, [the owner] is liable. [If] a little boy or girl, a slave boy or a slave girl [fell into it], he is exempt [from paying a ransom].

The matter of responsibility is refined. If there are two owners, they share liability. But that point is modified by the matter of responsibility. The partner who most recently has passed the pit is responsibility for ensuing damage. One has to take action to cover the pit properly. Here is a principle that once more pertains to a wide variety of cases, not only the matter of the pit. Scripture's rule that the owner of the pit is responsible for damages is vastly extended beyond the limits of the case and the principle of culpability.

M. Baba Qamma 5:7 All the same are an ox and all other beasts so far as (1) falling into a pit, (2) keeping apart from Mount Sinai [Ex. 19:12], (3) a double indemnity [Ex. 22:7], (4) the returning of that which is lost [Dt. 22:3, Ex. 23:4] (5), unloading [Ex. 23:51, (6) muzzling [Dt. 25:4], (7) hybridization [Lev. 19:19, Dt. 22:10], and the (8) Sabbath [Ex. 20:10, Dt. 5:14]. And so too are wild beasts and fowl subject to the same laws. If so, why is an ox or an ass specified? But Scripture spoken in terms of prevailing conditions.

Here the Mishnah explicitly acknowledges that Scripture's cases are exemplary, not particular. Here is an implicit judgment upon Scripture as formulated.

DAMAGES DONE BY THE CROP-DESTROYING BEAST

"When a man causes a field or vineyard to be grazed over or lets his beast loose and it feeds in another man's field, he shall make restitution from the beast in his own field and in his own vineyard" (Ex. 22:5)

Damages done by one's property — herds or flocks here — to someone else's property must be compensated — so much for the Book of the Covenant, another simple and undeveloped declaration.

M. Baba Qamma 6:1 He who brings a flock into a fold and shut the gate before it as required, but [the flock] got out and did damage, is exempt. [If] he did not shut the gate before it as required, and [the flock] got out and did damage, he is liable. [If the fence] was broken down by night, or thugs broke it down, and [the flock] got out and did damage, he is exempt. [If] the thugs took [the flock] out, [and the flock did damage], the thugs are liable.

If one has taken appropriate precautions, he is not held responsible for unforeseeable accidents. If one has not carried out his responsibility to prevent damage, he is liable. If his precautions were rendered null by damages he could not foresee or prevent ("thugs broke it down"), he is not liable. If a third party caused his property to inflict damages, the third party is liable. Scripture's case now yields a governing rule that pertains to any number of cases, the rule is extended into an abstract law of responsibility.

M. Baba Qamma 6:2 [If] he left it in the sun, [or if] he handed it over to a deaf-mute, idiot, or minor, and [the flock] got out and did damage, he is liable. [If] he handed it over to a shepherd, the shepherd takes the place of the owner [as to liability]. [If the flock] [accidentally] fell into a vegetable patch and derived benefit [from the produce], [the owner must] pay compensation [only] for the value of the benefit [derived by the flock]. [If the flock] went down in the normal way and did damage, [the owner must] pay compensation for the [actual] damage which [the flock] inflicted.

If the owner handed the flock out to an incompetent guardian, he is responsible, but if he employed a qualified shepherd, the shepherd assumes responsibility. If the flock accidentally did damage, the owner is liable only for the benefit enjoyed by the flock. But if this happened in an ordinary manner ("the normal way"), then the compensation must cover all damages. Here again the circumstances govern the compensation that is owing — a consideration not raised by Scripture.

M. Baba Qamma 6:3 He who stacks sheaves in the field of his fellow without permission, and the beast of the owner of the field ate them up, [the owner of the field] is exempt. And [if] it was injured by them, the owner of the sheaves is liable. But if he had put his sheaves there with permission, the owner of the field is liable.

The owner of the field where one has stacked his sheaves without permission is not responsible to guard the interloper's crops from his own beasts. The interloper is responsible for damage done to the field owner's animals. But if the owner gave permission, he assumes full responsibility. That is a point that once more extends to a variety of cases. The exposition of the genus, damages done by fire, presents no surprises.

DAMAGES DONE BY FIRE

"When fire breaks out and catches in thorns so that the stacked grain or the standing grain or the field is consumed, he that kindled the fire shall make full restitution" (Ex. 22:6)

One who initially creates a cause of damages is responsible for the secondary damages that are done.

M. Baba Qamma 6:4 He who causes a fire to break out through the action of a deaf-mute, idiot, or minor, is exempt from punishment under the laws of man, but liable to punishment under the laws of heaven. [If] he did so through the action of a person of sound senses, the person of sound senses is liable. [If] one person brought the flame, then another person brought the wood, the one who brings the wood is liable. [If] one person brought the wood and the other person then brought the flame, the one who brought the flame is liable. [If] a third party came along and fanned the fire, the one who fanned the flame is liable. [If] the wind fanned the flame, all of them are exempt. He who causes a fire to break out, which consumed wood, stones, or dirt, is liable.

The one who acts through a third party is not responsible for the third party's actions. But if he acts through party not responsible for his own actions, he bears no legal, actionable responsibility for that party's actions. The deaf-mute, idiot, or minor is not capable of culpable intentionality. But the one who is responsible for what they have done also is not liable in an earthly court for what they have done, but is answerable to Heaven. In a sequence of actions culminating in damages, the person who has completed the process bears responsibility. Thus if one person brought wood and then another flame, the latter is liable; if one person brought the flame and then another the wood, the latter is liable. If a third party fanned the flame, so increasing the damages, he is responsible. If the wind did so, all parties are exempt. The final statement recapitulates Scripture's principle, pure and simple. The upshot is, the case of Scripture is not only turned into an exemplification of a transaction not limited to the case at hand, it also is made to yield abstract principles of culpability that vastly transcend the issue of property damage.

M. Baba Qamma 6:6 A spark which flew out from under the hammer and did damage — [the smith] is liable. A camel which was carrying flax and passed by in the public way, and the flax it was carrying got poked into a store and caught fire from the lamp of the storekeeper and set fire to the building — the owner of the camel is liable.

One is responsible for the foreseeable damage that he has done, an obvious point that serves to set the stage for what is not self-evident, the matter of the camel. If the animal has caused foreseeable damages — its flax poked into the stores along the sides and caught fire — the owner of the camel is liable, the storekeeper has done nothing that requires compensation; he is not responsible for damages.

The syllogistic character of the Mishnah contrasts with the episodic formulation of the Book of the Covenant. At every point at which Scripture and the Mishnah take up the same subject, the Book of the Covenant sets forth a governing rule for a case, while Mishnah-tractate Baba Qamma finds a way of exemplifying a governing rule. That is because an analytical program animates the Mishnah's presentation of the law. It is not simply the Mishnah's capacity to present the rules as exemplary. It is also, and especially, the Mishnah's implicit theoretical framework that generates syllogisms extending far beyond the case at hand.

III. MISHNAH-TRACTATE BABA QAMMA AGAINST THE BOOK OF THE COVENANT

The Mishnah's judgment of the counterpart passages of Scripture comes to realization in the exemplary passages just now surveyed. The Mishnah has revolutionized the presentation of the specified topics that are shared with Scripture. That is in two aspects. First, Scripture's cases — ox, pit, crop-destroying beast, fire — are turned into exemplifications of types of damage, animate and inanimate, active and passive, for example. These cases furthermore illustrate the types of responsibility assigned for damages and contain a deeper analysis of types of causes, all in the manner of natural philosophy. The cases then yield rules. Each is treated as a genus, capable of speciation, and in due course the Talmud would compare and contrast the four genera and refine matters. But the analytical work of types of generative causes of damages is done in the Mishnah.

More important, second, the rules that are so worded as to exemplify and pertain to agricultural circumstances are translated into generalizations that govern all manner of transactions, a wide variety of topics. The generative concept is the abstraction, responsibility. Responsibility is framed in eloquent language: "In the case of anything of which I am liable to take care, I am deemed to render possible whatever damage it may do. If I am deemed to have rendered possible part of the damage it may do, I am liable for compensation as if I have made possible all of the damage it may do." That formulation transcends the cases and the classifications yielded by the cases and turns the law into jurisprudence. By the criterion of formulating the law with the power to extend and amplify itself beyond the case at hand and even past the limits of the transaction that the law explicitly describes, one must judge as unique the Mishnah's counterpart to passages in the Book of the Covenant that are explicitly encompassed by the Mishnah. The intellectual ambition that culminated in the hierarchization of degrees of responsibility marks the Mishnah as the outcome of a remarkable imagination.

THE DAMASCUS COVENANT (CD)
AND MISHNAH-TRACTATE SHABBAT

Among the various heirs of Scripture the Rabbinic sages who produced the Mishnah were not alone in compiling normative rules into compositions and composites, or, in conventional categories, "laws" into "codes."[6] I limit my comparison to the Damascus Covenant. That is because both the Mishnah and the Damascus Covenant bear in common systematic accounts of the Sabbath.

I.   TOPICAL COGENCY AND COMPREHENSIVENESS

Like Deuteronomy, the Damascus Covenant,[7] found first in the Cairo Geniza a century ago and then in the library of Qumran a half-century ago, is divided into an admonition and laws.[8] The laws are set out topic by topic, so Professor Chaim Rabin:[9]

"The work is clearly not a comprehensive handbook of Halakhah, but a series of Halakhic statements, roughly arranged by subjects...Several solemn concluding sections...suggest that it is a ...record of decisions taken at various sessions of the Meeting of the Camps. In contrast to the marriage laws..., most of the regulations...closely resemble Rabbinic Law; where it differs, that difference is in most cases hardly of greater importance than divergences of opinion found within the Tannaitic School itself...." (Rabin, x-xi).

The composite of laws alone concerns us here. "The laws," in Rabin's edition begin *in medias res:* "As for every case of devoting, namely, that a man be devoted so that he ceases to be a living man, he is to be put to death by the ordinances of the gentiles" (Rabin, p. 44). The order of topics, as articulated in the document itself, is as follows: [1] "concerning the oath," [2] "the order of the judges of the congregation," [3] "concerning the purification with water," [4] "concerning the Sabbath, to guard it according to its rule," concluding:

Thus far the order of the meeting of the cities of Israel concerning these rulings, so as to distinguish between the unclean and the clean and to make known the distinction between the holy and the profane. And these are the ordinances for the wise man in which to walk with every living being according to the ruling proper for every occasion. And according to this ruling shall the seed of Israel walk, and they shall not be cursed (Rabin, p. 62/ XV 19-22).

The document proceeds: "And this is the order of the meeting of the camps," "and this is the order of the camp overseer:" then:

Thus far the order of the meeting of the camps for the whole epoch of wickedness, and they that will not hold face to these will not be fit to dwell in the land when the Messiah of Aaron and Israel comes in the end of days," (Rabin, p. 66/l. 20-21)

Then: "and the order of the meeting of all camps," "and this is the order of the many for preparing all their requirements," then a systematic sequence: "concerning a woman's oath," "concerning the rules for freewill gifts, and so on. Viewed whole, the topical program is as follows, as outlined by VanderKam and Flint:

1.   For the priests
2.   On skin diseases, bodily discharges, childbirth
3.   For business and betrothal

4.	On measurements, offerings, gentile meat
5.	On oaths, becoming a member of the Yahad community, making vows
6.	On property and restitution
7.	On witnesses and judges
8.	On purification, Sabbath, sacrifices, holiness of the sanctuary and city
9.	On the demon-possessed, gentiles, impure foods
10.	Rules for those in camps, for the overseer, for relationships with outsiders
11.	Punishments for breaking rules[10]

Clearly, the topical program is comprised by items deemed immediately pertinent to the community as it was. The contrast to the Mishnah's topical program, so out of phase with the practical realities of the Israelite situation that pertained after 70, cannot be missed. It underscores the Mishnah's focus on the future restoration of the Israelite commonwealth, government, Temple, priesthood and all. So far as topical cogency is evaluated by the fit between the topical program and the social world contemplated by that program, the Damascus Covenant — so all scholarship concurs — responds to the world conceived by its compilers. That is not the case with the Mishnah.

The arrangement of the laws of CD by topics will not have surprised the framer of the Priestly Code (Lev. 1-7 in particular).[11] Still, if the parts of the collection are topically cogent, the construction as a whole is not. The principle of organization and the sequence of topics conform to no principle I can discern. Any other topical sequence will have served, and — more to the point — there is little rationality that accounts for the groupings of the topics, though No. 11 forms a fitting conclusion to the whole.

The cogency, accordingly, should not be overstated. The topical expositions are free-standing, not ordinarily organized in large topical expositions, so:

> Concerning a woman's oath: Forasmuch as he said, "It is for her husband to annul her oath," (Num. 30:14) let no man annul an oath of which he does not know whether it ought to be carried out or annulled. If it is such as to lead to transgressing of the covenant, let him annul it and not carry it out. Likewise is the rule for her father.
>
> Concerning the rules for freewill-gifts: Let no man vow to the altar anything unlawfully acquired. Also the priests should not take from Israel anything unlawfully acquired...and let no man declare holy the food of his mouth to God, for that is what he said, 'They trap each man his neighbor with a vow" (Micah 7:2: "Each hunts his brother with a net [Hebrew: herem]" (Rabin, p. 76)

But when we do have a large topical exposition, it consists of sets of unrelated, free-standing rules, not expositions of principles, thus, for a single example of a topical miscellany:

Concerning the Sabbath, to guard it according to its rule: Let no man do work on the Friday from the time when the orb of the sun is distant from the gate by its own fullness, for that is what he said, "Guard the Sabbath day to keep it holy" (Dt. 5:12).

And on the Sabbath day let no man speak a lewd or villainous word. Let him not lend anything to his neighbor. Let them not shed blood...

Let him not speak of matters of labor and work to be done on the morrow...Let no man walk about in the field on the Sabbath in order to do the work he requires after the Sabbath ends. Let him not walk about outside his town above one thousand cubits.

Let no man eat on the Sabbath day except that which has been prepared. And of that which is lying about in the field let him not eat. And let him not drink water unless it is in the camp" (Rabin, p. 52).

We shall return to the exposition of Sabbath-law presently. For the moment it suffices to point out that any other order of the sub-topics will have produced the same miscellany; there is no principle that dictates what comes first, what then follows. So too "purification with water" yields two random rules:

Let no man bathe in water that is dirty or that is less than the quantity that covers up a man. Let him not purify a vessel in it.

And as for every rock pool in a rock in which there is not the quantity that covers up a man which an unclean person has touched: he renders its water unclean with the uncleanness of water in a vessel (Rabin, p. 50).

That, sum and substance, fills the classification, media of purification. The contrast with Mishnah-tractate Miqvaot is intimidating.

Scripture is alluded to throughout: "It often comments upon a biblical law..." (Rabin, p. x). Occasionally, Scriptural law is explicitly cited and glossed:

"And as to that which he said, "You shall not take vengeance nor bear rancor against the children of thy people," (Lev. 19:18), every man of the members of the covenant who brings against his neighbor an accusation without reproving before witnesses and brings it up when he grows angry or tells his elders to make him contemptible, he is one who takes vengeance and bears rancor...." (Rabin, p. 44)

So too some cases are systematically introduced, "As to that which he [Moses] said...," thus Rabin, p. 44 2/2, 9/3, 52/14. Professor Lawrence H. Schiffman, cited presently, reconstructs the exegesis of Scripture that accounts for some of the Sabbath-laws and is able to show links with Scripture that are not made explicit in the text. Note the judgment of Lawrence H. Schiffman, "The laws contained in the Zadokite Fragments [=CD] are based, for the most part, on language derived from biblical verses. It is those verses that are being interpreted, although only rarely are the verses themselves explicitly quoted."[12]

As to cogency then: the construction of the document, with its admonition serving as a prologue to the laws, suggests that the topical program is not random but focused. The very cogency of the admonition and the laws then suggests the document is conceived to stand on its own, not presupposing other codes or extensions of its legal program. It sustains the judgment that the compilers contemplated a free-standing account of the norms of the community, much as the Mishnah presupposes no compilation of laws outside its own limits except for Scripture and even recapitulates those put forth in Scripture.

As to the comprehensive character of the topical program, it is difficult to form a definitive judgment. On the one side, CD treats a variety of subjects. On the other, set side by side with that of the Mishnah, five times more numerous in the subjects that are expounded, its table of contents is paltry. The upshot is, so far as a judgment can be made concerning the comprehensiveness of the Damascus Covenant, we must find in the Mishnah's favor: a much more encompassing, well-constructed compilation of laws. But these judgments are merely formal. What about the substance of matters: the purposive construction of facts that generate principles as against the random collection and miscellaneous arrangement of inert information?

II. Syllogistic Character: Comparing Components of the Damascus Covenant and Mishnah-Tractate Shabbat

What of the capacity of the code to cover cases or problems not articulated in its laws, to yield principles capable of extension and amplification even beyond the subject at hand? The syllogistic character of the Mishnah will now stand in contrast with the inert character of the laws of the Damascus Covenant. To begin with, two minor cases show what is at stake.

It is simple enough to point to the intimidating comparison of Mishnah-tractate Kelim and the first of the two items cited below, or Mishnah-tractate Ohalot and the second:

And all the wood and the stones and the dust which are defiled by man's impurity, while with stains of oil in them, in accordance with their uncleanness will make whoever touches them impure (CD A xii.16)

And every utensil, nail or peg in the wall which is with a dead person in the house [Num. 19] shall be unclean with the same uncleanness as tools for work...(CD A xii.17)

The thirty chapters of Mishnah-tractate Kelim, dealing with the susceptibility to uncleanness of objects made of wood, stone, or earthenware, the chapters of Mishnah-tractate Ohalot that expound the formal and functional traits of the "tent," viewed as an abstraction — these quite overwhelm in intellectual density the simple statements above. Consider in contrast with CD A xii.17 the opening chapter of Mishnah-tractate Ohalot:

CORPSE-UNCLEANNESS, ITS AFFECTS ON MAN AND UTENSILS

A. THE MATTER OF REMOVES

M. Ohalot 1:1 Two are unclean through a corpse [which is a Father of Fathers of Uncleanness]. One [who touches the corpse itself] is unclean with the uncleanness of seven [days] [as a Father of Uncleanness], and one [who touches him] is unclean with the uncleanness [that passes at] evening. Three are unclean through a corpse. Two are unclean with the uncleanness of seven [days], and one is unclean with the uncleanness [that passes at] evening. Four are unclean through a corpse. Three are unclean with the uncleanness of seven [days], and one is unclean with the uncleanness [that passes at] evening. How so [for] two? A man who touches the corpse is unclean with the uncleanness of seven [days], and a man who touches him is unclean with the uncleanness [that passes at] evening.

M. Ohalot 1:2 How so [for] three? Utensils which touch the corpse and utensils [which touch other] utensils are unclean with the uncleanness of seven [days]. The third, whether man or utensils, is unclean with the uncleanness [that passes at] evening.

M. Ohalot 1:3 How so [for] four? Utensils which touch the corpse, and a man [who touches] utensils, and utensils [which touch] man are unclean with the uncleanness of seven [days]. The fourth, whether man or utensils, is unclean with the uncleanness that passes in the evening.

The two issues introduced at the outset, the matter of removes of uncleanness, the variables that affect man and utensils as objects susceptible to uncleanness, corpse- and other sources of uncleanness as causes, are beyond the imagination of the Damascus Covenant's counterpart rules.

Readers may properly object that the miscellany on uncleanness set forth by the Damascus Covenant does not truly represent the capacity of the compilers of that document. Turn, they will say, to the elaborate code of laws for the Sabbath and build the comparison there. Fortunately, we have a reliable and systematic exposition of those laws, in Lawrence H. Schiffman, *The Halakhah at Qumran*.[13] These may be set in comparison with the Mishnah's counterpart exposition of Sabbath laws, with a single question in mind: does the Mishnah's topical exposition yield occasions for syllogistic analysis, and does the counterpart exposition of the Damascus Covenant do the same?

First, let us follow Schiffman's portrayal, then examine the Mishnah's counterpart. Schiffman maintains that the unit is complete.[14] I am not certain what he means in saying so, but my guess is, he deems the repertoire to exhaust the document's representation of the subject. Here is a fine opportunity to test the syllogistic possibilities of a systematic topical exposition outside the framework of the Mishnah but on a topic that is primary to the Mishnah and to the document adduced in comparison. I reproduce Schiffman's translation.

At issue, I emphasize, are not parallels between the two compilations of Sabbath laws, let alone points of intersection with other law codes produced by Jews, whether in antiquity or in medieval times. These are systematically reprised by Schiffman and have no bearing on our problem. What concerns me is the quality of the representation of the Sabbath-law, the capacity of that law to generate principles that extend to other topics entirely or at least to establish guidelines for solving further problems connected with Sabbath observance. That is what I mean in comparing the syllogistic possibilities of the Mishnah and those of the other ancient Israelite codes.

CD 10:14-17 CONCERNING THE SABBATH, to observe it according to its regulation: No one shall do work on Friday from the time when the sphere of the sun is distant from the gate by the sun's diameter, for this is the import of that which he said, "Observe the Sabbath day to sanctify it" (Deut. 5:12).

CD 10:17-19: DISCUSSION OF BUSINESS. And on the Sabbath day no one shall speak a wicked or vain word. Let him not lend his neighbor anything. Let him not dispute about wealth or profit. Let him not speak of things relating to the work and the labor to be done the next morning.

Adding to the time sanctified as the Sabbath and not speaking about mundane matters may join together as provisions for the protection of the Sabbath holiness. But the one does not lead into the next, and joined together the rules do not generate further issues.

CD 10:20 WALKING IN THE FIELD No one shall walk about in the field to do his desired work on the Sabbath
CD 10:21 A ONE THOUSAND CUBIT SABBATH LIMIT: Let him not walk about outside of his city more than a thousand cubits.

Once more we have free-standing items. The exact meaning of CD 10:20 is unclear, as Schiffman notes. The probable sense is, one should not plan on the Sabbath work to be done later on, after the Sabbath. If so, that has no bearing on the Sabbath limit, here 1,000 cubits, to which one may walk; these are distinct principles.

CD 10:22 PREPARATION OF FOOD BEFORE THE SABBATH No one shall eat anything on the Sabbath day except that which has been prepared in advance or from that which is decaying in the field.
CD 10:23 EATING AND DRINKING WITHIN THE CAMP Let him not drink or eat except if he or that which is in the camp.
CD 11:1f. DRINKING AND WASHING ON A JOURNEY On the road, if he goes down to wash, let him drink where he stands, but let him not draw water into any vessel.

Cooking on the Sabbath is forbidden. One may not carry into the camp what is located outside. One may not draw water on the Sabbath, but may kneel down and drink from a water source. The operative consideration at 10:22 is not violating the Sabbath repose by cooking, explicitly forbidden at Ex. 16:5, 23. At issue with the decaying fruit is that it not have fallen on the Sabbath; because it is decaying, it clearly has fallen before hand (Schiffman, p. 100). The reading, "that which" links to the foregoing; the food in the camp is made ready before the Sabbath, that in the field is not (Schiffman, p. 101). That reading presents us with two rules that cohere and can generate secondary amplification. The third item then stands on its own, having to do with a different subject.

CD 11:2 PERFORMANCE OF SABBATH WORK BY A NON-JEW Let him not send a foreigner to do his desire on the Sabbath

Schiffman, p. 106, interprets, "The sectarian may not spend the Sabbath among non-Jews [11:14], and he may also not send them to violate the Sabbath on his behalf." Since in his exposition he links the present law with the one we reach only later on, he may underscore the incoherence characteristic of the topical miscellany. The principle that links the two rules is not permitted formally to manifest itself. A talmud would accomplish that labor of extension and amplification, but the Qumran library contains nothing that resembles or suggests the traits of a talmud.[15]

CD 11:3f. THE CLEANLINESS OF SABBATH GARMENTS No one shall put on filthy garments or those put in storage unless they have been washed with water or are rubbed with frankincense.
CD 11:4f. ENTERING A PARTNERSHIP No one shall enter partnership by his own volition on the Sabbath.

No principle links the foregoing two items, which are free-standing and yield nothing more than each its own point. The point of CD 11:4 is that the law prohibits "declaring on the Sabbath any private property to be available for communal use."

CD 11:5-7 PASTURING ANIMALS No one shall walk after an animal to pasture it outside his city more than two thousand cubits. Let him not raise his hand to strike it with a fist. If it is stubborn, let him not take it out of his house.

Schiffman recognizes the coherence of the item: "This set of regulations must be taken as a group, since all three parts deal with the problem of pasturing animals on the Sabbath." He explains, "The normal Sabbath limit for a man at Qumran was one thousand cubits. In pasturing his animals, the sect allowed a man to walk an additional one thousand cubits." It was not permitted to drive animals (Schiffman, p. 112). Animals can be pastured if they will remain within the specified limit; if not, they were to be kept in the house (Schiffman).

CD 11:7-9 CARRYING FROM DOMAIN TO DOMAIN No one shall carry anything from the house to the outside or from the outside into the house. And if he is in the Sukkah, let him not carry anything out from it or bring anything into it.

The prohibition against carrying from private to public domain is familiar from M. Shabbat 1:1, but we shall see a remarkably different formulation of the matter, with a variety of secondary considerations articulated by the Mishnah but unnoted here.

CD 11:9 OPENING A SEALED VESSEL Let him not open plastered vessel on the Sabbath

Here is a good instance of the contrast between an inert and a generative rule. Here no reason is in play, no further considerations figure. The contrary rule in the Mishnah, at M. Shabbat 22:3, permits opening a jar sealed with plaster: A person breaks a jar to eat dried figs from it, on condition that he not intend [in opening the jar] to make it into a utensil. What principle is instantiated by this rule? It is permitted to destroy on the Sabbath, only forbidden to build (Schiffman, pp. 115-116). Hence the act of destruction is allowed. The stated rule then embodies an abstract principle that is capable of generating laws on a range of subjects, not only the present one. The rule becomes an example of a principle, a realization of an abstract conception that bears a myriad of consequences. The Mishnah's laws are exemplary and generic, the counterpart ones here are limited to their own case and sui generis.

CD 11:9f WEARING OF PERFUME BOTTLES No one shall carry spices on himself whether to go out or to come in on the Sabbath

The Mishnaic law goes over the present matter as follows:

M. 6:3 A woman should not go out with (1) a needle which has a hole, (2) with a ring which has a seal, (3) with a cochleae broach, (4) with a spice box, or (5) with a perfume flask.

M. 6:5 A woman goes out in hair ribbons, whether made of her own hair or of the hair of another woman or of a beast; and with (1) headband, (2) head bangles sewn [on the headdress], (3) a hair-net, and (4) wig, in the courtyard; (1) with wool in her ear, (2) wool in her sandals, (3) wool she has used for a napkin for her menstrual flow; (1) pepper, (2) a lump of salt, and (3) anything she puts into her mouth, on condition that she not first put it there on the Sabbath. And if it fell out, she may not put it back.]

M. 6:6 She goes out with a sela coin on a bunion. Little girls go out with threads and even ships in their ears. Arabian women go out veiled. Median women go out with cloaks looped up over their shoulders. And [so is the rule] for any person, but sages spoke concerning prevailing conditions.

M. 6:7 She weights her cloak with a stone, a nut, or a coin, on condition that she not attach the weight first on the Sabbath.

The contrast between the elaborate exposition of the Mishnah and the brief reference of CD is noteworthy. We need not dwell on the outcome of the cases of M. Shab. 6:3, 5-7; the Talmud does its work well. It suffices to note that the

Mishnah yields exemplary principles, not all of them limited to the topic or case at hand, and it shows how to generate further rules out of these same exemplary principles. CD does not.

CD 11:10f. HANDLING ROCKS AND EARTH Let him not handle rock or earth in a dwelling house.
CD 11:11 CARRYING INFANTS Let the parent not carry the infant to go out or to come in on the Sabbath.

The issue of CD 11:10 and that of the preceding and following entries do not intersect. CD 11:9 and 11:11 have to do with carrying. But the principle in play at 11:10 is what may not be used on the Sabbath, e.g., not handling what one cannot utilize. So a single principle does not inhere in the paragraphs.

CD 11:12 ENCOURAGING A SERVANT TO LABOR No one shall urge on his servant, his maidservant, or his hireling on the Sabbath

How this item relates to CD 11:2, performance of Sabbath work by a non-Jew, is not self-evident. Schiffman's discussion seems to me ample. But what is clear is that a principle of topical coherence has not dictated the ordering or arrangement of the laws, which are miscellaneous in their subject and also in the principles that they embody.

CD 11:13f CARING FOR DOMESTICATED ANIMALS No one shall deliver an animal on the Sabbath day. And if it fall into a cistern or pit, let him not lift it out on the Sabbath.

Schiffman states, "Here are presented two laws dealing with help that one might desire to give to domesticated animals on the Sabbath." One may not deliver on the Sabbath the offspring of a domestic beast. One may not remove an animal from a pit.

CD 11:14 SPENDING THE SABBATH AMONG GENTILES No one shall rest in a place close to the gentiles on the Sabbath.
CD 11:15 VIOLATION OF THE SABBATH FOR THE SAKE OF WEALTH No one shall violate the Sabbath for the sake of wealth or profit on the Sabbath.
CD 11:16f. SAVING OF LIFE And as to any human being who falls into a place of water or into a reservoir, no one shall bring him up with a ladder, rope, or instrument.

The second and third items form a pair. CD 11:15 forbids violating the Sabbath in order to preserve property, e.g., from fire. One may save a life, but without the use of equipment that is not set aside for that purpose in advance of the Sabbath (Schiffman, p. 126). If that is the sense of the law, then the juxtaposition of the two entries, 11:15 and 11:16 is purposive, with a clear contrast being drawn, yielding a variety of secondary rules and extensions. That exemplifies how in CD as much as in the Mishnah laws may generate principles, underscoring how uncommonly that takes place in CD.

CD 11:17 SACRIFICES No one shall offer anything upon the altar on the Sabbath except the burnt-offering of the Sabbath, for thus is it written, "except your Sabbaths" (Lev. 23:38).

The final item is a singleton. For the substance of the matter, see Schiffman, pp. 128-131.

The comparison of CD on the Sabbath with Mishnah-tractate Shabbat is made possible by the following annotated reprise, which reproduces the main compositions of the tractate.

I. DIMENSIONS: SPACE, TIME AND THE SABBATH

A. SPACE
M. 1:1 [Acts of] transporting objects from one domain to another [which violate] the Sabbath (1) are two, which [indeed] are four [for one who is] inside, (2) and two which are four [for one who is] outside. How so? [If on the Sabbath] the beggar stands outside and the householder inside, [and] the beggar stuck his hand inside and put [a beggar's bowl] into the hand of the householder, or if he took [something] from inside it and brought it out, the beggar is liable, the householder is exempt. [If] the householder stuck his hand outside and put [something] into the hand of the beggar, or if he took [something] from it and brought it inside, the householder is liable, and the beggar is exempt. [If] the beggar stuck his hand inside, and the householder took [something] from it, or if [the householder] put something in it and he [the beggar] removed it — both of them are exempt. [If] the householder put his hand outside and the beggar took [something] from it, or if [the beggar] put something into it and [the householder] brought it back inside, both of them are exempt.

B. TIME
M. 1:2 A man should not sit down before the barber close to the afternoon [prayer], unless he has already prayed. Nor [at that time] should a man go into a bathhouse or into a tannery, nor to eat, nor to enter into judgment. But if they began, they do not break off [what they were doing]. They do break off [what they were doing] to pronounce the recitation of the *Shema*. But they do not break off [what they were doing] to say the Prayer.

M. 1:3 A tailor should not go out carrying his needle near nightfall, lest he forget and cross [a boundary]; nor a scribe with his pen. And [on the Sabbath] one should not search his clothes [for fleas], or read by the light of a lamp. Nonetheless they state: [On the Sabbath] a teacher sees [by the light of a lamp] where the children are reading, but he does not read.

M. 1:10 They do not roast meat, onions, and eggs, unless there is time for them to be roasted while it is still day. They do not put bread into an oven at dusk, nor cakes on the coals, unless there is time for them to form a crust [even] on the top surface while it is still day.

M. 1:11 They lower the Passover-offering into an oven at dusk [when the fourteenth of Nisan falls on a Friday]. And they light the fire in the fireplace of the House of the Hearth. But in the provinces, [they do so only if] there is sufficient time for the flame to catch over the larger part of [the wood].

II. PREPARING FOR THE SABBATH: LIGHT, FOOD, CLOTHING

A. THE SABBATH LAMP

M. 2:1 With what do they kindle [the Sabbath light] and with what do they not kindle [it]? They do not kindle with (1) cedar fiber, (2) uncarded flax, (3) raw silk, (4) wick of bast, (5) wick of the desert, (6) or seaweed; or with (1) pitch, (2) wax, (3) castor oil, (4) oil [given to a priest as heave-offering which had become unclean and must therefore be] burned, (5) [grease from] the fat tail, or (6) tallow.

M. 2:2 All kinds of oils are permitted: (1) Sesame oil, (2) nut oil, (3) fish oil, (4) colocynth oil, (5) tar, and (6) naphtha.

M. 2:3 With nothing which exudes from a tree do they light [the Sabbath light], except for flax. And nothing which exudes from a tree contracts uncleanness [as a tent] through overshadowing [a corpse] except for flax.

M. 2:4 A person should not pierce an eggshell with oil and put it on the opening of a lamp so that [the oil] will drip [out and sustain the lamp], even if it is made out of earthenware, But if the potter joined it to begin with [to the lamp], it is permitted, because it is one utensil. A person may not fill a dish with oil and put it beside a lamp and place the head of the wick into it, so that it will draw [oil from the dish of oil].

M. 2:5 He who puts out a lamp because he is afraid of gentiles, thugs, a bad spirit, or if it is so that a sick person might sleep, is exempt [from liability to punishment]. [If he did so], to spare the lamp, the oil, the wick, he is liable.

M. 2:7 Three things must a man state in his house on the eve of Sabbath at dusk: (1) "Have you tithed?" (2) "Have you prepared the symbolic meal of fusion [to unite distinct domains for purposes of carrying on the Sabbath]?" (3) "[Then] kindle the lamp [for the Sabbath]."

M. 2:7 [If] it is a matter of doubt whether or not it is getting dark, (1) they do not tithe that which is certainly untithed, (2) and they do not immerse utensils, (3) and they do not kindle lamps. (1) But they do tithe that which is doubtfully tithed produce, (2) and they do prepare the symbolic meal of fusion [to unite distinct domains for purposes of carrying on the Sabbath], (3) and they do cover up what is to be kept hot.

B. FOOD FOR THE SABBATH

M. 3:1 A double stove that [people] have heated with stubble or straw – they put cooked food on it. [But if they heated it] with peat or with wood, one may not put [anything] on it until he has swept it out, or until he has covered it with ashes.

M. 3:2 An oven which [people] have heated with stubble or with straw — one should not put anything either into it or on top of it. A single stove which [people] have heated with stubble or with straw, lo, this is equivalent to a double stove. [If they heated it] with peat or with wood, lo, it is equivalent to an oven.

M. 3:3 They do not put an egg beside a kettle [on the Sabbath] so that it will be cooked. And one should not crack it into [hot] wrappings. And one should not bury it in sand or in road dirt so that it will be roasted.

M. 3:4 A *miliarum* which is cleared of ashes — they drink from it on the Sabbath. An antikhi [boiler], even though it is clear of ashes — they do not drink from it.

M. 3:5 A kettle [containing hot water] which one removed [from the stove] — one should not put cold water into it so that it [the cold water] may get warm. But one may put [enough cold water] into it or into a cup so that [the hot water] will cool off. The pan or pot which one has taken off the stove while it is boiling — one may not put spices into it. But he may put [spices] into [hot food which is] in a plate or a dish.

M. 3:6 [On the Sabbath] they do not put a utensil under a lamp to catch the oil. But if one put it there while it is still day, it is permitted. But they do not use any of that oil [on the Sabbath], since it is not something which was prepared [before the Sabbath for use on the Sabbath]. They carry a new lamp, but not an old one. They put a utensil under a lamp to catch the sparks. But [on the Sabbath] one may not put water into it, because he thereby puts out [the sparks].

M. 4:1 With what do they cover [up food to keep it hot], and with what do they not cover up [food to keep it hot]? They do not cover with (1) peat, (2) compost, (3) salt, (4) lime, or (5) sand, whether wet or dry. or with (6) straw, (7) grape skins, (8) flocking [rags], or (9) grass, when wet. But they do cover up [food to keep it hot] with them when they are dry. They cover up [food to keep it hot] with (1) cloth, (2) produce, (3) the wings of a dove, (4) carpenters' sawdust, and (5) soft hatcheled flax.

M. 4:2 They cover up [food to keep it hot] with fresh hides, and they carry [handle] them; with wool shearings, but they do not carry them. What does one do? He [simply] takes off the cover, and [the wool shearings] fall off [on their own]. [If] he did not cover up [the food] while it is still day, he should not cover it up after dark. [But if] he covered it up and it became uncovered, it is permitted to cover it up again. One fills a jug [on the Sabbath with cold food or liquid] and puts it under a pillow or a blanket [to keep it cool].

C. ORNAMENTS FOR ANIMALS, CLOTHING FOR PERSONS

A. ANIMALS

M. 5:1 With what does a beast (Ex. 20:10) go out [on the Sabbath], and with what does it not go out? (1) A camel goes out with its curb, (2) a female camel with its nose ring, (3) a Libyan ass with its bridle, (4) and a horse with its chain. And all beasts which wear a chain go out with a chain and are led by a chain, and they sprinkle on the [chains if they become unclean] and immerse them in place [without removing them].

M. 5:2 An ass goes out with its saddle cloth when it is tied on to him. Rams go out strapped up [at the male organ]. And female [sheep] go forth (1) strapped over their tails, (2) under their tails, or (3) wearing protective cloths.

M. 5:3 And with what does [a beast] not go out? (1) A camel does not go out with a pad, nor (2) with forelegs bound together [or: hind legs bound together] or (3) with a hoof tied back to the shoulder. And so is the rule for all other beasts. One should not tie camels to one another and lead them. But one puts the ropes [of all of them] into his hand and leads them, so long as he does not twist [the ropes together].

M. 5:4 (1) An ass does not go out with its saddle cloth when it is not tied to him, or with a bell, even though it is plugged, or with the ladder yoke around its neck, or with a strap on its leg. And (2) fowl do not go forth with ribbons or straps on their legs. And (3) rams do not go forth with a wagon under their fat tail. And (4) ewes do not go forth protected [with the wood chip in their nose]. And (5) a calf does not go out with its rush yoke. Or (6) a cow with a hedgehog skin [tied around the udder], or with a strap between its horns.

B. PERSONS

M. 6:1 With what does a woman go out, and with what does she not go out? A woman should not go out with (1) woolen ribbons, (2) flaxen ribbons, or (3) with bands around her head (4) or with a headband, (5) head bangles, when they are not sewn on, (6) or with a hair-net, into the public domain. Nor [should she go out] (1) with a [tiara in the form of] a golden city, (2) a necklace, (3) nose rings, (4) a ring lacking a seal, or (5) a needle lacking a hole. But if she went out [wearing any one of these] she is not liable for a sin-offering.

M. 6:2 A man should not go out with (1) a nail-studded sandal, (2) a single sandal if he has no wound on his foot, (3) Tefillin, (4) an amulet when it is not by an expert, (5) a breastplate, (6) a helmet, or (7) with greaves. But if he went out [wearing any one of these], he is not liable to a sin-offering.

M. 6:3 A woman should not go out with (1) a needle which has a hole, (2) with a ring which has a seal, (3) with a cochleae brooch, (4) with a spice box, or (5) with a perfume flask.

M. 6:4 A man should not go out with (1) a sword, (2) bow, (3) shield, (4) club, or (5) spear. And if he went out, he is liable to a sin-offering. A garter is insusceptible to uncleanness, and they go out in it on the Sabbath. Ankle chains are susceptible to uncleanness, and they do not go out in them on the Sabbath.

M. 6:5 A woman goes out in hair ribbons, whether made of her own hair or of the hair of another woman or of a beast; and with (1) headband, (2) head bangles sewn [on the headdress], (3) a hair-net, and (4) wig, in the courtyard; (1) with wool in her ear, (2) wool in her sandals, (3) wool she has used for a napkin for her menstrual flow; (1) pepper, (2) a lump of salt, and (3) anything she puts into her mouth, on condition that she not first put it there on the Sabbath. And if it fell out, she may not put it back.]

M. 6:6 She goes out with a sela coin on a bunion. Little girls go out with threads and even ships in their ears. Arabian women go out veiled. Median women go out with cloaks looped up over their shoulders. And [so is the rule] for any person, but sages spoke concerning prevailing conditions.

M. 6:7 She weights her cloak with a stone, a nut, or a coin, on condition that she not attach the weight first on the Sabbath.

M. 6:8 A cripple's knee pads (1) are susceptible to uncleanness imparted by pressure [to something upon which a Zab may lie or sit], (2) they go forth with them on the Sabbath, and (3) they go into a courtyard with them. His chair and its pads (1) are susceptible to uncleanness imparted by pressure, (2) they do not go out with them on the Sabbath, and (3) they do not go in with them into a courtyard. An artificial arm is insusceptible to uncleanness, and they do not go out in it.

M. 6:9 Boys go out in garlands, and princes with bells. [And so is the rule] for any person, but sages spoke concerning prevailing conditions.

We come to the high point of the tractate, Mishnah-tractate Shabbat Chapter Seven, its systematic exposition of the governing principles expressed through generalizations in the Mishnah's best manner. No other Judaic law code of antiquity comes close to the standard set here (as at Mishnah-tractate Baba Qamma Chapter One) for topical cogency and comprehensiveness attained through syllogistic exposition.

III. PROHIBITED ACTS OF LABOR ON THE SABBATH: NOT TRANSPORTING OBJECTS FROM ONE DOMAIN TO ANOTHER

A. THE GENERATIVE CATEGORIES OF PROHIBITED ACTS OF LABOR

M. 7:1 A governing principle did they state concerning the Sabbath: Whoever forgets the basic principle of the Sabbath and performs many acts of labor on many different Sabbath days is liable only for a single sin-offering. He who knows the principle of the Sabbath and performs many acts of labor on many different Sabbaths is liable for the violation of each and every Sabbath. He who knows that it is the Sabbath and performs many acts of labor on many different Sabbaths is liable for the violation of each and every generative category of labor. He who performs many acts of labor of a single type is liable only for a single sin-offering.

M. 7:2 The generative categories of acts of labor [prohibited on the Sabbath] are forty less one: (1) he who sows, (2) ploughs, (3) reaps, (4) binds sheaves, (5) threshes, (6) winnows, (7) selects [fit from unfit produce or crops], (8) grinds, (9) sifts, (10) kneads, (11) bakes; (12) he who shears wool, (13) washes it, (14) beats it, (15) dyes it; (16) spins, (17) weaves, (18) makes two loops, (19) weaves two threads, (20) separates two threads; (21) ties, (22) unties, (23) sews two stitches, (24) tears in order to sew two stitches; (25) he who traps a deer, (26) slaughters it, (27) flays it, (28) salts it, (29) cures its hide, (30) scrapes it, and (31) cuts it up; (32) he who writes two letters, (33) erases two letters in order to write two letters; (34) he who builds, (35) tears down; (36) he who puts out a fire, (37) kindles a fire; (38) he who hits with a hammer; (39) he who transports an object from one domain to another — lo, these are the forty generative acts of labor less one.

B. DOMAINS AND THE PROHIBITION OF TRANSPORTING OBJECTS FROM ONE DOMAIN TO ANOTHER

M. 7:3 And a further governing rule did they state: Whatever is suitable for storage, which people generally store in such quantity as one has taken out on the Sabbath — he is liable to a sin-offering on its account. And whatever is not suitable for storage, which people generally do not store in such quantity as one has taken out on the Sabbath – only he is liable on its account who stores it away [and who then takes it out].

M. 7:4 He who takes out a quantity of (1) straw sufficient for a cow's mouthful; (2) pea stalks sufficient for a camel's mouthful; (3) ears of grain sufficient for a lamb's mouthful; (4) grass sufficient for a kid's mouthful; (5) garlic or onion leaves, ([if] fresh, a dried fig's bulk), [and if] dry, sufficient for a kid's mouthful is liable,] and they do not join together with one another [to form a quantity sufficient for culpability], because they are not subject to equivalent measures. He who takes out foodstuffs [for a human being] in the volume of a dried fig is liable. And they do join together with one another [to form a quantity sufficient for culpability], because they are subject to equivalent measures, except for their (1) husks, (2) kernels, (3) stalks, (4) coarse bran, and (5) fine bran.

M. 8:1 He who takes out (1) wine — [is culpable if it is] enough to mix a cup; (2) milk — enough for a gulp; (3) honey — enough to put on a sore; (4) oil — enough to anoint a small limb; (5) water — enough to rub off an eye salve; and (6) of all other liquids, a quarter-log; (7) and of all slops [refuse], a quarter-log.

M. 8:2-4 He who takes out (1) rope — enough to make a handle for a basket; (2) reed cord — enough to make a hanger for a sifter or a sieve — (3) paper — enough to write on it a receipt for a tax collector. And he who takes out (1) a receipt for a tax collector is liable; (2) used paper — enough to wrap around a small perfume bottle. (3) Leather — enough to make an amulet; (4) parchment — enough to write on it a small pericope of the Tefillin, which is "Hear O Israel"; (5) ink — enough to write two letters; (6) eye shadow — enough to shadow one eye. (7) Lime — enough to put on the head of a lime twig; (8) pitch or sulfur — enough for making a small hole; (9) wax — enough to put over a small hole; (10) clay — enough to make the [bellow's] hole of the crucible of a goldsmith. (11) Bran — enough to put on the mouth of the crucible of a goldsmith; (12) quicklime — enough to smear the little finger of a girl.

M. 8:5 Earth for clay — enough to make a seal for a letter. (2) Manure or (3) fine sand — enough to manure a cabbage stalk, enough to manure a leek. (4) Coarse sand — enough to cover a plasterer's trowel; (5) reed — enough to make a pen. And if it was thick or broken — enough to [make a fire to] cook the smallest sort of egg, mixed [with oil] and put in a pan.

M. 8:6 (1) Bone — enough to make a spoon. (2) Glass — enough to scrape the end of a shuttle; (3) pebble or stone — enough to throw at a bird.

M. 9:5 He who brings out wood — [is liable if he carries out] enough to cook a small egg; spices — enough to spice a small egg; and they join together with one another [to make up the requisite quantity to impose liability]. (1) Nutshells, (2) pomegranate shells, (3) woad, and (4) dyer's madder — enough to dye a garment as small as a hair-net; (5) urine, (6) soda, (7) soap, (8) cimolian earth, or (9) lion's leaf — enough to launder a garment as small as a hair-net.

M. 9:6 (1) Pepper in any quantity at all; (2) tar in any quantity at all; (3) various sorts of spices and metal tools in any quantity at all; (1) stones of the altar, (2) dirt of the altar, (3) worn-out holy books, and (4) their worn-out covers — in any quantity at all. They store them away in order to hide them [for permanent storage].

M. 9:7 He who takes out a peddler's basket, even though there are many different sorts of things in it, is liable only for a single sin-offering. Garden seeds — less than a dried fig's bulk. [The standard measures for the following are:] (1) for cucumber seeds — two, (2) gourd seeds — two, (3) Egyptian bean seeds — two; [the standard measure for] (1) a clean, live locust — in any quantity whatsoever; [the standard measure for] (2) a dead one — the size of a dried fig; [the standard measure for] (3) 'a vineyard bird' [a kind of locust] whether alive or dead — in any quantity at all, for they store it away for [later use as] a remedy.

M. 10:1 He who put [something] away for seed, for a sample, or for a remedy and [then] took it out on the Sabbath is liable in any amount whatsoever. But any [other] person is liable on that same account only in the specified measure pertinent to [that sort of thing]. [If the person] went and put it back, he is liable [should he take it out again] only in the specified measure pertinent to it.

C. THE PROHIBITION OF CARRYING ON THE SABBATH ACROSS THE LINES OF DOMAINS

M. 10:2 He who takes out food and puts it down on the threshold, whether he then went and took it out, or someone else took it out, is exempt [from liability to a sin-offering], for he has not [completely] performed his prohibited act of labor at one time. A basket which is full of produce, which one put on the outer [half of the] threshold, even though the larger quantity of the produce is outside — he is exempt, unless he takes out the entire basket.

M. 10:3 He who takes [something] out, (1) whether in his right hand or in his left, (2) in his lap or (3) on his shoulder, is liable, for so is the manner of carrying [an object] by the children of Kohath (Num. 7:9). [If he takes something out] (1) on the back of his hand, (2) on his foot, (3) in his mouth, (4) in his elbow, (5) in his ear, or (6) in his hair, (1) in his wallet with its mouth downward, (2) between his wallet and his cloak, (3) in the hem of his cloak, (4) in his shoe, (5) in his sandal, he is exempt [from liability to a sin-offering]. For he has not carried [the object] out the way people [generally] carry out [objects].

M. 10:4 He who intends to take out something before him, and it slipped behind him is exempt. [If he intended to carry it out] behind him and it slipped in front of him, he is liable. Truly did they say, A woman who wore drawers [and took something out in them], whether in front of her or behind her, is liable, for they are likely to be moved around.

M. 10:5 He who takes out a loaf of bread into the public domain is liable. [If] two people took it out, they are exempt. [If] one person could not take it out, but two people took it out, they are liable. He who takes out food in a volume less than the specified measure in a utensil is exempt even on account of [taking out] the utensil, for the utensil is secondary to it [the food]. [He who takes out] a living person in a bed is exempt even on account of [taking out] the bed, for the bed is secondary to him. [If he took out] a corpse in a bed, he is liable. And so [one who takes out] an olive's bulk of corpse matter and an olive's bulk of carrion and a lentil's bulk of a dead creeping thing is liable.

M. 10:6 He who pares his fingernails with one another, or with his teeth, so, too, [if he pulled out the hair of] his (1) head, (2) moustache, or (3) beard — and so she who (1) dresses her hair, (2) puts on eye-shadow, or (3) rouges her face — these acts are prohibited because of [the principle of] Sabbath rest. He who picks [something] from a pot which has a hole [in the bottom] is liable. [If he picks something from a pot] which has no hole [in the bottom], he is exempt.

D. THROWING OBJECTS FROM ONE DOMAIN TO ANOTHER

M. 11:1 He who throws [an object] from private domain to public domain, [or] from public domain to private domain, is liable. [He who throws an object] from private domain to private domain, and public domain intervenes is exempt from penalty. How so? Two balconies opposite one another [extending] into the public domain — he who stretches out or throws [an object] from this one to that one is exempt. [If] both of them were [different private domains on the same side of the street and] at the same story, he who stretches [an object over] is liable, and he who throws from one to the other is exempt. For thus was the mode of labor of the Levites: Two wagons, one after the other, in the public domain — they stretch beams from this one to that one, but they do not throw [them from one to the other].

M. 11:2 The bank of a cistern and the rock ten handbreadths high and four broad
— he who takes [something] from that area or who puts something onto that area is liable.
[If they were] less than the stated measurements, he is exempt [from any penalty for such
an action].

M. 11:3 He who throws [something from a distance of] four cubits toward a
wall — [if he throws it] above ten handbreadths, it is as if he throws it into the air [which
is public domain]. [If it is] less than ten handbreadths, it is as if he throws an object onto
the ground [which is private domain]. He who throws [an object to a distance of] four
cubits on the ground, is liable. [If] he threw [an object] within the space of four cubits and
it rolled beyond four cubits, he is exempt. [If he threw an object] beyond four cubits and
it rolled back into four cubits, he is liable.

M. 11:4 He who throws [an object to a distance of] four cubits into the sea is
exempt. If it was shallow water and a public path passed through it, he who throws [an
object for a distance of] four cubits is liable. And what is the measure of shallow water?
Less than ten handbreadths in depth. [If there was] shallow water, and a public path goes
through it, he who throws into it to a distance of four cubits is liable.

M. 11:5 He who throws [an object] (1) from the sea to dry land or (2) from dry
land to the sea, or (3) from the sea to a boat, or (4) from a boat to the sea, or (5) from one
boat to another, is exempt. [If] boats are tied together, they move [objects] from one to the
next. If they are not tied together, even though they lie close together, they do not carry
[objects] from one to the other.

M. 11:6 He who throws [an object] and realizes [remembers what he has done]
after it leaves his hand, [if] another person caught it, [if] a dog caught it, or [if] it burned
up in a fire [intervening in its flight path] — he is exempt. [If] he threw it intending to
inflict a wound, whether at a man or at a beast, and realizes [what he has done] before it
inflicted the wound, he is exempt. This is the governing principle: All those who may be
liable to sin-offerings in fact are not liable unless at the beginning and the end, their [sin]
is done inadvertently. [But] if the beginning of their [sin] is inadvertent and the end is
deliberate, [or] the beginning deliberate and the end inadvertent, they are exempt — unless
at the beginning and at the end their [sin] is inadvertent.

IV. PROHIBITED ACTS OF LABOR

A. WHAT CONSTITUTES A WHOLE ACT OF LABOR

M. 12:1 He who builds — how much does he build so as to be liable [on that
count]? He who builds — in any measure at all. He who hews stone, hits with a hammer
or adze, bores — in any measure at all is liable. This is the governing principle: Whoever
on the Sabbath performs a forbidden act of labor and [the result of] his act of labor endures
is liable.

M. 12:2 He who ploughs — in any measure whatsoever, he who (1) weeds, he
who (2) cuts off dead leaves, and he who (3) prunes — in any measure whatsoever, is
liable. He who gathers branches of wood — if [it is] to improve the field — in any measure
at all; if [it is] for a fire — in a measure [of wood] sufficient to cook a small egg, [is
liable]. He who gathers herbs if [it is] to improve the field — in any measure at all; if it is
for cattle [to eat] — in the measure of a lamb's mouthful, [is liable].

M. 12:3 He who writes two letters, whether with his right hand or with his left, whether the same letter or two different letters, whether with different pigments, in any alphabet, is liable.

M. 12:4 He who writes two letters during a single spell of inadvertence is liable. [If] he wrote with (1) ink, (2) caustic, (3) red dye, (4) gum, or (5) copperas, or with anything which leaves a mark, on two walls forming a corner, or on two leaves of a tablet, which are read with one another, he is liable. He who writes on his flesh is liable.

M. 12:5 If] one wrote with (1) fluids [blood, water, milk, honey, (2) fruit juice, (3) dirt from the street, (4) writer's sand, or with anything which does not leave a lasting mark, he is exempt. (1) [If he wrote] with the back of his hand, with his foot, mouth, or elbow, (2) [if] he wrote one letter alongside a letter already written, (3) [if] he wrote a letter on top of a letter [already written], (4) [if] he intended to write a het and wrote two zayins, (5) [if he wrote] one on the ground and one on the beam, (6) [if] he wrote [two letters] on the two walls of the house, on the two sides of a leaf of paper, so that they cannot be read with one another, he is exempt.

M. 13:2 He who makes two meshes for the heddles or the sley [of a loom], [or two meshes] in a sifter, sieve, or basket, is liable. He who sews two stitches [is liable]. And he who tears in order to sew two stitches [is liable].

M. 13:3 He who tears [his clothing] because of his anger or on account of his bereavement, and all those who effect destruction, are exempt. But he who destroys in order to improve — the measure [for] his [action] is the same as for him who improves.

M. 13:4 The measure for one who bleaches, hackles, dyes, or spins is a double sit. And he who weaves two threads — his measure is a sit.

M. 13:5 [He who drives] a bird into a tower trap, or a deer into a house, into a courtyard, or into a corral is liable. This is the governing principle: [If] it yet lacks further work of hunting, he [who pens it in on the Sabbath] is exempt. [If] it does not lack further work of hunting, he is liable.

M. 13:6 A deer which entered a house, and someone locked it in — he [who locked it in] is liable. [If] two people locked it in, they are exempt. [If] one person could not lock the door, and two people did so, they are liable.

M. 13:7 [If] one of them sat down at the doorway and did not completely fill it [so that the deer could yet escape], but a second person sat down and finished filling it, the second person is liable. [If] the first person sat down at the doorway and filled it up, and a second one came along and sat down at his side, even though the first one got up and went along, the first remains liable, and the second exempt. lo, to what is this equivalent? To one who locks his house to shut it up [and protect it], and a deer turns out to be shut up [and trapped] inside.

M. 14:1 The eight creeping things mentioned in the Torah [the weasel, mouse, great lizard, gecko, land crocodile, lizard, sand lizard, and chameleon] — he who hunts them or wounds them is liable. And as to all other abominations and creeping things, he who wounds them is exempt. He who hunts them for use is liable. [He who hunts them] not for use is exempt. A wild beast and a bird which are in his domain — he who hunts them is exempt. He who wounds them is liable.

M. 14:2 They do not make pickling brine on the Sabbath. But one makes salt water and dips his bread in it and puts it into cooked food.

B. HEALING ON THE SABBATH

M. 14:3 They do not eat Greek hyssop on the Sabbath, because it is not a food for healthy people. But one eats pennyroyal or drinks knot grass water. All sorts of foods a person eats [which serve for] healing, and all such drinks he may drink, except for palm tree water [purgative water] or a cup of root water, because they are [solely] for jaundice. But one may drink palm tree water [to quench] his thirst. And one anoints with root oil, [if it is] not for healing.

M. 14:4 He who has tooth problems may not suck vinegar through them. But he dunks [his bread] in the normal way, and if he is healed, he is healed. He who is concerned about his loins [which give him pain], he may not anoint them with wine or vinegar. But he anoints with oil — not with rose oil. Princes [on the Sabbath] anoint themselves with rose oil on their wounds, since it is their way to do so on ordinary days.

C. KNOT-TYING, CLOTHING AND BEDS

M. 15:1 On account of [tying] what sorts of knots [on the Sabbath] are [people] liable? (1) A camel driver's knot, and (2) a sailor's knot. And just as one is liable for tying them, so he is liable for untying them.

M. 15:2 You have knots on account of which they are not liable, like a camel driver's knot and a sailor's knot. A woman ties (1) the slit of her shift, (2) the strings of her hair-net and of her belt, (3) the thongs of a shoe or sandal, (4) [leather] bottles of wine or oil, and (5) a cover over meat. They tie a bucket with a belt but not with a rope.

M. 15:3 They fold up clothing even four or five times. And they spread beds on the night of the Sabbath for use on the Sabbath, but not on the Sabbath for use after the Sabbath.

V.   ACTIONS THAT ARE PERMITTED ON THE SABBATH

A. SAVING OBJECTS FROM A FIRE ON THE SABBATH

M. 16:1 All Holy Scriptures — do they save from fire, whether they read in them or do not read in them. And even though they are written in any language [besides Hebrew], [if they become useless] they require storage [and are not to be burned]. And on what account do they not read in [some of] them? Because of the neglect of the [proper study of the Torah in the] study house. they save the case of the scroll with the scroll and the case of the phylacteries with the phylacteries, even though there is money in them. And where do they [take them to] save them? To a closed alley [which is not open as a thoroughfare and so is not public domain].

M. 16:2 They save food enough for three meals — [calculated from] what is suitable for human beings for human beings, what is suitable for cattle for cattle. How so? [If] a fire broke out on the night of the Sabbath, they save food for three meals. [If it broke out] in the morning, they save food for two meals. [If it broke out] in the afternoon, [they save food for] one meal.

M. 16:3 They save a basket full of loaves of bread, even if it contains enough food for a hundred meals, a wheel of pressed figs, and a jug of wine. And one says to others, "Come and save [what you can] for yourselves [as well]." Now if they were intelligent, they come to an agreement with him after the Sabbath. Where do they [take them to] save them? To a courtyard which is included within the Sabbath limit that fuses the area into a single domain [erub].

M. 16:4 And to that place [M. 16:3F-H] one takes out all his utensils. And he puts on all the clothing which he can put on, and he cloaks himself in all the cloaks he can put on. And he goes back, puts on clothing, and takes it out, and he says to others, "Come and save [the clothing] with me."

M. 16:6 A gentile who came to put out a fire — they do not say to him, "Put it out," or "Do not put it out," for they are not responsible for his Sabbath rest. But a minor [Israelite child] who came to put out a fire — they do not hearken to him [and let him do so], because his Sabbath rest is their responsibility.

M. 16:7 They cover a lamp with a dish so that it will not scorch a rafter; and the excrement of a child; and a scorpion, so that it will not bite.

M. 16:8 A gentile who lit a candle — an Israelite may make use of its light. But [if he did so] for an Israelite, it is prohibited [to do so on the Sabbath]. [If a gentile] drew water to give water to his beast, an Israelite gives water to his beast after him. But [if he did so] for an Israelite, it is prohibited [to use it on the Sabbath]. [If] a gentile made a gangway by which to come down from a ship, an Israelite goes down after him. But [if he did so] for an Israelite, it is prohibited [to use it on the Sabbath].

B. HANDLING OBJECTS ON THE SABBATH IN PRIVATE DOMAIN

M. 17:1 All utensils are handled on the Sabbath, and their [detached] doors along with them, even though they were detached on the Sabbath. For they are not equivalent to doors of a house, for the [latter] are not prepared [in advance of the Sabbath to be used].

M. 17:2 One handles (1), a hammer to split nuts, (2) an ax to chop off a fig, (3) a saw to cut through cheese, (4) a shovel to scoop up dried figs, (5) a winnowing shovel or (6) a fork to give something thereon to a child, (7) a spindle or (8) a shuttle staff to thrust into something, (9) a sewing needle to take out a thorn, (10) a sack maker's needle to open a door.

M. 17:3 A reed for olives, if it has a knot on its top, receives uncleanness. And if not, it does not receive uncleanness. One way or the other, it is handled on the Sabbath.

M. 17:4 All utensils are handled in case of need and not in case of need.

M. 17:5 All utensils which are handled on the Sabbath — fragments deriving from them may be handled along with them, on condition that they perform some sort of useful work [even if it is not what they did when they were whole]: [So how large must these fragments be to be regarded as useful for some work, if not the work they originally did?] (1) fragments of a kneading trough — [must be sufficiently large on their own] to cover the mouth of a barrel, (2) glass fragments — [must be sufficiently large on their own] to cover the mouth of a flask.

M. 17:6 A stone in a gourd shell [used for weighting it] — if they draw water in it and it does not fall out, they draw water with it [the gourd shell]. And if not, they do not draw water with it. A branch tied to a pitcher — they draw water with it on the Sabbath.

M. 17:7 The window shutter [stopper of a skylight] — they shut the window with it."

M. 17:8 All utensil covers which have handles are handled on the Sabbath.

M. 18:1 They clear away even four or five baskets of straw or grain on account of guests, or on account of [avoiding] neglect of the house of study. But [they do] not [clear away] a storeroom. They clear away (1) clean heave-offering, (2) doubtfully tithed produce, (3) first tithe the heave-offering of which has been removed, (4) second tithe and (5) consecrated produce which have been redeemed; and dried lupine, for it is food for poor people; but [they do] not [clear away] (6) produce from which tithes have not been removed, (7) first tithe the heave-offering of which has not been removed, (8) second tithe and (9) consecrated produce which have not been redeemed; arum, or mustard.

M. 18:2 Bundles of straw, branches, or young shoots — if one prepared them for food for cattle, they handle them, And if not, they do not handle them. They turn up a basket for chickens, so that they may go up [into the hen house] and down on it. A chicken that fled — they drive it along until it goes back [into the chicken yard]. They pull calves or young asses in the public way. A mother drags along her child.

M. 18:3 They do not deliver the young of cattle on the festival, but they help out. And they do deliver the young of a woman on the Sabbath. They call a midwife for her from a distant place, and they violate the Sabbath on her [the woman in childbirth's] account. And they tie the umbilical cord.

C. CIRCUMCISION ON THE SABBATH

M. 18:3 And all things required for circumcision do they perform on the Sabbath.

M. 19:1 Any sort of labor [in confection with circumcision] which it is possible to do on the eve of the Sabbath does not override [the restrictions of] the Sabbath, and that which it is not possible to do on the eve of the Sabbath does override [the prohibitions of] the Sabbath.

M. 19:2 They do prepare all that is needed for circumcision on the Sabbath: they (1) cut [the mark of circumcision], (2) tear, (3) suck [out the wound]. And they put on it a poultice and cumin. If one did not pound it on the eve of the Sabbath, he chews it in his teeth and puts it on. If one did not mix wine and oil on the eve of the Sabbath, let this be put on by itself and that by itself. And they do not make a bandage in the first instance. But they wrap a rag around [the wound of the circumcision]. If one did not prepare [the necessary rag] on the eve of the Sabbath, he wraps [the rag] around his finger and brings it, and even from a different courtyard.

M. 19:3 They wash off the infant, both before the circumcision and after the circumcision, and they sprinkle him, [If the sexual traits of the infant are a matter of] doubt, or [if the infant] bears the sexual traits of both sexes, they do not violate the Sabbath on his account.

M. 19:4 He who had two infants, one to circumcise after the Sabbath and one to circumcise on the Sabbath, and who forgot [which was which] and circumcised the one to be circumcised after the Sabbath on the Sabbath, is liable. [If he had] one to circumcise on the eve of the Sabbath and one to circumcise on the Sabbath, and he forgot and on the Sabbath, circumcised the one to be circumcised on the eve of the Sabbath,

M. 19:5 An infant is circumcised on the eighth, ninth, tenth, eleventh or twelfth day [after birth], never sooner, never later. How so? Under normal circumstances, it is on the eighth day. [If] he was born at twilight, he is circumcised on the ninth day. [If he was born] at twilight on the eve of the Sabbath, he is circumcised on the tenth day [the following Sunday]. In the case of a festival which falls after the Sabbath, he will be circumcised on the eleventh day [Monday]. In the case of two festival days of the New Year, he will be circumcised on the twelfth day [Tuesday]. An infant who is sick — they do not circumcise him until he gets well.

M. 19:6 These are the shreds [of the foreskin, if they remain] which render the circumcision invalid: flesh which covers the greater part of the corona — and such a one does not eat heave-offering. And if he was fat [so the corona appears to be covered up], one has to fix it up for appearance's sake. [If] one circumcised but did not tear the inner lining [the cut did not uncover the corona, since the membrane was not split and pulled down], it is as if he did not perform the act of circumcision.

D. PREPARING FOOD FOR MAN AND BEAST

M. 20:1 (1) On the festival they do not spread out a strainer, and (2) on the Sabbath they do not pour [wine] into one which is spread out. But on the festival they pour [wine] into one which is spread out.

M. 20:2 They pour water over wine dregs so that they will be clarified. And they strain wine in cloths or in a twig basket. And they put an egg into a mustard strainer. And they prepare honeyed wine on the Sabbath.

M. 20:3 They do not soak asafoetida in warm water. But one puts it into vinegar. And they do not soak vetches or rub them. But one puts them into a sieve or a basket. They do not sift chopped straw in a sifter. Nor does one put it on a high place so that the chaff will fall out. But one takes it in a sieve and pours it into the crib.

M. 20:4 They take [fodder] from before one beast and put it before another beast on the Sabbath.

M. 20:5 The straw which is on the bed — One should not shift it with his hand. But he shifts it with his body. And if it was food for a beast, or if there was a cushion or a sheet on it, he may shift it with his hand. A press used by householders do they loosen but do they not tighten. And one of laundrymen one should not touch [at all].

M. 21:1 A man takes up his child, with a stone in [the child's] hand, or a basket with a stone in it. And they handle unclean heave-offering along with clean heave-offering or with unconsecrated food.

M. 21:2 A stone which is over the mouth of a jar — One tilts [the jar] on its side and [the stone] falls off. [If] it [the jar] was among [other] jars, one lifts it [the jar] up and [then] turns it on its side, so that it [the stone] falls off. Coins which are on a pillow — One shakes the pillow, and they fall off. [If] there was snot on it, one wipes it off with a rag. [If] it was made of leather, they pour water on it until it [the snot] disappears.

M. 21:3 They remove from the table crumbs less than an olive's bulk in size, pods of chick-peas, and pods of lentils, because it is food for a beast. A sponge, if it has a handle — they wipe with it. And if not, they do not wipe with it.

M. 22:1 A jar which broke [on the Sabbath] — they save from it[s wine] enough sustenance for three meals. And one says to others, "Come along and save some for yourself" on condition that one not sponge it up. They do not squeeze pieces of fruit to get out the juice. And if the juice came out on its own, it is prohibited [for use on the Sabbath]. Honeycombs which one broke on the eve of the Sabbath and [their liquids] exuded on their own — they are prohibited.

M. 22:2 Whatever is put into hot water on the eve of the Sabbath — they soak it [again] in hot water on the Sabbath. And whatever is not put into hot water on the eve of the Sabbath — they [only] rinse it in hot water on the Sabbath, except for pickled fish, small salted fish, and Spanish tunny fish, for rinsing them is the completion of their preparation [for eating].

M. 22:3 A person breaks a jar to eat dried figs from it, on condition that he not intend [in opening the jar] to make it into a utensil. And they do not pierce it on the side. And if it was pierced, one should not put wax on it, because he would [have to] spread it over [which is a prohibited act].

M. 22:4 They put a cooked dish in a cistern so that it may be preserved, and [a vessel containing] fresh water into foul water to keep it cool, and cold water into the sun to warm it up. He whose clothing fell into water on the way goes along in them and does not scruple. [When] he reaches the outer courtyard, he spreads them out in the sun. But [this he does not do] in front of people.

M. 22:5 He who bathes in cave water or in the water of Tiberias and dried himself, even with ten towels, may not then carry them in his hand. But ten men dry their faces, hands, and feet with a single towel and bring it along in their hand.

M. 22:6 They anoint and massage the stomach. But they do not have it kneaded or scraped. They do not go down to a muddy wrestling ground. And they do not induce vomiting. And they do not straighten [the limb of] a child or set a broken limb. He whose hand or foot was dislocated should not pour cold water over them. But he washes in the usual way. And if he is healed, he is healed.

E. SEEMLY AND UNSEEMLY BEHAVIOR ON THE SABBATH

M. 23:1 A man [on the Sabbath] asks for jugs of wine or oil from his fellow, provided that he does not say to him, "Lend [them] to me." And so a woman [borrows] loaves of bread from her neighbor. And if one does not trust the other, he leaves his cloak with him and settles with him after the Sabbath. And so is the case on the eve of Passover in Jerusalem when that day coincides with the Sabbath: One leaves his cloak with him and takes his Passover lamb and settles with him after the festival.

M. 23:2 A man may count the number of his guests and the finger food portions orally, but not by what is written down. And he casts lots with his children and the members of his household at the table [to decide who gets which portion], on condition that he not intend to offset a larger portion, against a small one, because of [the prohibition of playing with] dice [on the Sabbath]. And they cast lots on a festival day for [which priest gets which part of] Holy Things, but not for the portions.

M. 23:3 A man should not hire workers on the Sabbath. And a man should not ask his fellow to hire workers for him. They do not wait at twilight at the Sabbath limit to hire workers, or to bring in produce. But one may wait at the Sabbath limit at twilight to guard [produce, and after nightfall] he brings back the produce in his hand. A governing principle did Abba Saul state, "Whatever I have the right to say [to another person to do], on that account I have the right to wait at twilight at the Sabbath limit."

M. 23:4 They wait at the Sabbath limit at twilight to attend to the business of a bride, and the affairs of a corpse, to bring it a coffin and wrappings. A gentile who brought wailing pipes on the Sabbath — an Israelite should not make a lament with them, unless they came from a nearby place, [If] they made for him [a gentile] a coffin and dug a grave for him, an Israelite may be buried therein. But if this was done for an Israelite, he may not ever be buried therein.

M. 23:5 They prepare all that is needed for a corpse. They anoint and rinse it, on condition that they not move any limb of the corpse. They remove the mattress from under it. And they put it on [cool] sand so that it will keep. They tie the chin, not so that it will go up, but so that it will not droop [further]. And so in the case of a beam which broke — they support it with a bench or the beams of a bed, not so that it will go up, but so that it will not droop further. They do not close the eyes of a corpse on the Sabbath, nor on an ordinary day at the moment the soul goes forth. And he who closes the eyes of a corpse at the moment the soul goes forth, lo, this one sheds blood.

M. 24:1 He who was overtaken by darkness on the road gives his purse to a gentile. If there is no gentile with him, he leaves it on an ass. [When] he reaches the outermost courtyard [of a town], he removes [from the ass] those utensils which may be handled on the Sabbath. And [as to] those [utensils] which are not to be handled on the Sabbath, he unloosens the ropes, and the bundles fall by themselves.

M. 24:2 They loosen bundles of hay in front of cattle, and they spread out bunches, but not small bundles. And they do not chop up unripe stalks of corn or carobs before cattle, whether large or small [beasts].

M. 24:3 They do not stuff food into a camel or cram it [into its mouth]. But they put food into its mouth. And they do not fatten calves [with food against their will], but they put food into their mouths [in the normal way]. And they force-feed chickens, They put water into the bran, but they do not knead it, And they do not put water before bees or doves which are in dovecotes. But they do put it before geese, chickens, and Herodian doves.

M. 24:4 They cut up gourds before cattle, and carrion meat before dogs.

M. 24:5 They abrogate vows on the Sabbath. And they receive questions concerning matters which are required for the Sabbath. They stop up a light hole. And they measure a piece of stuff and an immersion pool.

The details make the case, and the upshot is easily stated: we see not only a far more detailed exposition but a topically far more extensive one, which exhibits cogency and comprehensiveness. It is hardly necessary to note that the Mishnah systematically yields syllogisms, while CD does so only episodically. But to this point, we deal with a mass of data and articulate only the impression that those data are purposive and propositional. It is now my task to demonstrate that the Mishnah-tractate is coherent in its syllogistic repertoire: that through all its rich corpus of details it sets forth a few comprehensive principles. That demonstration establishes by the Mishnah's own criteria the superiority of the Mishnah over the Damascus Covenant in the presentation of the law of the Sabbath. By objective criteria, what is shown is the uniqueness of the Mishnah in Israelite context.

III. MISHNAH-TRACTATE SHABBAT AGAINST THE DAMASCUS COVENANT

What differentiates Mishnah-tractate Shabbat from the Damascus Covenant composite on the Sabbath and marks the former as different from the latter is now self-evident. In the setting of the shared topic, the Sabbath, the treatment by the Damascus Covenant is neither comprehensive nor cogent. It furthermore yields no syllogisms and manifests through its detail no encompassing propositions. And it does not lead beyond its topic to abstract principles of philosophy, theology, or law that govern through an entire system of norms on diverse subjects and relationships and transactions. But the Mishnah's tractate on the Sabbath possesses all these qualities.

It articulates in acute detail only a few generative conceptions, which I shall specify. And these encompass the whole. The handful of implicit governing principles, readily grasped through the details that are given, transforms into a cogent composition what on first glance appear to be bits and pieces of incoherent data no different from those of the Damascus Covenant in their miscellaneous quality.

We shall now see that the result of the applied reason and practical logic, most, though not all, of the Mishnah's concrete rulings that we have surveyed in section ii embody those few conceptions. To be sure, because of the promiscuous character of the Mishnah's illustrative compositions, which I have cited at tedious length, the Mishnah's Sabbath-Halakhah appears prolix. But in fact it is intellectually quite economical. Admittedly, the Mishnah-tractate's presentation of the Halakhah serves the dual purpose of setting forth governing conceptions through exemplary cases, on the one side, and supplying information required for the correct observance of the Sabbath, on the other. But the former task — instantiating, through exemplary cases, the generative conceptions of a broad and fundamental character — vastly predominates.

The repertoire of cases in the Mishnah merely serves as a medium for the concretization in normative action of certain large and encompassing conceptions, bearing no counterpart in CD's Sabbath laws. These implicit conceptions emerge when we survey the details of the law, specifying the passages of the Mishnah that through concrete cases work out the requirements of abstract principles that inhere. There are only six principles in all, and we find a place among those six generative principles for nearly the whole of the Halakhah before us. In my catalogue that follows I specify at the right-hand margin the Mishnah-compositions that recapitulate the problematics under discussion, so readers can test the validity of that claim. In my item-by-item survey I find only the following that fall entirely outside of the six comprehensive principles that govern throughout: M. 2:1, 3:1, 3:2, 4:1, 20:1-4, 23:1-2 — a negligible proportion of the whole. My catalogue of illustrations of no more than six governing principles thus covers nearly the entire Mishnah-tractate.

The conceptions are of two types, the one distinctive to the Sabbath, the other pertinent to a broad spectrum of Halakhic categories but here illustrated by cases involving the Sabbath. We begin with the more general. The latter type supplies the larger number of generative conceptions, concerning, first, intentionality, second, causality (cause and effect), and, third, how many things are one and one many. These constitute philosophical, not theological problems.

Let us consider the recurrent concerns that transcend the Sabbath altogether, starting with intentionality:

1. INTENTIONALITY: THE CLASSIFICATION OF AN ACTION IS GOVERNED BY THE INTENTION BY WHICH IT IS CARRIED OUT, SO TOO THE CONSEQUENCE:

A. One is not supposed to extinguish a flame, but if he does so for valid reasons, it is not a culpable action; if it is for selfish reasons, it is. If one deliberately violated the Sabbath, after the Sabbath one may not benefit from the action; if it was inadvertent, he may. We consider also the intentionality of gentiles. One may not benefit indirectly from a source of heat. But what happens *en passant,* and not by deliberation, is not subject to prohibition. Thus if a gentile lit a candle for his own purposes, the Israelite may benefit, but if he did so for an Israelite, the Israelite may not benefit.

B. If one did a variety of actions of a single classification in a single spell of inadvertence, he is liable on only one count.

C. In the case of anything that is not regarded as suitable for storage, the like of which in general people do not store away, but which a given individual has deemed fit for storage and has stored away, and which another party has come along and removed from storage and taken from one domain to another on the Sabbath — the party who moved the object across the line that separated the two domains has become liable by reason of the intentionality of the party who stored away this thing that is not ordinarily stored.

D. The act must be carried out in accord with the intent for culpability to be incurred. The wrong intention invalidates an act, the right one validates the same act. Thus a person breaks a jar to eat dried figs from it, on condition that he not intend [in opening the jar] to make it into a utensil.

M. 2:5, T. 2:16, T. 2:14, T. 2:17-18, 21,
M. 7:1-2, 10:4, 22:3-4

The principle that we take account of what one plans, not only what one does, and that the intentionality of an actor governs, yields at least four quite distinct results, none of them interchangeable with any of the others, but all of them subject to articulation in other contexts altogether, besides Shabbat.

To begin with, we deal with a familiar principle. Intentionality possesses taxonomic power. The status of an action — culpable or otherwise — is relative to the intent with which the action is carried out. That encompasses a gentile's action; he may not act in response to the will of an Israelite. But if he acts on his own account, then an Israelite *en passant* may benefit from what he has done.

If the intention is improper, the action is culpable, if proper, it is not. But so far as inadvertence is the opposite of intentionality, second, the result of the failure to will or plan is as consequential as the act of will. If one acts many times in a single spell of inadvertence, the acts are counted as one. This too is an entirely familiar notion.

The third entry is the most profound. To understand it, we have to know that the Halakhah in general takes account of what matters to people but treats as null what does not. Hence a sum of money or a volume of material deemed negligible is treated as though it did not exist.[16] If one deliberately transports a volume of material of such insufficient consequence that no one would store that volume of that material, no violation of the law against transporting objects has taken place. Transporting objects from one domain to the other matters only when what is transported is valued. What, then, about a volume of material that people in general deem null, but that a given individual regards as worth something? For example, people in general do not save a useless shard or remnant of fabric. But in a given case, an individual has so acted as to indicate he takes account of the shard. By his action he has imparted value to the shard, even though others would not concur. If then he has saved the negligible object, he has indicated that the shard matters. If someone else takes the shard out of storage and carries it from one domain to another, what is the result? Do we deem the one person's evaluation binding upon everyone else? Indeed we do, and the second party who does so is liable. The reason that ruling is not particular to the Sabbath becomes clear in the exegesis of the law, which carries us to a variety of other Halakhic topics altogether, e.g., what is susceptible to uncleanness must be deemed useful, and what is held of no account is insusceptible, and what a given person deems useful is taken into account, and the rest follows.

The fourth matter involving intentionality is a commonplace of the Halakhah and recapitulates the principle of the first. If someone acts in such a way as to violate the law but the act does not carry out his intent, he is not culpable; if he acts in accord with his intent and the intent is improper, he is culpable. So the match of intention and action serves to impose culpability.

In these ways, the particular law of Shabbat embodies general principles of intentionality that pertain to many other Halakhic rubrics. While these four exercises in the practical application of the theory of intentionality encompass the Halakhah of the Sabbath, none required the topic at hand in particular to make the point it wished to make; the applied reason and practical logic of intentionality yield only measured insight into the problematics of Shabbat.

The matter of causality produces a number of cases that make the same point, which is, we take account of indirect consequences, not only direct causality. But the consequences that we impute to indirect causality remain to be specified.

2.   NOT ONLY DIRECT, BUT INDIRECT CONSEQUENCES ARE TAKEN INTO ACCOUNT.

A. Since one may not perform an act of healing on the Sabbath, one may not consume substances that serve solely as medicine. But one may consume those that are eaten as food but also heal. One may lift a child, even though the child is holding something that one is not permitted to handle or move about; one may handle food that one may not eat (e.g., unclean) along with food that one may eat. One may not ask gentiles to do what he may not do, but one may wait at the Sabbath limit at twilight to do what one may ask another person to do. Thus: they do not go to the Sabbath limit to wait nightfall to bring in a beast. But if the beast was standing outside the Sabbath limit, one calls it and it comes on its own.

> M. 3:3, 4, 5, M. 4:2, M. 14:3-4,
> 16:7-8, 21:1-3, 23:3-4, 24:1-4

Once we distinguish indirect from direct causality, we want to know the degree to which, if at all, we hold a person responsible for what he has not directly caused; what level of culpability, if any, pertains? The point is that what comes about on its own, and not by the direct action of the Israelite adult, is deemed null. If one is permitted to eat certain foods, then those foods may be eaten on the Sabbath even though they possess, in addition to nourishment, healing powers. Indirect consequences of the action are null. One may carry a child, even though the child is holding something one may not carry. We impose a limit on the effects of causation, taking account of direct, but not indirect, results of one's action. One may make the case that the present principle places limits upon the one that assigns intentionality taxonomic power; here, even though one may will the result, if one has not directly brought about the result, he is still exempt from liability. In no way is this law particular to the Sabbath.

The third generative conception that in no way limits itself to Sabbath law involves assessing the manner in which we classify actions and the definition thereof. It invokes the rules of classification, e.g., when does an action encompass many episodes, and when does a single deed stand on its own? Sages conceive that a single spell of inadvertence, covering numerous episodes or transactions, constitutes one unitary action, the episodes being joined by the inadvertence of the actor, the actions then being treated as indivisible by reason of a single overarching intentionality, as we have already noted. They further conceive that numerous actions of a single type entail a single count of guilt, the repeated actions of the same classification constituting one protracted deed. On the other hand, by reason of consciousness, the performance of many actions entails guilt on each count, for each action on its own carries out the actor's intentionality. The larger problem of the many and the one forms the generative problematic of entire tractates, e.g., tractate Keritot, and enormous, interesting compositions of Halakhah are devoted to the way in which many things fall into a single classification, or a single category yields many subdivisions, e.g., tractate Peah (for land). In the present Halakhic rubric, the generative conception generates an elegant composition, but not a rich body of exegesis.

3. IN ASSESSING CULPABILITY FOR VIOLATING THE HALAKHAH OF THE SABBATH, WE RECKON THAT AN ACTION NOT ONLY MAY BE SUBDIVIDED BUT ALSO MAY BE JOINED WITH ANOTHER ACTION, SO THAT MULTIPLE ACTIONS YIELD A SINGLE COUNT OF CULPABILITY.

A. Thus whoever forgets the basic principle of the Sabbath and performs many acts of labor on many different Sabbath days is liable only for a single sin-offering. He who knows the principle of the Sabbath and performs many acts of labor on many different Sabbaths is liable for the violation of each and every Sabbath.

B. He who knows that it is the Sabbath and performs many acts of labor on many different Sabbaths is liable for the violation of each and every generative category of labor. He who performs many acts of labor of a single type is liable only for a single sin-offering.

M. 7:1-2, 22:5

Clearly, the principle that an act on its own is classified, as to culpability, by the considerations of intentionality, on the one side, and the classification of actions, on the other, cannot limit itself to the matter of the Sabbath. And we shall meet it many times in other areas of law altogether, e.g., oaths, acts of the contamination of the Temple (one or many spells of inadvertence, one or many types of action), and so on without limit.

A program of questions of general applicability to a variety of topics of the Halakhah clearly shaped the problematics of Shabbat. Intentionality, causality, and classification of the many as one and the one as many — these standard themes of philosophical inquiry turn out to shape the presentation of the Halakhah at hand, and, as my references indicate, the exegetical problems deemed to inhere in the topic at hand transform much of the Halakhah into an exercise in analytical thinking carried out in concrete terms — applied reason and practical logic of a philosophical character. If we were composing a handbook of Halakhic exegesis for a commentator intent on covering the entire surface of the Halakhah, the issue of the many and the one would take its place, alongside the issues of causality, direct and indirect, and the taxonomic power of intentionality. But the specificities of the Mishnah's Halakhah of the Sabbath in no way provided more than the occasion for a routine reprise of these familiar foci of exegesis.

If we had to stop at this point and generalize upon our results, we should conclude that the Mishnah's Halakhah on the Sabbath serves as a mere vehicle for the transmission of philosophical principles of general applicability. Cases of applied reason and practical logic sustain concrete illustration of abstractions, occasions for solution, in detail, of the working of axiomatic givens, governing postulates in the solution of problems of theory set forth in matters of fact. No problematics distinctive to the topic at hand precipitates deep thought that surfaces, in due course, in the formulation of specific problems and cases. Were we to close the matter where we now stand, then, the Mishnah's Halakhah of the Sabbath would appear to have no bearing upon the theme of the Sabbath, and that theme would appear to be interchangeable with any other for the purposes of the exegesis of abstract principles. Then, if we distinguish the philosophical, deriving from principles of general applicability based on analysis of everyday things, from the theological, deriving from distinctive conceptions based on divinely revealed conceptions, we should consequently assign the Halakhah a philosophical, but not a theological, task.

Such a result even merely on the face of things would prove dubious. For we should be left with a body of law disconnected from the religious life that accords to that law origins in revelation and authority in God's will. The Halakhah would emerge as the concretization of philosophical reflections that bear no consequence for the knowledge of God and what God has in mind for holy Israel. A mere medium of concretization of abstract thought, the Halakhah would contain within itself no deep thought upon theological principles, thought deriving from the revealed Torah. But as we shall now see, alongside systematic thinking about philosophical problems subject to generalization throughout the law, Mishnah-tractate Shabbat states in practical terms a set of conceptions deriving from a close reading of the Written Torah's account of the Sabbath.

These conceptions, framed in the same manner of concretization — practical logic and applied reason — embody deep thought about issues particular to the Sabbath. They yield conclusions that form the foundations of a massive theological structure, one built out of what is conveyed by revelation and implicit in the Torah's account of matters. These conclusions can have emerged only from the topic at hand. And the statement that sages wished to set forth can have come to systematic expression only in the particular setting defined by that topic. I cannot overstate matters. The Sabbath, and only the Sabbath, could produce a suitable statement of the conclusions sages set before us. And once in hand, the same conclusions turn out to delineate a vast world of cogent construction: the rules of creation as God intended it to be, translated into conduct in the here and now. When people study the details of the Halakhah, they encounter the concretization of governing conceptions revealed in the Torah in connection with the topic at hand and in no other conception.

Let me now specify what I conceive to be the encompassing principles, the generative conceptions that the laws embody and that animate the law in its most sustained and ambitious statements. They concern three matters, already signaled in my outline in section ii: [1] space, [2] time, and [3] activity, as the advent of the Sabbath affects all three.

The advent of the Sabbath transforms creation, specifically reorganizing space and time and reordering the range of permissible activity. First comes the transformation of space that takes effect at sundown at the end of the sixth day and that ends at sundown of the Sabbath day. At that time, for holy Israel, the entire world is divided into public domain and private domain, and what is located in the one may not be transported into the other. What is located in public domain may be transported only four cubits, that is, within the space occupied by a person's body. What is in private domain may be transported within the entire demarcated space of that domain. All public domain is deemed a single spatial entity, so too all private domain, so one may transport objects from one private domain to another. The net effect of the transformation of space is to move nearly all permitted activity to private domain and to close off public domain for all but the most severely limited activities; people may not transport objects from one domain to the other, but they may transport objects within private domain, so the closure of public domain from most activity, and nearly all material or physical activity, comes in consequence of the division of space effected by sunset at the end of the sixth day of the week.

1.   SPACE: On the Sabbath the household and village divide into private and public domain, and it is forbidden to transport objects from the one domain to the other:

A. Private domain is defined as at the very least an area ten handbreadths deep or high by four wide, public domain, an unimpeded space open to the public. There one may carry an object for no more than four cubits, which sages maintain is the dimension of man.

B. The sea, plain, *karmelit* [neutral domain], colonnade, and a threshold are neither private domain nor public domain. They do not carry or put [things] in such places. But if one carried or put [something into such a place], he is exempt [from punishment].

C. If in public domain one is liable for carrying an object four cubits, in private domain, there is no limit other than the outer boundaries of the demarcated area of the private domain, e.g., within the walls of the household.

D. What is worn for clothing or ornament does not violate the prohibition against carrying things from private to public domain. If one transports an object from private domain to private domain without bringing the object into public domain, e.g., by tossing it from private to private domain, he is not culpable.

M. 1:1, M. 6:1-9, 11:1-6

The point of the division into private and public domain emerges in the exposition of the distinction; it concerns transporting objects. One may cross the line, but not carry anything in so doing — hence the concern for what may or may not be worn as clothing. The same point emerges in the rule that one may move an object from one private domain to another, so long as public domain does not intervene. Carrying within public domain forms an equally important consideration; one may do so only within the space occupied by his very body, his person. But the four cubits a person occupies in public domain may be said to transform that particular segment of public domain into private domain, so the effect is the same. The delineation of areas that are not definitively public domain but also not private domain — the sea and the plain, which are not readily differentiated, the space within a colonnade, a threshold — simply refines and underscores the generative distinction of the two distinct domains.

So when it comes to space, the advent of the Sabbath divides into distinct domains for all practical purposes what in secular time is deemed divided only as to ownership, but united as to utilization. Sacred time then intensifies the arrangements of space as public and private, imparting enormous consequence to the status of what is private. There, and only there, on the Sabbath, is life to be lived. The Sabbath assigns to private domain the focus of life in holy time: the household is where things take place then.

Second comes the matter of time and how the advent of sacred time registers. Since the consequence of the demarcation on the Sabbath of all space into private and public domain effects, in particular, transporting objects from one space to the other, how time is differentiated will present no surprise. The effects concern private domain, the household. Specifically, what turns out to frame the Halakhic issue is what objects may be handled or used, even in private domain, on the Sabbath. The advent of the Sabbath thus affects the organization of space and the utilization of tools and other objects, the furniture of the household within the designated territory of the household.

The basic principle is simple. Objects may be handled only if they are designated in advance of the Sabbath for the purpose for which they will be utilized on the Sabbath. But if tools may be used for a purpose that is licit on the Sabbath, and if those tools are ordinarily used for that same purpose, they are deemed ready at hand and do not require reclassification; the accepted classification applies. What requires designation for Sabbath use in particular is any tool that may serve more than a single purpose, or that does not ordinarily serve the purpose for which it is wanted on the Sabbath. Designation for use on the Sabbath thus regularizes the irregular, but is not required for what is ordinarily used for the purpose for which it is wanted and is licitly utilized on the Sabbath.

2. TIME: WHAT IS TO BE USED ON THE SABBATH MUST BE SO DESIGNATED IN ADVANCE.

A. For example, on the Sabbath people do not put a utensil under a lamp to catch the oil. But if one put it there while it is still day, it is permitted. But they do not use any of that oil on the Sabbath, since it is not something which was prepared [before the Sabbath for use on the Sabbath.

B. What one uses on the Sabbath must be designated in advance for that purpose, either in a routine way (what is ordinarily used on the Sabbath, e.g., for food preparation, does not have to be designated especially for that purpose) or in an exceptional manner. But within that proviso, all utensils may be handled on the Sabbath, for a permitted purpose. If something is not ordinarily used as food but one designated it for that purpose, e.g., for cattle, it may be handled on the Sabbath.

M. 3:6, 17:1-8, 18:2, 20:5, 22:2

The advent of sacred time calls into question the accessibility and use of the objects and tools of the world, but with a very particular purpose in mind. That purpose emerges when we note that if an object is ordinarily used for a purpose that is licit on the Sabbath, e.g., for eating, it need not be designated for that purpose for use on the Sabbath. Since on the Sabbath it is used for its ordinary, and licit, purpose, that suffices. So the advent of the Sabbath requires that things licit for use on the Sabbath be used in the manner that is standard. If one wishes to use those things for a given purpose that is licit on the Sabbath, but that those objects do not ordinarily serve, then in advance of the Sabbath one must designate those objects for that purpose, that is, regularize them. That rule covers whole, useful tools, but not broken ones or tools that will not serve their primary purpose.

The Sabbath then finds all useful tools and objects in their proper place; that may mean, they may not be handled at all, since their ordinary function cannot be performed on the Sabbath. Or it may mean, they may be handled on the Sabbath exactly as they are handled every other day, the function being licit on the Sabbath. Or it may mean, they must be designated in advance of the Sabbath for licit utilization on the Sabbath. That third proviso covers utensils that serve more than a single function, or that do not ordinarily serve the function of licit utilization on the Sabbath that the householder wishes them to serve on this occasion. The advent of the Sabbath then requires that all tools and other things be regularized and ordered.

The rule extends even to utilization of space, within the household, that is not ordinarily used for a (licit) purpose for which, on the Sabbath, it is needed. If guests come, storage-space used for food may be cleared away to accommodate them, the space being conceived as suitable for sitting even when not ordinarily used for that purpose. But one may not clear out a store room for that purpose. One may also make a path in a store room so that one may move about there. One may handle objects that, in some way or another, can serve a licit purpose, in the theory that that purpose inheres. But what is not made ready for use may not be used on the Sabbath. So the advent of the Sabbath not only divides space into public and private, but also differentiates useful tools and objects into those that may or may not be handled within the household.

We come to the third generative problematics that is particular to the Sabbath. The affect upon activity that the advent of the Sabbath makes concerns constructive labor. I may state the generative problematics in a simple declarative sentence:

In a normal way one may not carry out entirely on his own a completed act of constructive labor, which is to say, work that produces enduring results.

That is what one is supposed to do in profane time. What is implicit in that simple statement proves profound and bears far-reaching implications. No prohibition impedes performing an act of labor in an other-than-normal way, e.g., in a way that is unusual and thus takes account of the differentiation of time. Labor in a natural, not in an unnatural, manner is prohibited. But that is not all. A person is not forbidden to carry out an act of destruction, or an act of labor that produces no lasting consequences. Nor is part of an act of labor, not brought to conclusion, prohibited. Nor is it forbidden to perform part of an act of labor in partnership with another person who carries out the other requisite part. Nor does one incur culpability for performing an act of labor in several distinct parts, e.g., over a protracted, differentiated period of time. The advent of the Sabbath prohibits activities carried out in ordinary time in a way deemed natural: acts that are complete, consequential, and in accord with their accepted character.

3.   ACTIVITY: ON THE SABBATH ONE IS LIABLE FOR THE INTENTIONAL COMMISSION OF A COMPLETED ACT OF CONSTRUCTIVE LABOR, E.G., TRANSPORTING AN OBJECT FROM ONE DOMAIN TO THE OTHER, IF ONE HAS PERFORMED, IN THE NORMAL MANNER, THE ENTIRE ACTION BEGINNING TO END.

A.   If one has performed only part of an action, the matter being completed by another party, he is exempt. If one has performed an entire action but done so in an-other-than-ordinary manner, he is exempt. If one transports an object only to the threshold and puts it down there, he is exempt, even though, later on, he picks it up and completes the transportation outward to public domain.

B.   He one performed a forbidden action but did not intend to do so, he is exempt. If one performed a forbidden action but in doing so did not accomplish his goal, he is exempt: If one transported an object or brought an object in — if he did so inadvertently, he is liable for a sin offering. If he did so deliberately, he is subject to the punishment of extirpation.

C. All the same are the one who takes out and the one who brings in, the one who stretches something out and the one who throws [something] in — in all such cases he is liable. By observing Sabbath prohibitions prior to sunset, one takes precautions to avoid inadvertent error.

D. One is liable for constructive, but not destructive acts of labor, and for acts of labor that produce a lasting consequence but not ephemeral ones.

E. One is liable for performing on the Sabbath classifications of labor the like of which was done in the tabernacle. They sowed, so you are not to sow. They harvested, so you are not to harvest. They lifted up the boards from the ground to the wagon, so you are not to lift them in from public to private domain. They lowered boards from the wagon to the ground, so you must not carry anything from private to public domain. They transported boards from wagon to wagon, so you must not carry from one private domain to another.

F. But moving the object must be in the normal manner, not in an exceptional way, if culpability is to be incurred.

G. An entire act of labor must involve a minimum volume, and it must yield an enduring result. An act of destruction is not culpable. Thus, as we recall, he who tears [his clothing] because of his anger or on account of his bereavement, and all those who effect destruction, are exempt.

H. Healing is classified as an act of constructive labor, so it is forbidden; but saving life is invariably permitted, as is any other action of a sacred character that cannot be postponed, e.g., circumcision, saving sacred scrolls from fire, saving from fire food for immediate use, and tending to the deceased, along with certain other urgent matters requiring a sage's ruling.

M. 1:1, 2, 3, 10-11, 2:7, 8, 7:2, M. 7:3-4,
M. :1-6, 9:5-7, 10:1, 10:2-4, 10:5-6, 12:1-5,
M. 13:2-7, 14:1-2, 15:1-3, 16:1-8, 18:3, 19:1-6,
T. 15:11ff., M. 22:1, 22:6, 23:5, 24:5

This systematic, extensive, and richly detailed account of the activity, labor, that is forbidden on the Sabbath but required on weekdays introduces these considerations, properly classified:

A.   PRECONDITIONS

    1.   intentionality: the act must carry out the intention of the actor, and the intention must be to carry out an illicit act of labor

    2.   a single actor: culpability is incurred for an act started, carried through, and completed by a single actor, not by an act that is started by one party and completed by another

    3.   analogy: an act that on the Sabbath may be carried out in the building and maintenance of the tabernacle (Temple) may not be performed in the household, and on that analogy the classification of forbidden acts of labor is worked out

B.   CONSIDERATIONS

1. routine character: the act must be done in the manner in which it is ordinarily done
2. constructive result: the act must build and not destroy, put together and not dismantle; an act of destruction if not culpable

C.   CONSEQUENCES

1. completeness: the act must be completely done, in all its elements and components
2. permanent result: the act must produce a lasting result, not an ephemeral one
3. consequence: to impart culpability, a forbidden act of labor must involve a matter of consequence, e.g., transport of a volume of materials that people deem worth storing and transporting, but not a negligible volume

What is the upshot of this remarkable repertoire of fundamental considerations having to do with activity, in the household, on the holy day? The Mishnah's Halakhah of the Sabbath in the aggregate concerns itself with formulating a statement of how the advent of the Sabbath defines the kind of activity that may be done by specifying what may not be done. That is the meaning of repose, the cessation of activity, not the commencement of activity of a different order. To carry out the Sabbath, one does nothing, not something. And what is that "nothing" that one realizes through inactivity? One may not carry out an act analogous to one that sustains creation. An act or activity for which one bears responsibility, and one that sustains creation, is [1] an act analogous to one required in the building and maintenance of the tabernacle, [2] that is intentionally carried out [3] in its entirety, [4] by a single actor, [5] in the ordinary manner, [6] with a constructive and [7] consequential result — one worthy of consideration by accepted norms. These are the seven conditions that pertain, and that, in one way or another, together with counterpart considerations in connection with the transformation of space and time, generate most of the Halakhah of Shabbat.

This construction in the richness and density of generative principles, both those focused on the Sabbath and the ones that are pertinent to a wide variety of venues of the Israelite social order, stands in contrast with the fragmentary and miscellaneous composite set forth by CD. It proves beyond any doubt not so much the conceptual as the logical and formal superiority, by the stated Mishnaic criteria, of the Mishnah over the Damascus Covenant in the aspect of the Sabbath, the single topic expounded in some detail by the Damascus Covenant Once more, we find the Mishnah unique in the diachronic context of Israelite law-codes. By the criteria of the Mishnah itself, nothing prior compares.

The comparison of the Mishnah with prior law codes, four in Scripture and two in the library found at Qumran, yields perspective on the Mishnah in diachronic context. The work produces a uniform outcome. Some of the codes we have examined are systematic and well-organized, as is the Mishnah. Other codes provide a comprehensive account of the Israelite social order that they contemplate, as does the Mishnah. But none undertakes the systematic, analytical program that everywhere marks as unique the Mishnah's systematic presentation of its topical program.

What we have seen is simple: when the Mishnah takes a topic treated by earlier codes, in density and complexity and profundity it formulates an utterly new statement. It is a presentation that transforms the topic and transcends its boundaries, treating facts as exemplary and identifying principles that govern other subjects as well as the one at hand. Generative logic prevails throughout, inert facts rarely define discourse. Six times over the same process of comparing the syllogistic aspect of biblical or Qumran codes with the Mishnah's topical counterpart has yielded the same result. And that result was not trivial nor did it rest on a singleton-proof. The systematic, philosophical reading of the law characteristic of the Mishnah alone in the Israelite setting before its time and imparted by the Mishnah upon continuation-documents in that same setting afterward distinguishes the Mishnah from all other law codes of the communities of Judaism.[17]

Indeed, so different is the Mishnah from the received collections of rules ("law codes") that we must classify it as a different kind of document altogether. If the Bible and Qumran have produced law-codes, then by the definition of law code that is realized in them, the Mishnah is something other than a law-code: not only larger in quantity but different in quality. Professor Cooper quite astutely comments, "I should say that the Mishnah is the first actual 'law code,' and that it is a misnomer to use that designation for any of the Mishnah's precursors." How to explain the difference represented by the Mishnah? We may account for the innovation in legal discourse in more than one way. History, theology, culture — all modes and models of explaining the result of comparison and contrast present plausible and promising approaches to our problem.

HISTORY: The Mishnah is to be seen as a response to the events of 70 and 132-135: the end of the Temple and the closure of Jerusalem to Israelites. The historical approach has to show that the Mishnah could not have been written had the Temple not been destroyed. The Mishnah belongs and responds to the aftermath of the cataclysmic event that defined its age, the destruction of the Temple in ca. 70 C.E. Its foci — emphasis on regularity and order, for example — stand in contrast against, and so correlate, with the destabilizing and disruptive effects of that event. Without the destruction of Jerusalem there can have been no Mishnah. That represents an historical model of explanation.

It is an appealing model. Since the Mishnah came to closure many centuries after the counterpart composites of the Bible and Qumran, we should be tempted to appeal to that much later age and quite different context in which the Mishnah took shape. The Mishnah came to closure, it is generally assumed, in ca. 200, that is, a bit more than a century after the destruction of Jerusalem and the Second Temple in 70 and about three generations after the end of the rebellion of 132-135 confirmed the result of 70. Consequently, the historical, political context promises to explain the characteristics of the document.

But though the explanation stands to reason, verisimilitude cannot be confused with actuality. A rigorous examination of the Mishnah's treatment of the topic represents the first step in testing the proposed explanation. And that examination must encompass comparison and contrast with other documents of the Rabbinic canon, with the same question in hand. So a historical explanation is plausible but unproven.

THEOLOGY: in this same context one may ask, in the language of Martin Pickup, "Is the reason for the formal and logical difference of the Mishnah due to any discernible difference in terms of eschatology, state-of-anticipation, or other religious conceptions between the framers of the Mishnah and the Qumran covenanters or biblical code authors?" The theology defined by the larger context, whether Scripture or other documents of the Qumran library, is thereby invoked, and fairly so. So a systemic approach is proposed. Work on how the various library documents of Qumran coalesce into a coherent system has not yet evolved to the point at which we may invoke the whole to account for the character of some of the parts. But if it is premature to appeal to theological context established by the Qumran library for its components, it is still a challenging model of explanation.

For the Mishnah takes its position in a larger context of conviction than is defined by its table of contents. Scripture and its authority, God and his plans for Israel, Israel and its task in humanity — all three components of a Judaic theological system impinge upon the character of the social order contemplated by the document. The Mishnah adumbrates a theological system and structure involving Torah, God, and Israel, and its traits ought to realize in literary and legal detail the main lines of that structure and system. How the theological system animating the Mishnah generates the formal and logical inquiry that distinguishes the Mishnah forms a source for explaining those traits that have so impressed us.

AMBIENT CULTURE: then what about shifts in the cultural setting, specifically, fundamental changes, from the ancient Near Eastern world in which Scripture locates itself, and which has supplied analogies and genres for biblical writing, to the world of Graeco-Roman late antiquity? Shifts in the prevailing practice of the making of law codes can account for the difference in codes produced at successive stopping points in the Israelite context.

The Bible's codes belong to a different, earlier world from the Mishnah's cultural context. The scriptural codes form, in the language of Stephen A. Kaufman,[18] referring to the Holiness Code "an extended collection of sizable citations from the traditional priestly legal lore intended to complete and correct omissions and errors in the other legal traditions included in the Torah, with a major leitmotif of 'you should be holy.'"

How the Qumran codes compare with those of the Mishnah awaits investigation. The Qumran code we examined does not vastly differ in gross formal and logical traits from the biblical code we considered. But the Mishnah does not adapt for itself the model of Scripture and its codes. It differs because overall it ignores the available Torah and recapitulates its expositions either whole or in part — a free-hand, free-standing formulation of its own. Then the difference between the Mishnah and (in this case) the Holiness Code is explained by reference to the program of the compilers, the one, constructing a systematic and complete statement not to complete Scripture but to replace it; the other, filling gaps and correcting errors.

A different approach to the description of the received codes is supplied also by Kaufman: "More important is the recognition of the role of the Holiness Code in the overall structure of the Torah. The literary structural norms of the ancient Near East created works that are constructed as nested chiasms with the climax at the precise center of the structure. Leviticus is the center of the Torah. The Holiness code is the center of Leviticus. Chapter 19 is the center and climax of the Holiness Code. The Golden Rule is the center and climax of Leviticus Nineteen."[19] In that case, the Mishnah is seen to have made a complete break from the received program of formulation of rules, their organization and articulation.

That differentiation of the Mishnah from the context of ancient Near Eastern law codes that accommodates Scripture's several codes is underscored by Alan Cooper,[20] who says, "No ancient Near Eastern collection of laws is comprehensive or coherent, nor were they intended to be. The promulgation of law manifests divine or royal authority, provides exemplary cases for judges and legal scholars, and establishes basic principles of justice. But the texts that we have should be read as works of literature, related only tangentially to day-to-day legal practice."

All three approaches to the explanation of the character of a cultural artifact — historical-political context, theological system, the setting of prevailing culture — promise illuminating results.

The contemporary context of historical explanation makes the first approach self-evidently plausible. Thus the social changes produced by political, institutional change ("catastrophe") demand attention, their effects strike the heirs of the mid-twentieth-century calamity of the Jews as obvious. But not all Jews of antiquity focused the social order in which they made their lives upon Jerusalem and the Temple. Not only so, but the Mishnah is remarkably obsessed with issues that do not intersect with the theology of the Temple and its destruction, issues of sorting out mixtures for one example, the interplay of action and intention for another. So the historical explanation awaits testing: at what point, in what documents, does the destruction of the Temple in 70 form the center of interest, and how do those documents compare with the Mishnah's treatment of the same matter?

The theological explanation, linking parts to a center and a whole, yields a satisfying sense that all things cohere in a few overriding theological affirmations, susceptible of infinite extension and amplification. But the Mishnah takes its program from natural philosophy more than from theology, and we should be hard put out of internal evidence only to reconstruct its theological principles and their secondary articulation solely with reference to the Mishnah. As to codification, comparisons between Graeco-Roman law codes and the Mishnah yield contrasts, seldom commonalities.[21] As in the ancient Near Eastern setting, so in late antiquity, if the Mishnah be defined as a law code, then it is unique in context — no other law codes exhibit comparable indicative qualities. That on the surface is an implausible outcome. So the upshot is, how to account for the vitality of the Mishnah's imagination: its capacity to see all things fresh and new, whether historical, theological, or cultural in character? It is never easy to explain what is unique.

ENDNOTES

[1] I have systematically examined the data in the following: *Scripture and the Generative Premises of the Halakhah. A Systematic Inquiry.* I. *Halakhah Based Principally on Scripture and Halakhic Categories Autonomous of Scripture.* Binghamton, 2000: Global Publications. ACADEMIC STUDIES IN ANCIENT JUDAISM series. *Scripture and the Generative Premises of the Halakhah. A Systematic Inquiry.* II. *Scripture's Topics Derivatively Amplified in the Halakhah.* Binghamton, 2000: Global Publications. ACADEMIC STUDIES IN ANCIENT JUDAISM series. *Scripture and the Generative Premises of the Halakhah. A Systematic Inquiry.* III. *Scripture's Topics Independently Developed in the Halakhah. From the Babas through Miqvaot.* Binghamton, 2000: Global Publications. ACADEMIC STUDIES IN ANCIENT JUDAISM series. *Scripture and the Generative Premises of the Halakhah. A Systematic Inquiry.* IV. *Scripture's Topics Independently Developed in the Halakhah. From Moed Qatan through Zebahim.* Binghamton, 2000: Global Publications. ACADEMIC STUDIES IN ANCIENT JUDAISM series. Second printing, revised and condensed: under the title, *The Torah and the Halakhah: The Four Relationships.* Lanham, 2003: University Press of America.

[2] M. Greenberg, "Exodus, book of," *Encyclopaedia Judaica* (Jerusalem, 1971), 6:1050ff. Passage cited: cols. 1056-7/ I also consulted Jeffrey H. Tigay, "Exodus. Introduction and Annotations," in Adele Berlin and Marc Zvi Brettler, *The Jewish Study Bible* (New York, 2002: Oxford University Press), pp. 102-202.

[3] Frank Cruesemann, *The Torah. Theology and Social History of Old Testament Law.* Translated by Allan. W. Mahnke. Minneapolis, 1996: Fortress Press), p. 109.

[4] Martin Noth, *Exodus, A commentary.* London, 1962: SCM Press, p. 173.

[5] These are directed towards all free Israelites who had to discuss and decide together in the local legal assembly. The principal aim of these requirements is to protect the poor and the weak against a partial judgment in favor of the rich and the powerful (Noth, p. 188).

[6] I add quotation marks to stress that the category-formations, "laws" and "codes," are used only because they are conventionally applied. I do not mean to suggest I classify the data at hand in so formal a manner, thus "rules" and "compositions" or "composites" strikes me as more neutral language.

[7] My starting point is Florentino García Martínez and Elbert J. C. Tigchelaar, *The Dead Sea Scrolls, Study Edition. Leiden, 1999: Brill.* For the Damascus Document, pp. 550ff., with a basic bibliography.

[8] I consulted Geza Vermes, *The Dead Sea Scrolls. Qumran in Perspective.* Minneapolis, 1977: Fortress; Michael A. Knibb, *The Qumran Community.* Cambridge, 1987: Cambridge University Press; James C. VanderKam, *The Dead Sea Scrolls Today* (Grand Rapids, 1994:

William B. Eerdmans Publishing Co.); Lawrence H. Schiffman, "Jewish Law at Qumran," in Jacob Neusner and Alan J. Avery-Peck and Bruce D. Chilton, eds., *Judaism in Late Antiquity*, Part Five. *The Judaism of Qumran. A systemic Reading of the Dead Sea Scrolls*. Section One. *Theory of Israel* (Boston and Leiden, 2001: Brill), pp. 75-90; Shemaryahu Talmon, *The World of Qumran from Within. Collected Studies*. Jerusalem & Leiden, 1989: Magnes Press, the Hebrew University and E. J. Brill. Note especially in Talmon, "Between the Bible and the Mishnah," *The World of Qumran from Within*, pp. 11-52, in particular pp. 36-38: "The formulations of Qumran enactments bear a close resemblance to the characteristic style and structure which mark the Pentateuchal legal compilations. The similarity shows both in the extrapolation and amplification of biblical laws and in the wordings of new ordinances which pertain in particular to the Yahad membership" (P. 36). So too: "Qumran legislation is sometimes couched in wordings which resemble the biblical casuistic mode..." "Practically all formula which Qumran authors apply in the expansion and amplification of biblical laws are also applied in the distinctive yahad legislation...." "The roster of purity laws in the Halakhic compilation 4QMMT is arranged in units of itemized related phenomena, each introduced by the protasis al. The same superscription is found in the Zadokite Documents...A similar purpose in the organization of legal materials is served by the standard phrase zeh haserekh...In contrast, Rabbinic legal literature is predominantly cast in the form of shaqla vetarya, the presentation and evaluation of discordant views leads to the promulgation of normative statements based on majority decisions or on past pronouncements of acknowledged authorities. Unlike Qumran tradition, the style and procedures which denote thee Rabbinic debates are fundamentally distinct from the ones which predominate in the legal corpora of the Hebrew Bible." (p. 37-8). See also Lawrence H. Schiffman, *The Halakhah at Qumran* (Leiden, 1975: E. J. Brill), cited extensively below.

[9] Chaim Rabin, *The Zadokite Documents. I. The Admonition. II. The Laws* (Oxford, 1954: Clarendon), pp x-xi. Sop too Vermes States, "The Statutes...consists of laws arranged according to their subject matter: on vows and oaths, on the tribunal, on witnesses and judges, on purification by water, on Sabbath observances, on ritual cleanness and uncleanness...rules relating to the organization and institutions of the Community are also included." See also Charlotte Hempel, *The Laws of the Damascus Document: Sources, Traditions, and Redaction* (Leiden, 1998: E. J. Brill), who divides the laws into the categories, Halakhah and Community Organization (Hannah K. Harrington, review, H-Net Reviews).

[10] James VanderKam and Peter Flint, *The Meaning of the Dead Sea Scrolls*, San Francisco, 2002: HarperSanFrancisco, p. 216,

[11] Compare Lawrence H. Schiffman op. cit., pp. 82-3.

[12] Lawrence H. Schiffman, "Jewish Law at Qumran," in Jacob Neusner and Alan J. Avery-Peck and Bruce D. Chilton, eds., *Judaism in Late Antiquity*, Part Five. *The Judaism of Qumran. A systemic Reading of the Dead Sea Scrolls*. Section One. *Theory of Israel* (Boston and Leiden, 2001: Brill), pp. 75-90, p. 83.

[13] Op. Cit.

[14] Op. Cit., p. 77.

[15] Compare my *Judaism and Zoroastrianism at the Dusk of Late Antiquity. How Two Ancient Faiths Wrote Down Their Great Traditions*. Atlanta, 1993: Scholars Press for South Florida Studies in the History of Judaism. Now: Lanham, University Press of America. There I contrast the presentation of the same law in the same form in a Judaic and a Zoroastrian law code, differentiating the Judaic account of the topic by reference to the Talmudic amplification and analysis of the rule, something the Zoroastrian counterpart lacks.

[16]So too a shard that can serve some useful purpose is taken into account; it is subject to uncleanness; one that can serve no useful purpose is treated as null, useless and hence not subject to uncleanness. How we assess usefulness is subject to much interesting reflection in other chapters of the Halakhah, which need not detain us here. My point is only that the considerations operative here encompass vast areas of Halakhah, which, in practical detail, otherwise scarcely intersect.

[17] But compare the Zoroastrian counterparts, in my *Judaism and Zoroastrianism at the Dusk of Late Antiquity. How Two Ancient Faiths Wrote Down Their Great Traditions.* Atlanta, 1993: Scholars Press for South Florida Studies in the History of Judaism. Now: Lanham, University Press of America.

[18] E mail, May 13, 2004.

[19] Same source.

[20] E-mail, May 13, 2004.

[21] See my "The Mishnah in Roman and Christian Contexts," based on Steven Stertz, "The Second Century: Roman Legal Codification," both published in J. Neusner and Alan Avery-Peck, editors, *The Mishnah in Contemporary Study*. Volume One. Leiden, 2002: E. J. Brill, pp. 121-166.

2

Is Scripture the Origin of the Halakhah?

Judaism in its formative canon, from the Mishnah, ca. 200 C.E. through the Bavli, ca. 600 C.E., persists in seeking the foundations of its normative laws, or Halakhah, in the Hebrew Scriptures of ancient Israel, particularly in the Pentateuch.[1] That represents a theological apologetic that attributes to God's revelation to Moses at Sinai the laws that the Rabbinic sages set forth.

When I ask whether Scripture is the origin of the Halakhah, I inquire about the beginning of the Halakhic system *viewed whole.* That is because the Halakhic system embodied in detail in the Mishnah and the Tosefta and amplified in the two Talmuds and in the Tannaite Midrash-compilations is no mere catalogue of facts. It is comprised by much more than random rulings about this and that lacking all syllogistic promise. Rather, the system constitutes a coherent construction comprised by category-formations defined by topics purposively amplified. These category-formations everywhere pursue a cogent analytical program, addressing to diverse subjects, treated systematically, a single set of questions of definition and analysis.

Diverse details are formed into topical compositions, which are framed to impart to data coherence in accord with an overriding analytical program. The whole coalesces into a comprehensive set of rules. The Halakhic system embodies analytical procedures capable of generating further rules and responding to new problems — but, as the facts show, incapable of generating important new category-formations. These traits of data formed into a remarkably stable structure of the social order signal the advent of the Halakhic system. Hence the urgent question: Is Scripture the origin of the Halakhic system, which defines the norms of Judaism?

In asking about the system viewed whole, I signal that at stake is not the starting point of discrete bits of legal data. Some of these have been shown to derive from Sumerian, Akkadian, Babylonian, Canaanite, Ugaritic and other ancient Near Eastern venues. Others originate in Scripture. Still others come from unknown sources. The discrete facts thus originate hither and yon. But that fact has no bearing on our problem. At issue, then, is the origin of the comprehensive *structure* comprised by the Halakhic category-formations, by these topics and no others.[2]

Scripture, in particular, the Pentateuch, forms the natural starting point for any inquiry into origins in Judaism. The question answered here derives from a simple fact: the Pentateuch is privileged within the Rabbinic system, which links as much of the Halakhah to the Pentateuchal law codes as it possibly can. So it is quite natural to treat Scripture as the base-line, the Halakhic category-formations as the variable, in seeking the origin of the system. But what happens when we treat the system as the base-line, and Scripture as the variable? Then we see that the Halakhic system viewed as a coherent statement does not originate in Scripture. Important parts — category-formations/tractates — of that statement do, important parts do not. Then the system viewed whole does not. That is the fact, even though the system reckoned comprehensively accommodates nearly the entirety of Scripture's legal data, which the system organizes and proportions in its own framework.[3] That is shown in two aspects, first, the identification of principal topics required for the system and not deriving from Scripture, second, the articulation of those topics. I refer to the Halakhah's definition of what, in those topics, requires exposition and the identification of the abstract principles in play in that exposition.

Where do we now find the system's governing, topical category-formations? In rich detail, the organizing topics are set forth in the topical program of the tractates of the Mishnah (ca. 200 C.E.), and that same program governs in the Tosefta (ca. 300), the Yerushalmi (ca. 400), and the Bavli (ca. 600)[4] — the entire legal corpus of normative Judaism in its formative age.[5] The category-formations of the Halakhah come to definitive expression in the Mishnah and the Tosefta, the topics of which constitute the category-formations of the Halakhah. By far the greater part of the details of the Halakhah registers in the Mishnah and the Tosefta. The two Talmuds and the Tannaite exegetical compilations, Mekhilta Attributed to R. Ishmael for Exodus, Sifra for Leviticus, Sifré for Numbers, and Sifré for Deuteronomy, analyze the details but do not organize data in the Halakhic category-formations. Consequently, the evidence for the origin of the Halakhah will emerge from the category-formations of the Halakhah as these are set forth in rich detail by the Mishnah with the Tosefta's complementary data.[6]

But our task of uncovering the Halakhic system at its conceptual foundations transcends mere description and paraphrase of the program of the Mishnah and the Tosefta. That is because the Mishnah and the Tosefta speak primarily in small matters. They take up a discourse of details. The concrete rulings of law are positioned many removes from the generative conceptions that impart cogency and order upon the data. The Mishnah and the Tosefta, accordingly, set forth the exegesis that results from the topical hermeneutics of the Halakhic system. Our task in quest of origins is to make the journey from exegesis to hermeneutics, from detail to the problematics and the principle. That is why we ask about the foundations, in Scripture or elsewhere, of that hermeneutics.[7]

That diverse Halakhic category-formations — topics systematically expounded in Mishnah-tractates and extended in the corresponding ones of the Tosefta, Yerushalmi, and Bavli — bear various relationships to the Torah of Moses presents no surprise. It was recognized by the Rabbinic sages themselves. They stated the matter explicitly. Some laws have little basis in Scripture and "hover in the air." Some elaborate statements relate to Scripture only episodically. And some have much on which to depend. The statement as set forth, then amplified, follows:

A. The absolution of vows hovers in the air, for it has nothing [in the Torah] upon which to depend.

B. The laws of the Sabbath, festal offerings, and sacrilege — lo, they are like mountains hanging by a string,

C. for they have little Scripture for many laws.

D. Laws concerning civil litigations, the sacrificial cult, things to be kept cultically clean, sources of cultic uncleanness, and prohibited consanguineous marriages have much on which to depend.

E. And both these and those [equally] are the essentials of the Torah.

Mishnah-tractate Hagigah 1:9

Let us consider how the Tosefta amplifies the Mishnah's statements, which are now given in italics:

A. *The absolution of vows hovers in the air, for it has nothing upon which to depend in the Torah* [M. Hag. 1:8A].

B. But a sage loosens a vow in accord with his wisdom.

C. *The laws of the Sabbath, festal-offerings, and sacrilege are like mountains hanging by a string, for they have little Scripture for many laws* [M. Hag. 1:8B].

D. They have nothing upon which to depend.

F. *Laws concerning civil litigations, the sacrificial cult, things to be kept cultically clean, sources of cultic uncleanness, and prohibited consanguineous marriages* [M. Hag. 1:8D],

G. and added to them are laws concerning valuations, things declared *herem,* and things declared sacred —

H. for them there is abundant Scripture, exegesis, and many laws.

I. *They have much on which to depend [M. Hag. 1:8D].*

J. Abba Yosé b. Hanan says, "These eight topics of the Torah constitute *the essentials of the laws* [thereof] [T. Er. 8:24]" [M. Hag. 1:8D-E].

Tosefta Hagigah 1:9

Accordingly, we find topics, the expositions of which form a mere reprise of Scripture's facts. Scripture entirely accounts for the presentation of the topic. We also meet category-formations that are introduced by Scripture but do not wholly depend on Scripture for their extenuation and amplification. These are topics introduced by Scripture but amplified independently of Scripture. Finally come those topics for which Scripture provides no Halakhic foundations at all — the ones that we should not, upon the basis of Scripture alone, anticipated finding among the Halakhic category-formations.

How are we to proceed? With the Mishnah and the Tosefta as our focus and variable and the category-formations as the base-line, we proceed to ask whether Scripture is the origin of the topical expositions, the tractates, of the Halakhah. We then sort out the category-formations by the criterion of the relationship of Scripture's data to the data of the respective topical formations.

There are cases in which the Halakhah addresses a topic that Scripture simply does not raise at all. Second, the systemic category-formation may take a topic that Scripture does treat and investigate questions important in that topic that Scripture does not raise at all; the Halakhah may find important in a given subject matters that Scripture scarcely acknowledges. Third, the Halakhic system may treat systematically what Scripture deals with in a haphazard and unorganized way. But, fourth, some category-formations do originate in Scripture and simplify amplify Scripture's data.

Logically, the whole — the Halakhic system — seems to me phenomenologically prior to Scripture's bits and pieces, even those Scriptural fragments that in places adumbrate the shape and structure of the whole. In the mythic language of Judaism, the oral part of the Torah is prior to the written part. I did not anticipate such a result when I began this work, and I do not offer it as a historical judgment.

And at issue, then, is when the articulation of the category-formation beyond the limits of Mishnah-Tosefta is mere exegesis, called for by the details of the Halakhah as given by Mishnah-Tosefta, and when is the articulation of the category-formation beyond Mishnah-Tosefta generated by the inner logic of the category-formation, not by the (mere) exegetical requirements of the Mishnah-Tosefta's formulation of matters. In other words, the same notion set forth here in saying that the Halakhic category-formations look like what is fundamental, the Scriptural counterparts look like mere summaries of some details, comes into play again there. It is easy to answer the question of when do we have in Yerushalmi and Bavli, or in Tosefta vis à vis Mishnah, mere exegesis, and where we have the outcome of generative logic working autonomously ("pure reason"), once we ask the question.

I.   No, Scripture is Not the Origin of the Halakhah

The Halakhic system does not originate in Scripture. Drawing upon Scripture for data, the system frames and shapes in accord with its own principles and plans of category-formation those received data and all other facts it finds useful, whatever the origin. The characteristic traits of the Halakhic system govern, not those of Scripture. Its rhetoric and logic of coherent discourse and analysis and the development of the topical program scarcely intersect with Scripture's indicative traits. To be sure, Scripture's laws are utilized by the Halakhic system. None is neglected. But the Halakhic system ventures into territories untouched by Scripture. And — more important — even where Scripture and the Halakhah go over the same ground, it is rare that the Halakhic system simply pursues lines of inquiry that Scripture has set forth. A set of specific considerations sustains this proposition.

First, take the Halakhah's systemic components in their relationship to Scripture. Ten of the sixty category-formations ignore Scripture altogether. And these form integral parts of the system. That is because they intersect with the principal divisions of the Halakhic system, the first, second, third, fifth, and sixth divisions, to be precise. We can have formed a theory of the program of the whole from these parts that are autonomous of Scripture. But we cannot have formed an account of the Halakhic system in its principal parts with the evidence in hand only of the tractates that recapitulate Scripture.

More to the point still: thirty-three Halakhic category-formations address topics dealt with in Scripture but raise issues not contemplated by Scripture. And these cover all six divisions. The upshot is decisive. No less than two-thirds of the Halakhic system's category-formations pursue their own topics, or expound Scripture's topics in their own way. By contrast, seven category-formations simply paraphrase what Scripture says about their topics, and another eleven remain within the limits of the topics as Scripture outlines them, eighteen in all. So viewed simply as a composite, forty three tractates pursue their own programs, in part on topics of their own choosing, while eighteen recapitulate Scripture's topics in Scripture's own way, for a total of sixty-one topical tractates in all. Accordingly, roughly two-thirds of the category-formations originate elsewhere than in Scripture's topics and respond to a hermeneutical program not defined by Scripture. And, it goes without saying, on the strength of these forty-three category-formations we certainly can reconstruct the system as a whole.

Can we not posit, second, that Scripture is the starting point, and the system moves out from Scripture's topics to topics that are made necessary by the logic of Scripture? I think not. The Halakhic system viewed whole exhibits traits of cogency that Scripture does not define. The analytical program that characterizes the articulation of the category-formations — analysis of language, inquiry into the impact of intentionality, concern for questions of teleology, to name three routine issues — never intersects with Scripture. That is because Scripture does not ask these questions at all, and its data do not respond to them even implicitly. The Halakhic analysis therefore does not originate in Scripture and does not intersect with Scripture. In some details Scripture's facts and narratives figure, but these do not impart coherence to the category-formations in which they figure. I cannot overstate the simple fact before us: the Halakhic system coheres within its own logic, it raises recurrent considerations characteristic of its own philosophy, its very topical program encompasses topics far beyond the program of Scripture and raises issues in no way responsive to the facts supplied by Scripture.

Where Scripture's facts figure, the Halakhic system imparts to those facts an importance, a problematic, that Scripture in no way suggests. So we can reconstruct the main outlines of the Halakhic system to which the parts cohere. But, by contrast, were we to begin without knowledge of the structure as a whole, we could never guess at what is needed to complete the principal parts of the system. Horayot, Negaim, Pesahim, Shebuot, Sotah, Sukkah, and Yoma on their own do not signal a coherent Halakhic system, not the one we have, not any other.

What they signal is that they form pieces of a system but they do not point to what that system requires beyond the indicated topics. Because they are odd, episodic entries, they do not connect to one another. What I mean is, what has Pesahim to do with Sotah and Yoma, and what encompassing conception — a plan for the social order for example — is contemplated in the seven units? True, Pesahim, Sukkah, and Yoma point to a system of appointed times. But Sotah on its own, Horayot by itself, Shebuot without a court system, for example, lead nowhere. And even if we were to play fast and loose with the topic and claim that Sotah points to a system that treats marriages, or Horayot adumbrates a civil administration and a Temple, or Shebuot a court system, we still could not theorize out of Sotah the necessity of a Ketubot and Qiddushin, which have no Scriptural foundations whatsoever and are not hinted at by the marriage-compositions of Scripture — and so for the rest.

The category-formations that originate in Scripture and remain within the bounds of Scripture's facts and interests do point to a system. But it is not the one at hand. And in any event that system that Scripture on its own produces proves remarkably out of balance, dealing with only one aspect of the temple and not another. For, we must ask, what has become of the rules of cultic cleanness? Scripture is the origin of the expositions on Negaim, but what of Kelim, Ohalot, Miqvaot, Parah — the heart and soul of the Halakhic system? The upshot is now self-evident: Scripture is not the origin of the Halakhic system.[8]

II. But Yes, without Scripture There Is No Halakhic System

But without Scripture, which defines a third of the category-formations and supplies the facts to most, though not all, of the rest of them, there is no Halakhic system. So Scripture also makes a massive contribution, and we have now to situate that contribution in its larger systemic context.

Seven category formations of the Halakhic system of the Mishnah-Tosefta-Yerushalmi-Bavli accomplish little more than the amplification of their counterparts in Scripture: Horayot, Negaim, Pesahim, Shebuot, Sotah, Sukkah, and Yoma. Does Scripture set forth as what we should call distinct categories, demarcated in literary terms, the themes and generative propositions of those categories? Lev. 4, Lev. 13-14, Ex. 12, Lev. 5, Num. 5, and Lev. 16, answer that question in the affirmative for all but Sukkah. In those six cases, everything important to the category of the

Halakhic system emerges in an explicit and sustained, coherent and complete statement of Scripture — thus, category matches category, point by point, in detail. The presentation of Tabernacles at Lev. 23 covers nearly all of the information on which Sukkah depends, but the Halakhah further draws upon, and organizes, the data of Numbers 29:12-38, the offerings on the occasion of the festival of Sukkot, and Deuteronomy 16:13-15 the use of the booth. Here the category of the Halakhic system depends entirely on Scripture for its topical program, though Scripture does not present a single, sustained disquisition on the subject.

Now, when we classify the seven specified category-formations as Halakhah based on Scripture, the criteria prove exact: [1] a well-defined category of Scripture which [2] defines the topical program and further [3] dictates the generative premises that come to realization in the counterpart category-formation of the Halakhic system .

The paramount role of Scripture becomes blatant when we note that some categories take shape within their own framework. Neither for topic and expository program for said topic nor, all the more so, for generative premises, do Berakhot, Demai, Ketubot, Qiddushin, Taanit, Tamid, Tohorot, and Uqsin look to Scripture. The Halakhah in those categories finds its own topic, identifies the problematic of the topic, works out the concrete exegetical program, and identifies the implicit principles of cogency, all within a rationality and a logic that Scripture has not suggested. We may propose that the system, with its interest in marriage and family, required Ketubot and Qiddushin; with its interest in the Temple and its offerings it required Tamid, Middot, and Qinnim; with its interest in the Israelite social order and its diversity it required Demai and Tohorot; and the like. So we may identify systemic interests that generated the non-scriptural category-formations. In the specified tractates, the topic proves integral to the Halakhic system, which generates its own category-formations, not only reworking topics contributed by Scripture.

That is not to suggest the autonomous constructions of the Halakhah utterly ignore the Pentateuch and raise questions unimagined within Scripture's larger narrative and legal repertoire. Scripture speaks of the cleanness of foods, though Tohorot and Uqsin, on domestic matters, stand on their own. Scripture concerns itself with questions of marital relationships (we need go no further than Sotah to make that point!). But Qiddushin and Ketubot ask their own questions about relationships that Scripture for its part does not take up in juridical terms. Scripture values piety outside of the Temple and its offerings, though Berakhot and Taanit pursue that of the individual and the village, never addressed in Scripture. Scripture defines the issues of tithing, and in that context, Demai's issue — doubtfully-tithed produce — finds a place for itself. And the daily whole offering is explicitly called for by Scripture, though the category-formation set forth by Tamid's narrative finds no counterpart therein.

Compare the autonomy of the seven free-standing tractates with the dependency of the seven subordinated ones. We see the full extent of the independence of the one set from Scripture when we contemplate the full extent of the reliance of the other set upon Scripture. If we were told in advance that wherever Pentateuchal law makes a large and coherent programmatic statement, bearing an implicit set of principles and judgments, there the Halakhah will produce a corresponding category, clarifying, amplifying, and augmenting the category as set forth by Scripture, we should readily have selected the categories represented by Negaim (Leviticus 13-14) and Sotah (Numbers 5) and the rest as candidates for systematic exposition by the Halakhic system. But with the entirety of the Pentateuchal Law in hand, we should have had little basis on which to fabricate category-formations corresponding to Qiddushin and Ketubot, Uqsin and Tohorot, Demai (for one set of reasons) and Taanit (for another set). And Tamid with Middot and Qinnim is a special case.

Scripture can tell us why we have the Halakhic categories based on Scripture, but it cannot tell us the reason we have the free-standing ones. Scripture is necessary to the Halakhic system, but Scripture is not sufficient to the formulation of that system.

III. IF NOT FROM SCRIPTURE, THEN WHENCE THE SYSTEM?

The Halakhic system that presents itself whole and complete in the Mishnah with the Tosefta, Yerushalmi, and Bavli, its category-formations fully defined, its generative problematic everywhere definitive, is born of the union of topic, logic, and rhetoric. It forms the outcome of the meeting of a singular message, method, and medium. It comes into being when the message of Scripture (if not that alone) is subjected to the method of analysis of natural philosophy that classifies topics in accord with the teleology of things, and is expressed in the medium of conveying large principles through the examination of exemplary cases and details.

The Halakhic system self-evidently comes to expression in the Mishnah, therefore by ca. 200 C.E. But what is its starting point? The answer is, when the three necessary elements of the system came together: message, method, and medium.

The message — the topical program — requires Scripture but transcends Scripture. It cannot have come into existence without Scripture. But it is incomplete when stated only within the limits of Scripture. So the system begins within the world in which Scripture took shape. Its message correlates with that of Scripture; its category-formations encompass those defined or contained by Scripture. But its message, whole and complete, so transcends Scripture's boundaries that we must say, either Scripture presupposes the Halakhic system, or the Halakhic system presupposes Scripture — or both. Accordingly, I propose a starting point for the message of the Halakhic system within the period in which Scripture's Halakhic statements were taking shape.[9] We return to this matter in due course.

So much for message, what of method? The method of the Halakhic system is defined by a focus on the organization of data by topics and the exposition of the respective topics by the criteria of teleology and intentionality. The method of the Halakhic system requires asking what is the purpose and end of an object or a transaction, what is the governing attitude and intentionality of that which brings about an object, action or transaction? That is the method of natural history as formulated by Aristotle.[10] A brief summary of the matter is supplied by Professor Robert Berchman, the key point being his treatment of intentionality:

> The questions Aristotle raises in his natural philosophy may be reduced to four heads: [1] Does this thing exist?; [2] does this event occur?; [3] If the thing exists, precisely what is it?; and [4] If the event occurs, why does it occur?
>
> Science does not occur unless it can advance from the solution of the first two questions to that of the latter two. Science is no mere catalogue of things and events. It consists of inquiries into the "real essences" and characteristics of things, and the laws of connection between events.
>
> When we ask "does such a thing exist" or "does such an event happen" we are asking is there a middle term which can connect the thing or event in question with the rest of known reality? Since it is the rule of the syllogism that the middle term must be taken universally, at least once in the premises, the search for middle terms may also be described as the search for universals, and we may speak of science as knowledge of the universal connections between facts and events.
>
> Intentionality plays a central role in Aristotle's and later Aristotelian systems. Beliefs and other mental states exhibit intentionality, and in a derived way so do sentences and books. The adjective "intentional" in this philosophical sense is a technical term not to be confused with the more familiar sense, characterizing something done on purpose. Beliefs and mental states are *about* various things.
>
> Intentionality means 'to point at' or 'aim at' or 'extend toward' phenomena. Phenomena with intentionality thus point outside of themselves to something else - whatever they are or about. Thus, intentionality defines the distinction between the mental and the physical; all and only mental phenomena exhibit intentionality.
>
> An example could be "hammering." "Hammering" is for making a cradle or a bookcase. In this sense the hammer is not merely a phenomenon with substance and attributes. It is defined in reference to its [mental] intentionality.
>
> The crucial move here is from intentionality to knowledge [science/*episteme*].
>
> Finally, Aristotle uses the 10 categories to define things. Briefly, primary substance is the individual thing. Secondary substance are the genera, species, and differentia of a thing. Accidents or properties are the quantity, quality, relation, place, time, position, possession, action, affection. Things are said to be because they are either quantities, qualities, or some other such category. Hence, the inquiry into the criteria

of what it means to be anything is transformed into an inquiry into the character possessed by a thing.

The categories display the grammatico-logical and ontological status of a thing or the general forms or ways in which being can be predicated. They are also determinations of being regarded as an object of thought, and consequently as a matter of speech.

There are four ways then to speak of a thing: 1] being by accident; 2] in the true way; 3] by potentiality; and 4] according to the schema of the categories.

It is clear that these aspects of Aristotle's system are basic to the Halakhic system.

To be sure, the conception of purposive nature, of things being meant for a particular purpose, is hardly alien to Scripture, from Genesis 1 onward. Scripture moreover recognizes the priority of intentionality in distinguishing murder from manslaughter. So while I have argued that the Mishnah's method follows Aristotle's principles of natural history, I recognize that some of the components of that analytical system can have been discerned in Scripture's own narrative and law. But in Scripture these considerations are episodic and notional, and to the Halakhic system they are essential and in it they are ubiquitous.

The medium of the Halakhic system as it reaches us in the form of the Mishnah (with the Tosefta, Yerushalmi, and Bavli) requires the formulation of abstract conceptions in concrete cases, prefers to deal with tertiary stages in the unfolding of the principles and not to engage in conflict on primary principles at all. This is in two aspects. First, the concrete details turn out to embody abstract positions. I have shown this for the Mishnah in *The Philosophical Mishnah*.[11] Second, the range of disputes focuses on subordinate details, the principal propositions being affirmed by all parties.[12]

Now directly to answer the question, if not from Scripture, whence the system and when?

When [1] the message of Moses met [2] the method of Aristotle framed in [3] the medium of concrete cases of law, the Halakhic system originated. Triangulating among the three points — message, method, medium — produced hermeneutics that defined the category-formations of the Halakhah ultimately set forth in the Mishnah's exegesis of the Halakhic system, item by item.

The first, the message or topical program of the Halakhah, in the main — all but a handful of tractates, for which we must account by appeal to the system's own generative logic and program[13] — derives from Scripture.

Second, the method, or modes of thought that define the way in which topics are expounded, corresponds to modes of the analytical inquiry of Aristotle into natural philosophy. (That judgment is stated within the qualification just now expressed.) Such issues for example encompass being and becoming, actuality and potentiality, the taxonomic power of intentionality, the teleology of objects and actions, and similar abstract analytical problems.

Third, the medium involves the translation, into details in the exposition of Moses's topics, of issues framed by Aristotle's analytical principles. The genius of the Halakhic system expresses in concrete terms of detailed laws deriving principally from Scripture the abstract issues of natural philosophy.

Before proceeding, let me give a single, simple example of triangulation of message, method, and medium, specifically, of the way in which details of the law originating in Scripture express in concrete terms abstract issues of natural philosophy. The message derives from Leviticus 11:34, 37, which we met at Makhshirin. The Rabbinic exegetes read those verses to mean that what is dry is insusceptible to uncleanness, while what has been wet down deliberately is susceptible. Consequently, the message concerns the status of liquid: wanted or unwanted, subject to the desire of a person or not subject to that desire. The method in the exposition to follow addresses the matter of intentionality, which carries with it on-going reflection on when action is required to confirm intention. The medium is a dispute on the status of honey in honeycombs: when does it become susceptible to uncleanness?

The triangulation of message, method, and medium require a simple instance. It occurs in the form of a dispute at Mishnah-tractate Uqsin 3:11. Here are the contending views:

A.   Honeycombs — from what point are they [is the honey-liquid] susceptible to uncleanness as liquid?

B.   The House of Shammai say, "When one will smoke out [the bees therefrom]."

C.   And the House of Hillel say, "When one will have broken [the honeycombs to remove the honey]."

The message is now self-evident. Liquid is susceptible to uncleanness when it is wanted (so Leviticus 11:34, 37, as the sages read those verses), that is, when it serves man's purposes, and it is not susceptible to uncleanness when man does not regard it as bearing consequence.

What is the method that defines what is at stake here? The important distinction is, is liquid deliberately applied to produce? Then dry produce, insusceptible to uncleanness, has been deliberately wet down, and because of man's deliberate action has been brought into the system of uncleanness and rendered susceptible. But how does the case frame the issue of intentionality?

That brings us to the medium, the particular case. When the bee-keeper smokes out the bees from the honey-combs, he exhibits his intentionality for some time in the future of taking and using the honey. So that is the point at which susceptibility to receive uncleanness affects the liquid honey, or, in the correct context, it is the point at which the honey if applied to dry produce imparts to the produce that puissant moisture that imparts susceptibility — that is to say, liquid deliberately put onto the produce. So far as the House of Shammai are concerned, therefore, a secondary cause (smoking out the bees) serves as readily as a primary cause (actually breaking the honeycombs). But the House of Hillel insists, and the Halakhah with them, that one actually must have carried out an action that directly confirms the intentionality. Secondary causation does not suffice; primary causation is required.

The Halakhah makes judgments about the effect of man's intentionality, as philosophy classifies causes into diverse classifications, e.g., primary and derivative, as in the present case. Here the religious issue — how do we sort out the intentions of man as Heaven responds to those intentions — joins together with the philosophical one — how do we classify types of causality, efficient versus secondary and derivative — to produce the Halakhah at hand. The position of the Halakhah about the character of man cannot be missed: whatever they intend or say, wait to see what they do — as in Eden, before and after the fall.

IV. WHEN? AN ANSWER FROM HISTORY

When did this triangulation of natural history and received law, producing category-formations in accord with philosophical principles of analysis, take place? To ask the question of when the coherent, comprehensive Halakhic system emerged, we work back from the completed account set forth in the Mishnah. We seek the context in which to set the origins of the Judaic legal system: [1] the category-formations (message), [2] their generative problematic (method), [3] the detailed articulation of the result of the method in coherent constructions of concrete, exemplary cases (medium).

The beginning point for much information and some category-formations is readily available. There can have been no Halakhic system without Scripture. So the *terminus a quo* is marked by the advent of Scripture's laws in Scripture's own context: whether in 1200 or 450 B.C.E. or at some point in between. Then important components of the topical program of the Halakhic system in the main reached formulation. But that self-evident observation sidesteps the question, when does the *entire* message emerge in its whole and complete form, in its analytical category-formations? Scripture cannot define the starting point of the comprehensive construction, only of discrete components.

Here my insistence on considering three elements, message, method, and medium, registers. Scripture defines some category-formations in a topical way, e.g., types of offerings, types of sources of uncleanness (the latter: Leviticus 11, 12-15), as we have already noted. But Scripture does not analyze those category-formations in accord with the Halakhic-systemic method. The comparison of Scripture's program for its topics with the Halakhic system's program for those same topics is telling. When it presents the case of the wife accused of adultery in Sotah, it concerns itself with the Temple rite, not the issue of justice. When it takes up the issues of Shebuot, Leviticus 5-6, Scripture's message concerns the Temple rites and offerings that are subject to classification. We have already noted that the category-formation on oaths, Shebuot covers two distinct subjects, [1] imparting uncleanness to the sanctuary and its Holy Things and [2] oaths. They are joined only by reason of Scripture's formulation of matters; the focus there is on common penalties for diverse sins or crimes. In Leviticus, then, Scripture organizes topics around classes of offerings associated with said topics. The guilt offering governs at Leviticus 5-6, and the category-formation Shebuot joins two distinct topics. The same contrast emerges when we compare Horayot and Leviticus 4. So even though the systemic message — the topic — belongs to Scripture, the analytical method does not. *When* does the message match the method?

The historical question finds its answer, then, when the organizing principle by topics and their indicative traits, is established and when the main lines of generative analysis are defined. The work of topical organization for teleological analysis of those laws is likely to have begun after the advent of the approach to natural history set forth by Aristotle, in the fourth century B.C.E. Then traits of data assembled along topical lines were analyzed along teleological lines. Hence (once more with the qualification expressed just now) the Halakhic system as we know it originated some time after the fourth century B.C.E., the *terminus a quo*. But there is a more precise date. Professor Robert Berchman comments, "Andronicus of Rhodes, first century B.C.E., was the editor of Aristotle's treatises. Before Andronicus there was no *editio princeps*. After Andronicus, Aristotle became widely known. Alexander of Aphrodisias, second century C.E., was the first Aristotelian to publish a number of commentaries on Aristotle's treatises based on the Andronican edition of Aristotle. These were widely read by Plotinus and his school, third century onwards."[14] It would seem to me to follow that the analytical approach to topical category-formation characteristic of the Mishnah and of natural philosophy made its impact in the first century B.C.E., at which point the unknown sages of the law of Judaism read Scripture analytically and crossed its topical boundaries as well, yielding the system viewed whole.

The end-point is equally self-evident: the Mishnah states the categorical system of the Halakhah whole and complete, the terminus ante quem. *No new category-formation would arise for many centuries after 200 C.E. (Neusner, 2003).*[15]

But when in the span of six hundred years — between the fourth century B.C.E. and the second century C.E. — did the work get underway?

My answer — a mere guess, really — is, sometime between 300 and 100 B.C.E. In that span of time Scripture's laws — the data, the message — fully registered, and the topical-teleological method of natural philosophy circulated. To be sure, it is easier to reconstruct processes of thought than to situate those processes in a particular century or determinate context. There is no external evidence that settles the question. Indeed, without the Mishnah and its successor documents closely linked to the Mishnah, we have no evidence that points to the existence of the Halakhic system. All we have, e.g., in the Christian writings, is bits and pieces of topical category-formations, e.g., Sabbath-law, uncleanness law, and tithing law. The Gospels of Mark, Matthew, and Luke attest to a Pharisaic corpus of rules on those topics. But whether these form components of a Halakhic system, let alone the Halakhic system embodied in the Mishnah, is not a question readily settled.

But there are two indicators that register. They point to an origin in the earlier part of the period of time under consideration.

First, the final articulation of the Halakhic category-formations by the Mishnah attributes numerous statements to named masters who flourished over the two centuries from ca. 50 B.C.E. to ca. 200 C.E. We cannot validate these attributions or verify that they were said by those to whom they are assigned at the specific points at which we assumed the named authorities flourished. But if, for a moment, we suspend critical judgment, an observation about the character of what is attributed does emerge.

These statements ordinarily register disagreements or disputes about subordinated details of the law, matters of refinement for example, and they confirm the consensus of sages on the basic principles in play. It is uncommon for a fundamental issue to engage the named sages, but routine for some minor application of an established law or principle to engage the contending sages. What lies at the foundations seldom precipitates dispute between named authorities. When it does, as in the case of M. Uqsin 3:11 given above, the named authorities stand for fixed differences concerning governing criteria built into the category-formation itself, in the present case the relationship of intention and action, the potential and the actual, and so on. I take that fact, shown in Contours of Coherence. The Dispute in Rabbinic Judaism,[16] *to bear a simple implication. It is to indicate that, prior to the process of recording the topical category-formations in detailed expositions of secondary and tertiary problems, a consensus on generative issues had emerged. Then, and only then, the work of presentation of the Mosaic message and philosophical method through the medium of minor, illustrative cases produced the main lines of the Mishnaic systematization of the Halakhic category-formations. In that process, named authorities played a primary role.[17]*

Second, and concomitantly, deep layers of systematic thought, the successive stages of which we are able to replicate at least in theory, underlie the subordinated, secondary and tertiary details, such as preoccupy the Mishnah's presentation of the Halakhic category-formations (all the more so, the Tosefta's and the Talmuds' continuation thereof). These dispositions of contingent detail — in the form of disputes about what are commonly rather minor matters for example — surface only in the categorical expositions attributed to authorities of the first century C.E. More to the point: refinements of detail dominate in the portrayal of the Halakhah by the Mishnah in the second century (Neusner, 2004). These facts attest to the prior formulation of a massive and cogent legal-philosophical system, fully in place and entirely realized. By the first century C. E., it seems to me, the Halakhic system had come to its full categorical formation, inclusive of the definition of the generative problematics of the respective category-formations. That is not in details but in its main outlines. By that point the Halakhah constituted a system in being, comprised by topics and rules of the analysis and exposition of those topics in accord with enduring issues of a philosophical character.[18]

I do not know how long a span of time can have been required for these deep layers of thought to accumulate around a corpus of facts and to germinate in that corpus, yielding a coherent composition. How long does it take to formulate the Halakhic category-formations of the complete Halakhic system, fully articulated but for the layer of discourse about concrete transactions and problems that would express the Halakhic system in all its specificity in the Mishnah (and related documents)? I cannot say. But it seems to me that some time long before the destruction of the Temple in 70 the system had attained its fundamental formulation, that triangulation of which I spoke: [1] organize by topics, specifically, [2] *these* topics, the result of [3] a long process of analytical reflection yielding concrete expression. That protracted spell of continuous thought accommodates the transition from abstract to concrete discourse. It takes account of the movement from principle to exemplary illustration. It allows for the transformation of the philosophical system in all its grandeur into the bits and pieces of particular information that could translate the whole into bits and pieces of easily-digestible truth.

So I venture to guess that some time between ca. 300 B.C.E. and ca. 100 B.C.E. the Halakhic system, its category-formations defined, came into being, with the main lines of its message, method, and medium fully realized. Thereafter the system would refine and polish itself, but because the category-formations had come to definition, it would not change in any fundamental aspect. By then principal category-formations of the Halakhah will have come to definition, the hermeneutics that generated the exegesis,[19] the animating issues, will have reached fruition, and the secondary development in minor practical matters that surface in the earliest strata of the Mishnah's Halakhah will have attained logical urgency. Some of these minor details can be shown play a role in the Gospels' narratives that touch on the Pharisaic Halakhah, so confirming for some category-formations a *terminus ante quem* of 70 C.E.

What is at issue, I cannot overemphasize, is *the fully-realized system*, not random details. These are not at issue but come to the fore as moot points only very late in the Halakhic process. The system originates when the Halakhic category-formations that would ultimately constitute the Mishnah had accomplished their task. That was to systematize Scripture's free-floating data into an orderly, comprehensive construction of topics, to define what was worth knowing about those data, and to generate the further categories that would fill gaps in the topical articulation of the system begun in Scripture. So at the heart of the Halakhic system as formed by the sages is the identification of that logic that inheres in Scripture's laws, the principles of coherence and order that transform the details into an encompassing, cogent theory of the social order.[20]

The governing thesis arising from historical considerations therefore is easy to set forth. At some point the principles of natural philosophy in thinking about the cases of the Mosaic law produced the determination to translate the result of philosophical systematization into exemplary, ordinarily secondary or tertiary, formulations of detail. Thinking philosophically about the normative data of Scripture and tradition produced topical category-formations that embodied principles in cases. Then the questions that animate the exposition of those formations would take over. The Halakhic categories would be so constituted as to process for a thousand years an unlimited flow of diverse data in a systematic manner. From 200 to 1200 C.E., when the new Aristotelianism of Maimonides took over the Halakhah and renewed the process of category-formation and articulation, the categorical work of the early centuries B.C.E. would govern.

But historical perspectives do not exhaust the matter. When we stand back and ask whether Scripture is not only necessary but entirely sufficient to the Halakhic system and whether the Halakhic system is not only necessary but entirely sufficient to Scripture, matters shift in focus.

v. Why Not? An Answer from Theology

Scripture is not the origin of the Halakhah. Why not? Because of this paradox:

Scripture is necessary for the Halakhic system. But Scripture is insufficient for the Halakhic system.

The Halakhic system is necessary for Scripture. The Halakhic *system* is sufficient without Scripture. It requires only Scripture's facts — *and these on their own form no system.*

Scripture is necessary to the Halakhic system. But it now is clear that Scripture also is insufficient for that system. Absent the Halakhic system, in message, method, and medium, Scripture comes up short. That is because, measured against the Halakhic system, on its own Scripture does not yield a coherent and comprehensive account of Israel's social order. Some category-formations form a silent but definitive testimony to the inadequacy of Scripture's counterpart design for Israel's social order — however generously we interpret the data Scripture does provide. Only the Halakhic system provides a coherent and encompassing composition for Israel as a sacred social entity.[21] And that phenomenological observation yields the theological reason why. Scripture — *the* [written part of the] *Torah* in the native category of Judaism — did not suffice but required the complement of the Halakhic system, fully realized. And that is why Scripture is necessary to the Halakhic system but insufficient for that system.

But should Scripture through its various legal compositions in Exodus, Leviticus, Numbers and Deuteronomy be expected to yield an encompassing statement? Indeed it should and promises to. By providing laws, not only history and prophecy and exhortation but social norms ("You shall be holy, for I the Lord your God am holy"), Scripture signals the intent of setting forth an account of the norms of the Israelite social order. Its rhetoric ("kingdom of priests and holy people") and myth ("you have seen...") promise no less. And, we must not forget, prophecy consistently invoked the imperative of justice, encompassing just law. But we have seen concrete reason to conclude that the details of what is provided fall far short of what is required. Scripture then presupposes not only a corpus of facts but a set of category-formations very much akin to the one before us but fails to provide some of what is needed and, more tellingly, hardly articulates what is essential for the greater part of the topics it does introduce.

A simple case suffices to make the point clear. The civil code conveyed by Baba Qamma-Baba-Mesia-Baba Batra draws upon Scripture for some of its critical points, but finds nothing in Scripture to support others that are equally essential to the comprehensive construction of the civil code. We cannot doubt that the Babas presuppose Scripture, because critical components of the tri-partite category formation, particularly the first half, are incomprehensible without Scripture. But Scripture seems to me to presuppose the Babas. For it intersects with them, takes as its constructive problem important elements that they cover — and yet contains legislation on some of the Babas' topics but not others! So we must wonder, did Scripture contemplate a law code that dealt with damages but not real estate, illicit commercial transactions but not licit ones? Or did Scripture, with its focus on the Israelite social order and the rule of justice therein — presuppose complementary law beyond its limits? The corpus of Scriptural passages that function in the Babas points to the latter alternative.

Not only so, but when we set Negaim and Sotah and Nazir side by side with Leviticus 13-14 and Numbers 5 and Numbers 6, respectively, we must ask a comparable question. Is not the analytical program of the Halakhic category-formation essential to the full exposition of what is implicit in, or — more to the point, — required by, Scripture's data on the *mesora*, the wife accused of infidelity, and the Nazirite vow? Indeed so.

Scripture never contemplated its statement of the law as sufficient, only as necessary (for reasons we need not pursue). Then Scripture always presupposes complementary law beyond its limits. That outcome matches the one with which we commenced: just as the Halakhic system presupposes Scripture but moves beyond Scripture's limits, so Scripture presupposes Halakhic expositions beyond its expositions of the law. Scripture indeed not only presupposes them, but demands them and, as in the case of the Babas (and not there alone) is impossible, is incomplete, without them. No wonder the outcome of centuries of rigorous thought yielding the Halakhic system, a process that we have tried in these pages to reconstruct, would be given the position of "Torah" in the Rabbinic tradition: the oral part of the revelation of Sinai. But that is to claim more than is needed to answer the question of this book. At issue is not literary or social history but the phenomena of religion read philosophically to yield theology.

So, to conclude with the main point: Scripture is necessary to the Halakhic system but insufficient for that system. Absent Scripture, however, does the Halakhic system accomplish its goals? Indeed it does. The answer is jarring. Apart from the facts that Scripture provides, e.g., topics fully articulated by Scripture and taken over by the Halakhic system whole, as well as the topics amplified by the Halakhic system wholly within the framework of Scripture's facts, the Halakhic system stands on its own. It does not take as its model Scripture's system, ignoring its method and its medium. It only utilizes its message, meaning here, Scripture's data.

Seen on its own, the Halakhic system does yield a coherent and comprehensive account of Israel's social order. The Halakhic system — its category-formations and their exposition — proves coherent, cogent, and comprehensive. That is why Scripture is necessary but insufficient to the Halakhic system, while the Halakhic system stands on its own, not only necessary but sufficient unto itself. Scripture is not only not the origin of the Halakhic system, it also is not the sine qua non *of that system seen whole. The systematization of received facts, the extension of those facts, the recapitulation of those facts into topical expositions of generative principles — all was the work of the Halakhic system. No other compilation of social norms ("law code") of Judaic antiquity attempted what the Halakhic system of the Mishnah and the Tosefta accomplished.*

ENDNOTES

[1] I summarize the findings set forth in detail of *Is Scripture the Origin of the Halakhah?* Lanham, 2005: University Press of America.

[2] That the components of the system as a whole are purposively selected can be shown only through an exercise of comparison and contrast with other systemic documents produced in one or another Judaism, that is, in the context of Scripture..

[3] The facts set forth in this study were entirely familiar to the Rabbinic sages, who formulated the narrative of the dual Torah, part in writing, part orally formulated and orally transmitted, to accommodate the facts that, as we shall see in a moment, they themselves recognized. See my *What, Exactly, Did the Rabbinic Sages Mean by "the Oral Torah"? An Inductive Answer to the Question of Rabbinic Judaism.* Atlanta, 1999: Scholars Press for South Florida Studies in the History of Judaism. Now: Lanham, MD: University Press of America. A comparison of the law codes of Scripture, the Dead Sea library, and the Mishnah-Tosefta is set forth in *The Vitality of Rabbinic Imagination: The Mishnah against the Bible and Qumran.* Lanham, 2005: University Press of America.

[4] But the topical category-formation does not govern in the Tannaite Midrash-compilations, Mekhilta, Sifra, and the two Sifrés.

[5] No category-formations beyond those of the Mishnah and the Tosefta function in the classical statements of the law to frame exposition and provoke systematic analysis. I have pursued this matter in *Why This, Not That? Ways Not Taken in the Halakhic Category-Formations of the Mishnah-Tosefta-Yerushalmi-Bavli.* Lanham, 2003: University Press of America.

⁶The Mishnah and the Tosefta set forth the Halakhic category-formations and the bulk of the generative law, the Yerushalmi and the Bavli contributing mere details to the topical program, but dense analysis of that program. That is the result of my *The Halakhah: An Encyclopaedia of the Law of Judaism.* (Leiden, 1999: E. J. Brill. The Brill Reference Library of Judaism, I-V. I give a precis of the law document by document, Mishnah, Tosefta, Yerushalmi, and Bavli, and show that the bulk of the details of the law are set forth in the Mishnah and the Tosefta, with little of substance, but much of analytical consequence, contributed by the Yerushalmi and the Bavli. The use of different type faces for each document's contribution to a given topic highlights that fact.

⁷ I point to *The Hermeneutics of the Rabbinic Category-Formations: An Introduction.* Lanham, 2000: University Press of America. Studies in Judaism SERIES. *The Comparative Hermeneutics of Rabbinic Judaism.* Volume One. *Introduction. Berakhot and Seder Mo'ed.* Binghamton, 2000: Global Publications. ACADEMIC STUDIES IN ANCIENT JUDAISM series *The Comparative Hermeneutics of Rabbinic Judaism.* Volume Two. *Seder Nashim.* Binghamton, 2000: Global Publications. ACADEMIC STUDIES IN ANCIENT JUDAISM series. *The Comparative Hermeneutics of Rabbinic Judaism.* Volume Three. *Seder Neziqin.* Binghamton, 2000: Global Publications. ACADEMIC STUDIES IN ANCIENT JUDAISM series. *The Comparative Hermeneutics of Rabbinic Judaism.* Volume Four. *Seder Qodoshim.* Binghamton, 2000: Global Publications. ACADEMIC STUDIES IN ANCIENT JUDAISM series. *The Comparative Hermeneutics of Rabbinic Judaism.* Volume Five. *Seder Tohorot.* Part *Kelim through Parah.* Binghamton, 2000: Global Publications. ACADEMIC STUDIES IN ANCIENT JUDAISM series. *The Comparative Hermeneutics of Rabbinic Judaism.* Volume Six. *Seder Tohorot. Tohorot through Uqsin.* Binghamton, 2000: Global Publications. ACADEMIC STUDIES IN ANCIENT JUDAISM series. *The Comparative Hermeneutics of Rabbinic Judaism.* Volume Seven *The Generic Hermeneutics of the Halakhah. A Handbook.* Binghamton, 2000: Global Publications. ACADEMIC STUDIES IN ANCIENT JUDAISM series. Volumes One through Seven: Second printing, condensed, under the title, *Halakhic Hermeneutics,* Lanham, 2003: University Press of America. *The Comparative Hermeneutics of Rabbinic Judaism.* Volume Eight. *Why This, Not That? Ways Not Taken in the Halakhic Category-Formations of the Mishnah-Tosefta-Yerushalmi-Bavli.* Binghamton, 2000: Global Publications. ACADEMIC STUDIES IN ANCIENT JUDAISM series. Second printing, revised; under the title, *Why This, Not That? Ways Not Taken in the Halakhic Category-Formations of the Mishnah-Tosefta-Yerushalmi-Bavli.* Lanham, 2003: University Press of America.

⁸ But the Halakhic system in relationship to Scripture takes up a fundamental position, and when we compare Scripture's version of a coherent set of laws to that of the Halakhic system for those same laws, Scripture appears subordinate, a summary of a more fully articulated system, and that is a summary that presupposes for realization the data of the Halakhic system. That argument has been invoked to show the dual media of the Torah, written and oral, with the written part of the Torah presupposing data set forth only in the oral part. I need not introduce the mythic formulation of matters to register the same point. We return to this matter in a more systematic way in a moment.

⁹ I do not invoke the mythic language of the Judaic narrative and speak of the oral part of the Torah and the written part of the Torah, but it is readily supplied.

¹⁰ I need not repeat the systematic inquiry of *Judaism as Philosophy. The Method and Message of the Mishnah.* Columbia, 1991: University of South Carolina Press.

¹¹ *The Philosophical Mishnah.* Volume I. *The Initial Probe.* Atlanta, 1989: Scholars Press for Brown Judaic Studies. Now: Lanham MD: University Press of America. *The Philosophical*

Mishnah. Volume II. *The Tractates' Agenda. From Abodah Zarah to Moed Qatan.* Atlanta, 1989: Scholars Press for Brown Judaic Studies. . Now: Lanham MD: University Press of America. *The Philosophical Mishnah.* Volume III. *The Tractates' Agenda. From Nazir to Zebahim.* Atlanta, 1989: Scholars Press for Brown Judaic Studies. . Now: Lanham MD: University Press of America. *The Philosophical Mishnah.* Volume IV. *The Repertoire.* Atlanta, 1989: Scholars Press for Brown Judaic Studies. Now: Lanham MD: University Press of America.

[12] That is the point of *Contours of Coherence. The Dispute in Rabbinic Judaism.* Leiden, 2004: E. J. Brill.

[13] And that would suggest a layered process of definition of category-formations, the completely independent ones coming to the fore only in a secondary process of completing the system's topical repertoire. But a systematic inquiry into the unfolding of the system, the sequence of systemic formulation, can only follow a systematic study of the diverse Judaic Halakhic systems, Scripture's and those of other writings, which I project in due course.

[14] Personal letter, April 4, 2004.

[15] See my *Why This, Not That? Ways Not Taken in the Halakhic Category-Formations of the Mishnah-Tosefta-Yerushalmi-Bavli.* Lanham, 2003: University Press of America.

[16] Leiden, 2005: E. J. Brill.

[17] We do not need to affirm that the named authorities of the Mishnah really said, in exactly the words attributed to them, what is assigned. I have shown that what is assigned to a later authority takes up an issue dependent upon the point registered in the name of an earlier authority — when we have attributed statements to successive generations of sages on the same topic. The work of what I call "verification" — showing that an earlier authority does not take for granted what is attributed to a later authority — rarely yields anomalies. And that extends to those Amoraic authorities of the Bavli where probes have been completed. That does not prove attributions are reliable, only that where we can test them, they commonly prove plausible. See Neusner, 2005.

[18] That category-formations concerning the Sabbath, tithing, and cultic cleanness in the domestic venue functioned in the first century C.E. is suggested also by the concurrence of the Rabbinic traditions assigned to pre-70 authorities and the sayings attributed to Jesus concerning Pharisees, where in both sets of traditions there is thematic intersection. I pursued that problem in my *Rabbinic Traditions about the Pharisees before 70* (Leiden, 1971: E. J. Brill) I-III.

[19] I do not need to recapitulate the findings of the following: *The Hermeneutics of the Rabbinic Category-Formations: An Introduction.* Lanham, 2000: University Press of America. Studies in Judaism SERIES. *The Comparative Hermeneutics of Rabbinic Judaism.* Volume One. *Introduction. Berakhot and Seder Mo'ed.* Binghamton, 2000: Global Publications. ACADEMIC STUDIES IN ANCIENT JUDAISM series. *The Comparative Hermeneutics of Rabbinic Judaism.* Volume Two. *Seder Nashim.* Binghamton, 2000: Global Publications. ACADEMIC STUDIES IN ANCIENT JUDAISM series. *The Comparative Hermeneutics of Rabbinic Judaism.* Volume Three. *Seder Neziqin.* Binghamton, 2000: Global Publications. ACADEMIC STUDIES IN ANCIENT JUDAISM series. *The Comparative Hermeneutics of Rabbinic Judaism.* Volume Four. *Seder Qodoshim.* Binghamton, 2000: Global Publications. ACADEMIC STUDIES IN ANCIENT JUDAISM series. *The Comparative Hermeneutics of Rabbinic Judaism.* Volume Five. *Seder Tohorot.* Part *Kelim through Parah.* Binghamton, 2000: Global Publications. ACADEMIC STUDIES IN ANCIENT JUDAISM series. *The Comparative Hermeneutics of Rabbinic*

Judaism. Volume Six. *Seder Tohorot. Tohorot through Uqsin.* Binghamton, 2000: Global Publications. ACADEMIC STUDIES IN ANCIENT JUDAISM series. *The Comparative Hermeneutics of Rabbinic Judaism.* Volume Seven *The Generic Hermeneutics of the Halakhah. A Handbook.* Binghamton, 2000: Global Publications. ACADEMIC STUDIES IN ANCIENT JUDAISM series. Volumes One through Seven: Second printing, condensed, under the title, *Halakhic Hermeneutics,* Lanham, 2003: University Press of America. *The Comparative Hermeneutics of Rabbinic Judaism.* Volume Eight. *Why This, Not That? Ways Not Taken in the Halakhic Category-Formations of the Mishnah-Tosefta-Yerushalmi-Bavli.* Binghamton, 2000: Global Publications. ACADEMIC STUDIES IN ANCIENT JUDAISM series. Second printing, revised; under the title, *Why This, Not That? Ways Not Taken in the Halakhic Category-Formations of the Mishnah-Tosefta-Yerushalmi-Bavli.* Lanham, 2003: University Press of America.

[20] I leave for another study the question of whether the category-formations reached definition in a cogent, determinate process or in an agglutinative process. Whether a vision of the whole dictated the articulation of the parts is a question that requires reflection in its own right, not in the present context, because it involves the comparison and contrast of Judaic systems, the Halakhic one of the Mishnah with counterparts, both Scriptural and otherwise. My *History of the Mishnaic Law* (Leiden, 1974-1986) in forty-three volumes and its consequent *Judaism: The Evidence of the Mishnah* (Chicago, 1981) pursued this question along historical lines, tracing the unfolding of the category-formations of the Mishnah with the Tosefta from before 70 to the closure of the Mishnah. But a phenomenological approach is called for.

[21] That is, the Halakhic system is unique among the Judaic religious systems of antiquity, a matter to be demonstrated in the comparison and contrast of the Halakhic system and the legal compositions of such venues as the Jewish community of Elephantine, the Dead Sea Library, and the Samaritan law codes. Among all of the Israelite legal writings produced in antiquity, only the Halakhic system served beyond its day and accommodated later ages and circumstances within its message, method, and medium. But the claim of uniqueness requires testing in its own terms. It is carried out in Chapter One, which is an epitome of my *The Vitality of Rabbinic Imagination: The Mishnah against the Bible and Qumran.* Lanham, 2005: University Press of America

3

How Important Was the Destruction of the Second Temple in the Formation of Rabbinic Judaism?

I. CONTEXT

Since I propose to assess the importance, in the context of Rabbinic Judaism in its formative centuries, the first through the sixth C.E., of the destruction of the Second Temple, I have to answer a basic question. It is, What marks a corpus of thought as important? First, the set of ideas will make its presence felt in both native categories of Rabbinic Judaism, Halakhah and Aggadah. An idea paramount in Aggadic writings but without a Halakhic counterpart is not primary to the Rabbinic system. Second, an important idea or doctrine will come to the surface in diverse settings, being invoked finally to solve a broad variety of fresh questions. The destruction of the Second Temple in 70 is treated in both the Halakhic and the Aggadic sectors of the Rabbinic canon. The topic surfaces in a variety of Halakhic settings and plays a role in a range of Aggadic expositions as well. So on the face of the matter, we deal with a significant matter. But how important?

As to the topics, 586, the destruction of the first Temple, 70, the destruction of the Second Temple, and 132-135, the disaster of the Bar Kokhba War: in the presentation of these events in the Rabbinic writings we possess a fairly simple set of ideas, elaborately instantiated. What I show is that the Rabbinic reading of the destruction of the Second Temple merely recapitulates in a fresh context quite commonplace ideas of Scripture, Ezekiel for the ultimate restoration of the cult, and Lamentations, for the reading of the destruction as a penalty for violating the Torah, for example. The Rabbinic reading of 70 continues the scriptural-prophetic reading of 586. It is thus difficult to affirm that the destruction of the Second Temple marked an important turning in the formation of Rabbinic Judaism. Rather, it is continuous with Scripture and scarcely does more than adapt a received scriptural conception to a new context. So we form the impression of a secondary recapitulation of an established and conventional construction of ideas. We deal in the Rabbinic reading of the destruction of the Second Temple with familiar forms imposed on fresh facts: adaptation, not innovation. The established system of Scriptural prophecy shaded over into a Rabbinic recapitulation of the same system. The event of 586 governs, the event of 70 conforms to the received paradigm, and the events of 132-135 scarcely register except for propositions meant to account for the disaster and exculpate the Rabbinic sages from responsibility therefor.

II. THE HALAKHIC PERSPECTIVE

The Halakhic component of my argument is simply stated:

The Halakhah of the Mishnah in its articulation of its category-formations absorbs the pattern of catastrophe into its encompassing system but does not permit that pattern to shape the Mishnah's own structure of category-formations. These presuppose in form and substance that the Second Temple, priesthood, altar and its blood-rite of atonement all flourish; that the principal locus of celebration of appointed times is the Temple in Jerusalem; that the priests continue to receive God's share in the produce of the Land; that nothing has changed that matters.

All this is implicit in the formulation of Mishnah-tractate Hullin and articulated in a wide range of category-formations of cultic topics. Let us consider once more the Mishnah's eloquent statement that Israel's sanctification endures without regard to the temporal or locative context.

Mishnah Hullin 5:1
The prohibition against slaughtering on the same day it and its young, Lev. 22:28, applies (1) in the Land and outside the Land, (2) in the time of the Temple and not in the time of the Temple, (3) in the case of unconsecrated beasts and in the case of consecrated beasts.
Mishnah Hullin 6:1
The requirement to cover up the blood applies in the Land and abroad, (2) in the time of the Temple and not in the time of the Temple, (3) in the case of unconsecrated beasts, but not in the case of Holy Things.
Mishnah Hullin 7:1
The prohibition of the sinew of the hip sciatic nerve, Gen. 32:32, applies (1) in the Land and outside of the Land, (2) in the time of the Temple and not in the time of the Temple, (3) to unconsecrated animals and to Holy Things.
Mishnah Hullin 10:1
The requirement to give to the priests the shoulder, the two cheeks, and the maw, Dt. 18:3, applies (1) in the Land and outside of the Land, (2) in the time of the Temple and not in the time of the Temple, (3) to unconsecrated beasts, but not to consecrated beasts.
Mishnah Hullin 11:1
The requirement to give to the priest the first of the fleece, Dt. 18:41, applies (1) in the Land and outside of the Land, (2) in the time of the Temple and not in the time of the Temple, (3) to unconsecrated beasts but not to consecrated beasts.

Mishnah Hullin 12:1

The requirement to let the dam go from the nest, Dt. 22:6-7, applies (1) in the Land and outside of the Land, (2) in the time of the Temple and not in the time of the Temple, (3) to unconsecrated birds but not to consecrated ones.

The sanctity of Israel, expressed here in the Halakhic system, endures beyond the loss of the holy city, the holy *Temple*, and, ultimately, the holy Land. The events of 132-135 registered in the same context. As to fundamental facts of the social order, Israel remains holy after 70 as before 70 and beyond the bounds of the Holy Land as much as within the Land.

Mishnah-tractate Hullin shows what the Mishnah could have accomplished had its framers wished articulately to legislate for the interim without the *Temple*. Between Mishnah-tractate Rosh Hashanah and Mishnah-tractate Taanit, a tractate on the 9th of Ab and the *Temple* after that event takes shape, and one need not tax the imagination to conceive of other candidates. But the Rabbinic sages did not choose to legislate for what they did not plan to acknowledge. Nowhere else are we told about how to conduct affairs both now and then, both here and there, both with and without a building, a working priesthood, a corps of Levites, and all Israel assembled for the pilgrimage to see God on the festival.

For one example, Bikkurim, on the presentation of firstfruits, does not explain how absent the *Temple* one hands over to the priest the firstfruits of the Land. Is that rite suspended now, and are the priests deprived of the firstfruits of the Land? The Mishnah's topical exposition does not respond. Mishnah-tractate Tamid on the daily whole-offering does not propose a surrogate for the present age or acknowledge that today differs from yesterday and, it is hoped, also from tomorrow. Mishnah-tractate Yoma Chapters One through Seven describe the progression of the rite of atonement on the Day of Atonement, without taking note that "in this time" it is null. Only its exposition of repentance and self-affliction as media of atonement, Mishnah-tractate Yoma Chapter Eight, shades over into an answer to the question of Israel in the here and now of deprivation. Mishnah-tractate Sheqalim describes the management and financial arrangements of the *Temple* as though the enterprise was in full swing. No one makes provision for the utilization of the half-sheqel offering for the public sacrifice of atonement in the age in which at sunrise and sunset there is no public offering. Perhaps everybody knew the Romans were collecting it from 70. But there is a great deal else that everybody knew but that the Mishnah records: 70 did happen, and the conditions brought about by the war of 132-135 continued to define the politics of Israel in the Land of Israel, beginning with the status of Jerusalem.

What difference in the norms of conduct then did the destruction make? For the law of the Mishnah the destruction of the Second Temple formed an established fact bearing obvious liturgical consequences. These were deemed transient and trivial, readily coped with. When it comes to the destruction of the Second Temple in 70, the Mishnah concerns itself with these issues: Sukkot after

70; the Shofar after 70; taking testimony of the New Moon; the 17th of Tammuz and the ninth of Ab and rules covering the categories in which each falls; the status of Nazirites after 70, signs of mourning for the Second Temple after 70 (with stress on avoiding excessive asceticism); and the status of new produce on the 15th of Nisan after 70. These few items add up to very little. To repeat, they do not comprise a Halakhic category-formation, but rather footnotes to received category-formations, details of a larger whole.

How does the Mishnah place into its distinctive perspective the historical moments of 586, 70, and 132-135? Once more to review a familiar passage:

Mishnah Taanit 4:6

A. Five events took place for our fathers…on the 9th of Ab:

C. On the 9th of Ab (1) the decree was made against our forefathers that they should not enter the land, (2) the First Temple and (3) the second [Temple] were destroyed, (4) Betar was taken, and (5) the city was ploughed up [after the war of Hadrian].

In the Halakhic system, with its stress on the classification of actions and transactions and events and the rule governing all those that fall into a single classification, history loses all weight. Events abandon their singularity, their individual implications. They are homogenized into a classification of events and yield not markers of time but timeless laws for the enduring social order. They bear not consequences unique to themselves but rules common to a given type. History thus loses its specificity and becomes a source of exemplary data yielding social rules that predict the consequence of actions. The events of 586, 70, and 132-135 in the Mishnah are treated as not unique — that is, as turning points in the cosmos — but exemplary. They registered not the end of time but mere symptoms of the human condition of Israel, merely deplorable turnings in Israel's condition, to be responded to in accord with the Torah's enduring lessons.

The happenings brought about changes, to be sure, but they left intact that pattern of sanctification in Israel's way of life that the Mishnah defines in its systematic manner. And the Mishnah's Halakhic category-formations affirm the cult, priesthood, Temple, Jerusalem — the whole institutional system of sanctification that succeeded the destruction of the First Temple in 586. A superficial survey of the Mishnah, accordingly, yields the generalization that 70 and 132-135 do not define decisive events in the supernatural life of holy Israel, which is lived beyond time and above history. In the language of the Mishnah and of the Tosefta nothing has changed in 70 and 132-135, except for Israel's circumstance, and that change is transient. What endures is the corpus of rules that, when realized, bring about sanctification.

The Mishnah, reaching closure perhaps two generations after 132-135, describes an Israelite social order centered on the Temple and its rites, governed by priest and king (Mishnah-tractate Sanhedrin Chapter Two). The focus of the Mishnah on the Temple and priesthood forms a definitive fact: the destruction is for the moment, the holy place and its sacrifices are for all time. To express this conviction in form, not only in substance, the Halakhah employs a rhetoric of an eternal present tense: this is how things are and how they are perpetually done. Its narratives of specific Temple rites form scripts for recapitulation of permanent liturgical or ritual patterns. That about which the Mishnah is silent is not the events of 586, 70, and 132-135, but about the destruction of the Temple and the cessation of its blood rite of atonement. That fact is shown in both affirmative and negative facts.

The affirmative fact is that the greater part of the Mishnah — four of its six divisions — explicitly focuses on the Temple: support for the priesthood (all of Zeraim), its rites for Appointed Times (most of Moed), the conduct of the offerings and the upkeep of the Temple (all of Qodoshim), and cultic purity, sacerdotal and domestic alike (Tohorot). Strictly speaking, then, an account of the Rabbinic canonical account of the events of 70 and 132-135 must begin with the massive record of remembered rules and rites of the Temple. The way to the restoration lay open, fully mapped.

The whole describes how things are done, not conceding that this is a record out of the past. The rhetoric on the liturgies of the Temple speaks of the Temple as it is, not as it was or will be. If we permitted the allegations of a document and the language that conveys them to dictate the venue in which a document was written, then the Mishnah was written when the Second Temple was standing and in operation. For Mishnah-tractates Yoma, Negaim, Parah, Sotah, Menahot, Sheqalim, and others contain elaborate, continuing-present-tense narratives about what at specific liturgical turnings the priest does and says, where he goes or does not go, what he does or does not do. These narratives of the Second Temple are the only ones in the Mishnah that exhibit the indicative formal traits noted just now. When the Mishnah's writers devote themselves to the conduct of the Second Temple, its management and its offerings and its upkeep, the whole is scripted, word and deed alike, for an abiding portrait, a motionless tableau. Slight provision is made for the present age, lacking a Second Temple and an altar. And, more to the point, there is no narrative counterpart for any other rites than the Second Temple's and the priesthood's, for example, involving the synagogue on a given occasion or the public life of the Rabbinic sages themselves, to the ritualization of which much attention is paid in the later Halakhic compilations.

What might we have anticipated had 70 denoted a decisive turning? An obvious candidate is an account of the life and affairs of the synagogue, supposedly the surrogate for the ruined Temple, its rites replacing, for the interim, the altar's offerings. For one striking instance, the Halakhah in the Mishnah's category-formations never provides for rites to replace those of the Temple during the interim of the Temple's ruin. Prayer is supposed to be the surrogate, but that is a generic judgment, not made specifically in the context of a particular prayer corresponding to a particular offering. True, the canon contains sayings that the study of the laws of sacrifice yields the same result as if one had actually made the offering. But when it comes to practice, these allegations yield nothing. Study of the Torah is not characterized by any Halakhic category-formation as the substitution for the Temple offerings.

For example, we have not got in the Rabbinic canon a single story or saying about a master who unintentionally violated the law of the Sabbath and consequently studied Mishnah-tractate Zebahim. Rather, we have the following:

Tosefta Shabbat 1:13

A. Said R. Ishmael, "One time I read by the light of a lamp, and [forgetfully,] I wanted to tilt it [to get more oil on the wick].

B. "I said, 'How great are the words of sages, who rule, 'They do not read on Sabbath nights by the light of a lamp.'"

C. R. Nathan says, "He [Ishmael] most certainly did tilt it."

D. "And written on his notebook is the following: 'Ishmael b. Elisha tilted a lamp on the Sabbath.

E. "'When the sanctuary will be rebuilt, he will bring a sin-offering.'"

So much for the standing of claims that studying the law of the Torah of sacrifice is tantamount to making the sacrifice. They have no Halakhic standing whatsoever, because they generate no specific rules. And as to prayer taking the place of sacrifice, the rites of the synagogue in no way replaced, but only corresponded with, the rites of the Temple as in the case of the Additional Service on Sabbaths and Festivals. More to the point, in the Mishnah the synagogue prayers centered on the declamation of the Torah figure casually and in severely limited aspects, for example in Mishnah-tractate Megillah. The liturgical wording and regulations figure in Mishnah-tractate Berakhot. In neither instance does substitution of prayer for sacrifice in the ruined Temple figure as a motivation.

The Mishnah's Halakhic system, indeed, never acknowledges the synagogue with a category-formation at all, for example, and legislates for the synagogue only partially, for its presentation of the declamation of the Torah. The latest Rabbinic documents contain statements that prayer takes the place of animal sacrifice, acts of loving kindness substitute for atonement-offerings, study of Torah forms the counterpart of sacrifice, and the like. But no Halakhic consequences follow from these statements; there is no Halakhah, let alone a Halakhic category-formation, to realize the conception that loving kindness serves as atonement as the Temple sacrifice once did. I cannot point to a single Halakhic ruling that realizes the beautiful idea that acts of loving kindness atone as sin-offerings atone, e.g., the sage said to him, "Go, atone by an act of altruism."

I stressed the probative standing of the category-formations of the Halakhah as systemic indicators. The synagogue offers a striking case: there is a tractate Middot to describe the architecture of the Second Temple and a tractate Tamid to portray its liturgy. There is no counterpart tractate devoted to the building *used* for a synagogue (one cannot speak of a synagogue-building), nor does the Mishnah assign to the synagogue the unique locus for the recitation of prayers, the Shema and the Prayer, for example. These may be recited nearly anywhere. Why not provide rules for synagogue buildings and their liturgy? To provide for buildings and rites uniquely performed in them would have required acknowledging the loss of the holy house and its atonement-rites. That the Mishnah declined to do, and with that decision, the Halakhic categorical system for a thousand years took shape.

The opposite is the case. In the Mishnah's vast, detailed account of Israel's holy life portrayed in the building blocks of large-scale, topical expositions, the priesthood has not lost its position at the side of the altar and the Levites have not fallen off their platform for singing. The sacerdotal estate continues to receive its holy rations from the Land of Israel and to eat its food in a state of cultic cleanness, as if in the Second Temple, as if in Jerusalem. Nor is this only in the realm of imagination. The Halakhah provides for the priests to continue to receive their holy rations, as Mishnah Hullin says in so many words noted earlier, and as is implicit in Mishnah-tractates Maaserot and Terumot and elsewhere. Jerusalem is still the metropolis and goal of pilgrimage, as Mishnah-tractate Maaser Sheni indicates. There is no thought given to other loci for pilgrimage. No one suggests — or troubles to condemn — spending Passover at the Temple of Onias in Egypt, for example.

Consider the alternative, which is, the formation of the Mishnah without the Second Temple as a paramount motif. If we were to remove from the Mishnah every paragraph, every chapter, every tractate that describes the status quo of an Israel restored to its holy place and holy vocation, of Jerusalem and its Temple offerings, we should be left with bits and pieces, shards and remnants of this and that — but the Halakhic system as we know it would be lost. It would consist of the larger part of the division of women and much of the division of damages (civil law). But lacking all supernatural connection, what is left would form no system at all, only components awaiting further required parts for composition into one. More to the point: we should have nothing like the recognizable ruins of the Mishnah as we know it. The discernible pattern would disappear, the system not only diminished but also destroyed, and the surviving ruins in their chaotic incoherence would not allow for its recovery.

To state the matter simply: the Mishnah, the first document of Rabbinic Judaism beyond Scripture, without its account of the working cult of the Temple, without its lines of structure and order radiating out into the Land of Israel and into the life of the people of Israel in the villages and in the fields, in time and out of time, the Mishnah is something other, utterly beyond imagining. For every passage that for local exigencies acknowledges the destruction of the Second Temple, the cessation of the cult, and the loss of Jerusalem, as at such passages as at Mishnah Hullin 5:1 or Mishnah Taanit 4:6, there are tens, indeed, hundreds of passages that describe the sanctification of Israel in its priesthood, cult, holy place, and holy city in an ideal present tense of realized eternity.

What proposition is presented in the law and its normative narratives? The obvious answer is, *denial, denial, denial.* Nothing has happened that cannot be corrected: Israel endures holy and unique. That is why the destruction of the Second Temple cannot claim a primary place in Rabbinic Judaism's Halakhic statement. To the Halakhah the destruction of the Second Temple in 70 is temporary and superficial and raises only some few minor questions of accommodation. That is because in the conception of the Halakhic system and in its paramount rhetoric, the

Second Temple still stands. It has not been, and cannot be, razed. It forms the heart and center of the legal system realized in rich detail in the Mishnah and the Tosefta and the articulation of the Halakhah. That is why the destruction of the Second Temple in 70 cannot be assigned a critical place in the formative history of Rabbinic Judaism. It was more than a footnote, but less than a principal text: to be coped with, not to be confirmed let alone affirmed as enduring.

What about adaptations to the new situation? Mishnah-tractate Rosh Hashanah Chapter Four (and parallels) logs in changes in the Halakhah by reason of the destruction of the Second Temple, and these concern the conduct, after the 9th of Ab in 70, of Temple-rites on festivals. Mishnah-tractate Hullin Chapters Five through Seven and Ten through Twelve catalogues rules governing food and insists that they continue even after 70. By any criterion the changes in the Halakhah, transient to begin with, are vastly outweighed in practical importance by the rules that survived the Second Temple's ruin. The Mishnah's Halakhic system acknowledges that the Temple is for the moment inaccessible but does not recognize as the end of Israel's story that temporary circumstance. The Halakhic system not only trivializes in its principal category-formations the destruction of the Second Temple but in its affirmative statements denies that beyond the lamentable facts known to all, anything much has changed.

Now briefly to answer out of the Halakhah the question, how important was the destruction of the Second Temple to Rabbinic Judaism? The Halakhic answer is, nothing that matters has permanently changed. The sanctification before 70 of city, people, and Land, sacrifice, priesthood, and Temple, endures afterward. The destruction of the Second Temple in 70 recapitulated the lessons of 586 and yielded no new ones: it cannot be judged as important to the Halakhic system of Rabbinic Judaism, where the systemic theology came to realization in norms of conduct. When we come to the matter of norms of conscience, beliefs not behavior, the picture changes, but the outcome is the same.

III. THE AGGADIC PERSPECTIVE

The components of the Rabbinic response to 586, 70, and 132-135 all together set forth the following Aggadic proposition, summarizing the theological components of the system:

1. The destruction in each case (586, 70) and the disaster of 132-135, came about because of Israel's own failings or sins, chief among them arrogance. For this Israel can atone by humility expressed through repentance, on the one side, study and fulfillment of the Torah, inclusive of acts of loving kindness, keeping the Sabbath, and other specified remedies, on the other.

2. Meanwhile Israel mourns appropriately, but, as in Aqiba's construction of matters, finds hope for the restoration in the realization of the prophetic admonitions.

3. All in all, Israel preserves its uniqueness among the nations.

The pattern is clear: sin, punishment, repentance, atonement, reconciliation — all possible because of God's own passionate engagement with Israel. The premises of the statement derive from the Torah, e.g., the second paragraph of the *Shema*: "If you will earnestly heed the commandments...I will favor your land...Take care lest you be tempted to forsake God and turn to false gods...for then the wrath of the Lord will be directed against you" (Dt. 11:113ff.) When Israel meets misfortune, it is because of the violation of the Torah. The destruction of the Temple in 586, then in 70, represents the loss of the medium for the atonement of sin — the last step in total estrangement. Yet, in line with the message of prophecy, the Rabbinic response reaffirms Israel's place in the relationship with God: sin punished by suffering produces repentance, atonement, and reconciliation. The lesson of 586, repeated in 70, animates the Rabbinic response throughout. But the event of 70 taught no lessons not already imparted in 586.

That statement presents as general propositions of theology the particular allegations of Aggadic exposition and exegesis. The Tosefta, beyond its Halakhic program, sets forth these Aggadic propositions: the destruction effected atonement for sins, the Temple was destroyed for Israel's sins, the restoration of Jerusalem will take place in the end of days, and until that point a curse affects the world. There are valid reasons to account for what has happened, first, idolatry, licentiousness, and bloodshed, second, avarice or neglect of Torah. If we take together the Mishnah's Halakhic program in response to the destruction and the Tosefta's supplementary theological program, accordingly, we find in hand the entire Rabbinic system, lacking only Aggadic refinements and theological amplifications, e.g., the matter of martyrdom. The next set of documents, the Tannaite Midrash-compilations, would address that matter and would in addition state the eschatological doctrine that completes the construction.

Are we able to position in time the set of ideas just now summarized? If we follow conventional opinion and date the Mishnah to 200, the Tosefta to 250 and the Tannaite Midrash-compilations to 300, we may say that the entire system had emerged fully exposed within the framework of the Mishnah and the Tosefta, that is, not before 150 (the martyrs of the post-135 repression are integral), not after 250. And — returning to our question, how important was 70 — of what did that system consist? In its generative principles, stressing God's justice and focusing on theodicy, it represented nothing more than a reprise of the original statement of Moses and the prophets: the Temple was burned for Israel's faults, but Israel remained holy and possessed the means of reform.

The Aggadic corpus answers the question, how and what is Israel to think between Temples, the Second and the Third and last? And the answer proves blatant: Israel is to think precisely how and what Moses and the other prophets had taught them to think. Rabbinic Judaism recapitulates the prophetic theology of sin and repentance, atonement and forgiveness, in response to the loss of the Land and the Metropolis and the holy altar. True, the details vary. But the received theological principles describing the just God govern, with their contemporary realizations fully exposed.

Matters do not conclude with the doctrine of Israel's enduring sanctification. The Aggadic contribution encompassed the status of all of humanity. That is because the Aggadah reflected on the event of 70 in the setting of the entire narrative of Scripture. The loss of the Temple and city figured for the Rabbinic sages not only in Israel's own setting — as the Halakhah in all its interiority would have it — but in reflection on the entire history of humanity from Eden onward. What happened, in the later phases in the formation of the Rabbinic system in its late antique canon, was the recasting of the system into an account of Israel as counterpart to humanity. The condition of humanity in cosmic proportions encompasses the experience of not only Adam but also Israel, and the experience of the one is deemed paradigmatic for that of the other. That universal vision of God in relationship to humanity in general and Israel in particular is captured by the exile of Adam and Eve from Eden, with its counterpart, the exile of Israel from Jerusalem (and God from the Temple). The Aggadic perspective that shaped the vision of the Tosefta and the Tannaite Midrash-compilations thus crossed the boundaries of Israel's circumstance and drew that analogy that marked the fulfillment of monotheism: the comparison of Adam and Israel.

The events of 586, 70, and 132-135 then serve to make concrete the condition of exile to which the Aggadic narrator refers. But the Rabbinic theologians, particularly of the fifth and sixth centuries C.E., simply assessed the condition of Israel in the aftermath of 70 and 132-135: the loss of the Land comparing with Adam's loss of Eden. We find that statement precisely where it should be located, which is in their systematic exegesis of the book of Lamentations in Lamentations Rabbah IV.i.1 (but not only there, also at Genesis Rabbah XIX:IX.1-2 = Pesiqta deRab Kahana XV:I.1.):

LAMENTATIONS RABBAH IV.I.1 (GENESIS RABBAH XIX:IX.1-2 = PESIQTA DERAB KAHANA XV:I.1.):

1.   A.   R. Abbahu in the name of R. Yosé bar Haninah: "It is written, 'But they [Israel] are like a man [Adam], they have transgressed the covenant' (Hos. 6:7).

     B.   "'They are like a man,' specifically, like the first man. [We shall now compare the story of the first man in Eden with the story of Israel in its land.]

     C.   "'In the case of the first man, I brought him into the garden of Eden, I commanded him, he violated my commandment, I judged him to be sent away and driven out, but I mourned for him, saying "How..."'[which begins the book of Lamentations, hence stands for a lament, but which, as we just saw, also is written with the consonants that also yield, 'Where are you'].

D. "'I brought him into the garden of Eden,' as it is written, 'And the Lord God took the man and put him into the garden of Eden' (Gen. 2:15).

E. "'I commanded him,' as it is written, 'And the Lord God commanded...' (Gen. 2:16).

F. "'And he violated my commandment,' as it is written, 'Did you eat from the tree concerning which I commanded you' (Gen. 3:11).

G. "'I judged him to be sent away,' as it is written, 'And the Lord God sent him from the garden of Eden' (Gen. 3:23).

H. "'And I judged him to be driven out.' 'And he drove out the man' (Gen. 3:24).

I. "'But I mourned for him, saying, "How...".' 'And he said to him, "Where are you"' (Gen. 3:9), and the word for 'where are you' is written, 'How....'

J. "'So too in the case of his descendants, [God continues to speak,] I brought them [Israel] into the Land of Israel, I commanded them, they violated my commandment, I judged them to be sent out and driven away but I mourned for them, saying, "How...."'

K. "'I brought them into the Land of Israel.' 'And I brought you into the land of Carmel' (Jer. 2:7).

L. "'I commanded them.' 'And you, command the children of Israel' (Ex. 27:20). 'Command the children of Israel' (Lev. 24:2).

M. "'They violated my commandment.' 'And all Israel have violated your Torah' (Dan. 9:11).

N. "'I judged them to be sent out.' 'Send them away, out of my sight and let them go forth' (Jer 15:1).

O. "'....and driven away.' 'From my house I shall drive them' (Hos. 9:15).

P. "'But I mourned for them, saying, "How...."' 'How has the city sat solitary, that was full of people' (Lam. 1:1)."

Appropriately, this climactic response to 586/70, placing the condition of Israel as counterpart to the condition of all humanity, comes to expression in Lamentations Rabbah, in the context of the book of Lamentations, the writing of mourning attributed to Jeremiah and produced after the destruction of the Temple in Jerusalem in 586 by the Babylonians. Here we end where we began, Israel in exile from the Land, like Adam in exile from Eden. But the Torah is clear that there is a difference: Israel can repent. Jerusalem and Eden, Israel and Adam — this ultimate interpretation of 586 places the event of 70 in the center of universal history: the entire human race is involved in Israel's fate, and Israel in humanity's. The Mishnah, Tosefta, and Tannaite Midrash-compilations, accordingly, invite the theologization of the destruction of the Temple, invoking the case of 586 to find the rule for 70. Then the late Rabbah-Midrash compilations and Pesiqta deRab Kahana would complete the process.

IV. HOW IMPORTANT WAS THE DESTRUCTION OF THE SECOND TEMPLE IN THE FORMATION OF RABBINIC JUDAISM?

Now to answer the question of the essay: To the formation of that prophetic-Rabbinic Judaism how important was the event of 70? The answer lies right on the surface. God had dwelt in the Temple but now has abandoned it. What could lay claim to greater importance than that event of cosmic consequence? The destruction of the Temple in 586, as interpreted in the Torah and prophets, defines the precipitating event in the composition of the Rabbinic system: sin, punishment, repentance, atonement, reconciliation as the prophets had admonished but also promised, all realized in that event and its aftermath. So if we ask, how important was the destruction of the Second Temple in the formation of the prophetic-Rabbinic Judaism, of necessity we respond: which Temple, First or Second? The event of 586 precipitated the construction of model to which the Rabbinic system too conformed. The event of 70 merely confirmed the original paradigm. Without that confirmation, however, the paradigm still governed.

Which Temple mattered? As to the Temple destroyed in 586: nothing in the Rabbinic canon does more than explore the implications embedded in the original construction of 586 as laid out in the Torah and the Prophets. That point is best illustrated by the repertoire, beginning with the Tosefta's, of reasons for the loss of the Temple, the bulk of them located in the flaws and failures of the Israelite social order as the prophets before and after 586 would have it. So much for 586.

As to the Second Temple destroyed in 70: to answer the question, how important? a mental experiment is required. We must commit an act of imagination. To do so we begin with the premise contained in another question: what if Israel had not raised a rebellion against Rome and what if the Second Temple had not been destroyed by the Romans in 70? The answer is clear: nothing new would have happened, the Second Temple offerings would have continued for centuries. For the established system in response to 586 had made its points. It had met the challenge of change by recasting its statement, never intact, but always unimpaired, from the formation of the Torah-book and the prophetic collections forward.

If, in the prophetic-Rabbinic system, nothing much changed with the destruction of the Second Temple, nothing in the established paradigm would have changed by reason of the Second Temple's continuing to flourish for a long time to come. The prophetic-Rabbinic Judaism reinforced by the Temple's powerful presence would have endured because it had the power to accommodate new challenges and respond to new crises. The Halakhic category-formations and Aggadic theology accommodated the Temple, whether standing or whether in ruins or whether restored once more. The event of 70 brought no new challenge to the system. And without that event, the received system with category-formations that matched the social order of pre-70 Jerusalem and the people of Israel surrounding the metropolis, served perfectly well.

That is not to suggest that absent the Zealots and their wars against Rome the Jerusalem Temple would have survived indefinitely. Only when the Roman Empire had definitively adopted Christianity as the state religion in the fifth century (not merely as a licit religion, which Constantine accomplished in the early fourth century) and campaigned to destroy paganism and its Temples would the Israelite Temple in Jerusalem been endangered, as synagogues in various cities were. At that time synagogue buildings suffered assaults, so why not the very Temple itself? But who knows what might have happened had the Second Temple stood for three or four more centuries than it did?

So had Yohanan ben Zakkai's nephew opposed the Zealots and, taking over, sued for peace, the original message of 586 and Ezekiel would have persisted unaffected. The enduring Second Temple, the on-going sacrificial system — these would have lasted so long as the narrative of 586 and the restoration that followed enjoyed prominence in Israel's politics and culture. The reading of 586 will have yielded the lesson: Israel has kept the Torah, so God has kept Israel. How far distant was that celebration of grace from its opposite: Israel has not kept the Torah, so God has punished Israel?

True, that view of the Second Temple and Jerusalem as media of the relationship did not enjoy universal assent. Groups of Israelites turned their backs on the Temple and its offerings, Jerusalem and its pilgrimages. For still others, distance had the same consequence as doctrinal difference. The Samaritans, the community represented by the Dead Sea library, the Israelites in Egypt who sacrificed in the Temple of Onias and the Christians all found — in the language of Yohanan ben Zakkai to Joshua b. Hananiah — a means of atonement that yielded the same result as the atonement offerings set forth morning and night: another metropolis, another Israel. And the Jews of the distant Diasporas, Babylonia and Rome, for example, of necessity found other centers for their encounter with God and other media of atonement and conciliation, besides Jerusalem and its offerings.

In that context, the destruction of the Second Temple in 70 cannot be deemed an important, let alone a unique, event in the history of Judaism. For those components of Israel that did not value the Second Temple, the destruction confirmed their negative judgment of Jerusalem and its offerings, and for those that did, the destruction produced no theological consequences that had not already come to full exposure in Scripture. How important was the destruction of the Second Temple in 70? To those to whom it was important, it mattered only to confirm what they already knew, to others, it also confirmed what they already knew. For neither sector of Israelite opinion did the destruction of 70 matter much, make much difference.

That does not complete matters, for we have to ask also about what importance the Bar Kokhba fiasco made in the formation of Rabbinic Judaism. To be sure, without 70 there was no 132-135. But 70 did take place, so we are constrained to ask, what can we say if matters had turned out differently in 132-

135? Specifically, would Rabbinic Judaism as we know it in the Mishnah and the Tosefta, the exegetical compilations of Midrashim and the Talmuds, have come to systemic fulfillment had Bar Kokhba won the second war against Rome? That is to say, what would have followed the destruction of the Second Temple *and its restoration three generations later, under the auspices of Bar Kokhba*?

Had Bar Kokhba rebuilt the Second Temple in 135, I do not think the Rabbinic system would have made a statement substantially different from the one that it made in the Mishnah, which better suits an age of restoration than an age of repression. On the contrary, had Bar Kokhba won, the Mishnah would all the more so have organized the Israelite social order within its familiar category-formations. For the Mishnah's category-formations will have better matched the configuration of the Israelite social order in the Land of Israel with a Temple than without.

But would not the Rabbinic sages have faced a political calamity in the victory of Bar Kokhba, in some narratives represented as a Messiah, a matter on which the Rabbinic sages took conflicting positions? The Rabbinic sages are represented by the Mishnah as clerks in the patriarchal government from 70 forward. The government organized by Rome after 70 and governed by the patriarch sponsored by Rome would have been discredited had Bar Kokhba won. So what would have happened in the aftermath of a Zealot victory to what we call prophetic-Rabbinic Judaism as portrayed by the Mishnah and the Tosefta?

We cannot take at face value the narrative of Aqiba's recognition of Bar Kokhba as a Messiah. But for the present speculation, we do not have to. It suffices to observe that the Rabbinic sages did not require political hegemony in order to accomplish their systemic goals of social reconstruction of Israel in the model of the Torah. They worked with the patriarchate of the Land of Israel and the exilarchate of Babylonia and ultimately subverted both institutions to their purpose. And Bar Kokhba's post-war administration required trained clerks too. The archaeology of the war has yielded well-prepared documents, and someone had to have written them and would be needed in the future. Where better to find scribes and lawyers than in the ranks of masters of the Torah out of whose circles — if the martyrologies are to be believed — martyrs in the recent war had emerged?

So how important was the destruction of the Second Temple in the formation of Rabbinic Judaism? Two facts answer the question. The destruction of the First Temple marked the beginning of the Rabbinic system, law and theology alike. And the destruction of the Second Temple precipitated the recapitulation of the original event. The first time presented a crisis, the second merely an opportunity to confirm the systemic outcome of the original crisis. The war of Bar Kokhba whether won, whether lost, made, and could have made, no difference in the Rabbinic sages' progress to power.

We may then wonder whether that outcome — the destruction of the Second Temple was not an important event in the formative history of Rabbinic Judaism — is not counter-intuitive. After all, the destruction of the Second Temple surely is treated in the formative canon as a critical, epoch-making event. But a second look at the question, what importance did Rabbinic Judaism impute to the destruction of the Second Temple? produces a different result. Just as the Halakhah treats as trivial and transient the effects of 70, so the Aggadah affords evidence of a balanced, moderate reading of matters. Rabbinic Judaism represented by Joshua and Ishmael in their meetings with mourners of Zion did not treat 70 as an apocalyptic caesura in the history of God's relationships with humanity through the extended family of Israel. Rather, the Rabbinic sages took the middle path, between dismissing as null the event of 70 and 132-135 (as did the Christians) and designating the destruction of the Second Temple as the end of days.

Rabbinic Judaism represents a very particular reading of 586, 70, and 132-135. It self-evidently dismisses the Christian interpretation of the destruction as the signal of God's rejection of the old Israel. But it also rejects the judgment of those who deem the destruction to mark the end of days. The Rabbinic view that matches the Halakhic evaluation of matters surfaces in a composition in the Tosefta. It makes explicit the Rabbinic rejection of the rejectionist position: not to mourn "too much." The Rabbinic sages thereby deny that the destruction of the Second Temple and cessation of its cult mark the end of days for Israel. But the Halakhic statement of matters is probative. As we have seen, the governing category-formations recognize liturgical problems in the context of a recapitulation of the entire, enduring sacrificial system. The implication of that fact is readily seen: in the Rabbinic system the destruction of the Second Temple in 70 constitutes a mournful event but not a unique catastrophe and not a caesura in the life of still- and eternally-holy Israel. And that position on the meaning of a historical catastrophe simply repeats the lessons of 586: suffering and repentance, exile and return.

The Temple did not have to suffer destruction for the lessons of 586 to be incorporated into a Judaic system for Israel's social order, and in 70 the prophetic-Rabbinic system in Judaism did not have to come into being to teach them. The destruction of the Second Temple made no difference in the received system and was readily absorbed into the established structure of law and theology. The received category-formations of the law easily accommodated the new data presented by history, the established dialectics of the ancient theology encompassing with facility the renewed task of theodicy. The prophetic-Rabbinic Judaism began not in 70 but in the aftermath of 586 with the formation, by the priests of the Temple, of Scripture — the Torah of Moses and the teachings of the prophets. In its late antique canon prophetic-Rabbinic Judaism would simply recapitulate the theology of the Torah of Moses and its law. To that enterprise of reiteration the destruction of the Second Temple presented an occasion to recapitulate, to enunciate merely a chronic and recurrent concern, not an acute crisis. The emergence of Rabbinic Judaism did not depend upon, and was not precipitated by, the destruction of the Second Temple in 70, but the destruction of the First Temple in 586 and its restoration afterward.

4

How Pivotal Is Yavneh
in the History of Judaism?

How a given subject is represented, not by successive documents but within its own framework forms the initial question.[1] To begin with, a demonstration of how the same subject provokes various responses of law and narrative is required to illustrate the problem at hand. When we address the diversity of the records that pertain to one and the same person, place, and thing, a particular topic defines the program. So we follow the treatment of that topic through a number of Rabbinic documents and attempt a synthesis of the data yielded by the several documents: an account of the subject viewed whole. Utter confusion follows. When we collect and analyze everything the canonical documents set forth on a given topic, without regard to its documentary origin, we find a mishmash of incoherent data. What emerges from topical synthesis is the complete chaos that the canonical documents reveal: everything and its opposite that pertains to the stated topic. What is required is not synthesis but analysis, and among the tools of analysis the inquiry into documentary traits proves promising.

Later on the differentiating boundaries provided by the documents and their respective foci in due course will be shown to bring order to the chaos of conflicting information circulated by the canonical writings read not as purposive composites but as a mass of undifferentiated compositions.

I. To What does "Yavneh" Refer?

To examine how a given person, place, and thing may be variously represented in the Rabbinic canonical documents, I take up the accounts of what happened in 70 in a particular place, to a particular person, with distinctive and important consequences. That is a key-testimony to show how people answered the question, why did "it" — the loss of Jerusalem, the destruction of the Temple — matter?

THE PERSON is Rabban Yohanan ben Zakkai, principal figure in the transfer of "the Torah" from fallen Jerusalem to the new age and location. Shortly before 70, in the summer of 68 (so conventional histories report on the basis of materials compiled four or five centuries later) Yohanan ben Zakkai, a leading Rabbinical sage of Jerusalem, disciple of the masters who flourished in the last century before 70 C.E. Shammai and Hillel, and teacher of those who would dominate in the first century afterward, Eliezer and Joshua, for example, abandoned the besieged city and secured permission from the Roman general to move to Yavneh and to found a school there. That school secured the continuity of the chain of tradition that had begun at Sinai and flourished in Jerusalem.

THE PLACE is an inland settlement off the southern coast of the Land of Israel. Yavneh (Greek: Jamnia) acquired importance in the history of Judaism in the First Rebellion against Rome, when Rabbinic sages established there the administrative court that exercised such authority as the Romans had left in Jewish hands. The legacy of the place secured continuity for the Judaism portrayed in the Torah as interpreted by the Rabbinic sages who settled there.

THE PERIOD of Yavneh refers to the time of reconstruction and renewal, in the decades after 70, marked by the adaptation of the law of the Torah to the condition — temporary, it was hoped — when the Temple no longer stood, a time of reconstruction and accommodation. The legacy of the period sustained the Jewish people because it revealed the power of the Torah to adapt to crisis and catastrophe and to renew itself.

THE CIRCUMSTANCE is defined by catastrophe and reconstruction, surviving the loss of a principal medium of the holy life of Israel, the Jewish people, and overcoming the sense of caesura in time that has taken place.

The entire issue is captured in a single story, which states succinctly the event and its meaning as the Rabbinic tradition would sort matters out:

THE FATHERS ACCORDING TO RABBI NATHAN IV:V.2

One time [after the destruction of the Temple in August, 70] Rabban Yohanan ben Zakkai was going forth from Jerusalem, with R. Joshua following after him. He saw the house of the sanctuary lying in ruins.

R. Joshua said, "Woe is us for this place that lies in ruins, the place in which the sins of Israel used to be atoned for."

He said to him, "My son, do not be distressed. We have another mode of atonement, which is like [atonement through sacrifice], and what is that? It is deeds of loving kindness.

"For so it is said, 'For I desire mercy and not sacrifice, and the knowledge of God rather than burnt offerings' (Hos. 6:6)."

Yavneh is not mentioned, but for Judaism, by which I mean the religious tradition that calls itself "the Torah," the age we call "the period of Yavneh" is defined here. The issue is theological, not secular: Israel's relationship to God, an issue made acute by the destruction of the Temple. The destruction of the Temple and cessation of its daily atonement offerings deprived Israel of its medium of atonement at just the moment that its sins had brought about catastrophe, so that the age demanded Israel's atonement for sin, but Israel could not comply. The resolution is emphasis on deeds of loving kindness, self-sacrifice in place of animal sacrifice. But this represents only one Rabbinic view. We shall see others.

What of other definitions of the problem of that place, circumstance, and age? In politics the surviving people had to face the end of its autonomous political standing, at least for a time. In interior life it had to reorganize the administration of the Jewish life of the country. In religion it had to adapt to the loss of its principal mode of serving God. And concomitantly, in theology it had to contemplate Israel's on-going relationship with God when the means of atonement provided for by the Torah for a thousand years no longer served. So for Judaism, "Yavneh" defines the age in which the Torah adapted itself to deal with the acute problem of repentance in an age persuaded that Israel's own sin had brought about calamity, as the prophets had warned. Then the pressing problem was atonement, and Yohanan ben Zakkai taught that atonement was attained through deeds of loving kindness.

II. Diverse Views of What Happened in 70 and its Meaning: Yavneh and Other Foci

We have to take account not only of pictures of Yavneh as the center of the story of the destruction of the Jerusalem sanctuary in 70, but also of accounts of the events of 70 that make no reference to Yavneh at all. Now, when we ask the Rabbinic writings, what, exactly, happened in 70, and why if at all does Yavneh figure? the answer depends upon whom we ask, or, more precisely, which Rabbinic document.

The representation of what happened in and after 70 and of the meaning of the events varies from one document to another. That is not as to details but as to the main point. These are the results we may anticipate from a survey of how Rabbinic writings represent the destruction of the Temple and is consequences — either/or:

1. Beyond 70 Yavneh was the place of continuation, indeed the very heir of Jerusalem. Or: Beyond 70 Yavneh does not figure.

2. Beyond 70 Yavneh happened to be where Rabbinic sages gathered and conducted a court. Or: Beyond 70 the law ignored Yavneh.

3. A variation of the foregoing: Yavneh was heir of, and corresponded to, Jerusalem. As God left Jerusalem for the heavens, so the Torah left Jerusalem for Yavneh. It found its location on the chain of holy places beginning at Sinai and ending in Jerusalem restored. Or: Yavneh does not figure at all.

4. The Messiah is a principal issue made acute by the destruction of the Temple. Or: The Messiah does not figure at all after 70. The sage is the principal actor of 70. All that matters is Israel's own attitude, which the sages shape in accord with the pattern of the Torah.

5. We tell the story of the continuation of the Torah beyond the first 9th of Ab without invoking the activity of Yohanan ben Zakkai in Yavneh at all. Or we tell

the story with Yohanan ben Zakkai at the heart of the matter. In the former, Yavneh provides the link, the next step in the sacred history of Israel the Jewish People. Yavneh does not figure, and 70 stands for *other continuities* altogether than those critical in the narrative of Yavneh.

Clearly, the canonical documents sustain a variety of views. Let us now survey the more important of them.

III. Yavneh at the Center: Torah Mediates Life out of Death

The most famous story of all sets forth the most extreme claim in behalf of Yavneh as the heir of Jerusalem, the place where the Torah took refuge after the destruction, the nexus of the continuity of Judaism and the Jewish People. It portrays Yohanan ben Zakkai as the Rabbinic sage who, in the model of Jeremiah before the first destruction, in 586 B.C.E., perceived the coming calamity and took action to save what could be saved, which is, the activity of study of the Torah, oral and written, by the Rabbinic sages. They would succeed to the position of leadership taken by the zealots who precipitated the hopeless war against Roman rule of the Land of Israel. Yohanan ben Zakkai then embodies the paradigm defined by Jeremiah in the first destruction, who had counseled submission to Babylonia and after the destruction of the Temple and Jerusalem in August, 586, embodied such recognition as the Jewish people received from the Babylonian conquerors. The upshot is, the two destructions form a pattern, and the pattern yields public policy for Israel, the Jewish people.

The Fathers According to Rabbi Nathan IV.VI.1

A. Now when Vespasian came to destroy Jerusalem, he said to [the inhabitants of the city,] "Idiots! why do you want to destroy this city and burn the house of the sanctuary? For what do I want of you, except that you send me a bow or an arrow [as marks of submission to my rule], and I shall go on my way."

B. They said to him, "Just as we sallied out against the first two who came before you and killed them, so shall we sally out and kill you."

C. When Rabban Yohanan ben Zakkai heard, he proclaimed to the men of Jerusalem, saying to them, "My sons, why do you want to destroy this city and burn the house of the sanctuary? For what does he want of you, except that you send him a bow or an arrow, and he will go on his way."

D. They said to him, "Just as we sallied out against the first two who came before him and killed them, so shall we sally out and kill him."

E. Vespasian had stationed men near the walls of the city, and whatever they heard, they would write on an arrow and shoot out over the wall. [They reported] that Rabban Yohanan ben Zakkai was a loyalist of Caesar's.

F. After Rabban Yohanan ben Zakkai had spoken to them one day, a second, and a third, and the people did not accept his counsel, he sent and called his disciples, R. Eliezer and R. Joshua, saying to them, "My sons, go and get me out of here. Make me an ark and I shall go to sleep in it."

G. R. Eliezer took the head and R. Joshua the feet, and toward sunset they carried him until they came to the gates of Jerusalem.

H. The gate keepers said to them, "Who is this?"

I. They said to him, "It is a corpse. Do you not know that a corpse is not kept overnight in Jerusalem."

J. They said to them, "If it is a corpse, take him out," so they took him out and brought him out at sunset, until they came to Vespasian.

K. They opened the ark and he stood before him.

L. He said to him, "Are you Rabban Yohanan ben Zakkai? Indicate what I should give you."

M. He said to him, "I ask from you only Yavneh, to which I shall go, and where I shall teach my disciples, establish prayer [Goldin: a prayer house], and carry out all of the religious duties."

N. He said to him, "Go and do whatever you want."

O. He said to him, "Would you mind if I said something to you."

P. He said to him, "Go ahead."]

Q. He said to him, "Lo, you are going to be made sovereign."

R. He said to him, "How do you know?

S. He said to him, "It is a tradition of ours that the house of the sanctuary will be given over not into the power of a commoner but of a king, for it is said, *And he shall cut down the thickets of the forest with iron, and Lebanon* [which refers to the Temple] *shall fall by a mighty one* (Is. 10:34)."

T. People say that not a day, two or three passed before a delegation came to him from his city indicating that the [former[Caesar had died and they had voted for him to ascend the throne.

U. They brought him a catapult and drew it up against the wall of Jerusalem.

V. They brought him cedar beams and put them into the catapult, and he struck them against the wall until a breach had been made in it. They brought the head of a pig and put it into the catapult and tossed it toward the limbs that were on the Temple altar.

W. At that moment Jerusalem was captured.

X. Rabban Yohanan ben Zakkai was in session and with trembling was looking outward, in the way that Eli had sat and waited: "Lo, Eli sat upon his seat by the wayside watching, for his heart trembled for the ark of God" (1 Sam. 4:13).

Y. When Rabban Yohanan ben Zakkai heard that Jerusalem had been destroyed and the house of the sanctuary burned in flames, he tore his garments, and his disciples tore their garments, and they wept and cried and mourned.

This sublime narrative, paramount in all histories of the Jews and of Judaism, demands more attention than we can give it. It provides a key to the entire system and structure of Rabbinic Judaism. We shall consider it in documentary context when we reach The Fathers According to Rabbi Nathan in Chapter Fourteen. For the present purpose it suffices to note four points.

First, Yohanan ben Zakkai weighs in the balance against the war-party, the zealots. He alone has the perspicacity to foresee the destruction and its gratuitous cause: mere submission in symbolic gesture.

Second, the motif of Jeremiah dominates. Before the destruction of the first Temple by the Babylonians in 586, the prophet Jeremiah had taught that Israel should submit, not resist. He survived the war and the Babylonians recognized his wisdom. Now Yohanan ben Zakkai follows suit. So Yohanan has recapitulated the model of the prophet set forth in the Torah.

Third, the disciples save the master's life through their knowledge of the Torah about not keeping a corpse in the city overnight.

Fourth, Yohanan's knowledge of the Torah produces his prediction of Vespasian's coming rise to imperial power. The story then tells how mastery of the Torah defines Israel's fate. It forms the source of sound public policy. More than that, it allows the sage to predict the future. And it constitutes the source of life over death, the medium of resurrection: as the sage escaped from dying Jerusalem in a bier and rose from the coffin to life, so from Yavneh the people of Israel surpassed calamity. Torah then defines the lesson, the legacy of Yavneh.

That is the lesson of the Fathers According to Rabbi Nathan. We note, too, that the story of Joshua's question and Yohanan's answer, "We have a means of atonement that is comparable, deeds of loving kindness," derives from the same document. So the lesson of that document is, the Torah defines Israel's relationship with God, dictates Israel's public policy, determines what is to happen in the future — all through the medium of the Rabbinic sages' mastery thereof.

The Fathers according to Rabbi Nathan presents a commentary on tractate Abot, the Sayings of the Fathers. In light of the character of that document, we cannot find surprising the present approach to Yavneh and Torah and the Temple. That is because tractate Abot portrays the sages as forming links in the chain of oral tradition from Moses at Sinai to the Rabbinic sages of the Mishnah itself. In its expansion of Tractate Abot, to which it forms a systematic amplification, the Fathers According to Rabbi Nathan applies to the destruction of the Temple, which is not mentioned in tractate Abot, the theological lessons of tractate Abot. The chain of tradition represented by the link of Yohanan ben Zakkai and his disciples establishes continuity through the chain of tradition from before to after the destruction. It is hardly surprising that the activity carried on by Yohanan in Yavneh is Torah-study, the public policy he advocates replicates that of Jeremiah, and he mourned the loss of the Temple as Eli mourned for the ark of God.

What is noteworthy is what the Fathers According to Rabbi Nathan's story of Yohanan ben Zakkai on the 9th of Ab does not introduce, and that is, the account of Jeremiah's book of Lamentations. Introducing Eli and the ark of God instead of a verse that pertains to Jerusalem and the Temple such as Lamentations can have provided contains its own lesson. It is imparted by the emphasis not on the place, Jerusalem, but on the ark, not a locative object by definition, but one that endows a place with holiness by reason of its presence. The ark compares, then, to the Torah. So Yavneh can succeed Jerusalem, because the place does not matter, the activity carried on — Torah-study — there does. And that activity — so the composite of the Fathers according to Rabbi Nathan stresses — is atonement, for which sacrifice is useful but not essential and which can be replaced by a superior medium of atonement, moral and ethical conduct. By altruistic deeds of good not bad, right not wrong, Israel enters into the right relationship with God.

IV. YOHANAN BEN ZAKKAI WITHOUT YAVNEH

Another, intersecting account of the same moment — Yohanan ben Zakkai and the transfer from Jerusalem before the catastrophe — yields a picture of Yohanan ben Zakkai without reference to Yavneh as a place or as a period. Issues shift in this account, which I shall show responds to the program of the document that presents the story.

Let us start with a preview of what we miss in the story as told about Yohanan rising from the grave, embodying the resurrection of the Jewish people in the person of its principal sage. What we do not find critical in the account of the Fathers according to Rabbi Nathan is the events that precipitate the crisis: the conduct of the zealots in endangering the Temple and Jerusalem. The principal actors are Yohanan and his disciples; Vespasian plays a supporting role. In this other, different picture of the destruction and Yohanan ben Zakkai's activities in that connection, [1] Yavneh is not mentioned; [2] Vespasian is given an active role; [3] other enemies figure; [4] Yohanan enters the action not because of his own volition but because his grandson is a leader of the war party. And [5] the climactic figure weighed in the balance as weightier than even the Roman general become emperor, is a virtuous sage other than Yohanan.

This picture, which broadens the focus from the sage at the center to the contending parties at the heart of the narrative, derives from Lamentations Rabbah, a commentary on the book of Lamentations. That work sets forth what are conceived to be Jeremiah's (and others') response to the 9th of Ab in 586 when the first Temple was destroyed. There, in Lamentation Rabbah,[2] we get a different picture of the same event, now with other emphases.[3]

LAMENTATIONS RABBAH XXXIX:II.

1.   **A.   For three and a half years Vespasian surrounded Jerusalem, with four generals with him: the general of Arabia, Africa, Alexandria, and Palestine.**
     B.   What was the name [of the general of Arabia}?

      C.   Two Amoraic authorities:

      D.   One said, "His name was Illam."

      E.   The other said, "His name was Abgar."

2.   **A.**   **In Jerusalem were three rich men, any one of whom had the resources to feed the city for five years: Ben Sisit, Ben Kalba-Shabua, and Naqdimon Ben Gurion.**

      B.   And there also was Ben Battiah, son of Rabban Yohanan b. Zakkai's daughter, who was in charge of the stores.

      C.   He went and burned all the stores.

      D.   Rabban Yohanan ben Zakkai heard and cried, "Woe!"

      E.   People went and said, "Lo, your friend said, 'woe.'"

      F.   He sent and summoned him, saying to him, "Why did you cry, 'woe'?"

      G.   He said to him, "I did not say 'woe' but 'wow.'"

      H.   He said to him, "Why did you say 'wow'?"

      I.   He said to him, "I was thinking that so long as the stores were available, the people of the city would not give themselves up to make sorties and do battle and engage the enemy."

      J.   Through the difference between "woe" and "wow," Rabban Yohanan ben Zakkai was saved.

      K.   This verse of Scripture applies to him: "The excellency of knowledge is that wisdom preserves the life of the one who has it" (Qoh. 7:12).

3.   **A.**   **Three days later Rabban Yohanan ben Zakkai went out to stroll in the market, and he saw people boiling straw and drinking the water.**

      B.   He said, "Can people who boil straw and drink the water stand before the armies of Vespasian? The simple fact is that I have to get myself out of here."

      C.   Rabban Yohanan sent to Ben Battiah, "Get me out of here."

      D.   He said to him, "We have agreed that no one is going to get out except for a corpse."

      E.   He said to him, "Get me out as a corpse."

      F.   R. Eliezer carried him at the head, R. Joshua at the feet, and Ben Battiah walked in front. When they got to the gates, the guards wanted to stab the corpse. Ben Battiah said to them, "Do you want people to say that when our teacher died, they stabbed his body?" They let them pass.

      G.   When they had passed the gates, they carried him to the cemetery and left him there and went back to the city.

4.   **A.**   **Rabban Yohanan b. Zakkai emerged and went among Vespasian's troops, saying to them, "Where is the king?"**

      B.   They went and told Vespasian, "A Jew wants you."

      C.   He said to them, "Bring him along."

      D.   When he came in, he said, *"Vive domine Imperator!"*

      E.   Vespasian said to him, "You greet me as a king but I am not, and if the king hears, he will assassinate me."

     F.   He said to him, "If you are not a king, you will be, because the temple will be destroyed only by the power of a king: 'And Lebanon shall fall by a mighty one' (Isa. 10:34)."

5.   **A.**   **They took [Rabban Yohanan ben Zakkai] and put him inside the innermost of seven rooms and asked him what time of night it was.**

     B.   He told them.

     C.   They asked him, "What time of the day is it?"

     D.   He told them.

     E.   How did he know it?

     F.   From his study [he kept repeating traditions, and these told him the passage of time].

6.   **A.**   **They took [Rabban Yohanan ben Zakkai] and put him inside the innermost of seven rooms and asked him what time of night it was.**

     B.   He told them.

     C.   They asked him, "What time of the day is it?"

     D.   He told them.

     E.   How did he know it?

     F.   From his study [he kept repeating traditions, and these told him the passage of time].

7.   **A.**   **Three days later Vespasian went to wash at Gophna. After he had bathed, he came out and put on his shoes. But when he had put on one of his shoes, they brought him a writing from Rome that the king had died and the citizens of Rome had crowned him king.**

     B.   He wanted to put on the other shoe and he could not put it on his foot.

     C.   He sent for Rabban Yohanan ben Zakkai and asked, "Can you tell me why all these years I have been able to put on these shoes, but when I put on one of them and wanted to put on the other, it would not go on my foot?"

     D.   He said to him, "You have heard good news: 'A good report makes the bones fat' (Prov. 15:30)."

     E.   "And what shall I do to get it on?"

     F.   He said to him, "If you have an enemy, or some one you owe, let him walk in front of you, and your flesh will shrink: 'A broken spirit dries bones' (Prov. 17:22)."

8.   **A.**   **The generals began to speak in parables before him: "As to a cask in which a snake has nested, what is to be done with it?"**

     B.   He said to him, "Bring a charmer and charm the snake."

     C.   Said Amgar [Pangar], "Kill the snake and break the cask."

     D.   "If a snake nested in a tower, what is to be done with it?"

     E.   "Bring a charmer and charm the snake, and leave the tower be."

     F.   Said Amgar, "Kill the snake and burn the tower."

G. Said Rabban Yohanan ben Zakkai, "All neighbors who do injury do it to their neighbors: Instead of defending us, you argue for the prosecution against us."

H. He said to him, "By your life! It is for your benefit that I have said what I said. So long as the temple is standing, the nations will envy you. But if it is destroyed, they will not envy you."

I. Said to him Rabban Yohanan ben Zakkai, "The heart truly knows whether it is woven or crooked [that is, what your intention really is]."

9. **A.** **Vespasian said to Rabban Yohanan ben Zakkai, "Ask for something, and I shall give it to you."**

B. He said to him, "I ask you to leave the city and go away."

C. He said to him, "The citizens of Rome did not make me king except to carry out public policy, and you tell me to leave the city and go away?! Ask something else, and I will do it."

D. He said to him, "I ask you to leave the western gate, which leads to Lydda, and spare everyone who leaves up to the fourth hour."

10. **A.** **After he had come and conquered the city, he said to him, "If you have a relative there, send and bring him out."**

B. He sent R. Eliezer and R. Joshua to bring out R. Saddoq, whom they found at the city gate.

C. When he came, Rabban Yohanan stood up before him.

D. Vespasian asked, "Are you honoring this emaciated old man?"

E. He said to him, "By your life, if in Jerusalem there had been one more like him, even though your army were twice as big, you would not have been able to take the city."

F. He said to him, "What is his power?"

G. He said to him, "He eats a single fig, and on the strength it gives him, he teaches a hundred sessions at the academy."

H. "Why is he so thin?"

I. "Because of his many abstinences and fasts."

J. Vespasian called physicians, who fed him little by little with food and drink until he recovered his strength.

K. [Saddoq's] son, Eleazar, said to him, "Father, give them their reward in this world, lest they have merit on your account in the world to come."

L. He gave them calculation by fingers and scales for weighing.

11. **A.** **When they had conquered the city, he divided the destruction of the four ramparts to the four generals, with the western one to Pangar.**

B. Heaven had decreed that the western wall should never be destroyed.

C. The three other generals destroyed their parts, but he did not destroy his.

D. He sent and summoned him and said, "Why did you not destroy your part?"

E.   He said to him, "If I had destroyed my part as the others destroyed theirs, the kingdoms that will arise after you would never know about the great glory of what you have destroyed. But when people look [at the western wall], they will say, 'See the power of Vespasian from what he destroyed!'"

F.   He said to him, "By your life, you have spoken well. But because you have disobeyed my orders, I decree for you that you go up and throw yourself off the top of the gate. If you live, you live, if you die, you die."

G.   He went up, threw himself off, and died.

H.   So did the curse of Rabban Yohanan ben Zakkai come to realization.

What we see is that in the battle for Jerusalem Yohanan is a bit-player, not the focus, which rests upon the pagan emperor and his allies. Now the sage has no particular standing but proves his worth by referring to the Torah in predicting the future. Yavneh does not figure at all, and the story contains no program for the future. Yohanan responds to events, but does not command their course.

The story begins with Vespasian and the four generals, balanced against the three rich men of Jerusalem. Yohanan b. Zakkai enters the picture via his grandson, who pays no respect to the Torah of his grandfather. Yohanan sees the war as hopeless, and that secular perception, not guidance from the Torah, accounts for his fleeing, to save his own life. Ben Battiah now saves his grandfather's life, he is party to the conspiracy. The disciples drop Yohanan off in the cemetery and go back to the city, there is no plan to build a school and maintain the chain of tradition of the Torah.

Yohanan has no special standing. He has to prove himself. This he does, for the emperor, by appeal to the Torah (Isa. 10:34). Yohanan's capacity to tell time even out of sight of light underscores the power he exercises through knowledge of the Torah. On that same basis he is able to counsel the Roman general when he cannot put on his shoes. Then the generals speak in parables, defending the war against Jerusalem. Only then, having proved his supernatural wisdom, does Yohanan get to ask a favor of Vespasian. He tries to spare the people the horrors of a brutal capture of the city. The next unit has Eliezer and Joshua reappear, now to rescue Saddoq from the capture, and once more Vespasian is exposed to the supernatural power of the Rabbinic sage. At the end, after the conquest, which is not described, the Roman ally gets his comeuppance.

The comparison of this picture of matters with that of the Fathers According to Rabbi Nathan highlights negatives. Unlike that version of events, here the sage, Yohanan ben Zakkai, reacts to events but does not guide their course; there are other players. He is not at the center of matters. Unlike the first picture, Yavneh does not figure. A center for the study of Torah and the practice of the commandments and the teaching of disciples is not contemplated and is not the consequence of the account. Rather, the climax is the virtue of Sadoq, whose humility and piety can have saved the city.

Those negatives yield some idea of the interest of the narrator. It is on the course of events, the execution of public policy, the conduct of the enemy as much as of the sage. The context in which the story of Jerusalem and Yohanan ben Zakkai is introduced in Lamentations Rabbah provides the key to the story. It is an attachment to a specific verse, which speaks of the enemy. Lamentations 1:5 reads, "Her foes have become the head, her enemies prosper.." The rise of the enemies to power forms the center of interest. That is reinforced by two readings of the verse. The first is as follows:

LAMENTATIONS RABBAH XXXIX.I.

1. A. **"Her foes have become the head:"**
   B. Said R. Hillel b. Berekhiah, "Whoever comes to torment Jerusalem is made head,
   C. "for it is written, 'Her foes have become the head.'
   D. "You find that before Jerusalem was destroyed, no city was regarded as important. Afterward, Caesarea became a metropolis, Antipatris, a city, and Neapolis a colony."

The verse is translated into a generalization, "Whoever comes to torment...." Then — as is common in the context of Rabbinic generalizations — a particular case is given and that bring us to our tale:

2. A. **Another reading of "Her foes have become the head:"**
   B. this refers to Nebuchadnezzar.
3. A. **"Her foes have become the head:"**
   B. this refers to Nebuzaradan.
4. A. **Another interpretation of the phrase "Her foes have become the head:"**
   B. this refers to Vespasian.
   C. "her enemies prosper:"
   D. this refers to Titus.

Now we find the key to this other version. The interest is in Vespasian in the model of Nebuchadnezzar. What is important in the transaction is how the events of 586 define a pattern for 70. There is no place here for the intrusion of a new refuge (Yavneh), let alone a surrogate for the Temple and its atonement-offerings. The principal players now are not sages qualified by Torah-learning but rather secular figures, Vespasian on the Roman side, the three rich men and Ben Battiah on the Israelite side. Yohanan does not govern the course of events and does not play the leading part in the narrative — until a new form of power is introduced. That is the supernatural power accruing to knowledge of the Torah, which is exemplified in two distinct and important compositions within the composite, Yohanan's telling time, his disposition of the parables of the enemies. The end and climax of the story matches the beginning: the power of the ascetic sage outweighs the power of Vespasian: If in Jerusalem there had been one more like him, even though your army were twice as big, you would not have been able to take the city." And his power lies in his abstinence, his strength in his weakness.

So Lamentations Rabbah tells the story of power, the balance of saint against general being at the heart of the matter. But who are the embodiments of power? The story is explicit: Vespasian against *Sadoq*! So we ask, How does this version of the event carry forward the program of Lamentations Rabbah, the document that preserves the account? The clear intent is to illustrate the statement of Lamentations, "Her foes have become head," which makes the promotion of Vespasian to the throne of Rome the key. But the document wishes to comment, the pagan becomes head by reason of Israel's own failings. Israel possesses within its numbers an unrealized power that exceeds the power of the pagan emperor. So the focus is on the exhibition of the pagan power, the potential power of the Torah illustrated by Yohanan ben Zakkai, and then, at the climactic moment, the true power, which is the power of the sage's own virtue, is shown to be embodied in Sadoq. Yohanan is a secondary figure because the story expresses the primary theme: secular power versus true power, which is virtue.

How does that proposition figure in the larger program of Lamentations Rabbah?[4] The theme of Lamentations Rabbati is Israel's relationship with God, and the message concerning that theme is that the stipulative covenant still and always governs that relationship. Israel is not helpless before its fate but controls its own destiny. So at stake is the matter of power: that of the gentiles and that of Israel. Israel's power lies in its virtue, inclusive of its devotion to study of the Torah. This is the one and whole message of Lamentations Rabbah, and it is the only message that is repeated throughout; everything else proves secondary and derivative of the fundamental proposition that the destruction of the Temple in Jerusalem in 70 C.E. — as much as in 586 B.C.E. — proves the enduring validity of the covenant, its rules and its promise of redemption. Lamentations Rabbah argues that when Israel has attained the merit that accrues through the Torah, God will redeem Israel. God's unique relationship with Israel, which is unique among the nations, works itself out even now, in a time of despair and disappointment. The resentment of the present condition, recapitulating the calamity of the destruction of the Temple, finds its resolution and remission in the redemption that will follow Israel's regeneration through the Torah — that is the program, that is the proposition, and in this compilation, there is no other. In that context the contrast between Vespasian and Sadoq bears a critical lesson. And to the presentation of that lesson the activities of Yohanan ben Zakkai prove necessary but not sufficient. What is necessary is what lies before us. What is left out of the account of Lamentations Rabbah but included in the Fathers According to Rabbi Nathan is what is not necessary to the picture drawn by Lamentations Rabbah and its purpose — beginning with Yavneh itself!

v. Yavneh without Yohanan ben Zakkai

As Lamentations Rabbah encompasses Yohanan ben Zakkai and omits reference to Yavneh, so in a *baraita* — a composition attributed to Tannaite authority responsible for the Mishnah but not contained in the Mishnah — cited at Bavli Rosh Hashanah 31a-b, "Yavneh" figures without Yohanan ben Zakkai. The leading figure of Yavneh is the Sanhedrin or Rabbinic supreme court. At issue in this narrative is the comparison of the Sanhedrin to the Shekhinah, or God's presence. The Sanhedrin is treated as counterpart to God's presence, so I take it the Sanhedrin stands for the Torah — another emanation of God in the world. Then what is the point of what we shall follow? Just as the Presence of God took leave of the Temple and Jerusalem, so the presence of the Torah in the Sanhedrin departed as well.

Now Yavneh enters into the chain of tradition because to that place the Rabbinic sages in 68 C. E. fled before the destruction of the Second Temple in August of 70. So Yavneh represents the continuity of the tradition of the Torah, a continuity embodied in the chain of tradition of the Sages of the Rabbinic Sanhedrin. Yohanan ben Zakkai plays no role in the presentation of Yavneh.

Bavli Rosh Hashanah 4:4 I.6/31a-b

[I.6 A] Said R. Judah bar Idi said R. Yohanan, "The divine presence [Shekhinah] made ten journeys [in leaving the land and people of Israel prior to the destruction of the first Temple]. [That is, "The Divine Presence left Israel by ten stages" (Simon, p. 147)]. [This we know from] Scripture. And corresponding to these [stages], the Sanhedrin was exiled [successively to ten places of banishment]. [This we know from] tradition."

[B] The divine presence [Shekhinah] made ten journeys [in leaving Israel prior to the destruction of the first Temple]. [This we know from] Scripture: [It went] (1) from the ark-cover to the cherub; [delete: and from (one) cherub to the (other) cherub;] (2) and from the cherub to the threshold [of the Holy-of-Holies]; (3) and from the threshold to the [Temple-] court; (4) and from the court to the altar; (5) and from the altar to [Temple-] roof; (6) and from the roof to wall; (7) and from the wall to the city; (8) and from the city to the mountain; (9) and from the mountain to the wilderness; (10) and from the wilderness it ascended and dwelled in its place [in heaven, as it is said (Hos. 5:15): "I will return again to my place, [until they acknowledge their guilt and seek my face]."

[E] "And corresponding to these [stages through which the divine presence left Israel], the Sanhedrin was exiled [successively to ten places of banishment; this we know from] tradition." [The Sanhedrin was banished] (1) from the Chamber of Hewn Stone [in the inner court of the Temple] to the market; and (2) from the market into Jerusalem [proper], and (3) from Jerusalem to Yavneh, [31b] and (4) from Yavneh to Usha, and (5) from Usha [back] to

Yavneh, and (6) from Yavneh [back] to Usha, (7) and from Usha
to Shefar, and (8) from Shefar to Beth Shearim, and (9) from Beth
Shearim to Sepphoris, and (10) from Sepphoris to Tiberias.

This is a puzzling composition in the details, but the main point is self-evident. I cannot claim to know what the framer had in mind in having the Sanhedrin locate itself from Jerusalem to Yavneh and then leave and return to Yavneh. The comparison of the Shekhinah and the Sanhedrin is the main point. Then the Rabbinic court in Yavneh is distinguished from all other Rabbinic courts and continues to exercise the authority formerly vested in the Rabbinic court in Jerusalem — and that is what is at issue in the setting of Mishnah-tractate Rosh Hashanah 4:1-4, which we meet in detail in a moment. That composite sets forth Mishnah's discussion of the ordinances decreed by Yohanan ben Zakkai in the aftermath of the destruction of Jerusalem, Mishnah-tractate Rosh Hashanah 4:1-4. The Halakhic discussion centers on the standing of Yavneh in the age in which Jerusalem Temple no longer afforded the location of the Sanhedrin or Rabbinical court. The view of the passage before us intersects with the treatment of Yavneh in the Halakhic documents, the Mishnah and the Tosefta. There the issue important here, how Yavneh relates to Jerusalem, is worked out in the context of normative conduct of the law.

VI. YAVNEH IN THE HALAKHAH OF THE MISHNAH-TOSEFTA

That brings us to the other half of the Rabbinic writings, the Halakhic part. The Halakhah, or law, sets forth norms of behavior, in distinction from the Aggadah, or narrative, which sets forth norms of belief. To this point we have surveyed documents of the Aggadah and their take on the destruction of the Temple and the age that succeeded. The Halakhah is contained principally in the Mishnah, a law code of ca. 200 C.E., and the Tosefta, a collection of complements and supplements to the Mishnah, of ca. 300 C.E. In both documents, Yavneh appears *en passant* and stands for the location of an important Rabbinic court. A brief survey suffices. In all items but one, Yavneh bears no special importance except for the presence of the Rabbinic sages. But the Halakhah, as we shall see in a moment, also contains the viewpoint that Yavneh is the heir of Jerusalem, its authorities carry forward the power of the Sanhedrin, and its court succeeds the court of Jerusalem. So by reason of not only location and circumstance but the continuity of the authority of the Torah, embodied in Yohanan ben Zakkai in particular, Yavneh stands in the normative law in its day for what Jerusalem embodied in its glory — a very considerable claim.

But first we rapidly survey the sizable corpus of routine references to Yavneh as a place among other places, not as a period and a moment in the sacred history of holy Israel, God's people.

A. THE MISHNAH: In the Mishnah Yavneh is the location of a court, which decided cases: M. Bekh. 5:6, 6:8 (an expert, like Ila in Yavneh). Yavneh further is the location of an appellate court, to which people referred difficult decisions: M. Kel. 5:4B (Fire broke out among the ovens of Kefar Signa, and the matter came to Yavneh, and Rabban Gamaliel declared them unclean); M. Par. 7:6D (One went to Yavneh three festival seasons, and at the third festival season they declared it fit for him-as a special dispensation); M. Sanh. 11:4A (They put him to death not in the court in his own town or in the court which is in Yavneh, but they bring him up to the high court in Jerusalem) M. R.H. 2:8D, 2:9H (Yavneh is the location of Rabban Gamaliel). That leaves the one important discussion, in the context of the law, of the standing and authority of Yavneh, which we meet in a moment.

B. THE TOSEFTA: In the Tosefta's amplification of the Mishnah, Yavneh is the location of a court, which decided cases (T. Bekh. 4:11; T. Kel. B.B. 5:6A; T. Kil. 1:3, 1:4; T. Nid. 4:3; T. Nid. 6:6; T. Mak. 3:15; T. Mid. 1:17). Yavneh formed the model for proper liturgical practice (T. R.H. 2:11). It was called the vineyard in Yavneh: T. Yeb. 6:6, 10:3: Said R. Ishmael b. R. Yohanan b. Beroqa, "I heard in the vineyard in Yavneh...." The "vineyard in Yavneh" served as the sages' gathering place:

T. EDUYYOT 1:1

1:1 A. When sages came together in the vineyard at Yavneh, they said, "The time is coming at which a person will go looking for a teaching of Torah and will not find it,

B. "a teaching of scribes and will not find it,

C. "since it is said, 'Behold, the days are coming, says the Lord Cod, when I will send a famine on the land; not a famine of bread, nor a thirst for water, but of hearing the words of the Lord. They shall wander from sea to sea and from north to east, they shall run to and fro, to seek the word of the Lord, but they shall not find it' (Amos 8:12).

D. "'The word of the Lord' refers to prophecy.

E. "'The word of the Lord' refers to [knowledge of] the end.

F. "'The word of the Lord' means that not one word of the Torah is the same as another word of the Torah."

G. They said, "Let us begin from Hillel and from Shammai."

Yavneh is the location of an appellate court, to which people referred difficult decisions (T. Mak. 7:4). The head of the Rabbinic sages after the death of Yohanan b. Zakkai, the principal figure of the Rabbinic administration, Gamaliel, continued the residence at Yavneh, thus Gamaliel presided at Yavneh (T. Ber. 2:6):

TOSEFTA SANHEDRIN 8:1

E . Said R. Eleazar b. R. Sadoq, "When Rabban Gamaliel sat in session in Yavneh, my father and one other were at his right hand, and elders were at his left hand."

F. And on what account does one sit in rank of age at his right hand? Because of the honor owing to age.

So too, sages assembled in Yavneh:[5]

TOSEFTA SOTAH 7:9, 13:4:

T. Sot. 7:9 A.   R. Yohanan b. Beroqah and R. Eleazar Hisma came from Yavneh
to Lud and they greeted R. Joshua in Peqiin.

B.   Said to them R. Joshua, "What was new in the school-house today?"

T. Sot. 13:4 A.   Then another time they were in session in Yavneh and heard an
echo saying, "There is among you a man who is worthy to receive
the Holy Spirit, but the generation is unworthy of such an honor."

B.   They all set their eyes upon Samuel the Small.

Other passages where Yavneh figures are routine and do not change the
picture.[6] In them Yavneh forms part of the inert background, the place where Rabbinic
sages gathered to do their work.

But in the Mishnah and its companion the Tosefta there is one Halakhic
passage at which the occasion of the destruction of Jerusalem and the Temple figures
— and where Yohanan ben Zakkai appears as well. Now Yohanan ben Zakkai takes
that leading role in events that we last witnessed in The Fathers According to Rabbi
Nathan: the founder and unmatched authority of the period following the destruction.
And the standing of Yavneh is connected to the destruction, just as in the passage of
Bavli Rosh Hashanah that compares the Sanhedrin and the Shekhinah. Here are the
two Halakhic presentations of Yavneh as the location of the heir to the authority of
Jerusalem, with Yohanan ben Zakkai at the center, heir of Moses and principal of
the transmission of the oral part of the Torah of Sinai:

MISHNAH-TRACTATE ROSH HASHANAH 4:1, 2.

4:1   A.   The festival day of the New Year which coincided with the Sabbath

B.   in the Temple they would sound the shofar

C.   But not in the provinces.

D.   When the Temple was destroyed, Rabban Yohanan ben Zakkai
made the rule that they should sound the shofar in every locale in
which there was a court.

E.   Said R. Eleazar, "Rabban Yohanan b. Zakkai made that rule only
in the case of Yavneh alone."

F.   They said to him, "All the same are Yavneh and every locale in
which there is a court."

4:2   A.   And in this regard also was Jerusalem ahead of Yavneh:

B.   in every town which is within sight and sound [of Jerusalem], and
nearby and able to come up to Jerusalem, they sound the shofar

C.   But as to Yavneh, they sound the shofar only in the court alone.

The issue of sounding the shofar on a Sabbath that coincided with the
New Year presumably arose within a brief time after August, 70. Yohanan ben
Zakkai decreed that just as in the Temple, they had sounded the Shofar, so wherever
there was a Rabbinic court, they should do the same now. So the Rabbinic court in

this age continued the standing and authority of the Temple. No wonder the compositors of the Talmud of Babylonia included in their commentary to the Mishnah chapter before us the explicit claim that the Presence of God in heaven found its counterpart in the Sanhedrin, that is, the Rabbinic court on earth. Then the law states in its way what the narrative says in its idiom: the Temple has lost its central position in the economy of the sacred, the Temple has found its successor in the Rabbinic court.

The Mishnah-passage contains a schismatic opinion, Eleazar's, which wished to arrogate to Yavneh the position of sole heir of the Temple. It is not sufficient that Rabbinic courts in general succeed, Yavneh stands by itself. That is separate from the normative rule, that the shofar is sounded on the New Year that coincides with the Sabbath where there was a court. It particularizes the Torah to Yavneh. I cannot imagine a more extreme claim. It occurs only in the present context. But the normative law, as we shall now see, treats Yavneh as inferior in the law's hierarchical classification of holy places to Jerusalem:

MISHNAH-TRACTATE ROSH HASHANAH 4:3

4:3 [A] In olden times the lulab was taken up in the Temple for seven days, and in the provinces, for one day.

[B] When the Temple was destroyed, Rabban Yohanan b. Zakkai made the rule that in the provinces the lulab should be taken up for seven days, as a memorial to the Temple;

The celebration of the Festival of Festivals, Sukkot, or Tabernacles, involved the rite in the temple of taking up the palm branch, or lulab, for seven days, done in the provinces only on the first day. The difference was once more the Sabbath. Now Yohanan arrogates to the provinces the rite of taking up the lulab on all seven days — as a memorial to the Temple. This assigns to the local places of prayer, the synagogues, the status of heir of the Temple, just as M. R.H. 4:1-2 have treated the Rabbinic court as enjoying the status of the Temple. Now we come to the third of the tripod of posts on which the Judaic administration rested, the patriarch, in addition to the Rabbinic court and the synagogue. The patriarch, Yohanan in his time, Gamaliel as successor in the house of Hillel, enjoyed Roman recognition as the ethnarch, the principal authority of the Jews.

MISHNAH-TRACTATE ROSH HASHANAH 4:3C, 4

4:3 [C] and that the day [the sixteenth of Nisan] on which the omer is waved should be wholly prohibited [in regard to the eating of new produce; M. Suk. 3:12].

4:4 [A] At first they would receive testimony about the new moon all day long.

[B] One time the witnesses came late, and the Levites consequently were mixed up as to [what] psalm [they should sing].

[C] They made the rule that they should receive testimony [about the new moon] only up to the afternoon offering.

[D] Then, if witnesses came after the afternoon offering, they would treat that entire day as holy and the next day as holy [too].

[E] When the Temple was destroyed, Rabban Yohanan b. Zakkai made the rule that they should [once more] receive testimony about the new moon all day long.

[F] Said R. Joshua b. Qorha, "This rule too did Rabban Yohanan b. Zakkai make:

[G] "Even if the head of the court is located somewhere else, the witnesses should come only to the location of the council [to give testimony, and not to the location of the head of the court]."

At issue at M. 4:3C, 4A-D, E, is how to deal with the timing of rites formerly carried on in the Temple and now no longer realized. The first item, conduct on the sixteenth of Nisan, requires a word of explanation. The Torah prohibited the utilization of the new crops until the waving of the sheaf of first grain of the barley harvest, called the 'omer, at noon on the sixteenth of Nisan, that is, the day after the advent of Passover at the full moon or fifteenth of Nisan. Then people could make use of the new crop, within the tithing season now begun. When the Temple stood, people were able to take for granted that the priests of the Temple, punctilious at their sacred task, would make the offering on time, so from noon of the 16th they would feel free too make use of the new crops. With the temple in ruins and no offering in hand, they waited out the entire day.

The issue at M. 4:4 concerns receiving testimony as to the advent of the new moon in connection with determining the calendar. This affected the offerings of the Temple, dictating what was required that day and the next. Yohanan provided for the interim in which the Temple offerings were suspended. What is important is the schismatic view of Joshua b. Qorha: wherever the head of the court, the nasi or patriarch was located, the collegium of sages who formed the court was what counted. The patriarch was not the key to the procedure, the Rabbinic court was. So Yohanan ben Zakkai is represented as treating the patriarch as a footnote, the Rabbinic sages as the text.

The Tosefta's complement presents no surprises. To show how the Tosefta cites and glosses the Mishnah, I present the Mishnah in italics, the Tosefta's own materials in plain type. Yavneh is comparable to Jerusalem.

Tosefta Rosh Hashanah 2:8

2:8 A. *And in this regard also was Jerusalem ahead of Yavneh: In every town which is within sight and sound, near, and [with folk] able to come up to Jerusalem [they sound the shofar]* [M. R.H. 4:2A-B]—

B. [if] these three things apply to it, *they sound the shofar in it.*

C. *But as to Yavneh, they sound the shofar only in the court alone* [M. R.H. 4:2C].

T. 2:9 A.   *R. Eleazar b. R. Sadoq says, "If it did not appear in its expected*
            time, they do not sanctify it, for Heaven has already declared it
            sanctified" [M. R.H. 2:7D].

B.   R. Simeon b. Eleazar says, "If it did not appear in its expected
     time, they do not sanctify it, for the prior month already has declared
     it sanctified."

C.   Simeon, son of the prefect, says, "If witnesses came after the
     afternoon offering, they would sound the *shofar.* But they do not
     add the offerings unless they actually declared the new moon
     sanctified" [cf. M. R.H. 4:4A-D].

D.   Said R. Joshua b. Qorha, "These rules did Rabban Yohanan b.
     Zakkai make after the Temple was destroyed.

E.   "Now when it is rebuilt, — quickly in our times! — matters will
     return to their original state" [cf. M. R.H. 4:4F-G].

Joshua b. Qorha's statement at the end is jarring: the only allusion to the
restoration of the Temple to its glory, the priesthood to its service, the altar to its
appointed task. We shall return to this matter in due course. It is the one of the few
points at which the legacy of Yavneh encompasses the theme of the end of days.[7]

What the Tosefta adds that interests us is at T. 2:9E, matters will return to
their original state when the temple is rebuilt. What the Tosefta adds is the necessary
affirmation that the adaptations of the law to the circumstance of the destruction
represents a temporary expedient, but in the end the Temple will be restored, and
with it the law will revert to its original perfection.

The representation of Yavneh, the place and the occasion, by the Mishnah
and the Tosefta obviously conforms to the larger program of the Halakhic documents.
These compilations collect a vast corpus of details and organize them by topics,
and they do not ordinarily pursue problems of theology of history, such as have
occupied us to this point. Nor do they make provision for individual figures; when
named authorities are cited, it is to mark their opinions as schismatic. In that context
we cannot anticipate finding deep reflection on the meaning of the destruction of
the Temple, except its practical consequences, or on the importance of Yohanan
ben Zakkai and the Rabbinic gathering at Yavneh.

Yet we find both. First, the law does adapt the liturgy to the destruction of
the Temple. Second, Yohanan's work at Yavneh is recognized as epochal. So in its
idiom, the classical law underscores the basic point: we cannot contemplate the
calamity and the Judaic response, in the Halakhah as much as in the Aggadah,
without invoking the figure of Yohanan ben Zakkai, the Rabbinic court at Yavneh,
and the basic affirmation that something important happened in 70 — and changed
everything from then on. But in other Halakhic and Aggadic ones as well, the event
of 70 and the advent of Yavneh in the person of Yohanan ben Zakkai do not figure
at all.

VII. Catastrophe without Yavneh.
A. The Halakhic Account of the Meaning of 70

Specifically, we find massive Halakhic expositions that respond to 70 and the destruction without Yavneh. These do not minimize the catastrophe of the destruction, but they do show appreciation for what has endured. They do not portray how God has left Jerusalem but rather how Israel the people remains holy — and much else does to. We encounter enormous Aggadic ones that define the normative response to disaster without highlighting the figure of the Rabbinic sage as the key and the matter of Torah-study as primary, such as defines the responses to catastrophe of the Mishnah and the Tosefta with their appreciation for the comparability of Jerusalem and Yavneh, the priestly labor and the sages' work, not to mention the Fathers according to Rabbi Nathan and Lamentations Rabbah. Our picture of the legacy of Yavneh would not be complete without an account of matters where Yavneh does not figure at all, and where the destruction of the Temple is negotiated without the sense of that dramatic caesura that governed in the documents considered to this point.

To this point we have surveyed several documents' treatment of the catastrophe of 70 as that treatment encompassed the figure of Yohanan ben Zakkai and the role of Yavneh as heir of Jerusalem. But the circumstance signified by "Yavneh" — the destruction of the Temple, the reconstruction of life after the ruin — encompasses deep thought on the meaning of the event and the age represented by Yavneh: what happened in 70, and what did not happen. What happened was the destruction of the Temple. What did not happen was the annihilation of Israel, the Jewish people. The Halakhah addresses that fact. The Halakhic account in so many words asks whether Israel, the people, is still holy without the Temple and responds that it is. A program of sanctification of Israel's life is explicitly situated in relationship to the loss of the Temple and even exile from the Land. The Halakhah turns out to embody in deed the results of profound deliberation about fundamental issues of theology.

These are engaged with through the Halakhic exposition of Israel's relationship with God beyond the loss of the Temple — that very same issue that Joshua presented to Yohanan ben Zakkai in The Fathers According to Rabbi Nathan. The Halakhic presentation concerns the laws for slaughtering animals for domestic consumption, that is, for use in the Israelite household. To understand how the Halakhah addresses the issue of whether or not Israel the people retains its sanctity beyond 70 and loss of the Temple is made easy by the framing of the law. A sequence of rules is cited, and in each case, a single formula is applied to them.

Mishnah-tractate Hullin — the triumph of the Mishnah — sets forth the explicit statement that meat prepared for Israelites is subject to rules that express its sanctification even outside of the Land, when the Temple is in ruins, and for beasts that to begin with have not been sanctified for the altar. The recurrent formula, the law of such and such applies "(1) in the Land and outside the Land, (2) in the time of the Temple and not in the time of the Temple, (3) in the case of unconsecrated beasts and in the case of consecrated beasts," insists that these rules transcend boundaries of space, time, and circumstance.

What theological principle follows. It is this: The eternity of Israel transcends the ephemerality of the Temple; Israel's table remains sanctified and therefore subject to the rules of cultic slaughter, even after God's table has been desecrated. Where is the theology in all this? It lies right at the surface. *Israel is God's abode even when there is no Temple.* The Mishnah makes that statement in so many words when it says that the laws that apply to the altar and the table apply to the table even when the altar is destroyed. Here is the language of the law that says so.

MISHNAH-TRACTATE HULLIN 5:1

[The prohibition against slaughtering on the same day] "it and its young" (Lev. 22:28) applies (1) in the Land and outside the Land, (2) in the time of the Temple and not in the time of the Temple, (3) in the case of unconsecrated beasts and in the case of consecrated beasts. How so? He who slaughters it and its offspring, (1) which are unconsecrated, (2) outside [the Temple courtyard] — both of them are valid. And [for slaughtering] the second he incurs forty stripes. [He who slaughters] (1) Holy Things (2) outside — [for] the first is he liable to extirpation, and both of them are invalid, and [for] both of them he incurs forty stripes. [He who slaughters] (1) unconsecrated beasts (2) inside [the Temple courtyard] — both of them are invalid, and [for] the second he incurs forty stripes. [He who slaughters] (1) Holy Things (2) inside — the first is valid, and he is exempt [from any punishment], and [for] the second he incurs forty stripes, and it is invalid.

The pattern is established by speaking specifically of the holiness of the Land, the time of the Temple, and consecrated beasts, and insisting that the Israelite table at home takes priority in the level of sanctification over the Land, Temple-times, and beasts sanctified for the altar.

MISHNAH-TRACTATE HULLIN 6:1

[The requirement to] cover up the blood (Lev. 17:13-14) applies in the Land and abroad, (2) in the time of the Temple and not in the time of the Temple, (3) in the case of unconsecrated beasts, but not in the case of Holy Things. And it applies (4) to a wild beast and a bird, (5) to that which is captive and to that which is not captive. And it applies (6) to a *koy*, because it is a matter of doubt [whether it is wild or domesticated]. And they do not slaughter it [a *koy*] on the festival. But if one has slaughtered it, they do not cover up its blood.

Now the issue is covering up the blood, and the outcome is the same. The other items are self-evident.

MISHNAH-TRACTATE HULLIN **7:1, 8:1, 10:1-2, 11:1, 12:1**

M. 7:1 [The prohibition of] the sinew of the hip [sciatic nerve, Gen. 32:32] applies (1) in the Land [of Israel] and outside of the Land, (2) in the time of the Temple and not in the time of the Temple, (3) to unconsecrated animals and to Holy Things. It applies (1) to domesticated cattle and to wild beasts, (2) to the right hip and to the left hip. But it does not apply (3) to a bird, because it has no hollow [of the thigh or spoon-shaped hip And its fat is permitted. Butchers are believed (1) concerning it and (2) concerning the [forbidden] fat (Lev. 3:17, 7:23).

M. 8:1 [As to the separation of milk and meat (Ex. 23:19, 34:26, Dt. 12:21)]: Every [kind of] flesh [i.e., meat, of cattle, wild beast, and fowl] is it prohibited to cook in milk, except for the flesh of fish and locusts. And it is prohibited to serve it up onto the table with cheese, except for the flesh of fish and locusts. He who vows [to abstain] from flesh is permitted [to make use of] the flesh of fish and locusts.

M. 10:1 [The requirement to give to the priests] the shoulder, the two cheeks, and the maw (Deut. 18:3) applies (1) in the Land and outside of the Land, (2) in the time of the Temple and not in the time of the Temple, (3) to unconsecrated beasts, but not to consecrated beasts. For it [the contrary] might have appeared logical: Now, if unconsecrated animals, which are not liable for the breast and thigh [which are taken from peace offerings for the priests, (Lev. 7:31)], are liable for the [priestly] gifts [of the shoulder, cheeks, and maw], Holy Things, which *are* liable for the breast and thigh, logically should be liable to the priestly gifts. Scripture therefore states, "And I have given them to Aaron the priest and to his sons as a due for ever" (Lev. 7:34) — he has a right [in consecrated beasts] only to that which is explicitly stated [namely, the breast and thigh].

M. 11:1-2 [The laws concerning the obligation to donate to the priest] the first shearings [of wool from the sheep of one's flock (Deut. 18:4)] apply both inside the Land of Israel and outside the Land of Israel, in the time the Temple [in Jerusalem stands] and in the time the Temple does not [stand]. [And the laws apply] to [the fleece of] unconsecrated [animals] but not to [the fleece of animals that were] consecrated [to the Temple]. A stricter rule applies to [the obligation to give to the priest] the shoulder, the two cheeks and the maw [of one's animals] than to [the obligation to give to the priest] the first shearings [of wool from the sheep of one's flock]. For [the obligation to give to the priest] the shoulder, the two cheeks and the maw [of one's animals] applies both to the [large] animals of one's herd and to the [small] animals of one's flock.

M. 12:1 [The requirement to] let [the dam] go from the nest [Deut. 22:6-7] applies (1) in the Land and outside of the Land, (2) in the time of the Temple and not in the time of the Temple, (3) to unconsecrated [birds] but not to consecrated ones. A more strict rule applies to covering up the blood than to letting [the dam] go from the nest: For the requirement of covering up the blood applies (1) to a wild beast and to fowl, (2) to that which is captive and to that which is not captive. But letting [the dam] go from the nest applies only (1) to fowl and applies only (2) to that which is not captive. What is that which is not captive? For example, geese and fowl which make their nest in an orchard. But if they make their nest in the house (and so Herodian doves), one is free of the requirement of letting the dam go.

The law of the Mishnah here states in so many words what it wants to know. That is whether [1] the destruction of the Temple and cessation of the offerings, [2] the degradation of the Land of Israel — its loss of its Israelite residents — and

[3] the exile of the holy people, Israel, from the Holy Land, affect the rules of Israelite sustenance in the model of the nourishment of God, Israel's domestic food is prepared in accord with rules that apply to God's sanctified food. Is that only in the Temple, only in the Land, only of food deriving from the Land? The question pertains to three venues: [1] in the Temple, [2] in the Land, [3] among the holy people.

The answer is, whatever the condition of the Temple and its altar, whatever the source — the Holy Land or unclean gentile lands — of animals, and whatever the location of the people Israel — whether in the Holy Land or not — one thing persists. And that is the sanctification of Israel, the people. That status of holiness imputed to the social entity (Israel) and to each individual (Israelite) therein — endures [1] in the absence of the cult and [2] in alien, unclean territory and [3] whatever the source of the food that Israel eats.

Israel's sanctity is eternal, unconditional, absolute. The sanctification that inheres in Israel, the people, transcends the Land and outlives the Temple and its cult.

Since the sanctity of Israel, the people, persists beyond the Temple and outside of the Land, that sanctity stands at a higher point in the hierarchy of domains of the holy that ascend from earth to heaven and from humanity to God.[8] The status of Israel — in the Land or abroad, possessed of the Temple or excluded therefrom — in preparing meat, whether for God or for Israel itself address the condition of corporate Israel after 70. They represent an articulate response to the catastrophe of that year and its sequel, 132-135, which we shall meet in a moment. The law of the Mishnah, to make its statement about the eternal sanctification of the people, Israel, explicitly responds to three facts: [1] Israelites live not only in the holy land but abroad, in unclean lands; [2] the Temple has been destroyed and not yet rebuilt; [3] and, consequently, animals are slaughtered not only in the Temple in the Land but in unconsecrated space and abroad, and the meat is eaten not only in a cultic but in a profane circumstance.

Here the circumstance of Yavneh, with its question of Israel's standing in Heaven now that its holy place has perished from the earth, finds its explicit response. Holy, corporate Israel's sanctification endures beyond the Land, beyond the Temple, and beyond the age in which the active source of sanctification, the altar, functions. It continues when the other sources of sanctification do not. How then do we hierarchize Temple, Land, and corporate Israel? The desuetude of the one, the abandonment of the other — neither ultimately affects the standing of the Israel. The Land and the Temple have lost that sanctity that infused them when Israel dwelt on the Land and the Temple altar was nourished by Israel's priesthood and produce. But the sanctification of Israel itself endures through history, eternal and untouched by time and change. And when Israel returns to the Land and rebuilds the Temple, the sanctification of the Land and the Temple will once more be realized.

Anyone who wonders — as does the author of the book of Lamentations attributed to Jeremiah in the aftermath of the destruction of 586 — whether the law of the Mishnah that applied to the Temple and the home when the Temple was standing and Israel was in the Land of Israel continues to apply with the Temple in ruins and Israel in exile here finds the answer. And every meal at which the Israelite eats meat embodies that answer in a most active form: the menu itself. Although the sanctity of the Temple stands in abeyance, the sanctity of the Israelite table persists. Although Israel is in exile from the Holy Land, Israel remains holy. Although in the Temple rules of uncleanness are not now kept, they continue in force wherever Israelites may be. Birds and animals that flourish outside of the Land, when prepared for the Israelite table, are regulated by the same rules that apply in the Land and even (where relevant) at the altar. So Israel, the people, not only retains sanctity but preserves it outside of the Land, and the sanctity of Israel transcends that of the Temple and its altar. Corporate Israel is endowed with a higher degree of sanctity than the Temple and the Land — and, in the hierarchy of the sacred, stands at the apex, closest to God.

WHY HULLIN IN PARTICULAR? Why is it particularly the law of Mishnah-tractate Hullin — food for the Israelite table, not for the table of the Lord inn the Temple of Jerusalem — that makes the statement that Israel is holier than the Land and even than the Temple, even endowing with sanctity animals slaughtered to nourish the people? That theological proposition comes to the fore in particular here because the written Torah supplies the law that contains the entire message. It does so when it imposes the same requirements that pertain to slaughter of an animal sacrifice for the altar in Jerusalem and to killing an animal for the use of Israel at home, specifically, burying the blood or draining it. That means that the meat Israel eats is subject to the same regulations that apply to the meat that God receives on the altar-fires. That very law states that meat for those who are not holy, that is, for gentiles or idolaters, is not subject to the same rules (Ex. 22:30, Dt. 14:21). So, it is unmistakable: food for God and for Israel must be prepared in comparable manner, which rule does not apply to food for gentiles.

History enters in when we ask how that principle affects animals raised abroad. *The laws of Hullin apply to them, because the laws apply to unconsecrated animals as much as consecrated ones.* The purpose in nature — nourishing Israel — is alone what counts. The beast intended for Israelite consumption at the table even in a foreign country must be prepared as though for God on the altar in Jerusalem, and that can only mean, since the beast is intended (by the act of correct slaughter) for Israel, the use of the beast by Israel sanctifies the beast and necessitates conformity with the rules of slaughter for God in the Temple. Israel, even abroad, renders the food that it eats comparable to food for the altar.

WHAT ABOUT THE TEMPLE IN RUINS? Then comes the matter of the Temple and its condition. We ask, What has food-preparation to do with the consideration of location? The rule that permits slaughter of meat outside of the Temple (Dt. 12:20-24) explicitly states that it speaks of corporate Israel outside of the Temple in Jerusalem. So, even if the act of slaughter does not take place in Jerusalem, the act must conform, because the focus is on Israel, wherever Israel is located — even far from Jerusalem (for so the law is formulated in Scripture). The law of the Mishnah-tractate before us simply carries the same conception forward in a logical way: the same considerations govern even so far from Jerusalem as territory that to begin with is laden with corpse-uncleanness, that is, foreign soil; and even in an age in which Jerusalem is no more; and, it goes without saying, even in connection with a beast that has not been consecrated for the altar.

Since Scripture itself has separated the act of slaughter from the rite of sacrifice in the Temple, the law of the Mishnah has done little more than explore the consequences of that rule when it states that the requirements of slaughter in the cult pertain also outside of the cult, thus wherever Israelites are located, and whenever the act takes place — even outside of the Land altogether, even during the time that the Temple is no longer standing. If an Israelite people outside of Jerusalem is contained within the logic set forth by the Torah at Deuteronomy 12:20-24, then the next step, and it is not a giant step, is to contemplate an Israel outside of the Land altogether, not to say a Temple in ruins.

The integral connection of slaughter of animals and sacrifice at the altar having been broken when all cultic activity was focused by Deuteronomy within Jerusalem, all that the law of the Mishnah has done is to address in so many words the extreme consequences of that situation. If the rules apply even to unconsecrated beasts, and even to the Land beyond Jerusalem, and even outside of the Temple, then by the same token, logic dictates a utopian consequence. The same laws apply even when no animals are being consecrated at all, and they apply even once the Temple no longer stands, and they pertain even abroad.

So the Torah sets the stage by addressing the situation of slaughter not in behalf of the transaction at the altar and not in the setting of the holy place. And, consequently, the law of the Mishnah worked out in the critical details of the sustenance of life, the conviction that Israel the people forms the locus of sanctification. What follows is that this allegation about the enduring, ubiquitous sanctification inherent in Israel the people — even outside of the Land, even in the time of the Temple's destruction — pervades the exposition of the laws in detail. It is an amazing statement in its insistence upon the priority and permanence of the sanctity of Israel — whatever may become of the holiness of the altar and of the Land.

LOCATION, OCCASION, THE CHARACTER OF THE ENCOUNTER, IN GOD'S CONTEXT, OF GOD AND THE ISRAELITE: Affirming the unique holiness of the Temple and the Land of Israel, Mishnah-tractate Hullin still wants to show how the holiness of the people, Israel, retains its own integrity. Israel's enduring sanctification transcends location and occasion because it is realized at the moment at which life-blood is spilled in the preservation of life. Thus, the law of the Mishnah establishes in practical ways that Israel remains holy even outside of the Land, even in the age without the Temple. Meat prepared for Israel, wherever the meat has itself been nourished, even on gentile ground, must be prepared as though for the altar in Jerusalem. Then Israel's sanctity persists, even when that continuum in which it stood, the chain of continuity with the Temple altar in Jerusalem (as the formulation of Deuteronomy 12:20-24 framed matters), has been disrupted. Israel's sanctity endows with sanctity even animals raised in unclean ground, so powerful is the sanctification that transforms Israel.

VIII. CATASTROPHE WITHOUT YAVNEH. B. THE MESSIAH THEME AND THE AGGADIC PICTURE OF WHAT IS TO BE DONE IN RESPONSE TO THE DESTRUCTION

If the Halakhah can systematically raise the issues of Yavneh — ruin and renewal — without introducing Yavneh at all, what of the Aggadah? Should we not expect the Messiah-theme to figure? That is a prominent topic in Judaic writings other than the Rabbinic ones we have considered.

The fact is that in neither the Halakhic nor the Aggadic writings that concern Yavneh with or without Yohanan ben Zakkai does the Messiah-theme play a role. Specifically, we have just seen how the Temple's restoration can be discussed without inclusion of the Messiah's role in the restoration of Jerusalem, Temple, and sacrifices. We have already passed by a Halakhic allusion to the restoration. The Halakhic reference to what is to resolve the crisis of Yavneh is elliptical and allusive. We noticed it in the exposition of the ordinances of Yohanan ben Zakkai at Yavneh:

TOSEFTA ROSH HASHANAH 2:8

D.   Said R. Joshua b. Qorha, "These rules did Rabban Yohanan b. Zakkai make after the Temple was destroyed.

E.   "Now when it is rebuilt, — quickly in our times! — matters will return to their original state" [cf. M. R.H. 4:4F-G].

This explicit reference to the restoration of Jerusalem and the rebuilding of the Temple provokes us to wonder, what has become of the figure of the Messiah, and where does the Messiah-theme figure in the legacy of Yavneh? So the question arises, how does the Aggadic corpus deal with the future, beyond 70, with stress on the ultimate outcome.

The Messiah-theme plays no role of consequence in the Aggadic corpus pertaining to Yavneh and its reconstruction. The restoration of the Temple can be discussed without introducing the Messiah-theme. And when it is, the focus is on the end of days. The Mishnah's judgment is expressed in the following saying:

MISHNAH-TRACTATE SOTAH 9:15 MM

R. Pinhas b. Yair says, "Heedfulness leads to cleanliness, cleanliness leads to cleanness; cleanness leads to abstinence, abstinence leads to holiness, holiness leads to modesty, modesty leads to the fear of sin, the fear of sin leads to piety, piety leads to the Holy Spirit, the Holy Spirit leads to the resurrection of the dead, and the resurrection of the dead comes through Elijah, blessed be his memory, Amen."

So we must ask ourselves, does the legacy of Yavneh include no doctrine of the coming of the Messiah and what is to be done to hasten the day?

To find the answer, we turn to responses to the catastrophe of 70 attributed to other actors than those who flourished at Yavneh or in the age of Yavneh. There in the context of stories on an explicit effort at restoration of Jerusalem and its holy place the figure of the Messiah comes to the fore. That is in the setting of Rabbinic comments on the figure of Bar Kokhba, leader of the Second War against Rome in 132-135. So the destruction of the Temple encompasses a Messiah-doctrine, an attitude and a policy that concern the end of days and how to hasten its advent.

A principal authority of Yavneh, Aqiba, is described as regarding Bar Kokhba as the Messiah, and other Yavneh-figures rejected that view.

YERUSHALMI-TRACTATE TA'ANIT 4:5 VII.1

[G] R. Simeon b. Yohai taught, "Aqiba, my master, would interpret the following verse: 'A star (kokhab) shall come forth out of Jacob' (Num. 24:17) — 'A disappointment (Kozeba) shall come forth out of Jacob.'"

[H] R. Aqiba, when he saw Bar Kozeba, said, "This is the royal Messiah."

[I] Said to him R. Yohanan ben Toreta, "Aqiba! Grass will grow on your cheeks, and the Messiah will not yet have come!"

What follows is that part of the legacy of Yavneh — coming to the fore at the time of the Second War against Rome — is a debate on the Messiah-theme. But nothing in the heritage of sayings attributed to Yavneh-authorities or stories told about them places the Messiah-theme at the head of the agenda of law or theology. The contrast with the narratives of the Second War against Rome is drawn by the account of Aqiba and Bar Kokhba. Stories about that war underscore why Bar Kokhba was not, and could not have been, the Messiah.

IX. ANALYSIS, NOT SYNTHESIS

The internal evidence for differentiating canonical documents gives its best service in the contrast between the accounts concerning Yohanan's escape from besieged Jerusalem provided by The Fathers according to Rabbi Nathan and Lamentations Rabbah, respectively. There we could explain the differences in the picture of Yohanan ben Zakkai by appeal to the documentary programs of the respective compilations. These differences were recognized by the great Israeli Talmudic historian, G. Alon, and explained by him in the historical framework: different views of what happened, each with its own politics. For Alon and three generations of Talmudic historians who followed him, at stake in the sources always was the historical events preserved within them. The premise always maintained that the husk of the narrative always contained a kernel of historical truth. I take a different path in accounting for the conflicting picture, appealing to the program of the two documents that present the conflicting pictures. Historical analysis presupposes the presence of details that afford access to things that really happened.

But narratives preserved in documents that came to closure many centuries after the events they purport to describe afford reliable information only on the imagination of the narrators. The prerequisites of historical fact, eye-witness accounts, transcripts of things really said or written down by the principals, for example, hardly characterize the kinds of evidence set forth in the Rabbinic canon. Historical synthesis of the two accounts proves hopeless and leads nowhere. There is no way to validate or falsify as historical fact any allegation contained within the Rabbinic literature but one. The people who compiled the documents thought they had good reason to record matters as they did. But whether or not that reason pertained to history as contemporary history is formulated — an account of how things actually were — remains to be demonstrated. I do not think it can be demonstrated.

We now start again, this time with a document, not a topic to be addressed to a group of documents. To the principal parts of each document I address a fixed set of questions. [1] How do we know that a composition refers to 70 and/or 132-135? [2] What is important about the person, place, or thing that pertains? [3] What proposition is presented in the law or narrative? At the end of the presentation of a document's relevant compositions and composites, I ask how the treatment of the topic carries forward the perspective of the document that sets forth that topic in just that way.

ENDNOTES

[1] This essay originated as a lecture at the University of Hartford. My thanks go to my hosts at the Greenberg Center of Jewish Studies, in particular Dr. Richard Freund, and to the sponsor of the event, Mr. Ricky Greenfield of the *Connecticut Jewish Ledger.*

[2] A complementary and congruent version of the Lamentations Rabbah story is at Bavli Gittin 56b. I deal with the Bavli's data in due course.

[3] The comparison of the two versions, that of the Fathers according to Rabbi Nathan and the one of Lamentations Rabbah, was first carried out by Gedaliah Alon, the grand master of Talmudic history, in his *Studies in Jewish History* I, II (in Hebrew), Tel Aviv, 1957, 1958, I:238-251. My critique of Alon's view is in my *Life*, pp 124ff. The comparison carried out here has no bearing on the empirical facts of history at issue in Alon's, and my original, reading of the topic.

[4] The version of the story at Bavli Gittin 56b is not relevant at this point. Its place in the Bavli's program is best defined by the context in which the Bavli presents the narrative. A comparison of the two versions — Bavli's and Lamentation Rabbah's — shows the latter to have been corrected in light of the former, but that need not detain us. We should need a clearer picture of the Bavli's larger intent in the context of its exposition of Mishnah-tractate Gittin. It suffices here to say that the Bavli introduces the story to supply background

information. It forms a small part of a huge topical miscellany on the two great wars, 66-73 and 132=135. The miscellany has been compiled for thematic reasons and inserted to clarify a detail of the Mishnah's law, For further discussion of the topical miscellanies, see *The Bavli's Massive Miscellanies. The Problem of Agglutinative Discourse in the Talmud of Babylonia.* Atlanta, 1992: Scholars Press for South Florida Studies in the History of Judaism. Now: Lanham, University Press of America.

[5] T. Yad. 2:16

[6] Yavneh is a desert-area: T. Ar. 2:8C. The majority of those who stored produce n the storehouse of Yavneh were Samaritans T. Dem. 1:14 (in the case of a storehouse of [produce belonging to] Israelites and Samaritans, they follow the [status of the] majority… They said to him, "[Thus do you rule] after having taught us that [produce in] the storehouse of Yavneh, which is inside the [city] wall, is [held to be] *Dema'i!"* — and the majority of it was [produce of] Samaritans.)

[7] In their death scenes Yohanan ben Zakkai and Eliezer b. Hyrcanus are given veiled allusions to the coming of the Messiah, cf. Bavli Berakhot 28a.

[8] Mishnah-tractate Kelim Chapter One and its Toseftan complement particularize the hierarchization of the holy. In the present context we do not require the details of uncleanness and holiness that are given there.

5

The Kingdom of Heaven
in Kindred Systems, Judaic and Christian

I. WHY DOES THE FORMULA, "KINGDOM OF HEAVEN," FIGURE IN THE SYSTEMIC COMPARISON OF CATEGORY-FORMATIONS?

Theological systems of social thought produced by diverse heirs of the Hebrew Scriptures concur on generative category-formations, Israel/gentiles, sin-repentance-atonement, for example. These are critical not only to the Aggadic theology that structures the Rabbinic system but, appropriately adapted, to the theological constructions that animate other canonical communities. But a component deriving from Scripture that figures prominently in one Judaic system may form part of the background of another or play no role whatsoever in a third. So the comparison and contrast of Judaisms begins with the available theological category-formations: generative or inert.[1]

"The Kingdom of Heaven" provides one such case. It is generative in one continuator-system of Scripture, inert in another. When, specifically, we come to the theme, the Kingdom of Heaven (in Rabbinic writings) or the Kingdom of God (in Christian ones), we find what forms to the one an inert reference-point, lacking systemic mission or position, and to the other, a category-formation integral to the construction and the working of entire compositions of thought. In the Aggadic system it is one way of referring to God's dominion — that alone. In the Christian system set forth in the Synoptic Gospels it defines the heart of Jesus' message. Indeed, it is so systemically active that a particular literary medium the parable, is designated as principal medium for the message. That surely justifies classifying the conception as a generative category-formation by the evidence of the systemic writings themselves.

To define what is at issue, we begin with the simple question: how, in framing a hypothesis of matters, do we intuit the activity of any given category-formation? The answer implicit throughout is, we rely on the signals of the language of our documents, beginning with the words they use to deal with transactions deemed comparable or congruent, or with actors of the same sort: Israel stands for Israelites and corporate Israel, sin-repentance-atonement covers a variety of actions characterized by the same attitude. So the choice of words such as Israel or gentile, or of the complex, sin-repentance-atonement, forms the first indication of the presence and activity of a candidate for defining a systemic category-formation.

But the task transcends concordance-work. For a single word on its own does not stand for a systemic category-formation. In the theological grammar of the Rabbinic Aggadah, we may say, a head-noun presents us with a candidate for designation as a category-formation, but on its own does not establish its claim to play a considerable role in its system. That qualification — a noun is not a category-formation, it is only a noun — we shall see in connection with the Messiah-theme, which divides itself among and contributes to a variety of fundamental and generative category-formations but which possesses no integrity or autonomy within the Aggadic theological system, for reasons to be explained.

That brings us to our problem, which is, the systemic standing of the conception of "Kingdom of Heaven" in the Aggadic theological system, comparable to "Kingdom of God " elsewhere. "Kingdom of God" stands for a collection of related notions, God is King, God rules, God exercises dominion, God's politics govern, God commands and Israel obeys, Israelites are God's slaves, and so on. The language provides a way of referring to those integrated conceptions. What we want to know is how the language of the Aggadic compilations and compositions presents in the formula "Kingdom of Heaven" the idea of divine governance and whether the usages of that formula signal an integral and generative conception or an inert and passive, neutral one. That it is a ubiquitous notion is proved self-evident by the formulation of the Qaddish, which beseeches the prompt advent of "his Kingdom." But where and how, in the Aggadic system, the conception of God's dominion figures as a generative category-formation, not merely part of the background of givens, is not equivalently self-evident. God's dominion both pervades the system and leaves no categorical mark upon the composition and workings of the system.

Now that observation points to what is at stake in this exercise. It is how and whether "Kingdom of Heaven" functions as a category-formation in the Aggadic theology as it does in the Evangelists' account of Jesus' teaching and the media framed to bear that message. In Aggadic and Halakhic contexts, by contrast, the theme of God's rule pervades, but the particularization of that theme as "Kingdom of Heaven" forms no more than an inert category-formation, one that figures as part of the background of ideas that everywhere inhere but nowhere take an active, generative role.

II. What does "Kingdom of Heaven" look like when it is systemically generative — active and integral?

When it is generative, the "Kingdom of Heaven" will come to realization within the unfolding of the mythic narrative of the system, link to other principal parts of the system to provoke fresh thought about new problems, find a literary expression in context that accords to the conception particular emphasis. These conditions are met by the category-formation, sin-repentance-atonement, and Israel/gentiles.

Let us begin with an elementary question: Why should we suppose the Kingdom of Heaven presents a candidate for identification as a category-formation? To answer that question for "Kingdom of Heaven," we need more than a case in which God's rule registers in some categorical role. Such a case does not qualify as systemically consequential — generative in the way in which sin-repentance-atonement generate new thought about fresh problems, exercise predictive power. We deal here with a generality, not a systemic particularization, in a working set of category-formations, of a generalization.

So to legitimate invoking the Kingdom of God as a generative category-formation, I have to show that in a competing system constructed by heirs of the same Scripture, that topic does function as active and principal. So we need to begin with the demonstration that an idea such as God's dominion, at the foundations everywhere, sustaining every system that privileges the Hebrew Scriptures, can rise to the surface of systemic discourse and form the center of that discourse. Does an entire working set of category-formations derive energy from that particularization of a general conception, as, for example, the Rabbinic Aggadic system does from sin-repentance-atonement? Such an example from some Scripturally-founded system other than the Rabbinic one will validate the supposition that "the Kingdom of Heaven" can serve as a generative category-formation. With that picture in hand, we gain perspective on the counterpart data of the Aggadic writings: if this is what a generative categorical expression of the concept of divine rule looks like, then how shall we classify the counterpart expression in the Rabbinic writings?

I suppose that the "Kingdom of Heaven" presents a candidate for identification as an Aggadic category-formation in Rabbinic theology, resting as it does on deep foundations in Scripture, because in the Synoptic Gospels' accounts of Jesus' teaching, saturated as they are in the heritage of Israelite Scripture, "Kingdom of Heaven" or "Kingdom of God " not only defines the central motif. It also is given its own literary medium for carrying the message, the parable in Evangelical formulation.[2] The simple fact is, as represented by the Gospels, the system of thought set forth in the teaching attributed to Jesus centers on the Kingdom of God.

Reading the vast and compelling literature on the subject of the Kingdom of God, Bruce D. Chilton and J. I. H. McDonald state matters in a decisive way,

"The programmatic center of Jesus' ministry was...that of God's rule. The Synoptic Gospels make it evidence that his essential purpose was to promulgate the announcement that God's Kingdom had come near (see Matt. 4:17; Mark 1:15, Luke 4:43)."[3] So too they state:

> Jesus' stated purpose in the Gospels is to preach the Kingdom [of God] and hereby to win his hearers' repentance in the face of God's imminent action...In a number of cases, Jesus' parables — which largely concern the Kingdom — portray a situation of eschatological crisis, be it as harvest...as surprising transformation...as amazing discovery...or as final reckoning...[4]

The meaning of "Kingdom of God" in the Gospels is defined by Chilton and McDonald in the following language:

> ...if Jesus' initial proclamation is of the 'imminence' of the Kingdom, the performance of the message...effects the present crisis in time...the encounter with the Kingdom. The Kingdom that intersects time is 'at hand' in the sense that it may be entered (p. 61)...
>
> [Jesus] has brought the Kingdom within our reach and created space for us to move into God's realm and feel its power...(p. 62)

Chilton and McDonald also point out that the bulk of the parables that distinguish the traditions of Jesus' teaching focus on the kingdom of God:

> The parables articulate and image a reality that can be discerned, encountered, and responded to in the midst of life...The Kingdom can be compared to the mysterious process of growth that calls for decisive human action at the critical moment, but is otherwise independent of human activity (Mark 4:26-9), or to th astonishing product of the tiny mustard seed (Mark 4:30) or to the fate of a seed sown in a field (Mark 4:3-9), or to the leavening process (Matt. 13:33, Luke 3:20), or to the budding fig tree (Mark 13:28). It may also be compared to the consequence of the sabotaging of a wheat field, and how the 'householder' deals with the weed-infested crops (Matt. 3:24-30). It is like finding treasure in a field (Matt. 13:44) or a pearl of great value (Matt. 13:45)...Again, it is like searching for a lost sheep (Matt. 18:12, Luke 15:4-7) or a lost coin (Luke 1:8)...The motifs...may be found in the complex world of human relations... (p. 64)...The Kingdom...has already broken in upon the human scene — not least in the parabler and the parables he tells...

The relevance of the parable to our inquiry should not be missed, since Chilton and McDonald make it explicit: Jesus is at the center of the Kingdom: "If the Kingdom is discerned in the interaction of people and world, Jesus himself is a catalyst of such interaction..." (p. 70), and in so many words:

> [Jesus'] performance of the Kingdom cannot be interpreted primarily in Christological terms; rather, Christology has to be understood in the light of his performance of the Kingdom. His ministry is now seen to follow a teleological pattern which leads through suffering and death to the life of 'resurrection.' Hence any attempt to capture the Kingdom of God within worldly sovereignty or power...will meet with either critical or ambivalent response, for the transcendent factor qualifies the alleged realization: while not denying worldly obligations, one always renders to God what belongs to him — including the Kingdom ("only God is King") (p. 71).

Chilton and McDonald's judgment suffices to make the point I wish to register. That is, any systemic account of Jesus' teaching will identify the Kingdom of God as a critical component of that system, articulately interacting with other components (with ethics, for Chilton and McDonald). The Kingdom of God constitutes a category-formation imparting energy and cogency to the message, indeed, defining its point of coherence. In that context, the focus upon the parable as medium for the message contributes a strong indication of the systemic centrality of the category-formation — not just a generalized theme or conception but a particular realization of matters. However broad and varied the range of academic debate on the Gospels and the religious system set forth by their principal, nearly all scholarship concurs on the critical role of the category-formation, Kingdom of God.

That is what "Kingdom of God " looks like when it constitutes a category-formation in a system grounded in the Hebrew Scriptures of ancient Israel, as is the Rabbinic system expressed in the Aggadic corpus. Let us now address the counterpart concretizations of the theme of God's dominion and ask whether these coalesce into an articulated component of the categorical structure and system as a whole.

III. How is the Kingdom of Heaven Defined?

I have first to show that "Kingdom of God " and "Kingdom of Heaven" are synonymous, and that the usages of the Aggadic writings are accurately portrayed in treating the two formulations as equivalent in all material ways. The evidence is abundant. "Heaven" routinely refers to God, and Kingdom of Heaven means, "Kingdom of God," as in the following examples of tractate Abot:

Tractate Abot

1:3 Á.   Antigonos of Sokho received [the Torah] from Simeon the Righteous. He would say, (1) Do not be like servants who serve the master on condition of receiving a reward, (2) but [be] like servants who serve the master not on condition of receiving a reward. (3) And let the fear of Heaven be upon you."

1:11 A. Abtalion says, (1) "Sages, watch what you say, Lest you become liable to the punishment of exile, and go into exile to a place of bad water, and disciples who follow you drink [bad water) and die, and the name of heaven be thereby profaned."

2:2 A. Rabban Gamaliel, son of R. Judah the Patriarch, says, "And all who work with the community — let them work with them for the sake of Heaven."

2:12 A. R. Yosé says, "…may everything you do be for the sake of Heaven."

4:4 B. R. Yohanan b. Beroqah says, "Whoever secretly treats the Name of Heaven as profane publicly pays the price. All the same are the one who does so inadvertently and the one who does so deliberately, when it comes to treating the name of Heaven as profane."

4:11.D. R. Yohanan Hassandelar says, "Any gathering which is for the sake of Heaven is going to endure. And any which is not for the sake of Heaven is not going to endure."

4:12 A. R. Eleazar b. Shammua says, "The honor owing to your disciple should be as precious to you as yours.

B. "And the honor owing to your fellow should be like the reverence owing to your master.

C. "And the reverence owing to your master should be like the awe owing to Heaven."

5:17 A. Any dispute which is for the sake of Heaven will in the end yield results, and any which is not for the sake of Heaven will in the end not yield results.

B. What is a dispute for the sake of Heaven? This is the sort of dispute between Hillel and Shammai.

C. And what is one which is not for the sake of Heaven? h is the dispute of Korach and all his party.

These cases all prove that by "Heaven" the Rabbinic authors mean God, and there can be no doubt whatsoever that "Heaven" forms a euphemism for God, pure and simple. Further, in the Mishnah we find reference to the liturgical formula, "the Name of his Kingdom, meaning, the Kingdom of God :

MISHNAH-TRACTATE YOMA 3:8

A. He came over to his bullock.

B. Now his bullock was set between the Porch and the Altar.

C. Its head was to the south and its face to the west.

D. And the priest stands at the east, with his face to the west.

E. And he puts his two hands on it and states the confession.

F. And thus did he say, "O Lord, I have committed iniquity, transgressed, and sinned before you, I and my house. 0 Lord, forgive the iniquities, transgressions, and sins, which I have done by committing iniquity, transgression, and sin before you, I and my house.

G. "As it is written in the Torah of Moses, your servant, For on this day shall atonement be made for you to clean you. From all of your sins shall you be clean before the Lord (Lev. 16:30)."

H. And they respond to him, "Blessed is the name of the glory of his Kingdom forever and ever."

"His Kingdom " here, as in the wording of the Qaddish-prayer, is synonymous with "Kingdom of God " and its equivalent, "Kingdom of Heaven."

These passages serve to demonstrate that "his Kingdom," "Kingdom of Heaven," and "Kingdom of God" refer to the same thing, which is God's rule over creation and humanity. But at the heart of the matter is, does the Rabbinic system, Halakhic and Aggadic, so formulate that conception as to highlight it, use it in the identification and resolution of problems, build the structure of society and define personal virtue in its terms? Do the components of the Rabbinic system viewed whole focus upon the Kingdom of Heaven, realize it and situate it as the centerpiece of systemic construction, in the way in which the Evangelists do in the Synoptic Gospels? Does the concretization of the conception, divine dominion, through "Kingdom of Heaven" generatively function in the Aggadic system in the way in which the Rabbinic thinkers treat sin-repentance-atonement as critical to the message of their system, and in the way in which the same thinkers find in Israel/gentiles the source of dynamics of their system?

IV. THE KINGDOM OF HEAVEN IN HALAKHIC FORMULATION

While we address what is principally an Aggadic category-formation, the Kingdom of Heaven does encompass normative actions, not only attitudes. The specific reference to "Kingdom of Heaven" at Mishnah-tractate Berakhot 2:1-2, 2:5 is the sole Halakhic point at which the matter is defined and invoked. The specific act that is involved concerns the recitation of the Shema', and what one must do is accept the Kingdom of God in the act of saying the opening lines of that creed. That view of matters emerges in Joshua b. Qorha's statement at M. 2:2H-I:

MISHNAH-TRACTATE BERAKHOT 2:1-2

H. Said R. Joshua b. Qorha, "Why does Shema' precede 'And it shall come to pass' [in the order of this liturgy]?

I. "So that one should first accept upon himself the yoke of the

Kingdom of Heaven and afterwards accept the yoke of the commandments.

J.   "[Why does] 'And it shall come to pass' [precede]: 'And the Lord said'?

K.   "For 'And it shall come to pass' is customarily [recited] by both day and night.

L.   "And 'And the Lord said' is customarily [recited] only by day.

M. 2:2

The norm is, when one recites the Shema', he accepts the yoke of the Kingdom of Heaven, meaning, God's dominion, and then the yoke of the commandments, meaning, the religious obligations imposed by God in the Torah. The former is made explicit in the following:

MISHNAH-TRACTATE BERAKHOT 2:5

A.   A bridegroom is exempt from the recitation of the Shema' on the first night [after the wedding] until after the Sabbath [following the wedding],

B.   if he did not yet consummate the marriage.

C.   M'SH B: Rabban Gamaliel who was married and recited the Shema' on the first night of his marriage.

D.   [His students] said to him, "Did our master not teach us: 'A bridegroom is exempt from the recitation of the Shema' on the first night'?"

E.   He said to them, "I cannot accede to you so as to suspend myself from [accepting] the Kingdom of Heaven [even] for one hour."

The sole counterpart reference in Tosefta is at T. Berakhot 2:1:

TOSEFTA BERAKHOT 2:1

2:1 A.   One who recites the Shema' must mention the exodus from Egypt [cf. M. Ber. 1:5] in [the benediction following the Shema' which begins] "True and firm."

B.   Rabbi says, "In it [that benediction] one must mention [God's] Kingdom ."

This is the locus classicus for the Rabbinic conception of the Kingdom of God /Kingdom of Heaven, so far as the Halakhic texts are concerned. Accepting the yoke of the Kingdom of Heaven involves an expression of one's attitude, regarding oneself as God's servant and acting in his service, living in his domain. It is an act of individual Israelites but characterizes the community of Israel as well.

The Babylonian Talmud's exposition of the Mishnah-passage is as follows. Italics signify Aramaic, plain type, Hebrew. I indent passages that are secondary and intruded, yielding a clear account of the main line of thought and argument. I limit my comments to points pertinent to our problem. What we shall see is the context in which the conception of the Kingdom of Heaven figures in the Halakhic framework. I eliminate passages where it does not pertain.

BAVLI BERAKHOT 2:1-2 IV.2/14B-15A

IV.2 A.   *Rab washed his hands, recited the Shema', put on phylacteries, and then said the Prayer.*

    B.   *How could he have done it this way?*

    C.   *And has it not been stated on Tannaite authority:*

    D.   He who digs a burial niche for a corpse in a grave-area is exempt from the requirement to recite the Shema' and from having to say the Prayer and from having to put on phylacteries and from all of the religious duties that are listed in the Torah. Once the time for reciting the Shema' comes, he comes up [out of the hole], washes his hands, puts on his phylacteries, recites the Shema' and says the Prayer.

    E.   *Lo, there is a contradiction in the cited passage itself, which announces at the beginning that one is exempt and at the end that he is obligated [to carry out the rites].*

    F.   *That indeed is no contradiction, since the latter part deals with a case in which there are two ditch-diggers, and the former part a case in which there is only one.*

    G.   *In any event the cited passage presents a contradiction to the position of Rab [at A].*

    H.   *Rab accords with R. Joshua b. Qorhah, who has said,* "First comes accepting the yoke of the Kingdom of Heaven and afterward comes accepting the yoke of the commandments [on which account the phylacteries, which serve to carry out a commandment, come after reciting the Shema']."

    I.   *Now I can well understand that R. Joshua b. Qorhah had the idea of reciting one passage before reciting another passage. But does he mean to imply that one should place a recitation of a passage before the actual carrying out of one's religious duty [with reference to the phylacteries]?*

    J.   *And, furthermore, does he really accord with the view of R. Joshua b. Qorhah?*

    K.   *And has not R. Hiyya bar Ashi said, "Many times I stood before Rab, and he would first of all wash his hands and say a blessing, then he would repeat our chapter to us, then he would put on his phylacteries, then recite the Shema'."*

    L.   *Now if you say that he referred to the time before the hour for reciting the Shema' had come, if that were the case, what would be the purpose of the testimony of R. Hiyya bar Ashi?*

    M.   *It would serve to exclude the position of one who maintains that it is not necessary to say a blessing in connection with Mishnah-study.*

N.   *Thus [Hiyya] has informed us that also for Mishnah-study it is
      required to say a blessing.*

O.   *In any event it is a contradiction to the position of Rab [outlined
      at the outset].*

P.   *His messenger was the one who made the mistake [and brought
      his phylacteries too late that day. Normally he put them on first.]*

I see no development of the notion of the Kingdom of Heaven, only an
allusion to the premise that in reciting the Shema', one accepts the yoke of God's
rule. The order of actions follows from that established fact. The same fact recurs
in the following at IV.3.C:

IV.3 A.   Said Ulla, "Whoever recites the Shema' without putting on
           phylacteries is as if he gave false testimony against himself."

B.   Said R. Hiyya bar Abba said R. Yohanan, "It is as if he brought a
           burnt-offering without added a meal-offering, or a sacrifice without
           drink-offerings."

C.   And R. Yohanan said, "He who wants to accept upon himself the
           yoke of the Kingdom of Heaven in a full way **[15A]** should first
           empty his bowel, then wash his hands, put on his phylacteries,
           recite the Shema', and say the Prayer, and this constitutes accepting
           the Kingdom of Heaven in a full way."

Now accepting the King of Heaven involves not only reciting the Shema'
but a variety of actions and rites.

D.   And R. Hiyya bar Abba said R. Yohanan said, "Whoever empties
           his bowel, then washes his hands, puts on his phylacteries, recites
           the Shema' and says the Prayer is regarded by Scripture as if he
           had built an altar and offering an offering on it.

E.   "For it is written, 'I will wash my hands in cleanliness and I will
           walk around your altar, O Lord" (Ps. 26:6)."

F.   *Said Raba to him, "Does not the master maintain that it is as if he
           had immersed,*

G.   "for it is written, 'I shall wash in cleanliness,' and not, 'I shall
           wash my hands.'"

Other Bavli-references to "Kingdom of Heaven" are these. They do nothing
to change the picture of a rite involving a gesture in affirmation of God's rule — a
way of referring to God's dominion over Israel that concerns the affirmative action
of a private person:

BAVLI BERAKHOT 1:2 I.16/10B

I.16. L.   And R. Isaac said R. Yohanan said R. Yosé b. R. Hanina said in the
            name of R. Eliezer b. Jacob, "Whoever eats, drinks, and only then

says his prayers is regarded by Scripture as follows: 'And me have you cast beyond your back' (1 Kgs. 14:9).

M.   "Do not read the letters as though they say 'your back' but rather, 'your pride.'

N.   "Said the Holy One, blessed be he, 'After this one has taken pride in himself, only then has he accepted the Kingdom of Heaven !'"

Once more we find "Kingdom of Heaven" an established fact, a matter of attitude, what one undertakes to accept through the recitation of the cited creed. The same is indicated in the following entries:

Bavli Berakhot 3:3 I.1/20a-b

A.   Women, and slaves, and minors are exempt from the recitation of the Shema' [20B] and from [the obligation of wearing] phylacteries,

B.   but are obligated [to recite] the Prayer,

C.   and [are obligated to post] the mezuzah and to recite Grace after meals.

I.1   A.   *As to [the exemption from reciting the Shema'] that is self-evident, since it is a religious duty of commission that has to be done at a particular time, and from the obligations to carry out religious duties of commission that have to be done at a particular time women are exempt.*

B.   *What might you have said? Since in the recitation of the Shema' is the act of accepting the Kingdom of Heaven, [they might be obligated to recite the Shema'] even though they are exempt from other religious duties in that classification].*

C.   *So we are informed that that is not the case.*

All we have is the reiteration of the established fact that when one recites the Shema', she accepts the Kingdom of Heaven. The same fact defines part of the background of the following narrative:

Bavli Berakhot 9:1-9 XVIII.2/61b

XVIII.2   A.   *Our rabbis have taught on Tannaite authority:*

B.   The wicked government once made a decree that the Israelites should not take up the study of Torah. Pappos b. Judah came and found R. Aqiba gathering crowds in public and taking up the study of Torah.

C.   He said to him, "Aqiba, aren't you afraid of the government?"

D.   He said to him, "I shall show you a parable. What is the matter like? It is like the case of a fox who was going along the river and saw fish running in swarms place to place."

E.   He said to them, "Why are you running away?"

F.   They said to him, 'Because of the nets people cast over us.'

G.   "He said to him, 'Why don't you come up on dry land, and you and I can live in peace as my ancestors lived in peace with yours?'

H.   "They said to him, 'Are you the one they call the cleverest of all wild beasts? You are not clever, you're a fool. Now if in the place in which we can live, we are afraid, in a place in which we perish, how much the more so [should we fear]!'

I.   "Now we too, if when we are in session and taking up the study of Torah, in which it is written, 'For it is your life and the length of your days' (Deut. 30:20), things are as they are, if we should go and abandon it, how much the more so [shall we be in trouble]!"

J.   They say that only a few days passed before they arrested and imprisoned R. Aqiba. They arrested and imprisoned Pappos b. Judah nearby. He said to him, "Pappos, who brought you here?"

K.   He said to him, "Happy are you, Aqiba, because you were arrested on account of teachings of Torah. Woe is Pappos, who was arrested on account of nonsense."

L.   The hour at which they brought R. Aqiba out to be put to death was the time for reciting the Shema'. They were combing his flesh with iron combs while he was accepting upon himself [in the recitation of the Shema'] the yoke of the Kingdom of Heaven.

M.   His disciples said to him, "Our master, to such an extent?"

N.   He said to them, "For my whole life I have been troubled about this verse, 'With all your soul' [meaning] even though he takes your soul. I wondered when I shall have the privilege of carrying out this commandment. Now that it has come to hand, should I not carry it out?"

O.   He held on to the word, "One," until his soul expired [as he said the word] "one." An echo came forth and said, "Happy are you, Rabbi Aqiba, that your soul expired with the word 'one.'"

P.   The serving angels said before the Holy One, blessed be he, "Is this Torah and that the reward? 'From them that die by your hand, O Lord' (Ps. 17:14) [ought to have been his lot]."

Q.   He said to them, "'Their portion is in life' (Ps. 17:14)."

R.   An echo went forth and proclaimed, "Happy are you, R. Aqiba, for you are selected for the life of the world to come."

Bavli-tractate Hagigah 1:2 VI.30/5B

30. A.   "But if you won't obey it, my soul shall weep in secret for the pride" (Jer. 13:17):

    B.   Said R. Samuel bar Inayya in the name of Rab, "The Holy One, blessed be he, has a place which is called 'Secret.'"

31. A.   *And what is the meaning of* for the pride?

    B.   Said R. Samuel bar Isaac, "Because of the pride of Israel that has been taken from them and handed over to the nations of the world."

    C.   R. Samuel bar Nahmani said, "Because of the pride of the Kingdom of Heaven."

The Bavli's repertoire of references to the Kingdom of God point to the conviction that God rules on earth, and that Israel responds to God's rule by accepting the yoke of his dominion, which they do by carrying out various religious obligations of omission and commission. That, sum and substance, defines the category. In the Halakhic context, accepting the yoke of God's Kingdom is associated with putting on phylacteries and reciting the Shema' — normative actions.

The Kingdom of Heaven, however, is no abstraction to be realized in individual consciousness alone. It is made concrete within the Halakhic system. God's court forms part of the system of enforcing the law of the Torah, and this is made explicit. No grasp of the category-formation, Kingdom of Heaven, is complete without a clear recognition of the concreteness of the conviction that God rules. Within the theory of sages, sages' courts govern concrete cases on earth, but only within a larger system in which the Heavenly court exercises jurisdiction over cases of another order. Certain concrete sins or crimes (the system knows no distinction between them) are referred to Heaven for judgment.

So Israel forms the this-worldly extension of God's heavenly Kingdom, and that is the fact even now. Not only so, but it is a fact that bears material and tangible consequences in the governance of the social order. That is why the heavenly court is assigned tasks alongside the earthly one. The sages' court punishes murder when the rules of testimony, which are strict and rigid, permit; when not, there is always Heaven to step in. Or when a man clearly has served as efficient and sufficient cause of death, the earthly court punishes him.

But what are the sorts of concrete actions left over for Heaven to punish — and to penalize as concretely as the earthly court does? These include, for example, the following:

TOSEFTA TRACTATE BABA QAMMA 6:16:

A.   He who frightens his fellow to death is exempt from punishment by the laws of man,

B.   and his case is handed to Heaven.

C.   [If] he shouted into his ear and deafened him, he is exempt.

D.   [If] he seized him and shouted into his ear and deafened him, he is liable.

E.   He who frightens the ox of his fellow to death is exempt from punishment by the laws of man,

F.   and his case is handed over to Heaven.

6:17 A.   [If] one force-fed [the ox of his fellow] with asafoetida, creeper-berries, a poisonous ointment, or chicken shit, he is exempt from punishment under the laws of man,

B.   and his case is handed over to Heaven.

C.   He who performs an extraneous act of labor while preparing purification-water or a cow for purification belonging to his fellow [thus spoiling what has been done] is exempt from punishment by the laws of man,

D.   and his case is handed over to Heaven.

E.   A court-official who administered a blow by the decision of a court and did injury is exempt from punishment by the laws of man,

F.   and his case is handed over to Heaven.

G.   He who chops up the foetus in the belly of a woman by the decision of a court and did damage is exempt from punishment by the laws of man,

H.   and his case is handed over to Heaven.

I.   A seasoned physician who administered a remedy by a decision of a court and did damage is exempt from punishment by the laws of man,

J.   and his case is handed over to Heaven.

The Heavenly court alone is asked for a final assessment of the motives behind an action, of the causation embodied in the action when the case is ambiguous, and other imponderables. What the sages' courts cannot discern, the Heavenly court will perceive. What is important in these rules emerges from the concrete character of the cases handed over to Heaven for adjudication. The Kingdom of Heaven embraces the here and now, and sages took for granted that God and God's agencies would carry out their responsibilities within the larger system of governance of holy Israel that sages contemplated.

But despite that fact, in the Halakhic system the Kingdom of God does not define a category-formation and does not surface in any established one. It forms part of the background of the Halakhic category-formations that do generate new questions and new answers and do sort out new data, that narrative that I set forth in organizing and rationalizing the Halakhic data into a system. The category is Halakhically inert, everywhere the premise, no where part of the proposition.

v. The Kingdom of Heaven in Aggadic Exposition

"The Kingdom of Heaven" in Aggadic settings provides one way, and not a dominant one, of saying that Israel is ruled by God. Here and now Israel forms the realm of God in this world, where God takes up presence, in synagogues and in school houses, where prayers are recited and the Torah studied, respectively. God's Kingdom, unlike the kingdoms of this world and age, is not locative, and it is also not tangible. It is a Kingdom that one enters by right attitude, through accepting the government and laws of that king and undertaking to obey his rules, the commandments. I find a fine definition for the Rabbinic Aggadic disposition of the matter of the Kingdom of God in Chilton and McDonald's language:

> [The Kingdom of God] is realized...not in the dream world
> of apocalyptic nor in temple cult, legalistic casuistry, ascetic discipline
> nor power politics, but in personal and community life that is responsive
> to the call of God (p. 79).

The martyrdom of Aqiba, in the midst of his recitation of the Shema' and acceptance of God's Kingdom, forms an appropriate illustration of the realization of God's dominion in personal and community life response to God's commandments. How is the matter articulated in Aggadic settings? The answer to that question affords the required data for situating the concept at hand within the larger Rabbinic system and determining its activity in that system: generative or inert. What we shall see is that the conception of God's dominion comes to expression in a variety of category-formations, not only the Kingdom of Heaven. The Rabbinic sages found a variety of categories for the expression of the notion that God governs Israel and the world, and some of these, such as the religious duties or commandments and associated formulas, markedly exceed in density and richness the Kingdom of Heaven.

First to express the general notion of God's dominion that is concretized and realized in the mythic logoumenon, Kingdom of Heaven: To be Israel in sages' model means to live in God's Kingdom, wherever one is located and whenever, in the sequence of the ages, one enjoys this-worldly existence. God's Kingdom forms the realm of eternity within time. Embodying God's Kingdom by obeying God's will, Israel was created to carry out religious duties and perform good deeds. These are what differentiate Israel from the gentiles-idolators.

What this means, concretely, is that God rules now, and those who acknowledge and accept his rule, performing his commandments and living by his will, live under God's dominion. To single out Israel, God sanctified the people by endowing them with numerous commandments. Carrying out these commandments, then, brings Israel into the Kingdom of Heaven, as they acknowledge the dominion of God. That merging of politics and theology emerges in the language of the formula for reciting a blessing before carrying out a commandment or religious duty, "Blessed are you, Lord our God, king of the world, who has sanctified us by his commandments and commanded us to...." That is the formula that transforms an ordinary deed into an act of sanctification, a gesture of belonging to God's Kingdom. But in that context the concretization of the matter in the language, "Kingdom of Heaven" does not figure. That signals the inert status of the language at hand.

The recitation of a blessing also entails recognition of God's kingship, with the phrase, "...king of the world, who has commanded us...," and that clause is deemed essential to any blessing:

YERUSHALMI TRACTATE BERAKHOT 9:1 I:3

A. R. Zeira and R. Judah in the name of Rab, "Any blessing which does not include [a reference to] God's Kingdom, is not a valid blessing."

B. Said R. Tanhuma, "I will tell you what is the basis [in Scripture for this rule]: 'I will extol thee my God and King' [Ps.145:1]."

God is addressed in the political metaphor because God's Kingdom is at hand not at one moment but at all times;[5] the "us" then embodies all Israel even in a single individual, and the critical language then follows: "who has given commandments," one of which is going to be carried out. That is how Israel is subject to the dominion of God and if properly motivated now lives in the Kingdom of Heaven. The Kingdom of Heaven is a phenomenon of this age as well as the world to come, and it involves tangible actions of everyday life, not only abstract existence. The doctrines in detail hold together in the conviction that God rules here and now, for those who, with a correct act of will and with proper conduct, accept his rule.

This is accomplished in various ways. First of all, as the Halakhic corpus has already shown us, it takes place through the declaration of the unity of God in the *Shema'*. In so doing, the Israelite accepts God's authority, then the commandments that are entailed by that authority:. The Halakhah suffices to state the matter, and there is no Aggadic iteration: A person should first accept upon himself the yoke of the Kingdom of Heaven i.e. recite the *Shema'* and then accept upon himself the yoke of the commandments e.g. the obligation to wear Tefillin or phylacteries (Mishnah-tractate Berakhot 2:2/I) The holy people has accepted God's kingship at Sinai and has not got the right to serve any other, so we recall the statement:

Tosefta tractate Baba Qamma 7:5

A. On what account is the ear among all the limbs designated to be pierced? Because it heard from Mount Sinai, "For unto me are the children of Israel slaves, they are my slaves" (Lev. 25:55).
B. Yet the ear broke off itself the yoke of Heaven and took upon itself the rule of the yoke of mortal man.
C. Therefore Scripture says, "Let the ear come and be pierced, for it has not observed the commandment which it heard."

In the following protracted exposition, we see how the conception of Israel's forming God's Kingdom plays itself out in the setting of Israel's current situation. Here we notice, therefore, the way in which the critical problematic — the anomaly of Israel's subordination to the idolatrous nations — governs discourse throughout:

Sifré to Numbers CXV:V.4

A. ["I am the Lord your God who brought you out of the land of Egypt to be your God"]:
B. Why make mention of the Exodus from Egypt in the setting of discourse on each and every one of the religious duties?

A parable makes the matter transparent:

C. The matter may be compared to the case of a king whose ally was taken captive. When the king paid the ransom [and so redeemed him], he did not redeem him as a free man but as a slave, so that if the king made a decree and the other did not accept it, he might say to him, "You are my slave."

D. When he came into a city, he said to him, "Tie my shoe-latch, carry my clothing before me and bring them to the bath house." [Doing these services marks a man as the slave of the one for whom he does them.]

E. The son began to complain. The king produced the bond and said to him, "You are my slave."

F. So when the Holy One, blessed be he, redeemed the seed of Abraham, his ally, he redeemed them not as sons but as slaves. When he makes a decree and they do not accept it, he may say to them, "You are my slaves."

G. When the people had gone forth to the wilderness, he began to make decrees for them involving part of the lesser religious duties as well as part of the more stringent religious duties, for example, the Sabbath, the prohibition against consanguineous marriages, the fringes, and the requirement to don *Tefillin*. The Israelites began to complain. He said to them, "You are my slaves. It was on that stipulation that I redeemed you, on the condition that I may make a decree and you must carry it out."

Israel accepts God's rule as a slave accepts his redeemer's authority; that is, Israel owes God allegiance and obedience. By carrying out God's will through the commandments, Israel enters God's dominion. But the concretization of the matter in the language "Kingdom of Heaven" does not contribute.

As the passage unfolds, the operative category-formation is Israel/nations, not "Kingdom of Heaven." Now the urgent question presents itself: since Israel is governed by the nations of the world, does that not mean that God has given up his dominion over them? Then Israel no longer is subject to God's authority and need not keep the commandments.

Sifré to Numbers CXV:V.5

A. "[So you shall remember and do [all my commandments and be holy to your God. I am the Lord your God who brought you out of the land of Egypt to be your God.] I am the Lord your God" (Num. 15:37-41):

B. Why repeat the phrase, "I am the Lord your God"?

C. Is it not already stated, "I am the Lord your God who brought you out of the land of Egypt to be your God"?

D. Why then repeat the phrase, "I am the Lord your God"?

E. It is so that the Israelites should not say, "Why has the Omnipresent given us commandments? Let us not do them and not collect a reward."

F. They do not do them, and they shall not collect a reward.

Now the precedent provided by Scripture shows the governing rule:

G.   This is in line with what the Israelites said to Ezekiel: "Some of the elders of Israel came to consult the Lord [and were sitting with me. Then this word came to me from the Lord: 'Man, say to the elders of Israel, This is the word of the Lord God: Do you come to consult me? As I live, I will not be consulted by you. This is the very word of the Lord God]'" (Ez. 20:1-3).

H.   They said to Ezekiel, "In the case of a slave whose master has sold him off, has not the slave left the master's dominion?"

I.   He said to them, "Yes."

J.   They said to him, "Since the Omnipresent has sold us to the nations of the world, we have left his dominion."

K.   He said to them, "Lo, in the case of a slave whose master has sold him only on the stipulation that later on the slave will return, has the slave left the dominion of the master? [Surely not.]"

L.   "When you say to yourselves, 'Let us become like the nations and tribes of other lands and worship wood and stone,' you are thinking of something that can never be. As I live, says the Lord God, I will reign over you with a strong hand, with arm outstretched and wrath poured out'" (Ez. 20:32-33).

M.   "...with a strong hand:" this refers to pestilence, as it is said, "Lo the hand of the Lord is upon your cattle in the field" (Ex. 9:3).

N.   "...with arm outstretched:" this refers to the sword, as it is said, "And his sword is unsheathed in his hand, stretched forth against Jerusalem" (1 Chr. 21:16).

O.   "...and wrath poured out:" this refers to famine.

P.   "After I have brought against you these three forms of punishment, one after the other, then 'I will reign over you'— despite yourselves.

Q.   That is why it is said a second time, "I am the Lord your God."

God will not relinquish his rule over Israel, and he enforces his dominion despite Israel's conduct. The moral order then plays itself out within the inexorable logic of God's will.

But for all their interest in matters of jurisprudence and politics, to which we referred a moment ago, for sages, the Kingdom of Heaven above all was realized in the ordinary world in which Israel performed the commandments. "Kingdom of Heaven" in the Halakhah does not introduce the notion of the Qaddish, "May your Kingdom come speedily and in our days...," that is, the temporal-ordinal view. Rather it stresses that the Kingdom of Heaven is a mark of the human condition, not a historical age. That concept plays slight role here; when the Rabbinic Aggadic documents wish to speak of the world or age to come, they invoked a different category-formation from Kingdom of Heaven, as in the category-formation, Resurrection, and the correlative but distinct category-formation, the World to Come. In that context, "Kingdom of Heaven" simply does not figure.

So "Kingdom of Heaven" is atemporal. When an Israelite carried out a positive commandment, or, more important, in obedience to Heaven refrained from a deed prohibited by a negative commandment, that formed the moment of realization of God's rule on earth. Then Israel through Israelites may bring about God's rule on earth. The commandments, originally emerging in small groups, mark the appearance of God's Kingdom on earth. But alone among nations Israel finally got all of them, 248 positive ones, matching the bones of the body, 365 negative ones, matching the days of the solar year. So Israel alone within humanity has the possibility, and the power, to bring about God's rule, which is fully realized in the restoration that marks the last things in the model of first things. Here the gradual delivery of the commandments is spelled out, the story of the sequential exposure of the concretizations of the Kingdom of Heaven in the life of humanity:

Pesiqta deRab Kahana XII:I.1ff.:

1. A. R. Judah bar Simon commenced discourse by citing the following verse: "Many daughters show how capable they are, but you excel them all. [Charm is a delusion and beauty fleeting; it is the God-fearing woman who is honored. Extol her for the fruit of her toil and let her labors bring her honor in the city gate]' (Prov. 31:29-31):

We start with the six commandments assigned to Adam, as the facts of Scripture indicate:

   B. "The first man was assigned six religious duties, and they are: not worshipping idols, not blaspheming, setting up courts of justice, not murdering, not practicing fornication, not stealing.
   C. "And all of them derive from a single verse of Scripture: 'And the Lord God commanded the man, saying, 'You may freely eat of every tree of the garden, [but of the tree of the knowledge of good and evil you shall not eat, for in the day that you eat of it you shall die]' (Gen. 2:16).
   D. "'And the Lord God commanded the man, saying': this refers to idolatry, as it is said, 'For Ephraim was happy to walk after the command' (Hos. 5:11).
   E. "'The Lord:' this refers to blasphemy, as it is said, 'Whoever curses the name of the Lord will surely die' (Lev. 24:16).
   F. "God: this refers to setting up courts of justice, as it is said, 'God [in context, the judges] you shall not curse' (Ex. 22:27).
   G. "the man: this refers to murder, as it is said, 'He who sheds the blood of man by man his blood shall be shed' (Gen. 9:6).
   H. "saying: this refers to fornication, as it is said, 'Saying, will a man divorce his wife' (Jer. 3:1).
   I. "'You may freely eat of every tree of the garden: ' this refers to the prohibition of stealing, as you say, 'but of the tree of the knowledge of good and evil you shall not eat.'

Noah inherited those six commandments and was given another:

J.   "Noah was commanded, in addition, not to cut a limb from a living
      beast, as it is said, 'But as to meat with its soul – its blood you
      shall not eat ' (Gen. 9:4).

Abraham got the seven and an eighth (though, elsewhere, it is alleged that
Abraham in any event observed all of the commandments):

K.   "Abraham was commanded, in addition, concerning circumcision,
      as it is said, 'And as to you, my covenant you shall keep '(Gen.
      17:9).
L.   "Isaac was circumcised on the eighth day, as it is said, 'And
      Abraham circumcised Isaac, his son, on the eighth day' (Gen. 21:4).

Jacob got a ninth, his son Judah a tenth:

M.   "Jacob was commanded not to eat the sciatic nerve, as it is said,
      'On that account the children of Israel will not eat the sciatic nerve'
      (Gen. 32:33).
N.   "Judah was commanded concerning marrying the childless
      brother's widow, as it is said, 'And Judah said to Onen, Go to the
      wife of your childless brother and exercise the duties of a levir
      with her' (Gen. 38:8).

But Israel got them all, matching the bones of the body to the days of the
year, the whole of life through all time:

O.   "But as to you, at Sinai you received six hundred thirteen religious
      duties, two hundred forty-eight religious duties of commission [acts
      to be done], three hundred sixty-five religious duties of omission
      [acts not to be done],
P.   "the former matching the two hundred forty-eight limbs that a
      human being has.
Q.   "Each limb says to a person, 'By your leave, with me do this
      religious duty.'
R.   "Three hundred sixty-five religious duties of omission [acts not to
      be done] matching the days of the solar calendar.
S.   "Each day says to a person, 'By your leave, on me do not carry out
      that transgression.'"

That Israel got them all and so entered God's Kingdom is what requires
explanation, and the explanation has to do with the union of the days of the solar
year with the bones of man: at all time, with all one's being, one obeys God's
commandments. The mode of explanation here does not require the introduction of

proof-texts, appealing rather to the state of nature — solar calendar, the bone-structure of man — to account for the facts. The Kingdom of Heaven, then, encompasses every day of the year and the components of the human body. The amplification at R-S cannot be improved upon.

But the concrete realization of God's Kingdom required constant encounter with the Torah, and that is not only because the Torah formed the source of the commandments that Israel was to carry out in obedience to its Heavenly Father and King. It also was because, within the words of the God's own "I," his self-manifestation, was eternally recorded and therefore always to be encountered. Torah-study constituted the occasion for meeting God, because the words of the Torah convey whatever man knows with certainty about God. If Israel meets God in the Torah, God therefore is present when the Torah is opened and studied; then God is present within Israel:

BAVLI TRACTATE MEGILLAH 4:4 I.14

A. Expounded Raba: What [is meant by what] is written, "Lord, you have been a dwelling place for us" (Ps. 90:1)?
B. These are the synagogues and academies.
C. Said Abbayye, "Initially I used to study at home and pray in the synagogue. After I heard what David said [namely], 'Lord, I loved the place of your house' (Ps. 26:8), I studied in the synagogue."

There the Holy Spirit comes to rest. What is striking here is that God's domain is defined without the Kingdom of Heaven being invoked. "The Kingdom of Heaven" comes to the surface in connection with an act of attitude — accepting the yoke of the Kingdom — and consequence actions of obedience, carrying out the commandments. But as that is at any time, so it is at any place, and "Kingdom of God" does not serve to identify school houses or synagogues.

That is not the only context in which, were Kingdom of Heaven a generative category-formation, the concept should be expected to play an important role. Another issue, ubiquitous in the Aggadic theology, concerns Israel's suffering and estrangement from God. Israel suffers for disobedience to the Torah, a critical component of the category-formation, Israel/gentiles. God's inaccessibility to Israel forms part of that category-formation, and it is explained by reference to Israel's sin, that is, by invoking yet another principal category-formation, sin-repentance-atonement. When the Aggadah turns to the image of God's hiding his face, we find no interest in the imagery or language of Kingdom of Heaven. No one says, for example, that God hides his face when Israel(ites) fail to accept the Kingdom of Heaven.

The way the matter is expressed encompasses the active category-formations, therefore, and omits the inert one. Thus although Israel is subject to God's rule, God is not always accessible to Israel, because of Israel's own doings. But that is only for a moment. Within the restorationist theology at hand, God may hide his face and make himself inaccessible to Israel by reason of evil, but in the end God will restore his presence to Israel:

> J.   R. Jacob bar Abbayye in the name of R. Aha brings proof of the same proposition from the following verse of Scripture: "I will wait for the Lord, who is hiding his face from the house of Jacob, and I will hope in him" (Is. 8:17).
>
> K.   There was never a more difficult hour for the world than that hour at which the Holy One, blessed be he, said to Moses, "And I will surely hide my face in that day [on account of all the evil which they have done, because they have turned to other gods]" (Deut. 31:18).

Now follows the entire theology of restoration: Israel's repentance, God's consoling forgiveness mark the return to perfection as at the beginning:

> L.   At that hour: "I will wait for the Lord," for thus did he say to him at Sinai, "[And when many evils and troubles have come upon them, this song shall comfort them as a witness,] for it will live unforgotten in the months of their descendants; [for I know the purposes which they are already forming, before I have brought them into the land that I swore to give]" (Deut. 31:21).
>
> M.   And to what end?
>
> N.   "Behold, I and the children whom the Lord has given me [are the signs and the portents in Israel from the Lord of hosts, who dwells on Mount Sinai]" (Is. 8:18).
>
> O.   Now were they really his children? And were they not his disciples?
>
> P.   But it teaches that they were as precious to him as his children, so he called them, "My children."

The articulation of the relationship of God to Israel as master to slaves makes no mark here. Now the relationship is father to children, pure and simple. So the natural metaphors in this context attest to the absence of the master-metaphor, Kingdom of Heaven.

Accordingly, Israel meets God not principally in obedience o the commandments that embody the yoke of the Kingdom but rather in Torah study, and the more one studies, the more one gains; there is ample occasion to learn by hearing the Torah:

Bavli-tractate Sukkah 4:7 IV.4/46A:

> M.   And R. Zira said, and some say it was R. Hanina bar Papa, "Come and see that the trait of the Holy One, blessed be he, is not like the trait of mortal man.
>
> N.   "In the case of mortal man, an empty vessel holds something, but a full vessel does not.

O.   "But the trait of the Holy One, blessed be he, [is not like that.] A full utensil will hold [something], but an empty one will not hold something.

P.   "For it is said, 'And it shall come to pass, if you will listen diligently' (Deut. 28:1). [One has to learn much and if he does, he will retain his knowledge.]

Q.   "The sense is, If you will listen, you will go on listening, and if not, you will not go on listening.

R.   "Another matter: If you hear concerning what is already in hand, you will also hear what is new.

S.   "'But if your heart turns away' (Deut. 30:17), you will not hear anything again."

So much for Israel's study of the Torah. It is the propaedeutic of prophecy, which leads to the encounter with the Holy Spirit.

The failure to invoke the category, Kingdom of God, proves still more blatant when we consider a statement of the system viewed whole: what are the consequences of Israel's humbly accepting the divine rule? What Israel must do is to accept God's will, carry out God's commandments, above all, humbly take up its position in the Kingdom of God. Israel's task is to accept its fate as destiny decreed by God, to be humble and accepting, and ultimately to triumph in God's time. Israel is similar to the dust of the earth, which is why Israel, like the dirt, will endure forever. That summary-formulation of matters manages to come to fulfillment without invoking the category-formation, Kingdom of Heaven, which is, when present, inert, and when absent, unremarkable, as we see in the following counterpart to a creedal construction:

Genesis Rabbah XLI:IX.1

A.   "I will make your descendants as the dust of the earth" (Gen. 13:16):

B.   Just as the dust of the earth is from one end of the world to the other, so your children will be from one end of the world to the other.

C.   Just as the dust of the earth is blessed only with water, so your children will be blessed only through the merit attained by study of the Torah, which is compared to water [hence: through water].

D.   Just as the dust of the earth wears out metal utensils and yet endures forever, so Israel endures while the nations of the world come to an end.

E.   Just as the dust of the world is treated as something on which to trample, so your children are treated as something to be trampled upon by the government.

F.   That is in line with this verse: "And I will put it into the hand of them that afflict you" (Is. 51:23), that is to say, those who make your wounds flow..

G. Nonetheless, it is for your good that they do so, for they cleanse you of guilt, in line with this verse: "You make her soft with showers" (Ps. 65:11).

H. "That have said to your soul, 'Bow down, that we may go over'" (Is. 51:23):

I. What did they do to them? They made them lie down in the streets and drew ploughs over them."

J. R. Azariah in the name of R. Aha: "That is a good sign. Just as the street wears out those who pass over it and endures forever, so your children will wear out all the nations of the world and will live forever."

The generative category-formation in this powerful creedal statement is, once more, Israel/nations. Israel will show acceptance and humility and so overcome the nations not by power nor by its own might but by means of winning God's help through Torah-study, obedience, and patience. These responses to God's rule do not require the category-formation, Kingdom of God, to register their point.

VI. GENERATIVE VERSUS INERT CATEGORY-FORMATIONS: THE CASE AT HAND

How does the category-formation, Kingdom of Heaven, qualify as inert and not generative? To answer that question we take up the criteria cited at the Introduction.

A. DOES THE CATEGORY KINGDOM OF HEAVEN DESCRIBE MOST OF THE DATA, HALAKHIC AND AGGADIC, THAT RELATE TO GOD'S DOMINION

The survey of Halakhic data yields a sparse result, one important item: reciting the Shema' marks acceptance of God's Kingdom; one striking, but tangential item, God's court in Heaven judges cases that the sages' court on earth cannot adjudicate. The Aggadic data prove diffuse. God's rule is everywhere acknowledged, but the category-formation, Kingdom of God does not form the principal medium for presentation of the conception of God's dominion, which does not suffice to cover all modes of expressing that one conception. "Kingdom" serves to refer to God's governance, but God's governance comes into play even when Kingdom is not invoked. The rather diffuse survey of Aggadic data just now completed hardly suggests that the category, Kingdom of Heaven, encompasses most of the Aggadic expressions of the conception that God rules. Where, as in the final instance, the creedal construction, we should have anticipated its presence, e.g., rule by nations versus Kingdom of Heaven, it is blatant for its absence.

B. **Does the Category Kingdom of Heaven Yield a Theory of the Future, possessing Predictive Quality**

The Kingdom of God is present-tense, and those that accept it live in the workaday world of the here and the now. Those who enter the Kingdom of God by reciting the Shema' carry out God's will, as we see in the story of Aqiba's martyrdom. But how that category permits projecting into the future one's aspirations or hopes is not self-evident to me. Perhaps it suffices to note that those that live in God's Kingdom inherit the world to come and eternal life. But that anticipation plays no part in the exposition of the category. In eschatological matters, we shall look in vain for utilization, in predicting the future, of the category, God's Kingdom. "The world to come" or the Garden of Eden and "God's Kingdom" rarely intersect in eschatological contexts, and a necessary connection between them is not expressed in the Aggadic materials reviewed here or there. Here the contrast with the Gospels' focus on Kingdom of God makes its mark. For the Kingdom of God yields a theory of the future and does possess predictive quality.

C. **Does the Category Kingdom of Heaven Yield Norms of Public Policy**

Sin-repentance-atonement encompass a public policy that favors humility over arrogance. Israel/nations likewise explains to Israel how it should act in history, as the creedal construction shows. Does Kingdom of Heaven contain within itself a definition of virtue spilling over into public life as does the category-formation already examined? The answer is obviously affirmative, for it is the same definition that flows from the category as it encompasses public policy of corporate Israel. But there is a difference. In the generative and active category-formation, sin-repentance-atonement, the definition of the public norms responds to the particularities of the details at hand: sin is the result of arrogance, repentance comes about through humility, and atonement embodies an act of contrition.

But what particular traits of God's kingdom comparably come to expression in the public policy defining virtue consequent upon the specific character of God's Kingdom as a category? The only narrative that has passed before us invokes the image of the slave, Israel, carrying the master's towel and clothing to the bath house — not a mark of humility of will and spirit but of acceptance of the status of slavery. So if sin-repentance-atonement produce a guide to public policy — social virtue, for example — that matches the main lines of the category-formation and embodies what is implicit in the myth embodied therein, then by that criterion we cannot affirm the same outcome here.

VII. What Indicates the Inert, as against the Generative, Category-formation?

What this exercise has demonstrated is now clear. The generative category-formations function within a complete and effective system of the social order of the Israel contemplated by the Aggadic writings viewed whole. They process data of diverse kinds within a single paradigm, and one category-formation requires others, fore and aft, to accomplish its part of the systemic task. By contrast, here what we see is how a theme in a particular realization of that theme forms part of the background, not acting upon, or in concert with, other ideas but expressive of the outcome of that action. That God, creator of the world and revealer of the Torah, exercises dominion in the world enjoys the standing of self-evidence.

But in the Aggadic system the realization of that conception in the image and language "Kingdom of Heaven" proves routine and commonplace. It provokes no deep thought on, e.g., how God exercises dominion, or on why at some points God declines to intervene, while at others, he does. These and similar indicators of systemic generativity do not make an appearance in the Aggadic record. But when we deal with active and generative Aggadic category-formations, we do find deep thought on, e.g., how God rules through the gentiles and how Israel commands its own fate, through an act of humility and self-abnegation.

What makes the system work is its power to identify new questions and generate new responses, all the time within the established paradigm. A category-formation of a generative order imparts dynamism to the system, always repeating itself in fresh ways and in response to new cases. An inert one merely repeats the same cases and says nothing new. The difference has come to full exposition in the contrast between the generativity of the Kingdom of God in the Synoptic Gospels and the inert status of the Kingdom of Heaven in the Halakhic context and its striking absence where it can have done good service in the Aggadic setting.

The upshot is an account of how the system expresses a conception integral to its logic — God rules the world is surely the absolute premise of all religious thought in Scripture and in every writing of every heir of Scripture — that furthermore is incidental to the generativity of that logic in systemic context. When we come to the category-formation, Israel/gentiles, we see how God exercises dominion, the particular media that serve his purpose, and the systemic consequences of his eternal governance of the humanity made in his image. To that context, we now realize, the Kingdom of Heaven belongs in perspective but never participates in proposition. But in the counterpart, Gospels' system, the Kingdom of Heaven everywhere dominates, as Chilton and MacDonald make clear, at the very heart of matters.

The main point is simple. Comparison among category-formations and compositions set forth by heirs to a common Scripture provides the key. What is inert in the Rabbinic system is generative in its Gospels' counterpart. The Christian heirs of Israelite Scripture subordinate much else to the Kingdom of God, to which (even) the generative Rabbinic category-formations, sin-repentance-atonement and Israel/nations submit. The Rabbinic heirs find at the heart of matters sin/repentance/ atonement, to which (even) Israel/gentiles and Kingdom of Heaven accommodate themselves. When we know what category-formation adapts itself to what other, we know the difference in systemic category-formations between the inert and the generative, subordinate and primary.

ENDNOTES

[1] For an elaboration of the analytic issues raised here, see my *Comparing Theological Category-Formations in Rabbinic Judaism. Generative versus Inert, Primary versus Subordinate*. Leiden, 2004: E. J. Brill. I compare Generative Versus Inert Category-Formations: Generative Category-Formations: The Synergy of Sin, Repentance, and Atonement and An Inert Category-Formation: The Kingdom of Heaven. Then I compare Primary versus Subordinate Category-Formation: Primary Category-Formations: Israel/ Gentiles and The Messiah-Theme: Its Diverse Roles in the Eschatological Narrative of the Resurrection of the Individual Israelite and the Advent of the world to Come for Corporate Israel.

[2] For an account of the diverse representations and utilizations of parabolic writing see my *Rabbinic Narrative. A Documentary Perspective*. Volume Four. *The Precedent and the Parable in Diachronic View*. Leiden, 2003: E. J. Brill. The Brill Reference Library of Judaism.

[3] Bruce D. Chilton and J.I.H. McDonald, *Jesus and the Ethics of the Kingdom* (Grand Rapids, 19887: Eerdmans), p. 3.

[4] *Ibid.*, p. 5.

[5] That signals the incompatibility of the category-formation, "Kingdom of God/Heaven," as defined and instantiated and utilized in the Synoptic Gospels and in the Rabbinic Aggadic writings respectively. The parables of Jesus all treat "Kingdom of God" in temporal terms — that which is about to break into time, for which people are to make themselves ready (through repentance) — comparable to the judgment to which Mishnah-tractate Sanhedrin 10:1 refers, meaning in that context, the world or age to come or the restoration to Eden. But in the Rabbinic setting "kingdom of Heaven" is present in the here and now, not a matter of temporal order but of existential condition. The parables of Jesus and their counterparts in the Rabbinic writings are not only incompatible, they are mutually unintelligible, even where in detail they intersect.

6

The Mishnah's Conception of the Priesthood:
The Aggadah versus the Halakhah

The Rabbinic literature divides into two parts, each with its own task, logic, and rhetoric: lore (Aggadah) and law (Halakhah), the one dealing with the exegesis of Scripture and the amplification of its narratives and prophecy, the other with the normative law and its detailed rules. Each sets forth its own message about a topic common to them both, a division we see most clearly in connection with the Temple priesthood, its integrity and reliability.

One and the same document, the Mishnah, a philosophical law code that reached closure in ca. 200 C.E., presents contradictory accounts of the priesthood of the Jerusalem Temple. Legal passages rest on one set of premises, narrative passages on another, contradictory set. The rhetoric of the law bears no relationship to that of the lore, the one concise and declarative, the other fully spelled out and discursive. The logic of coherent discourse of the legal passages is syllogistic and propositional, that of the narrative passages is teleological. And the messages conflict.

When the Mishnah portrays the priesthood in normative law (Halakhah), it affirms the priest's unique power to mediate between God and Israel. Not only so, but the picture that the law draws of the priest in the premises of the law portrays him as punctilious and principled. The premise of the entire Halakhic structure of sacrifice confirms that the priest functions with correct intentions and makes provision for occasional error. It does not control for the deliberate and systematic violation of the law, whether in action or intention, by the priesthood. The intentionality of the priesthood always matches the sacred task, barring a rare error.

That the normative law deems the priesthood to be virtuous and a suitable instrument of divine service presents a surprise, because the counterpart narratives (Aggadah) take the contrary view that the priesthood acts in a self-interested and arbitrary manner, is comprised by ignoramuses, and when it does its job properly, simply serves as the puppet of the sage. The Aggadic narratives of the Mishnah (and its complement, the Tosefta) portray the priest-automaton, the priest-ignoramus, the priest unworthy of his charge. From these stories we should not have formed a picture of the priest upon whose correct intentionality Israel's and the Israelite's relationship with God depends. To what is at stake in the Halakhah, which is reconciling God and the erring Israelite through an act of will on the part of the ever-faithful priest, the stories about the capricious and unreliable priest are monumentally irrelevant.

The disjuncture between the Halakhic premises concerning the priesthood and the Aggadic narratives about the same is complete and beyond reconciliation. In the premise of the Halakhah, holy Israel has placed its entire fate into the hands of the priesthood, a premise that is beyond imagining were the priesthood corrupt and not to be trusted. Since I derive from a family of the priesthood, a family tradition through the male line that extends backward for many generations and has now been confirmed by DNA studies of the priesthood in the state of Israel for a sizable sample of the contemporary priesthood, I am not an unbiased observer. Each sector of the Rabbinic canon carries out its assignment, the one — the Halakhic — facing inward and portraying the interiority of Israelite existence with God, the other — the Aggadic — turned outward and portraying the external politics of the Israelite social order.

1. The Aggadic Indictment of the Priesthood of Temple Times

A brief survey of the Aggadic portrait of the Temple priesthood commences beyond the limits of the Mishnah and the Tosefta, to that *summa* of the Rabbinic canon, The Fathers according to Rabbi Nathan, which as is often the case states the Rabbinic position in a concrete and succinct way. In the present instance the document states in a few words the Aggadic judgment of the priesthood:

The Fathers According to Rabbi Nathan IV: VI. 2

A. Scripture says, "Open your doors, O Lebanon, that the fire may devour your cedars" (Zech. 11:1).

B. That verse refers to the high priests who were in the sanctuary [on the day it was burned].

C. They took their keys in their hands and threw them upward, saying before the Holy One, blessed be he, "Lord of the world, here are your keys which you entrusted to us, for we have not been faithful custodians to carry out the work of the king and to receive support from the table of the king."

"We have not been faithful custodians" — how more incisively can the Rabbinic sages have laid down the judgment upon the priesthood as slothful and slovenly!

In the Aggadic account set forth by the Mishnah amplified by the Tosefta, Rabbinic Judaism both acknowledges the sacerdotal hegemony of the priesthood and imposes the sages' priority and authority upon the priesthood. No wonder then that the sages represent the priest as worthy only of carrying out their orders, as at Mishnah-tractate Negaim. Here, when the person afflicted with the skin-ailment has brought his condition to the priest as Scripture requires, the sage evaluates the case and tells the priest what to say:

MISHNAH-TRACTATE NEGAIM 3:1
B.   All are suitable to examine the plagues.
C.   But the [actual declaration of] uncleanness and cleanness is in the hands of a priest. They say to him, "Say, 'Unclean,'" and he says, "Unclean." Say, "'Clean,'" and he says, "Clean."[1]

Scripture provides that the marks of the skin-ailment be brought for the priest's evaluation, and the sages honor the letter of the law, but that alone. "All are suitable" for the examination *who know the law,* as is stressed at Tosefta's counterpart, but the priest reserves the right to declare the decision reached by others: he is a puppet.

The Aggadic formulations of the Mishnah articulate the judgment that the priest is subordinate to the disciple of the sage because the disciple of the sage knows the Torah and the priest does not. This claim of the priority of the sage over others is formulated in two contexts, each of them striking for its radical claim, the one involving the high priest, the other the father, both of them subordinate to the sage:

MISHNAH-TRACTATE HORAYOT 3:8
A.   A priest takes precedence over a Levite, a Levite over an Israelite, an Israelite over a *mamzer, a mamzer* over *a Netin, a Netin* over a proselyte, a proselyte over a freed slave.
B.   Under what circumstances?
C.   When all of them are equivalent [in mastery of the Torah].
D.   But if the *mamzer* was a disciple of a sage and a high priest was an *am haares,* the *mamzer* who is a disciple of a sage takes precedence over a high priest who is an *am haares.*

This same conception is given still more extreme form in the following, which explains the reward of Torah-learning: life of the world to come.

MISHNAH-TRACTATE BABA MESIA 2:11
A.   [If he has to choose between seeking] what he has lost and what his father has lost,
B.   his own takes precedence.
C.   . hat he has lost and what his master has lost,
D.   his own takes precedence.
F.   ...what his father has lost and what his master has lost, that of his master takes precedence.

G.   For his father brought him into this world.

H.   But his master, who taught him wisdom, will bring him into the life of the world to come.

I.   But if his father is a sage, that of his father takes precedence.

J.   [If] his father and his master were carrying heavy burdens, he removes that of his master, and afterward removes that of his father.

K.   [If] his father and his master were taken captive,

L.   he ransoms his master, and afterward he ransoms his father.

M.   But if his father is a sage, he ransoms his father, and afterward he ransoms his master.

The Mishnah leaves no doubt as to what is at stake, which is, entry into eternal life, which learning in the Torah makes possible. In these ways the Rabbinic sages lay claim to their hegemony over the priestly caste.

In the conduct of the Temple rites, the Mishnah and Tosefta claim, the Rabbinic sages governed when and where they could. Thus we have an explicit claim that when the priesthood ventured out of the Temple to perform a rite, the sage exercised authority. One such case among many in which the Aggadah portrays the sages as running things concerns the conduct of the rite, outside of the temple, of burning the red cow for the making of ashes to be utilized in the purification-water to remove corpse-uncleanness.

TOSEFTA-TRACTATE PARAH 3: 7-8

3: 7 D.   And they made the priest who burns the cow unclean,

E.   because of the Sadducees, so that they should not say that it is done by someone upon whom the sun has set for the completion of his purification.

3: 8 A.   WM'SH B: A certain Sadducee had awaited sunset [for purification] and [then] came to burn the cow.

B.   And Rabban Yohanan ben Zakkai became cognizant of his intention, and he came and placed his two hands on him and said to him, "My lord, High Priest. How fitting are you to be high priest! Now go down and immerse one time."

C.   He went down and immersed and emerged. After he came up, he [Yohanan] tore (on) his ear [rendering him unfit to serve]

D.   He said to him, "Ben Zakkai — when I have time for you."

E.   He said to him, "When you have time."

F.   Not three days passed before they put him in his grave.

G.   His father came to Rabban Yohanan ben Zakkai and said to him, "Ben Zakkai, my son did not have time."

The priests maintained that the highest level of purification pertained even outside of the Temple precincts, and the sages held that the rite was performed by a priest in a lower level of purification, one who had immersed but awaited sunset to complete the purification-rite. That view took into account that the rite of burning the cow took place outside of the Temple court, on the mount of Olives. For our inquiry the point is, the sage controlled the operation.

And why not, when the priests cared more for matters of purification than issues of morality, as the Mishnah and the Tosefta make explicit in a truly disturbing narrative;

Mishnah-tractate Yoma 2:1

2:1 A. At first whoever wants to take up the ashes from the altar does so.

B. And when they are many [who wanted to do so], they run up the ramp.

C. And whoever gets there before his fellow, within four cubits of the altar, has acquired the right to do so.

D. And if the two came at the same time, the one in charge says to them, "Choose up [by raising a finger."

2:2 A. M'SH S: There were two who got there at the same time, running up the ramp.

B . And one shoved his fellow.

C. And he [the other] fell and broke his foot.

D. When the court saw that the matter was dangerous, they ordained that the right of clearing off the ashes from the altar should be apportioned only by lot.

This story is radically redirected in the Tosefta's amplification and turned into an indictment of the priesthood and its management of the Temple:

Tosefta Kippurim 1:12

A. M'SH B: There were two who got there at the same time, running up the ramp. One shoved the other [M. Yoma 2:2A-B], within four cubits [of the altar]. The other then took out a knife and stabbed him in the heart.

B. R. Sadoq came and stood on the steps of the porch and said,

C. "Hear me, O brethren of the house of Israel! Lo, Scripture says, 'If in the land which the Lord your Cod gives you to possess, any one is found slain, lying in the open country, and it is not known who killed him, then your elders and your judges shall come forth, and they shall measure the distance to the cities which are around him that is slain' (Deut. 21:1-2).

D. "Come so let us measure to find out for what area it is appropriate to bring the calf, for the sanctuary, or for the courts!"

E. All of them moaned after his speech.

F. And afterward the father of the youngster came to them, saying, "O brethren of ours! May I be your atonement. His [my] son is still writhing, so the knife has not yet been made unclean."

G. This teaches you that the uncleanness of a knife is more grievous to Israelites than murder. And so it says, "Moreover Manasseh shed very much innocent blood, till he had filled Jerusalem from one end to the other" (11 Kings 21:16).

H.   On this basis they have said, "Because of the sin of murder the Presence
of God was raised up, and the sanctuary was made unclean."

So much for the explicit, Aggadic judgment of the Temple priesthood.
The Tosefta's concluding statement — God left an unclean sanctuary by reason of
the corruption of values, with greater concern for cultic uncleanness affecting a
knife than for murder — captures the Aggadic bias.

The polemic of the Aggadah stresses three points. First, the priest is not a
sage and must be instructed in the Torah. The priest enjoys caste preference, but
that priority is set aside in favor of the status conferred by Torah-learning. The sage
dictates the conduct of the cult outside of the Temple, in decisions concerning the
skin-ailment, in the conduct of the rite of burning the red cow on the Mount of
Olives. Second, the priests exaggerate matters of cultic cleanness and ignore those
of morality. That then yields the third point, the disproportion that destroyed the
Temple: "Because of the sin...." These polemical points leave ample space for
what the Halakhic treatment of the topic will stress: the priests' punctiliousness
about their task, their reliability. Their fault lay in an excess of punctiliousness,
insufficiency of Torah-learning. But that other premise of the Halakhah, that what
made a sage a sage is mastery of Torah, leading to eternal life, forms the foundation
of the entire Halakhic system, not just the law of the priesthood alone.

2. THE HALAKHIC EMPOWERMENT OF THE PRIESTHOOD

The Mishnah and its supplement in the Tosefta do not register their
judgments only or mainly in narrative. They form coherent statements of a theological
system set forth in normative statements of conduct, not conviction, behavior, not
belief, action, not attitude. So when we ask about the premises of the law vis a vis
the priesthood, we find our way into the interior precincts of the system: its rulings
on concrete matters.

The Halakhah set forth in the Mishnah recapitulates facts of Scripture and
raises its own issues as well. Where the Halakhah contributes more than the
systematization and hierarchization of received facts of Scripture, it commonly
pursues problems of the interplay between the Israelite's, the priest's, and God's
will and plan for the blood-rite in any particular circumstance. The particular issues
inherent in the blood-rite that engage the Halakhah of the Mishnah involve those
considerations of the relationship of intention and action that everywhere embodies
Israel's encounter with God. And those issues yield a picture of the attitudes imputed
by the Mishnah to the priesthood, the intentions with which they carry on their
sacerdotal rites.

Specifically, God pays the closest possible attention to the attitude and
purpose of the Israelite and also the priestly participant in any cultic transaction,
the one donates, the other delivers, the offering. What each party has in mind in the

exchange must coincide with the thought of the other. The action bears consequence by reason of the attitude that animates it. And here, the Israelite and the priest must concur on the meaning of what is done; then the message intended by the action may register. Much of the efficacy of the rites depends upon the harmonies of intentionality that animate the participants in the offering. And then God concurs.

3. INTENTIONALITY IN THE SACRIFICIAL SYSTEM

The link between Israel and God is effected by the attitude or intentionality of the Israelite and of the priest, each in his position in the transaction. God responds to the Israelite's and the priest's feelings and plans, and the offering is acceptable to him only so far as these are correct in a particular, specific way. At what points, in connection with what specific actions, does the intentionality of the donor and the priest register? The Halakhah makes its statement solely through its cases, and here, by what it says, it also eliminates many possibilities.

The offering is offered for six purposes, and the priest acting in behalf of the donor must have in mind the proper attitude concerning all six. The attitude of the officiating priest governs, and if the priest expresses no improper attitude, that suffices to validate the offering on these points. For the sake of six things is the animal offering sacrificed: (1) for the sake of the animal offering, (2) for the sake of the one who sacrifices it, (3) for the sake of the Lord, (4) for the sake of the altar fires, (5) for the sake of the odor, (6) for the sake of the pleasing smell. And as to the sin offering and the guilt offering, for the sake of the sin expiated thereby. That is to say, the officiating priest has to have in mind the particular offering at hand, offering a burnt-offering as a burnt-offering and not as peace-offerings. The one who sacrifices it is the donor of the animal, who benefits, e.g., from the expiation. The intent must be for God, not for an idol (!). The intent must be to roast the meat on the fire of the altar, not at any other location. One must intend an odor to ascend from the roast. And in the case of the sin- or guilt-offering, the particular sin that is expiated must be in mind. As to the particular actions at which these six aspects of intentionality must conform, they involve these deeds: cutting the pertinent organs, collecting the blood in a bowl, conveying the blood to the altar, and tossing the blood on the altar.

The priest is required for preparation of an offering; a non-priest cannot carry out the critical procedures of the blood-rite. An invalid priest likewise spoils the rite by his participation, e.g., one who was unclean, improperly dressed, and the like. But if the status of the priest weighs heavily on the rite, the attitude of the priest carries still greater consequence. Specifically, as just now noted, four processes integral to the rite, killing the beast, collecting the blood, conveying the blood to the altar, and tossing the blood on the altar, must be carried out by the officiating priest in accord with the intentionality of the *sacrifier* — a technical term referring to the person who benefits from the offering, as distinct from the *sacrificer*, the priest who carries out the offering. There must be an accord between the will of the sacrifier in designating the beast and the will of the sacrificer in carrying out the rite. Should the priest declare that he carries out the action for some purpose other than the designated one, e.g., conveying the blood of a lamb for the purpose of peace-offerings when it is the fourteenth of Nisan and the beast has been designated for a Passover, the rite is spoiled.

Why does the attitude of the officiating priest bear so heavily on the matter? To find the answer, we take the classic case of how intentionality invalidates a deed. What we see is that what one intends before the fact governs the status of the act itself, and even though one performs the act correctly and ultimately acts in accord with the law, the initial intentionality still dictates the outcome. I can think of no more powerful way of stating that what one intends in advance, and not what one does in fact, dictates the outcome of a transaction. Before us then is an extreme position, one that imposes its own perspective upon all else: the intentionality that motivates an action, not what is really done, governs. The way this is said is not complicated. It involves a rule about the priest's consuming the meat of the offering that he presents and how, at the moment of slaughter (encompassing the other phases of the blood rite) he intends to eat that meat: when and where.

Specifically, the meat of the offerings that the priests receive must be eaten by them within a specific span of time, two nights and the intervening day. If the priest when slaughtering the beast (or wringing the neck of a bird) says that he will eat the meat later on, that very act of intentionality suffices to render the act of slaughter one of abomination, and the status of the offering is determined — without any action whatsoever on the priest's part. Now we see what it means to evaluate what happens solely by reference to what one intends to make happen: not what one actually does after the fact, but what one is thinking in advance of it. The rule is framed in terms of not what the priest does but what he is thinking of doing later on: He who slaughters the animal offering intending to toss its blood outside of the Temple court, to burn its sacrificial portions outside, , to eat its meat outside, or to eat an olive's bulk of the skin of the fat tail outside — it is invalid. He who slaughters the animal offering, intending to toss its blood on the next day, to burn its sacrificial portions on the next day, to eat its meat on the next day, or an olive's bulk of the skin of the fat tail on the next day — it is refuse. And that is without regard to the actual deed of the priest. If he after the fact of the declared intention, he did the deed at the correct time or place, it changes nothing. With such remarkable power over the status of the beast that the mere intention to eat the meat outside of its proper time or to dispose of it outside of the proper place suffices to ruin the offering, the priest's intentionality in connection with immediate, concrete actions in other aspects of the offering will make a massive difference as well.

What about the transaction of the priest in behalf of the sacrifier? Here too, the action is evaluated by the intention, so that even if all the rites are correctly carried out, if the priest does not do them with the right attitude, the sacrifier loses out. This is expressed in the formulation that follows. If a beast, designated as sanctified by its own for a particular classification of offering, is actually slaughtered for a purpose other than that for which it was originally designated, what is the result? If the officiating priest does not carry out the intention of the Israelite who purchased and sanctified the beast, the offering remains valid; the blood is collected, conveyed to the altar, and tossed there. So far as the beast is concerned, the act of sanctification is irrevocable. So far as the householder is concerned, his obligation has not yet been carried out; he must present another animal to accomplish his purpose, e.g., to present a sin-offering or carry out a vow. There are two exceptions to this rule. If on the afternoon of the fourteenth of Nisan an Israelite's animal, designated to serve as a Passover offering, is offered for some other purpose, e.g., as peace-offerings, it is null. So too an animal designated as a sin-offering must be presented for that purpose and for no other. In both cases, the specificity of the occasion — the Passover, the sin — takes over; the animal that has been mis-classified by the priest is lost.

Here the initial designation is indelible and the animal that has been destined for the specified purpose may then serve no other. If an animal sanctified as a Passover- or sin-offering is slaughtered for some other purpose, it too is unfit. This principle of specificity is broadened by the generalization that follows: If one slaughtered them for the sake of that which is higher than they, they are valid. If one slaughtered them for the sake of that which is lower than they But if under the name of a lower grade, they are invalid. How so? Most Holy Things which one slaughtered for the sake of Lesser Holy Things are invalid. Lesser Holy Things which one slaughtered for the sake of Most Holy Things are valid. The firstling and tithe which one slaughtered for the sake of peace offerings are valid, and peace offerings which one slaughtered for the sake of a firstling, or for the sake of tithe, are invalid.

4. INTENTIONALITY IN INVALIDATING THE RITE: WHEN IT MATTERS, WHEN IT DOES NOT MATTER

Intentionality bears, also, upon the effectiveness of the rite. But there are limits, and these show us the boundaries of the rite, indicating what, in the entire procedure, bears consequence. What matters is the blood-rite, that alone. Much else can go wrong and not matter. So long as the blood is properly tossed, the rest of the sacrifice may be burned or eaten, as the case requires. If this is done properly and the sacrifice is not spoiled by some other invalidating element before the tossing of the blood, then the liability to extirpation applies. The intentionality that prevails at that point dictates the classification of the act.

This is expressed in the following language: How is what renders the offering permissible offered in accord with its requirement? If one slaughtered in silence lacking improper intent, but received the blood and conveyed the blood and sprinkled the blood intending to eat or burn the flesh outside of its proper time, or if one slaughtered intending to eat or burn the flesh outside of the proper time, received the blood and conveyed the blood and sprinkled the blood in silence lacking improper intent, or if he slaughtered, received the blood, and conveyed the blood and sprinkled the blood intending to eat or burn the flesh outside of its proper time — this is a case in which what renders the offering permissible is offered in accord with its requirement. In the foregoing case, then, the blood rite has not been invalidated. How is what renders the offering permissible not offered in accord with its requirement? If one slaughtered intending to eat or burn the flesh outside of its place, received the blood and conveyed the blood and tossed the blood intending to eat or burn the flesh outside of its time, or if one slaughtered intending to eat or burn the flesh outside its proper time, received the blood and conveyed the blood and tossed the blood intending to eat or burn the flesh outside of its place, or if one slaughtered, received the blood and conveyed the blood and tossed the blood intending to eat or burn the flesh outside of its place — this is a case in which what renders the offering permissible is not offered in accord with its requirement.

Intentionality invalidates only if what is subject to improper intention concerns eating the meat or burning the sacrificial parts outside its proper place or outside its proper time, and, in respect to the Passover and the sin offering, improper intention invalidates when this involves slaughtering them not for their own name not for the purpose for which the beast was originally designated as a Holy Thing.

The details present their own surprises, once more underscoring the narrow definition of the range at which intentionality registers. If he slaughtered it on condition that he intended (1) to sprinkle it on the ramp, not at the foundation of the altar, (2) to sprinkle those which are to be sprinkled below, above, (3) or those which are to be sprinkled above, below, (4) those which are to be sprinkled inside, outside (5) or those which are to be sprinkled outside, inside — (1) that unclean people eat it, (2) that unclean people offer it up, (3) that uncircumcised priests eat it, (4) that uncircumcised priests offer it up, (1) to break the bones of the Passover, (Ex. 12: 9), (2) or to eat of it while it is raw, (3) to mix its blood with the blood of unfit beasts — it is valid. Furthermore, the intentionality that invalidates must concern the routine and ordinary. If one forms an improper intentionality that departs from the norm, that idiosyncratic plan has no consequences. He who slaughters the animal sacrifice intending to eat something which is not usually eaten, to burn something which is not usually burned — the offering nonetheless is valid. He who slaughters female consecrated animals intending to eat the foetus or the afterbirth outside the proper place or time has not rendered the sacrifice refuse for these are not usually eaten.

5. The Halakhah's Governing Premise concerning the Character of the Temple Priesthood

The Halakhah imputes to the priesthood considerable power in determining the relationship between the Israelite and God. The Israelite's intention for an offering must define that of the officiating priest, who can ruin the rite by improper intentionality, as we have seen. But we look in vain for evidence of distrust of the priesthood. No provision is made for the priest's having to compensate the sacrifier for ruining the offering through improper intentionality. All the priest had to do was state, "Lo, I offer this animal for such-and-such a purpose," or "Lo, I act with the intention of eating the meat beyond the specified span of time in which it may be eaten or tossing the blood at the wrong time," and the investment was lost. But the Halakhah does not provide for such a possibility. The trust of the priests' good will, not only their technical facility at butchering the beast and tossing its blood, is implicit everywhere. The upshot is, the attitude or intention, which is intangible and not necessarily accessible to the sacrifier, takes priority in the validation of the rite over the actualities of deed.

6. THE INTEGRITY OF THE PRIESTHOOD MATCHING THE INTEGRITY OF ISRAEL

Why the stress on intentionality, and what outcome for Israel's relationship with God do we discern? The simple fact is, the Israelite has the power to change the status of a beast from secular to sacred, and this he does by an act of will. He designates a beast as sacred, specifying the purpose of the act of sanctification. So the entire process of presenting personal offerings (as distinct from the public ones) depends upon the act of will effected by the individual Israelite. And since the rites are carried out at the critical turnings by the priest, the attitude that governs his activities likewise must register. Neither the Israelite nor the priest is portrayed as an automaton, nor do the actions of the two parties emerge as coerced or automatic. What the Israelite does realizes his will, which is why the deed makes a difference, and, the Halakhah takes for granted, the priest too engages through an act of will. Both are deemed to have, and to make, choices, and these choices respond to the intentionality that motivates the entire transaction, start to finish. So the Halakhah portrays the cult as the stage on which Israel — priest and Israelite alike — work out in concrete actions the results of their interior reflections.

Since, as with the daily whole-offerings of all Israel all together, the entire rite is time and again represented as an exercise in expiation of sin, even though a variety of offerings serves another purpose altogether (e.g. celebration, service, and the like), we do well to recall the principal (but not sole) occasion for individual participation:

MISHNAH-TRACTATE KERITOT 1:2

For those [thirty-six classes of transgressions] are people liable, for deliberately doing them, to the punishment of extirpation, and for accidentally doing them, to the bringing of a sin offering, and for not being certain of whether or not one has done them, to a suspensive guilt offering [Lev. 5:17] — [except for] the one who blasphemes, as it is said, "You shall have one law for him that does anything unwittingly" (Num. 15:29) — excluding the blasphemer, who does no concrete deed.

The cult expiates sin only when the sin is inadvertent; deliberate sin is expiated through the sacrifice of years of life ("extirpation"). Then the entire transaction at the altar, so far as the expiation of sin forms the center, concerns those actions that one did not intend to carry out but nonetheless has done. The intentionality governing the deed therefore proves decisive, and we may not find surprising the focus upon attitude accompanying the action of sacrifice.

Just as the offering expiates an inadvertent sin, so the attitude that motivates the sacrifier (and, correspondingly, the priest too) will define matters: it is for this particular sin, that I did not mean to do, that I have deliberately designated as holy that particular beast. An unintentional, sinful act then provokes an intentional act of expiation. Then what God follows with close anticipation is how this act of will is realized — confirmed in actuality; that occasion of acute advertence is what concludes the transaction begun inadvertently. And that means in the concrete arrangements of the cult, how the actions of the priest conform in the priest's intentionality to the original act of sanctification brought about by the Israelite's intentionality. The entire relationship between Israel and God works itself out as a match of the intentions of the several parties, each of them qualified to form an independent act of will, all of them conforming to bring about the successful result, the expiation of sin or the fulfillment of commitment.

Accordingly, in the offerings of the altar, the Israelite relates to God by an act of will in designating as sacred for a specific purpose defined as acceptable by God for purposes of propitiation an animal and related materials. The priest then mediates this act of will by realizing, in actions resulting in the tossing of the animal's blood on the altar, the intentionality of the Israelite. And God relates to the Israelite, in that same transaction, by paying closest possible attention to the interplay of the Israelite's initial intentionality in the act of sanctification and the concrete outcome, in the priest's realization of that same intentionality, in the act of offering.

We should not miss the negative, for it yields a positive result: the implicit judgment of the integrity of the priesthood. It is not enough that the Israelite designate the animal; God must know that the priest has prepared it in accord with the definition of the sanctification that has taken hold of that animal by reason of the Israelite's act of sanctification: the priest must carry out the action within the same framework of purpose established by the Israelite for the beast. So it does not suffice for the priest to impose his judgment upon the disposition of the beast; the initial act of sanctification has imposed limits upon his purpose. The Israelite requires priestly conformity to his, the Israelite's, act of will in designating the beast. The priest effects the correct offering only when he subordinates his will to that of the Israelite. The Israelite attains atonement and reconciliation with God only when, after an unintended violation of the Torah, he demonstrates that, in giving something back (whether a costly beast, whether a bird of no account), he subordinates his will to that of God. We find matched acts of willful and deliberate subordination — the priest's to the Israelite's, the Israelite's to God's.

The sequence of acts in conformity with the will of another having been worked out, God then accepts the actions that come about by reason of right thought and responds by accepting the blood-offering as an act of propitiation and atonement, on the one side, or of fulfillment of obligation, on the other. What is required in a valid act of fulfillment of the Israelite's act of consecration is uniform conformity of deed to will. When it comes to characterizing Israel's relationship with God, what counts, then, is that God follows this sequence of steps, this process leading the beast from the secular herd to the sacred altar, its blood turned into the reagent to wash away the inadvertent sin of the sacrifier. Everyone must concur in sequence, the sacrifier, the sacrificer, and God in confirmation to the correct intention of both. It is as though God wished to set up a system carefully to monitor the will of successive participants in the process, each exposing for God's inspection the contents of his hearts.

7. THE PRECISE SYMMETRY OF THE PRIEST'S AND THE ISRAELITE'S INTENTIONALITY IN THE SACRIFICIAL RITES

The premise of the Halakhah is fully exposed here: God closely attends to the match of deliberation and deed, and only when the Israelite's intent and the priest's intent coincide does God confirm his gracious acceptance of the result, propitiation resulting. So while the presentation of offerings superficially places the human side of the transaction at the center — it is the Israelite's, then the priest's parts that effect the relationship — in fact, it is God's engagement with the same transaction, his close and careful surveillance of the match of intent and action, word and deed, that makes all the difference. In the cult Israel relates to God intimately and concretely. Once the Israelite undertakes by an act of will to engage in a deed of sanctification, God's participation in the process, step by step, his close attention to the interior of the activities consequence upon the undertaking — these responses embody God's intense interest in the Israelite's attitude, to which God responds.

That is why "intentionality" takes on very concrete and specific meanings in the setting of the offering to God of the gifts of the Land, meat, wine, oil, grain and the like. When an Israelite expresses his intentionality to sanctify a particular animal for a specified offering that consecrates the beast for God's service at the altar. But the intentionality of the Israelite then requires a corresponding attitude on the part of, with a confirming action by, the officiating priest. If he does the deeds of the sacrifice for some purpose other than the announced one of the Israelite, he denies the Israelite the benefit of confirmation of his intentionality by a cultic action. What is the result of the priest's mis-conceiving of matters? Where the beast can serve for some appropriate cultic purpose, it does so. That is to say, the original action of the Israelite in sanctifying the beast is not nullified by the contradictory intentionality of the priest. But where the beast is designated for a very particular purpose and can then serve no other, the sacrificial act is lost. Such a system defies the imagination, if the priesthood is not to be trusted.

8. BEFORE 70?

What conclusions are we to draw for the actualities of the priesthood before the destruction of the Temple in 70 C.E.? Debates in the name of authorities of 70-130, after the destruction, concerning details of the matters treated here — Eliezer and Joshua and Aqiba are primary players — suggest that before 70, the Halakhic conceptions that form the foundations of the Mishnah's construction were laid down. Not only so, but the probability that the attributions to Eliezer, Joshua, Aqiba and their generation of secondary refinements of that primary, established law are plausible can be tested. Do the authorities of the generation following, from 130 to 170, after the Bar Kokhba War and repression following, raise fundamental questions or take for granted the principles attributed to the prior generation and respond to subordinate and secondary issues? A systematic comparison of the match between the generation to which an issue is attributed and the standing of that issue in the logical unfolding of the system produces a one-sided result. What is assigned to a prior generation concerns a primary issue, and what is assigned to the later generation addresses secondary and derivative issues.[2] So the fundamental principles of the Halakhah of Zebahim come are established before 70 and subject to secondary development and refinement afterward.

Whether the pre-70 authorities of the Halakhah portray the priesthood as it was or only as the logic of their theology dictated they should imagine it to be, we cannot say on the basis of what is before us. As I said at the outset, I am a *Kohen,* and I like to conceive that my ancestors proved worthy of their sacred calling. But I also am a rabbi, and I aspire to be worthy of that still higher vocation.

References Cited

Neusner, Jacob
1979   *A History of Mishnaic Law of Holy Things*. Pt. 1: *Zebahim: translation and explanation*. Leiden: Brill. (Studies in Judaism in Late Antiquity, 30)
1980   *A History of Mishnaic Law of Holy Things*. Pt. 6: *The Mishnaic System of sacrifice and Sanctuary.* Leiden: Brill. (Studies in Judaism in Late Antiquity, 30)

ENDNOTES

[1] The Tosefta assumes that the priest masters the law and speaks of his reaching a decision, not only announcing one:

TOSEFTA NEGAIM 1:2

A.   R. Eliezer b. Jacob said in the name of R. Hananiah b. Kina'i, who said in the name of R. Aqiba, "How do you know that a priest who is an expert in plagues and not in itches, in itches and not in bald spots, in man and not in clothing, in B. "Scripture states, 'This is the Torah for every plague of leprosy: for the itch, and for leprosy of the garment and in the house, and for the swelling and for the eruption, and for the spot and to teach [when it is unclean and when it is clean. This is the law for leprosy]' [Lev. 14:5]."

[2] This is worked out in detail in Neusner 1979; Neusner 1980.

7

Does Classical Judaism Yield a Doctrine of Tolerance?

There are no theological foundations for tolerance in classical Judaism, only eschatological intimations that at the end of days all humanity will know the one true God — but that is not the same thing as a theological basis for tolerating of error or those that commit error. In the here and now there are no doctrines that accord recognition to religions other than Judaism. And Classical Judaism contains no doubt as to the outcome of history in the end-time: God will see to it that all of humanity accords recognition to him as the one true God, and on that basis, now as part of the Israel that knows God, the ex-gentiles will inherit the world to come.

Let me begin with one detail and then turn to the comprehensive issues that require attention. The entire issue of toleration is captured by a dispute that concerns eschatological tolerance of gentiles, defined as idolaters as against Israelites, defined as those who know God: Does the gentile at the end of days rise from the grave, stand in judgment, and gain a portion in the world to come, as do nearly all Israelites? The matter is subject to debate:

A. R. Eleazar says, "None of the gentiles has a portion in the world to come, as it is said, ''The wicked shall return to Sheol, all the gentiles who forget God' (Ps. 9:17). The wicked shall return to Sheol' — these are the wicked Israelites. 'And all the gentiles who forget God' — these are the nations."

B. Said to him R. Joshua, "If it had been written, 'The wicked shall return to Sheol — all the gentiles,' and then nothing further, I should have maintained as you do. Now that it is in fact written, 'All the gentiles who forget God,' it indicates that there are righteous people among the nations of the world who do have a portion in the world to come."

Tosefta Sanhedrin 13:2

What makes a gentile righteous is that he does not forget God. But remembering God entails acknowledging him and that makes the gentile into an Israelite. That is in line with the prophetic vision, recapitulated in the *Alenu* prayer, that in the end of days the whole of humanity will know God as Israel does now. All Israel has a portion in the world to come (M. San. 11:1) yields, "All who have a portion in the world to come are Israel." So eschatological tolerance raises a prospect that, on second glance, does not yield toleration at all: gentiles enjoy eternal life, but only as Israelites — and that is Joshua's view. Eliezer, for his part, does not dissimulate. But even if we treat Joshua's opinion as normative, we have no category, idolatry, or a religion devoted to a god other than the God who made himself known to Abraham,, to which toleration is accorded. The category-formation, tolerable religion other than that of the Lord, does not present itself in the classic Rabbinic law and theology.

That is because the systemic category-formation that defines the social order that Judaism constitutes, called "Israel," precipitates the formation of its opposite, "non-Israel," outsider, and the "non-Israel" is defined as God's enemy: the idolater. The entire system aims at demonstrating God's justice and mercy, and in that context, the outsider is justly excluded. There are nuances to the exposition of the matter that we shall consider, but the basic point registers: there are no theological foundations for toleration of idolatry or the idolater in classical Judaism.

Neither the philosophical nor the exegetical nor the mythic formulation sets forth a doctrine that validates difference from the monotheist norm. Monotheism by its nature begins with the intolerant position that there is only one God, so all other gods are false, and those that worship other gods than the God who made himself known in revelation — in the Instruction, or Torah, of Sinai, — are enemies of God. To uncover the foundations for a policy of toleration we must enter into the complexity of the law, theology, and narrative of classical Judaism.

For Scripture, the starting point of Judaism, the community at large forms the focus of the law, and idolatry is not to be negotiated with by the collectivity of holy Israel. In its Land Israel is to wipe out idolatry, even as a memory. Scripture is clear that Israel is to obliterate all mention of idols (Ex. 23:13), not bow down to gentiles' gods or serve them but overthrow them and break them into pieces (Ex. 23:24): "You shall break down their altars and dash in pieces their pillars and hew down their Asherim and burn their graven images with fire" (Dt. 7:5). Israelites are commanded along these same lines:

> "The graven images of their gods you shall burn with fire;
> you shall not covet the silver or the gold that is on them or take it for
> yourselves, lest you be ensnared by it; for it is an abomination to the
> Lord your God. And you shall not bring an abominable thing into your
> house and become accused like it" (Dt. 7:25-26).
> "You shall surely destroy all the places where the nations
> whom you shall dispossess served their gods, upon the high mountains

and upon the hills and under every green tree; you shall tear down their altars and dash in pieces their pillars and burn their Asherim with fire; you shall hew down the graven images of their gods and destroy their name out of that place" (Dt. 12:2-3).

Accordingly, so far as the Written Torah supplies the foundations for the treatment of the matter by the Rabbinic canon of the formative age, the focus of discourse concerning the gentiles is idolatry. Scripture's Halakhah does not contemplate Israel's co-existing, in the land, with gentiles and their idolatry.

The canon of classical Judaism comprised by Scripture and the Rabbinic legal and exegetical complements to Scripture came to closure by the seventh century C.E. The Rabbinic law, contained in the Mishnah, ca. 200 C.E., a philosophical law code, the Tosefta, ca. 300 C.E., complements to the Mishnah, the Yerushalmi or Talmud of the Land of Israel, ca. 400 C.E., a commentary to thirty-nine tractates of the sixty-one topical expositions of the Mishnah and the Tosefta, and the Bavli or Talmud of Babylonia, ca. 600 C.E., a commentary to thirty-seven tractates of the Mishnah and the Tosefta. The whole is constructed in dialogue with the law, narrative, and prophecy of Scripture, with a privileged standing accorded to the Pentateuch or Torah of Moses.

The Rabbinic sages of late antiquity set forth a religious system of the culture and social order of the community of which they speak, which they call "Israel," those concerning whom Scripture tells its stories and to whom Scripture addresses its law and prophecy. That religious system defines the way of life and the world view of the Israel that embodies the one and explains itself in accord with the other. The world — all humanity — is divided, in accord with the Judaic system, into two classifications of persons, the gentiles and Israel. So our question becomes, what are the theological resources for tolerance of gentiles that classical Judaism nurtures? Why should gentiles enjoy the toleration of Israelites, meaning, why does God accommodate in the world that he made and now governs the presence of gentiles as well as Israelites?

The Halakhic system of the Mishnah, Tosefta, Yerushalmi, and Bavli speaks to a world that is not so simple. The Land belongs to Israel, but gentiles live there too — and run things. And Israel no longer forms a coherent collectivity but a realm made up of individuals, with their distinctive and particular interests. The Halakhah of the Rabbinic canon of the formative age commences its treatment of the same subject with the opposite premise: gentiles live side by side (whether or not in the Land of Israel) with Israelites, and Israelites have to sort out the complex problems of co-existence with idolatry. And that co-existence involves not whole communities, the People, Israel, and the peoples, whoever they may be, but individuals, this Israelite living side by side with that gentile.

Not only so, but the Rabbinic documents use the occasion of idolatry to contemplate a condition entirely beyond the imagination of Scripture, which is the hegemony of idolatrous nations and the subjugation of holy Israel. The topic of idolatry forms the occasion for the discussion of Israel's place among the nations of the world and of Israel's relationships with gentiles. Furthermore, the Rabbinic system's theory of who Israel is finds its context in the contrast with the gentiles. The meeting point with the Written Torah is defined by the indicative trait of the gentiles, which is their idolatry; that is all that matters about them.

i. Why Is Humanity Divided between Israel, the unique community of humanity that knows God, and the Gentiles, no community at all, who do not know God?

We turn to the mythic explanation of why there are gentiles in the world and how they are to be assessed by Judaism. It is a narrative of the story of humanity in relationship to the one and only God of creation. The story recapitulates the history of Adam and Eve and their successors, ten generations from Adam to Noah that God found rebellious:

A.	The generation of the flood has no share in the world to come,
B.	and they shall not stand in the judgment,
C.	since it is written, "My spirit shall not judge with man forever" (Gen. 6:3)
D.	neither judgment nor spirit.
E.	The generation of the dispersion has no share in the world to come,
F.	since it is said, "So the Lord scattered them abroad from there upon the face of the whole earth" (Gen. 11:8).
G.	"So the Lord scattered them abroad" — in this world,
H.	"and the Lord scattered them from there" — in the world to come.
I.	The men of Sodom have no portion in the world to come,
J.	since it is said, "Now the men of Sodom were wicked and sinners against the Lord exceedingly" (Gen. 13:13)
K.	"Wicked" — in this world,
L.	"And sinners" — in the world to come.

Mishnah-tractate Sanhedrin 10:3

God wiped out the children of Adam, leaving only Noah — "righteous in his generation" — to re-generate the human race. The children of Noah, all humanity, are subject to seven religious obligations or commandments, for which violations are punished. Israel, whom we meet in a later chapter of the same narrative, is obligated to hundreds (the conventional number is 613, the combination of the days of the solar year and the bones of the body).

God tolerates the children of Noah so long as they keep the commandments assigned to them. God does not neglect the gentiles or fail to exercise dominion over them. For even now, gentiles are subject to a number of commandments or religious obligations. God cares for gentiles as for Israel, he wants gentiles as much as Israel to enter the kingdom of Heaven, and he assigns to gentiles opportunities to evince their acceptance of his rule. One of these commandments is not to curse God's name:

> A.   "Any man who curses his God shall bear his sin" (Lev. 24:15).
> B.   It would have been clear had the text simply said, "A man."
> C.   Why does it specify, "Any"?
> D.   It serves to encompass idolaters, who are admonished not to curse the Name, just as Israelites are so admonished.
>
> > Bavli Sanhedrin 7:5 I.2/56a

Not cursing God, even while worshipping idols, seems a minimal expectation.

But, in fact there are seven such religious obligations that apply to the children of Noah. If they observe these commandments, they are in good standing with God . It is not surprising — indeed, it is predictable — that the definition of the matter should find its place in the Halakhah of Abodah Zarah:

> ### Tosefta-tractate Abodah Zarah 8:4-6
> T. 8:4 A.   Concerning seven religious requirements were the children of Noah admonished:
> > B.   setting up courts of justice, idolatry, blasphemy [cursing the Name of God], fornication, bloodshed, and thievery.

We now proceed to show how each of these religious obligations is represented as applying to gentiles as much as to Israelites:

> C.   Concerning setting up courts of justice — how so [how does Scripture or reason validate the claim that gentiles are to set up courts of justice]?
> D.   Just as Israelites are commanded to call into session in their towns courts of justice.
> E.   Concerning idolatry and blasphemy — how so? ...
> F.   Concerning fornication — how so?
> G.   "On account of any form of prohibited sexual relationship on account of which an Israelite court inflicts the death-penalty, the children of Noah are subject to warning," the words of R. Meir.
> H.   And sages say, "There are many prohibited relationships, on account of which an Israelite court does not inflict the death-penalty and the children of Noah are [not] warned. In regard to these forbidden relationships the nations are judged in accord with the laws governing the nations.
> I.   "And you have only the prohibitions of sexual relations with a betrothed maiden alone."

The systemization of Scripture's evidence for the stated proposition continues:

T. 8:5 A.   For bloodshed — how so?

        B.   A gentile [who kills] a gentile and a gentile who kills an Israelite are liable. An Israelite [who kills] a gentile is exempt.

        C.   Concerning thievery?

        D.   [If] one has stolen, or robbed, and so too in the case of finding a beautiful captive [woman], and in similar cases:

        E.   a gentile in regard to a gentile, or a gentile in regard to an Israelite— it is prohibited. And an Israelite in regard to a gentile— it is permitted.

T. 8:6 A.   Concerning a limb cut from a living beast— how so?

        B.   A dangling limb on a beast, [which] is not [so connected] as to bring about healing,

        C.   is forbidden for use by the children of Noah, and, it goes without saying, for Israelites.

        D.   But if there is [in the connecting flesh] sufficient [blood supply] to bring about healing,

        E.   it is permitted to Israelites, and, it goes without saying, to the children of Noah.

As in the case of Israelites, so the death penalty applies to a Noahide, so b. San. 7:5 I.4-5/57a: On account of violating three religious duties are children of Noah put to death: on account of adultery, murder, and blasphemy.'" R. Huna, R. Judah, and all the disciples of Rab say, "On account of seven commandments a son of Noah is put to death. The All-Merciful revealed that fact of one of them, and the same rule applies to all of them." But just as Israelites, educated in the Torah, are assumed to exhibit certain uniform virtues, e.g., forbearance, so gentiles, lacking that same education, are assumed to conform to a different model.

Gentiles, by reason of their condition outside of the Torah, are characterized by certain traits natural to their situation, and these are worldly. Not only so, but the sages' theology of gentiles shapes the normative law in how to relate to them. If an Israelite is by nature forbearing and forgiving, the gentile by nature is ferocious. That explains why in the Halakhah as much as in the Aggadah gentiles are always suspect of the cardinal sins, bestiality, fornication, and bloodshed, as well as constant idolatry. The Judaic theology of the gentiles, which sees them as an undifferentiated phalanx of enemies of God, who worship idols deliberately ignoring the truth, leaves little basis for affirming altruistic conduct toward "others." On the contrary, even ordinary transactions that express simple compassion are subjected to doubt:

        A.   They do not leave cattle in gentiles' inns,

        B.   because they are suspect in regard to bestiality.

        C.   And a woman should not be alone with them,

        D.   because they are suspect in regard to fornication.

E.   And a man should not be alone with them,

F.   because they are suspect in regard to bloodshed.

G.   An Israelite girl should not serve as a midwife to a gentile woman,

H.   because she serves to bring forth a child for the service of idolatry.

I.   But a gentile woman may serve as a midwife to an Israelite girl.

J.   An Israelite girl should not give suck to the child of a gentile woman.

K.   But a gentile woman may give suck to the child of an Israelite girl,

L.   when it is by permission.

Mishnah-tractate Abodah Zarah 2:1

A.   They accept from them healing for property,

B.   but not healing for a person.

C.   "And they do not allow them to cut hair under any circumstances," the words of R. Meir.

D.   And sages say, "In the public domain it is permitted,

E.   "but not if they are alone."

Mishnah Abodah Zarah 2:1-2

The prevailing attitude of suspicion of gentiles derives from the definition of gentiles: idolaters, enemies of God. One should not anticipate a rich repertoire of rulings on how one must sacrifice for the welfare of the gentile-other. I cannot point to narratives that suggest one must, let alone laws that obligate it.

That view of matters is embodied in normative law, as we have seen. The law of the Mishnah corresponds to the lore of scriptural exegesis; the theory of the gentiles governs in both. Beyond the Torah there not only is no salvation from death, there is not even the possibility of a common decency. The Torah makes all the difference. The upshot may be stated very simply. Israel and the gentiles form the two divisions of humanity. The one will die but rise from the grave to eternal life with God. When the other dies, it perishes; that is the end. Moses said it very well: Choose life. The gentiles sustain comparison and contrast with Israel, the point of ultimate division being death for the one, eternal life for the other.

If Israel and the gentiles are deemed comparable, the gentiles do not acknowledge or know God, therefore, while they are like Israelites in sharing a common humanity by reason of mythic genealogy — deriving from Noah — the gentiles do not receive in a meritorious manner the blessings that God bestows upon them. So much for the points of stress of the Aggadah. When it comes to the Halakhah, as we have seen, the religious problematics focuses not upon the gentiles but upon Israel: what, given the world as it is, can Israel do in the dominion subject to Israel's own will and intention? That is the question that, as we now see, the Halakhah fully answers. For the Halakhah constructs, indeed defines, the interiority of an Israel sustaining God's service in a world of idolatry: life against death in the two concrete and tangible dimensions by which life is sustained: trade and the production of food, the foci of the Halakhah. No wonder Israel must refrain from engaging with idolatry on days of the festivals for idols that the great fairs embody

— then especially. The presentation of the Halakhah commences with the single most important, comprehensive point — as usual.

The gentiles deprived themselves of the Torah because they rejected it, and, showing the precision of justice, they rejected the Torah because the Torah deprived them of the very practices or traits that they deemed characteristic, essential to their being. That circularity marks the tale of how things were to begin with in fact describes how things always are; it is not historical but philosophical. The gentiles' own character, the shape of their conscience, then, now, and always, accounts for their condition — which, by an act of will, as we have noted, they can change. What they did not want, that of which they were by their own word unworthy, is denied them. And what they do want condemns them. So when each nation comes under judgment for rejecting the Torah, the indictment of each is spoken out of its own mouth, its own-self-indictment then forms the core of the matter. Given what we know about the definition of Israel as those destined to live and the gentile as those not, we cannot find surprising that the entire account is set in that age to come to which the gentiles are denied entry.

When they protest the injustice of the decision that takes effect just then, they are shown the workings of the moral order, as the following quite systematic account of the governing pattern explains:

BAVLI TRACTATE ABODAH ZARAH 1:1 I.2/2A-B:

A. R. Hanina bar Pappa, and some say, R. Simlai, gave the following exposition [of the verse, "They that fashion a graven image are all of them vanity, and their delectable things shall not profit, and their own witnesses see not nor know" (Isa. 44:9)]: "In the age to come the Holy One, blessed be He, will bring a scroll of the Torah and hold it in his bosom and say, 'Let him who has kept himself busy with it come and take his reward.' Then all the gentiles will crowd together: 'All of the nations are gathered together' (Isa. 43:9). The Holy One, blessed be He, will say to them, 'Do not crowd together before me in a mob. But let each nation enter together with [2B] its scribes, 'and let the peoples be gathered together' (Isa. 43:9), and the word 'people' means 'kingdom': 'and one kingdom shall be stronger than the other' (Gen. 25:23)."

We note that the players are the principal participants in world history: the Romans first and foremost, then the Persians, the other world-rulers of the age:

C. "The kingdom of Rome comes in first."

H. "The Holy One, blessed be He, will say to them, 'How have you defined your chief occupation?'

I. "They will say before him, 'Lord of the world, a vast number of marketplaces have we set up, a vast number of bathhouses we have made, a vast amount of silver and gold have we accumulated. And all of these things we have done only in behalf of Israel, so that they may define as their chief occupation the study of the Torah.'

J.   "The Holy One, blessed be He, will say to them, 'You complete idiots! Whatever you have done has been for your own convenience. You have set up a vast number of marketplaces to be sure, but that was so as to set up whorehouses in them. The bathhouses were for your own pleasure. Silver and gold belong to me anyhow: "Mine is the silver and mine is the gold, says the Lord of hosts" (Hag. 2:8). Are there any among you who have been telling of "this," and "this" is only the Torah: "And this is the Torah that Moses set before the children of Israel' (Dt. 4:44)." So they will make their exit, humiliated.

The claim of Rome — to support Israel in Torah-study — is rejected on grounds that the Romans did not exhibit the right attitude, always a dynamic force in the theology. Then the other world rule enters in with its claim:

K.   "When the kingdom of Rome has made its exit, the kingdom of Persia enters afterward."

M.   "The Holy One, blessed be He, will say to them, 'How have you defined your chief occupation?'

N.   "They will say before him, 'Lord of the world, We have thrown up a vast number of bridges, we have conquered a vast number of towns, we have made a vast number of wars, and all of them we did only for Israel, so that they may define as their chief occupation the study of the Torah.'

O.   "The Holy One, blessed be He, will say to them, 'Whatever you have done has been for your own convenience. You have thrown up a vast number of bridges, to collect tolls, you have conquered a vast number of towns, to collect the corvée, and, as to making a vast number of wars, I am the one who makes wars: "The Lord is a man of war" (Ex. 19:17). Are there any among you who have been telling of "this," and "this" is only the Torah: "And this is the Torah that Moses set before the children of Israel" (Dt. 4:44).' So they will make their exit, humiliated.

R.   "And so it will go with each and every nation."

As native categories, Rome and Persia are singled out, "all the other nations" play no role, for reasons with which we are already familiar. Once more the theology reaches into its deepest thought on the power of intentionality, showing that what people want is what they get.

But matters cannot be limited to the two world-empires of the present age, Rome and Iran, standing in judgment at the end of time. The theology values balance, proportion, seeks complementary relationships, and therefore treats beginnings along with endings, the one going over the ground of the other. Accordingly, a recapitulation of the same event — the gentiles' rejection of the Torah — chooses as its setting not the last judgment but the first encounter, that is, the giving of the Torah itself. In the timeless world constructed by the Rabbinic canon of the formative age, what happens at the outset exemplifies how things always happen, and what happens at the end embodies what has always taken place. The basic thesis is identical — the gentiles cannot accept the Torah because to do so they would have to deny their very character. But the exposition retains its interest because it takes its own course.

Now the gentiles are not just Rome and Persia but others; and of special interest, the Torah is embodied in some of the ten commandments — not to murder, not to commit adultery, not to steal; then the gentiles are rejected for not keeping the seven commandments assigned to the children of Noah. The upshot is that the reason that the gentiles rejected the Torah is that the Torah prohibits deeds that the gentiles do by their very nature. The subtext here is already familiar from Chapter Three: Israel ultimately is changed by the Torah, so that Israel exhibits traits imparted by their encounter with the Torah. So too with the gentiles, by their nature they are what they are; the Torah has not changed their nature.

Once more a single standard applies to both components of humanity, but with opposite effect:

SIFRÉ TO DEUTERONOMY CCCXLIII:IV.1FF.:

1. A. Another teaching concerning the phrase, "He said, 'The Lord came from Sinai'":
   B. When the Omnipresent appeared to give the Torah to Israel, it was not to Israel alone that he revealed himself but to every nation.
   C. First of all he came to the children of Esau. He said to them, "Will you accept the Torah?"
   D. They said to him, "What is written in it?"
   E. He said to them, "'You shall not murder' (Ex. 20:13)."
   F. They said to him, "The very being of 'those men' [namely, us] and of their father is to murder, for it is said, 'But the hands are the hands of Esau'"(Gen. 27:22). 'By your sword you shall live' (Gen. 27:40)."

At this point we cover new ground: other classes of gentiles that reject the Torah; now the Torah's own narrative takes over, replacing the known facts of world politics, such as the earlier account sets forth, and instead supplying evidence out of Scripture as to the character of the gentile group under discussion:

   G. So he went to the children of Ammon and Moab and said to them, "Will you accept the Torah?"
   H. They said to him, "What is written in it?"
   I. He said to them, "'You shall not commit adultery' (Ex. 20:13)."
   J. They said to him, "The very essence of fornication belongs to them [us], for it is said, 'Thus were both the daughters of Lot with child by their fathers' (Gen. 19:36)."

K.   So he went to the children of Ishmael and said to them, "Will you accept the Torah?"

L.   They said to him, "What is written in it?"

M.   He said to them, "'You shall not steal' (Ex. 20:13)."

N.   They said to him, "The very essence of their [our] father is thievery, as it is said, 'And he shall be a wild ass of a man' (Gen. 16:12)."

O.   And so it went. He went to every nation, asking them, "Will you accept the Torah?"

P.   For so it is said, "All the kings of the earth shall give you thanks, O Lord, for they have heard the words of your mouth" (Ps. 138:4).

Q.   Might one suppose that they listened and accepted the Torah?

R.   Scripture says, "And I will execute vengeance in anger and fury upon the nations, because they did not listen" (Mic. 5:14).

At this point we turn back to the obligations that God has imposed upon the gentiles; these obligations have no bearing upon the acceptance of the Torah; they form part of the ground of being, the condition of existence, of the gentiles. Yet even here, the gentiles do not accept God's authority in matters of natural law:

S.   And it is not enough for them that they did not listen, but even the seven religious duties that the children of Noah indeed accepted upon themselves they could not uphold before breaking them.

T.   When the Holy One, blessed be He, saw that that is how things were, he gave them to Israel.

Now comes another parable, involving not a king but a common person:

2. A.   The matter may be compared to the case of a person who sent his ass and dog to the threshing floor and loaded up a *letekh* of grain on his ass and three *seahs* of grain on his dog. The ass went along, while the dog panted.

B.   He took a seah of grain off the dog and put it on the ass, so with the second, so with the third.

C.   Thus was Israel: they accepted the Torah, complete with all its secondary amplifications and minor details, even the seven religious duties that the children of Noah could not uphold without breaking them did the Israelites come along and accept.

D.   That is why it is said, "The Lord came from Sinai; he shone upon them from Seir."

Along these same lines, the gentiles would like to make a common pact with Israel, but cannot have a share in God:

Sifré to Deuteronomy CCCXLIII:IX.2:

A.   Thus the nations of the world would ask Israel, saying to them, "'What is your beloved more than another beloved' (Song 5:9)? For you are willing to accept death on his account."

B. For so Scripture says, "Therefore they love you to death" (Song 1:3).

C. And further: "No, but for your sake are we killed all day long" (Ps. 44:23).

Now comes the envy of the gentiles, their desire to amalgamate with Israel, and Israel's insistence upon remaining a holy people, a people apart:

D. [The nations continue,] "All of you are handsome, all of you are strong. Come and let us form a group in common."

E. And the Israelites answer, "We shall report to you part of the praise that is coming to him, and in that way you will discern him:

F. "'My beloved is white and ruddy...his head is as the most fine gold...his eyes are like doves beside the water-brooks...his cheeks are as a bed of spices....his hands are as rods of gold....His legs are as pillars of marble....His mouth is most sweet, yes, he is altogether sweet' (Song 5:10-16)."

G. When the nations of the world hear about the beauty and praiseworthy quality of the Holy One, blessed be He, they say to them, "Let us come with you."

H. For it is said, "Where has your beloved gone, O you fairest among women? Where has your beloved turned, that we may seek him with you" (Song 5:1).

Israel's is not the task of winning over the gentiles. That is God's task, and it will be done in God's own good time:

I. What do the Israelites answer them? "You have no share in him: "'I am my beloved's and my beloved is mine, who feeds among the lilies" (Song 6:3).

The various gentile nations rejected the Torah for specific and reasonable considerations, concretely, because the Torah prohibited deeds essential to their being. This point is made in so many words, then amplified through a parable. Israel, by contrast, is prepared to give up life itself for the Torah. But that is because Israel is transformed by the Torah into a kingdom of priests and a holy people.

II. In the classical sources of Judaism, what is the role of other religions?

The Halakhah finds difficult the differentiation of pagans into distinct nations, treating all gentiles as equivalent in connection with idolatry, on the one side, and cultic uncleanness, on the other. All gentiles constitute sources of uncleanness analogous to corpses, all with uniform consequences. And, along these same lines, Rabbinic Judaism affords through differentiation no recognition to other religions. All form media of idolatry, and while the Rabbinic sages know that diverse idols are served through diverse liturgies, all other religions fall into the same category. None is worse than any other. The Aggadic narratives differentiate Babylonia, Persia, Greece, and Rome, in constructing a theology of history that places Israel at the fifth and final phase of human history, once more, the eschatological resolution of all matters in favor of one God, who made himself known at Sinai to the children of Abraham, Isaac, and Israel. But when those narratives do differentiate one nation and its gods from another, it is only to impute to all of them the same wicked qualities, as at Leviticus Rabbah 13:5.

III. ARE DIFFERENT RELIGIONS ACKNOWLEDGED, REJECTED, MERELY ENDURED, OR RELIGIOUSLY CONSTRUCTIVE? ARE OTHER RELIGIONS TREATED GENERICALLY OR DIFFERENTIATED?

Since other religions are treated generically and not differentiated from one another, classical Judaism face the task of explaining the presence in the world of idolatry that defined the everyday context of Israel's existence. First, they maintained, gentiles act as though they do not really mean to honor idols. By the standard of respect shown by Israel to God, gentiles fail. Second, gentiles cannot transform the natural world into an object prohibited for Israelite use by reason of its forming an idol.

MISHNAH-TRACTATE ABODAH ZARAH 3:4-5

A. Peroqlos b. Pelosepos "Pericles the Philosopher". asked Rabban Gamaliel in Akko, when he was washing in Aphrodite's bathhouse, saying to him, "It is written in your Torah, 'And there shall cleave nothing of the devoted thing to your hand' (Deut. 13:18). How come you're taking a bath in Aphrodite's bathhouse?"

B. He said to him, "They do not give answers in a bathhouse."

C. When he went out, he said to him, "I never came into her domain. She came into mine. They don't say, 'Let's make a bathhouse as an ornament for Aphrodite.' But they say, 'Let's make Aphrodite as an ornament for the bathhouse.'

D. "Another matter: If someone gave you a lot of money, you would never walk into your temple of idolatry naked or suffering a flux, nor would you urinate in its presence.

E. "Yet this thing is standing right at the head of the gutter and everybody urinates right in front of her.

F. "It is said only, '...their gods' (Deut. 12:3) — that which one treats as a god is prohibited, but that which one treats not as a god is permitted."

M. A.Z. 3:4

A. Gentiles who worship hills and valleys —

B. these hills or valleys. are permitted, but what is on them is forbidden for Israelite use.

C.   as it is said, "You shall not covet the silver or gold that is upon them not take it."
D.   R. Yosé says, "Their gods are on the mountains, and the mountains are not their gods. Their gods are in the valleys, and the valleys are not their gods."
E.   On what account is an *asherah* prohibited? Because it has been subject to manual labor, and whatever has been subject to manual labor is prohibited.
F.   Said R. Aqiba, "I shall explain and interpret the matter before you:
G.   "In any place in which you find a high mountain, a lofty hill, or a green tree, you may take for granted that there is an idol there."

M. A. Z. 3:5

Idolatry is rejected, not acknowledged, but the action of the idolater imparts the status of idolatry to what is in fact neutral. It is all a matter of intentionality. That is, the pagan imparts power to the idol by reason of his own will, which is therefore corrupt and corrupting. Here are the norms set forth by Mishnah-tractate Abodah Zarah 4:4-6, joined with Tosefta's complement as indicated. The Mishnah-text is given in bold face type, so to differentiate it from the Tosefta's amplification.

MISHNAH-TRACTATE ABODAH ZARAH 4:4-6

M. 4:4   **An idol belonging to a gentile is prohibited forthwith [when it is made]. And one belonging to an Israelite is prohibited only after it will have been worshipped. A gentile has the power to nullify an idol belonging either to himself or his fellow gentile. But an Israelite has not got the power to nullify an idol belonging to a gentile.**

T. 5:6   The pedestals which gentiles set up during the persecution [by Hadrian] — even though the time of persecution is over — Lo, these are forbidden. Is it possible that an idol which a gentile nullified — is it possible that it should be deemed prohibited? Scripture says, "The graven images of their gods you shall burn with fire" (Deut. 7:25). That which he treats as a god is prohibited. And that which he does not treat as a god is permitted. Is it then possible that an idol which a gentile nullified should be deemed permitted? Scripture says, The graven images of their gods . . .— Whether he treats it as a god or does not treat it as a god, it is forbidden.

T. 5:7   How does one nullify [an idol]? A gentile nullifies an idol belonging to himself or to an Israelite. But an Israelite does not nullify an idol belonging to a gentile [cf. M. A.Z. 4:4C-D].

T. 5:9   At what point is it called 'set aside [for idolatrous purposes]'? Once some concrete deed has been done to it [for that purpose].

T. 5:10   What is one which has been worshipped? Any one which people worship — whether inadvertently or deliberately. What is one which has been set aside? Any which has been set aside for idolatry. But if one has said, "This ox is for idolatry," "This house is for idolatry," he has said nothing whatsoever. For there is no such thing as an act of consecration for idolatry.

M. 4:5   How does one nullify it? [If] he has cut off the tip of its ear, the tip of its nose, the tip of its finger, [if] he battered it, even though he did not break off [any part of] it, he has nullified it. [If] he spit in its face, urinated in front of it, scraped it, threw shit at it, lo, this does not constitute an act of nullification.

T. 5:8   A pedestal, the greater part of which was damaged — lo, this is permitted. One the whole of which was damaged is prohibited until one will restore it. That belonging to him is permitted, and that belonging to his fellow is prohibited. Before it has been sanctified, it is prohibited. After it has been sanctified, it is permitted.

M. 4:6   An idol, the worshippers of which have abandoned it in time of peace, is permitted. [If they abandoned it] in time of war, it is forbidden. Idol pedestals set up for kings — lo, these are permitted, since they set [images up on them only] at the time kings go by.

What emerges is the distinction between the Israelite's and the idolater's relationship to the idol. The gentile is assumed to be an idolater and once the idol is manufactured, it automatically is prohibited. But if it is made for an Israelite, it is assumed to be a piece of wood until the Israelite commits an act of worship. Then he, like the pagan, exercises his power of will to impart to the piece of wood the status of a false god. The gentile's idol lies outside of the Israelite's power of intentionality. To nullify it, the Israelite must acquire possession of it and then treat it as his own property. The gentile's power of intentionality governs, for example, when we assess whether an idol has been abandoned willingly or under duress. If the latter is the case, it is not nullified. The laws suffice to demonstrate that paganism and idolatry are not acknowledged but rejected and it goes without saying are assigned no constructive task.

IV. HOW DO THE CLASSICAL JUDAIC SOURCES JUSTIFY, OR ACCOUNT FOR, THE EXISTENCE AND PERSISTENCE OF OTHER RELIGIONS? ARE THE OTHER RELIGIONS SEEN AS ERRORS, ACCIDENTS, THE CONSEQUENCE OF EVIL, A CONSTRUCTIVE PART OF REALITY, OR SOME COMBINATION OF VARIATION OF THESE OPTIONS?

The normative sources do not justify idolatry. They account for its persistence only by appeal to God's plan for nature. God condemns the idolater, the gentile, for the blasphemous intentionality exhibited by the idol that he makes:

BAVLI TRACTATE ABODAH ZARAH 4:6 I.2FF./54B-55A:

I.2 A.   A philosopher asked Rabban Gamaliel, "It is written in your Torah, 'For the Lord your God is a devouring fire, a jealous God' (Dt. 4:24). How come he is more jealous against the worshippers of the idol than against the idol itself?"

> B. He said to him, "I shall give you a parable. To what is the matter to be compared? To a mortal king who had a single son, and this son raised a dog for himself, which he called by his father's name, so that, whenever he took an oath, he exclaimed, 'By the life of this dog, my father!' When the king heard, with whom was he angry? Was he angry with the son, or what he angry with the dog? One has to say it was with the son that he was angry."

At this point the question of the substantiality of the idol emerges; the debate to this point is framed to presuppose the sages' position. Now we ask how one can dismiss the power of idols in their own right:

> C. [The philosopher] said to him, "Are you going to call the idol a dog? But there is some substance to it."
> D. He said to him, "What makes you say so?"
> E. He said to him, "One time a fire broke out in our town and the entire town burned up, but that temple was not burned up."
> F. He said to him, "I shall give you a parable. To what is the matter to be compared? To a mortal king against whom one of the provinces rebelled. When he makes war, with whom does he do it? With the living or with the dead? You must say it is with the living he makes war."
> G. He said to him, "So you're just calling it names — a dog, a corpse. In that case, then let him just destroy it out of the world."

If God exercises so much power, then why not simply wipe out idolatry? Here we once more ask a fundamental question, which receives a reasonable response:

> H. He said to him, "If people worshipped something of which the world had no need, he certainly would wipe it away. But lo, people worship the sun, moon, stars, and planets, brooks and valleys. Now do you think he is going to wipe out his world because of idiots?
> I. "And so Scripture says, [55A] 'Am I utterly to consume all things from off the face of the ground, says the Lord, am I to consume man and beast, am I to consume the bird of the heaven and the fish of the sea, even the stumbling blocks of the wicked' (Zeph. 1:2).
> J. "Now simply because the wicked stumble on account of these things, is he going to destroy them from the world? Don't they also worship the human being, 'so am I to cut off man from off the face of the ground'?"

Nonetheless, Scripture itself attests to God's own recognition of the substantiality of idolatry. He is jealous of idolatry, and that shows he himself concedes that idols compete. In the same line of questions figures, also, the possibility that idols do some good. As before, the argument is framed through parables.

I.3 A. General Agrippa asked Rabban Gamaliel, "It is written in your
Torah, 'For the Lord your God is a devouring fire, a jealous God'
(Dt. 4:24). Is there jealousy, except on the part of a sage for another
sage, on the part of a great athlete for another great athlete, on the
part of a wealthy man for another wealthy man?"

B. He said to him, "I shall give you a parable. To what is the matter
to be compared? To a man who married a second wife. If she is
more important than she, she will not be jealous of her. If she is
less than she, she will be jealous of her."

So much for the matter of gentile idolatry: to be a gentile means to be an
idolater.

But cannot idolators point to the great deeds of their gods in their temples?
We turn now to concrete cases in which both parties concede something happens in
a temple of an idol, whether healing, whether some other sort of supernatural event.
The first of the two cases involves a rather complex parable. In the second, since
sages form the conversation, texts of Scripture are introduced and accepted as self-
evident proof.

I.4 A. Zeno asked R. Aqiba, "In my heart and in your heart we both
know that there is no substance whatsoever in idolatry. But lo, we
see people go into a shrine crippled and come out cured. How
come?"

B. He said to him, "I shall give you a parable. To what is the matter to
be compared? To a reliable person who was in a town, and all the
townsfolk would deposit their money into his care without
witnesses. One man came and left a deposit in his charge with
witnesses, but once he forgot and left his deposit without witnesses.
The wife of the reliable man said to him, 'Come, let us deny it.' He
said to her, 'Because this idiot acted improperly, shall we destroy
our good name for reliability?' So it is with troubles. When they
send them upon a person, they are made to take the oath, 'You
shall come upon him only on such-and-such a day, and you shall
depart from him only on such-and-such a day, and at such-and-
such an hour, through the medium of so-and-so, with such-and-
such a remedy.' When it is time for them to take their leave, it just
happened that the man went to a temple of an idol. So the afflictions
plea, 'It is right and proper that we not leave him and go our way,
but because this fool acts as he does, are we going to break our
oath?'"

From the parable, we turn to concrete cases in the everyday world:

I.5 A. Raba b. R. Isaac said to R. Judah, "There is a temple to an idol in
our locale. When there is need for rain, the idol appears in a dream

and says to them, 'Kill someone for me and I shall bring rain.' So
they kill someone for her, and she brings rain."

B.   He said to him, "If I were dead, no one could tell you this statement
which Rab said, 'What is the meaning of the verse of Scripture,
"...which the Lord your God has divided to all the peoples under
the whole heaven" (Dt. 4:19)? [Since the letters of the word
'divided' may be read as 'smooth,' the verse means this:] this
teaches that he made them smooth talkers, so as to banish them
from the world."

C.   That is in line with what R. Simeon b. Laqish said, "What is the
meaning of the verse of Scripture, 'Surely he scorns the scorners,
but he gives grace to the lowly' (Prov. 3:34)? If someone comes
along to make himself unclean, they open the gate for him. If he
comes along to purify himself, they also help him do so."

To summarize: the rationality of God's attitudes requires explanation. He
despises idolators more than the idol because the idolators act as though there were
substance to the idol. He does not concede any substance to the idol and therefore
bears the object no special malice. God does not destroy things gentiles worship,
since that would prove disproportionate.

The world order is defined by rationality, which finds its substance in the
rule of justice. Then the moral order of justice enters at just this point. Having
established that idolators subject themselves to God's hatred by reason of their
attitudes and consequent actions, we ask about the matter of fairness. To explain
matters, we turn to an account of how things came about — a reason we should call
historical but sages would classify as paradigmatic. That is, the sages' explanation,
framed in terms of a narrative of something that happened, turns out to be a picture
of how things now are — a characterization of the established facts as these are
realized under all circumstances and at any time, the tenses, past, present, or future,
making no difference.. So when we ask, why to begin with have gentiles entered
the category of death, we take up a tale that casts in mythic-narrative form what
constitutes an analysis of characteristic traits. Not only so, but the narrative explicitly
points to the enduring traits, not a given action, to explain the enduring condition of
the gentiles: that is how they are, because that is how they wish to be.

So now the question becomes urgent: how has this catastrophic
differentiation imposed itself between Israel and the gentiles, such that the gentiles,
for all their glory in the here-and-now, have won for themselves the grave, while
Israel, for all its humiliation in the present age, will inherit the world to come? And
the answer is self-evident from all that has been said: the gentiles reject God, whom
they could and should have known in the Torah. They rejected the Torah, and all
else followed. The proposition then moves in these simple steps:

[1] Israel differs from the gentiles because Israel possesses the Torah and
the gentiles do not;

[2] because they do not possess the Torah, the gentiles also worship idols instead of God; and

[3] therefore God rejects the gentiles and identifies with Israel.

V. SINCE WE KNOW THAT WITHIN RELIGIONS THERE ARE DIVERGENT, SOMETIMES OPPOSED, VIEWS OF OTHER RELIGIONS, WHAT ARE THE DOCTRINAL FAULT LINES WITHIN THE RELIGION THAT PRODUCE THIS DIVERGENCE? WHICH TEACHINGS WITHIN THE SOURCES OF JUDAISM JUSTIFY TOLERANCE OF OTHER RELIGIONS, AND WHICH JUSTIFY INTOLERANCE?

One teaching of the classical Rabbinic canon justifies tolerance of gentiles, if none validates tolerance of idolatry; It is captured at our starting point: the eschatological resolution of the matter, so that gentiles too may enjoy the resurrection and eternal life that represent Israel's destiny, requires attention. It is the one point in the system at which systemic thought about the other or the outsider comes into play. We engage with that thought when we ask, What about gentiles in general? All depends upon their own actions. Since the point of differentiation is idolatry as against worship of the one God, gentiles may enter into the category of Israel, which is to say, they recognize the one God and come to serve him. That means, whether now or later, some, perhaps many, gentiles will enter Israel, being defined as other Israelites are defined: those who worship the one and only God. The gentiles include many righteous persons. But by the end of days these God will bring to Israel:

YERUSHALMI BERAKHOT 2:8 I:2:

A. When R. Hiyya bar Adda, the nephew of Bar Qappara, died Resh Laqish accepted [condolences] on his account because he [Resh Laqish] had been his teacher. We may say that [this action is justified because] a person's student is as beloved to him as his son,

B. And he [Resh Laqish] expounded concerning him [Hiyya] this verse: "My beloved has gone down to his garden, to the bed of spices, to pasture his flock in the gardens, and to gather lilies" [Song 6:2]. It is not necessary [for the verse to mention, 'To the bed of spices']. [It is redundant if you interpret the verse literally, for most gardens have spice beds.]

C. Rather [interpret the verse as follows:] My beloved — this is God; has gone down to his garden — this is the world; to the beds of spices — this is Israel; to pasture his flock in the gardens — these are the nations of the world; and to gather lilies — these are the righteous whom he takes from their midst.

Now a parable restates the proposition in narrative terms; having chosen a different mode of discourse from the narrative one that dominates in the Authorized History, Genesis through Kings, sages reintroduce narrative for an other-than-historical purpose, as here:

D.   They offer a parable [relevant to this subject]. To what may we compare this matter [of the tragic death of his student]? A king had a son who was very beloved to him. What did the king do? He planted an orchard for him.

E.   As long as the son acted according to his father's will, he would search throughout the world to seek the beautiful saplings of the world, and to plant them in his orchard. And when his son angered him he went and cut down all his saplings.

F.   Accordingly, so long as Israel acts according to God's will he searches throughout the world to seek the righteous persons of the nations of the world and bring them and join them to Israel, as he did with Jethro and Rahab. And when they [the Israelites] anger him he removes the righteous from their midst.

It follows that Israel bears a heavy burden of responsibility even for the gentiles. When Israel pleases God, the righteous among the gentiles are joined to them, and when not, not. So while gentiles as such cannot inherit the world to come, they too can enter the status of Israel, in which case they join Israel in the world to come. And that is precisely what sages expect will happen.

This the gentiles will do in exactly the way that Israel attained that status to begin with, which is by knowing God through his self-manifestation in the Torah, therefore by accepting God's rule as set forth therein. In this way the theology of Rabbinic Judaism maintains its perfect consistency and inner logic: the Torah determines all things. That point is made explicit: If a gentile keeps the Torah, he is saved. But by keeping the Torah, the gentile has ceased to be gentile and become Israelite, worth even of the high priesthood. First comes the definition of how Israel becomes Israel, which is by accepting God's dominion in the Torah:

Sifra CXCIV:ii.1

1. A.   "The Lord spoke to Moses saying, Speak to the Israelite people and say to them, I am the Lord your God":

B.   R. Simeon b. Yohai says, "That is in line with what is said elsewhere: 'I am the Lord your God [who brought you out of the land of Egypt, out of the house of bondage]' (Ex. 20:2).

C.   "'Am I the Lord, whose sovereignty you took upon yourself in Egypt?'

D.   "They said to him, 'Indeed.'

E.   "'Indeed you have accepted my dominion.'

F.   "'They accepted my decrees: "You will have no other gods before me."'

G.   "That is what is said here: 'I am the Lord your God,' meaning, 'Am I the one whose dominion you accepted at Sinai?'

H.   "They said to him, 'Indeed.'

I.   "'Indeed you have accepted my dominion.'

J. "'They accepted my decrees: "You shall not copy the practices of the land of Egypt where you dwelt, or of the land of Canaan to which I am taking you; nor shall you follow their laws."'"

I cite the passage to underscore how matters are defined, which is by appeal to the Torah. Then the true state of affairs emerges when the same definition explicitly is brought to bear upon the gentiles. That yields the clear inference that gentiles have the power to join themselves to Israel as fully-naturalized Israelites, so the Torah that defines their status also constitutes the ticket of admission to the world to come that Israel will enter in due course. Sages could not be more explicit than they are when they insist, the gentile ceases to be in the status of the gentile when he accepts God's rule in the Torah:

Sifra CXCIV:ii.15

A. "...by the pursuit of which man shall live":
B. R. Jeremiah says, "How do I know that even a gentile who keeps the Torah, lo, he is like the high priest?
C. "Scripture says, 'by the pursuit of which man shall live.'"
D. And so he says, "'And this is the Torah of the priests, Levites, and Israelites,' is not what is said here, but rather, 'This is the Torah of the man, O Lord God' (2 Sam. 7:19)."
E. And so he says, "'open the gates and let priests, Levites, and Israelites will enter it' is not what is said, but rather, 'Open the gates and let the righteous nation, who keeps faith, enter it' (Is. 26:2)."
F. And so he says, "'This is the gate of the Lord. Priests, Levites, and Israelites...' is not what is said, but rather, 'the righteous shall enter into it' (Ps. 118:20).
G. And so he says, "'What is said is not, 'Rejoice, priests, Levites, and Israelites,' but rather, 'Rejoice, O righteous, in the Lord' (Ps. 33:1)."
H. And so he says, "It is not, 'Do good, O Lord, to the priests, Levites, and Israelites,' but rather, 'Do good, O Lord, to the good, to the upright in heart' (Ps. 125:4)."
I. "Thus, even a gentile who keeps the Torah, lo, he is like the high priest."

What is at issue is no genealogy ("high priest") but keeping the Torah. To be "Israel" represents not an ethnic but a theological classification. That is not to suggest God does not rule the gentiles. He does — whether they like it or not, acknowledge him or not. God responds, also, to the acts of merit taken by gentiles, as much as to those of Israel. The upshot is, "gentile" and "Israel" classify through the presence or absence of the same traits; they form taxonomic categories that can in the case of the gentile change when that which is classified requires reclassification by criteria of a supernatural character.

VI. ARE THERE HISTORICAL, POLITICAL, AND/OR BEHAVIORAL FACTORS THAT
CORRELATE WITH THE EXPRESSION OF TOLERANCE IN JUDAISM? WITH
INTOLERANCE? HOW DO YOU EXPLAIN THE CHOICES MADE WITHIN
THE RELIGION FOR TOLERANCE AND INTOLERANCE?

Normative Judaism in its formative canon did not have the last word on the matter at hand or on any other. A long and complex history of exegesis and amplification yielded other Aggadic-theological perspectives, other Halakhic rulings. A massive complication intervened in the form of Christianity and Islam. These represented challenges to not only the Judaic account of self-manifestation in the Torah but also the Judaic classification of humanity into those that know God and those that do not, monotheists and idolaters. As to God's instruction, Christianity both affirmed Scripture and added to the Torah the New Testament and produced the Bible. For its part Islam acknowledged the revelation of the Bible and deemed the Quran to be the last, best word that God set forth. So neither conformed to the paradigm of Classical Judaism: in or out. And both monotheist religions explicitly rejected idolatry just as did Judaism. Indeed, Christians accepted martyrdom for the sake of sanctifying God's name (in the categories of Judaism) by rejecting pagan sacrifices. So, in medieval and modern times, the classical version of matters confronted facts it could not with facility dismiss or explain away.

If we leap over the centuries that intervene between the Rabbinic canon of the first six hundred years of the Common Era and our own day, we find an effort to construct an affirmative theology of Christianity (and by implication of Islam). A close look at the effort by Professor Jon D. Levenson suffices to summarize the outcome:

> *Dabru Emet* [the statement of a Judaic reading of Christianity that differentiates Christianity from other religions] essentially consists of eight theses of one sentence apiece (each of which is then followed by a brief explanatory paragraph):

1	Jews and Christians worship the same God.
2	Jews and Christians seek authority from the same book—the Bible (what Jews call "Tanakh" and Christians call the "Old Testament").
3	Christians can respect the claim of the Jewish people upon the land of Israel.
4	Jews and Christians accept the moral principles of Torah.
5	Nazism was not a Christian phenomenon.
6	The humanly irreconcilable difference between Jews and Christians will not be settled until God redeems the entire world as promised in Scripture.

| 7 | A new relationship between Jews and Christians will not weaken Jewish practice. |
| 8 | Jews and Christians must work together for justice and peace.[1] |

The claim that "Jews and Christians worship the same God" is more daring and more innovative than appears at first glance. Historically, it would not, to be sure, have met with much dissent among Christians. However much they have believed Jewish modes of worship to be literal, carnal, and obsolete, Christian orthodoxy early on anathematized the belief that theirs was a higher (and thus different) God from that of the Jews and their scriptures. But here – as generally in Jewish-Christian relations – asymmetry reigns, and simple reciprocity is a dangerous course indeed. For historically, Jews have not always been convinced that Christians worship their God. Maimonides, for example, the great Sephardic legal authority and philosopher of the twelfth century, explicitly classifies Christianity as idolatry, thus forbidding contact with Christians of the sort permitted with practitioners of other, non-idolatrous religions.[2] In the medieval Ashkenazic world as well, some authorities interpreted the monotheistic affirmation of the *Shema'*, the mandatory daily declaration of Jewish faith, as an outright denial of the Christianity doctrine of the Trinity.[3]

At issue is whether Christianity and Islam are to be differentiated from other religious traditions and accorded recognition as authentic monotheisms in line with the revelation of the Torah at Sinai. Self-segregationist Judaism, in closed communities, maintains the integrity of the classical traditions, But other communities of Judaism take up diverse positions on that issue. Conservative, Modern/integrationist Orthodox, Reform, Reconstructionist, New Age, Jewish Renewal, and other Judaisms do take up a more tolerant position vis-à-vis Christianity and Islam than does the normative canon. Some find authoritative foundations for differentiating Christianity and Islam from the idolatry so rigorously rejected by God in the Torah.

But the classical position challenges theological toleration within Judaisms. The Torah is God's word, by the criterion of which all other claims to speak for God are to be assessed — and by which in one aspect or another, all are found wanting. Accordingly, while, in part for political reasons, in part out of genuine conviction, Jews (whether practicing Judaism or not) express attitudes of tolerance and tolerate other religions, the classical response to the modern and contemporary challenge of religious toleration endures. That is, Judaism finds it difficult to validate those attitudes when its normative sources are interrogated. One would face formidable obstacles in attempting to compose out of the sources of the Halakhah and of the Aggadah a Judaic theology of Christianity and of Islam. A single narrative articulates the theological foundation of intolerance: the criterion of God's honest truth:

A.   The books of the Evangelists and the books of the minim they do not save from a fire. But they are allowed to burn where they are,

B.   they and the references to the Divine Name which are in them.

C.   R. Yosé the Galilean says, "On ordinary days, one cuts out the references to the Divine Name which are in them and stores them away, and the rest burns."

D.   Said R. Tarfon, "May I bury my sons, if such things come into my hands and I do not burn them, and even the references to the Divine Name which are in them.

E.   "And if someone was running after me, I should go into a temple of idolatry, but I should not go into their houses [of worship].

F.   "For idolators do not recognize the Divinity in denying him, but these recognize the Divinity and deny him.

G.   "And about them Scripture states, 'Behind the door and the doorpost you have set up your symbol for deserting me, you have uncovered your bed' (Is. 57:8)."

H.   Said R. Ishmael, "Now if to bring peace between a man and his wife, the Omnipresent declared that a scroll written in a state of sanctification should be blotted out by water, the books of the minim, which bring enmity between Israel and their Father who is in heaven, all the more so should be blotted out,

I.   "they and the references to the Divine Name in them.

J.   "And concerning them has Scripture stated, 'Do I not hate them that hate thee, O Lord? And do I not loathe them that rise up against thee? I hate them with perfect hatred, I count them my enemies' (Ps. 139:21-22)."

Tosefta Shabbat 13:5

There are ways of nurturing attitudes of respect and toleration for religious difference — including the right of the other to err — out of the resources of Judaism. But compromise and dissimulation and negotiation of matters of truth do not form one of them.

ENDNOTES

[1] Ibid., xvii-xx. All citations from *Dabru Emet* in this article are taken from these pages.

[2] Commentary on the Mishnah, *Abodah Zarah* 1:1.

[3] See Jacob Katz, *Exclusiveness and Tolerance: Studies in Jewish-Gentile Relations in Medieval and Modern Times* (Springfield, New Jersey: Behrman House, 1961), 18-19.

8

Does Classical Judaism Yield a Doctrine of Altruism?

Let me commence with a rough and ready definition of altruism, which permits us to begin with concrete data. That definition is simple: altruism is unselfish, un-rewarded behavior that benefits others at a cost to oneself. The many refinements and complexities of the matter will enter in due course. It is difficult to imagine that a critical position for altruism will present itself in a religious tradition that takes as its watchword, "You will love your neighbor as yourself" (Lev. 19:18), meaning, not more than yourself, and which teaches, "Your life takes priority over the life of another." In Judaism one is expected to give up one's life for God, "for the sanctification of God's name," which means, accept death as a martyr rather than publicly commit idolatry, murder, or sexual impropriety. Accepting martyrdom under less exalted auspices than God's is difficult to validate. For example, the law assigns priority to the life of a woman in childbirth over that of the foetus until the baby is born:

A.   The woman who is in hard labor — they chop up the child in her womb and they remove it limb by limb, because her life takes precedence over his life.

B.   If its greater part has gone forth, they do not touch him, for they do not set aside one life on account of another life.

Mishnah-tractate Yebamot 7:6

Here at the very critical transaction of childbirth, an act of self-sacrifice is not demanded of the mother, even as it cannot be demanded of the foetus. We should not anticipate that the religious system represented by these rulings and comparable ones altruism meaning more than a generous spirit toward others will find form a dominant motif. But a more systematic account of Judaism is required for characterizing the normative position. What we shall see is that for systemic theological reasons, altruism in any rigorous definition — meaning, anything beyond mere philanthropy in a broad sense — does not apply. If it finds a natural home in Christianity, that too is for systemic reasons, particular to the theological narrative of Christianity, not to the generic religiosity characteristic of all religious traditions, if we may speak of the generic in the context of religion at all.

i. IDENTIFYING NORMATIVE DOCTRINE IN LAW AND THEOLOGY OF JUDAISM

When we want to identify the normative doctrine of a particular religion, we have first of all to explain how we go about the task. Like the other enduring religions that appeal to the authority of canonical documents, Judaism sets forth a mass of opinions, in law and theology alike, and over time these opinions change. Not only so, but matters of context and proportion demand consideration, since interpreting data demands attention to the circumstance in which an opinion registers and the importance, relative to the religious system as a whole, of a particular ruling. Issues of taste and judgment also enter in, therefore, when we wish to describe, analyze, and interpret particular laws and doctrines of a given religious tradition.

In the case of Judaism, moreover, the absence of central institutions, e.g., an authority comparable to the papacy, and the reliance on consensus of the faithful form massive obstacles to defining normative doctrine. That is still more complicated because the ethnic group, the Jews, tends to confuse itself with the religious tradition, Judaism, so that people define Judaism as the religion of the Jews. That definition does not serve since the Jews, like other ethnic groups, exhibit diverse and contradictory convictions on matters of religion. And even by "Judaism" diverse communities mean diverse and conflicting things. Any account of a particular doctrine must therefore specify the source for the normative rule — whether theological or legal — and its context in the particular, encompassing and larger system to which reference is made.

Since our problem in the matter of altruism focuses on issues of definition and systemic coherence, I represent the doctrine of Judaism in its classical context, provided by the Hebrew Scriptures of ancient Israel as mediated by the Rabbinic authorities of the first six centuries of the Common Era. Their writings of legal exposition and Scriptural interpretation form a coherent system of law and theology, and they have defined the norm for Judaism from antiquity to modern times. Diverse Judaic religious systems from the nineteenth century forward have evaluated the Classical writings in diverse ways, but for most, though not all, of the Judaisms of contemporary times continue to consult those writings and accord to them normative standing, if in some instances allowing them only a vote but not a veto on contemporary practice and belief. The "classical Judaism" under discussion here, therefore, is comprised by the legal and theological system that animates the Rabbinic canon.[1] Any account of a Judaic doctrine must encompass two different types of writing, legal or Halakhic and theological or Aggadic. For my exemplary cases of altruism, I have chosen a theological narrative and a legal exposition of the hierarchy of philanthropic conduct, respectively.

II. ALTRUISM AS UNSELFISH BEHAVIOR TO THE BENEFIT OF OTHERS IN JUDAIC THEOLOGY

Narratives of singular acts of altruistic conduct do circulate in the formative canon of normative Judaism. What we shall now see is a set of stories about how heavenly favor is shown to a simple man by reason of his self-sacrifice for which no reward was anticipated. Important in these stories is that no articulated religious obligation — mitzvah or commandment — is thereby carried out. It is supererogatory conduct. Through deeds that the law of the Torah cannot require but must favor one commits an act of altruism: beyond the measure of the law. This encompasses what one does on one's own volition, beyond a commandment of the Torah that embodies God's volition:

YERUSHALMI TAANIT 1:4.I.

L.   A certain ass driver appeared before the rabbis the context requires: in a dream and prayed, and rain came. The rabbis sent and brought him and said to him, "What is your trade?"

M.   He said to them, "I am an ass driver."

N.   They said to him, "And how do you conduct your business?"

O.   He said to them, "One time I rented my ass to a certain woman, and she was weeping on the way, and I said to her, 'What's with you?' and she said to me, 'The husband of that woman me is in prison for debt, and I wanted to see what I can do to free him.' So I sold my ass and I gave her the proceeds, and I said to her, 'Here is your money, free your husband, but do not sin by becoming a prostitute to raise the necessary funds.'"

P.   They said to him, "You are worthy of praying and having your prayers answered."

The ass-driver clearly has a powerful lien on Heaven, so that his prayers are answered, even while those of others are not. What he did to get that entitlement? He did what no law could demand: impoverished himself to save the woman from a "fate worse than death." He had no expectation of reward. He did not ask the Rabbinic sages about his power to pray for rain, they asked him. His act of altruism was to give up his means of making a living.

YERUSHALMI TAANIT 1:4.I.

Q.   In a dream of R. Abbahu, Mr. Pentakaka "Five sins" appeared, who prayed that rain would come, and it rained. R. Abbahu sent and summoned him. He said to him, "What is your trade?"

R.   He said to him, "Five sins does that man I do every day, for I am a pimp: hiring whores, cleaning up the theater, bringing home their garments for washing, dancing, and performing before them."

S.   He said to him, "And what sort of decent thing have you ever done?"

T.   He said to him, "One day that man I was cleaning the theater, and
            a woman came and stood behind a pillar and cried. I said to her,
            'What's with you?' And she said to me, 'That woman's my husband
            is in prison, and I wanted to see what I can do to free him,' so I
            sold my bed and cover, and I gave the proceeds to her. I said to her,
            'Here is your money, free your husband, but do not sin.'"

U.   He said to him, "You are worthy of praying and having your prayers
            answered."

The second story moves us still further, since the named man, a reprobate,
has done everything sinful that one can do, and, more to the point, he has done and
does wicked deeds every day. So we are shown the singularity of the act of altruism,
which suffices if done only one time to outweigh a life of sin. Here too the man sold
the necessities of life to spare the woman a life of sin.

These narratives meet the requirements of our preliminary definition: action
that is unselfish and gratuitous, carried out, without anticipated reward, to the actor's
disadvantage. Whether the set of stories qualifies by a more rigorous definition
remains to be seen. The set occurs in an authoritative document, and it is clearly
intended to encourage self-sacrifice in behalf of another.

The issue of context and proportion, however, presents itself. May we
characterize the system that values these stories as an altruistic one? In the context
of Rabbinic Judaism, with its emphasis on the priority of learning in the Torah as a
means of acquiring merit, the two players — the unlettered man, the woman in each
story — represent outsiders. The system's norms — mastery of the Torah, consistent
conformity to the law, maleness — are not met. Neither is represented as a master
of Torah-learning. In the setting of Rabbinic Judaism, with its stress on the long-
term disciplines of the law, leading to a life of piety lived out in consistent daily
discipline, the stories' make a further point. A single action accomplishes what an
entire life of piety and Torah-learning accomplishes.

In both cases — the unlettered man, the woman excluded by definition,
and also the single action outweighing a life of sin — we therefore deal with a
systemic reversal: outsiders who do not keep the law acting beyond the outer
requirements of the law. The transvaluation of values accomplished by the narratives
indicates we have located the very heart of the system: provision for the spontaneous
in the midst of the routine. And that singular act, which outweighs all else, embodies
what God cannot command but what man can freely give: un-compensated self-
sacrifice. In the setting of the creed, "You will love the Lord your God with all your
heart, soul, and might," altruism conforms to the paradigm of the relationship for
which God yearns but which only human beings can realize of their own free will:
love, which cannot be commanded and coerced, only responded to, by God. So
much for an Aggadic representation of altruism. But altruism cannot be represented
as the norm.

What about a Halakhic formulation? The system makes its normative statements in law, not in narrative, and so we have to turn to a legal document for an authoritative picture of the way in which our rough-and-ready definition of altruism guides us to a view of Judaism on that matter. I turn to part of the definition of proper philanthropy — the Hebrew word is *tzedakah*, righteousness — that is set forth by Moses Maimonides (1135-1204), who codified the law of the Talmuds, commentaries, and existing codes, in a highly systematic and rational statement. He sets forth "the eight stages of Tzedakah." What we wish to identify is a place for altruism in the transactions of philanthropy:

> There are eight degrees of tzedakah, each one superior to the next.
>
> 1. Than which there is none higher, is the one who upholds the hand of an Israelite reduced to poverty by handing that person a gift or loan, or by entering into a partnership with him or her, or by finding that Israelite work, in order to strengthen that person's hand, so that she or he will have no need to beg from others. Concerning such a person it is stated, You shall uphold that one, as a stranger and a settler shall that person live with you — meaning, uphold that person, so that she or he will not lapse into want.
>
> 2. Below this is one who gives alms to the poor in such a way that the giver knows not to whom the alms are given, nor does the poor person know from whom the alms are received. This constitutes the fulfilling of a religious duty for its own sake, and for such there was a chamber of secrets in the Temple, where the righteous would contribute sums secretly, and where the poor of good families would draw their sustenance in equal secrecy. Close to such a person is the one who contributes directly to the charity fund.
>
> 3. Below this is the person who knows the one receiving while the poor person knows not from whom the gift comes. Such a donor is like the great among the sages who would set forth secretly, throwing money before the doors of the poor. This is an appropriate procedure, to be preferred if those administering charity funds are not behaving honorably.
>
> 4. Below this is the instances in which the poor knows the identity of the donor, but remains unknown to the donor. The giver is thus like the great among the sages who would place money in the folded corner of a linen sheet, throw the sheet over their shoulders, and allow the poor to come up form behind them and remove the money without being subject to humiliation.
>
> 5. Below this is the one who hands charity directly to the poor before being asked for it.
>
> 6. Below this is the one who hands charity to the poor after the poor has requested it.
>
> 7. Below this is the one who gives to the poor less than what is appropriate, but gives it in a friendly manner.

8. Below this is the one who gives charity with a scowl.

At what point does an act of philanthropy qualify as altruistic? It enters in at the seventh stage, when the donor is anonymous and gets no public credit for his action, and when the donor also does not know to whom the funds have gone. Then the self-sacrificial act — the surrender to the other of scarce resources — is done "for its own sake," not for the sake of a reward. That is the second highest level of philanthropy. But the donor pleases Heaven and furthermore gains satisfaction from knowing that he has helped some poor person, if not a particular one. He has carried out an obligation to Heaven, such as philanthropy embodies. It is difficult to represent the transaction as true altruism, un-rewarded self-sacrifice. That systemic representation of virtuous actions in response to God's commandments leaves little space indeed for truly altruistic conduct in the normative Judaism.

The highest has no bearing on our problem but embodies a social philosophy for philanthropy beyond altruistic limits. The highest form of philanthropy is attained through rendering philanthropy altogether unnecessary: giving a fish hook, not a fish. That matter has no bearing on our problem, so we stop at the seventh level. On the surface, therefore, we may say that Classical Judaism does set forth a doctrine of altruistic behavior: acts of love for the other that are not only not done for the sake of a reward but that also exact a cost in the resources or circumstances of the altruistic actor. Let us turn to the analytical program that animates this exercise and broaden the frame of reference. For the examples offer merely suggestive, not probative evidence for altruism in normative Judaism.

It remains to ask, how does Judaism represent the act of self-sacrifice for the good of the community at large? Does such an act qualify as unselfish self-sacrifice for the public welfare? Can Judaism say, no greater merit attaches to any deed than to giving up one's life for one's fellow, for the public good? We have such a case described in the setting of Joshua's exchange with Achan. In the description of how the death penalty was inflicted, the law of the Mishnah invokes the case of Achan in connection with the confession. Specifically, Joshua 7 tells the story of how the Israelites lost a skirmish in conquering the Land and blamed it on a sin committed in their midst. Joshua located Achan, who had violated the divine instruction on the disposition of the spoils of war, and this is how the Mishnah represents the transaction:

A.   When he was ten cubits from the place of stoning, they say to him, "Confess," for it is usual for those about to be put to death to confess.

B.   For whoever confesses has a share in the world to come.

C.   For so we find concerning Achan, to whom Joshua said, "My son, I pray you, give glory to the Lord, the God of Israel, and confess to him, and tell me now what you have done; hide it not from me." And Achan answered Joshua and said, "Truly have I sinned against

the Lord, the God of Israel, and thus and thus I have done" (Josh.
7:19). And how do we know that his confession achieved atonement
for him? For it is said, "And Joshua said, Why have you troubled
us? The Lord will trouble you this day" (Josh. 7:25) — *This day
you will be troubled, but you will not be troubled in the world to
come.*

D.   And if he does not know how to confess, they say to him, "Say as
follows: 'Let my death be atonement for all of my transgressions.'"

M. Sanhedrin 6:2

At issue is the welfare of the community. Achan sacrifices himself for its
future relationship with God. But it is to his own advantage. He enjoys a very
concrete reward: atonement and reconciliation with God, leading to eternal life.
Within the very center of the Halakhic exposition comes the theological principle
that the death-penalty opens the way for life eternal. Achan pays the supreme penalty
but secures his place in the world to come. This is not an act of altruism at all, but
an act of repentance committed to Achan's own advantage.

III. IN THE SOURCES OF JUDAISM IN ITS CLASSICAL CANON, WHAT ARE THE MAJOR
CATEGORIES OF BEHAVIOR FOR THE WELFARE OF OTHERS?

Now when we turn to the agenda of issues of altruism addressed to the
principal religious traditions of humanity, we place into systemic context the episodic
lessons just now set forth. What we have seen is, we can find narratives that value
altruistic behavior conventionally defined. But do these represent a systemic
component of critical consequence? In context does altruistic behavior define a
norm of everyday conduct, or an exception to what is expected in ordinary
circumstances? We answer the question by asking how the system that tells these
stories provides for the welfare of others in a workaday world of common folk, not
in a world of transvaluation and exceptional conduct. We begin with classifications
for the welfare of others. Judaism does not leave to the vagaries of human initiative
and volition the systematic maintenance of the poor, needy, and disempowered. It
provides obligatory support and does so as a matter of routine. It is a religious duty
to support the poor, and this is in concrete and detailed patterns. Altruism does not
enter in to action for the welfare of others, conventionally construed, which is
commanded and not self-initiated.

To ask the Halakhic system of Judaism how it makes provision for the
welfare of others is to demand a comprehensive survey of the system viewed whole.
For the Halakhic system portrays a comprehensive account of the social order, all
things in proper place, all transactions yielding a proportionate outcome. What the
individual component of the social order, the private person, does must take account
the rights of others in that same society. The law covering economic transactions
— the disposition of scarce resources — rests on a theory of distributive economics

that prohibits one party to an exchange from emerging with more value than he brought to the transaction, another with less. The system understands by welfare, moreover, relationships of not only a social but a supernatural character. The conduct of the Temple offerings yields atonement for the collective sin of all Israel, the holy people, and forms a critical component of the public welfare.

But the conventional category of "welfare of others" addresses the support of the poor, the landless, the unempowered. That encompasses in the case of the Halakhic system the priests and Levites, who are landless, as well as the poor. What is important is that the same procedures apply. God and the householder are deemed partners in the ownership of the Land of Israel, and when the householder lays claim on his share of the crop, God's interest in the crop is provoked, and his share is to be set aside. Then the householder must set aside God's share of the crop to be given to the priesthood for their rations and to the poor for their support. Professor Roger Brooks states the matter definitively:

> Tractate Peah asserts that needy Israelites are entitled to a portion of each crop that grows on the Land of Israel. The householder must designate some of his produce to meet this entitlement, while other gifts become the property of the poor entirely through processes of accident. What these various types of food have in common is the fact that they are reserved for the poor alone—no one else may eat them. So the fundamental claim of this tractate is that the poor should receive some bit of the Land's yield for their exclusive use. This notion of poor-relief emerges through Mishnah's discussion of the procedures for designating and distributing the several poor-offerings mentioned in Scripture. Tractate Peah deals with each offering specified in the Mosaic Codes in the order in which they are separated during the harvesting process: that which grows in the rear corner of the field (*peah*; Lev. 19:9; 23:22), gleanings (Lev. 19:9; 23:22), forgotten sheaves (Deut. 24:19), separated grapes (Lev. 19:10), defective clusters (Lev. 19:10; Deut. 24:21), and poorman's tithe (Deut. 26:12). In sum, the tractate takes as its topic the entire repertoire of Scriptural references to poor-offerings....
>
> What conception stands behind this analogy between the poor and the priests? It is their common claim on God for protective support. Because neither group possesses a portion of the Land of Israel, neither can produce the food it needs. The priests, for their part, are forbidden by Scriptural law to own land (see Deut. 18:1-5). Instead, they act as God's servants in the Temple and are accorded food on that account. Similarly, the poor have lost whatever portion of the Land they may have possessed, and so are entitled to receive some of its yield. God supports both the priests and the poor because they neither own land nor attain the economic prosperity promised to all Israelites who live in the Land (see Deut. 8:7-10).
>
> These claims on God are satisfied through the action of the ordinary Israelite householder. As a tenant farmer, he works God's Land

and enjoys its yield, with the result that a portion of all that he produces belongs to God. In order to pay this obligation, Israelites render to the priests grain as heave offering, tithes, and other priestly rations. Similarly, a specific portion of the Land's yield is set aside, by chance alone, for the poor. So underlying the designation of both priestly rations and poor-offerings is a single theory: God owns the entire Land of Israel and, because of this ownership, a portion of each crop must be paid to him as a sort of sacred tax (see Lev. 27:30-33). According to Mishnah's framers, God claims that which is owed him and then gives it to those under his special care, the poor and the priests.[2]

The support for the poor and the priesthood cannot be classified as altruistic. It is routine, not spontaneous; it is exacted as an obligation, it does not fall beyond the measure of the law; above all, it yields a benefit to the donor, who thereby acquires access to the portion of the crop that God, as landowner, assigns the householder, as tenant farmer, for his share. The absence of intentionality is striking: the selection of the portion of the crop for the priests' rations and the poor is done by chance.

We have now eliminated from the realm of altruistic conduct three classifications of activity for the welfare of others: donations to the sacrificial service in the Temple, exchanges of scarce resources in commercial transactions, broadly construed, and donations to the support of scheduled castes, the priesthood and the poor. All these represent areas in which the criteria of altruistic conduct do not pertain. On the contrary the good that is done for others produces a commensurate advantage for the one who does the deed.

Does nothing correspond? A saying in the collection of wise sayings, The Sentences of the Fathers (tractate Pirqé Abot), captures the matter:

A.	There are four sorts of people.
B.	(1) He who says, "What's mine is mine and what's yours is yours" — this is the average sort.
C.	(And some say, "This is the sort of Sodom.")
D.	(2) "What's mine is yours and what's yours is mine" — this is a boor,
E.	(3) "What's mine is yours and what's yours is yours" — this is a truly pious man.
F	(4) "What's mine is mine and what's yours is mine" — this is a truly wicked man.

Tractate Abot 5:10

Here we find ourselves near the conception of altruistic conduct: un-rewarded, unselfish sacrifice for another. It comes with the truly pious man, who does not take but gives and is truly pious. The conduct of Mr. Five-Sins would qualify — if he knew that Heaven would ignore his behavior and acted deliberately on condition that he not be compensated. The story does not suggest whether or not those conditions have been met.

IV. BEHAVIOR FOR THE WELFARE OF OTHERS: WHAT IS MEANT BY "OTHERS"? WHAT DOES THE RELIGION MEAN BY "OTHERS" BOTH DOCTRINALLY AND HISTORICALLY? FOR EXAMPLE, IN THE CLASSICAL TEXTS, DO "OTHERS" INCLUDE PEOPLE OUTSIDE OF THE RELIGIOUS COMMUNITY?

Who is the "other" who is the object of altruistic conduct? Our opening narratives assume we deal with Israelites in an interior transaction. The support for the poor outlined in tractate Peah and described by Professor Brooks sustains Israel's scheduled castes. The systematization of levels of philanthropy explicitly refers at the highest level to making it possible for an Israelite to support himself. The four types of possessors in tractate Abot recapitulate the same assumption, that we speak of transactions within the community of Israel. The Judaic theology of the gentiles, which sees them as an undifferentiated phalanx of enemies of God, who worship idols deliberately ignoring the truth, leaves little basis for affirming altruistic conduct toward "others." On the contrary, even ordinary transactions that express simple compassion are subjected to doubt:

A	They do not leave cattle in gentiles' inns,
B	because they are suspect in regard to bestiality.
C	And a woman should not be alone with them,
D	because they are suspect in regard to fornication.
E	And a man should not be alone with them,
F	because they are suspect in regard to bloodshed.
G	An Israelite girl should not serve as a midwife to a gentile woman,
H	because she serves to bring forth a child for the service of idolatry.
I	But a gentile woman may serve as a midwife to an Israelite girl.
J	An Israelite girl should not give suck to the child of a gentile woman.
K	But a gentile woman may give suck to the child of an Israelite girl,
L	when it is by permission.

Mishnah-tractate Abodah Zarah 2:1

A	They accept from them healing for property,
B	but not healing for a person.
C	"And they do not allow them to cut hair under any circumstances," the words of R. Meir.
D	And sages say, "In the public domain it is permitted,
E	"but not if they are alone."

Mishnah Abodah Zarah 2:1-2

The prevailing attitude of suspicion of gentiles derives from the definition of gentiles: idolaters, enemies of God. One should not anticipate a rich repertoire of rulings on how one must sacrifice for the welfare of the gentile-other. I cannot point to narratives that suggest one must, let alone laws that obligate it. There is motivation to sacrifice for the outsider: one supports the poor of the gentiles "for the sake of peace:

L.   They do not prevent poor gentiles from collecting produce under the laws of Gleanings, the Forgotten Sheaf, and the Corner of the Field, in the interests of peace.

                                        Mishnah-tractate Gittin 5:8

1.   And they inquire after their [gentiles'] welfare,

J.   in the interests of peace.

                                        Mishnah-tractate Gittin 5:9

This is not un-rewarded behavior, carried out gratuitously. It is a matter of sound public policy, leading to communal peace and amity. "They do not prevent...," "they inquire after their welfare" — minimal gestures of common courtesy prevent needless enmity. They accommodate the gentile-other, they do not accord selfless love to him. Altruism within Judaism is embodied in stories that presuppose the Israelite identification of the actors and beneficiaries. Judaism sets forth a social system that distinguishes, in humanity, those that know and love God from those that serve idols and hate God.

v. How does Judaism assess the meaning of behavior for the welfare of others? For instance, does it assess such behavior in terms of its impact on the recipient, in terms of the action itself, in terms of the motivation or intention of the actor, or some combination of the above? If the actor's intention or motivation is a factor in determining the action's meaning, how is intention or motivation known and assessed? Does the actor determine what motivated the action, or is there some other source that makes such a determination?

To answer these questions, we turn back to the narratives of extraordinary, altruistic conduct set forth at the outset. We begin with a reprise of one of the two stories; the other follows the same pattern.

Yerushalmi Taanit 1:4.I.

Q.   In a dream of R. Abbahu, Mr. Pentakaka "Five sins" appeared, who prayed that rain would come, and it rained. R. Abbahu sent and summoned him. He said to him, "What is your trade?"

R.   He said to him, "Five sins does that man I do every day, for I am a pimp: hiring whores, cleaning up the theater, bringing home their garments for washing, dancing, and performing before them."

S.   He said to him, "And what sort of decent thing have you ever done?"

T.   He said to him, "One day that man I was cleaning the theater, and a woman came and stood behind a pillar and cried. I said to her,

'What's with you?' And she said to me, 'That woman's my husband is in prison, and I wanted to see what I can do to free him,' so I sold my bed and cover, and I gave the proceeds to her. I said to her, 'Here is your money, free your husband, but do not sin.'"

U.   He said to him, "You are worthy of praying and having your prayers answered."

Let us now take up each of the questions in turn. How does Judaism assess the meaning of behavior for the welfare of others? The story before us values conduct for the welfare of others. This valuation is attributed to heaven. When Mr. Five Sins prayed for rain, rain would follow. The context in which the capacity to pray for rain and elicit a response from Heaven is defined by the public liturgy for communal prayers, as follows:

A.   (1) For the first [ending] he says, "He who answered Abraham on Mount Moriah will answer you and hear the sound of your cry this day. Blessed are you, 0 Lord, redeemer of Israel."

B.   (2) For the second he says, "He who answered our fathers at the Red Sea will answer you and hear the sound of your cry this day. Blessed are you, 0 Lord, who remembers forgotten things."

C.   (3) For the third he says, "He who answered Joshua at Gilgal will answer you and hear the sound of your cry this day. Blessed are you, 0 Lord, who hears the sound of the shofar."

D.   (4) For the fourth he says, "He who answered Samuel at Mispeh will answer you and hear the sound of your cry this day. Blessed are you, 0 Lord, who hears a cry."

E.   (5) For the fifth he says, "He who answered Elijah at Mount Carmel will answer you and hear the sound of your cry this day. Blessed are you, 0 Lord, who hears prayer."

F   (6) For the sixth he says, "He who answered Jonah in the belly of the fish will answer you and hear the sound of your cry this day. Blessed are you, 0 Lord, who answers prayer in a time of trouble."

G.   For the seventh he says, "He who answered David and Solomon, his son, in Jerusalem, will answer you and hear the sound of your cry this day. Blessed are you, 0 Lord, who has mercy on the Land."

Mishnah-tractate Taanit 2:6

Able to pray for run and evoke a response from Heaven, Mr. Five-Sins now finds his classification in the great saints of Israel's history, saints acknowledged by Heaven's favor in precisely the same way in which Mr. Five-Sins' virtue is acknowledged.

To the second question: does the law of Judaism assess such behavior in terms of its impact on the recipient, in terms of the action itself, in terms of the motivation or intention of the actor, or some combination of the above? I find here a matter of judgment. The act is valued for its impact on the woman. But I think the narrator also admires the self-sacrifice that leads Mr. Five-Sins to give up his livelihood in favor of the woman. So the selfless action, joined to pure intention ("for its own sake") and its desired result, the saving of the woman from a fate worse than death, join together.

If the actor's intention or motivation is a factor in determining the action's meaning, how is intention or motivation known and assessed? I think the narrative takes for granted the intention and motivator of the actor: the capacity to make the trouble facing the other into one's own concern, the power to turn sympathy into empathy.

Does the actor determine what motivated the action, or is there some other source that makes such a determination? The narrator creates the entire transaction. The act is — and to qualify as altruistic must be — self-motivated, not in response to a religious duty or divine commandment, for there is no religious commandment in Judaism that imposes the obligation to sacrifice in behalf of the other. The important participant is the divine witness, God, who values that love that cannot be coerced or commanded but only elicited by one's own capacity for empathy and empathetic response. God knows what motivated the action. That is because God's record, in the context of responding to the prayers of Abraham at Moriah, Israel at the Sea, Joshua at Gilgal, Samuel at Mispeh, Elijah at Carmel, Jonah in the fish, and David and Solomon at Jerusalem — God's record is what is replicated by Mr. Five-Sins. He has acted like God in responding to pathos, and his selfless service is what a human being can do to act like God.

VI. DOES JUDAISM CREATE A CONTEXT IN WHICH IT IS POSSIBLE THAT INTENTIONAL ACTION FOR THE WELFARE OF OTHERS CAN HAVE ONLY A NEUTRAL OR NEGATIVE CONSEQUENCE ON THE ACTOR? IS IT POSSIBLE FOR ACTION ON BEHALF OF OTHERS TO HAVE NO BENEFICIAL CONSEQUENCE FOR THE ACTOR?

Nothing in this rapid review of some high points of the Judaic law and narrative of service to others suggests that action on behalf of others to have no beneficial consequence for the actor. On the contrary, the one who intentionally commits an act of altruism — selfless un-rewarded service to others at considerable cost to oneself — by definition cannot produce neutral, let alone negative, results for himself. Self-sacrifice for others elicits God's empathy. That is why it is not possible for an action for others to produce no consequence for the actor, such a possibility lies beyond the imaginative power of the system.

Once God craves but cannot coerce one's love, God's own record intervenes. What one gives freely, to one's own cost, is bound to win God's recognition and appreciation. The only difference between a good deed for others that is commanded by God, such as support for the poor, and a good deed that cannot be commanded by God, such as support for the poor that is beyond the measure of the law, is the greater response, in proportion, provoked in Heaven by authentic altruism on earth. But then, with such a reward in prospect, as the narrative at hand underscores, self-sacrifice is not an act of altruism. Heaven itself, by its very nature, renders null the very category, selfless action for another's benefit without beneficial consequence for the actor. God is always present to assure appropriate response: "pray and one's prayers for rain are answered," for example. Altruistic conduct is difficult to locate in the classical statements of law and theology of Judaism. That is because the category-formations of that Judaism, with their stress on human obligation to carry out the divine will, with reward or punishment the consequence of obedience or rebellion, make no provision for a critical role of unselfish, un-rewarded behavior that benefits others at a cost to oneself. Altruism so defined is a-systemic, and I think, anti-systemic, since it turns virtuous conduct into supererogatory action, while the commandments govern: greater is the action of one who is commanded and acts than the one who is not commanded but acts, in context, to carry out a virtuous deed.

ENDNOTES

[1] The normative canon is comprised by the Mishnah, a philosophical law code of the late second century, and its documents of amplification and exegesis, the Tosefta, a collection of supplements to the Mishnah, of ca. 300 C.E., the Talmud of the Land of Israel, a commentary to thirty-nine of the Mishnah's sixty-three topical expositions or tractates, of ca. 400 C.E., and the Talmud of Babylonia, a comparable commentary to thirty-seven of the Mishnah's tractates, of ca. 600 C.E.; and about a dozen large compilations of exegesis of law and theology of Scripture called "Midrashim," which originate from the third to the seventh centuries. It is carried forward in later times by a continuous tradition of exegesis of law and Scripture.

[2] *The Law of Agriculture in the Mishnah and the Tosefta. Translation, commentary, theology.* Leiden, 2004-2006: E. J. Brill. II. *Peah.* Translation and commentary by Roger Brooks, p. 4.

9

A Documentary Reading of Rabbinic Compositions on 586, 70, and 132-135 in the Formative Canon

The documentary thesis of the Rabbinic canon of late antiquity maintains that the several canonical compilations, from the Mishnah through the Bavli, represent coherent viewpoints, each speaking for its compilers of its composites and authors of its compositions. A history of ideas of Rabbinic Judaism reconstructs the sequence of representations of ideas on a common theme set forth document by document. That approach represents a way around the reliance upon attributions to classify sayings in temporal sequence and produces a different kind of history.

The familiar approach to the history of Rabbinic Judaism in its normative canon takes up themes and collects and arranges whatever we find on a given theme from any Rabbinic source, early, middle, or late, or, indeed, goes so far as to collect and arrange anything located in any document attributed to Jewish authorship.

I maintain that topical collections obscure and do not illuminate the data. Let me first give a simple example of the futility of collecting and arranging whatever we find in the Rabbinic corpus of late antiquity on a given topic, the unwisdom of ignoring the documentary venue in which a given allegation makes its appearance. Now, to take a single problem, if we ask the Rabbinic sources, what, exactly, happened in 70, and why does Yavneh figure? the answer depends upon whom we ask, or, more precisely, what Rabbinic document we consult. The representation of what happened in and after 70 — and the meaning of the events — varies from one document to another — not as to details but as to the main point. In asking how Judaism responded to the catastrophe of 70 we do well to take account not only of pictures of Yavneh as the center of the story of the destruction of the Jerusalem sanctuary in 70, but also of accounts of the events of 70 that make no reference to Yavneh at all.

These are the results we may anticipate from a survey of how Rabbinic writings represent the destruction of the Temple and is consequences — either/or:

1. Beyond 70 Yavneh was the place of continuation, indeed the heir of Jerusalem. Or: Beyond 70 Yavneh does not figure.

2. Beyond 70 Yavneh happened to be where Rabbinic sages gathered and conducted a court. Or: Beyond 70 the law ignored Yavneh.

3. Yavneh was heir of, and corresponded to Jerusalem. As God left Jerusalem for the heavens, so the Torah left Jerusalem for Yavneh. It found its location on the chain of holy places beginning at Sinai and ending in Jerusalem restored. Or: Yavneh does not figure at all.

4. The Messiah is a principal issue made acute by the destruction of the Temple. Or: The Messiah does not figure at all after 70. The sage is the principal actor of 70. All that matters is Israel's own attitude, which the sages shape in accord with the pattern of the Torah.

5. We tell the story of the continuation of the Torah beyond the first 9th of Ab without invoking the activity of Yohanan ben Zakkai in Yavneh at all. Or we tell the story with Yohanan ben Zakkai at the heart of the matter. In the former, Yavneh provides the link, the next step in the sacred history of Israel the Jewish People. Yavneh does not figure, and 70 stands for *other continuities* altogether than those critical in the narrative of Yavneh.

All these alternatives and others too are made explicit in one source of another. What we see is that each narrative conveys a viewpoint. Every one of them offers the outcome of sustained thought about the topic, Judaism from 70, historical-political, religious-theological, and so on. So the multiple legacies of Yavneh — from enormous to null — emerge when we read each narrative, each composite of laws, on its own and in the context of the particular document that contains it. In the relationship between the picture of the world beyond 70 drawn by a particular story and the larger focus and interest of the document that contains that picture we are able to sort out the conflicts and make sense of the diversity of our sources on that one topic.

Such an analytical program represents an innovation in the study of formative Judaism. Until recently, we have tended to synthesize references to persons, places, and things scattered across the various Rabbinic writings of the formative age of Judaism, from the Mishnah through the Bavli. Taking everything at face value, people have defined as their task the rendition in a single continuous, coherent narrative of evidences that in fact convey diverse viewpoints. But since these not only conflict but derive from different periods, authorities, and writings, we miss the point of the diversity: the several modes of thought about, and consequent accounts of, what happened in and after the destruction of the Temple: the continuity of Israel, the Jewish people, and the Torah.

Now to the problem at hand, which is, how do the Rabbinic documents treat the events of 586, 70, and 132-135. What I investigate in the documentary thesis of the Rabbinic canon, illustrated here in connection with the destruction of the First Temple, 586, the second Temple, 70, and the Bar Kokhba War, 132-135, is the way in which the several successive components of the Rabbinic canon that address the matter of 586, 70 and 132-135 represent events and explain their consequence. The narratives that are selected and the foci and emphases that define them differ from document to document. One document dwells on the catastrophe, another pretends it never happened. A third lays its emphasis on a systematic statement through norms of conduct and conviction alike, a fourth treats the topic episodically and routinely. The character of a given document's treatment of 586, 70 and 132-135 forms an indicator of the program of that document itself. It corresponds to the document's animating theology, expressed in narrative, exegesis, and law.

What is at stake in this protracted survey of the entirety of a corpus of sayings and laws? The first and the more accessible result is to refine our understanding of the reading of 586, 70, and 132-135 in the formation of Rabbinic Judaism. We follow the discussions of those events set forth in successive documents and assess their importance in documentary context. The second outcome concerns how we are to reconstruct the history of ideas of Rabbinic Judaism. The problem addressed here — diverse documentary dispositions of the same persons, places, and things — fits into the theory I have advanced for some decades that Rabbinic documents of the late antique canon, first through seventh centuries, express the purposes and program of their respective compilers. They respond to the circumstances of the work of compilation. They set forth propositions, in emphasis and proportion congruent to those circumstances, to the program of the successive documents.

These questions predominate: What, exactly, did the compilers of the pertinent data in a given compilation encompass as an account of the war against Rome, the destruction of the Temple, and the consequences in law and theology for the community of Israel? What accounts for the inclusion of the matter of 586, 70 and of 132-135 in a given document, what message did the document wished to convey through its account of events (broadly defined, cultural as well as political), and why did the program of that document found it necessary to encompass the events at hand? I want to find out, in detail, what in the opinion of the compilers of this document happened in those fateful years, 586, 70 and 135, why in documentary context it mattered, and how that representation of matters advanced the program of the compilers of the document at hand. The narrative of how a document represents the events of 586, 70 and 132-135 bears a clear answer to the question of meaning and importance. The events of those years were widely known and long remembered. The ubiquity of knowledge that Jerusalem is lost and the Temple ruined is why to each document in its principal divisions I am able to address the same questions.

I. LOGGING IN THE TREATMENT OF 586, 70, AND 132-135, DOCUMENT BY DOCUMENT IN SEQUENCE

Now we undertake to characterize the Rabbinic treatment of the events of 586, 70, and 132-135. Here we survey the main points that register and gain perspective on the contents of the entire corpus. The characterization requires two exercises: recapitulation in succinct form of the entire corpus, ordering of the corpus document by document, by the criterion of successive documents' contributions to the unfolding of the complete repertoire of laws and theology.

First, we review the entries and identify the contribution made by each to the corpus of law and theology pertinent to the events under consideration. Where a given proposition first occurs, there I log it into my catalogue of responses to these specific catastrophes. Where it occurs later on, I simply note the document in which the narrative, exegesis, or proposition additionally makes its appearance. I treat as a single entry narratives or expositions that go over the same ground, ignoring the differences in detail. Thus the escape of Yohanan b. Zakkai, for example, constitutes a single entry on my master-list, even though it occurs in three (late) documents, Lamentations Rabbah, Fathers According to Rabbi Nathan, and the Bavli, each with its own detailed formulation of the incident.

The second step is to analyze in documentary sequence, item by item, the whole corpus of compositions and composites in which the events of 586, 70, and 132-135 figure. I list each idea in order of documentary appearance, then in the same point on my chart I indicate where it occurs in subsequent documents. That procedure affords a picture of the documentary history of the response to the destruction of the Temple recorded in the Rabbinic canon from the Mishnah through the Bavli. By that I mean, we can relate a component of the corpus of laws and propositions to the particular compilation that first puts forward said component: the program, policy, predilections of the compilers of that document.

I.	II.	III.	IV.	V.	VI.	VII.	VIII.	IX.	X.
Mish	Tan.	Yer.	Gen.	Lev.	PRK	Est.R	Lam.R	ARN	Bavli
Tos.	Mid.		R.	R.		Ruth.			
Abot	Mekh.					R.			
	Sifra					Song			
	Sif.					R.			
	Num.								
	Sif.								
	DT.								

	I.	II.	III.	IV.	V.	VI.	VII.	VIII.	IX.	X.

Items that first surface in the Mishnah

[The Mishnah's Halakhic items all recur in Tosefta, Yerushalmi, and Bavli.]

	I.	II.	III.	IV.	V.	VI.	VII.	VIII.	IX.	X.
1. Sukkot after 70	*	*	*							*
2. Shofar after 70	*	*	*							*
3. New Moon testimony	*	*	*							*
4. 17 Tammuz 9 Ab, events on	*	*	*							*
5. Nazirites after 70	*	*	*							*
6. Signs of mourning after 70; tear garment; make memorial mark. Excessive asceticism Discouraged.	*	*	*							*
7. Temple destruction marks an era for marking time.	*	*	*							*
8. New produce after 70	*	*	*							*
9. After 70, in Exile food taboos continue valid	*	*	*							*

	I.	II.	III.	IV.	V.	VI.	VII.	VIII.	IX.	X.

Items that first surface in the Tosefta or Abot

[These are in column one but differentiated here.]

	I.	II.	III.	IV.	V.	VI.	VII.	VIII.	IX.	X.
10. Destruction of Jerusalem effected atonement for its sins.	*			*	*					
11. Temple was destroyed for Israel's sins; including patriarchs' sins.		*	*	*	*					
12. On 9th of		*								

	I.	II.	III.	IV.	V.	VI.	VII.	VIII.	IX.	X.

Items that first surface in the Tosefta or Abot

[These are in column one but differentiated here.]Ab that falls

	I.	II.	III.	IV.	V.	VI.	VII.	VIII.	IX.	X.
on Sabbath one does not fast.										
13. Restoration* of Jerusalem will take place in the end of days.				*	*					
14. From the day on which the Temple was destroyed, there is no day on which there is no curse.		*								
15. Reason for destruction: Jerusalem's first building, on what account was it destroyed? Because of idolatry. licentiousness bloodshed But as to the latter building On what account did they go into exile? Because they love money and hate one another. Other reasons adduced in the same pattern, e.g., Sabbath, neglect Of children's education. Narratives convey the matter as well. This is a staple of the system.		*		*					*	*

	I.	II.	III.	IV.	V.	VI.	VII.	VIII.	IX.	X.

Items that first surface in Mekhilta, Sifra, or the two Sifrés
[These are situated in column II.]

	I.	II.	III.	IV.	V.	VI.	VII.	VIII.	IX.	X.
16. Three things* were given conditionally: the land of Israel, the house of the sanctuary, and the monarchy of the house of David										
17. They did not* want to count time in accord with the building of the sanctuary let them count time in accord with the date of its destruction; elaborated upon in story of how wealthy woman was destitute.								*		*
17. Martyrdom* of Ishmael & Simeon b. Gamaliel							*			
18. Israelites are* not to say, "Since we have gone into exile among the gentiles, let us act like them"										
19. Just the words* of Uriah have been Carried out, so in the end the words of Zechariah will come about							*			
20. Martyrdom* of Hanina b. Teradion; other Sages; various martyrs; martyrs get eternal life.		*			*	*	*		*	

	I.	II.	III.	IV	V.	VI.	VII.	VIII.	IX.	X.

Items that first surface in Yerushalmi.

[These are situated in column III.]

	I.	II.	III.	IV	V.	VI.	VII.	VIII.	IX.	X.
21. Messiah born on day Temple was destroyed			*							
22. Temple was destroyed when offerings ceased	*									
23. Any generation in the time of which the Temple is not rebuilt — Scripture regards it as if that generation itself had destroyed it	*									
24. God facilitated the Romans' war against the Jews (Tronianus); Babylonians too.	*			*			*			
25. God went into exile with Israel; nature too.			*			*		*		
26. Israel takes charge of its own fate: If Israel keeps a single Sabbath in the proper way, the son of David will come, and what is at stake is repentance and Sabbath rest.			*							
27. Bar Kokhba was arrogant and overconfident. He murdered a great sage in an act of temper.			*					*		
28. Burning of the Temple matched by the burning of the school houses	*				*					

	I.	II.	III.	IV.	V.	VI.	VII.	VIII.	IX.	X.

Items that first surface in Genesis Rabbah.
[These are situated in column IV.]

	I.	II.	III.	IV.	V.	VI.	VII.	VIII.	IX.	X.
29. Destruction of the Temple was part of God's plan for Creation.			*		*					
30. Israel constantly prays for rebuilding of the Temple.				*						
31. Romans permitted Israel to rebuild Temple but then reneged.					*					

	I.	II.	III.	IV.	V.	VI.	VII.	VIII.	IX.	X.

Items that first surface in Leviticus Rabbah.
[These are situated in column V.]

	I.	II.	III.	IV.	V.	VI.	VII.	VIII.	IX.	X.
32. Study laws of offerings equivalent to making the offerings.					*					
33. On the day on which the first Temple was dedicated, the sin committed that day persuaded God to destroy that Temple					*					
34. Israel is sick by reason of its separation from the Temple					*					

	I.	II.	III.	IV.	V.	VI.	VII.	VIII.	IX.	X.

Items that first surface in Pesiqta deRab Kahana.
[These are situated in column VI.]

	I.	II.	III.	IV.	V.	VI.	VII.	VIII.	IX.	X.
35. Rite of red cow read as a paradigm of Israel's loss of Temple.						*				
36. Babylonia was prepared in advance for Israel's exile.					*				*	
37. God mourned destruction like a mortal king					*		*			
38. God sent prophets to comfort Jerusalem						*				
39. Nations that destroyed Jerusalem will be destroyed						*				
40. Temple made a place for many more righteous ones when it was destroyed than it did when it was standing					*	*				
41. One who carries out penitence is regarded it as though he had gone up to Jerusalem, built the house of the sanctuary, built the altar, and offered on it all required offerings						*				

I.	II.	III.	IV.	V.	VI.	VII.	VIII.	IX.	X.

**Items that first surface in Esther Rabbah,
Ruth Rabbah, and Song of Songs Rabbah.**

[These are situated in column VII.]

42. The oath is imposed upon Israel that they not rebel against the yoke of the kingdoms. And the oath is imposed upon the kingdoms that they not make the yoke too hard for Israel. For if they make the yoke too hard on Israel, they will force the end to come before its appointed time – vs. Bar Kokhba.   *

43. GOD'S PLAN ENCOMPASSED DESTROYING THE TEMPLE AND REBUILDING IT. ISRAELITES WERE PUNISHED, BUT SO TOO WERE THE BABYLONIANS   *

44. GOD WILL PUNISH THE ROMANS FOR WHAT THEY DID IN BETHAR.   *

45. IF THE ISRAELITES HAD GONE UP LIKE A WALL FROM BABYLONIA, THE HOUSE OF THE SANCTUARY THAT THEY BUILT WOULD NOT HAVE BEEN DESTROYED A SECOND TIME.   *

	I.	II.	III.	IV.	V.	VI.	VII.	VIII.	IX.	X.

Items that first surface in Lamentations Rabbah.

[These are situated in column VIII.]

	I.	II.	III.	IV.	V.	VI.	VII.	VIII.	IX.	X.
46. GOD PUNISHED MOAB AND AMMON FOR TAUNTING ISRAEL BY ACCUSATIONS OF IDOLATRY							*			
47. ISRAEL LOST THE PRIESTHOOD AND THE MONARCHY BY REASON OF THE GOLDEN CALF								*		
48. ISRAEL IS ISOLATED AMONG THE NATIONS.							*			
49. THE ENTIRE CORPS OF PATRIARCHS AND MATRIARCHS AND PROPHETS ASSEMBLE AT THE DESTRUCTION, AND GOD RESPONDS TO THEIR PLEA BY PLEDGING TO RACHEL THAT HE WILL BRING THE ISRAELITES BACK TO THEIR LAND.							*			
50. God left Temple in ten stages.								*		*
51. Yohanan b. Zakkai escaped from Jerusalem and went over to Vespasian.							*	*	*	
52. God's demands for exclusiveness embittered Israel's relationships with her neighbors and closed their borders to Israel when it went in search of refuge.								*		
53. God took out his wrath on the building, not on the people, to whom he is still devoted.								*		

	I.	II.	III.	IV.	V.	VI.	VII.	VIII.	IX.	X.
54. Israelites' mutual enmity brought on the loss of the Temple and of the Jews' stronghold.							*			

	I.	II.	III.	IV.	V.	VI.	VII.	VIII.	IX.	X.

Items that first surface in Fathers According to Rabbi Nathan.

[These are situated in column IX.]

	I.	II.	III.	IV.	V.	VI.	VII.	VIII.	IX.	X.
55. We have another mode of atonement, which is like atonement through sacrifice — deeds of loving kindness. Torah-study as well.									*	*

	I.	II.	III.	IV.	V.	VI.	VII.	VIII.	IX.	X.

Items that first surface in the Bavli.

[These are situated in column X.]

	I.	II.	III.	IV.	V.	VI.	VII.	VIII.	IX.	X.
56. When Israelites go into synagogues and schoolhouses and respond, "May the great name be blessed," the Holy One shakes his head and says, "Happy is the king whom they praise in his house in such a way! What does a father have who has exiled his children? And woe to the children who are exiled from their father's table!"										*

The documents stand for themselves: the opinions of their compilers and the authors of the compositions that have been chosen. We do not know the state of opinion, either in the Rabbinic estate or in the Israelite population at large, either in the Land of Israel or in Babylonia (or Egypt and other parts of the Roman diaspora of Israel). What we gain is two things. First we acquire a sense for the relative positioning of pertinent propositions in the Rabbinic writings as they came to closure one by one. Second, and more to the point, we are able to identify the marks of a particular documentary interest in a given datum, first occurring in said document: why did this particular compilation emphasize this particular proposition? At stake is portrayal, as a cogent whole, of the bits and pieces that comprise the parts. My question concerns the generative logic that produced the particular details: what sense of self-evidence, what compelling principles of thought, stimulated the Rabbinic sages before us to make the concrete comments that they have set forth in particular contexts?

For the present purpose I have compiled a chart. It shows the provenance of each item of the fifty-six singular propositional or topical entries I have identified pertinent to 586, 70, and 132-135, from the Mishnah through the Bavli. In a few words, down the left hand column I allude to an idea, a law, an opinion or exegesis, in which 586, 70, or 132-135 figure, following the specified order. The vertical log makes possible the horizontal entries. In this way I show the order of appearance of specific topical or propositional items, and the later distribution of the same items among subsequently-closed documents.

I group the documents as follows: I. Mishnah-Tosefta-Abot; II. the Tannaite Midrash-compilations, Mekhilta, Sifra, and the two Sifrés; III. Yerushalmi; IV. Genesis Rabbah; V. Leviticus Rabbah; VI. Pesiqta de Rab Kahana; VII. Esther Rabbah, Ruth Rabbah, and Song of Songs Rabbah; VIII. Lamentations Rabbah; IX. Abot deRabbi Natan; X. Bavli. The documents thus are organized in likely sequence of closure. I am confident of the order of the items in groups I-VI and X, but am less certain of the order or even period of closure of the Rabbah-Midrash-compilations and Abot deRabbi Natan, VII-IX. I separate Lamentations Rabbah at VIII from the Rabbah-items fore and aft because of the volume of materials located in that document.

I stipulate in advance that Halakhic items in the Mishnah recur in the Tosefta, Yerushalmi, and Bavli. These are sustained and continuous discussions of a given Halakhic ruling, nearly all of them commencing in the Mishnah and continued in one way or another through the Tosefta, Yerushalmi, and Bavli. I do not trace the exegetical unfolding of the Halakhic compositions of the Mishnah (or the Tosefta).

I find fifty-six distinct entries, consisting of laws or narratives or theological propositions that contain a fundamentally fresh conception. I do not list ancillary items, generic references to the destruction of the Temple, for example.

II. MAIN PROPOSITIONS OF THE RABBINIC CORPUS

What do these fifty-six items add up to? I find the following propositions, which accommodate all the entries in my log:

1. After 70, adjustments and adaptations in the Halakhah took account of the destruction of the Temple, but the basic Halakhah endured: 1, 2, 3, 4, 5, 8, 9

2. Certain rites of mourning and repentance were adopted to respond to the destruction of the Temple, which was a time of penalty: 6, 7, 14, 34, 35

3. After 70, Israel could atone for sins through various means: 12, 32, 41, 51, 55

4. Destruction was part of God's plan from creation. The Temple was destroyed and Jerusalem was lost by reason of Israel's sins and failures; God facilitated the enemies' efforts; recriminations (e.g., what Israel did not do while

Temple stood they had to remember when it was in ruins): 11, 15 (elaborate presentation), 17, 22, 24, 29, 33, 43, 47, 53 (God punished the building, not the people), 54 (enmity brought about destruction)

5. Jerusalem will be restored at the end of days, when the Messiah will come and rebuild the Temple, land of Israel, temple, monarchy all were given conditionally and will be restored; just as prophecies of doom have been realized, so promises of restoration will be realized, when Israel keeps the Torah/Sabbath properly, all will follow: 13, 19, 21, 26, 30 (Israel prays for rebuilding), 38 (prophets comfort Jerusalem); 42 (Israel is not to hasten the coming of the Messiah but must wait patiently, and gentiles must not oppress Israel too much), 45 (when the time comes, respond en masse) 49 (patriarchs and matriarchs got God to pledge to restore Israel to the Land), 56 (God regrets exile)

6. Martyrs for God and Torah-study remembered, including those lost in burning of the schools: 17, 20, 28

7. Exile is no place to imitate gentiles; it is a place for Torah-study and penitence: 18, 36, 52 (separation from gentiles embitters relationships)

8. Any generation in which the Temple is not rebuilt is one responsible for Temple's destruction; Romans permitted rebuilding but reneged: 23, 31

9. God went into exile with Israel, left the Temple, mourned for the destruction and for Israel's suffering, and will punish the gentiles for their deeds: 25, 37, 39, 44, 46, 48, 50

10. Bar Kokhba and his fighters were arrogant toward God: 27

We may compose these data into a few fundamental propositions, which accommodate them all:

HALAKHAH: The law adjusts to the temporary inaccessibility of the Temple and suspension of its rites and provides for rites of mourning and atonement (1, 2, 3).

AGGADAH: What has happened to Israel expresses God's will, in particular God's response to Israel's own failings, such as neglect of the Torah, arrogance (10), and various sins against the social order. When Israel sins, it is punished by the nations, whom God uses as the rod of his wrath; when Israel atones through repentance, it may look forward to restoration (4, 5). Meanwhile, Israel shows its love for God through martyrdom for the sake of the Torah (6), remaining unique among the nations (7). God for his part shows his humanity by sharing Israel's suffering and mourning Israel's losses (9).

III. DOES THE DOCUMENTARY DISTRIBUTION BEAR SIGNIFICANCE?

Is the documentary distribution random or significant? And if significant, what does it signify? To answer that question, we must reconsider the data of the log. Our question now is, at what point does the documentary distribution of the components of the Rabbinic sages' treatment of the events of 586, 70, and 132-135 suggest a particular documentary venue for a distinctive idea or proposition?

Clearly, some documents have adopted and shaped for their larger program the theme of 586, 70, and 132-135 and treated that theme in a manner congruent with their purpose. That is the main upshot of the documentary analysis contained in the foregoing log.

That exercise of the documentary program in connection with the presentation of the particular events under review is certainly so in the case of the Mishnah, which treats the destruction, particularly in reference to 70 and 132-135, as an event to be noted. The Mishnah is uniformly Halakhic, and the Halakhah serves as its theological medium. The upshot is simply stated. The law of the Mishnah adapts itself to the consequences of the destruction (a matter to which we shall return in this evening's lecture).

The Tosefta is true to its character as a mixed bag, partly Mishnah-augmentation, partly Mishnah-exegesis, and partly an Aggadic supplement to the Mishnah. Here is where the enduring system of Scripture registers. The Aggadic component of the Tosefta sets forth the main theological response to the destruction: the Temple was destroyed by reason of Israel's sins, but will be restored at the end of days, and until then Israel must repent and responds to misfortune through repentance. In the two documents, the Mishnah and the Tosefta, we find the entire response to the calamities of 586, 70, and 132-135 put forth by Rabbinic Judaism in its formative canon viewed whole. Everything else would supply details within that established framework of sin, punishment, repentance, reconciliation and restoration.

To that fully articulated system, column II adds the recrimination that what Israel did not do willingly when it was in favor it now does in woeful circumstances. The prophetic admonitions have been realized, the consolation is sure to follow. Aqiba's invocation of the prophecies of punishment, which have been realized, as evidence of the reliability of the prophecies of restoration and reconciliation, does little more than articulate in the particular context of 70 the received prophetic heritage of Scripture.

The Yerushalmi, column III, introduces elaborate compositions on the Messiah-theme. That is not surprising, since the Yerushalmi is the first Rabbinic document in sequence to develop and naturalize the messiah-theme in the context of the Rabbinic system: if all Israel keeps a single Sabbath, the Messiah will come, "today, if you want." God facilitated the work of the enemies of Israel, but God went into exile with Israel. In the end Israel is in charge of its own fate and can bring the Messiah by keeping the Torah. Israel also brings down upon itself misfortune by reason of arrogance. The Yerushalmi's contributions prove cogent on their own and coherent with the received corpus of ideas.

The one important addition of Genesis Rabbah, column IV, is predictable: the introduction of the Temple's destruction into the larger plan for creation that

God had originally devised. Consistent with its predecessor, Leviticus Rabbah, column V, is equally well matched to Leviticus, with its interest in the offerings and the Temple and the plan for destruction in response to sins committed at its building.

Pesiqta deRab Kahana, column VI, draws us close to Lamentation Rabbah in its exposition of God's humanity, both his mourning for the Temple and his provision of a place for Israel's exile that would accommodate the people well, as well as his sending the prophets to comfort Jerusalem. Indeed, every item that first surfaces here is included in response to a lectionary occasion involving the 9th of Ab, the Sabbaths fore and aft, and the themes inherent on those Sabbaths of admonition and consolation. So the inclusion of the events of 586 and 70 and 132-135 forms part of the documentary program of Pesiqta deRab Kahana, which is to expound the lectionary cycle of special Sabbaths, encompassing those that commemorate the catastrophes of Jerusalem.

The entries for column VII, deriving from Esther Rabbah, Ruth Rabbah, and Song of Songs Rabbah, strike me as random and episodic. I see no documentary program that has shaped their treatment of the theme of the destruction.

Lamentations Rabbah, VIII, covers a vast amount of ground, even while contributing the portrait of the humanity of God, his weeping and mourning for Israel's suffering and loss. Its unique materials stand out for their elaborate character. Fully articulated narratives involving the destruction, God's abandonment of the Temple, the response of the patriarchs, matriarchs, and prophets to the event of 586/70 — these compositions and composites have no counterpart in any other document. The documentary program of a commentary on the book of Lamentations accounts for the unique focus of Lamentations Rabbah on 586/70/132-135.

The Fathers According to Rabbi Nathan, column IX, sets forth only one new item, an important one, which provides for substitutes for the Temple offerings when the Temple is in ruins. These involve those standards of Rabbinic Judaism, Torah-study and acts of loving kindness, the one quintessentially Rabbinic, the other adopted from prophecy. Since the Fathers According to Rabbi Nathan amplifies tractate Abot, the Fathers, we cannot find surprising the utilization of the theme of 70 in the exposition of the theme of tractate Abot, Torah study as the center of Israelite existence.

I see only a single item new to our corpus contributed by the Bavli, column X, and that continues the established theme of God's mourning for his children that Lamentations Rabbah has so elegantly articulated. It is not surprising that the Bavli, at the end, found little need to innovate but, as the Bavli's participation in many prior entries shows, much to recapitulate.

The documentary distribution cannot account for each compilation's contributions to the corpus of law, narrative, and theology devoted to the theme of the destructions of Jerusalem. But it does show a correlation between most of the several documents and their contributions to the articulation of the theme at hand.

IV. WHAT DID THE RABBINIC SAGES CONTRIBUTE?

The Rabbinic canon yields a coherent religious system for (theoretical) Israel's social order: *prophetic-Rabbinic Judaism*. The results to this point raise the next question: Can we characterize the Rabbinic sages' contribution as fundamental, or does the corpus of their responses to the destruction of the Temple and loss of Jerusalem appear derivative, a mere adaptation of received theological principles? And, in that very context, we wonder, whence the generative logic that animates the fifty-six detailed components of the log before us?

In my judgment, what the Rabbinic sages have accomplished is to recapitulate the prophetic theology of Jeremiah at the time of the first destruction in 586, which rests on the theodicy put forth by Moses for Ezekiel in Leviticus and for Jeremiah in Deuteronomy. And the generative logic in play is that of Moses and the prophets, who found a correlation between Israel's faithfulness to the covenant with God and Israel's fate in the Land and among the nations. It is a theology that focuses on theodicy: manifesting the justice of God in times of calamity. But, we cannot forget, the Rabbinic sages' manifest goal is not merely to justify God but to comfort suffering Israel and endow God's people with enduring hope: to enlist the patriarchs, matriarchs, and prophets in the task of restoring Israel's soul, as we see in Lamentations Rabbah.

To explain the answer to the question of the context, in the received Scriptures, of the Rabbinic theodicy, we ask, where have we heard, in prior documents, the conceptions that Israel is punished for its sins but rewarded for its humble obedience to God — the basic logic that animates the bits and pieces of our log? Moses in the admonitions of Leviticus 26 and Deuteronomy 34, Isaiah, Jeremiah, Ezekiel, and the Twelve prophets — wherever we turn we come across the basic pattern of stipulation and covenant that comes to the fore in the Rabbinic response to the events of 586, 70 and 132-135. It is no accident that that response attaches itself to Lamentations Rabbah in particular, forming of the commentary to Lamentations a veritable encyclopaedia of Rabbinic theodicy. The theodicy is, moreover, remarkable for its subtlety. For it does not suffice to recriminate and so register the justice of God in punishing Israel and the mercy of God in promising to respond to repentance, atonement, and a new beginning. Lamentations Rabbah is the document that registers the humanity of God, who shares in Israel's suffering and beyond recrimination undertakes to mourn for Israel's condition.

If in all this I had to specify the single contribution that the Rabbinic sages have made in this unfolding corpus of thought about what in our own times we have learned to call "the Shoah," it would not be the theodicy of justice, which draws all but minor details from Moses's teaching in Leviticus and Deuteronomy. It is, rather, the invocation, in consoling Israel, of God's broken heart. Rabbinic Judaism in its formative canon offered God's people the portrait of God as suffering with Israel and for Israel. It was that broken-hearted God sharing Israel's sorrow beyond all recrimination that was the chief endowment for the ages. Song of Songs Rabbah and Lamentations Rabbah, starkly contrasting with and complementing one another, together comprise the Rabbinic message of the God of passion and of tears. I cannot think of a corpus of Judaic writing prior to that of the Rabbinic sages — not in Philo, not in the Dead Sea Library, not in the Enoch-writings, not in Hebrew, Greek, or Aramaic — that portrays the patriarchs and matriarchs and prophets, and the very sages themselves, bearing witness to those tears. It was the humanity of God that for the ages persuaded Israel to rest its burden and its hope on the divinity of God.

10

Rabbinic Literature and the Christian Scriptures

I. THE STATE OF THE QUESTION

Because they share a common Scripture, the writings of early Christianity and of Rabbinic Judaism intersect. They form an ideal arena for the comparative study of religions: enough alike to validate comparison, enough unlike to yield interesting contrast. Each represents a choice that Scripture affords and each provides perspective upon the other.

What conclusions do people draw, however, from the intersection of teachings? Take for example one attributed to Jesus and to Hillel. Citing Leviticus 19:18, Jesus said as the Golden Rule, "You will love your neighbor as yourself." Citing the same verse, Hillel said, "What is hateful to yourself do not do to your neighbor; that is the entire Torah; all the rest is commentary; now go forth and learn." From the intersection of these two responses to Leviticus 19:18, scholars have set forth such conclusions as, "Jesus's formulation was superior because...," or "Hillel's was superior because...," or "Jesus was not original, because Hillel said it first...," or "Jesus was nothing more than a rabbi, like any other," and so on — comparative study in the service of religious polemics. But reciprocity prevails. Rabbinic literature may contribute to the study of the Christian Scriptures a keen perspective upon the choices the competing and opposing system embodies. And Christian writings offer counterpart illumination of Rabbinic Judaism. When for instance in discussing Genesis Rabbah we referred to Eusebius and Augustine, we asked Christianity to testify to issues faced by the fourth and fifth century Rabbinic sages.

But there are problems. Comparing and contrasting sayings and stories that first reached documentary closure in the third or fifth or seventh centuries with those of the letters of Paul and of the Gospels requires us to treat as first century writings what manifestly belong to much later centuries. That formidable objection can be overcome in one of two ways.

First, we undertake the act of faith that affirms all attributions as valid. In that case, why not give up the so-called critical quest for the historical Jesus — meaning, what he really said among the sayings attributed to him — and believe it all?

Or, second, we may redefine our quest altogether, asking for data of an-other-than-synchronic character to provide a perspective of a different kind from the narrowly-historical one. Work that yields little of value in the synchronic setting produces much of interest in the diachronic one.

Specifically, if we seek to characterize an entire religious system and structure — Rabbinic Judaism that records its Oral Torah in the score of documents from the Mishnah through the Talmud of Babylonia, the Christianity that reaches written form in the Gospels, the letter of Paul, the Church Fathers — diachronic work vastly helps. For characterizing wholes — the whole of one structure and system — gains nuance and detail when brought into juxtaposition with comparable wholes.

But how would such diachronic comparison of whole systems work? The basic premise of systemic description, analysis, and interpretation here enters in. The premise of systemic study of religions maintains that details contain within themselves and recapitulate the system as a whole, so that, from the parts, we can reconstruct much of the entirety of the structure, much as do anthropologists and paleontologists dealing with details of culture or of mammals, respectively. That premise flows from the very notion of a system — an entire structure that imparts proportion and cogency to details and that holds the whole together in a single cogent statement.

II. Comparing Gospels and Rabbinic Writings: An Aggadic Instance

For single concrete case I have chosen a parable that occurs in the Synoptic Gospels and in the Talmud of Babylonia, the one in the name of Jesus, the other of Yohanan ben Zakkai, who is assumed to have lived in the first century. Early on, people recognized that the parable set forth in Yohanan's name looks something like the one set forth in Jesus's, and they therefore asked Yohanan to clarify the sense and meaning of Jesus. But later on, most people conceded that a parable attributed to a first century authority in a seventh century compilation cannot be taken at face value to record what really was said and done on that singular day in the first century to which reference is made.

Diachronic reading of religious systems leads us past the impasse. But we learn then about the Christian system of the Gospels, the Judaic system of the Talmud of Babylonia. The shape and structure of Christianity and of Judaism then come under study and into perspective. Narrowly historical questions give way to broad and encompassing ones concerning the religious order. The parable allows for the comparison and contrast of religions.

What we shall see is how finding what Christian and Judaic canonical documents share permits a process of first comparison but then contrast. Likeness takes priority. When we see how matters are alike, we perceive the differences as well, and having established a solid basis for comparison, contrast proves illuminating. The parable concerns a king who gave a feast, but did not specify the time. Some people responded to the invitation wisely, some foolishly. Some were ready when the time came, some were not. The parable in that form contains no determinate message and does not hint at its own interpretation. That is all that the two religions have in common: the shared parable of the king who gave a banquet but did not specify the time. Everything else, as we shall see, is particular to the two religious traditions that utilized the parable, each for its own message. The contrast then permits us to show where each differs from the other, what each really wishes to say — no small point of clarification when it comes to the description and analysis of religions.

Let us consider, first, how the naked components of the parable are clothed in the formulation attributed to Jesus:

> And again Jesus spoke to them in parables, saying, "The kingdom of Heaven may be compared to a king who gave a marriage feast for his son and [1] sent his servants to call those who were invited to the marriage feast, but they would not come.
>
> "Again [2] he sent other servants, saying, 'Tell those who are invited, behold I have made ready my dinner, my oxen and ,my fat calves are killed, and everything is ready; come to the marriage feast.' But they made light of it and went off, one to his farm, another to his business, while the rest seized his servants, treated them shamefully and killed them. The king was angry, and he sent his troops and destroyed those murderers and burned their city. Then he said to his servants, 'The wedding is ready, but those invited were not worthy.
>
> "'[3] Go therefore to the thoroughfares and invite to the marriage feast as many as you find.' And those servants went out into the streets and gathered all whom they found, both bad and good, so the wedding hall was filled with guests. But when the king came in to look at the guests, he saw there a man who had no wedding garment, and he said to him, 'Friend, how did you get in here without a wedding garment?' And he was speechless. Then the king said to the attendants, 'Bind him hand and foot and cast him into the outer darkness; there men will weep and gnash their teeth. For many are called but few are chosen.'"
>
> Matthew 22:1-14/Luke 14:15-24 (RSV)

As Jesus shapes the parable, it tells a rather protracted and complicated story. That is because, read as a unitary formulation, the story of the king's feast is told thrice, and each version makes its own point. First, the king has issued invitations, but no one will come. This is made deliberate and blameworthy: people reject the invitation, and they do so violently: The wedding is ready, but those invited were not worthy. Then the king issues new invitations. People now come as they are. They had no choice, having been summoned without notice or opportunity to get ready. Those who are unready are punished: they should have been ready.

Then is tacked on a new moral: many are called but few are chosen. But no version of the parable of the king's fiasco matches that moral. The first version has many called, but those who are called either will not come (to the original feast) or are not worthy (of the second feast) but reject the invitation altogether. So in the first set of stories, many are called but nobody responds. In the third go-around, many are called and do show up, but a few — one man only — is unready. So the triplet is rather odd.

But the point is clear: the Kingdom of Heaven is at hand. Jesus is the son. People reject the invitation to the marriage feast, that is, the Kingdom of Heaven. The invitation is repeated: everything is ready. The invited people now reject the invitation violently and are themselves unworthy. In the third go-around there is no choice about coming; people are dragooned. Now the kingdom is at hand and people must enter. Some are ready, some not. All are judged in accord with their condition at the moment of the invitation — ready or not.

That is the point at which the Rabbinic version of the same story — the story about the king who made a feast and invited people — intersects with the Christian use of the parable. But to examine it in its context, we have to consider the text that utilizes the parable, not just the parable, which is not free-standing. If the context of the parable as Jesus utilizes it is the kingdom of Heaven and its sudden advent, the context in the Rabbinic version is everyday life, the here and now and the death that comes to everyone. That is what happens without warning, for which people must be ready. The text commences with generalizations: one should repent one day before he dies, and that means, every day. One should be ever-ready. This is linked to a verse in Qohelet 9:8, "Let your garments be always white and don't let your head lack ointment," which is taken to refer to keeping one's body in condition as a corpse, that is, dressed in white garments, the color of death in the Rabbinic writings, and properly anointed, as the corpse is anointed for burial.

The compositor of the construction of the Talmud of Babylonia has then added the parable of the king who invited people to a banquet. He set no specific time. Some kept themselves in readiness, some did not. Now the parable illustrates the teaching that one should be ready for the banquet that God will call at any moment — which is to say, one should be ready for death through a life of perpetual repentance:

B. SHABBAT 153A/M. SHAB. 23:5K-M I.44-45[1]

I.45 A.	*We have learned in the Mishnah there:* **R. Eliezer says, "Repent one day before you die"** [M. Abot 2:10D].
B.	His disciples asked R. Eliezer, "So does someone know just what day he'll die?"
C.	He said to them, "All the more so let him repent today, lest he die tomorrow, and he will turn out to spend all his days in repentance."

D.   And so, too, did Solomon say, "Let your garments be always white and don't let your head lack ointment" (Qoh. 9:8).

I.46 A.   ["Let your garments be always white and don't let your head lack ointment" (Qoh. 9:8)] — said R. Yohanan b. Zakkai, "The matter may be compared to the case of a king who invited his courtiers to a banquet, but he didn't set a time. The smart ones among them got themselves fixed up and waited at the gate of the palace, saying, 'Does the palace lack anything?' [They can do it any time.] The stupid ones among them went about their work, saying, 'So is there a banquet without a whole lot of preparation?'

B.   Suddenly the king demanded the presence of his courtiers. The smart ones went right before him, all fixed up, but the fools went before him filthy from their work. The king received the smart ones pleasantly, but showed anger to the fools.

C.   He said, 'These, who fixed themselves up for the banquet, will sit and eat and drink. Those, who didn't fix themselves up for the banquet, will stand and look on.'"

The passage bears a gloss, as follows:

D.   R. Meir's son in law in the name of R. Meir said, "They, too, would appear as though in attendance. But, rather, both parties sit, the one eating, the other starving, the one drinking, the other in thirst: 'Therefore thus says the Lord God, behold, my servants shall eat, but you shall be hungry, behold, my servants shall drink, but you shall be thirty, behold, my servants shall rejoice, but you shall be ashamed; behold, my servants shall sing for joy of heart, but you shall cry for sorrow of heart' (Isa. 65:13-14)."

A further treatment of the base-verse, Qoh. 9:8, transforms the emphasis upon the attitude of repentance in preparation for death to the practice of the faith, the reference to garments now alluding to show-fringes, and to the head to phylacteries:

E.   Another matter: "Let your garments be always white and don't let your head lack ointment" (Qoh. 9:8) —

F.   "Let your garments be always white": This refers to show fringes.

G.   "And don't let your head lack ointment": This refers to phylacteries.

Clearly, we have moved a long way from the triple banquet that Jesus has the king hold, and the parable serves remarkably disparate purposes. All that is shared is the common motif, the king who gave a feast and was disappointed in the result because people are unready. There are some corresponding developments, specifically, [1] diverse responses to the invitation, and [2] consequently, some are ready when the hour strikes, some not. Otherwise the versions of the parable scarcely intersect, as the following comparison shows:

Jesus	Yohanan ben Zakkai
"The kingdom of Heaven may be compared to <u>a king who gave a marriage feast</u> for his son	"The matter may be compared to the case of <u>a king who invited his courtiers to a banquet,</u> but he didn't set a time."
and sent his servants to call those who were invited to the marriage feast, but they would not come. Again he sent other servants, saying, 'Tell those who are invited, behold I have made ready my dinner, my oxen and ,my fat calves are killed, and everything is ready; come to the marriage feast.'	
But they made light of it and went off, one to his farm, another to his business, while the rest seized his servants, treated them shamefully and killed them. The king was angry, and he sent his troops and destroyed those murderers and burned their city. Then he said to his servants, 'The wedding is ready, but those invited were not worthy. Go therefore to the thoroughfares and invite to the marriage feast as many as you find.'	The smart ones among them got themselves fixed up and waited at the gate of the palace, saying, 'Does the palace lack anything?' [They can do it any time.] The stupid ones among them went about their work, saying, 'So is there a banquet without a whole lot of preparation?' Suddenly the king demanded the presence of his courtiers. The smart ones went right before him, all fixed up, but the fools went before him filthy from their work.
And those servants went out into the streets and gathered all whom they found, both bad and good, so the wedding hall was filled with guests.	
But when the king came in to look at the guests, he saw there a man who had no wedding garment, and he said to him, 'Friend, how did you get in here without a wedding garment?' And he was speechless. Then the king said to the attendants, 'Bind him hand and foot and cast him into the outer darkness; there men will weep and gnash their teeth For many are called but few are chosen.'"	The king received the smart ones pleasantly, but showed anger to the fools. He said, 'These, who fixed themselves up for the banquet, will sit and eat and drink. Those, who didn't fix themselves up for the banquet, will stand and look on.'"

The upshot is simple: the parable shared by Christianity and Judaism concerns a king who gave a banquet with unhappy results — that alone. But that shared motif (for all we have in common is a motif, not a fully-executed tale) suffices to validate comparing the ways in which the two religious worlds have utilized the motif. And that produces striking contrasts, which turn our attention from the detail — the case at hand — and toward the large-scale systems that have imposed their respective paradigms upon the detail of the (proto-)parable: the shared motif of the king who gave a banquet for people who were unwilling or unready to attend, the shared lesson that one has to be ready on the spur of the moment, and the common conviction that that for which one must be forever prepared is nothing less than entry into God's kingdom. But what is that kingdom? On that the two heirs of the common Scripture differ radically.

III. CONTEXTS OF COMPARISON

What do we learn from the contrast? We may speak of religious systems represented in the detail of a parable and gain perspective on the whole from the part. Christianity, in the case at hand, defines God's kingdom around the advent of Jesus Christ. The formulation in the Gospels concerns itself with the rejection of Jesus and the Kingdom he inaugurates. People do not wish to respond to the invitation. Or people are not ready to respond. At stake is God's rule, which is at hand, but which comes when least expected. But the net result is the same. Christianity in the statement of the Gospels then sets forth a religious system focused upon the figure of Jesus in the advent of God's rule. Rabbinic Judaism, in the case at hand, centers its interest on the moral conduct of everyday life. That is where God's kingdom is realized, in the quotidian world of the here and the now. How to accept God's rule, together with the unpredictable occasion at which God will exercise his dominion? People living in ordinary times must engage in a constant process of repentance, to be ready for the event — God's intervention and assertion of his dominion — that is inevitable but unpredictable, death.

The parable in Matthew emphasizes the apologetic that Christianity required. Jesus and his rule proved unacceptable to Jesus' own people: those who reject the rule of God through Jesus may be more numerous than those who accept Jesus, but the rejection of Jesus is inexcusable. The Rabbinic parable, by contrast, makes the point that while the people desire the Kingdom of God, they lack the willingness to expend the daily effort to be ready for it in their moral conduct. The Rabbinic parable is fundamentally admonitory in function, the Christian parable apologetic.[2]

Through working on the same motif of the king and the banquet and the guests who are not ready, and through insisting upon the same message, which is one has to be ready every moment for the coming of the kingdom, the two systems say very different things. Perspective on the character and emphases of each is gained from the contrast with the other, made possible by the shared motif, which generates two comparable, but contrasting parables. The humble detail — a few lines of narrative in the respective documents — proves to contain within itself much of what we require to differentiate the one reading of the shared Scripture from the other.

"Our sages of blessed memory" read Scripture as the account of how God's kingdom on earth is to take shape, how holy Israel is to realize the rules that govern the everyday and the here and now of the kingdom Heaven in which, through obedience to the Torah, priests and the holy people is to make its life, so declaring every morning and every night with the rising and setting of the sun, the regularity of nature, in the recitation of the Shema proclaiming God's rule. "Jesus Christ" received the same heritage as an account of not the enduring present but the now-realized future: the climax is at hand, the kingdom of Heaven marks not a lasting condition, matching nature with supernature in Israel's obedience, but the acutely present moment. And obedience is to the king, who has made a banquet — in Judaism, for his courtiers = Israel (or, all humanity for that matter), in Christianity, for his son = Jesus Christ. Where else but at the intersection of like parables could we have encountered so jarring a collision: everyday Israel versus Jesus Christ! At every point likeness underscores difference, but only diachronic comparison sustains the encounter, synchronic reading forbidding it.

True, we end up where just we started, but now enlightened on where we stand. The reciprocal reading of the rabbis' and the Gospels' parables, like the comparative-contrastive reading of much else, yields two religions, each constructing upon, but asymmetrical to, the same foundation, buildings remarkable for their symmetry, but also for their utter incongruity.

IV. COMPARING GOSPELS AND RABBINIC WRITINGS: A HALAKHIC INSTANCE

What we see when we turn to Halakhic compositions for comparison and contrast is that the same topic, healing on the Sabbath, in the Gospels makes one point, in the Halakhah of the Mishnah and the Tosefta makes an entirely different point, and treating the same subject the two bodies of tradition simply part company. But that fact affords striking insight into the issues that inhere in the whole of the two religious systems, respectively.

Matt. 12:9-14=Mark 3:1-6=Lk. 6:6-11 show Jesus challenged to heal on the Sabbath. Mark has, "Is it lawful on the Sabbath to do good or to do harm, to save life or to kill?" In Matthew he answers, "What man of you, if he has one sheep and it falls into a pit on the Sabbath, will not lay hold of it and lift it out? Of how much more value is a man than a sheep. So it is lawful to do good on the Sabbath." The premise throughout is, it is lawful on the Sabbath to save life, as indeed, the law of the Mishnah and the Tosefta and the exegetical readings of the pertinent passages in the Written Torah all concur is the fact. But saving life is not at issue in the story, only doing good.

And that brings us to the specific premise in the version of Matthew, that one may lift a sheep out of a pit on the Sabbath. The Tosefta (among many documents) is explicit that one saves life on the Sabbath, and any show of piety is hypocrisy:

TOSEFTA-TRACTATE SHABBAT 15:11-12

T. Shabbat 15:11   They remove debris for one whose life is in doubt on the Sabbath. And the one who is prompt in the matter, lo, this one is to be praised. And it is not necessary to get permission from a court. How so? [If] one fell into the ocean and cannot climb up, or [if] his ship is sinking in the sea, and he cannot climb up, they go down and pull him out of there. And it is not necessary to get permission from a court.

T. Shabbat 15:12   If he fell into a pit and cannot get out, they let down a chain to him and climb down and pull him out of there. And it is not necessary to get permission from a court. A baby who went into a house and cannot get out — they break down the doors of the house for him, even if they were of stone, and they get him out of there. And it is not necessary to get permission from a court. They put out a fire and make a barrier against a fire on the Sabbath [cf. M. Shab. Chap. 16]. And one who is prompt, lo, this one is to be praised. And it is not necessary to get permission from a court.

But that brings us to the Halakhic premise of the statement of Jesus: what about the animal in a pit?

TOSEFTA-TRACTATE SHABBAT 14:3

L.   For a beast which fell into a pit they provide food in the place in which it has fallen, so that it not die, [and they pull it up after the Sabbath].

The rule is given anonymously; it is not subject to dispute but is normative. But then how are we to understand the certainty with which Jesus asks, "What man of you, if he has one sheep and it falls into a pit on the Sabbath, will not lay hold of it and lift it out? Of how much more value is a man than a sheep. So it is lawful to do good on the Sabbath." The Halakhic definition of doing good on the Sabbath is feeding the beast in the pit, not raising it up.

Clearly, for the synoptic picture of Jesus deems the critical issue to concern whether or not it is lawful to do good on the Sabbath, and the answer is, it is indeed lawful to do good, and the Pharisees do not understand the law. But what if, to the framers of the Mishnah[3] the Sabbath involves other issues entirely, so that when they speak of the Sabbath, the use a theological language that simply does not intersect with the language of doing work on the Sabbath or doing good on the Sabbath? After all, even the parallelism, do good or do harm, save life or kill, hardly is commensurate; sages concur, one must save life, and everyone knows, one may never murder, not on a week day, not on the Sabbath. So the framing of the question, sensible in the setting of Jesus's teaching, proves disingenuous in the setting of the sages' system. But then in what context do sages consider healing on the Sabbath? It is not a matter of (excess) labor — and the story strikingly does not represent Jesus as having done an act of labor, for no labor is involved in the healing. The catalogue of the thirty-nine classifications of labor does not register. Jesus tells the man, "Come here." He said to the man, "Stretch out your hand." He stretched it out, and his hand was restored. In fact, Jesus has done nothing; *labor is not the issue.* What is at issue is violation of the sanctity of the Sabbath not in order to save life, and that is a distraction from the holiness of the Sabbath day. The opposition to Jesus does not concede his supernatural standing and does not distinguish his act of healing from that of any other human being, but for the Christian narrative that is the very heart of the matter: "For the Son of man is Lord of the Sabbath." He is a higher authority — not because of his claim properly to interpret and apply the Sabbath prohibition, but because of Jesus's own status.

What defines the issues of the Sabbath for the Rabbinic tradition of the Torah? With regard to the Sabbath, the Halakhah of the Mishnah, Tosefta, and Talmuds concerns three matters, [1] space, [2] time, and [3] activity, as the advent of the Sabbath affects all three. The advent of the Sabbath transforms creation, specifically reorganizing space and time and reordering the range of permissible activity. First comes the transformation of space that takes effect at sundown at the end of the sixth day and that ends at sundown of the Sabbath day. At that time, for holy Israel, the entire world is divided into public domain and private domain, and what is located in the one may not be transported into the other. What is located in public domain may be transported only four cubits, that is, within the space occupied by a person's body. What is in private domain may be transported within the entire demarcated space of that domain. All public domain is deemed a single spatial entity, so too all private domain, so one may transport objects from one private domain to another. The net effect of the transformation of space on the Sabbath is to move nearly all permitted activity to private domain and to close off public domain for all but the most severely limited activities; people may not transport objects from one domain to the other, but they may transport objects within private domain, so the closure of public domain from most activity, and nearly all material or physical activity, comes in consequence of the division of space effected by sunset at the end of the sixth day of the week.

When it comes to space, the advent of the Sabbath divides into distinct domains for all practical purposes what in secular time is deemed divided only as to ownership, but united as to utilization. Sacred time then intensifies the arrangements of space as public and private, imparting enormous consequence to the status of what is private. There, and only there, on the Sabbath, is life to be lived. The Sabbath assigns to private domain the focus of life in holy time: the household is where things take place then. When, presently, we realize that the household (private domain) is deemed analogous to the Temple or tabernacle (God's household), forming a mirror image to the tabernacle, we shall understand the full meaning of the generative principle before us concerning space on the Sabbath.

Second comes the matter of time and how the advent of sacred time registers. Since the consequence of the demarcation on the Sabbath of all space into private and public domain effects, in particular, transporting objects from one space to the other, how time is differentiated will present no surprise. The effects concern private domain, the household. Specifically, what turns out to frame the Halakhic issue is what objects may be handled or used, even in private domain, on the Sabbath. The advent of the Sabbath thus affects the organization of space and the utilization of tools and other objects, the furniture of the household within the designated territory of the household. The basic principle is simple. Objects may be handled only if they are designated in advance of the Sabbath for use for the purpose for which they will be utilized on the Sabbath. But if tools may be used for a purpose that is licit on the Sabbath, and if those tools are ordinarily used for that same purpose, they are deemed ready at hand and do not require reclassification; the accepted classification applies. What requires designation for Sabbath use in particular is any tool that may serve more than a single purpose, or that does not ordinarily serve the purpose for which it is wanted on the Sabbath. Designation for use on the Sabbath thus regularizes the irregular, but is not required for what is ordinarily used for the purpose for which it is wanted and is licitly utilized on the Sabbath.

The Sabbath then finds all useful tools and objects in their proper place; that may mean, they may not be handled at all, since their ordinary function cannot be performed on the Sabbath; or it may mean, they may be handled on the Sabbath exactly as they are handled every other day, the function being licit on the Sabbath; or it may mean, they must be designated in advance of the Sabbath for licit utilization on the Sabbath. That third proviso covers utensils that serve more than a single function, or that do not ordinarily serve the function of licit utilization on the Sabbath that the householder wishes them to serve on this occasion. The advent of the Sabbath then requires that all tools and other things be regularized and ordered. The rule extends even to utilization of space, within the household, that is not ordinarily used for a (licit) purpose for which, on the Sabbath, it is needed. If guests come, storage-space used for food may be cleared away to accommodate them, the space being conceived as suitable for sitting even when not ordinarily used for that purpose. But one may not clear out a store room for that purpose. One may also make a path in a store room so that one may move about there. One may handle objects that, in some way or another, can serve a licit purpose, in the theory that that purpose inheres. But what is not made ready for use may not be used on the Sabbath. So the advent of the Sabbath not only divides space into public and private, but also differentiates useful tools and objects into those that may or may not be handled within the household.

Third, we come to the generative problematics particular to the Sabbath. The affect upon activity that the advent of the Sabbath makes concerns constructive labor. In a normal way one may not carry out entirely on his own a completed act of constructive labor, which is to say, work that produces enduring results. That is what one is supposed to do in profane time. What is implicit in that simple statement proves profound and bears far-reaching implications. No prohibition impedes performing an act of labor in an other-than-normal way, for example, in a way that is unusual and thus takes account of the differentiation of time. Labor in a natural, not in an unnatural, manner is prohibited. But that is not all. A person is not forbidden to carry out an act of destruction, or an act of labor that produces no lasting consequences. Nor is part of an act of labor, not brought to conclusion, prohibited. Nor is it forbidden to perform part of an act of labor in partnership with another person who carries out the other requisite part. Nor does one incur culpability for performing an act of labor in several distinct parts, for example, over a protracted, differentiated period of time. The advent of the Sabbath prohibits activities carried out in ordinary time in a way deemed natural: acts that are complete, consequential, and in accord with their accepted character.

What is the upshot of this remarkable repertoire of fundamental considerations having to do with activity, in the household, on the holy day? The Halakhah of Shabbat in the aggregate concerns itself with formulating a statement of how the advent of the Sabbath defines the kind of activity that may be done by specifying what may not be done. That is the meaning of repose, the cessation of activity, not the commencement of activity of a different order. To carry out the Sabbath, one does nothing, not something. And what is that "nothing" that one realizes through inactivity? One may not carry out an act analogous to one that sustains creation. An act or activity for which one bears responsibility, and one that sustains creation, is [1] an act analogous to one required in the building and maintenance of the tabernacle, [2] that is intentionally carried out [3] in its entirety, [4] by a single actor, [5] in the ordinary manner, [6] with a constructive and [7] consequential result — one worthy of consideration by accepted norms. These are the seven conditions that pertain, and that, in one way or another, together with counterpart considerations in connection with the transformation of space and time, generate most of the Halakhah of Shabbat.

Like God at the completion of creation, so is Israel on the Sabbath: the Halakhah of the Sabbath defines the Sabbath to mean to do no more, but instead to do nothing. At issue in Sabbath rest is not ceasing from labor but ceasing from labor of a very particular character, labor in the model of God's work in making the world. Then why the issues of space, time, and activity? Given the division of space into public domain, where nothing much can happen, and the private domain of the household, where nearly everything dealt with in the law at hand takes place, we realize that the Sabbath forms an occasion of the household in particular. There man takes up repose, leaving off the tools required to make the world, ceasing to perform the acts that sustain the world. The issue of the Sabbath is the restoration of Eden, the realization of Eden in the household of holy Israel.

To that issue, the matter of how much effort is involved in saving the beast proves monumentally irrelevant. Nor can sages have grasped what someone meant in saying, "The son of man is the Lord of the Sabbath." When set alongside the Gospels' framing of issues, we realize, the two pictures of the Sabbath and the issues that inhere therein scarcely intersect. But knowing that fact affords perspective on both the figure of Jesus and the Torah of the sages that seeing each on its own does not provide. Small details turn out to recapitulate large conceptions, and that, in the end, ought to define the hermeneutics, and the consequent exegetics, of the next phase of study of both the Gospels and the Mishnah.

The Rabbinic literature may be read in its own terms and framework, and so too the early Christian writings. But when the two bodies of writing are drawn into a relationship of comparison and contrast, both of them take on deeper meaning. The differences are sharpened. The details of each, emerging as part of a coherent and cogent system, make sense as part of a coherent whole. The Gospel asks the Sabbath to serve as a medium to express the dominion of Jesus Christ over the Torah, and the Rabbinic Halakhah expresses the theology of the restoration of the perfection of Creation that animates much of the Rabbinic system. The two readings of the same matter intersect and part company.

What is to be learned is perspective and proportion, the perspective that discerns choices systems make, the proportion that indicates what matters in one system, what matters in another. Without perspective and proportion, we simply recapitulate what the texts say. With, we can begin to reflect on their meaning: what is at stake in the irrepressible conflict between the two heirs of Scripture. The issues of religious truth then come to the fore.

ENDNOTES

[1] A medieval treatment of the same verse in Qohelet completes the exposition by referring to the trilogy, commandments, good deeds, and Torah-study:

> Does Scripture speak literally about garments? But how many white garments do the pagans have? And if Scripture literally speaks of good oil, how much good oil do the pagans have! But Scripture speaks only of the performance of the commandments, good deeds, and the study of the Torah" (Qohelet Rabbah 9:8).

Here we see how the medieval documents of Rabbinic Judaism clearly continue and carry forward with great precision the teachings of the classical writings. Nothing has intervened in the unfolding of the Rabbinic system, which amplifies and refines the initial statement, absorbs new ideas and naturalizes them, but which continues an essentially straight path from antiquity forward.

[2] I owe this formulation to Professor Martin Pickup, Florida College, Tampa FL, my former student at the University of South Florida.

[3] The role of Pharisees before 70 in the framing of Rabbinic Judaism afterward carries its own set of problems, which I have discussed in *Eliezer ben Hyrcanus. The Tradition and the Man.* Leiden, 1973: Brill, I-II.

11

The Divergent Discourses of Rabbinic Judaism
How Halakhic and Aggadic Documents Treat the Bestiary Common to Them Both

Judaism's two native categories, theology and law, parable and praxis, Aggadah and Halakhah — form two distinct modes of discourse. The one expounds norms of attitude and belief, the other, norms of action and behavior. Joined together, they complete and complement one another, forming a remarkably coherent statement. Until we grasp how the two form a coherent statement, we cannot fully describe, analyze, and interpret Rabbinic Judaism as a religious system.

The problem is that these categories exhibit a peculiar trait: each follows its own rules of thought and presentation, vocabulary and grammar and syntax. When Halakhah or law defines the subject, one set of questions is asked and answered in a particular rhetoric, and when theology forms the issue in presenting the very same subject, a different set of questions governs, a distinct corpus of language-rules comes into play. So the generative native categories of Judaism function in such a way that the *same* topic produces two distinct modes of thought and expression; even the category-formations that encompass the same data — here, animals — scarcely intersect, for lions or snakes or oxen stand for one thing in Halakhic discourse, another in Aggadic. There is no single bestiary in Rabbinic Judaism, but we find two distinct ways of thinking and speaking about animals, as about much else.[1]

How the Aggadah and Halakhah relate is here examined through the survey of the treatment by each of a topic common to them both, the bestiary. Animals form an ideal control, because in the Rabbinic setting of late antiquity, the formative documents show that there is little at stake in how they are presented. There is no agenda that Halakhic discourse is constrained to articulate, no narrative to which Aggadic discourse must adhere. By contrast the shared topic, Land of Israel, involves narrative and law in an exposition of how Eden is replicated, along with Adam, in the Land of Israel and in Israel the people. There is much at stake. So too, time imposes on the Halakhah a vast program of differentiation, e.g., time and space on the Sabbath, and upon the Aggadah an equally complex task of composition, e.g., expounding the interplay of nature and Israelite paradigmatic history. Here, by contrast, when animals enter in, the two distinct modes of discourse function unmediated by extrinsic, systemic considerations, for example, an overriding myth. Animals represent little more than themselves throughout. Hence we find at hand an ideal opportunity to examine without intervening variables the workings of the two media of thought and expression as they address a single systemically neutral category-formation: animals.

We shall see how that single topic — the morality and law of the animal kingdom — in the Rabbinic canon of the formative age, like all other ubiquitous topics encompassed in that canon, produces two distinct vocabularies of analysis. These two distinct realms of thought and speech on the same subject yield lessons of two separate classifications of the order of nature and society. How the two media of expression intersect and part company in a single case permits us to characterize the two Judaic modes of discourse in general. That labor of general characterization of the interplay of Halakhah and Aggadah defines the interior dynamics of Rabbinic Judaism and forms the principal task of systemic analysis of that Judaism. In the Rabbinic manner, here we work our way from the case to the rule.

When the documents of the law discuss norms of conduct, animals figure in a finite program and contribute in a particular manner, and when the documents of theology and exegesis take up norms of conviction, e.g., the deeper meanings of Scriptural stories, animals are discussed from a quite different perspective, with commensurate results. The comparison of the two Talmuds, the only documents that extensively treat both Halakhic and Aggadic subjects, proves that the difference is not documentary but governed by genre: the topic and the context in which the topic is taken up. So the question presents itself: what conventions govern the topic, animals, in the Halakhic writing, and how do these conventions shift in the Aggadic kind?

I. PRAXIS: HOW HALAKHIC DOCUMENTS TREAT THE BESTIARY

Are there particular Halakhic topics served by the bestiary? To find the answer to that question, a quick review of the topics in which the bestiary figures will serve, with the question in mind: why here, not there?

A. THE THEOLOGICAL BESTIARY OF THE MISHNAH

What in the Mishnah is important about animals, and how, consequently, are they classified? The answer for the Halakhah, from the Mishnah through the Bavli, is the same: the Halakhic category-formations govern in the classification of beasts, and rarely do the traits of the species of the particular beasts themselves figure in the taxonomic exercises of hierarchical classification that comprise the Halakhic enterprise. Stated simply: the goal of Halakhic discourse is to generalize diverse species into a common genus, and that requires homogenization. Hence what is important is not the distinctive traits of the dog, lion, or snake, but what links them together in a given legal context, e.g., types of causation.

The method of the Mishnah entails the classification of data by a governing taxonomy, yielding a rule covering a variety of cases and a general principle to be extended to new cases and the solution of new problems. That method governs in the amplification of the Halakhah and extends to beasts, which rarely form distinct species and still less commonly a single genus. The category-formations are defined principally but not invariably on Scripture's terms. The Mishnah classifies Scripture's data, it does not interpret them. That is shown in a simple fact. Scripture assigns particular beasts to the expiation of particular sins, e.g., why the goat for the expiation of inadvertent acts of idolatry. But no one in the Mishnah suggests what traits of the goat match those idolatrous deeds. If Scripture invokes the heifer for specific purposes in line with the narrative of the golden calf, the Mishnah has not made its own and utilized that correlation for drawing lessons and composing a bestiary. Scripture's classifications of beasts in the cult thus has yielded for the Mishnah a variety of facts, but no propositions, no effort whatsoever at deciphering Scripture's meanings. The Mishnah also does not advance its own distinctive perspective on matters, if indeed it possessed one.

As the Mishnah goes, so go the further documents of the Halakhah in their category-formations from the Mishnah through the Bavli. We cannot say that the Mishnah yields a bestiary at all, so far as a bestiary imputes traits to beasts that differentiate one species of beast from another by reason of said traits, e.g., virtues or particular traits of mind or body. The indicative qualities that in the Mishnah's legal system distinguish beast from beast derive not from the animal itself but from extrinsic circumstance, the happenstance of deeds committed upon the beast for example. In that case the cow, lion, sheep, panther, goat or bear fall into a single category, e.g., having been worshipped or not having been worshipped, having been subjected to sexual relations with a human being or not having been so subjected. True, the differentiation between the animals that are attested dangers from those deemed harmless extends to traits of beasts: man and snake as against sheep and goat. But no conclusions are drawn from that fact.

The bull, sheep, and goat yield to the authors of Leviticus Rabbah the lesson: Do not make offerings before me from those animals that pursue, but from those that are pursued. The list in Baba Qamma comprised by man and dog, lion and snake, does not produce a counterpart lesson based on the distinctive traits of dog, lion, snake, or man but on those shared in common. The pig is rarely in play. The law set forth by the Mishnah in its systematization of Scripture utilized facts pertaining to animals. The *koy* is the best example of the Mishnah's method in this context of the bestiary, but the general rules of hybridization compete. In that context, so far as a bestiary produces edifying lessons, the Mishnah contains no bestiary at all. That fact takes on meaning when we meet successive documents of the Aggadah, in which animals and their indicative traits become media for moral instruction and bear the compilations' systemic message.

B. THE THEOLOGICAL BESTIARY OF THE TOSEFTA

What in the Tosefta us is important about animals, and how, consequently, are they classified? The question I should ask is *not* why here, not there, but why nowhere in the Halakhic corpus do we find evidence of thought about moral meaning in the context of nature? The Tosefta here and there contains odds and ends that carry us beyond the Mishnah's approach to the relevant data. If deciphering Scripture's (or some other) bestiary code defined the problem addressed in the law, we have found not a trace of evidence of that fact. The same taxonomies that the Mishnah's law generated govern in the Tosefta, and with one exception I found nothing new beyond them, only refinement and clarification of the received law.

The Tosefta's he-goat and the ram stand for sages, not for virtues or social traits or historical players. I note a variety of traits imputed to the dog, the koy remains interstitial, and the pig plays no role to speak of. The lion, bear, leopard, panther, snake and other types of animate creatures that play a part in the exposition of types of causation in the law represent little more than dangers to life and limb. The cow, sheep, goat, and other beasts and subsets of those beasts that play a role are classified, as in the Mishnah's law, by what is done to them, not by what they do or represent or embody; they are not generative metaphors. The Halakhah in the Tosefta's supplement does not form a promising source of bestiary parables; beasts stand for themselves, with little indication of deeper meanings imputed to them.

We come to a unique and unprecedented item, one that represents a new mode of thought entirely and would surface in Aggadic compilations but not in other Halakhic ones.

T. Miqvaot
7:11   A.   A cow which drank purification-water, and one slaughtered it within twenty-four hours —
       B.   This was a case, and R. Yosé the Galilean did declare it clean, and R. Aqiba did declare it unclean.
       C.   R. Tarfon supported R. Yosé the Galilean. R. Simeon ben Nannos supported R. Aqiba .
       D.   R. Simeon b. Nannos dismissed [the arguments of] R. Tarfon. R. Yosé the Galilean dismissed [the arguments of] R. Simeon b. Nannos.
       E.   R. Aqiba dismissed [the arguments of] R. Yosé the Galilean.
       F.   After a time, he [Yosé] found an answer for him ['Aqiba].

G. He said to him, "Am I able to reverse myself?"

H. He said to him, "Not anyone [may reverse himself], but you [may do so], for you are Yosé the Galilean."

I. [He said to him] "I shall say to you: Lo, Scripture states, 'And they shall be kept for the congregation of the people of Israel for the purification-water. '

J. "Just so long as they are kept, lo, they are purification-water, and not when a cow has drunk them." [The water has suffered reclassification by being drunk by the cow.]

K. This was a case, and thirty-two elders voted in Lud and declared it clean.

L. At that time R. Tarfon recited this verse:

M. "'I saw the ram goring westward and northward and southward, and all the animals were unable to stand against it, and none afforded protection from its power, and it did just as it liked and grew great' (Dan. 8:4) —

N. "[this is R. Aqiba .

O. "'As I was considering, behold, a he-goat came from the west across the face of the whole earth, without touching the ground; and the goat had a conspicuous horn between his eyes.

P. "'He came to the ram with the two horns, which I had seen standing on the bank of the river, and he ran at him in his mighty wrath. I saw him come close to the ram, and he was enraged against him and struck the ram and broke his two horns' — this is R. Aqiba and R. Simeon b. Nannos.

Q. "'And the ram had no power to stand before him' — this is 'Aqiba.

R. "'But he cast him down to the ground and trampled upon him' — this is R. Yosé the Galilean.

S. "'And there was no one who could rescue the ram from his power' — these are the thirty-two elders who voted in Lud and declared it clean."

A-J+K form an elaborate report of a dispute, with its contradictory rulings, B-E, and then a set of arguments based on scripture to validate the ruling that the cow was not contaminated by drinking the purification water, because it is not properly kept as purification water. All of this is unconnected to what follows.

Then comes the reading of Dan. 8:4 as an account of the conflict of the sages. The ram goring in all directions is Aqiba; no one can withstand his reasoning. The ram then represents the aggressive dialectician of the law. But Yosé the Galilean, the he-goat, overcomes the ram and breaks his horns, that represent Aqiba, and the elders adopted his position. The he-goat overcomes the ram.

Here the bestiary of the apocalyptic vision of Daniel 8:4 is translated into the figures of the Rabbinic sages. The animals embody named sages. Aqiba is the ram, Yosé the Galilean, the he-goat, and the narrative of Daniel's vision now is realized in the sages' conflict. This is an absolutely unique exercise for the Mishnah and the Tosefta and represents a different mode of thought about the meaning of animals from any we have seen to this point. But the traits of beasts and the lessons to be learned from them do not figure. The he-goat and the ram embody traits of the named rabbis. The named rabbis do not represent the he-goat or the ram. Animals then serve as metaphors for sages, but the choice of the particular beast that stands for a specific sage appears arbitrary. The Tosefta remains well within the boundaries set by the Halakhah of the Mishnah.

c. The Theological Bestiary of Sifra

Sifra contains one important innovation, but it is not followed up. What has happened at Sifra XCIX:I is that someone has asked a question not asked earlier in the Mishnah, Tosefta, or nearly all of Sifra: *what do these particular beasts used for offerings signify?* The question was asked because an answer — they signify thus and so — presented itself: the provisions for the sacrificial service.

How come the Israelites have to present an offering more than Aaron?
He said to them, "As to you, you bear responsibility both at the outset [with the incident of Joseph, which brought Israel down to Egypt], and also at the end [with the incident with the golden calf].

"At the outset: 'They slaughtered a kid' (Gen. 37:31) [in connection with the affair with Joseph, dipping the ornamented tunic in the blood].
"At the end: 'They made for themselves a molten calf' (Ex. 32:8).
"Let a kid come and effect atonement for the matter of the kid, and let a calf come and effect atonement for the matter of the molten calf."

Here is material for a true bestiary. Types of beasts for particular classes of offerings bear meaning. That meaning awaits discovery in the details of the Torah's narrative. Why in Sifra in particular? Because much of the book of Leviticus concerns itself with the types and procedures of sacrifice, and all of it devotes itself to the sanctification of Israel. Why not in the Mishnah or, therefore, in its companion, the Tosefta? Because neither document took as its task an exegetical inquiry into questions of meaning and significance. Such questions imposed particularity on data deemed to conform to a single rule. A type is a philosophical category, the result of classification of data uniformly. It yields no singular meanings — by definition. Matching meaning and significance to events and meaningful moments differentiated what was uniform and specified the singular and the significant in a piece of data broken out of its taxon altogether. Let me explain.

With the Tosefta following the example of the Mishnah, the authors and compilers of both documents took as their task the organization, by topic and speciation by indicative traits, of masses of data, not the quest for the context in society of nature's facts, not for the situating in history of the imperatives of the cultic celebration of the natural world of the Land of Israel. Once Leviticus comes into view, with its persistent contextualization of the imperatives of Israel's sanctification within the setting of Israel's salvation, as Leviticus 26 states explicitly, the issue of the suitable match and meaning made its appearance. Then the inquiry into the correspondence of a particular species of beast with a particular event — of nature to history — produced the question at hand: what do these particular beasts signify? And the rest followed.

The Mishnah and the Tosefta embodied that pure rationality that deemed all things subject to governing rules, which we can discern with adequate knowledge of the facts of classification, inclusive of hierarchization. To that rationality of abstract thinking about the traits of things particularization and contextualization proved monumentally irrelevant. After all, how is a calf differentiated by historical context, what traits intrinsic in the heifer respond to a particular event? *Hierarchical classification depends upon the uniformity of data,* not upon its heterogeneity, established by one-time happenings. We face, then, a conflict at the deepest foundations of reason: classification versus ad hoc interpretation, the uniform condition of nature versus the vagaries of society and history, with their differentiation of all things by appeal to action specific to an occasion. The critique, which I illustrated only once, by Sifra's authors of the Mishnah's system of classification by logic — the logical hierarchy of indicative traits of classes of things, in favor of their advocacy of the specificity of scripture's own system of classification by divine decree — now takes on further consequence. Once generative thought opposes the Mishnah's and the Tosefta's mode of analysis, of the classification of things by appeal to intrinsic traits and their uniformity and hierarchy, everything changes. Then the particularization of the general indicative traits by appeal to special characteristics of components of a species defined by general traits raises questions unthinkable in natural history: the majesty of the lion, the duplicity of the pig, the nobility of the sheep, goat, and cow. Then not all lions, pigs, sheep, goats or cows are like all others. Incidents intervene.

These theoretical remarks bring us back, by a circuitous route, to the advent of a bestiary full of lessons of virtue and morality. The premise of the question is that beasts bear signification, because a rationality, consisting of the self-evidence of a given indicative quality, governs. But that signification transcends the data of nature. It appeals to the data of the Israelite narrative: the facts of the human condition and how particular events have embodied those facts. The particular bestiary exercise before us — majestic but lonely in canonical context — consists of the following premises that the situation of Leviticus conveys: [1] a rationality infuses the laws of the cult; [2] that rationality consists in the justice that comes to expression in the match between the particular beast employed for a determinate purpose in the cult and the decisive deeds of Israel in relationship with God.

[3] That brings us to the humble entry before us: "Let a kid come and effect atonement for the matter of the kid, and let a calf come and effect atonement

for the matter of the molten calf." The cult responds to the particular incident, the golden calf at Sinai, and its details then match the details of that incident. The key is why an atonement offering is invariably demanded, and the lock that is opened is the mystery of the cult, in all its complex details, instituted n the aftermath of Sinai. That leads to the final lesson implicit in the indicated bestiary proposition.

The calf serves, among others beasts, as a sign that [4] God is just and the principle of measure for measure governs divine justice. But God is merciful and provides a medium of atonement: the particular beast of the atonement offering (and not that offering only) signifies the right action toward that very same species by which Israel had sinned and so corrupted its relationship with God at the very moment of initiation.

The conflict between the Mishnah's insistence on the rationality of all things, conforming as they do to a uniform rule and ignoring the particularities of time and circumstance, and Sifra's critique of the Mishnah's purity of logic in the classification and hierarchization of all things, produces this document. But the singular item does not fit into that argument or the Halakhic-exegetical program of the document.

Rather, an incident has intervened to differentiate beast from beast, to explain why this beast for this category of offering, and to do so by appeal to a singular event. So Israel's social world, its history and its narrative, break into the integrity of the natural world and its coherence. No longer do all beasts form a common genus, e.g., clean or unclean. Now the particularities of the lion and the snake, the calf and the goat, come to the fore. Once the lion differs from the goat by its leonine qualities, the same modes of thought would come to bear upon the flock and the herd. And ultimately particular species of beasts would embody the traits of nations, and the Israelite bestiary would supply a mode of thinking about history — the ultimate outcome of Judaism's theological bestiary and the reversion of Rabbinic thought to the apocalyptic mysteries captured in Daniel's charging ram in the setting of Rabbinic debate. But we have gotten well ahead of our story. It will be some time before we have completed our survey of Halakhic discourse on animals and compared them with the Aggadic counterpart and so shown beyond any doubt that the two modes of Rabbinic thought and expression, the Halakhah and the Aggadah, are to be differentiated as to their indicative traits by how they speak, also, of animals.

D. THE THEOLOGICAL BESTIARY OF SIFRÉ TO NUMBERS

As in the case of other Halakhic compilations, so here too I see rare and episodic references awaiting collection and disposition. I do not find implicit a comprehensive bestiary. The reason is certainly not the character of the book of Numbers, with its extensive exposition of procedures and requirements of the cult and its animal offerings. A simple fact emerges: Halakhic discourse invites little attention to the indicative traits of animals, seeking to generalize the particular, not interpret it.

E. THE THEOLOGICAL BESTIARY OF SIFRÉ TO DEUTERONOMY

If we had to rely on Sifré to Deuteronomy, we should conclude no system of thought focused on animals emerges from Rabbinic Judaism, which manages to make its complete statement without moralizing on the traits of animals in particular. That such moralizing is routine has been demonstrated: all nature responds to the creator's plan and imperative — mountains and oxen — but only Israel behaves contrary to nature. Scripture takes that position and the Rabbinic exegetes replicate it.

Accordingly, I find nothing that sustains the inquiry into Rabbinic categorization of beasts. Everything lies exposed, on the surface. The items in section ii are routine and commonplace: big snakes. Where animals figure, they do not form an autonomous taxon but participate in a classification — obedient to God's plan for creation, not obedient — utterly indifferent to beasts' distinctive taxic indicators I cannot overstress the main finding: Sifré to Deuteronomy CCCVI:I.1 classifies in a single category heaven, earth, gentiles, mountains, oxen, fowl, domesticated beasts, wild beasts, and ants, because all fit the indicated pattern. Beasts, furthermore, live up to their natural condition, do not decline to pull the plough or bear a burden. In none of these items and their companions do animals yield a lesson beyond their natural limits. Where a taxic program does enter in, at the food laws, Scripture has laid down the conclusions that the exegetes draw: clean food is for holy Israel, unclean for the idolatrous gentiles. What Deuteronomy says, the Rabbinic exegetes repeat. That conforms to the Halakhic program of amplification and extenuation and generalization, not metaphorization and moralization.

F. THE THEOLOGICAL BESTIARY OF MEKHILTA ATTRIBUTED TO R. ISHMAEL

Sifra, the two Sifrés and Mekhilta attributed to R. Ishmael replicate a single result: where Halakhah is at issue, as is mostly the case in all four compilations, the focus of interest is not in particular beasts and their distinctive qualities, whether moral, whether zoological, but in classes of beasts, undifferentiated as to species. Two distinct realms of thought and speech characterize beasts, the Halakhic and the Aggadic. The program of the Aggadic is readily discerned: animals represent nations or types of persons, and animals' traits may be transferred from nature to the social order. The program of the Halakhic is equally blatant: generalization and homogenization, that is, a process of hierarchical classification.

G. The Theological Bestiary of the Yerushalmi's Halakhah

The Halakhic sector of the Yerushalmi, which predominates in the document, carries forward the traits of discourse concerning beasts that characterize the Mishnah, Tosefta, and Tannaite Midrash-compilations. Particular species rarely figure, beasts form categories indicated by traits extrinsic to their *animal-ness*, e.g., unclean/clean, large/small — matters that differentiate pots and pans as much as pigs and goats, sheep and lions. The Halakhic treatment of beasts differs from the Aggadic, not only in the Halakhic interest in classification and hierarchization. It differs also in the Aggadic interest in the particularities of the species, their moral traits, and in the concomitant Aggadic interest in how animals may stand for, or embody transactions analogous to those of human beings.

H. The Theological Bestiary of the Bavli's Halakhah

What in the Bavli is important about animals corresponds to the concerns of the Halakhic system in general: the classification of animals and the hierarchization of the classes. The Bavli's Halakhic compositions that introduce the topic of animals prove routine, never treating animals as metaphors, asking them to stand for more than themselves. Thus lions and snakes occur where the narrative requires them: real lions, camels, snakes behave in accord with their nature and are subject to routine speciation. General rules govern all of them, e.g., the principle that pertains to what they may bear on the Sabbath. What is not a burden but an ornament is differentiated by species only by a principle common to them all and illustrated by each one respectively. So the classification does not derive from bestiary considerations.

The taxic process, rather, homogenizes species, e.g., at B. Shab. 1:9. IV.3 C: As to a goat kept for milk, a ewe for shearing, a fowl for eggs, oxen for ploughing, and dates for trading, Rab forbids handling them on the Sabbath, Samuel permits doing so. Goat/ewe/fowl/oxen/dates — animate and inanimate categories — are subject to a single differentiating principle. We see the same at B. Shab. 16:7 II.1 C: fly/hornet/scorpion/snake/mad dog, differentiated by location but not by species.

The character of the Halakhic category-formations involving beasts is revealed at B. Hagigah 2:1 IV.15B: lion/ox/eagle/man form a single taxon. That once more shows the interest of the Halakhah: generalization, not differentiation, homogenization, not particularization. The bestiary scarcely registers, except in routine contexts. Where species are distinguished from one another, the genus is homogeneous: "dangerous beasts vs. benign ones," "large beasts vs. small ones." Scorpions and snakes form a common genus, then speciated, while types of snakes or scorpions do not give way to detailed speciation. So too, the manner in which various genera and species give birth differentiates only in a larger process of systematization of data.

Where we find speciation, e.g., among types of snakes, the indicative traits of one species distinct from another derive from the Rabbinic system, thus snakes that serve the rabbis as against those that do not (B. Shab. 14:3 III.2 B). Another common genus is sin-offering, which serves to form an encompassing category-formation for lambs and goats, turtledoves and pigeons. That forms another category-formation that treats as null the traits of particular species of beasts and that takes shape around Halakhic considerations only. So too, small cattle comprise chickens and goats. Attested dangers as distinct from beasts deemed harmless until proven otherwise encompass wolf/lion/bear/leopard/panther/serpent — and man! The upshot is, the Halakhic taxonomy of beasts is constructed out of traits important to the Rabbinic Halakhic system, its points of differentiation, classification, and hierarchization, and not the taxic traits defined by nature.

What I have shown on the basis of the Bavli's taxonomy applies to all the Halakhic documents: the Rabbinic system does not appeal to a bestiary in the formation its classification-system and the hierarchization of its category-formations. The traits of beasts that register make their mark by reason of their conformity to the concerns of the Rabbinic system overall, e.g., snakes that carry out the tasks of the Rabbis versus those that do not, big beasts versus small ones, attested dangers versus those deemed harmless. The speciation of the genus, lions, by contrast, seldom registers. And conversely, where animate creatures are formed into category-formations, e.g., lambs/goats, turtledoves/pigeons, it is their common function on the altar that dictates the definitive characteristics of the category-formation. A fine example of the operative considerations is at B. B.M. 2:5 I.1:

> *Said Raba, "How come Scripture specified* 'ox,' 'ass,' 'sheep, and 'garment' [at Dt. 22:1-3]?
> *"All these had specifically to be named. For if Scripture had referred only to garment, I might have concluded that the rule pertains to a case in which there is the possibility of attestation of the garment or if the garment bears distinguishing traits on its own. But as to an ass, if there is attestation of the character of its saddle, or if the saddle bears distinguishing traits, [but not the ass itself], we are not obligated to return it the ass. So Scripture specified the ass, indicating that even if the ass is recognized only by the distinguishing traits, [one still has to return the beast]."*

The distinguishing characteristics do not derive from nature but from the Halakhic system's own taxic indicators, the Rabbinic-systemic criteria that have nothing to do with beasts' own traits: possibility of attestation in the present instance. Rare indeed is the taxic power of natural traits invoked, e.g., at B. Bekhorot 1:2I-K I.4, where hybridization is instantiated by the domestic goose and the wild goose, traits of nature thus forming taxic indicators. There a theological principle registers: nature differentiates between animate and inanimate categories, fauna and flora, only to match fauna and flora as corresponding classes. And that theological judgment dismisses as taxic indicators natural differences of a fundamental order.

II. PARABLE: HOW AGGADIC DOCUMENTS TREAT THE BESTIARY

A parable narrates one thing in terms of something else, a transaction among human beings in a story about animals, a set of relationships among nations embodied by beasts. For the present purpose, the parable represents a broad variety of Aggadic writing: narrative, exegesis, exhortation, all beyond the norms of conduct and focused on conscience and conviction. We pursue Aggadic data to answer the following questions: Does a determinate program of topics and propositions underlie the Aggadic corpus of the bestiary? What are the problems of an Aggadic character that predominate when animals figure, and are these random or does a pattern emerge? Why do animals come to the fore?

A. THE THEOLOGICAL BESTIARY OF GENESIS RABBAH

In Genesis Rabbah we encounter a reprise of Halakhic discourse, now in the Aggadic context, alongside a mode of thought — parabolization, metaphorization — and expression entirely divorced from those characteristic of the Halakhah. It follows that the Aggadic thought first of all follows the patterns of the Halakhic, representing a shift in subject-matter but not in analytic procedures, e.g., analogical-contrastive reasoning, the search for resemblances and patterns. Furthermore, the Halakhic category-formations, e.g., unclean/clean beasts, operate routinely in Aggadic settings. A third characteristic shared by Aggadic and Halakhic discourse surfaces. Both Aggadic and Halakhic writing, e.g., as portrayed by Genesis Rabbah and the Mishnah, treat animals as inert facts, categorically neutral and incidental in context. The snake at Gen. R. XIX:IV.2 stands for itself in the context of Scripture's narrative. It yields no transcendent lessons. Finally, just as Halakhic inquiry is governed by logic, not by the facts of the social order, so the Aggadic inquiry draws upon received data, not tested against the facts of nature, e.g., in the account of the phoenix, Gen. R. XIX:V.3.

Where taxic indicators establish categories, Gen. R. encompasses Halakhic issues, as at Gen. R. VII:II.1, fish are subject to ritual slaughter like mammals; VII;IV.2, fish are subject to the prohibition of hybridization; we differentiate domesticated animals from wild beasts from fowl (Gen. R. XXXII:V.3). The analogical-contrastive method is articulated at Gen. R. LXV:III.1, the status of the starling. Here facts of nature are invoked to resolve the matter. The Aggadic theological proposition, all things carry out God's purposes, encompassing fleas, gnats, flies, not to mention snakes, scorpions, and frogs. A series of probative cases suffices to make that point stick. But much of the speciation of animals yields lessons neither for Halakhic nor for Aggadic propositions. Overall, Genesis Rabbah contains a high proportion of compositions that systematize data without propositional consequence, whether Aggadic or Halakhic, as at the elaborate exposition of Gen. R. XLIV:XIV.2.

Where Aggadic discourse exhibits its own distinctive traits is in parabolic thinking about beasts. There traits of animals are imputed to human beings or vice versa, and where a range of questions of the meaning of history and the theological implications of events registers. In standing for world empires, species of animals — pig/bear for example — make possible systematic and organized thought about matters that vastly transcend Halakhic systematization of the social order. When the Rabbinic sages thought about world-history, the succession of pagan empires, they resorted to parabolic and allegorical thought because they had no other available medium for the organization and interpretation of the data: the rise and fall of Israel, Babylonia, Media, Greece, Rome — yielding the final ascent of Israel.

No category-formation of the social order could accommodate propositions making sense of, deriving from, world-historical events. Daniel's visions showed the way, first tentatively, as at Tosefta Miqvaot, then fully recapitulated, as in Genesis Rabbah and Leviticus Rabbah. So the allegorization and parabolization of the bestiary carried forward Daniel's apocalyptic vision, but the Rabbinic sages, true to their Halakhic training, identified the marks of system and order in the chaos of natural history. That yields an answer to the question, why here, not there? Halakhic category-formations present no opportunity for thinking about world-historical events, centered as they are upon the interiorities of the Israelite social order. A different mode of thought was required. When the Rabbinic sages took up the challenge of theology of history, they adopted the model of Daniel (and not Daniel alone), which they adapted to their larger system by systematic processing of data through classification and hierarchization. The classification was world-empires, the species, the hierarchization was Babylonia/Media/Greece/Rome — all the time aiming at Israel the holy people. For the purpose of speciation and hierarchization of world-empires, the precedent of Daniel presented itself, poorly executed where incongruous (as with the sages of Yavneh at Tosefta Miqvaot), brilliantly realized where commensurate (as here). And once the metaphorization of beasts as world-empires took over, other metaphors claimed attention.

Allegorical representation of animals registers at Gen. R. LXIV:X.3, where the lion represents cynical wisdom to yield the point, it is enough for us that we dealt with this nation whole and came forth whole. The snake embodies the proposition that what he wanted was not given to him and what he had was taken away from him. The destruction of the snake yields a lesson concerning the fall of Babylonia, Gen. R. XX:V.1. The pig is a metaphor for Cain/Rome Gen. R. XXII:XIII. So too Gen. R. LXXVIII:VII.1 has a comparable parable about how the beasts tried to conciliate the lion but forgot their wisdom as they drew near. Then it was *sauve qui peut.*

Gen. R. XLII:III.2 registers the elaborate metaphorization in the name of Ahaz:

If there are no kids, there will be no he-goats. If there are no he-goats, there will be no flock. If there is no flock, there will be no Shepherd, if there is no Shepherd, there will be no world.

If there are no children, there will be no adults. If there are no adults, there will be no disciples. If there are no disciples, there will be no sages. If there are no sages, there will be no elders. If there are no elders, there will be no prophets. If there are no prophets, the Holy One, blessed be he, will not allow his presence to come to rest in the world...

Gen. 15:9, "bring me a heifer...," treats animals as representatives of Babylonia, Media, Greece, and Rome (Edom), so XLIV:XV.1. Rome , Gen. R. LXV:I.1, is compared to the swine of the wood, bearing the qualities of hypocrisy: pretending to be a clean beast but lacking the indicators of cleanness. So too, Israel is compared to the ram caught in a thicket by his horns, Gen. R. LVI:IV.1, but in the end will be redeemed by the horns of a ram. Gen. R. LIV:IV.1 uses the ewe lambs in a different way, now they stand for seven generations by which the joy of Israel will be postponed. To animals are imputed human piety and virtue in the story of the ass of Phineas b. Yair.

But animals are not the unique media for metaphorization and the generation of parables, Gen. R. LXX:VIII.2 treats a well in the field, three flocks of sheep, a stone on the well's mouth, and the like; animals form merely a component of the vocabulary of metaphorization. Even our random sample of other sources of metaphors shows that fact. Nor do animal-metaphors bear a distinctive task of exposition or instantiation. They form a small part of a large and diverse vocabulary of metaphors, though their task seems fixed, e.g., serving as a standard metaphor for Babylonia, Media, Greece, Rome. Gen. R. LXXVI:VI.1 forms a variation on that same theme. Gen. R. XVIX:II.1 compares the tribes to animals to kingdoms, Benjamin/Media/wolf, a more elaborate approach to the same topic.

To conclude: where does the Aggadah recapitulate Halakhic modes of analysis — analogical-contrastive reasoning in a process of classification and hence hierarchization — and where does it pursue its own modes of thought? Where exposition of the Aggadic topic involves a variety of probative cases, the Aggadic composition offers a generalization sustained by a variety of illustrations, factual proofs drawn from Scripture, in the manner of the Halakhic writings. The two best examples are the propositions that strong emotions disrupt the status quo and that Israel compares with Adam.

Where Aggadic discourse shifts into its own modes of thought and analysis a particular topic predominates: the meaning of history, the interpretation of the rule of world-empires, the patterning of events. There animals are made to serve as metaphors for world-empires, and parabolic thinking takes over. Babylonia/Media/Greece/Rome — these persistently are embodied by animals, and their traits as empires are deemed comparable to those of beasts. The pattern shifts, the one at hand involving Babylonia/Judah, a lion; Medea/Benjamin, a wolf; Greece/Levi, Rome/Joseph, a bullock, other instances comparing Rome to the lion or to the pig, depending on context. For the purpose of conceptualizing the world empires and their sequence, Daniel's apocalyptic thinking, resorting to beasts to represent empires, provides a model for the Rabbinic exegetes of Genesis Rabbah, who classify in the manner of the Mishnah but who explain in the medium of a mode of thought — parabolic, metaphorical — particular to their Aggadic context.

B. THE THEOLOGICAL BESTIARY OF LEVITICUS RABBAH

Rather than commenting on sequences of verses of a base-text, as at, e.g., Genesis or Numbers or Deuteronomy as expounded by Genesis Rabbah and the two Sifrés, Leviticus Rabbah sets forth propositions demonstrated and amplified through probative cases. The compilers made no pretense at a systematic exegesis of sequences of verses of Scripture, abandoning the verse by verse mode of organizing discourse They struck out on their own to compose a means of expressing their propositions in a more systematic and cogent way.

That documentary program permits us to assess the remarkable component of the document contributed by the bestiary, with its profound reflections on Israel as comparable to the sheep (Lev. R. IV:VI.1), the massive exercise in bestiary thinking at Lev. R. XIII:V.1, "the prophets foresaw what the pagan kingdoms would do to Israel," with the river-system of Eden and the animals that represent the kingdoms providing analogies in the theology of history, and its account of the meaning of the selection of animals for Israelite virtue ("God favors the victim, not the pursuer"). So too, the bull, sheep, and goat match the merits of the patriarchs (Lev. R. XXI:XI.1). The ram embodies Israel trapped among the nations and entangled among the kingdoms (Lev. R. XXIX:XI.1). We found in the Halakhic documents and in Genesis Rabbah among the Aggadic ones little comparable in depth and comprehensiveness to these compositions and their companions. Clearly, the shift from verse-by-verse exegesis of details to large constructions of syllogistic compositions changed the fundamental approach to the reading of Scripture on the part of the Rabbinic sages. In that shift the possibilities of the metaphorization of animals, the formation of analogies to yield from the traits of beasts examples of virtues for Israel, vastly expanded. Above all, animals provided the medium for reflection on the theology of history in a time of crisis — the advent of the Christian empire, for Leviticus Rabbah came to closure about a century after the legalization of Christianity and its subsequent adoption as state religion.

These historical events precipitated thought on the meaning of history and its direction. The Rabbinic sages possessed models of the conduct of such thought in Scripture, both in the Authorized History from Genesis through Kings, and, more to the point of this study, in the representation of historical actors as beasts in the apocalyptic book of Daniel. Clearly, the model of Daniel Chapter Seven has stimulated thought on how beasts embody the traits of world-empires. But the apocalyptic vision of Daniel gives way to the Rabbinic mode of analytical thought. Daniel's vision involved beasts of fable, not fact. It set forth fantasies of beasts out of all relationship with the bestiary of nature — the lion with eagles' wings, the bear with three ribs in its mouth, the leopard with four wings of a bird, and the fourth beast with iron teeth, different from all before it, with ten horns… (Daniel 7:4-7). And while Daniel's intent is to speak through mystery and obscurity, the Rabbinic exegetes aimed at a clear and readily accessible statement of their meaning.

While the Rabbinic theologians of history may have found inspiration in Daniel's model, beasts representing historical empires, they thus followed their own mode of thought and articulate expression in making beasts into the media of theological expression. The Rabbinic counterpart drew upon the traits of beasts in the order of nature, the lion without wings, the bear lacking ribs in its mouth, and so on. Rather, the natural traits of lion/bear, so too bull, sheep, goat — these govern and embody the lessons that are to be learned. The beasts' traits represent the kingdoms' traits, not arbitrary fantasies of their qualities and conduct.

Accordingly, there is a correspondence between the natural conduct of the pig and the qualities of Rome, and so throughout. Evoking the figure of this beast or that in deciphering the meaning of events involved an entirely rational sifting of facts of this-worldly conduct, parallel patterns of behavior between pig and Rome, to take a commonplace analogy. Indeed, the parallel of beast and empire corresponded to the analogical-contrastive reasoning that classified the starling (Genesis Rabbah LXV:III.1) or settled the question of whether or not fish require an act of slaughter. The mode of thought of Leviticus Rabbah in connection with beasts (and much else, self-evidently) accounts for the way in which beasts embody the message that the document's framers wish to impart. With its sifting of the facts of nature and the social order and its bias in favor of the comparability of nature and nurture in the Torah, Rabbinic bestiary thought originates in the Rabbinic system, not in Daniel's model.

To place the use of the bestiary into its larger documentary context, we have to stand back and look at the document whole. The message of Leviticus Rabbah — congruent with that of Genesis Rabbah — is that the laws of history may be known out of Scripture's narratives, as these yield regularities and order, and that these laws, so far as Israel is concerned, focus upon the holy life of the community. If, as Moses made articulate in Leviticus and Deuteronomy, Israel obeys the laws of society aimed at Israel's sanctification, then the foreordained history, resting on the merit of the ancestors, will unfold as Israel hopes. So there is no secret to the meaning of the events of the day, and Israel, for its part, can affect its destiny and effect salvation. The authorship of Leviticus Rabbah has thus joined the two great motifs, sanctification and salvation, by reading Leviticus, the biblical book that is devoted to the former in the light of the requirements of the latter. In this way they made their fundamental point, which is that salvation at the end of history depends upon sanctification in the here and now. Nature and the Israelite social order guarantee that outcome. Then the bestiary is essential to the proposition of the document, and the truly remarkable compositions of the bestiary originate in response to the larger documentary program of Leviticus Rabbah.

To prove these points about the match society and nature, the authors of the compositions made lists of facts that bear the same traits and show the working of rules of history. Among those lists is the bestiary that asks geography and the bestiary to account for the future history of Israel as the prophets contemplated that history. It follows that the mode of thought brought to bear upon the theme of history remains exactly the same as in the Mishnah: list-making, with data exhibiting similar taxonomic traits drawn together into lists based on common monothetic traits or definitions. These lists then through the power of repetition make a single enormous point or prove a social law of history.

This brings us back to the bestiary and the metaphorical, parabolic thought processes that yield the remarkable expositions of the present document. Comparing empires to animals juxtaposes history and nature. As we find the rules of nature by identifying and classifying facts of natural life, in the traits of beasts, so we find rules of history by identifying and classifying the facts of the nations. So too as we find God's preference as to virtue in his choice of animals for the altar — pursued, not pursuers — so we compare Israel to the lamb or the ram and identify passivity as its virtue. Once discovered in the revealed bestiary of the altar, the social rules of Israel's national life yield explicit statements, such as that God hates the arrogant and loves the humble. That explains why the theological bestiary of Leviticus Rabbah attains the success we have encountered: why here, why now in particular. It is not because of the promise of the bestiary — the geology of rivers works equally well. Rather, it is because of the power of Leviticus Rabbah to precipitate for the Rabbinic exegetes parabolic and metaphorical thought in the encounter with the book of Leviticus. That mode of thought worked well with the bestiary and produced the results I have found so admirable. That outcome is particular to Leviticus Rabbah, not in response to traits of the book of Leviticus, as Sifra, devoted to the same book of Scripture, amply demonstrates.

C. THE THEOLOGICAL BESTIARY OF PESIQTA DERAB KAHANA

The systematic exposition of nearly an entire composite marks the one significant difference between Leviticus Rabbah and Pesiqta deRab Kahana. The bestiary writing of Leviticus Rabbah takes the form of compositions, not an entire composite. By contrast, Pesiqta deRab Kahana contains more than episodic references to animals. A systematic reading of the cultic data produces a coherent account of their meaning, a composite, not merely episodic compositions. That is accomplished in Pisqa Four, devoted to the theme of the red cow (Numbers 19), where a single approach to the reading of the bestiary produces a coherent result covering an entire composite.

We may say simply that absent the contribution of the bestiary to the exposition of Numbers 19, we should have no Pisqa Four to speak of. The opening item provides the model. Facts of Scripture are compared and contrasted to yield a generalization. Scripture indicts corporate Israel for the golden calf, and Scripture accords to corporate Israel the opportunity to atone for that sin. The red cow effects atonement for the sin of making the golden calf, a female responsible for her offspring, the rare offering that is not a male beast. What triggers the reading of matters is the choice of a female rather than a male, and the explanation follows — a fine case of deciphering the animal code of the altar. Pesiqta deRab Kahana IV:IX.1 then invokes the metaphors for the world empires, with Egypt tacked on to Babylonia/Media/Greece/Edom-Rome. The red cow embodies all of them. Thus a fixed repertoire of candidates is attached to the details of the red cow: heifer/red/ without defect/free of the yoke. Pesiqta deRab Kahana IV:IX.2 develops the metaphor for Edom/Rome. Pesiqta deRab Kahana IV:X.1 proceeds to metaphorize Israel in the red cow.

The rest is episodic. Pesiqta deRab Kahana VI:IV.1 continued by Pesiqta deRab Kahana VI:IV.2, 3, goes its own way, explaining the meaning of the lambs used for the regular daily whole offering: to remove the sins of corporate Israel. Pesiqta deRab Kahana XIII:I.3, XIII:XV.1, utilize the lion in contradictory ways, as a metaphor for Jerusalem and for Nebuchadnezzar. These represent compositions but do not effect the formation of a fully-executed composite.

Continuous with Leviticus Rabbah in metaphorical exploitation of the bestiary but still more systematic in its execution, Pesiqta deRab Kahana thus yields an entire pisqa devoted to beasts, delivering a massive message that depends on the bestiary for its realization. What Leviticus Rabbah commenced is carried to fulfillment: the reading of an entire passage of Scripture in the allegorical, metaphorical manner in exposition of the meaning in history for transactions of nature conducted in the Israelite cult.

D. THE THEOLOGICAL BESTIARY OF RUTH RABBAH

Ruth Rabbah contains nothing of consequence for our study, just a few standard animal-based metaphors, fox, dog, lion. The sample is so slight that we must conclude, reading the book of Ruth involved no thought on the promise of bestiary metaphors. That is because the issues of Ruth — the naturalization of an outsider to Israel by the Torah — in no way intersected with the matters illuminated by metaphors involved animals, e.g., the world-empires, the cult and its animal offerings as illustrative of virtue, and the like. That act points to one conclusion: the program of the document governed the selection of genres and media for the execution of that program. First comes the documentary vocation, then the media.

E. THE THEOLOGICAL BESTIARY OF ESTHER RABBAH I

We see that the representation of the four world-empires by animals here forms a convention. What is at stake at Song 5:2 to precipitate introduction of the nations into the reading of the Song is unclear to me. But the importance of the world-empires to the narrative of Esther is self-evident, and the possibility of encompassing Haman cannot have been missed.

F. THE THEOLOGICAL BESTIARY OF SONG OF SONGS RABBAH

The comparison of Israel or the patriarchs to the dove proves unique in context, the one truly successful exegesis based on the vocabulary of the bestiary. What we do not find now proves telling, for we can answer the question, why this, not that, when we turn to a blatant case in which the bestiary is not called upon in a way proportionate to its promise. When sages reading Song of Songs wished to refer to the nations of the world, they did *not* invoke the animals that stood for the world-empires, thus in one famous example we find:

SONG OF SONGS RABBAH XXIV:II

1. A. R. Yosé b. R. Hanina said, "The two oaths [Song 2:7: 'I adjure you, O daughters of Jerusalem,' and Song 3:5, 'I adjure you, O daughters of Jerusalem, by the gazelles or the hinds of the field'] apply, one to Israel, the other to the nations of the world.
   B. "The oath is imposed upon Israel that they not rebel against the yoke of the kingdoms.
   C. "And the oath is imposed upon the kingdoms that they not make the yoke too hard for Israel.
   D. "For if they make the yoke too hard on Israel, they will force the end to come before its appointed time."

SONG OF SONGS RABBAH XXIV:II

4. A. R. Helbo says, "There are four oaths that are mentioned here [Song 2:7, 'I adjure you, O daughters of Jerusalem,' Song 3:5, 'I adjure you, O daughters of Jerusalem, by the gazelles or the hinds of the field,' Song 5:8, 'I adjure you, O daughters of Jerusalem, if you find my beloved, that you tell him I am sick with love,' Song 8:4, 'I adjure you, O daughters of Jerusalem, that you not stir up nor awaken love until it please'], specifically,
   B. "he imposed an oath on Israel not to rebel against the kingdoms and not to force the end [before its time[, not to reveal its mysteries to the nations of the world, and not to go up from the exile by force.
   C. "For if so [that they go up from the exile by force], then why should the royal messiah come to gather together the exiles of Israel?"

SONG OF SONGS RABBAH XXIV:II

5. A.   R. Onia said, "The four oaths he imposed upon them corresponded to the four generations that forced the end before its time and stumbled in the effort.

   B.   "And what are they?

   C.   "Once in the days of Amram, once in the days of Dinai, once in the days of Kosiba, and once in the days of Shutelah son of Abraham: 'The children of Ephraim were as archers handling the bow' (Ps. 78:9)."

   D.   Some say, "One in the days of Amram, once in the generation of the repression, once in the days of the son of Kosiba, and once in the days of Shutelah son of Abraham: 'The children of Ephraim were as archers handling the bow' (Ps. 78:9)."

   E.   "For they were reckoning the hour from the time that the Holy One, blessed be He, made the decree when he speak with our father, Abraham, between the pieces [Gen. 15:13-17], but the time actually commenced from the moment at which Isaac was born.

   F.   "[Basing their actions upon this erroneous reckoning,] they assembled and went forth to battle and many of them fell slain.

   G.   "How come? 'Because they did not believe in the Lord and did not trust in his salvation' (Ps. 78:9),

   H.   "but they forced the end and violated the oath."

Here the Rabbinic exegetes wish to discuss the nations of the world, and we find no interest in animals as media of metaphorization. The representation of the nations by the lion, wolf, leopard, panther, and the like is ignored; the nations are undifferentiated. There is no interest in the bestiary as medium for thought and expression. I take that sequence of givens to explain itself: because the exegete did not plan to differentiate the nations, he also did not ask the conventional bestiary to contribute to his exposition. Every passage in which the world-empires are represented by beasts intends to distinguish one empire from another, to examine the distinctive traits of each — yielding a picture of Israel's distinction as well. That is not what is in play here.

Given the fundamental character of the Rabbinic reading of the Song of Songs as a metaphor, we must find puzzling the rather paltry result of this survey. The gazelles and hinds are compared with the patriarchs or the tribal progenitors. So too the patriarchs are compared to the dove, and also Israel is compared to the dove in an elaborate exposition, and to a ewe in a brief snippet. Man is the pride of animate creatures, eagle, ox, lion. The contrast with Genesis Rabbah and especially with Leviticus Rabbah and its companion, Pesiqta deRab Kahana, which found in animals a unique way of presenting theological reflection on Israel among the nations and on Israel's own virtue, proves blatant. The composition on the dove does not stand comparison with the counterpart, the propositional exposition on God favoring the pursued over the pursuer, shown by probative cases and by the conduct of the altar alike.

Song of Songs Rabbah contains nothing that compares with the fully realized metaphors of beasts for the world empires, beasts for the patriarchs, or beasts for models of virtue, as in Genesis Rabbah, Leviticus Rabbah, and Pesiqta deRab Kahana. For that purpose animals do not serve. Scripture offered an authoritative precedent for thinking of nations through animal-metaphors, with which the compilers of the document were preoccupied. By contrast, Midrash-exegesis in Song of Songs Rabbah turns to everyday experience — the love of husband and wife — for a metaphor of God's love for Israel and Israel's love for God. It is difficult to identify more than random precedents for metaphorization through the bestiary of emotional relationships. How they convey the intensity of Israel's love of God forms the point of special interest in this document. For it is not in propositions that they choose to speak, but in the medium of symbols. Beasts can have served — the loyalty of the male and female of a given species to one another for example. But established conventions intervened.

The Rabbinic sages here use language as a repertoire of opaque symbols in the form of words. They set forth sequences of words that connote meanings, elicit emotions, stand for events, form the verbal equivalent of pictures or music or dance or poetry. Through the repertoire of these verbal-symbols and their arrangement and rearrangement, the message the authors wish to convey emerges: not in so many words, but through words nonetheless. Sages chose for their compilation a very brief list of items among many possible candidates. They therefore determined to appeal to a highly restricted list of implicit meanings, calling upon some very few events or persons, repeatedly identifying these as the expressions of God's profound affection for Israel, and Israel's deep love for God. The message of the document comes not so much from stories of what happened or did not happen, assertions of truth or denials of error, but rather from the repetitious rehearsal of sets of symbols.

Given how well beasts served in the setting of stories of what happened or did not happen and in the context of world-historical movements, we cannot find surprising that beasts provided only episodic occasions for bearing the message of the document at hand. Conventions and implicit meanings governed, dictating what could and could not be done with inherited modes of thought and expression. In that context the very success of the bestiary in conveying the propositions of Genesis Rabbah, Leviticus Rabbah, and Pesiqta deRab Kahana concerning the world-empires imposed limitations on the bestiary's usefulness to portray in symbolic discourse the relationship of Israel and God. Other metaphors would have to serve. The very precise fit between the bestiary and the theology of history realized in the prior compilations placed severe limitations on what could be said in other contexts, for other purposes, through that same bestiary.

G. THE THEOLOGICAL BESTIARY OF LAMENTATIONS RABBAH

Why do the symbolic and metaphorical values of the bestiary provide so little of interest to the writers and compilers of Lamentations Rabbah? Recalling the settings in which the bestiary comes to the fore, we can have predicted its subordinated position here. The nations of the world do not take a primary position in the narrative of Lamentations Rabbah, which is devoted not to world-empires and their place in history but to God's relationship with Israel and Israel's with God. Where that theme calls forth an image of God bereft of Israel, the sparrow serves as the metaphor for Israel. And no beast can supply a metaphor for God's weeping for Israel, because God cannot be compared to an animal.

So the most ambitious compositions of Lamentations Rabbah involve God's mourning for Israel, recriminations for Israel's sorry condition, testimony to Israel's sin and explanation of its suffering. For that purpose no parabolic conventions built out of animal behavior presented themselves. God is never compared to an animal in the Rabbinic literature we have surveyed. The themes of Lamentations Rabbah accordingly are not encompassed by the metaphorical or symbolic vocabulary of the established bestiary. When we understand the tasks of the bestiary in Aggadic settings, we can also predict where it will not serve.

H. THE THEOLOGICAL BESTIARY OF THE FATHERS ACCORDING TO RABBI NATHAN

The serpent in The Fathers according to R. Nathan I:VIII.1ff. stands for itself, recapitulating its place in the narrative of Scripture. Along these same lines, the cattle of Abraham and the ass of Hanina b. Dosa embody the virtue of pious beasts, but they do not symbolize Israel. They offer exemplary cases of virtue that even a dumb animal realizes. They offer not metaphors but actors. So too the heifer well broken, the horse that has a bridle — these capture the virtue of the disciplined disciple of the Torah. Only the comparison of Rome to the boar out of the wood serves a theological purpose. But the message of the lesson in context is when Israelites do God's will, the nations of the world cannot rule over them, and to that message, the boar is an incidental figure. Its traits do not figure, only Israel's.

So the composite devoted to the exposition of tractate Abot presents no important metaphors drawn from the bestiary vocabulary of Rabbinic Judaism, only rarely reflecting the depth of thought contained within the metaphorization of animals in the theology of history that so impressed us at Genesis Rabbah, Leviticus Rabbah, and Pesiqta deRab Kahana. Tractate Abot, and hence its amplification in The Fathers According to R. Nathan, pursues no Halakhic program and also constructs no theology of Israelite history involving the world-empires, so the two principal types of discourse involving the theme of animals play no role. The exception, noted at the outset, proves the rule.

We see that the documentary program, whether Halakhic or Aggadic, governs the selection of compositions involving animals. But the genre, Halakhic or Aggadic, governs the execution: the kind of analysis, the mode of expression.

I. THE THEOLOGICAL BESTIARY OF THE YERUSHALMI'S AGGADAH

The important difference between the Yerushalmi's Halakhic and Aggadic writing on animals is that the Aggadic writing ignores the general taxonomic traits of beasts (pursued/pursuers), while the Halakhic one pays close attention to that same matter. That hardly surprises, since the Halakhic interest in the classification of data defines Halakhic discourse. By contrast, the Yerushalmi's Halakhic compositions ignore the unique traits of beasts, and the Aggadic ones find important lessons in the distinctive qualities of beasts, e.g., snakes carry out God's purpose (Y. Shab. 6:9 III:1, Y. Peah 1:1 XXVIII, 3:6 III) and the exemplary piety of the ass of Phineas b. Yair. All these items recapitulate themes and propositions that surface elsewhere in Aggadic documents. That rather general observation raises the question of whether the bestiary serves particular propositional purposes or makes itself available promiscuously for whatever tasks arise randomly.

J. THE THEOLOGICAL BESTIARY OF THE BAVLI'S AGGADAH

The contrast between the Bavli's Halakhic and Aggadic components recapitulates our result for the Yerushalmi. While the Bavli's Halakhic compositions aim at generalizations, the Aggadic ones stress the particular traits of beasts and their singular probative value. The one homogenizes and the other differentiates, the one presenting rules, the other singular cases of a theological or ethical proposition.

The Bavli's Aggadic materials fall into three categories. A portion takes up the theme of animals without demonstrating a proposition or proving a point or establishing a classification of beasts subject to a common theological proposition or Halakhic rule. When the theological proposition is that all species serve God's particular purpose, animals are bound to surface, but not alone, B. Shab. 8:1 III:3, 4. B. Ber. 5:1 I:28 makes a point not particular to animals, which is that prosperity leads to sin. More simply still, B. Shab. 6:4 II:13-114, dogs bite. Animals are incidental to the narrative, B. Ber. 9:1-5 XVII:2, that shows that whatever the All-Merciful does he does for good. These examples of an indeterminate intention in dealing with animals represent the following in addition: B. Ber. 9:1-5 XIX:16; B. Shab. 24:3 III:10 ("Israel is not subject to the stars"); B. Pes. 10:1 V:7; B. Hag. 2:1 IV:15; B. Git. 5:6 I:18; B. B.M. 8:1 I:20. In addition, singletons involve the delivery of wild goats (B. B.B. 1:6 IV:45 and the unique characteristics of Job's goats (B. B.B. 1:3 IV:27).

I here call attention to the enormous topical composite involving improbable beasts reported by Rabbah bar bar Hannah (B. B.B. 5:1A-D IV:7ff). I place it in the appendix because I do not know what to make of that composite. Each item is unique, so there is no taxic program. But only rarely does a composition in this group register a judgment, e.g., a moral imperative, on the basis of the reported beast and its traits and conduct. The topical composite stands outside the program of the Bavli in context; it is parachuted down, but has been collected for an other-than-theological (or Halakhic) purpose. I do not know what that purpose can have been, and I know of no comparable bestiary topical composite in the Bavli.

The second group, small in proportion to the whole, encompasses classifications of beasts that produce generalizations but that do not invoke distinctive qualities of specified beasts in the production of these generalizations. B. Hag. 2:1 IV:15, for instance, treats man and beast within a single, hierarchized classification: wild beasts/ox; fowl/eagle; and man/God. Snakes guard the burial places of sages and respond to the instructions of sages (B. B.M. 7:4 I;25). Large cattle and small cattle form subsets of cattle; it is forbidden to raise the former in the Land of Israel (B. Temurah 2:2 I:3). God is like a lion, but not like just any lion. God resembles a lion in his own unique way (B. Hullin 3:6-7 I:4). In general beasts here accord with the rules of nature; carry out God's will; have a particular purpose. Their distinctive traits rarely register.

The particular qualities of beasts dictate the classification in which they belong and produce something very like a conventional bestiary: lessons imparted by animals acting like human beings or analogous to them. These entries form by far the largest component of our log of references to animals. The significance of dreaming about various beasts, B. Ber. 9:1-5 I:32ff., imputes deeper meaning to the specified beasts, e.g., dreaming about an ox involves goring, biting, kicking, with diverse consequences. But animals are not the only occasions for dream-interpretation, and the category-formation is defined by a broader interest in symbolism.

Comparative zoology with close attention to particular traits of specific species figures at B. Shab. 8:1 III.5, 6. The former catalogues anomalies, where the weak frighten the strong beast, the latter, the comparison of goats, camels, and sheep. The issues derive from the natural traits of the species, yielding a genus that encompasses all of them. Adaptive evolution is implicit in the composition. B. Hor. 3:8 VII:3 compares a dog and a cat. The same interest in comparison figures at B. Shab. 19:1 II.7, the comparison now of Israel and a dove, a familiar theme. The category-formations, nations, animals, birds, small animals and trees yield comparisons as well, B. Bes. 3:3 I.4. So too B. Taanit 1:32E-H I.39 contains an implicit comparison among animals, lion, wolf, snake. Animals embody virtues, modesty, honesty, chastity, good manners, B. Er. 10:8A-E II:13. The apocalyptic representation of the nations by beasts at Dan. 8:21 and so forth recurs, now with Edom/Rome, Persia, Greece, B. Yoma 1:1 III:21, B. Meg. 1:13 IX.1, B. A.Z. 1:1 I:2. The traits of animals are matched with those of nations at B. Sot. 1:8-9 I:12, and with those of the Israelite tribal progenitors at B. Sot. 1:8-9 II:19.

The species are differentiated by their conduct in Noah's ark, B. San. 11:2A-CC I:20, 21. That again implies that sexual conduct of diverse species is to be classified. Beasts — dogs — yield a parable about alliances in the face of common enemies.

The world of nature exhibits the marks of God's perfection at creation, B. Hul. 9:6 II:3, II:4 (with its amplification at B. Bekh. 1:21K I:6):

> You have creatures that grow in the sea and you have creatures that grow on the dry land. Those that are in the sea, if they ever come up on dry land they immediately die. And those that are on dry land, if they ever go down into the sea they immediately die. You have creatures that grow in the fire and creatures that grow in the air. Those that are in the fire, if they ever go out to the air they immediately die. Those that are in the air, if they ever go down to the fire they immediately die. 'O Lord, how manifold are thy works!
>
> Every [kind of creature] that there is on dry land, there is a counterpart in the sea except for the weasel.

Here we conclude the Bavli's corpus with a clear statement that can have been made only in the Aggadic genre, not in the Halakhic one. The Aggadah finds in its particular cases the medium for its theological message, and we shall now ask about the particular forms of service, Halakhically and Aggadically, performed by the beasts of the Rabbinic corpus.

III. DIVERGENT DISCOURSES OF RABBINIC JUDAISM

What does the canonical corpus say through resort to animals that it could only express in the framework of a bestiary?

The Halakhah imposes a determinate program upon diverse topics, including animals. Specifically, it places animals into a single structure along with inanimate objects. What is important about animals is their capacity to inflict damage, and for that purpose, animals bear generic traits in common. They are not singular species, but a common genus. The Halakhic documents viewed whole introduce animals when they require classification in the context of the Halakhic program, e.g., M. B.Q. 1:1 and the like. When animals enter into the exposition, they are subjected to the analogical-contrastive process that overrides all else. They rarely serve as distinct analogies and do not generate parables to illustrate the law. Rather, they persistently represent themselves. For how many times did we find ample a simple comment: snakes bite, dogs bark! Not only so, but animals, we noted, commonly are formed into categories that find definition not in the differentiating traits of given species but in homogenizing traits that cover all species, e.g., the animal paid over as the fee for a dog or for a whore. The Halakhah does not differentiate among beasts because it seeks to identify what is common to diverse species, to find the genus that encompasses many species. In its work of hierarchical classification, animals figure only as themselves. That is why the Halakhah can have done its business without access to a bestiary bearing messages and meanings related to the indicative traits of its components.

The Aggadah speaks of other things altogether, and its interest in differentiation and speciation by appeal to indicative traits of distinction serves its larger task. We need not recapitulate the details, for a simple generalization serves.

The Aggadah asks animals to stand for something other than themselves, and it finds in their traits guidance in the identification of that something other: nations as beasts, nations as rivers, for example.

The Aggadah thus conducts a thought-process involving metaphorization, animals are like nations, nations are like animals. That fact emerges most effectively in the paramount metaphor that compares the world-empires to appropriate species of beasts. Rivers serve equally well, but without the particular effect attained by the explanation of what Persia has in common with a bear, or Rome with a pig, and so throughout.

Why then does Rabbinic Judaism resort to two modes of discourse? The answer appears to be, because there are propositions involving beasts — but not particular ones — that the system can express only in the context of Halakhic analysis, and that, in that context, only beasts serve to bear the message. The sacrificial cult represents one such context, the animate sources of damages, another. And there are issues that sages can investigate only through the medium of Aggadic narrative (whether in exegetical or expository form), about which they can think only within the bestiary and its facts and images, whether Scriptural or natural. The distinctive use of the bestiary in the Aggadic compilations, different from the approach of Daniel to the same beasts, for example, points to that fact. A single case, the dove, suffices to show how the Aggadah finds itself constrained to select a single species of animate being to express what it wishes to say about Israel. The traits of the dove in nature correspond with those of Israel in the social order of humanity.

If I had to identify the single most telling difference between Halakhic and Aggadic discourse on animals, it is that the Halakhic discourse seeks generalization and homogenization of species of beasts into category-formations that transcend beasts altogether, e.g., M. B.Q. 1:1, on which we have dwelt at length. Aggadic discourse, by contrast, asks animals to stand for things beyond themselves, most notably, world-empires, but also virtuous conduct (for one example), and treats animals in a metaphorical manner, through parables for example. Metaphorical thinking does not enter into the Halakhic area. There the limits of this world are reached. Dogs serve not as metaphors for loyalty but merely bite. Aggadic discourse crosses the boundaries into other modes of thought entirely, as illustrated by the shifts in the bestiary, where animals are subject to particularization, on the one side, and a massive process of extenuation through analogy and metaphor and parable, on the other. Stated simply: in Aggadah animals compare with other beings, embody virtue, represent world-empires, realize Israel.

IV. BESTIARY IN CONTEXT

Where in documentary context do we locate the shift from Halakhic to Aggadic modes of thought about beasts? The Halakhic documents come first, Mishnah and Tosefta before all else. They reached closure while the process of composing compositions for the Aggadic composite was still underway. In foundation-documents of the Halakhah, we now realize, animals stand for themselves and their species, awaiting classification in a common genus, e.g., clean/unclean, fit for the altar/not fit for the altar, hierarchically situated among causes of damages, animate and inanimate, and the like. That mode of thought persists in the Aggadic documents but another takes its place alongside.

That is the point at which the bestiary conveys a system of thought and meaning connected with animals and their taxic traits. Then emerges a morality best illuminated by beasts, but a morality pertinent to the human condition: nations and peoples for example. It surfaces in Genesis Rabbah and comes to its climactic expression in Leviticus Rabbah. But metaphorical thinking about the bestiary and its uses simply does not present itself in the Mishnah or the Tosefta or in the continuator documents of the Halakhah. The breakout into a taxic system drawing moral lessons from beasts thus comes in the compilations of the fifth century, with Genesis Rabbah at 400, Leviticus Rabbah at 450, and Pesiqta deRab Kahana, the single most fully realized statement, at 500. It was then that the Rabbinic sages were devoting profound thought to the theology of history, the meaning of events and the place of Israel among the empires. What the Aggadic compositions invoked was abstract thinking, the transformation of animals from particular instances of a species to representatives of traits that stand for more than a species of animals — much more.

But that process of treating as an abstraction a species of beast, of viewing animals as metaphors for men and nations, represents merely an extension of an already fully realized mode of abstract thinking to a new set of problems, those of the Aggadah represented by the theology of history. In fact, treating cases as representative of rules, concrete things as subject to abstraction and extension, already had established itself in the Halakhic framework. Before the Aggadic documents took shape, the Halakhic documents beginning with the Mishnah and the Tosefta had already explored the uses of abstraction and concretization in their analytical processes. This they did by speaking of concrete things in order to convey abstract principles, the consecration of a woman to a particular man as a concrete embodiment of the process of the transfer of title (Mishnah-tractate Qiddushin Chapter One), for example, or at Mishnah-tractate Baba Qamma Chapter One, sorting out the types of causation, from direct to remote, and consequent levels of responsibility by appeal to the four primary causes of damages and consequent responsibility in the remarkably homely formulation,

M. Baba Qamma

1:1   A.   [There are] four generative causes of damages: (1) ox [Ex. 21:35-36], (2) pit [Ex. 21:33], (3) crop-destroying beast [Ex. 22:4], and (4) conflagration [Ex. 22:5].

      B.   [The definitive characteristic] of the ox is not equivalent to that of the crop-destroying beast;

      C.   nor is that of the crop-destroying beast equivalent to that of the ox;

      D.   nor are this one and that one, which are animate, equivalent to fire, which is not animate;

      E.   nor are this one and that one, which usually [get up and] go and do damage, equivalent to a pit, which does not usually [get up and] go and do damage.

      F.   What they have in common is that they customarily do damage and taking care of them is your responsibility

      G.   And when one [of them] has caused damage, the [owner] of that which causes the damage is liable to pay compensation for damage out of the best of his land [Ex. 22:4].

The mode of thought represented by concretization of abstract principles or conceptions begins in the Halakhah and continues and is carried forward into the Aggadah. First comes the ox/pit/crop-destroying beast/conflagration, then the lion, bear, wolf, and leopard for the world-empires. The upshot is simply stated: Aggadic thought is continuous with Halakhic, adapting to its tasks the analytical method of analogical-contrastive thinking. Halakhic praxis and Aggadic parable, the divergent discourses of Rabbinic Judaism differ in subject-matter. But, the bestiary common to them both has shown, a single mode of thought and analysis animates throughout.

ENDNOTES

[1] The interplay of the Halakhah and the Aggadah is worked out in the sequence, *The Theology of the Oral Torah. Revealing the Justice of God.* Kingston and Montreal, 1999: McGill-Queen's University Press and Ithaca, 1999: Cornell University Press, and *The Theology of the Halakhah.* Leiden, 2001: E. J. Brill.

12

Pirqé Abot Read as a Coherent Theological Statement

Tractate Abot, conventionally dated at ca. 250 C.E.,1 on the surface appears to be a miscellaneous collection of sayings. But a second glance yields a different result. The document proves to form a theological system fully exposed. The sayings cohere and recapitulate the very category-formations that would define Rabbinic Judaism in the first six centuries of the Common Era.2

A claim for system and logic must set forth what is at the center of matters and holds the whole together.3 This collection of episodic aphorisms forms a melancholy meditation on the human condition of the individual Israelite. Corporate Israel and its historical fate never frame the issue. The problem facing the framer of the document — provoked by the logic of monotheism — is succinctly stated: "We do not have in hand an explanation either for the prosperity of the wicked or for the suffering of the righteous" (4:15). The resolution of the paradox of palpable injustice — the prosperity of the wicked more than the suffering of the righteous — is in the doctrine of life beyond the grave. Individual existence does not end in death. There is a world to come, which affords eternal life to the righteous but which excludes those who are wicked in this world.

In tractate Abot that eternal life is afforded in a juridical procedure, a trial, to individuals in response to their conduct in this life. "This world is like an antechamber before the world to come. Get ready in the antechamber, so you can go into the great hall." How to prepare? "Better is a single moment spent in penitence and good deeds in this world than the whole of the world to come. And better is a single moment of inner peace in the world to come than the whole of a lifetime spent in this world" (4:16-17). The world to come then forms the reward for those that live humbly and righteously.

Above all, Heaven knows what mortals do and keeps a record for each one, with consequences that follow from right conduct, and punishment for wrong. Thus "Be meticulous in a small religious duty as in a large one, for you do not know

269

what sort of reward is coming for any of the various religious duties. And reckon with the loss required in carrying out a religious duty against the reward for doing it, and the reward for committing a transgression against the loss for doing it. And keep your eye on three things, so you will not come into the clutches of transgression: Know what is above you: An eye which sees, and an ear which hears, and all your actions are written down in a book" (2:1). "And know before whom you work, for your employer can be depended Upon to pay your wages for what you can do" (2:14). God is an active presence everywhere, and prayer is addressed to a listening ear: "when you pray, don't treat your praying as a matter of routine. But let it be a plea for mercy and supplication before the Omnipresent, blessed be he" (2:13). The Israelite lives in an enchanted world, where everything he says and does counts.

Accordingly, a coherent, compelling picture of the human situation emerges. "Those who are born are destined to die, and those who die are destined for resurrection. And the living are destined to be judged — so as to know, to make known, and to confirm that he is God, he is the one who forms, he is the one who creates, he is the one who understands, he is the one who judges, he is the one who gives evidence, he is the one who brings suit, and he is the one who is going to make the ultimate judgment. Blessed be he, for before him are not guile, forgetfulness, respect for persons, bribe taking, for everything is his. And know that everything is subject to reckoning. And do not let your evil impulse persuade you that Sheol is a place of refuge for you. For despite your wishes were you formed, despite your wishes were you born, despite your wishes do you live, despite your wishes do you die, and despite your wishes are you going to give a full accounting before the King of kings of kings, the Holy One, blessed be he" (4:22). The key to the document's message thus is that there is justice and there is a judge, and all who live are subject to retribution for their deeds: "He saw a skull floating on the water and said to it, 'Because you drowned others, they drowned you, and in the end those who drowned you will be drowned.'"

Where is the justice in all this? A simple doctrine accounts for the responsibility of each individual for every action. Man is accountable for what he does because he has free choice: "Everything is foreseen, and free choice is given. In goodness the world is judged. And all is in accord with the abundance of deeds. All is handed over as a pledge, And a net is cast over all the living. The store is open, the storekeeper gives credit, the account book is open, and the hand is writing. Whoever wants to borrow may come and borrow. The charity collectors go around every day and collect from man whether he knows it or not. And they have grounds for what they do. And the judgment is a true judgment. And everything is ready for the meal (3:15-16)." I cannot imagine a more articulate statement of the system viewed whole than that statement of reward and punishment, foreknowledge and free will.

What guarantees the equity of God's governance therefore is that death is succeeded by life for those that merit it. "Don't give up hope of retribution" (1:7).

"And do not have confidence in yourself until the day you die... And do not say, 'When I have time, I shall study,' for you may never have time" (2:4). "It's not your job to finish the work, but you're not free to walk away from it. If you have learned much Torah, they will give you a good reward. And your employer can be depended upon to pay your wages for what you do. And know what sort of reward is going to be given to the righteous in the coming time" (2:16). Reward and punishment are tempered by God's mercy and patience with human shortcomings: everything is in the effort.

The human situation portrayed by tractate Abot therefore entails alert and conscious conduct and imposes humility and fear. Man is a nullity, yet is an actor responsible for his own fate, has no reason to take pride in his condition, yet is subject to God's acute concern: "Reflect upon three things and you will not fall into the clutches of transgression: Know from whence you come, whither you are going, and before whom you are going to have to give a full account of yourself. From whence do you come? From a putrid drop. Whither are you going? To a place of dust, worms, and maggots And before whom are you going to give a full account of yourself? Before the King of kings of kings, the Holy One, blessed be he" (3:1).

So much for the reward for good conduct and the punishment for bad. The system portrayed in tractate Abot defines principles of virtue that register as good conduct. Of what does virtue consist? Since the human condition depends on God's will, virtue consists in making one's own wishes conform to those of God: "Make his wishes into your own wishes, so that he will make your wishes into his wishes. Put aside your wishes on account of his wishes, so that he will put aside the wishes of other people in favor of your wishes" (2:4). Those wishes are known, for God, in the Torah. Hence the supreme act of virtue consists in study of the Torah. Knowledge of God and the human condition derive from the act of grace comprised by the Torah, which informs man of what he otherwise could not have surmised, which is that he is created in the image of God; and which informs Israel that they are the children of God: "Precious is Adam, who was created in the image of God. It was an act of still greater love that it was made known to him that he was created in the image of God, as it is said, For in the image of God he made man (Gen. 9:6). Precious are Israelites, who are called children to the Omnipresent. It was an act of still greater love that they were called children to the Omnipresent, as it is said, You are the children of the Lord your God (Dt. 14:1). Precious are Israelites, to whom was given the precious thing. It was an act of still greater love that it was made known to them that to them was given that precious thing with which the world was made, as it is said, For I give you a good doctrine. Do not forsake my Torah (Prov. 4:2)" (3:14).

Torah-study forms the definition of the human vocation. Man was created to study the Torah: "If you have learned much Torah, do not puff yourself up on that account, for it was for that purpose that you were created" (2:8). That claim is hardly excessive, since through Torah-study man meets God: "If two sit together and between them do not pass teachings of Torah, lo, this is a seat of the scornful, as it is said, Nor sits in the seat of the scornful (Ps. 1:1). But two who are sitting, and words of Torah do pass between them — the Presence is with them, as it is said, Then they that feared the Lord spoke with one another, and the Lord hearkened and heard, and a book of remembrance was written before him, for them that feared the Lord and gave thought to His name (Mal. 3:16). I know that this applies to two. How do I know that even if a single person sits and works on Torah, the Holy One, blessed be he, sets aside a reward for him? As it is said, 'Let him sit alone and keep silent, because he had laid it upon him' (Lam. 3:28)." Torah-study is analogous to prayer, with this difference: when the Israelite prays, he talks to God, but when he studies, God talks to him.

Accordingly, God is present where the Torah is studied, and the way to know God is to study the Torah. "Three who ate at a single table and did not talk about teachings of Torah while at that table are as though they ate from dead sacrifices (Ps, 106:28), as it is said, For all tables are full of vomit and filthiness if they are without God (Ps. 106:28). But three who ate at a single table and did talk about teachings of Torah while at that table are as if they ate at the table of the Omnipresent, blessed is he, as it is said, 'And he said to me, This is the table that is before the Lord' (Ez. 41:22)" (3:2-3). So too the matter is elaborated: "Among ten who sit and work hard on Torah the Presence comes to rest, as it is said, 'God stands in the congregation of God' (Ps. 82:1). And how do we know that the same is so even of five? For it is said, 'And he has founded his group upon the earth' (Am. 9:6). And how do we know that this is so even of three? Since it is said, 'And he judges among the judges' (Ps. 82:1). And how do we know that this is so even of two? Because it is said, 'Then they that feared the Lord spoke with one another, and the Lord hearkened and heard' (Mal. 3:16). And how do we know that this is so even of one? Since it is said, 'In every place where I record my name I will come to you and I will bless you' (Ex. 20:24)" (3:6).

But study of Torah bears with it two further obligations. The first is to make a living. One cannot rely on Torah-learning to provide for material wealth. Second, one must carry out the teachings that one studies. "Fitting is learning in Torah along with a craft, for the labor put into the two of them makes one forget sin. And all learning of Torah which is not joined with labor is destined to be null and cause sin. And all who work with the community — let them work with them for the sake of Heaven. For the merit of their fathers strengthens them, and their fathers' righteousness stands forever. And as for you, I credit you with a great reward, as if you had done all of the work required by the community on your own merit alone" (2:2). But Torah-study should be ceaseless and not interrupted by extraneous thoughts: "He who is going along the way and repeating his Torah tradition but interrupts his repetition and says, 'How beautiful is that tree! How beautiful is that ploughed field!' — Scripture reckons it to him as if he has become liable for his life" (3:7). This implacable judgment shocks and has sustained the softening of interpretation: if one deems the beauty of the tree or field to interrupt the continuity of Torah-learning, so failing to perceive the lessons of the Torah contained within nature, then the penalty accrues. But read on its own, its message is clear: the stakes in Torah-learning are cosmic.

The temptation to concentrate on Torah-study to the exclusion of virtuous deeds provokes concern. Practice of the Torah's teachings, not merely mastery of their content, counts. What of the tension between knowing and doing, the outcome of Torah-study? The result of Torah-study is proper conduct, and without proper conduct Torah-study is null: "If there is no learning of Torah, there is no proper conduct. If there is no proper conduct, there is no learning in Torah. If there is no wisdom, there is no reverence. If there is no reverence, there is no wisdom If there is no understanding, there is no knowledge. If there is no knowledge, there is no understanding. If there is no sustenance, there is no Torah learning. If there is no Torah learning, there is no sustenance" (3:17). "He who learns so as to teach — they give him a chance to learn and to teach. He who learns so as to carry out his teachings — they give him a chance to learn, to teach, to keep, and to do" (4:5). Torah study yields this-worldly rewards: "Whoever keeps the Torah when poor will in the end keep it in wealth. And whoever treats the Torah as nothing when he is wealthy in the end will treat it as nothing in poverty. Keep your business to a minimum and make your business Torah. And be humble before everybody. And if you treat the Torah as nothing, you will have many treating you as nothing. And if you have labored in Torah, God has a great reward to give you" (4:9-10). But study of the Torah is its own reward and should not be construed as a source of benefit in this-worldly terms: "Do not make Torah teachings a crown with which to glorify yourself or a spade with which to dig. Whoever derives worldly benefit from teachings of Torah takes his life out of this world" (4:5).

To whom does the document speak? The "you" of the document is all Israel. But among Israelites, the document speaks most explicitly to masters and disciples, masters called upon to make decisions in courts as judges, disciples preparing through imitation of the masters for the same public responsibility. Abot is a handbook for judges, lawyers, and disciples. The lessons of Torah-study focus on the conduct of masters called upon to judge cases and dispense justice "Be prudent in judgment. Raise up many disciples. Make a fence for the Torah" (1:2). "Don't make yourself like one of those who make advocacy before judges while you yourself are judging a case. And when the litigants stand before you, regard them as guilty. And when they leave you, regard them as acquitted, when they have accepted your judgment." (1:8). "Examine the witnesses with great care. And watch what you say, lest they learn from what you say how to lie" (1:9). "Do not serve as a judge by yourself, for there is only One who serves as a judge all alone. And do not say, 'Accept my opinion.' For they have the choice in that matter, not you." (4:8). "He who avoids serving as a judge breaks off the power of enmity, robbery, and false swearing. And he who is arrogant about making decisions is a fool, evil, and prideful" (4:7).

Israel seen whole, not merely the sector of judges, lawyers, and disciples, comes under consideration only generically. So far as the document sets forth a social philosophy, it covers the Temple, the Torah, and private acts of loving kindness (1:2). "On three things does the world stand: on justice, on truth, and on peace." "Love work. Hate authority. Don't get friendly with the government" (1:10). Virtue depends upon forming the right motivation for right action and invokes once more the issues of reward and punishment. "Do not be like servants who serve the master on condition of receiving a reward, but be like servants who serve the master not on condition of receiving a reward. And let the fear of Heaven be upon you" (1:3).

What doctrine of emotions emerges, defining the everyday outcome of virtue? The ideal Israelite accommodates, concedes, conciliates, gives way, forbears. Virtue requires perpetual patience, penitence and concern for the feelings and responses of others: "Let the respect owing to your fellow be as precious to you as the respect owing to you yourself. And don't be easy to anger. And repent one day before you die" (2:10). "The honor owing to your disciple should be as precious to you as yours. And the honor owing to your fellow should be like the reverence owing to your master. And the reverence owing to your master should be like the awe owing to Heaven" (4:12). One must not only forbear but actively conciliate his fellows: "Anyone from whom people take pleasure — the Omnipresent takes pleasure. And anyone from whom people do not take pleasure, the Omnipresent does not take pleasure" (3:10).

The right attitude then requires trembling and humility before God and man alike. Fear of sin is the key to virtuous conduct, even more than mastery of Torah-learning or wisdom: "For anyone whose fear of sin takes precedence over his wisdom, his wisdom will endure, And for anyone whose wisdom takes precedence over his fear of sin, his wisdom will not endure." Anyone whose deeds are more than his wisdom — his wisdom will endure. And anyone whose wisdom is more than his deeds — his wisdom will not endure" (3:9). Wisdom requires astuteness: "Who is a sage? He who learns from everybody. Who is strong? He who overcomes his desire. Who is rich? He who is happy in what he has. Who is honored? He who honors everybody" (4:1). "Do not despise anybody and do not treat anything as unlikely. For you have no one who does not have his time, and you have nothing which does not have its place" (4:3). So too, one must nurture the virtues of consideration and restraint: "Do not try to make amends with your fellow when he is angry, or comfort him when the corpse of his beloved is lying before him, or seek to find absolution for him at the moment at which he takes a vow, or attempt to see him when he is humiliated" (4:18).

Accordingly, a coherent message emerges from tractate Abot. It is in three parts. First, God is just and merciful, and those traits come to realization when every individual answers to him for conduct in this life, with reward or punishment awaiting in the world to come. Virtue, second, consists in obedience to God's wishes, the upright person making his wishes conform to those of God. The requirements of virtue, third, are known in the Torah, the ultimate act of divine grace, which the Israelite is charged with mastering and carrying out.

The document speaks for Rabbinic sages and expresses their concerns. Its compilers and authors of its sayings conceive Israel to form not a corporate community bearing political power, e.g., to inflict acts of legitimate violence, but a collection of individuals, each responsible for himself before God. Israel is made up of persons possessed of the Torah and endowed with personal free will to obey or disobey the Torah. It is that endowment that defines the dynamics of the system put forth in the collected sayings. All Israelites enjoy the freedom to choose that originates with Adam and accounts for the disaster brought on by his deed: death above all. The Torah provides the antidote to death: access to eternal life. And each individual Israelite determines for himself his fate beyond the grave, everyone accorded a trial on his own. Accordingly that shift in Israel's circumstance from the public and the political to the private and the personal requires a shift in focus to the power of the individual to make his wishes and will conform to God's — a decision of a profoundly personal nature.

The single preoccupation paramount in the program of the document occurs in its account of virtue as submission to God and conciliation of one's fellow man. These traits of the submissive, humble, accommodating individual point to a persons lacking all political aspirations, deprived of this-worldly capacity to realize their own will. Collective action is not contemplated. The individual Israelite makes God's will his own will, in hope that God will make his will that of the Israelite.

What is striking is not only the absence of a collective, communal conception of Israel as a political entity but its attribution to God of the virtues of the vanquished. The system assigns to Heaven the operating program: justice and judgment, recompense and retribution. The reward of restraint lies in submission: the surrender of free will, which brings about sin, and the subordination of one's own will to God's. As Israel is subject to the nations in the here-and-now, so the Israelite accepts God's will and conforms to his commandments. The reward for the Israelites in the world to come proves commensurate. Then this world matters only as the antechamber of the world to come, and what makes a difference in the here and now is solely submission: acceptance of the givens of this world. The document, preoccupied with the individual and his parlous existence, in fact speaks to corporate Israel about its collective situation. What we have before us is a social philosophy rendered, paradoxically, in private and personal terms. All who aspire to live forever in affirming the eternity of their individuality comprise a moral collectivity, each individual knowing God in the same way as all the others, through the Torah.

What is affirmed by Abot is an encompassing system, not merely a mélange of episodic allegations. That system responds to the problem of evil that forms the dynamic of monotheist theology: how can God be conceived to be both all-powerful and just when the condition of humanity is contemplated: the righteous suffer, the wicked prosper, and exact justice prevails only sometimes. The solution to the problem of evil encompasses three aspects: [1] the fate of the individual in this life and after death, [2] the study of the Torah in response to the human condition, and [3] the nurture of virtue consequent upon Torah-study. [2] Study of the Torah leads to [3] virtue, which defines [1] the righteous life worthy of eternity. The destiny of individuals is to die, with judgment and advent to the age to come for those that merit it. Study of the Torah invokes the presence of God. From Torah study the Israelite learns the lessons of the virtue that secures the world to come.

Implicit in the tripartite construction —Torah-study, virtue, resurrection — are norms of belief in principles so fundamental and generative that tractate Abot in all its specificity falls to pieces if any of these norms are defied. These norms define God, his character and conscience. The one, unique God who governs is just and merciful. That premise sustains the system. God is everywhere aware of what each individual in all of creation does at all times. Human beings, accordingly, live in an enchanted realm of the divine person's perpetual presence, subject to supervision yielding a detailed record of all their actions and attitudes. That record is examined when individuals die, with results that are articulated, as we have seen.

Before a single sentence in Abot can have been written, therefore, three convictions had to prevail. First, God, who forms a presence and a personality everywhere, is just, and rules of rationality pervade creation. Second, man is like God in possessing free will and is responsible for the choices that he makes. Third, the Torah forms the medium for the encounter with God in the world, especially at meals. In that context, heresy consisted of three contrary convictions. There is no judge and there is no justice. Man is not subject to retribution for his actions. The Torah forms a tradition, an act of culture, but not the record of the words of the living God. What is implicit in Abot and therefore attested as norms of conviction is made explicit as heresy:

A.   All Israelites have a share in the world to come,
B.   as it is said, "your people also shall be all righteous, they shall inherit the land forever; the branch of my planting, the work of my hands, that I may be glorified" (Is. 60:21).
C.   And these are the ones who have no portion in the world to come:
D.   He who says, the resurrection of the dead is a teaching that does not derive from the Torah, and the Torah does not come from Heaven; and an Epicurean [who denies divine judgment and retribution].

                                   Mishnah-tractate Sanhedrin 10:1

Here we find explicit statements of the norms implicit in tractate Abot: resurrection, judgment, and the Torah, all in the form of heresies: denial of the Torah, of judgment, and therefore of resurrection as critical to the Torah's construction of human existence.

ENDNOTES

1 But see now Guenter Stemberger, "Mischna Avot. Fruehe Weisheitsschrift, pharisaeisches Erbe, oder spaetrabbinische Bildung?" *Zeitschrift der neutestamentliche Wissenschaft*, 2005.

2 I here reproduce my translation, *Torah from Our Sages: Pirke Avot. A New American Translation and Explanation*. Chappaqua, 1983: Rossel. Paperback edition: 1987. In print: S. Orange, 2005: Behrman House.

3 Contrast the view of Amram Tropper, *Wisdom, Politics, and Historiography. Tractate Avot in the Context of the Graeco-Roman Near East* (Oxford and New York, 2004: Oxford University Press). Tropper situates Abot in diverse and otherwise unconnected cultural settings and yields complete chaos. My review of his book appears below.

13

The Two Stages in the Formation of Talmudic Judaism: The Literary Inquiry into a Historical question

The one whole Torah of Moses, our rabbi, written and oral, derives from — finds it life-situation in — the synagogue and the school-house (or study-circle, or profession of clerks), respectively. That is to say, that Judaism's principal literary divisions take shape around documents identified as fundamental and therefore subjected to searching, sustained and systematic exegetical re-presentation by the sages, whether in the synagogue or in the school-house.[1]

The difference between the one and the other concerns subject-matter. The synagogue selects the definitive organization provided in particular by books of Scripture that serve in the synagogue liturgy and are declaimed within the framework of synagogue worship.[2] These are the Pentateuch and the Five Scrolls, most of which in the formative age of Rabbinic Judaism receive large-scale compilations of an exegetical character. The school-house identifies the Mishnah-tractates that will be subjected to systematic study and in particular the distinctive, dialectical analysis that transforms the Mishnah's cases into governing laws and abstract principles, subject to generalization and extension.[3] Together, Scripture and the Mishnah thus provide the organizing structures — books of Scripture, tractates of the Mishnah — that hold together every kind of preserved writing produced, valued, sponsored, preserved, and handed on as tradition by our sages of blessed memory. No free-standing document except for those that are shaped around Scripture- or Mishnah-exegesis bears the traits that every document sponsored by these sages does: the ubiquitous, persistent citation of sages themselves.[4]

It follows that in this Judaism that appeals to the structure of the dual Torah, oral and written, as the one whole Torah of Moses our Rabbi, both Scripture ("the written part of the Torah") and the Mishnah ("the oral part of the Torah") enjoy a standing that is unique. That authority proves definitive and determinative of structure and order. These two documents in the Rabbinic canon uniquely serve to define the principles of formal and even propositional-associative coherence. We therefore must assign to the fact of the privileging of Scripture and the Mishnah the status of the generative event in the formation of the literature that sets forth the Judaism of the dual Torah in its initial statement.

Furthermore, it is to the Talmud of Babylonia, because of its remarkable power to hold together both Scripture- and Mishnah-exegesis — a power possessed by no other document in the Rabbinic canon except for the Talmud of the Land of Israel — that we may fairly assign a unique position by speaking of Talmudic Judaism. That phrase refers to the Judaic religious system that is set forth by the Talmud of Babylonia in particular. We need not — indeed, we *should* not — distinguish Talmudic Judaism from Rabbinic Judaism in general — that is, the Judaism laid out by the entirety of the Rabbinic canon. But an interest in the history of the formation of Rabbinic Judaism is well served by a focus upon the evidence of the Talmud in particular.[5]

That is because the Talmud is made up of two kinds of writing in the form of large-scale, constitutive components, only one of which realizes the definitive purposes of the document as a whole. The Talmud is formed as a systematic commentary to selected tractates of the Mishnah, and, as a matter of fact, most of the composites of which the Talmud is comprised serve that one purpose in providing Mishnah-exegesis and the amplification of the Mishnah's laws. But the Talmud contains another classification of composite, which does not conform to the document's definitive traits, and that is the kind of composite that ignores the Mishnah altogether. Neither the Mishnah's propositions, nor its language, nor even its topical program, is addressed in this other kind of composite, which holds together compositions on entirely other matters than those addressed by a tractate, a chapter, a paragraph, even a single line, of a Mishnah-passage under discussion in a determinate context or in any other context.

This other-than-Mishnah-exegetical classification of composite clearly took shape for some purpose other than the making of what we now know as the Talmud. The writers of its compositions and the compilers of those compositions into the composite as we have it concerned themselves with other matters entirely — systematic exegesis of Scripture, the presentation of virtue, the formulation of social policy beyond the realm of normative law, and the consideration of theological topics being the main categories into which those other matters fall. The Mishnah contains some systematic exegesis of Scripture, occasionally sets forth teachings concerning virtue, at some points lays out supererogatory, supra-legal norms, and here and there raises theological questions. But the free-standing composites to which reference is made utterly ignore those passages of the Mishnah, in no way respond to their character or specific contents, and bear no relationship with, let alone correspondence to, the Mishnah-passages on comparable themes.

II. THE PRIVILEGING OF THE MISHNAH AND THE TEMPORAL PRIORITY OF THE OTHER-THAN-MISHNAH-EXEGETICAL COMPOSITES OF THE TALMUD

That is the point at which considerations of priority enter in. A simple argument suffices. It serves specifically to establish the claim that the other-than-Mishnah-exegetical composites in the Talmud carry us into a time prior to the moment at which the Mishnah, along with Scripture, gained the privilege of defining the principles of coherence, association, and order, that would govern the entirety of the Rabbinic canon. That privileging so defined the entire canon that every document (with the specified exceptions) of Rabbinic Judaism would serve in the line of tradition and exegesis of Scripture, in the Midrash-compilations, or the Mishnah, in the Talmud.

That argument, first of all, encompasses these four points of established fact, upon which all else depends:

[1] the Talmud and Midrash-compilations take shape around the Mishnah and Scripture and so demonstrate the privileged positions of the Mishnah and Scripture (to be designated, the oral and the written components of the one whole Torah of Moses, our rabbi);

[2] so, as a matter of fact, completed writing, whether mere compositions or entire composites alike, that serves to amplify the sense or meaning or implications of verses of Scripture or paragraphs of the Mishnah will always, invariably, everywhere be given primary standing in the organization of compilations and priority in the order of materials that are selected;[6]

[3] and, concomitantly, completed writing that realizes some purpose other than Mishnah- or Scripture-exegesis will be assigned subordinate standing and preserved only tangentially, and for a purpose somehow deemed relevant to the principal work of Mishnah- or Scripture-exegesis, however remote or merely-formal;

[4] and, correlatively, the media for the preservation of that other-than-Mishnah- or Scripture-exegetical writing will be limited to the ones that serve the Mishnah or Scripture; no other medium for the organization and preservation of that other classification of preserved writing will take shape

Now these four facts yielded by the character of the Rabbinic canon that is now extant permit us to identify the necessary breaking point in the temporal sequence in which writing takes shape: before and after the privileging of the Mishnah. We may identify two periods in the writing of the materials now located in the Talmud and Midrash-compilation. Working from the known, the end-product, to the unknown, we begin with the latest: the second, and final period is the one in which the documentary requirements of the Talmud or Midrash-compilation governed. Then people knew that whatever writing they would produce would find its ultimate form in a Talmud-tractate or Midrash-compilation. After the Mishnah and Scripture had gained that privileged position that they were to enjoy from the formation of the Rabbinic canon to our own time, sages knew that whatever was to be formalized and transmitted would find its ultimate position in the chain of tradition only in an exegetical document that acknowledged that privileging. And, further, people also knew that it would be large-scale composites — whole documents — that would form the principal, probably the sole, medium for the transmission of tradition into the long future. Writing would therefore attain publication not in brief snippets — compositions, composites — but in huge documents. These then form the two effects of the privileging of the two pillars of the dual Torah:

[1] the type of writing that would predominate;

[2] the medium of publication that would alone serve.

In this regard, the privileging of the Mishnah and Scripture imposed on writing its own governing metaphor: like the Mishnah, or like Scripture, writing would cover the established program of the foundation-documents; and like them, writing would coalesce in very large formations, tractates or scrolls of components of the written Torah ("books"), respectively.

But what about the time — indeterminate, to be sure — *before* the privileging of the Mishnah and Scripture? Evidence that for some period of time, people assumed that other kinds of writing would find their place as authoritative among sages and would find media of transmission appropriate to said writing derives from the composites in the Talmud that presuppose a valid labor besides that of Mishnah- or liturgical-Scripture-exegesis. The matter takes both a negative and a positive formulation: what people could not have known, what their actions tell us they took for granted. Before the privileging of Scripture and the Mishnah, people could not have known that the finished compositions and (more to the point) composites that they would produce would find their final place only in a subordinated, often anomalous and awkward way, in the setting of the Mishnah- or Scripture-exegetical documents. And, by way of complement, they must have assumed that their writing would find an appropriate medium for transmission, whether in the form of large-scale compilations ("books" such as we now have) or in the form of episodic and random pieces of formalized doctrine, units not much larger than the composites (or even the free-standing compositions" themselves. Either way, we must assume that they took for granted what they wrote would find a future in some appropriate way,[7] and not in the inappropriate way by which the other-than-Mishnah-exegetical composites actually would reach their ultimate destination in the Rabbinic canon.

Now, as we realize, we have in the Talmud[8] an ample selection of such writing, though all together writing of that classification occupies only a negligible proportion of the Talmud.[9] That other than Mishnah-exegetical writing clearly presupposes that writing of an other-than-exegetical character, and writing on topics other than those presented by the Mishnah (and the same pertains to Scripture) would find its place. But the place that said writing now occupies also tells us that with the privileging of the two documents, that other kind of writing would make its way only around the edges of the primary literary enterprise and not at its center. It would emerge subordinate, random, occasional, and episodic; always tangential and never at the heart of matters, it would contribute information but only rare occasion for dialectical analysis.[10] It must follow that writing that serves a purpose other than that of Mishnah- or Scripture-exegesis presupposes also the availability of media for organization and preservation other than the media that in fact pertain, the Mishnah- or Scripture-commentaries. We cannot know whether sages anticipated other kinds of large-scale compilations besides those we have or no sort of large-scale compilation at all. That issue has no affect upon this argument.

To recapitulate: we now revert to the effects of the privileging of the specified documents. For, as to types of writing, prior to the determinate moment at which the future shape of the canon was defined, people can have written — and demonstrably did write — in a variety of ways other than those required by Mishnah- and Scripture-exegesis — as well as in the exegetical modes serving those two documents. Since they cannot have known that in the end only two kinds of documents would emerge, and these would take the shape only of exegesis or secondary amplification, and these would serve only the specified documents, they can certainly have written their compositions and formulated their composites within two other assumptions.

[1] Other documents, besides those of Mishnah- or Scripture-exegesis, will come into being for the large-scale formation and transmission of their compositions and composites. Hence, they can have imagined, documents devoted to Scripture-exegesis of books of the written Torah other than the liturgical ones that predominated will encompass their compositions and composites.

[2] No large-scale medium for the collection and organization of compositions and composites will emerge, so that these compositions and composites will circulate in that free-standing, self-contained version that the initial authors of the compositions or compilers of the composites have set forth. A medium other than that of publication in massive compilations — an oral one, for one example, or a fragmentary and episodic one, for another — will serve alongside the medium that serves the Mishnah and Scripture.

III. THE INITIAL PHASES? WHY THE OTHER-THAN-MISHNAH-EXEGETICAL COMPOSITES LEAD US INTO A PRIOR STAGE — NOT MERELY A DIFFERENT MODE — IN THE FORMATION OF THE TALMUD'S COMPONENTS

Either route we take, we find ourselves at the same final destination, one that places ourselves at a determinate point in establishing priority, *temporal* priority, in sorting out the kinds of writing now preserved in the Talmud. These for the Talmud fall into two classes: Mishnah-exegesis and everything else.

[1] MISHNAH-EXEGESIS: At any point in the formation of the Rabbinic canon, beginning, middle, and end, down to the final afternoon in the writing of the Talmud,

work on the exegesis of Scripture or the Mishnah can have gone forward; whether or not people assumed such work would be further formulated into massive composites, e.g., tractates or Midrash-compilations, hardly makes any difference. From the conclusion of the Mishnah, work on Mishnah-exegesis yielded compositions and compilations, and that sort of work can have gone forward even to the final stages in the ultimate compilation and closure of the Talmud.[11]

[2] THE OTHER-THAN-MISHNAH-EXEGETICAL COMPOSITES: But what about compositions and, in particular, compilations that take shape for an other-than-Mishnah-exegetical purpose? Since these cannot be distinguished on formal grounds from the compositions and compilations of a Mishnah-exegetical character, we must ask a question that differentiates said compilations in another way. It is this: do the compilers of these kinds of writing assume that their work will be preserved ("published")? Of course they do — by definition. Why write in the manner of those who write for publication if one does not assume that what he is writing also is going to be published?

Then do these particular writers know that their writing is not going to be published in massive compilations of a homogeneous character, as the Talmud's tractates compile formally and intellectually coherent material on the Mishnah and its law? Of course not. And, to ask the question in a different way, can they have conceived that they were engaged in a form of writing that would not then attain publication in the conventional manner (whatever that manner was)? Certainly not.

Why not? A simple fact requires that we answer both questions negatively. The same forms govern; the same authorities occur; the same language-patterns, word-choices, grammatical rules, and the like dictate the character of the prose. I cannot point to a single formal or rhetorical trait in the other-than-Mishnah-exegetical composites that is not shared by the Mishnah-exegetical ones. It is the simple fact that on formal grounds we cannot differentiate composites of the one sort from those of the other — composites addressed to the Mishnah from composites focused upon abstract theological problems, traits of virtue, or supererogatory social ideals, for instance, or even composites that hold together around sequences of verses of Scripture other than those in synagogue liturgy. In the pages of the Talmud, both kinds of composites exhibit the same qualities of formalization, rhetoric, logical coherence, and other documentary indicators.[12] The uniformity of traits of composition and composite-making characteristic of all kinds of writing in the Talmud indicates that those who wrote and preserved the one wrote and preserved the other; and it must follow from the simple, technical facts of the character of the writing, the expectations characteristic of those who wrote the one must also have animated those who wrote the other.

What, in my mind, follows? It is that the framers of Mishnah-exegetical units and those of other-than-Mishnah-exegetical units that exhibit the same indicative traits must also therefore have flourished at the same time, down to the point at which the Mishnah, along with Scripture, was privileged. And then, *at that point but not earlier,* the on-going, future formation of other-than-Mishnah-exegetical units would have imposed the requirement to solve this simple problem: for what kind of large-scale compilation, if any, do we now write? And, alongside, for what kind of publication do we now aspire for our writing? These questions draw us onward to the center of this argument in favor of the hypothesis set forth just now.

I see two answers, which yield two more answers, which in turn yield a single conclusion. The first set of answers is as follows:

[1] People stopped writing altogether these other-than-Mishnah-exegetical compositions and composites.

[2] Or they continued to write them, but anticipated publication in some medium other than has now survived.

We have no way of settling these questions. Without depending upon attributions, we cannot stratify the composites in periods by named sages. Then how are we to explain the data before us? I see three modes of explanation, one temporal-historical, the second, political, the third, adventitious.

[1] TEMPORAL-HISTORICAL: The other-than-Mishnah-exegetical compositions, but, especially, composites bring us into *a time prior* to the privileging of the Mishnah (and Scripture);

[2] POLITICAL: The other-than-Mishnah-exegetical compositions, but, especially, the composites carry us into circles that did not acknowledge the privileging of the Mishnah at all but continued to write within another premise as to publication altogether.

[3] ADVENTITIOUS: sages produced documents that did not survive. Those are the documents that contain the other-than-Mishnah-exegetical compositions and composites produced after the privileging of the Mishnah.

As among these three possible conclusions, I see only one — the first — that can sustain any kind of examination:

The other-than-Mishnah-exegetical writings derive from the time prior to the privileging of the Mishnah (and Scripture) and attest to initial phases in the formation of Talmudic Judaism.

That does the temporal-historical explanation strike me as the sole plausible one for the data that are before us, analyzed in the way that I have done. That is, why do I hold that the classification of writings just now defined expose conceptions held in a period prior to the time of the privileging of the Mishnah and Scripture? When we review the meaning of that privileging, the answer emerges. It is in two parts.

First, since we refer to the point at which the decision was to taken to organize and hand on for tradition in only a single form, the exegetical one, people who wrote in some other than an exegetical form — the propositional one characteristic of the larger part, though not the whole, of the other-than-Mishnah-exegetical composites will have then to have known that they were producing writing that would not conform to the character of the sole acceptable media for preservation and transmission of their writing. It seems to me far more likely that people will have produced writing for preservation and transmission than that they will have produced writing knowing that no one beyond themselves would benefit from their thoughts. For at stake in all writing was the Torah, and if, as their every word signifies, sages valued as Torah the teachings of the masters, then the goal of all authoritative writing had to have been publication. It must follow, the media of publication would dictate the character of the method of writing, encompassing (as the case would determine) the rhetoric, logic of coherent discourse, and topical and even propositional program.

Second, that privileging meant it would be around only two documents, Scripture and the Mishnah, that the entire antecedent corpus of preserved writing would be set forth. Here too, it seems to me unlikely that people will have continued a mode of writing that the decision to privilege the Mishnah rendered obsolete and anomalous. By making critical to the formation of the canon what formerly was only one mode of composition and composite-making among several, the sages who determined to privilege the Mishnah also subordinated all other modes of writing. The received heritage — presumably from the time of Rab and Samuel, Simeon b. Laqish and Yohanan — would then be differentiated; parts would receive priority of place and paramount status in sheer volume; other parts would find a place only with difficulty, as appendices and footnotes, for example. Here again, I find it difficult to point to large-scale enterprises of writing for a purpose other than the dominant one. Since the extant canon yields a negligible proportion of other-than-Mishnah-exegetical writing, it seems to me likely that either people produced less once the canon found its definitive form or people continued to produce a kind of writing that was allowed to atrophy and disappear. Either way, the result is the same.

Whether people stopped writing compositions and compiling composites of an other-than-exegetical character, or continued doing so but without result or impact upon the extant documents, the status of what we do have is unchanged. If they continued writing such composites, it was in defiance of the now-established convention and that would represent a political act of non-conformity that contradicts the character of the sages' culture. Not only so, but we should find in the other-than-Mishnah- and Scripture-exegetical compositions and composites a different and contradictory set of propositions and principles from those that operate in the Mishnah- and Scripture-exegetical ones. But, as we shall see in these four volumes, scarcely a line in the other-than-Mishnah- and Scripture-exegetical compositions and composites can be set against and opposite the forms and the propositions of the Mishnah- and Scripture-exegetical ones. If nothing differentiates the one type of composition and composite from the other, that fact must mean the framers of the one stand alongside the framers of the other on every issue that matters. The documents before us allege no less when they place the same names on the one type of composition and composite and on the other. Once more, the political reading of matters defies the character of the evidence, and the temporal-historical one conforms to it.

The upshot, in my judgment, is that the other-than-Mishnah- and Scripture-exegetical compositions and composites tell us about ideas held in the period prior to the privileging of the Mishnah (and Scripture).[13] In those composites we find our way into an earlier age than the one of formation, compilation, closure, that is, the conclusive redaction of the Talmud.[14] That judgment then forms the foundation of the claim to open the way to an earlier stratum of ideas than those set forth in the Talmud's final statement, at the point of closure and conclusion.

But — to complete the matter — what of the other possible conclusions? As to the third, what we cannot show, we do not know; we cannot therefore form the hypothesis of documents that collected material of a certain kind but did not survive, so we also cannot reasonably explain what we do have by (an utterly fatuous) appeal to what we do not have.

I have already shown why I reject the alternative proposition, that the other-than-Mishnah-exegetical composites speak for those who do not acknowledge the privileged position of the Mishnah once that position had been assigned to the Mishnah. It is equally unacceptable, because it contradicts the simple fact that these composites are preserved in the Talmud, the principal document that the privileging of the Mishnah brought into being. At no point can we identify a single proposition in other-than-Mishnah-exegetical composites that contradicts or in any detail comes into conflicts with a comparable or counterpart proposition in a Mishnah-exegetical composition or composite.[15]

Since that is the fact, it must follow that the other-than-Mishnah-exegetical compositions introduce us to conceptions held prior to the privileging of the Mishnah.16 Can we then claim that writing for composites of an other-than-Mishnah-exegetical classification came to an end? Indeed so, for, I maintain, once the work on the Mishnah gained priority, then, for the reasons spelled out earlier, with the same people producing both kinds of writing, it would have to follow, their work of the other kind — for some other document, or for no form of publication further contemplated — in due course, with all deliberate speed, drew to a close. The privileging of the Mishnah (and Scripture) carried in its wake both incentives to move forward with Mishnah-exegesis and also leave off the composition and compilation of composites for a purpose other than that of Mishnah-exegesis. Once the media for publication changed in character, the modes of composition would certainly shift among people who wrote — that is, committed thought to fixed and accessible, public form for the purpose of transmission to others now and later on. Since the most profound premise of all of Rabbinic writing, beginning to end, affirms both the value and the importance of publishing what sages received as the Torah, we have every reason to affirm that writing responded to the character of the media available for publication.

To conclude: we can find our way backward from the final stage in the formation of the Talmud to a prior stage through the Talmud's other-than-Mishnah-exegetical composites. And, it follows, that prior stage — earlier than documentary definition and ultimate formulation and redaction — of the document exposes components of the Judaic religious system — the Judaism — that the framers of the Talmud set forth. While we cannot identify the determinate time or place to which the phenomena of literary analysis point, we now can formulate an account of some of the principal, generative ideas that people held in the period before the decision was taken to assign privileged status to the Mishnah and its exegesis, alongside the liturgical units of Scripture and their exegesis.

IV. RECONSTRUCTING DOCUMENTS: FROM THE TALMUD'S MISHNAH-EXEGETICAL COMPOSITIONS AND COMPOSITES TO THE MISHNAH, FROM THE TALMUD'S OTHER-THAN-MISHNAH-EXEGETICAL COMPOSITES TO WHAT?

That small component of the Talmud takes shape in free-standing composites or compositions that respond to a different set of questions from those raised by the Mishnah. That is the definitive result of the analytical commentary on the Talmud's construction and cogency that I have now completed in *The Talmud of Babylonia. An Academic Commentary*[17] and its counterpart and summary, *The Talmud of Babylonia. A Complete Outline.*[18] In those complementary studies I identify the free-standing composites and explain why the compiler of the document has included them and positioned them where he has. This other, second set of composites and compositions is to be distinguished from the paramount component by a different presupposition altogether. And identifying the other-than-Mishnah-exegetical composites of the Talmud leads us to the problem of this systematic study of them.

Specifically, we have to begin the work of trying to imagine that other corpus of authoritative statements, besides the Mishnah, that these other sorts of composites and composites presuppose. That requires us to ask, how do these other-than-Mishnah-exegetical compositions and composites attain order, structure, and cogency, absent the Mishnah — or even a (formal) counterpart to the Mishnah? That is the question that provokes the sizable project: to work back from the parts to the whole — if there is a whole. And, it is self-evident, we have also to pursue the question, if not, why not?

To explain: just as out of the Talmud we should have to form the hypothesis that a prior document is presupposed and clearly generates the Talmud's own writing, most of which loses cogency and some of which becomes gibberish outside the framework defined by the Mishnah, so we ask whether the same is so of the Talmud's non-talmudic component a set of counterpart inquiries. The Mishnah-exegetical compositions and compilations of the Talmud follow a fixed program of inquiry. Do the others? The Mishnah-exegetical compositions and compilations generate systematic inquiries of enormous (sometimes run-on) volume, e.g., long dialectical arguments about the utilization of Scripture, or equivalently-spun-out analytical arguments about the conflict of legal principles, and the like.

The observation that the Talmud (a.k.a., Bavli, Talmud of Babylonia) is made up of cogent compositions ordinarily formed into large-scale composites.[19] Most of these focus upon the exegesis of the Mishnah and the amplification of its law. These define the documentary building-blocks and comprise, I estimate, in excess of 90% of the large-scale and systematic constituents of the Talmud overall, depending on the tractate. But the Talmud further contains completed compositions and even composites that do not carry out the Talmud's documentary program or conform to its definition. They rarely attend to legal topics at all, but ordinarily take up subjects paramount in compilations of Midrash-exegeses of Scripture and uncommon in the compilations of normative law, the Mishnah, the Tosefta and, as indicated, the two Talmuds themselves. In terms of the native categories of the Rabbinic system, comprising *halakhah,* law, and *aggadah,* theology, the other-than-Mishnah-exegetical compositions and composites that take their place in the Talmud fall into the category of *aggadah* and form that layer of the Talmud that addresses issues of theology, broadly construed.

By definition these already-completed writings originate among writers or compilers who undertook compositions and composites for a purpose other than that of Mishnah-exegesis, possibly for documents other than the one devoted to the amplification of the law as set forth in the Mishnah. In the present volumes I systematically analyze, within a uniform program of inquiry, the other-than-Mishnah-exegetical compositions and compilations of the Talmud of Babylonia.

These free-standing units of thought and expression take their place beyond the work of formulation and redaction that produced the Talmud as we know it. They invariably can be read on their own, outside of the context in which they now are situated. They attain cogency in a manner that simply has no bearing upon that redactional context that the ultimate compilers of the Talmud have defined for them. When we seek to explain the decision for including them, we sometimes find a clear answer, sometimes perceive none. They sometimes amplify the topic introduced by the Mishnah but ignore the law pertaining to said topic and disrupt the flow of Mishnah-exegesis; but they also may stand entirely aloof from the Mishnah to begin with, being inserted into the Talmud for reasons that on occasion prove difficult to discern.

These other-than-Mishnah-exegetical, free-standing, large-scale units of discourse form the layer of Talmudic Judaism — the Judaic religious system that the Talmud in particular sets forth — that stands apart from, and, as I have now argued at some length, possibly precedes the writing of the Talmud's own, paramount components. In due course, therefore, we shall want to examine in detail the solid evidence on the state of opinion separate from, and arguably prior to, the position of the Talmud's compilers (inclusive of the compilers of its paramount Mishnah-exegetical compositions and composites). We may hope to move a step behind, if not temporally before, the moment of the Talmud as we know it. That step leads us to the possibility of describing character of the layers of thought of the Judaic system to which these redactionally-distinct and conceivably prior components point.

v. TALMUDIC PHENOMENOLOGY

In the monograph, *Where the Talmud Comes From: A Talmudic Phenomenology. Identifying the Free-Standing Building Blocks of Talmudic Discourse* (Atlanta, 1995: Scholars Press for South Florida Studies in the History of Judaism), I set forth not only the arguments and evidence that sustain the foregoing propositions concerning the free-standing building blocks that ignore the Mishnah and its law, but also the basic taxonomy that governs. The four[20] parts, covering exegesis of Scripture, exemplary virtue, social ethics (broadly construed), and theology stand for the four thematic types of free-standing building blocks in the Talmud, beyond those devoted to Mishnah-exegesis and amplification, that set forth important elements of the religious system adumbrated by the Talmud.[21]

I. EXEGESIS OF SCRIPTURE: By "exegesis of Scripture," I mean a large-scale and formally coherent exercise in the reading of passages of Scripture. I do not refer to episodic allusions to verses of Scripture or to the utilization of verses of Scripture to demonstrate propositions extrinsic to the topic (e.g., a moral apothegm joined with a proof-text), but only to a composite that holds together because each component of the composite refers to a verse or sequence of scriptural verses, and because the whole holds together only or mainly by reference to said verse or sequence of verses.

II. EXEMPLARY VIRTUE: By "exemplary virtue" I mean, stories that in concrete terms illustrate virtue, moral excellence, proper attitude and action. These commonly present as their heroes named sages, but they cannot be classed as "biography," since no sage in the Talmud receives a full-length, systematic biography, and all biographical snippets turn out in context to form episodes in the life of the named sage that show exemplary actions resting on right emotions, attitudes, or modes of thought.

III. SOCIAL ETHICS: "Social ethics" covers those actions that the law cannot require but that the Torah as the sages represent it values, matters of social policy, principles of behavior not reduced to anecdotal law, and the like. It is not always easy to distinguish composites devoted to exemplary virtue from those that address in more abstract terms propositions governing supererogatory ethics, the requirements of action in the public interest that transcend the limits of the law. In general we shall class in the former category composites or compositions that play out their theme through narratives concerning persons, generally sages, and in the latter, those that formulate abstract propositions (even though in sequences of concrete cases).

IV. THEOLOGY: "Theology" encompasses compositions and composites that raise questions about God's love and justice, God and Israel, God's will for ordinary people, life after death, and that entire repertoire of conviction concerning the ultimate and transcendent questions of meaning, truth, and worth, the answers to which are contained in both the law, on the one side, and statements concerning the meaning of passages of Scripture, the requirements of virtue, and the supererogatory obligations of social ethics, on the other side.

VI. THE DOCUMENTARY FRAMEWORK OF TALMUDIC PHENOMENOLOGY. THE MATTER OF TEMPORAL PRIORITY OF NON-DOCUMENTARY WRITING RECONSIDERED

To explain why I use the word "initial" in the title, let me broaden the framework of discussion, beyond the particular problem before us. Up to this point I have set forth only in the setting of the Talmud (and Midrash-compilations) my hypothesis on the temporal priority of the other-than-Mishnah-exegetical composites. But we have now to state matters in broader and more theoretical terms. For the Talmud is not the only Rabbinic document that contains some elements of finished writing — compositions, perhaps even composites, that were not composed within the discipline of a document's own, particular program and plan.

To state the hypothesis in abstract language: I tend to think that writing that does not carry out a document's principal and definitive purpose was formed not only under different circumstances or auspices but also — so it is my opinion — earlier than the writing particular to said documents. For example, some sayings and stories, even composites, may float from one document to another. These writings by definition are extra-documentary and non-documentary. The reason is that these writings serve the purposes not of compilers (or authors or authorships) of distinct compilations, but the interests of a another type of authorship entirely. That is one that thought making up stories (whether or not for collections) itself an important activity; or making up exercises on Mishnah-Scripture relationships; or other such writings as lie beyond the imagination of the compilers of the score of documents that comprise the canon. When writings work well for two or more documents therefore they must be assumed to have a literary history different from those that serve only one writing or one type of writing, and, also, demand a different hermeneutic. Let me explain the matter and why I am inclined to suppose that non-documentary writing stands in a relationship of temporal priority, not merely phenomenological autonomy, to documentary writing.

To begin with, let me define the types of writing and how I classify them by appeal to objective, formal traits. We find in the various Rabbinic documents three classes of writing, each with its own traits. Then we classify the writing that comprises a document among these three classes and determine the character of the document's paramount components. The classification is as follows:

[1] writing that is entirely formed within the rules of the documents that now present that writing. In the present instance the Mishnah-exegetical compositions and compilations exemplify this kind of writing.

[2] writing that is not shaped by documentary requirements of the text before us but by some other document of the canon. In the present case the other-than-Mishnah-exegetical compositions and compilations supply examples of this kind of writing.

[3] writing that is not shaped by the documentary requirements of the canonical compilations we now have. Stories about events in the lives of sages would provide a case of this kind of extra-documentary writing for non-canonical compilations, since we have no gospels or biographies of sages; but we have ample cases of writing that can have gone into such non-extant documents.

It follows that — as a matter of hypothesis — in the Rabbinic texts are [2, 3] some writings that were formed independent of the plan of using them in a given compilation, alongside [1] the other writings that were formed in response to the program of the authorship of a given compilation. And that fact makes it possible to address the problem of the origin of writing that does not conform to the requirements of a particular document. In the present case, we take up writing that is in the Talmud but not of the Talmud.

The broader class of such writing encompasses those floating materials that progress from one document to another — some bearing names of authorities, some anonymous. Because they may serve any and all documents equally well (or poorly), these extra-documentary cognitive units and even whole compositions will guide us to that prior ("a priori") system that underlay all of the discrete documents of the canon of the Judaism of the dual Torah. And, within the framework of this monograph, that will constitute the answer to the question of where the Talmud comes from, besides its own compilers and the writers of its characteristic and necessary compositions.

To expand on this point: each of the score of documents that make up the canon of Judaism in late antiquity exhibits distinctive traits in logic, rhetoric, and topic, so that we may identify the purposes and traits of form and intellect of the authorship of that document. It follows that documents that exhibit coherent traits possess integrity and are not merely scrapbooks, compilations made with no clear purpose or aesthetic plan. But, as is well known, some completed units of thought — propositional arguments, sayings, and stories for instance — travel from one document to another. It further follows that the several documents intersect through shared materials. Furthermore, writings that peregrinate *by definition* do not carry out the rhetorical, logical, and topical program of a particular document. If they can fit in as well or as poorly wherever they end up, then they have not been composed with a particular document's definition in mind. Free-standing units of discourse then have to be classified in relationship to the document in which they appear, and it is that criterion, as I said, that dictates the context in which these compositions or composites are to be examined.

In framing a theory to accommodate the facts that documents are autonomous but also connected through such shared materials, therefore, we must account for the history of not only the documents in hand but also the completed pieces of writing that move from here to there. In fact documents stand in three relationships to one another and to the system of which they form part, that is, to Judaism, as a whole.

[1] Each document is to be seen all by itself, that is, as autonomous of all others.

[2] Each document is to be examined for its relationships with other documents universally regarded as falling into the same classification, as Torah.

[3] And, finally, in the theology of Judaism every canonical writing is equally and undifferentiatedly part of the Torah. That is to say, each document is to be allowed to take its place as part of the undifferentiated aggregation of documents that, all together, constitute the canon of, in the case of Judaism, the "one whole Torah revealed by God to Moses at Mount Sinai."

Simple logic makes self-evident the proposition that, if a document comes down to us within its own framework, as a complete book with a beginning, middle, and end, a book with its own logic in the ordering of materials, a logic we can identify, then, in preserving that book, the canon presents us with a document on its own and not solely as part of a larger composition or construct. So we too see the document as it reaches us, that is, as autonomous. If, second, a document contains materials shared verbatim or in substantial content with other documents of its classification, or if one document refers to the contents of other documents, then the several documents that clearly wish to engage in conversation with one another have to address one another. That is to say, we have to seek for the marks of connectedness, asking for the meaning of those connections. It is at this level of connectedness that we labor. For the purpose of comparison is to tell us what is like something else, what is unlike something else. To begin with, we can declare something unlike something else only if we know that it is like that other thing. Otherwise the original judgment bears no sense whatsoever. So, once more, canon defines context, or, in descriptive language, the first classification for comparative study is the document, brought into juxtaposition with, and contrast to, another document.

Finally, since the community of the faithful of Judaism, in all of the contemporary expressions of Judaism, concur that documents held to be authoritative constitute one whole, seamless "Torah," that is, a complete and exhaustive statement of God's will for Israel and humanity, we take as a further appropriate task, the description of the whole out of the undifferentiated testimony of all of its parts. These components in the theological context are viewed, as is clear, as equally authoritative for the composition of the whole: one, continuous system.

Some of these same documents draw upon materials that have been composed with the requirements of the respective documents in mind. The present monograph rests on the acknowledged fact that Rabbinic documents in some measure also draw upon a fund of completed compositions of thought that have taken shape without attention to the needs of the compilers of those documents. These constitute those free-standing cognitive units or composites of which we speak. Within the distinction between writing that serves a redactional purpose and writing that does not, we see four types of completed compositions of thought. Each type may be distinguished from the others by appeal to a single criterion of differentiation, that is to say, to traits of precisely the same sort. The indicative traits concern relationship to the redactional purpose of a piece of writing, viewed overall. This permits us to review the basic scheme that is set forth in this chapter:

[1] Some writings in a given compilation clearly serve the redactional program of the framers of the document in which those writings occur. In the case of the Talmud, defined as a Mishnah-commentary and amplification, that covers the great part of the document, most of which is given over to the document's definitive purpose.

[2] Some writings in a given compilation serve not the redactional program of the document in which they occur, but some other document, now in our hands. There is no material difference, as to the taxonomy of the writing of the classics in Judaism, between the first and second types; it is a problem of transmission of documents, not their formation. In the Talmud, we find abstracts of other documents, e.g., the Tosefta, the Sifra, and so on, and, when we do, these present themselves as distinctive in their indicative traits, so that we can always pick out what is primary to the Tosefta from what is primary to the Talmud, so too to Sifra or Sifré to Deuteronomy or the other documents upon which the compilers draw from time to time.

[3] Some writings in a given compilation serve not the purposes of the document in which they occur but rather a redactional program of a document, or of a type of document, that we do not now have, but can readily envision. One example would be, commentaries to passages of Scripture, read in sequence. In this category we find the possibility of imagining compilations that we do not have, but that can have existed but did not survive; or that can have existed and were then recast into the kinds of writings that people clearly preferred (later on) to produce.

[4] Some writings now found in a given compilation stand autonomous of any redactional program we have in an existing compilation or of any we can even imagine on the foundations of said writings. An example, out of the Talmud, is the formation of a theological demonstration or an ethical proposition, for the compilation of neither one of which we have any extant document.

The distinctions upon which these analytical taxonomies rest are objective, since they depend upon the fixed and factual relationship between a piece of writing and a larger redactional context.

[1] We know the requirements of redactors of the several documents of the Rabbinic canon, because I have already shown[22] what they are in the case of a

large variety of documents.[23] When, therefore, we judge a piece of writing to serve the program of the document in which that writing occurs, it is not because of a personal impulse or a private and incommunicable insight, but because the traits of that writing self-evidently respond to the documentary program of the book in which the writing is located. Enough systematic work on the Talmud makes unnecessary any further discussion of this point.

[2] When, further, we conclude that a piece of writing belongs in some other document than the one in which it is found, that too forms a factual judgment.

[3] A piece of writing that serves no where we now know may nonetheless conform to the rules of writing that we can readily imagine and describe in theory. For instance, a propositional composition, that runs through a wide variety of texts to make a point autonomous of all of the texts that are invoked, clearly is intended for a propositional document, one that (like the Mishnah) makes points autonomous of a given prior writing, e.g., a biblical book, but that makes points that for one reason or another cohere quite nicely on their own. Authors of propositional compilations self-evidently can imagine that kind of redaction. We have their writings, but not the books that they intended to be made up of those writings. Another example, as I have already pointed out, is a collection of stories about a given authority, or about a given kind of virtue exemplified by a variety of authorities. These and other types of compilations we can imagine but do not have are dealt with in the present rubric.

[4] And, finally, where we have utterly hermetic writing, sealed off from any broader literary context and able to define its own limits and sustain its point without regard to anything outside itself, we know that here we are in the presence of authorships that had no larger redactional plan in mind, no intent on the making of books out of their little pieces of writing.

I therefore offer public and accessible criteria for the classification of the data, and anyone is able to test my judgments against the actualities of the documents, their compositions and composites. Since no subjective judgment limits their use, these data of a wholly phenomenological character bear implications for both literary and intellectual description. First, this theory on the literary formation of the Rabbinic canon in general posits three stages in the formation of writing. Moving ordinally, not temporally, from the latest to the earliest,[24] one stage is marked by the definition of a document, its topical program, its rhetorical medium, its logical message. The document as we know it in its basic structure and main lines therefore comes at the end. It follows that writings that clearly serve the program of that document and carry it the purposes of its authorship were made up in connection with the formation of *that* document. What I have already said about the Talmud suffices to make this point clear.

Another, and I think, prior stage is marked by the preparation of writings that do not serve the needs of a particular document now in our hands, but can have carried out the purposes of an authorship working on a document of a *type* we now have. The existing documents then form a model for defining other kinds of writings worked out to meet the program of a documentary authorship.

But there are other types of writings that in no way serve the needs or plans of any document we now have, and that, furthermore, also cannot find a place in any document of a type that we now have. These writings, as a matter of fact, very commonly prove peripatetic, traveling from one writing to another, equally at home in, or alien to, the program of the documents in which they end up. These writings therefore were carried out without regard to a documentary program of any kind exemplified by the canonical books of the Judaism of the dual Torah. They form what I conceive to be the earliest in the three stages of the writing of the units of completed thought that in the aggregate form the canonical literature of the Judaism of the dual Torah of late antiquity.

That proposed order in the formation of the distinct types of writing explains why, when we wish to find out where the Talmud comes from, we turn to the free-standing components of the document, as those items that come from persons outside of the circle of writers of the Talmud's own materials or prior to the work of writing the Talmud's materials. It further explains why, when we want to describe layers of thought autonomous of, and arguably prior to, the thought represented by the Talmud, we turn to those same writings. Let me now take up the basis on which I have formed the opinion — not yet a hypothesis — just now set forth.

VII. Taxonomy and Temporal Priority

My "three stages" in ordinal sequence correspond, as a matter of fact, to a taxic structure, that is, three types of writing.

[1] The first — and last in assumed temporal order — is writing carried out in the context of the making, or compilation, of a classic. That writing responds to the redactional program and plan of the authorship of a classic.

[2] The second, penultimate in order, is writing that can appears in a given document but better serves a document other than the one in which it (singularly) occurs. This kind of writing seems to me not to fall within the same period of redaction as the first. For while it is a type of writing under the identical conditions, it also is writing that presupposes redactional programs in no way in play in the ultimate, and definitive, period of the formation of the canon: when people did things this way, and not in some other. That is why I think it is a kind of writing that was done prior to the period in which people limited their redactional work and associated labor of composition to the program that yielded the books we now have.

[3] The third kind of writing seems to me to originate in a period prior to the other two. It is carried on in a manner independent of all redactional considerations such as are known to us. Then it should derive from a time when

redactional considerations played no paramount role in the making of compositions. A brief essay, rather than a sustained composition, was then the dominant mode of writing.

My hypothesis is that people can have written both long and short compositions — compositions and composites, in my language — at one and the same time. But writing that does not presuppose a secondary labor of redaction, e.g., in a composite, probably originated when authors or authorships did not anticipate any fate for their writing beyond their labor of composition itself. If that reasoning be accepted, then we have grounds on which to suppose that writing exclusive of all redactional purpose and context would come not only separate from, but prior to, writing that acknowledges a redactional purpose and context.

The upshot is simple: whether the classification of writing be given a temporal or merely taxonomic valence, the issue is the same: have these writers done their work with documentary considerations in mind? I believe I have shown that they have not. Then where did they expect their work to makes its way? Anywhere it might, because, so they assumed, fitting in no where in particular, it found a suitable locus everywhere it turned up. But I think temporal, not merely taxonomic, considerations pertain.

Along these same lines of argument, this writing may or may not travel from one document to another. What that means is that the author or authorship does not imagine a future for his writing. What fits anywhere is composed to go nowhere in particular. Accordingly, what matters is not whether a writing fits one document or another, but whether, as the author or authorship has composed a piece of writing, that writing meets the requirements of any document we now have or can even imagine. If it does not, then we deal with a literary period in which the main kind of writing was ad hoc and episodic, not sustained and documentary.

Where does this leave us in our interest in finding out where the Talmud comes from? Extra- and non-documentary kinds of writing seem to me to derive from either [1] a period prior to the work of the making of compilations and the two Talmuds alike; or [2] a labor of composition not subject to the rules and considerations that operated in the work of the making of compilations and the two Talmuds. The second may be treated as a fact, beyond all question.

The first stands for a possibility and an opinion. If we ignore the attributions of sayings to named authorities from the beginning to the end of the sequence of the Talmud's sages' generations, then I should guess that non-documentary writing would come prior to making any kind of documents of consequence, and extra-documentary writing comes prior to the period in which the specificities of the documents we now have were defined. That is to say, writing that can fit anywhere or nowhere is prior to writing that can fit somewhere but does not fit anywhere now accessible to us, and both kinds of writing are prior to the kind that fits only in what documents in which it is now located. But just as we cannot validate attributions and so compose a history of the Talmud and of its sources that depends upon attributions, so we cannot demonstrate that they have no foundation in fact. We rely upon the fact in hand, but do not exclude other possibilities of description and analysis.

ENDNOTES

[1]That is not to maintain that authors other than sages represent the synagogue; sages manifestly dominate in both kinds of writing. It is only to classify the point to which reference is made, not the locus of origination. Nor is it self-evident that that division, on phenomenological grounds, carries in its wake principles of interpretation, let alone inexorable "historical" conclusions, *pace* Eliezer Segal, *The Babylonia Esther Midrash. A Critical Commentary* (Atlanta, 1994: Scholars Press for Brown Judaic Studies) I-III.

[2]That encompasses, also, Pesiqta deRab Kahana and Pesiqta Rabbati, which are quintessentially liturgical in their principles of selection and organization, built as they are around the liturgical calendar! No Midrash-compilation of the formative age treats a book of Scripture other than those declaimed in synagogue worship. But, as we see in this study, numerous passages of Scripture that have no place in synagogue liturgy are subjected to sustained exegesis in episodic compositions and even composites.

[3]There is no exception to this rule for the Rabbinic canon, since the Fathers According to Rabbi Nathan serves as a talmud for tractate Abot ("the Fathers"). I do not here deal with the so-called minor tractates, e.g., Soferim, Semahot, because it is not clear to me that they are integral to the canon as it reached definition by the closure of the Talmud at all. While we have a fine text-edition and suitable translations, critical-historical inquiry has yet to be undertaken. For the moment, therefore, the minor tractates will have to wait their turn. The generalizations set forth here cover all other documents in the Rabbinic canon, as defined by the indicative trait identified here: systematic appeal to sages' own authority, by name.

[4]That is not to claim that sages did not deem authoritative other documents besides those bearing the names of their acknowledged authorities. They cite the other books of Scripture besides those that figure in the liturgy of the synagogue; they refer to Ben Sira as authoritative; they preserve and systematically comment upon Megillat Ta'anit; they certainly accept the common forms of prayer and legislated concerning them. It is not clear that sages formulated the language of the statutory liturgy or selected, e.g., the verses of Scripture that comprise the Shema. The prayers specifically assigned to named sayings address a different life-situation from that of the synagogue. Not only so, but whether we may speak of not only formalized prayers but a prayer-book as a document seems to me an open question; and they may have accepted and valued the formalized statements classified as "mystical," though whether those statements derive from the period in which the Rabbinic canon took shape is not yet clear. For the most current statement on the classification of "mysticism" in relationship to the Judaisms of late antiquity, see Ithamar Gruenwald, "Jewish Mysticism," in Jacob Neusner, ed., *Handbuch der Orientalistik. Judaistik.* Leiden, 1994: E. J. Brill. Volume Two. *Judaism in Late Antiquity. Historical Syntheses*, pp. 1ff.

[5]It is quite routine in the documentary approach to the history of ideas that I have formulated to describe, analyze, and interpret the Judaic religious system put forth in a given document (should such a system inhere in a given document); no one would then imagine that the various documents stand autonomous of all other writings. But each stands on its own, and

it is necessary to read each document in its own terms, not only in the larger canonical context in which it is preserved and handed on as tradition. That accounts for my distinguishing the documentary Judaism, Talmudic Judaism, from its broader systemic framework, Rabbinic Judaism. For further explanation, see my *Rabbinic Judaism. The Documentary History of the Formative Age.* Bethesda, 1994: CDL Press.

[6]That has been proven for the Talmud of Babylonia in my *Complete Outline.* I state flatly that there is not a single exception to that rule in the entirety of the Bavli.

[7]The study set forth in *The Bavli's Massive Miscellanies. The Problem of Agglutinative Discourse in the Talmud of Babylonia* as well as the data assembled in these four volumes leave no doubt that the sages who produced the composites under study — and these were the same sages who produced the Mishnah-exegetical composites, if the recurrence of the same names in both types of writing proves anything — conformed to rules of agglutination, hence laws for the future preservation of their composites. That these rules differed from those that would operate in the Talmud then shows a different expectation for the future of their writing than the one that actually came about.

[8]And I am sure some of the Midrash-compilations as well as the other Talmud, but these await systematic study.

[9]I do not now know how large a proportion of any Midrash-compilation is made up of other than documentary writing; in Sifra, my impression is, it must form a very minimal part, while in Leviticus Rabbah and the later Midrash-compilations, documentary rules do not ubiquitously govern — or the documentary rules are different from those that operate in Sifra and (probably) the two Sifrés. But all that remains to be investigated. I am planning to do so in my projected *The Rabbinic Midrash-Compilations of Late Antiquity. Their Structure and System.* This will form for the Midrash-compilations the systematic counterpart to the *Talmud of Babylonia. An Academic Commentary,* and its planned counterpart for the Talmud of the Land of Israel.

[10]My *Complete Outline* bears out this observation, for it shows that while materials from the Tannaite compilations, the Tosefta and Sifra, for instance, commonly is subjected to the same persistent dialectical analysis as those from the Mishnah, the materials of the other-than-Mishnah-exegetical classification rarely receive analytical attention at all; they may be glossed, given appendices, or otherwise elaborated; but they do not ordinarily provoke systematic and sustained criticism, such as much of the Mishnah and a determinate, if not vast, part of the Tosefta receive.

[11]That is not to argue that without relying upon attributions of ipsissima verba, not subject to validation or falsification, we cannot identify several stages in the formation of Mishnah-commentary and legal amplification. Indicative data that yield hypotheses subject to testing, even to the formation of null-hypotheses, certainly inhere in the compositions and composites devoted to Mishnah-exegesis and legal amplification. These kinds of indicative data to begin with will be formal, but, further, will involve the construction of experiments of logical analysis, e.g., identification of conclusions that had to have been reached prior to the formulation of secondary and derivative questions, problems that had to have been solved before the identification of refinements and improvements, and the like. Such work has gone forward, but all of it is marred by the premise that the attributions a priori can supply data without further testing. A second fault, weightier than the first, is that the work to date is episodic and random, and not a single systematic and completed study has reached publication in any language known to me. My *History of the Mishnaic Law* (in forty-three volumes) did correlate the sequences of attributions by generations in the Mishnah with the

sequences of steps in the logical unfolding of a problem, so that what is assigned to earlier sages settles basic questions, and what is assigned to later sages takes for granted the results of that prior stage in analysis and reasoning. That general correlation yields not a single consequential exception. But it covers too limited a range of the law of the Mishnah to produce prima facie evidence in favor of matching the sequence of sages with the logical steps in the unfolding of a law. And, so far as I know, no counterpart work on the history of ideas executed through the analysis of the stages in the unfolding of logic has systematically addressed the more ample questions of Talmudic analysis of the law. The reason, it seems to me, is that the Talmudists take slight interest in problems of the history of ideas in the Talmud and take for granted that what is assigned to a named sage really was said by him, so the problem that concerns us will not concern those most engaged by study of the document.

[12]If the Mishnah-exegetical compositions provoke dialectical analysis and theological ones rarely follow suit, that must be regarded as a secondary and derivative fact, flowing from the intrinsic requirements of the one and not the other.

[13]I have already stressed that on the basis of an analysis along the lines of the one at hand we cannot make the same statement about the Mishnah-exegetical ones. But I am confident other sorts of analysis will produce a comparable result. The issue is not the generalization but the details: which Mishnah-exegetical compositions and composites take temporal priority over which others, and on what basis do we reach such judgments if we cannot appeal to the names of authorities attached to compositions or composites? The answer to the question of method is self-evident to me; but it is a different method from the one set forth here. It must appeal to internal traits of logic, not external ones of topic, which operate in the study of the other-than-Mishnah-exegetical compositions and composites. But that is appropriate to the character of the data themselves, which ultimately must govern throughout.

[14]I have no doubt that further inquiry will permit our differentiating among these materials by appeal to arguments on priority, hence we may hope for further temporal differentiation. But for the moment it suffices, on purely phenomenological grounds, to reach and explore the territory outlined here.

[15]That statement requires no demonstration at all, since every exegete of the Talmud, from the beginning to the present, concerns himself with the possibilities of contradiction or inconsistency of exactly that character!

[16]Let me settle an obvious, but wrong proposition: Is that to suggest that the other-than-Mishnah-exegetical composites stand in temporal priority in relationship to the Mishnah-exegetical ones? Not at all. Both kinds of writing were carried on from the closure of the Mishnah; as I said, the uniformity of the formal traits of the two classes of compositions and composites leaves no doubt on that score.

[17]Atlanta, 1994-5: Scholars Press for *USF Academic Commentary Series*. Thirty-six volumes.

[18] Atlanta, 1995: Scholars Press for *USF Academic Commentary Series*. Four volumes.

[19]For the distinction between composition and composite, see my *The Rules of Composition of the Talmud of Babylonia. The Cogency of the Bavli's Composite*. Atlanta, 1991: Scholars Press for South Florida Studies in the History of Judaism.

[20]I faced some difficulty in classifying a tiny number of important composites devoted to themes other than the four outlined here. These involve medical matters, for one major example; the Talmud preserves a few quite sizable composites on healing various ailments. They represent, by way of example, the types of composites that I altogether omit. The reason is that my interest is in a particular matter, which concerns the religious system that the Talmud presupposes. The taxonomy in play here focuses upon four principal components

of a religious system in the case of a Judaism: Scripture, virtue, the social order, and (obviously) the topics of theology narrowly construed. I have therefore omitted reference to that negligible number of sizable composites that, by the definition of religious system I have formulated, do not come under consideration at all. If my problem were narrowly literary, I should have found myself obligated to include them as well. It ought also to be said that the answers to the questions outlined in the concluding unit of this Introduction likely will prove uniform for both the other-than-Mishnah-exegetical composites pertinent to the history of religion and those that seem to me not to pertain.

[21]I tested this taxonomy for Bavli-tractate Moed Qatan in *Where the Talmud Comes From.* The test-case validated proceeding with the hypothesis that these four taxa encompass the candidates for analysis, but only in the fully-articulated survey of the present four volumes do we determine the correct taxonomy.

[22]One set of demonstrations is as follows: *The Integrity of Leviticus Rabbah. The Problem of the Autonomy of a Rabbinic Document.* Chico, 1985: Scholars Press for Brown Judaic Studies; *Canon and Connection: Intertextuality in Judaism.* Lanham, 1986: University Press of America. *Studies in Judaism* Series; *Midrash as Literature: The Primacy of Documentary Discourse.* Lanham, 1987: University Press of America *Studies in Judaism* series.

[23]The entire repertoire is summarized in my *Introduction to Rabbinic Literature.* N.Y., 1994: Doubleday. *The Doubleday Anchor Reference Library.*

[24]I underscore that at this point, I use these terms not in a temporal but only in an ordinal sense. That is, mere logic suggests the order in which steps have to have been taken; but these steps can have been taken in one afternoon of hard work, as much as in a hundred years of labor. The document is logically the latest stage, writings for it falling in line with it; the free-standing units that can fit into a document but not the one in which they are located forms a second stage; and the first stage is represented by compositions and even composites that fit some document the like of which we now do not have at all. In a moment I offer the opinion — not a hypothesis — that the ordinal sequence may stand for a temporal, that is, a historical one; but the considerations I introduce do not settle the matter even of formulating a hypothesis.

14

Do Types and Forms Yield
a Pre-history of the Bavli?

Testing the Results of Richard Kalmin

I. THE PROMISE OF FORM-ANALYSIS

The Talmud of Babylonia is a remarkably cogent document, exhibiting uniform traits of rhetoric and logic throughout. It speaks in one voice everywhere.[1] But the Talmud manifestly encompasses distinct compositions, in part forming a composite of ready-made writings.[2] So the question presents itself: do the types and forms of Mishnah-exegesis and Halakhah-analysis of the Bavli make possible a sequential history of the Talmudic knowledge, layer by layer, for example, generation by generation?

The distinctive forms and types of analytical discourse, bits and pieces of we know not what stand separate from the paramount and governing program of the document. These diverse exercises are subject to formal differentiation and also exhibit distinctive traits of logical inquiry, which distinguish one type from another. So the Bavli's one voice is the voice of a large choir, parts that sing each its own melody, even as all sing together and respond to a sole conductor.[3] The document itself claims no less. The ready-made compositions, distinct from the documentary plan, bear attributions to named authorities assumed to have flourished over centuries. What — short of gullibly taking at face value the attributions of sayings to named authorities — are we to make of the Bavli's Halakhic compositions that do stand distinct from the documentary program of the Bavli's compositors?

303

II. PRIOR WORK: THE DEBT TO RICHARD KALMIN

Happily, I am not the first to pursue the question raised here, and mine is not the first inquiry into the identification of the components of Talmudic knowledge that attributions and forms signal. Dr. Richard Kalmin, Professor of Talmud at the Jewish Theological Seminary of America, has undertaken a variety of studies,[4] yielding these results, based on his accompanying studies:[5]

1. "...formal aspects of Amoraic discourse provide evidence of generational contrast indicative of the diversity of talmudic source material....statements by later Amoraim are formally distinguishable from statements by earlier Amoraim..."[6]

2. We may adduce "differences between the introductory formulae introducing statements by early, later, and middle-generation Amoraim. These differences...support my claim regarding the presence of diverse sources in the Bavli, distinguishable along chronological lines..."[7]

3. "Middle generation Babylonian Amoraim [are] transitional...these transitional features may reveal the role of third – and fourth-generation Amoraim in the editing of earlier Amoraic statements..."[8]

These statements of Kalmin aim at a historical outcome: "...early Amoraic generations...played a role in the editorial process...."[9]

Kalmin's studies open the way to the present project,[10] which is systematically to find evidences of layers of knowledge that are preserved in the final, coherent statement of the Talmud at the end of its development.

One need not follow every detail of Kalmin's inquiry into the interplay of forms and attributions to appreciate his basic proposition, which is that the Bavli embodies the culmination of generations of cumulative results, and that we may follow the historical formation of the document by these layers. That history of the formation of the text defines Kalmin's purpose; are we able to replicate his results?

III. TYPES AND FORMS OF MISHNAH-EXEGESIS AND HALAKHAH-ANALYSIS OF BAVLI TRACTATE MOED QATAN

A survey of Bavli-tractate Moed Qatan[11] yields the following forms and types of Mishnah-exegesis, in the indicated proportions:

MISHNAH

Citation of a rule + gloss on the application of the rule	39	54%
Concession of a simple case, challenge to a complex one	2	3%
Consistency of versions of the law	3	4%
Identification of the Named Authority behind the Anonymous Rule	3	4%
Meanings of Words and Phrases	16	22%
Perfection of the Mishnah: No redundancy, perfect cogency	3	4%

Reason behind the Mishnah's law	2	3%
Whence in Scripture do we find an indication that....	5	6%
Total	73	100%

How shall we characterize the types and forms of Mishnah-exegesis in the Bavli-tractate sampled here? Over half of our sample of Mishnah-exegesis is comprised by the citation and gloss of the Mishnah, its language and its law. Nearly a quarter of the sample is made up of inquiries into the meaning of the language of the Mishnah, a subset of citation and gloss. Add to that the citation of the Mishnah and the question, "whence in Scripture do we find proof that...," and we have 82% of the whole. More to the point, we are able to classify with other-than-generic indicators (concession of a simple case, challenge to a complex one, perfection of the Mishnah, authority behind an anonymous rule, and the like) only a scattering of items. The types and forms of Mishnah-exegesis yield few indications of differentiation and many of homogenization.

HALAKHAH		
Clarification of what is subject to dispute	2	2%
Classification or clarification of an interstitial case	2	2%
Concession of an obvious case yielding a question on a complex one	2	2%
Declaration of a law and analysis thereof	84	86%
Declaration of the decided law	1	1%
Derivation of an inference of law from a clarification of a rule	1	.1%
Distinction between an action for a licit purpose and for an illicit one	1	1%
How the exegesis of a verse yields the rule at hand	2	2%
Limitation placed on the applicability of a general rule	1	1%
Reasoning behind the law	1	1%
Sorting out interstitial occasions	1	1%
Total	98	100%

The types and forms of Halakhah-analysis come down to a single item: citation of a law, set forth whether in the Mishnah or in the Tosefta or in a baraita, joined by a gloss. That generic type encompasses 86% of the sample. The glossing is miscellaneous and not readily classified by indicator traits. The other entries are episodic. They suggest the possibility of taxonomy of analytical initiatives but prove too random to sustain such an exercise. Some categories are identical to those of the Mishnah, e.g., how the exegesis of a verse yields the rule at hand, concession of an obvious case yielding a question on a complex one. Others have no clear counterpart in Mishnah-exegesis and validate the distinction between Mishnah-exegesis and Halakhah-analysis, e.g., reasoning behind the law, distinction between an action for a licit purpose and for an illicit one.

IV. THE DATA IN DETAIL: TYPES AND FORMS OF MISHNAH-EXEGESIS

WHENCE IN SCRIPTURE DO WE FIND AN INDICATION THAT....

1:1-2 VII.1-3+4 Whence do we find an indication in Scripture that
1:7-8 I.2.   And how on the basis of Scripture do we know that
3:5-6 I.5.   How on the basis of Scripture do we know that ...It derives from
          a verbal analogy based on the presence of the word...
3:5-6 I.12.   In session R. X/Y/Z ... This matter came up among them: "How
          do we know on the basis of Scripture that ... ? As it is written
3:5-6 I.22.   Our rabbis have taught on Tannaite authority: ... Said R. X, What
          is the scriptural basis for the position of R. Y? It is written, ... Said R. Z What is
          the scriptural basis for the position of R. W? It is written ...

PERFECTION OF THE MISHNAH: NO REDUNDANCY, PERFECT COGENCY

1:1 I.1   Since it is explicitly stated..., is it necessary to say...?
2:1 I.1   While the passage commences by discussing ..., it concludes solely
          with ...
2:2 I.1   It was necessary to give us the cases of ..., for had the first case
          alone been given to us, we might have supposed that it is in that case in particular
          that..., but in the case of ... I might say that he concurs ....And had we been given
          only the second case, it would have been in that case in particular that X took the
          position that he did, but as to the other, I might have said that he concurs Y. So
          both cases had to be set forth.

MEANINGS OF WORDS AND PHRASES

1:1 I.2   on what basis is it inferred that the meaning of the words...
1:1 III.1   What are...?
1:1 V.1   What is the meaning of..."
1:4 I.1   What is the definition of ...?
1:5C-G II.1   What is the sense of ...
1:6 I.1   What are ... and what are ...
1:6 III.1   What is a ...
1:7-8 IV.1   What is the definition ...
1:7-8 V.1   What does it mean to ...?
1:7-8 VI.1   What defines ...?
1:9 I.1   What is the meaning of ...?
1:10 I.1   What is the definition of ...?
2:5 I.1   R. X and R. Y differ [on the meaning of the usage of the
                    verb

2:5 II.1   Citation of the Mishnah + the question was raised: Does the
                language...mean...?
3:5-6 I.2   What is the meaning of + clause of the Mishnah?
3:5-6 I.13.   Our rabbis have taught on Tannaite authority + cited law +
                What defines ... and what defines ' ...?

IDENTIFICATION OF THE NAMED AUTHORITY BEHIND THE ANONYMOUS RULE SET FORTH IN
THE MISHNAH

1:1 I.3.   Who is the Tannaite authority who takes the position that
                work ...
2:2 I.2.   Who is the Tannaite authority who takes the view that...
3:1-2 II.1   Citation of the Mishnah-paragraph + Our Mishnah-paragraph's
                rule is not in accord with the position of R. X. For it has been taught on Tannaite
                authority

CITATION OF A RULE + GLOSS ON THE APPLICATION OF THE RULE

1:1 VI.1   X is all right but not Y
1:1-2 VII.6-7+8 Citation and light gloss of Tosefta
1:1-2 VIII.1   Citation of a clause of the Mishnah + but in fact...do we...but
                there is the following contradiction....
1:3 I.1-3   Citation of clause + said Rabbi X, [that applies] if....+so too it has been
                taught on Tannaite authority
1:4 III.1   They block up a breach: How is the breach blocked up?
1:6 II.1   But they ...How do they ...?
1:7-8 I.1   So if it's ..., what's so bad about that? [Challenge to the reason given by
                the Mishnah's rule]
1:7-8 II.2.   That rule applies only in the case of ... But as to ..., that is not
                so."
1:10 III.1   Citation of a law of the Mishnah + ... An objection was raised +
                There is no contradiction. There reference is made to ... here, it is to...
1:10 IV.1   Citation of a law of the Mishnah + report of a case illustrating the law
2:4A I.1   X raised this question to...He said to him, We have learned in the Mishnah
2:4B-E I.1   Citation of a clause of the Mishnah + But have you not said in the
                opening clause,
2:4B-E II.1   Said R. X, R. Y examined us + citation of a clause of the Mishnah
                + but by contrast + citation of a contradictory ruling
2:5 II.5   Ruling plus objection in the form of a citation of the Mishnah-rule
3:1-2 III.1   Citation of a clause of the Mishnah + Asked X, Is this
                concession permitted only where ...or is that the rule even if ...
3:1-2 IV.1   Proposition (said R. X said R. Y), he who... + objection
                based on verbatim citation of the Mishnah-rule

3:1-2 IV.2   As above

3:3 I.1. 2   Said X + proposition + may we say that the following supports his thesis + citation of the Mishnah-paragraph

3:5-6 I.1   Gloss: Uncited clause of the Mishnah + Said X, "... are nullified, but ... are not nullified. so said R. Z..., but R. Y said....

3:5-6 I.3   In accord with which authority is that which R. X said R/ Y said

3:5-6 I.9-11   Our rabbis have taught on Tannaite authority + citation of the Tosefta-rule + Said R. X said R. Y + gloss +Z said, "The decided law accords with the position of our Tannaite authority, who said, ...W came ... Said R V, "What is the decided law?" He said to him....

3:5-6 I.30-31   X says + rule + said R. Y said R. Z + W raised this question....

3:5-6 I.32   Rule plus gloss/case/said Abbayye...

3:5-6 I.33   Rule plus gloss

3:5-6 I.34   Rule + gloss

3:5-6 I.35   As above

3:5-6 I.36   Rule + gloss (what verse of Scripture)

3:5-6 I.37   Rule (unglossed)

3:5-6 I.38   R. X said + rule (2x)

3:5-6 II.1-2   Citation of the Mishnah-rule followed by x, y, these say...those say...+ an appended dispute + May we say that at issue is what is under debate among the Tannaite authorities in the following

3:5-6 II.3-5   X asked...he said to him... (with thematic composite tacked on)

3:5-6 II.6   Said X + rule, and Y said + rule

3:5-6 III.1   X says/citation of the Mishnah + the decided law accords with the position of R. Y.

3:5-6 IV.1   [Implicit reference to the Mishnah-rule +] X gave this + rule

3:5-6 IV.2   As above

3:5-6 IV.3   X appointed...and then gave this exposition + rule

3:7A-B I.1   [Implicit citation of the rule of the Mishnah +] Even in the case of ...? But has it not been taught on Tannaite authority:

3:7C-E 3:8A-C II.1   Citation of the Mishnah + Said R. X, "The consideration of ... does not stand in the face of ...all the more so ..."

3:7C-E 3:8A-C III.1   Citation of the Mishnah + said authority W + They have taught this rule only in connection with ...

CONCESSION OF A SIMPLE CASE, CHALLENGE TO A COMPLEX ONE

1:1 IV.1   There is no problem with respect to ..., since ...but why ever ... ?

1:10 II.1   Now if it is permitted to ..., is there any question that ... ?

THE REASON BEHIND THE MISHNAH'S LAW

1:1 IV.2   X repeated the Mishnah's law along with the reason, The reason is that ... but this presented a problem to him because of a contradiction ...

3:1-2 I.1   What is the reason that ...It is in line with that which we have learned in the Mishnah: What is the operative consideration that...

1:5A-B I.3.   The master has said, But has not the opposite between taught on Tannaite authority? It represents a conflict of Tannaite statements in respect to the position of ... One authority takes the view that ...And the other authority takes the view that

1:5C-G I.1   Citation of the rule + An objection was raised on the basis of the following: And in that connection said ... Said X, "Say the rule as follows:

1:6 IV.1   We have a Tannaite formulation along these same lines in that which our rabbis have taught on Tannaite authority:

V. THE DATA IN DETAIL: TYPES AND FORMS OF HALAKHAH-ANALYSIS

CLASSIFICATION OR CLARIFICATION OF AN INTERSTITIAL CASE

1:1 I.4-7   He who...on what count...

3:5-6 I.7.   X raised this question of Y ... He said to him ... He raised an objection based on the following

CONCESSION OF AN OBVIOUS CASE YIELDING A QUESTION CONCERNING A COMPLEX ONE

1:1 II.1   There is no trouble in understanding why ... since .... But what objection can there be to ..., since ...?

1:1 V.1   It is obvious that...but what about..."

DERIVATION OF AN INFERENCE OF LAW FROM A CLARIFICATION OF A RULE: WHAT IS AT STAKE IS... THAT LEADS TO THE INFERENCE THAT....

1:1-2 VIII.2   What makes...special...it is at that time that...that leads to the inference that....

LIMITATION PLACED ON THE APPLICABILITY OF A GENERAL RULE

1:4 III.2.   This rule [concerning repairing walls] has been taught only of..., but as to ...May we say that the following supports his position

CLARIFICATION OF WHAT IS SUBJECT TO DISPUTE

1:5A-B I.2   In the case of...all concur that not...in the case of...all concur that...where there is disagreement, it concerns....

1:5A-B I.4   Does that position...bear the implication that....

How the exegesis of a verse yields the rule at hand

1:5A-B I.5   How does the cited verse yield that conclusion? If the verse yielded
                          no such conclusion, Scripture would have written...[fully articulated dialectical
                          argument]
3:5-6 I.20   How on the basis of Scripture do we know ...?

Distinction between doing an action for a licit purpose and doing it for an illicit purpose

1:9 I.6.   One who ..., if it is with the purpose in mind of ..., that is
                          permitted; if it is with the purpose in mind of ..., it is forbidden

Sorting out interstitial occasions or situations: the comparison of the laws governing an interstitial categories

2:2 I.4   The laws governing the intermediate days of the festival are in the
                          same classification as the laws governing relationships with Kutim [Samaritans]."

The reasoning behind the law and the conflicting rulings yielded by that reasoning

3:1-2 I.2.   X raised this question: "If ...what is the law about ...? Since...he
                          may...Or perhaps, since the reason is not compelling, he may not...?"

Declaration of a law and analysis thereof

1:1 II.3   Our rabbis have taught on Tannaite authority...But that is so only if ...
                vs. Even though ...
1:4 I.2.   Our rabbis have taught on Tannaite authority ...And that is the case only if ...
I:4 II.1   Citation of the Mishnah-rule + Our rabbis have taught on Tannaite
                authority
1:7-8 II.1   Citation of a clause of the Mishnah + Our rabbis have taught on
                Tannaite authority:
1:7-8 III.1   Citation of a clause of the Mishnah + It has been taught on Tannaite
                authority:
2:3 I.1   Citation of a law of the Mishnah + It was taught as a Tannaite
                statement: that is with the stipulation that ...
3:1-2 II.2   Said Authority + legal proposition ... That rule applies only if...but
                if...
3:1-2 II.2   As above
3:1-2 II.4   Rule + as it is said
3:1-2 II.5   Rule + gloss (Said R. X....)
3:1-2 II.6   Rule plus gloss, as above
3:1-2 .II.7   Rule plus proof-text, gloss
3:1-2 .II.8   Rule plus proof-text

3:1-2 .II.9	Rule plus proof-text
3:1-2 II.10	Rule plus proof-text
3:1-2 II.11	Rule plus proof-text
3:1-2 II.12	Rule plus proof-text
3:1-2 II.13	Rule plus proof-text
3:1-2 II.14	Rule plus proof-text
3:1-2 II.15	Rule plus proof-text
3:1-2 II.16	Rule plus proof-text
3:1-2 II.17	Rule plus proof-text
3:1-2 II.18	Rule plus proof-text
3:1-2 II.19	Rule plus Tannaite law
3:1-2 II.20	How on the basis of Scripture do we know the rule that....(with secondary glosses at 3:1-2 II.21, 22
3:1-2 II.23	Our rabbis have taught on Tannaite authority + law
3:1-2 II.24	Said Rabbi X, plus declarative sentence of the law(with a secondary gloss at 3:1-2 II.25)
3:1-2 II.26	Declaration of a law
3:-2 II.27	How long does...for one day...
3:1-2 .II.39	Said X + statement of a rule + That is in line with that which has been taught on Tannaite authority
3:1-2 II.40	Said X + statement of a rule + a case
3:1-2 II.45	Said X + statement of a rule + said Y ....
3:1-2 III.2	A Tannaite statement + As to ..., what sort of case can be in mind? If we say
3:1-2 .III.3	Our rabbis have taught on Tannaite authority + Tannaite statement + But has it not been taught on Tannaite authority: they are forbidden? Said X, When that Tannaite formulation was set forth that they are allowed to do so, it speaks only of those who ...
3:1-2 .III.4.	Our rabbis have taught on Tannaite authority + dispute (2x)
3:4 I.1	Citation of a clause of the Mishnah + Our rabbis have taught on Tannaite authority:
3:4 II.1	Citation of a clause of the Mishnah + Our rabbis have taught on Tannaite authority:
3:5-6 I.6	Referring to a citation of a Tannaite dispute: All parties [even Abba Saul] concur that ... The decided law is in accord with the statement of
3:5-6 I.15	Said R. X, "If one so ...X repeated as a Tannaite statement, "If ... but by the end of the Sabbath it turns out to be classified as ..., he observes ...
3:5-6 I.16.	Does he ... or does he not ...? + dispute
3:5-6 I.17	Our Rabbis have taught on Tannaite authority + rule
3:5-6 I.21.	Our rabbis have taught on Tannaite authority + Rule + case that illustrates the rule
3:5-6 I.23-27	Our rabbis have taught on Tannaite authority + pronouncement of a law + gloss (But has it not been taught on Tannaite authority)
3:5-6 I.28-29	Our rabbis have taught on Tannaite authority + pronouncement of a law + gloss
3:5-6 I.40.	Our rabbis have taught on Tannaite authority + rule
3:5-6 I.41.	Our rabbis have taught on Tannaite authority + rule
3:5-6 I.42.	Our rabbis have taught on Tannaite authority + rule

3:5-6 I.43.	Our rabbis have taught on Tannaite authority + rule
3:5-6 II.7	Statement of a rule + and lo, they said to X...they said to Y...
3:5-6 II.8	Said X, your disciple Y said + it has been taught on Tannaite authority
3:5-6 II.9	Statement of a question on the prevailing rule + disagreement between X and Y + one said...the other said...
3:5-6 II.10	Said X + rule
3:7A-B I.16-20	Our rabbis have taught on Tannaite authority + rule + glosses of the rule + proof texts and amplifications, a continuous exposition
3:7A-B I.21	Our rabbis have taught on Tannaite authority + rule and amplification
3:7A-B I.22	citation of a clause of a rule + proof-text
3:7A-B I.23	citation of a clause of a rule + proof-text
3:7A-B I.28	Our rabbis have taught on Tannaite authority + rule + gloss
3:7A-B I.29	Our rabbis have taught on Tannaite authority + rule + gloss
3:7A-B I.30	Our rabbis have taught on Tannaite authority
3:7A-B I.31	Our rabbis have taught on Tannaite authority + dispute of conflicting opinions + the decided law
3:7A-B I.32	So too it has been taught on Tannaite authority:
3:7A-B I.33	Our rabbis have taught on Tannaite authority + gloss
3:7A-B I.34	To what extent + answer + proof-text
3:7A-B I.35	There was a dispute on this matter between R. X and R. Y... One said ...The other said...
3:7A-B I.36	Our rabbis have taught on Tannaite authority + rule
3:7A-B I.37	Our rabbis have taught on Tannaite authority + rule + gloss
3:7A-B II.1	Citation of the Mishnah + Our rabbis have taught on Tannaite authority
3:7A-B I.16-18	Our rabbis have taught on Tannaite authority + rule + glosses of the rule + proof texts and amplifications, a continuous exposition
3:7A-B II.3.	Our rabbis have taught on Tannaite authority + rule, without comment.
3:7A-B II.4.	Our rabbis have taught on Tannaite authority: At what point do they turn over the couches?
3:7A-B II.5.	Our rabbis have taught on Tannaite authority: When do they set the beds upright on the eve of the Sabbath? From the time of the offering at dusk and onwards.
3:7A-B II.6-7.	Our rabbis have taught on Tannaite authority: He who turns over his bed does not, in fact, turn over only his own bed, but he turns over all the beds that he has in the house, even if he has ten located in two places, he turns over all of them.
3:7A-B II.8	Our rabbis have taught on Tannaite authority: If ... he has not carried out his duty
3:7A-B II.9	Our rabbis have taught on Tannaite authority: They may ...
3:7C-E 3:8A-C I.1	Our rabbis have taught on Tannaite authority:
3:7C-E 3:8A-C I.2	Our rabbis have taught on Tannaite authority:
3:7C-E 3:8A-C II.3	Our rabbis have taught on Tannaite authority: He who ...
3:7C-E 3:8A-C II.4	Said R. X + rule (3x)

3:7C-E 3:8A-C II.5   Said R. X said Y + rule
3:7C-E 3:8A-C II.6   Our rabbis have taught on Tannaite authority: + rule
3:7C-E 3:8A-C II.9   Said X + rule
3:8D-E, 3:9 I.6. Said R. X + rule
3:8D-E, 3:9 I.7. Said R. X, "How on the basis of Scripture do we know that
3:8D-E, 3:9 I.10.And said R. Y, "He who ... should ... He who ... should ...

DECLARATION OF THE DECIDED LAW

3:5-6 I.8   When X came he said Y said...so too R. Z instructed + statement of the law

VI. THE DISTRIBUTION OF TYPES AND FORMS OF MISHNAH-EXEGESIS AND HALAKHAH-ANALYSIS AMONG NAMED AUTHORITIES OF BAVLI TRACTATE MOED QATAN

Do particular authorities of the Bavli specialize in particular types and forms of Mishnah-exegesis and Halakhah-analysis? Or do we find a random distribution of types and forms scattered among named authorities? The answer is, I discern no clear preference of a given authority for a type of exegesis or analysis. The catalogues of types and forms and how they are distributed that follow yield a one-sided result, with some noteworthy, but undemonstrated, tendencies.

Specifically, authorities who are assumed to have come early in the unfolding of the Talmud, such as Rab, Samuel, and Judah, do not predominate in the elementary initiatives, e.g., the search in Scripture for a foundation of a law, the explanation of the meanings of words and phrases. And authorities who are assumed to have flourished later on in the same process, such as Abbayye and Raba, are not excluded. There is a tendency to attribute to earlier figures, such as Judah, inquiries into the meanings of words and phrases. The key-category of Mishnah-exegesis and Halakhah-analysis, the citation of a law and the glossing and analysis of that law, encompasses authorities early, middle, and late. There is a tendency to attribute to later figures analytical initiatives.

But these two tendencies do not validate the proposition that the earlier authorities focused their attention on Mishnah-exegesis, with special attention to the meanings of words and phrases, the correct reading of the Mishnah-rules, and the scriptural foundations of the Mishnah-law. And they do not support the proposition that the middle- and later-authorities concentrated on the analysis of problems of law and legal theory, deeming the exegetical work to have been completed.

The catalogues that follow yield a negative conclusion, that there is no correlation between types and forms of Mishnah-exegesis and Halakhah-analysis in our probe.

VII. AUTHORITIES OF MISHNAH-EXEGESIS BY TYPES

WHENCE IN SCRIPTURE DO WE FIND AN INDICATION THAT....

1:1-2 VII.1-3+4 Simeon b. Pazzi/Rabina/Ashi; Abbahu; Abbayye; Pappa; Hinena; Joshua
      b. R. Idi; Mar Zutra; Ashi; Rabina; glossed by a free-standing composition that
      cites Joshua b. Levi
1:7-8 I.2. Anonymous
3:5-6 I.5. Anonymous
3:5-6 I.12 Hiyya bar Abba, Ammi, Isaac Nappaha
3:5-6 I.22. Mattenah/Ina

PERFECTION OF THE MISHNAH: NO REDUNDANCY, PERFECT COGENCY

1:1 I.1 Anonymous
2:1 I.1 Shisha b. R. Idi/Ashi
2:2 I.1 Anonymous

MEANINGS OF WORDS AND PHRASES

1:1 I.2 Anonymous
1:1 III.1 Judah
1:1 V.1 Abba
1:4 I.1 Judah/Raba bar Ishmael
1:5C-G II.1 Rab
1:6 I.1 Judah
1:6 II.1 Judah
1:6 III.1 Judah
1:7-8 IV.1 Yannai
1:7-8 V.1 Yohanan/Rabbah bar Samuel
1:7-8 VI.1 Dimi
2:5 I.1 Hiyya bar Abba/Assi
2:5 II.1 Anonymous
3:5-6 I.2 Anonymous
3:5-6 I.13. Said Rabbah bar bar Hanna said R. Yohanan

IDENTIFICATION OF THE NAMED AUTHORITY BEHIND THE ANONYMOUS RULE SET FORTH IN
THE MISHNAH

1:1 I.3. Huna, Pappa (Abbayye)
2:2 I.2. Isaac bar Abdimi
3:1-2 II.1 Raba
3:5-6 I.3 Amram/Rab
3:5-6 I.4 Abbayye (glosses foregoing: the decided law....)

CITATION OF A RULE + GLOSS ON THE APPLICATION OF THE RULE

1:1 II.3   Jeremiah, Abbayye
1:1 VI.1   Jacob/Yohanan. Ashi
1:1-2 VII.6-7+8 Anonymous. The passage is glossed by Judah/Samuel, Judah bar Ammi/
        Judah, Pappa
1:1-2 VIII.1   Eleazar/Yose bar Hanina
1:3 I.1-3   Judah; Huna
1:4 I.2.   Simeon b. Gamaliel/Yemar bar Shalamayya/Abbayye
I:4 II.1   Anonymous
1:4 II.2   Simeon b. Eleazar
1:4 III.1   Joseph
1:5C-G III.1   Kahana/Judah/Rab
1:7-8 I.1   Judah/Samuel, Eleazar/Oshaia or Hanina; Rabbah bar R. Huna + Abbayye
1:7-8 II.1   Hisda
1:7-8 II.2.   Hisda/Hina bar Hinnena
1:7-8 III.1   Judah
1:10 I.1   Joseph
1:10 III.1   Hisda
1:10 IV.1 Raba, Abbayye
2:2 I:5   Huna/Rabbah bar R. Huna
2:3 I.1   Anonymous
2:3 II.1   Jeremiah/Zira
2:4A I.1   Raba/Nahman
2:4B-E I.1   Abbayye
2:4B-E II.1   Pappa/Raba
2:5 II.5   Huna/Kahana
3:1-2 III.1   Jeremiah/Zira
3:1-2 III.2   Hisda/Rabina bar Shila
3:1-2 III.3   Hisda/Shila
3:1-2 III.4   Ulla
3:1-2 IV.1   Assi/Yohanan/Jeremiah
3:1-2 IV.2   Raba/Abbayye/Bar Hedayya
3:3 I.1   Samuel
3:4 I.1   Samuel glosses
3:4 II.1   Samuel glosses
3:5-6 I.1   Rab/Huna/Sheshet
3:5-6 I.9-11   Huna/Hiyya bar Abba/Yohanan; Raba/Rabina
3:5-6 I.21   Case involving Rabbah bar bar Hanna illustrates Tannaite teaching
3:5-6 I.23-27   Idi bar Abin (minor gloss)
3:5-6 I.28-29   Hiyya bar Abba/Yohanan
3:5-6 I.30-31   Hiyya bar Kameda/*colleague of R. Abba bar Hiyya/R. Abba/R. Zira*
3:5-6 I.32   Abbayye
3:5-6 I.33   Rabbah bar bar Hanna
3:5-6 I.34   Anonymous
3:5-5 I.35   Simeon b. Eleazar
3:5-6 I;36   Abbahu

3:5-6 I.37   Anonymous
3:5-6 I.38   Rabin-Yohanan/Hiyya bar Abba/Hisda
3:5-6 I.40   Joshua b. Qorhah
3:5-6 I.41   Anonymous
3:5-6 I.42   Pappa
3:5-6 I.43   Anonymous/gloss (3:5-6 I.44) Abbayye and Raba
3:5-6 II.1   Judeans, Galilaeans
3:5-6 II.2   Yohanan
3:5-6 II.3-4   Yohanan/Samuel
3:5-6 II.6   Samuel/Rab
3:5-6 III.1   Giddal bar Menassia/Samuel
3:5-6 IV.1   Annani bar Sasson/Ammi
3:5-6 IV.2   Sheshet
3:5-6 IV.3   Pappa
3:7A-B I.1   Anonymous (+3:7A-B I.2: Safira)
3:7C-E 3:8A-C II.1   Pappa
3:7C-E 3:8A-C III.1   The Nehardeans

CONCESSION OF A SIMPLE CASE, CHALLENGE TO A COMPLEX ONE

1:1-2 IV.1   Zira, Abba b. Mamel
1:10 II.1   Anonymous

THE REASON BEHIND THE MISHNAH'S LAW

1:1-2 IV.2   Amemar
3:1-2 I.1   Anonymous; glossed by Rabbah bar   bar Hanna

THE CONSISTENCY OF VERSIONS OF THE LAW OF THE MISHNAH OR TOSEFTA: CLARIFYING
CONFLICTING TRADITIONS

1:5A-B I.3.   Anonymous
1:5C-G   Abbayye

VIII. AUTHORITIES OF HALAKHAH-ANALYSIS BY TYPES

CLASSIFICATION OR CLARIFICATION OF AN INTERSTITIAL CASE

1:1 I.4   Rabbah, Joseph (Abbayye)
3:5-6 I.7   Abbayye/Rabbah

CONCESSION OF AN OBVIOUS CASE YIELDING A QUESTION CONCERNING A COMPLEX ONE

1:1 II.1   Ilaa/Yohanan v. Ashi
1:1 V.1   Anonymous. But a set of case-reports follows, with Abbayye, Jeremiah,
       and Ashi.

CITATION OF A RULE + GLOSS ON THE APPLICATION OF THE RULE: ONLY IF...EVEN IF....

1:1 II.3   Pappa vs. Ashi

DERIVATION OF AN INFERENCE OF LAW FROM A CLARIFICATION OF A RULE: WHAT IS AT STAKE IS... THAT LEADS TO THE INFERENCE THAT....

1:1-2 VIII.2   Jacob/Yohanan, Zebid, Mesharshayya

LIMITATION PLACED ON THE APPLICABILITY OF A GENERAL RULE

1:4 III.2.   Hisda

CLARIFICATION OF WHAT IS SUBJECT TO DISPUTE

1:5A-B I.2   Raba
1:5A-B 1:3   Anonymous
1:5A-B I.4   Glossed by Abbayye and Raba

HOW THE EXEGESIS OF A VERSE YIELDS THE RULE AT HAND

1:5A-B I.5   Abbayye/Raba
3:5-6 I.20   Ammi bar Hama

DISTINCTION BETWEEN DOING AN ACTION FOR A LICIT PURPOSE AND DOING IT FOR AN ILLICIT PURPOSE

1:9 I.6.   Raba

SORTING OUT INTERSTITIAL OCCASIONS OR SITUATIONS: THE COMPARISON OF THE LAWS GOVERNING AN INTERSTITIAL CATEGORIES

2:2 I.4   Hama bar Guria said Rab

THE REASONING BEHIND THE LAW AND THE CONFLICTING RULINGS YIELDED BY THAT REASONING

3:1-2 I.2.   Abbayye

DECLARATION OF A LAW AND ANALYSIS THEREOF

3:1-2 II.2   Samuel/Phineas/Ashi
3:1-2 II.2   As above
3:1-2 II.4   Anonymous
3:1-2 II.5   Joseph/Abbayye
3:1-2 II.6   Abbayye

3:1-2 II.7	Anonymous
3:1-2 .II.8	Joseph/Abbayye
3:1-2 II.9	Pappa
3:1-2 II.10	Joseph/Abbayye
3:1-2 II.11	Rab
3:1-2 II.12	Anonymous
3:1-2 II.13	Anonymous
3:1-2 II.14	Anonymous
3:1-2 II.15	Joseph
3:1-2 II.16	Joseph
3:1-2 II.17	Joseph
3:1-2 II.18	Joseph/Abbayye
3:1-2 II.19	Joseph/Abbayye
3:1-2 II.20	Raba
3:1-2 II.23	Anonymous
3:1-2 II.24	Hisda
3:1-2 II.39	R. Tanhum b. R. Hiyya of Kefar Akko said R. Jacob bar Aha said R. Simlai,
3:1-2 II.40	Joseph
3:1-2 II.45	Giddal/Rab, Pappa
3:5-6 I.6	Huna b. R. Joshua
3:5-6 I.15	Said R. Yose bar Abin/Adda of Caesarea-Yohanan
3:5-6 I.16.	Mani/Hanina
3:5-6 I.17	Tannaite citation, no attributed gloss
3:5-6 II.7	Samuel/Yohanan
3:5-6 II.8	Rabin bar Ada/Raba
3:5-6 II.9	Oshaia and Bar Qappara
3:5-6 II.10	Raba
3:7A-B I.16-20	No telling attribution
3:7A-B I.21	Anonymous
3:7A-B I.22	As above
3:7A-B I.23	As above
3:7A-B I.24	Helbo/Huna
3:7A-B I.26	Helbo/Ulla/Eleazar
3:7A-B I.27	Anonymous
3:7A-B I.28	Hisda
3:7A-B I.29	Hisda
3:7A-B I.30	Anonymous
3:7A-B I.31	Ulla
3:7A-B I.32	Anonymous
3:7A-B I.33	Nahman/Samuel
3:7A-B I.34	Anonymous
3:7A-B I.35	Mattenah & Mar Uqba
3:7A-B I.36	Anonymous
3:7A-B I.37	Pappa
3:7A-B II.1	Anonymous
3:7A-B II.3	Anonymous

```
3:7A-B II.4          Anonymous
3:7A-B II.5          Anonymous
3:7A-B II.6-7        Anonymous
3:7A-B II.8          Anonymous
3:7A-B II.9          Anonymous
3:7C-E 3:8A-C I.1       Anonymous
3:7C-E 3:8A-C I.2       Anonymous
3:7C-E 3:8A-C II.3      Anonymous
3:7C-E 3:8A-C II.4.     Yohanan
3:7C-E 3:8A-C II.5.     Judah/Rab
3:7C-E 3:8A-C II.6.     Anonymous
3:7C-E 3:8A-C II.9      Levi
3:8D-E, 3:9 I.6         Yohanan
3:8D-E, 3:9 I.7         Abbahu
3:8D-E, 3:9 I.10 Levi bar Haita
```

DECLARATION OF THE DECIDED LAW

3:5-6 I.8   Rabin/Yohanan; Eleazar, Pedat

IX. DOES BAVLI MOED QATAN YIELD INDICATIONS OF LAYERS OF TALMUDIC KNOWLEDGE?

When we attempt to correlate the types and forms of exegesis and analysis with the names of authorities invoked in the compositions surveyed here, we produce no pattern that sustains differentiating discourse by layers, e.g., of generations of sages. I see no patterns of attribution of a determinate type of composition to a particular authority or set of authorities. For the most part, we have come up with a single governing pattern: citation and gloss, whether in Mishnah-exegesis or Halakhah-analysis. The attributions of that governing pattern appear random and scattered.

If successive layers of writing accumulated in the process of the agglutination of the Bavli on Moed Qatan, we have been unable to find the detritus of that process: forms characteristic of one generation (a.k.a., group of names) but not of another. The thesis of a cumulative process produced a null hypothesis: if we deal with layers of knowledge, we should find formal indications thereof. But we found no evidence to sustain that hypothesis.

X. RICHARD KALMIN'S MAIN RESULTS COMPARED WITH THOSE YIELDED BY BAVLI MOED QATAN

This finding contradicts the statements of Richard Kalmin that we met at the outset:

"…formal aspects of Amoraic discourse provide evidence of generational contrast indicative of the diversity of talmudic source material….statements by later Amoraim are formally distinguishable from statements by earlier Amoraim…"[12]

Clearly, my form-analysis does not replicate Kalmin's result. His articles are richly documented, and this contradictory outcome requires an explanation.

I suspect he means by "formally distinguishable" something other than the kind of form-analysis that yielded the results summarized here. I went in search of recurrent patterns of a gross order, repeatedly characteristic of large blocks of writing, and I came up with one principal pattern, the citation and gloss of a passage of the Mishnah, Tosefta, or external Halakhic source. I did not attempt to distinguish one citation + gloss exegesis or analysis from another; to me they conform to a single pattern.

Kalmin proceeds to another claim I could not replicate in my sample:

We may adduce "differences between the introductory formulae introducing statements by early, later, and middle-generation Amoraim. These differences…support my claim regarding the presence of diverse sources in the Bavli, distinguishable along chronological lines…"[13]

Here Kalmin focuses on "introductory formulae," which I took to mean, "Our rabbis have taught on Tannaite authority" and similar rhetorical cliches. He clearly has in mind a much more refined set of criteria.

"Middle generation Babylonian Amoraim [are] transitional…these transitional features may reveal the role of third– and fourth-generation Amoraim in the editing of earlier Amoraic statements…"[14]

Here Kalmin produces a correlation that I could not replicate, let alone demonstrate. But the difference is in premise, not form-analysis. He seems to me to rely on attributions for his indicative data, working from the attribution to the classification of "early/middle/late." But I assume nothing about attributions, except that they represent data requiring verification. So Kalmin's path was closed to me by the question that precipitated the inquiry: do we find correlations of type or form and sequence of attributions? I could not assume at the outset what I set out to investigate.

Accordingly, I account for the contradictory results produced here in a simple way. First, in the first two of his three propositions Kalmin understands by form, and by form-analysis, much more refined data than the gross indicators that governed my classification. Second, Kalmin is less troubled than I am by the problem of testing the reliability and intent of attributions, a matter to which I return at the end.

XI. DOES AN EXEGETICAL PROGRAM GOVERN THROUGHOUT? DO ANALYTICAL
INITIATIVES OF A PARTICULAR TYPE RECUR?

Let me now articulate the outcome of my probe into the layers of Talmudic knowledge in Bavli Moed Qatan.

First, do the same types and forms of Mishnah-exegesis and of Halakhah-analysis persist throughout the Bavli-tractate probed here and in what proportions? Yes, citation and gloss, subdivided into a few specific types of exegetical inquiry, account for nearly the whole of the exegesis of the Mishnah. The counterpart exercises of the Halakhic analyses produce the same result. Nearly the whole of the Talmud's work of exegesis and analysis requires citation and gloss for its form, clarification of issues of consistency and coherence for its content. That is without regard to the names or provenience of the authorities to whom sayings are attributed.

Second, how do the several types and forms of Mishnah-exegesis and Halakhah-analysis relate: is it in fixed sequences, or not in a clearly indicated order? Mishnah-exegesis invariably takes priority over Halakhah-analysis. The program is fixed: first clarify the Mishnah, then pursue analytical questions of law. My reference system, with its ordinal enumeration of compositions, signals that result throughout.

Third, analytical initiatives of a particular type do recur and do predominate in all types of compositions and among all named authorities: citation of the received formulation of the law, whether in the Mishnah or in the Tosefta or in a collection external to both, then exposition or refinement of the law.

XII. DO DETERMINATE TYPES OF EXEGESIS AND ANALYSIS RECUR IN
PARTICULAR NAMES OR SETS OF NAMES?

Apart from some tendencies noted there, the indicated types of exegesis and analysis are randomly scattered among particular names or sets of names. This result is particularly troubling in light of Kalmin's contrary result.

It is also striking in light of the rules of composition that govern in the Mishnah and the Tosefta, which do not randomly sample names of particular sages. On the contrary, the Mishnah and the Tosefta are so composed as to permit the correlation of logic and attribution. What is assigned to an early authority is fundamental in logic, what is assigned to a later authority that intersects is subordinate in logic. With that result in hand, I asked in my probe of Bavli Moed Qatan, do we discern evidences of temporal sequence, signaled by successive generations of Rabbinic authorities in the Bavli? I wanted to know whether sets of authorities generally assumed to have flourished early in the period in which the Talmud took shape — Rab and Samuel, for example — pursue a logical inquiry that is primary in the unfolding of the Halakhic analysis, while sets of authorities generally supposed to have flourished later in that period — Rabbah, Raba and Abbayye, for instance

— pursue analytical problems that rest on a logic subordinate to that governing in the inquiry assigned to earlier figures?[15] The answer is negative.

Even if we were to follow Kalmin's lead in taking for granted that the Rabbinic sages really said what is attributed to them, we could not reconstruct an unfolding logic corresponding in its development from simplicity to complexity as successive generations of sages joined in the exegetical and analytical work. What the Mishnah and the Tosefta exposed — a correspondence between the sequence of generations and the unfolding from fundamental to secondary, primary to subordinate — the Bavli simply does not make manifest. That is not because discussions do not unfold in ever more refined and complex sequences of thought. Protracted dialectical arguments do just that.[16] But those dialectical arguments are constructed in response to an applied logic that transcends attributions to named authorities of particular components of the composition.

In general, in the Bavli, questions of a primary character may surface in the names of authorities, early, middle, and late. A survey of sayings attributed to "middle" and "late" authorities will sustain that claim.

But we need not invoke the alleged sequence of named generations. Rather, the Talmud's sustained and systematic expositions simply are not constructed in accord with, and do not take account of, sequences of generations. They pursue their own logic, their own dialectics, without matching primary to early names, subordinate to later ones. The Bavli exhibits its own traits of composition and the agglutination of composites, and its interest in attributions is for considerations not comparable to those that govern in the Mishnah and the Tosefta.

It is solely by paraphrasing the Talmud itself that we may indeed describe the generative logic of Talmudic analysis as that exegetical and analytical process unfolded in sequences signified by the requirements of a pure, atemporal dialectics. Stating the matter simply: the attributions of sayings to named authorities within a dialectical analysis of the law do not bear upon the exposition of the analytical process.

XIII. DECIPHERING THE ARCHITECTONICS OF TALMUDIC KNOWLEDGE: WHAT, EXACTLY, CAN WE MAKE OF ATTRIBUTIONS?

Kalmin aims at a historical outcome: "…early Amoraic generations…played a role in the editorial process…."[17] Thinking in historical terms, he has interpreted the data of attributions to yield historical results: order, correlation of time and sequence of intellectual events. I have not found it possible to replicate his results. I could not establish the correlations required to validate his results.

Two reasons account for the difference. First, as I said, I think each of us invokes for "form-analysis" different criteria for defining what is meant by "forms"

And second, what Kalmin takes as a datum I subject to doubt. He seems certain that attributions bear a fixed significance wherever they occur. But as I explained in the Introduction, that is false for the Mishnah, tractate Abot, and the Tosefta.[18] Each document uses attributions for a purpose particular to the documentary program at hand. In light of that fact, we must ask what an attribution signals in the Bavli: what sort of information is afforded by the attributive, "say/ said," and its counterparts? This extension of the documentary hypothesis of the Rabbinic canon to the problem at hand dictates the next problem that requires attention.

ENDNOTES

[1] See *The Bavli's One Voice: Types and Forms of Analytical Discourse and their Fixed Order of Appearance.* Atlanta, 1991: Scholars Press for South Florida Studies in the History of Judaism. Now: Lanham, MD: University Press of America; *How the Bavli Shaped Rabbinic Discourse.* Atlanta, 1991: Scholars Press for South Florida Studies in the History of Judaism; *The Bavli's Massive Miscellanies. The Problem of Agglutinative Discourse in the Talmud of Babylonia.* Atlanta, 1992: Scholars Press for South Florida Studies in the History of Judaism; *Sources and Traditions. Types of Composition in the Talmud of Babylonia.* Atlanta, 1992: Scholars Press for South Florida Studies in the History of Judaism; *The Law Behind the Laws. The Bavli's Essential Discourse.* Atlanta, 1992: Scholars Press for South Florida Studies in the History of Judaism; *The Bavli's Primary Discourse. Mishnah Commentary, its Rhetorical Paradigms and their Theological Implications in the Talmud of Babylonia Tractate Moed Qatan.* Atlanta, 1992: Scholars Press for South Florida Studies in the History of Judaism; *The Discourse of the Bavli: Language, Literature, and Symbolism. Five Recent Findings.* Atlanta, 1991: Scholars Press for South Florida Studies in the History of Judaism.

[2] The distinction between the composition and the composite comprised by compositions is spelled out in my *The Rules of Composition of the Talmud of Babylonia. The Cogency of the Bavli's Composite.* Atlanta, 1991: Scholars Press for South Florida Studies in the History of Judaism.

[3] I first introduced the metaphor of music to describe the Bavli in *Judaism's Theological Voice: The Melody of the Talmud.* Chicago, 1995: The University of Chicago Press.

[4] Collected in *Sages, Stories, Authors and Editors in Rabbinic Babylonia* (Atlanta, 1995: Scholars Press for Brown Judaic Studies).

[5] I checked with him this brief precis of his main results and he confirmed that it is an accurate account.

[6] "Unique formal characteristics of later Amoraic discourse," p. 111.

[7] "Quotation forms in the Babylonian Talmud," p. 127.

[8] "Middle-Generation Amoraim as among the editors of the Talmud," p. 169.

[9] *Sages, Stories*, p. 172.

[10] I know of no other systematic work on the problem, and his extensive notes in *Sages, Stories* do not suggest otherwise.

[11] I reproduce the reference-system of my *The Talmud of Babylonia. An Academic Commentary.* Atlanta, 1994-1996, 1999: Scholars Press for *USF Academic Commentary Series.* Now: Lanham, MD. University Press of America. XI. *Bavli Tractate Moed Qatan.*

[12] "Unique formal characteristics of later Amoraic discourse," p. 111.

[13] "Quotation forms in the Babylonian Talmud," p. 127.

[14] "Middle-Generation Amoraim as among the editors of the Talmud," p. 169.

[15] My *History of the Mishnaic Law* (Leiden, 1974-1986, in forty-three volumes) pursued a comparable problem. It is, can we correlate the attributions of sayings to authorities of the Mishnah assumed to have flourished early in the sequence of generations with the standing of what is attributed to them in the larger unfolding of the law? That is, do we find that what is assigned to early authorities concerns primary and generative conceptions of the law, while what attributed to later ones addresses secondary and derivative ones? If that is the case, then we have sequences of ideas matching sequences of sets of authorities, the order of authorities matching the logical standing of what is assigned to those same authorities. I found that that is the case where the inquiry is sustained by the evidence, that is, where we have sequences of authorities and sets of rules set forth in ordinal relationships of persons, bearing rulings that intersect and exhibit the traits of logical unfolding, there the process yields an affirmative result. It is most, most unusual for a saying assigned to an early authority to rest on premises attested only by sayings attributed to a later one. The great exception to that rule is the Houses of Shammai and Hillel, who are not uncommonly represented as disputing secondary and derivative issues otherwise first attested in disputes among mid-second century figures, Judah, Meir, Simeon, and the like. I showed that that is the case for the entirety of tractate Makhshirin in *Form Analysis and Exegesis: A Fresh Approach to the Interpretation of Mishnah.* Minneapolis, 1980: University of Minnesota Press.

[16] See my survey of the dialectical argument narrowly defined: *Talmudic Dialectics: Types and Forms.* Atlanta, 1995: Scholars Press for South Florida Studies in the History of Judaism. I. *Introduction. Tractate Berakhot and the Divisions of Appointed Times and Women; and Talmudic Dialectics: Types and Forms.* Atlanta, 1995: Scholars Press for South Florida Studies in the History of Judaism. II. *The Divisions of Damages and Holy Things and Tractate Niddah.*

[17] *Sages, Stories*, p. 172.

[18] I deal with the uses of attributions in the Mishnah, tractate Abot, and the Tosefta, in "What Use Attributions? An Open Question in the Study of Rabbinic Literature," in *When Judaism and Christianity Began, Essays in Memory of Anthony J. Saldarini,* ed. By Alan J. Avery-Peck, Daniel Harrington, and Jacob Neusner (Leiden, 2003: E. J. Brill), pp. 445-464.

15

The Second Temple Origins of the Halakhah of Besah

I. THE CATEGORY-FORMATION, BESAH, ITS ORIGINS AND ITS GENERATIVE PROBLEMATIC

The Halakhic category-formation, Besah (a.k.a., Yom Tob, festival), represented in the Mishnah, Tosefta, Yerushalmi, and Bavli, deals with the preparation of food on the festival day itself. Scripture explicitly permits doing so. The pertinent verse, allowing cooking on the festival days, lays the foundations for the category-formation. But the problematic of the legal topic emerges not from the base-verse but from the hermeneutics of the Rabbinic sages — we know not when or where they flourished nor do their names ever surface anywhere — and their mode of thought in interpreting Scripture's facts.

For once the Torah says that on the festival day (in context, Passover, but therefore also, Pentecost and Tabernacles) one may cook but not constructively work, the festival day is both treated as like the Sabbath (not work) but also not like the Sabbath (cook). This distinction is expressed in the language of Scripture, in the view of David Instone-Brewer:

> The origin of the distinction between work on a Sabbath and on a Yom Tob was originally based on Torah vocabulary. On Yom Tob the Torah prohibits 'servile labor' ('abad) but on Sabbath it also prohibits all other 'labor' (melakah). I am impressed by how consistent this distinction is in the Torah. The word 'abad appears several times with regard to Yom Tob (Lev.23.7f, 21, 25, 35f; Num.28.18, 25f; 29.1, 12, 35) while melakah is used only with regard to Sabbaths except re the Day of Atonement when both are prohibited, e.g., Lev.23.28-31.[1]

Scripture clearly recognizes the species of the genus, work, in its philology.

That philologically establishes a genus comprised by two species, and the processes of analogical thinking take over. Hence the category-formation, cooking on the festival-day, takes shape around the hermeneutics of comparison and contrast: how is the festival like the Sabbath, how unlike, and what are the issues that present themselves when we ask? What we have before us is a perfect model of how a category-formation takes shape in response to a theory of interpretation, a hermeneutics, that imparts structure and order and cogency to the category-formation. It is a hermeneutics that makes of the given information consequential knowledge, transforming facts into well-formed principles. I cannot point to a better example of the interplay of category-formation, hermeneutics, and the exegesis that is guided by hermeneutics and required to work out problems set forth within the category-formation at hand. Nor does it surprise that Besah is a great favorite of those that love Halakhic study.

How, exactly, does the hermeneutics of the category-formation take shape through a process of analogical-contrastive thinking? The answer is simple, and here we see the hermeneutics at work. Things are like one another, so follow the same rule, or they are unlike, so the rule for the one is opposite the rule for the other of the species of the genus. In the present case, the issue throughout is, how is the festival day different from the Sabbath, as the fact that one may cook on that day indicates it is different? Does the difference mean that the rules of sanctification that govern on the Sabbath do not pertain at all, or do they apply in a different (commensurate) way?

To state matters simply: the category-formation is defined by the topic, cooking on the festival. The hermeneutics derives form the analogical-contrastive thinking that generates the questions just now set forth.

II. The Hermeneutical Foundations of the Halakhah of Besah: The Thought Processes Reconstructed

What fuses the Halakhic data into a category-formation? For that purpose, we must reconstruct the thought processes that produced out of the datum of Scripture the category-formation of Besah. In that reconstruction, we shall encounter the work of the unnamed sages who, long before the Mishnah assembled the work of category-formation into a systematic law code, thought through in abstract terms what would take on concrete form only in the Mishnah (along with the Tosefta).

We deal with facts and modes of thought about those facts. Scripture provides the facts. The sages whose ideas were made concrete and specific in the Mishnah's Halakhah thought deeply about those facts and transformed them into the wherewithal of the category-formation before us.

What are the data and how are they interpreted? *The raw data derive from random rules about not using fire, hence not cooking, on the Sabbath. The interpretation, as is common in the Halakhah, rests on a procedure of comparison and contrast, that is, a process of analogical-contrastive thinking in a process of hierarchical classification.*

At the foundations of the matter is the simple fact that Scripture recognizes the genus, holy day (Sabbath, festival), on which servile labor may not be done, but — Scripture again speciates also. Specifically, it defines the two species of the genus, Sabbath and festival, on the one of which cooking may not be done, on the other of which, cooking may be done. So before us is an exercise in the analysis of speciation of a genus, the whole guided by the hermeneutics of comparison and contrast, as I said.

The governing principles are these: [1] food for use on the festival must be available and designated for that purpose, actually or potentially, prior to the festival. How does this relate to the matter of sanctification like that of the Sabbath? Just as one has to prepare food for the Sabbath in advance of the Sabbath, so one has to designate food for use on the festival in advance of the festival. Then cooking on the festival is not a secular act, done in a random manner, but an act of sanctification of the festival, as much as cooking in advance of the Sabbath is an act of sanctification of the Sabbath. Sanctification, by definition, requires an act of particularization: this and no other, for this act of sanctification, and no other.

Further, [2] may or may not one carry on the preparation of food on the festival in exactly the same way in which one does so on an ordinary day? Here again the hermeneutics of comparison and contrast yields the exegesis of the laws that comprise the category-formation. Is the festival day unlike the Sabbath and therefore the act of cooking is entirely secular? Or is it holy like the Sabbath, and therefore the act of cooking must be done in a manner that distinguishes it from the same act done on a weekday? Here again, the theory of interpretation that sets like beside like and under the same rule, and unlike opposite unlike and therefore under the contrasting rule, governs.

Next, [3] may or may not one prepare what is required for the preparation of food, that is, secondary or tertiary acts of labor, in the way in which one may do so on an ordinary day? Just as the differentiation between cooking on the festival and cooking on an ordinary day plays its role, so we ask about secondary or tertiary acts of labor: may these be done in the ordinary manner or must they be done in a differentiated way?

Finally, [4] may or may not one do such acts of labor at all? Here the issue is obvious. The Sabbath supplies the governing analogy. The tractate asks about distinguishing the actual preparation of food, which the Written Torah permits, from acts of labor required for food but not directly pertaining thereto; acts of labor indirectly involved in food preparation. The analogy of the Sabbath is ever present. And introducing that analogy represents the key initiative of hermeneutics.

Designating food before the festival for use on the festival, on the one side, and linking the status of the household to the status (e.g., as to location) of his possessions, on the other, form the principal laws that are worked out in detail here. In advance of the householder must designate for use on the festival what he is going to prepare on the festival. That, as we now have come to expect, represents an act of particularization, this batch of food for this festival in particular, and it is entirely familiar to us in another context altogether. The Temple and its offerings define that context, where, we recall from the Halakhah of Pesahim, the animal to be used for a Passover offering must be designated for that purpose. Once the animal is designated, without appropriate rite it cannot then be used for some secular purpose or some other sacred purpose. An animal for use as a sin-offering must be linked to that particular sin; the farmer who presents it must have in mind the inadvertent transgression that the animal expiates. A general statement that the animal expiates generic sin will not serve. Insisting on that same procedure in connection with the bulk of food and utensils for food preparation used for the festival treats the food for the table as comparable to the food for the altar. The same rule governs the identification and particularization of both, each for its respective purpose.

The hermeneutics begins with a philosophical question and shades over into reflection upon a theological issue. The philosophical question is, how do we classify what is potential? Do we deem it as actual, in that the acorn contains within itself the potentiality of the oak, so the acorn is classified as an oak in nuce? Or do we deem what is potential as distinct from what is actual? Readers familiar with Aristotle's deep thought about causation will find themselves right at home here. The Halakhah takes the position that the egg may not be eaten, meaning, we differentiate the potential from the actual.

Embedded in the same case, especially in Tosefta's rich amplification of it, is the Halakhah's recurrent stress on the particularity of intentionality. Here the principle is, one must in advance of the festival designate for use on the festival whatever one is going to utilize on that day. What about food? We impute to the householder the intent to prepare certain food comes to hand, therefore a calf born on the festival may be slaughtered and eaten on that same day. But the owner has to have known in advance that what he will eat on the festival in fact was available as food: even though the egg is edible, since the owner did not know, in advance, that the egg would be available, he did not designate it for eating on the festival, and so it is not available for that purpose. When it comes to things other than edibles, advance planning is absolutely required. These reflections on intentionality intersect with deep thought on the potential and the actual to create a complex grid of analysis of cases by appeal to the one principle or to the other. But they lead to a theological principle that the sacred, e. g., sacred time, must be designated and differentiated as an act of intentionality. One must prepare in advance for the advent of the festival by designating what is going to serve the legitimate tasks of that day. Once more the Tosefta states a case that bears the principle: Ashes from a fire which one lit on the festival day do they not use to cover blood of a beast slaughtered on that festival day, for they are not that which was made ready before the festival day.

III. THE THEOLOGY OF THE CATEGORY-FORMATION, BESAH:
WORKING BACK FROM CONCRETE RULE TO ABSTRACT REFLECTION

From the thought processes that yielded the Halakhah let us now turn to the identification of the theological issues that animated the Halakhic inquiry. Once more we find ourselves in a pre-literary realm, where we have neither named authorities nor texts, only the results in the Halakhic documents of rigorous theological reflection about abstract issues.

The theological question concerns the divisibility of the sacred time, which is to say, do we differentiate what is sacred for one reason from what is sacred for another, the time that is sacred as the Festival from that which is sacred as the Sabbath, in the present case? Or does the Festival flow naturally into the Sabbath? At issue is whether what is legitimate on the Festival may be done on the Festival for utilization on the Sabbath, a deeply-reflected on question indeed. The answer carries us into the conception of commingling. We recall that space may be commingled, so that on the Sabbath ownership may be shared to a common courtyard or alleyway; owners relinquish their private ownership for the common good of establishing a shared domain, and a fictive, symbolic meal of commingling accomplishes that task. In the case of commingling time, the Halakhah both differentiates the holiness of the Festival from the holiness of the Sabbath and also commingles them. It does so by treating them as not continuous but subject to melding. That yields a number of concrete rules, all of them based on the differentiation of contiguous spells of consecrated time.

First, one may prepare food on the festival, and what is left over may be used on the Sabbath, on which one of course does not prepare food. So the Halakhah is explicit. While on a festival day one is permitted only to prepare food for that same day. He may not prepare food for use after the festival, on the festival he may prepare food for the festival itself, and if he leaves something over, he has left it over for the Sabbath.

Second, one may not prepare on the festival food specifically for use on the Sabbath that follows immediately.

Third, if one starts preparing food on Thursday for the festival that falls on Friday, he may continue adding food to the mixture on Friday, leaving over more food for the Sabbath. And before the eve of the festival day that is, on Thursday he may prepare a cooked dish and rely on it to prepare food on Friday for the Sabbath. The preparation of this dish — the fusion-meal or 'erub-tabshilin — marks the beginning of the individual's cooking of food for the Sabbath. Once he has begun, on Thursday, to prepare food for the Sabbath, he may continue that preparation, even on the festival day itself. And for that purpose single dish is sufficient. That represents a commingling of time effected through a meal, comparable to the commingling of space effected through the meal.

Through these closely-linked rules, the Halakhah states that we respond both to the unity and the diversity of sacred time. All consecrated time bears the same traits, e. g., the prohibition of labor. But within that genus, we speciate sacred time on which one may prepare food from that on which one may not. Just as we noted in connection with the intermediate days of the festival, we move from the concrete to the abstract, so here too we do the same. That is, from the fact that on the intermediate days, festival offerings are presented, we proceed to the abstract conception that in some ways, these days on which it is permitted to work are differentiated from other days on which it is permitted to work because on these days offerings respond to the level of sanctification accorded to those intermediate days.

That is to say, the differentiation at the one point is generalized into elements of differentiation elsewhere. Here too we both treat as continuous and differentiate the sacred time marked by the festival, on the one side, and the Sabbath, on the other. Just as on the one occasion we may cook and on the other we may not — cooking then representing the indicator in the household, comparable to the offering in the Temple — so on the one occasion we may not prepare food for the other occasion. But we may both use on the Sabbath food left over from the festival and also prepare in advance a single stew or broth that will serve both. Preparation in advance of the festival for both the festival and, en passant, the Sabbath, is certainly permitted. In sum, we both differentiate and homogenize.

That leads us to a profound issue: doing actions connected with preparing food on a festival day in a different manner from on ordinary days. That is an issue familiar from the principle, in connection with the Sabbath, that if on the Sabbath one carries something from one domain to another in an other-than-ordinary manner, he is not culpable. Now, when it comes to food-preparation, encompassing bringing food from place to place, one brings jars of wine not in a basket but on his shoulder; And so too: he who takes straw should not hang the hamper over his back. But he brings it carrying it in his hand. What is at issue here? If we say that on the festival, those acts that are permitted may be carried out in a routine way, as they are done in ordinary time, then we maintain that the secular breaks into sacred time, the act of cooking on the festival (encompassing also secondary and tertiary stages in the process) is comparable to the act of cooking on a weekday. In this aspect the festival is distinguished from the Sabbath and therefore in this aspect is secular.

If we say that on the festival those acts that are permitted must be done in a manner different from the way they are done in ordinary time, we are saying that the sacred time of the festival is different from the sacred time of the Sabbath, but remains sacred time, subject to restrictions upon secular behavior even when actions in the category of the secular are permitted to be carried out. The law takes the latter view. It recognizes the genus, sacred time, and its species, Sabbath distinct from festival. That explains why many of the acts that are permitted in connection with food preparation must be carried out in a manner that distinguishes the same action from the way it is done on an ordinary day. We deal, then, with two subdivisions of sacred time, each sharing traits with the other, while distinguished from the other: we distinguish the sacred from the sacred.

That fact is underscored when we recall the counterpart rulings in connection with the performance of permitted labor during the intermediate days of the festival. There two principles govern.

First, if labor is permitted on the intermediate days of the festival, it may be carried out in the ordinary manner. They hunt moles and mice in a tree-planted field and in a field of grain, in the usual manner, on the intermediate days of a festival and in the Sabbatical Year. They may only block up a breach in the intermediate days of a festival. And in the seventh year the Sabbatical Year, one builds it in the normal way. And they do all public needs. What are public needs? They judge capital cases, property cases, and cases involving fines. And they burn a red cow. And they break the neck of a heifer in the case of a derelict corpse. And they pierce the ear of a Hebrew slave who wishes to remain with his master. And they effect redemption for pledges of personal valuation, for things declared herem, for things declared consecrated, and for second tithe through coins to be taken up to Jerusalem. And they untie a shoe from the last so long as one does not put it back.

Second, permitted labor may not be carried out in an excessively laborious manner. They do not dig cisterns, pits, or ditches on the intermediate days of a festival, but they refashion and repair them. These two principles treat the intermediate days of the festival at a lower level of sanctification than the first and final days of the festival; the latter are comparable to the Sabbath, but different, the former, to the profane weekdays, but different.

The difference between the holiness of the festival and the Sabbath is intrinsic and substantive. The difference between the intermediate days of the festival and utterly profane time is notional and circumstantial: hard work versus routine work — but work if done, then done in the usual way. The issue, then, is, how do we differentiate secular time that is distinguished at the cult from secular time that is not, hence the intermediate days of the festival from ordinary days? Here, by contrast, we differentiate the sacred from the sacred, and that explains why what work is permitted is done in a manner that registers the difference between the holy day on which it is performed and the manner of doing the same work on an ordinary day. When the Sabbath concludes, followed by a festival day, the liturgy that marks the distinction between the Sabbath and other time — the rite of differentiation or Habdalah — states the matter very simply. At the end of the Sabbath prior to a weekday, the prayer praises God for distinguishing the holy from the ordinary. At the end of the Sabbath prior to a festival day, the same prayer praises God for distinguishing the holy from the holy. The Halakhah says no less, but spells out the meaning of the theological distinction, which is shown in rich detail to make a huge difference.

IV. THE ORIGIN OF BESAH IN SECOND TEMPLE TIMES

The system of thought, the construction of the category-formation — all is complete in its theoretical, generative principles *before* the Mishnah, with the Tosefta, comes to detailed expression — long before. Once the category-formation has taken shape around the hermeneutics of analogy and contrast to the Sabbath, everything else coheres. And then, and only then, the concrete issues raised in the Mishnah come to the surface. The category-formation shows itself able to identify a boundless range of relevant problems and to solve those problems in a consistent way. I cannot point to a more perfect example of the workings of a well-crafted native category-formation, the power of a hermeneutics of such a category-formation to reproduce itself in case after case. And now, it suffices to observe, the Bavli's sages have in no way participated in this process. They have inherited its outcome and have made themselves worthy heirs indeed. But theirs is not the category-formation, theirs are not the generative principles that have given it shape, to them uniquely do not belong the modes of thought that have defined its particularization.

Prior to the translation, by the Mishnah, of theory into law, of hermeneutics into topics and the consequent topical exegesis, the thought-processes instantiated in the Halakhah had completed their work. These thought-processes originate in analogical-contrastive thinking, and they generally, if not invariably, focus on topics that, in general, sustain that inquiry, which accounts for Besah and explains, also, the inert character of Berakhot, an exception.

The governing and generative analogy — the festival day is like the Sabbath but not wholly so — then came to expression in concrete cases of an exemplary character. That is what shapes the entire presentation of the Halakhah, which, in organization and in detail is the work of the Mishnah, complemented in detail by the Tosefta. The details produce points of contention, where named sages figure, but the basic hermeneutics never changes and produces only cogent results. The uniformity of the exegetical problems, their close cohesion to the generative problematics of the category-formation, makes the presentation a model of coherent thought: mode, problematic, outcome.

No wonder the framers of some of the Tosefta's compositions, those that cross topical boundaries but hold together diverse illustrations of a single principle in common, put their best energies into showing the deeper unities of the law, those that penetrate beyond the surface of the topical divisions of the Mishnah. The character of the Halakhah itself, as set forth by Moses in the Torah and analyzed by the Rabbinic sages, invited just such an initiative. The category-formation, Besah, turns out to form a whole the sum of which is greater than the parts, with its remarkable power to invent new problems and propound deep questions, metaphysical questions of the sacred. The category-formation begins, as we saw earlier, in Scripture. But in the category-formation, Besah, we deal with one of the triumphs of the Halakhic hermeneutics of analogical-contrastive reasoning and the Rabbinic theological imagination.

The generative premises of the Halakhah outlined earlier, concerning intentionality, for example, form a natural connection to the topic at hand, but every one of them works well, also, in other contexts altogether, and none is particular to the topic, let alone insinuated by Scripture's meager statement on the topic, of festival cooking. What we have before us is a quite independent development of a subject rather casually stated by Scripture. All of the complexities, and the premises that generate them, derive from other minds altogether, even though, one may fairly claim, all of the participating intellects concur on everything important within the governing logic that comprehends the law of Scripture and the Halakhah commencing therein but not defined thereby.

What is relevant specifically to our inquiry is this simple fact: the entire thought process was fully articulated before a single concrete Halakhic rule of the Mishnah (or the Tosefta) was composed. That is why named sages play no role: the work was carried out in a generation remote from the first and second century authorities who gloss the details of the Mishnah and the Tosefta and are celebrated in the chain of tradition of tractate Abot Chapter One. Some time (using that chain as a reference point) between the men of the Great Assembly and the Houses of Shammai and Hillel, a vast enterprise of sustained, systematic thought transformed Scripture's data into the Halakhah's system, its fully-executed category-formations, and with that topical program in hand, the named sages of the first and second century attended to the details.

The category-formation, Besah, was fully designed, its Halakhic issues completely discerned, before — I think, long before — the composition of the Mishnah in ca. 200 C.E., and to a particular authority in Besah is attributed by name not a single one of the generative principles of the Halakhah. The Houses are given positions on the conflicting principles we outlined earlier; they are not credited with discovering those principles, only negotiating the conflicts between them. They identified the interstitial problems and solved them, leaving space for refinement and conflict about what did not really matter.

The judgment that, in the Halakhic structure, the system takes priority over the individual sage, that "self" of the title of this book, is now fully explained. The category-formation in its abstract principles and in its concrete expressions derives from unnamed sages, of whom we know nothing but the main thing. That is, to repeat: their work was long complete before named authorities in the Bavli, on whom we have concentrated in this probe, ever encountered the outcome, the Halakhah of the Mishnah-Tosefta.

Can we identify the stages in the process of Halakhic realization?

[1] Some time from the promulgation of the Torah, encompassing the law distinguishing cooking from other forms of labor and the festival from the Sabbath, theological issues of sanctification and differentiation within the realm of the sacred confronted the heirs of the Torah.

[2] They framed these issues within the analytical program of philosophy concerning intentionality and deed, the genus and the species, analogy and contrast, potentiality and actuality.

And [3] with the upshot — a system of thought calculated to guide the realization of thought in concrete social reality — the category-formation comprised by the topic, Besah, took shape in full rationality and in acute detail. When we do not know, but it is certainly a work of Second Temple times, probably early in that period, given the participation of the Houses of Shammai and Hillel and other first century authorities in the detailed exposition of the law. But in the end it is a labor of logic, therefore unbounded by particularities of time, space, and circumstance.

ENDNOTES

[1] E-mail, January 19, 2004. My thanks to him for his valuable observation.

16

The Integrity of the Rabbinic Law of Purity (Mishnah-Tractate Tohorot)

When the Rabbinic sages wished in Mishnah-tractate Tohorot to organize a basic category (retrospectively) called "purities" — Tohorot in Hebrew — as was their way, they identified data that, for reasons they discerned, cohered. These data were turned from rules into exemplifications of encompassing and systemic principles, with the result that through a repertoire of concrete laws, the sages produced a remarkably abstract statement of natural philosophy, a work of coherence and integrity. In tractate Tohorot they treat four problems. The connections that they draw between these four distinct categories of Halakhah having to do with purities then expose the rationality that animates their thinking throughout.

That fact becomes clear when we examine the outline of the tractate:

i. Principles of Uncleanness of Food: Meat. Fathers and Offspring of Uncleanness. The Matter of Removes
ii. Susceptibility to Uncleanness of Holy Things, Heave-Offering, and Unconsecrated Food
iii. Doubt in Matters of Uncleanness
iv. The *Haber* and the *'Am Ha'ares*
v. Concluding Miscellanies and Reprise. Uncleanness of Foods, Liquids, Connection

The important items are these:

1. the relationship between sources of uncleanness and removes or successive levels of sanctification;
2. the relationship between Fathers and Offspring of uncleanness;
3. sorting out matters of doubt and determining probabilities;
4. the relationship of the *haber* and the *'am ha'ares*.

These four categories derive from the systematic presentation of the Halakhah by the Mishnah and the Tosefta of Tohorot, the only sustained statements on the matter that we have from Rabbinic antiquity, the Talmuds falling silent here.[1] Stated in the indicated sequence, then, the four main foci of Tohorot hold together because to the sages they make a single continuous statement, from logical beginning to inexorable end, and the fixed order of the topics is essential and is critical to the message that is set forth.

The Rabbinic sages contemplate an intangible world of confusion between classes of things and persons that are both alike and not alike: things that may contract uncleanness but also attain sanctification; sources of uncleanness; things that may be unclean or clean; persons who are Israelites all together, but who may or may not keep certain laws of the Torah. What the Halakhah accomplishes in each case is to identify things that are to begin with alike — that stand along a single continuum, that bear traits in common — but that also exhibit differentiating qualities. Extrapolating from cases, the Halakhah then offers the governing rules that sort out these mixtures of things that are both alike and unlike. The Halakhah tells us how to differentiate the unlike among the like, so to sort out confusion and clarify the categories that pertain.

Take the categories one by one. Sources of uncleanness form a single classification; but we differentiate between the primary source and removes therefrom, that is, successive contacts: the source, what has touched the source, what has touched what has touched the source, and so on into the outer reaches of imagination. Thus, in philosophical terms, we distinguish what is primary from what is secondary and derivative, that is, between efficient and proximate causes. And again, sources of uncleanness form one category, but some sources are more virulent than others, that is to say, some sources of uncleanness produce powerful and long-lasting effects, others limited and transient ones; some affect many things, others only a few; some transmit uncleanness only if touched, others when overshadowed, or when carried even though not touched, and so on. The two points of engagement — removes, Fathers/offspring — clearly correspond, as we move from the source of uncleanness through the successive removes, and from the Father of uncleanness through the diminishing effects of the Offspring thereof. So much for differentiating between sources of uncleanness and among their effects: a labor of identifying the lines of order and structure that separate uncleanness from uncleanness and differentiate their affects upon food and drink and clothing at various levels of sanctification: this affects that, but not the other thing; this is affected by that, but not the other thing.

What about what is affected by sources of uncleanness? That question carries us from corpses, spit, and blood of certain origin, to food, drink, and human beings. The third subdivision of the Halakhah as set forth by the Mishnah and the Tosefta involves food and drink, the fourth, persons. In both cases we confront the same problem: how to deal with doubt as to the status, in respect to uncleanness, of food and drink, on the one side, and persons, on the other. What persons, food, and utensils have in common is that all may be made unclean, but, from the perspective of the Halakhah, they also may attain cultic cleanness, and, in the setting of the household as much as the Temple, ought to. That with which we have to reckon, then, is whether in an unguarded moment they have contracted uncleanness.

We resolve doubt as to the classification of food and drink by appeal to a variety of probabilities. It is more probable that the status quo has prevailed than that it has not; it is more probable that what is dragged, and so can touch something, has touched the thing than that what is tossed, and so cannot touch, has made contact. Common sense about the more or the less probable, however, is joined to certain principles that appear to be arbitrary. Because we want the householder to maintain a high state of alertness concerning sources of uncleanness, we declare that cases of doubt in private property are treated as unclean. Because the public domain contains many imponderables and cannot be closed off to the faithful, we declare cases of doubt in public property to be treated as clean. Now that position is counter-intuitive, since in the public domain circulate gentiles, whose persons and secretions are by definition unclean, as well as Israelites who do not keep this aspect of the Halakhah. And, given the distractions of crowds, one is more likely there than in private domain to step on unclean spit or urine deriving from gentiles. And who is to know the "history" of an object — what the one who touched it has touched, and what that has touched, backward for however many removes from the initial source of uncleanness? Reason therefore suggests that a case of doubt in public domain should be resolved in favor of uncleanness, and in private, cleanness. So here the system concerns itself with its larger goal — sanctifying the household and its table — and mitigates its more extreme possibilities. Where people can and should take care, they are held to a high standard. Where circumstances make difficult a constant state of alertness amid a barrage of occasions for contamination, they are not.

So much for food, drink, and utensils, what about persons? Here we classify the category of Israelites, differentiating the *haber* from the *'am ha'ares*, that is, those who prepare their ordinary food as though it were heave-offering or Holy Things from those who do not. The former take care not to contract uncleanness and are careful to remove its effects through immersion. The latter do not. Then how do the two classes of Israelites interact, and, more to the point, how do the ones who keep the purity-laws determine the status of their persons and property that has been subject to the disposition of those who do not keep those laws? Here again, as we have seen, a few comprehensive principles accommodate the cases and problems at hand; these have already been specified.

So we see four large composites, each laying out its own principles, all concerned with the same basic issue. What is that issue? Viewed from one perspective, it is how to differentiate the species of a given genus: on the side of contamination, source of uncleanness from removes, Father from Offspring; on the side of sanctification, what is subject to uncleanness of one virulence, what to another; what food or drink may or may not have contracted uncleanness; what Israelites may or may not have imparted uncleanness under specified circumstances of indeterminacy. Viewed from another perspective, we deal with a variety of persons and objects that have had each its own "history." Each must tell its own story, but the chapters are the same: is the person or object, food or drink, to be classified as unclean or clean? To answer that question, I need to know the following:

1. the level of sanctification for which the status of cleanness is required (how the person, object, food or drink has been subject to surveillance over time);

2. the character of the uncleanness to which the person or food may or may not have been exposed, primary or secondary, and the number of removes from exposure to that source at which the person or food stands: immediate contact, once-removed, and so on outward;

3. in what location (public, private domain), in what season (dry or rainy), and within what sort of transaction, the exposure is supposed to have taken place or not taken place;

4. what sort of instructions, conditions, and rules were articulated to the parties who may or may not have imparted uncleanness by touching the food or drink or utensils that are subject to doubt

In reaching a decision on how to classify a person, object, food or drink, each of these questions requires an answer, and at every stage in the process of interrogation, we have to reconstruct the story of what has happened to this person, object, food or drink in the context established by the inquiry into the status that pertains. And having come this far, we realize what holds the whole together: the four principal parts of the Halakhah before us contribute to the single, sustained narrative that encompasses the person or object, the food or drink, and that determines the taxonomic outcome of the process. The narrative tells us what things the person or object has touched, what things those things have touched, and so on through a sequence of removes; and it further tells us the status imputed to the food or drink (or, in line with Mishnah-tractate Hagigah, the person) by the attitude and intentionality of the principal player in the drama, the person affected by the considerations at hand: uncleanness at the one side, sanctification at the other. All of this, amplified by the consideration of removes, forms a small narrative of a cosmic transaction.

So much for the unfolding of a single coherent account, a sequence of facts concerning intangibles to make sense of which we have invoked the metaphor of history: the tale of sequential and coherent events, each of which causes the next in the chain of happenings that leads to the end-decision. But the components of the Halakhah hold together in a more intimate connection as well. Each component turns out to appeal, in the end, to a consideration that operates for them all, and, by this point in the exposition it is scarcely necessary to say, that is intentionality. In this unseen world the impalpable force of the attitude of responsible actors makes its impact everywhere. Uncleanness is relative to that which it affects, and the sensitivity to uncleanness of that which is affected by uncleanness depends upon the status imputed by man's will.

Stated simply: if man assigns food or drink to the status of Holy Things and so acts as to preserve the cleanness of what is sanctified in that status, then the sources of uncleanness affect the food or drink through successive removes, as many as three (and Mishnah-tractate Parah adds a fourth). If man's intentionality does not impart to the food or drink the standing of Holy Things but of ordinary, secular food or drink, then fewer removes from the source of uncleanness produce effects. It is the initial decision and attitude of man that makes the difference. If man is alert and capable of forming intentionality, if man can be interrogated in the assumption that he cares about contamination, then the rules of contamination are strictly enforced; if not, then they are null. A child cannot form an intention to preserve cleanness and, therefore, in a case of doubt, he also cannot be assumed to have imparted uncleanness. The *'am ha'ares* is assumed to touch whatever he can reach — unless he is instructed not to. Then his intentionality, to respect the wishes of the householder, is assumed to pertain and therefore to protect from uncleanness what the *'am ha'ares* can have touched but probably did not contaminate at all. At the critical turnings in the decision-making process, the taxonomic question finds its answer in the relativities of attitude and intention.

But one matter is not subject to the decision-making process of man, and one component of the system, one chapter of the narrative, does not find its dynamics in human will. That is the sources of uncleanness. These do function *ex opere operato* and do not depend upon man's will for them to bring about contamination. On the contrary, the corpse contaminates whatever is in the tent that overshadows it, and the contaminating power of flux (zob) depends upon its emerging naturally and not by artificial stimulus. That same insistence on the inexorability of the workings of sources of contamination emerges in the consideration of the distinction between Fathers and Offspring of uncleanness; at no point in that corpus of Halakhah do considerations of attitude intervene.

So when we contemplate the Israelite household as the Halakhah portrays it, we see a space marked off in three ways:

by [1] the family sanctified by reason of its descent from the holy seed of the patriarchs and by its avoidance of the marital relationships spelled out in the Written Torah,

which acts [2] on specified occasions of sacred time to sanctify the household by words and deeds and acts of restraint from deeds,

and which further acts [3] to preserve the cultic cleanness, therefore the potential sanctification, of the food and drink consumed in the household, and, consequently, to avoid cultic contamination of the clothing and utensils of those that live there.

Then what is the given and what marks change? The Halakhah rests on the foundations of a single condition: Israel is holy, wherever located; that is its natural condition. What removes Israel from its status as sanctified is unnatural to Israel, but a given of the world. Sanctification is the established condition for family and property (food, drink, clothing, utensils). What removes the family, its food, drink, clothing and utensils, from the status of sanctification interferes with what ought to be natural. Sources of uncleanness also come about by nature; sages adhere rigidly to the definition of those sources that Scripture establishes and do not add a single new source or extend an existing source in any consequential way.

Holy Israel, then, confronts round about the sources of contamination; its task is constantly to remain alert and watchful, lest those contamination affect Israel. And, we now see, that means, Israel must watch not only what it eats and drinks and wears and where it stands and sits and lies. Israel also must pay attention to what the food it eats may have touched, who may have stood or sat upon the clothing that it wears and the beds on which it takes a rest. To preserve the condition it ought always to enjoy, which is, the state of sanctification, Israel has then to maintain a constant surveillance of the present and past of the world in which it lives and the people among whom it makes its life. Marrying without carefully investigating the genealogy of the Israelite family into which one marries can produce mamzerim (ineligible for licit marriage), and sitting on a bench without finding out who has sat there before can produce uncleanness that can contaminate much else, and eating a piece of bread without knowing where it has been and who has touched it can diminish one's standing in the hierarchy of sanctification.

All this why? It is, as we now realize full well, to The family, the space occupied by it for the sacred occasions (each man in "his place"), and the property in the full sense of the word — real estate, personalty, and movables — furthermore are treated as analogous to the sacred space, the Temple, occupied by the consecrated caste, the priesthood and their staff, and what is kept therein. What establishes the analogy? The sources of change and disruption that threaten the cleanness, hence the sanctification of the Temple are the same sources that threaten the norm of cleanness of the household. If the same uncleanness affects the Temple and the table, then the only difference is one of degree, not of kind, as the Halakhah states explicitly. And the rest follows.

Now we see the context in which the texts that invoke intentionality find their place, the reason that the entire system treats cleanness and sanctification, or uncleanness and desacralization, as relative to the Israelite's attitude and will. What the Israelite values as food receives or conveys uncleanness as food. What he does not value does not contract or transmit uncleanness; only that to which an Israelite to begin with pays attention counts for anything in the system of watchfulness with which we deal. What the Israelite values as a useful utensil may contract uncleanness. What the Israelite deems an essential part of a piece of fruit or vegetable is integral to the fruit or vegetable, adds to its volume, contracts from, or transmits to, the fruit or vegetable such uncleanness as takes effect. What the Israelite holds inedible or disgusting even for dog-food does not contract uncleanness as food. When the Israelite subjects to the cleanness-regulations of consecrated food what is merely everyday edibles, the rules of consecrated food pertain — even though the substance of the food is unchanged. In these and numerous other details the relativity of all things to intentionality comes to full and rich instantiation. So the Halakhah manages to say the same thing about many things.

But we must ask ourselves, do they believe in the actuality of what they are saying, given the relativity of palpable and tangible things — liquids, bits of food, pieces of cloth (as Kelim shows) to matters that are intangible, such as how someone feels that minute, or where someone is located, or what someone intends for the liquids, food, and cloth? Is that to say sages do not believe in the material-reality of the system of uncleanness and sanctification of the household? Certainly sages deem palpable results to emerge from violation of the rules that protect Israel's status of sanctification. Violating the sanctity of the marriage bed produces mamzerim, and for generations to come the offspring of the union of two persons who are legally forbidden to wed suffer the result. That is hardly a matter relative to anyone's intentionality, even though the offspring come about by reason of an act of will. Meat destined for the Lord's altar that contracts uncleanness is burned, not eaten. That is not subject to negotiation or compromise, even though a principal source of disqualification of the meat of offerings is the improper intentionality formed and expressed by the officiating priest for the disposition of that meat.

So we may say, when it comes to certain matters of sanctification and contamination, genealogy on the one side, the Temple and its offerings, on the other, intentionality plays a role, but nothing that matters in issues of genealogy and cult is treated as relative. Absolutes govern: one may not marry his mother, one may not offer carrion upon the altar, and nothing complicates those simple rules. But when we deal with the household and its table, the Halakhah certainly does set aside considerations of intrinsic uncleanness and treats matters of status and taxonomy as relative to the intangibilities of attitude, plan, intentionality, and will. Everything now is made to depend upon the watchfulness, the alertness, of the householder and his ménage, their (likely) capacity to take note of what is taking place round about: a dead frog here, a menstruating woman there, a corpse in the neighbor's attached dwelling, under the same roof — the list is formidable.

But are these not practical matters, immune to considerations of relationship and circumstance (household vs. marketplace, for instance)? The law contains within itself its own judgment: the household is not the Temple, the table is not the altar. Something resembles, as treated as like, something else; the something is not the same thing as that something else. The household may be compared to the Temple, the table may be treated as analogous, in the ways amply spelled out here, to the altar, upon the same continuum, to revert to the language I have used. But that is not the same thing as saying the table here is the altar there. Sages think about the power of similitudes when they consider humanity: man is like God, so Scripture announces — but to be like God is not to be God! What differentiates that which is compared to the thing upon which the comparison is based is what separates the imitation from the real thing. And sages knew and valued that difference, and that is why the Halakhah in every line realizes that difference. And that makes all the more remarkable sages' extensive legislation to embody the imitation and realize it. If the table is like the altar in the way in which man is like God, then let us elaborate the meaning of the similitude, the uses of the analogy, the moral authority of the metaphor by reason of what generates the metaphor: the altar, God, respectively.

In the context at hand, with the Temple a vivid presence in the religious world-view of the framers of the Halakhah, the elaborate system carried its own messages, and to those within the system, these messages enjoyed the standing of self-evidence. No one formed an apologia for the to us obsessional laws about dead creeping things falling into dough and the like. In medieval times other views, a different rationality, would take over, and the entire system of cultic cleanness and uncleanness in the household would lose all purchase on rationality.[2] That is hardly surprising, given the fragility of the act of imagination that, for the brief period represented by the Halakhah of the Mishnah and the Tosefta, rendered a state of perpetual consciousness into the inner testimony of enduring sanctification. The message of the Halakhah — so long as Israel pays attention to its condition in regard to cleanness, it may aspire to the status of sanctification as well — could scarcely find a hearing where Israelites by definition lived in the condition of uncleanness, that is, on foreign soil. And even in the Holy Land itself, how many generations would have to pass before the Temple and the rules for entering it would lose all purchase and persist only as a sign for some future restoration. Then the analogy — marry with genealogical considerations in mind, like priests; eat food with cultic contamination in mind, like priests; in holy time form of the household a miniature Temple courtyard, like priests — would lose the power to animate and explain a pretend-reality.

To see what happens then, as rationalities shift, so what is obvious at one stage becomes implausible at another, we conclude with a story in a medieval compilation of Midrash-exegeses about a first-century authority, a story that adheres to the convictions of medieval philosophical rationalism, not late antique Halakhah and its powerful mode of analogical-contrastive thinking. In this story, a pagan confronts a sage, Yohanan ben Zakkai, on the hocus-pocus of the purity laws:

A. "These deeds that you do appear to me like hocus pocus. You bring a heifer and burn it, crush it, takes the ashes, and if one of you is defiled by a corpse, you sprinkle him on the third and seventh days after he has contracted uncleanness and say to him, 'You are purified.'"

B. He answered, "Has a wandering spirit every entered into you."

C. "No."

D. "But have you ever seen a man into whom a wandering spirit ever entered?"

E. "Yes."

F. "And what did you do for him?"

G. "You put smoking roots under him and threw water over him and the spirit flees."

H. He said, "Listen then with your ears to what your mouth speaks. This is the spirit of uncleanness, such as Zechariah speaks of (Zech. 13:2): 'And also I shall cause the spirit of uncleanness to pass away from the earth.' You sprinkle on him waters of purification and it flees."

I. After the man left, the disciples said to Yohanan, "Master, this man you have driven off with a broken reed. But what are you going to reply to us?"

J. He answered, "By your lives! It is not the corpse that imparts uncleanness nor the waters that purify, but the Holy One said, 'A statute have I enacted...an ordinance have I ordained, and you are not permitted to transgress my commandment, as it is said, 'This is the ordinance of the Torah' (Num. 19:1)."

Numbers Rabbah 19:4; Tanhuma, ed. Buber, Hukat 26

Now the story shows how the cleanness-laws have lost all purchase on rationality and are represented as a mere spiritual exercise. In the documents of the Oral Torah that reached closure in ancient times, the same view — certain religious duties cannot be accounted for within any accessible rationality, but represent a discipline to be accepted anyhow — did come to expression. But among those duties that transcend the limits of reason, the system of cultic purity and contamination does not find a place.

The contrast between the story about Yohanan in a medieval document and statements about the same problem in late antique compilations of the third and seventh centuries, respectively, which make the same point, is not to be missed:

A. R. Eleazar b. Azariah says, "How do we know that someone should not say, 'I do not want to wear mixed fibers, I don't want to eat pork, I don't want to have incestuous sexual relations.'

B. "Rather: 'I do want [to wear mixed fibers, I do want to eat pork, I do want to have incestuous sexual relations.] But what can I do? For my father in heaven has made a decree for me!'

C. "So Scripture says, 'and have separated you from the peoples, that you should be mine.'

D. So one will turn out to keep far from transgression and accept upon himself the rule of Heaven."

Sifra CCVII:II.13

Sifra's view, representing third century C.E. opinion, concerns obeying the morally-neutral commandments as an act of obedience, of subordinating one's own will to God's. In the Bavli's statement on the same matter, representing a sixth century document, Satan makes people wonder about certain other matters, including those having to do with cultic purification. But no one asks why the corpse contaminates:

3. A.   *Our rabbis have taught on Tannaite authority:*

   B.   "My ordinances you shall perform" (Lev. 18:4) — this refers to such matters that, were they not written in the Torah, it would be a matter of compelling logic that they be written, and these are they: the prohibitions against idolatry, fornication, bloodshed, robbery, and blasphemy.

   C.   "...and my statutes you shall keep" (Lev. 18:4) — this refers to such matters against which Satan brings objections, and these are they: the prohibition against eating pork, the prohibition against wearing mixed fabrics [linen and wool], the rite of removing the shoe to sever the relationship of a deceased childless brother's wife to a surviving brother, the purification of the person afflicted with the skin-ailment, and the rite of sending away the he-goat.

   D.   Might you imagine that these rites are empty rituals?

   E.   Scripture states, "I am the Lord" — [thus God speaks:] "I have made the decree, and you have no right to meditate too deeply about it."

                                        Bavli-tractate Yoma 6:6 IV.3/67b

The contrast between the late antique and the medieval formulation of matters tells us what demanded explanation, because none presented itself by the governing criteria at hand, and what did not. That is why we ought not ignore the character of the items on the list of what lies beyond worldly rationality in the mind of the earlier documents.

The Halakhah turns out to form the medium by which Israel's imagination of itself would be embodied in concrete, consequential forms: actions and relationships bearing consequence. The Halakhah — law — exposes the interiorities of the Oral Torah, the Aggadah — lore — the exteriorities. By encouraging faithful Israelites to cultivate an inner attitude of watchfulness, by making small things matter much, sages underscored in humble ways and in quotidian terms the reality of Israel's interior existence: holy people, holy land, holy Temple, all now reduced in worldly dimensions to the space of the humble household, but not by the transcendent standard that aspiration and hope measure. The Halakhah found plausibility by reason of its realization of the analogy of the household to the Temple and lost its footing when the Temple as a palpable place faded.

Then the fragile construction built upon the comparison of household to Temple and sustained by the act of supererogatory will of those that adopted the analogy and realized it in deed simply faded. The rules remained. Some would conduct profound and sophisticated analyses of their logic and governing rationality. But no one could penetrate the realm of sentiment and feeling, the extravagance of emotion and attitude, that imparted to the rules the urgency that, for a brief moment, made them systemically critical. The Halakhah of Tohorot would become a matter of theory — perhaps what its own relativization of matters dictated as its inevitable outcome.

The web of relationships between sanctification and uncleanness spins itself out into every corner of the Israelite household, where the system makes a difference. And it is the will of the householder that determines the difference that the distinction between clean and unclean is going to make. Everything is relative to the householder's will; he has it in his power to draw the household table into alignment with the altar in the Temple, that is to say, to place the table and the food set thereon into relationship, onto a continuum, with the altar and the Holy Things of the cult. This he can accomplish through an act of will that motivates an attitude of constant watchfulness for those very sources of contamination that Scripture identifies as danger to the Lord's altar in the Jerusalem Temple. Such an attitude of watchfulness then comes to realization in actions that confirm the attitude and embody the intentionality: take note, avoid, watch out for this, that, and the other thing. That is because the faithful of the Halakhah think of themselves as Temple priests but situate themselves in the ordinary world.

In the actual Temple avoiding sources of uncleanness, e.g., corpses, menstruating women, people suffering a flux, posed no enormous problems; most of the virulent sources of uncleanness were walled out to begin with. But in the village, the household and the marketplace who knows what can happen — and commonly does? And bumping into someone quite inadvertently forms a primary event, and yet who can trace the history of each person, his or her encounter with a corpse, her period, for instance, or with someone who has had such an encounter or sat on a chair on whom a menstruating woman or a man with flux has sat? The possibilities for cultic contamination, controlled in the cult, prove limitless outside. But then, the Halakhah aims at imposing order and a certain rationality, a well-construed assessment of probabilities, upon that chaos of the unclean and the profane.

ENDNOTES

[1] While law codes of other communities of Judaism refer to matters of cleanness and uncleanness, no other code compares in depth and density to the Mishnah's treatment of these topics (among all topics that are touched upon by Judaic systems of antiquity).

[2] With the important qualification that sexual purity and impurity remained a vital consideration throughout the history of Rabbinic Judaism to the present day! But the cleanness of the bed was not taken to pertain to preparation for participation in the cult, rather to the procreation of offspring in a state of purity. Exactly when that shift in the hermeneutics of the matter took place is not indicated in the sources I have studied.

17

Judaism and the Hebrew Language

1. THE LANGUAGE OF JUDAISM

Hebrew, an ancient northwest Semitic language, has served as the principal language of Judaism, even after the Jews ceased to speak Hebrew as their everyday language. The Hebrew Scriptures ("Old Testament," "written Torah") of ancient Israel were mainly in Hebrew. Brief sections of Ezra and Daniel are in Aramaic. The Scriptures were translated into Greek, Aramaic, and other languages, but in the synagogue were and are declaimed in Hebrew. The great commentaries to Scripture written by the Rabbinic sages of the first six centuries of the common Era all were written in Hebrew, and philosophy, poetry, and liturgy favored that language as well. That preference for Hebrew persisted, even though it was explicitly stated that translation of Scripture into Aramaic was allowed, and the use of the vernacular for various purposes made explicit.

The prophet Zephaniah (3:9) speaks of the future, in which "I (God) will change the speech of the peoples to a pure speech," meaning Hebrew. Called "lashon haqqodesh," or Holy Language, the Hebrew language is accorded religious status in Judaism. A community with roots deep in the past, diverse and widely scattered, affirms its coherence through privileging a single language, Hebrew. Hebrew is a way for "identifying one's original religious allegiance" (Aaron 2000a, p. 271). "By relating to their language as holy, Jews transformed Hebrew into a kind of ritual object, parallel...to the Torah-scroll itself...part of a religious system" (Aaron 2000a, p. 268-9).

2. LANGUAGE OF PRAYER; LANGUAGES OF DAILY LIFE

Even though Hebrew enjoyed the status of a religious artifact in Judaism, the languages of the Israelites in the Land of Israel in late antiquity were Aramaic and Greek. Leading Rabbinic sages knew Greek and encouraged some of their disciples to use it (Mishnah-tractate Abodah Zarah 3:4). While it was not the language of daily life, Hebrew enjoyed privileged standing in certain liturgical settings, but by no means throughout. But since not everybody knew Hebrew, provision was made for the recitation of obligatory prayers in any language, and these included the recitation of the creed, the Shema ("Hear O Israel, the Lord our God, the Lord is one") and the presentation of the Prayer ("Eighteen benedictions").

Mishnah-tractate Sotah 7:1-2

7:1 A. These are said in any language: (1) the pericope of the accused wife (Num. 5:19-22), and (2) the confession of the tithe (Dt. 26:13-15), and (3) the recital of the Shema, (Dt. 6:4-9), and (4) the Prayer, (5) the oath of testimony, and (6) the oath concerning a bailment.

7:2 A. And these are said (only) in the Holy Language (Hebrew): (1) the verses of the firstfruits (Dt. 26:3-10), (2) the rite of removing the shoe (Dt. 25:7), (3) blessings and curses (Dt. 27:15-26), (4) the blessing of the priests (Num. 6:24-26), (5) the blessing of a high priest (on the Day of Atonement), (6) the pericope of the king (Dt. 17:1420);

B. (7) the pericope of the heifer whose neck is to be broken (Dt. 21:7f.), and (8) (the message of) the anointed for battle when he speaks to the people (Dt. 20:2-7).

What is limited to Hebrew are few items, mostly involving texts supplied by Scripture, as indicated. Here the key is that the recitation must be verbatim, hence not only a fixed text, as in the Shema and the Prayer, but a set text that Scripture prescribes, in so many words, in Hebrew.

Translations of Scripture into Aramaic (called Targumim) and Greek were enunciated in public worship, but Scripture had to be read, first of all, in Hebrew. The following concerns the public declamation, on Purim, of the scroll of Esther, which had to be read in Hebrew, not in translation:

Mishnah-tractate Megillah 2:1

A. One who reads the Megillah (scroll of Esther) out of (its literary) sequence has not fulfilled his obligation.

B. (1) If he read it from memory, (2) if he read it in translation into any language, he has not fulfilled his obligation; (3) but one may read it to non-speakers of Hebrew (le 'uzot) in other languages. (4) And a speaker of another language who heard Ashurit (the text read from a scroll written in Hebrew language and in square script) has fulfilled his obligation.

But that is only one aspect of the matter of public worship and communal rites. When it comes to prayer, Hebrew was not privileged. The Shema, the Credo recited in worship, could be said in any language, so too the formal petitions or The Prayer par excellence were said in the vernacular. But in the history of Judaism from antiquity forward, the use of Hebrew in synagogue worship predominated.

Home rites, such the liturgy, Haggadah ("Narrative") recited at the Passover Seder, also were developed principally in Hebrew. Prayer other than in Hebrew, while licit, thus was discouraged: "When one petitions for his needs in Aramaic, the ministering angels do not listen to him, for they do not understand Aramaic" (Bavli Shabbat 112b). So too:

Aramaic was the everyday language of the Rabbis of the Judaic academies, but they produced in Hebrew the law code, the Mishnah, and its supplement, the Tosefta, and commentaries, the Talmud of the Land of Israel and the Talmud of Babylonia. Their Hebrew differed from that of Scripture. But education in the Hebrew of Scripture and of the Rabbinic writings was integral to the religious nurture of the young (see Sifre to Deuteronomy XLVI:I).

3. THE ROLE OF LANGUAGE ANALYSIS IN THE LAW OF JUDAISM

The legal literature of Judaism is written in Hebrew and in Aramaic. The law codes, the Mishnah, Tosefta, and related collections, are in Hebrew. The analytical work of commenting upon the law is in Aramaic. By their choice of the very language in which they would express what they wished to say on their own account they differentiated themselves from their antecedents. When it came to citations from prior, non-scriptural authorities, they used one formation of the Hebrew language, specifically, Middle, or Mishnaic, Hebrew; when it came to the conduct of their own analytical process, they used one formation of the Aramaic language, Eastern or Talmudic Aramaic. They never alluded to authoritative facts, they always cited them in so many words; but the indication of citation — in a writing in which the modern sigla of quotation marks and footnotes were simply unavailable — came to expression in the choice of language. In point of fact, the Talmud of Babylonia or Bavli is in one language, not two, and that language is Aramaic. The infrastructure of the document, its entire repertoire of editorial conventions and sigla, are in Aramaic.

When a saying is assigned to a named authority, the saying may be in Hebrew or in Aramaic, and the same named authority may be given sayings in both languages — even within the same sentence. But the editorial and conceptual infrastructure of the document comes to expression only in Aramaic, and when no name is attached to a statement, that statement is always in Aramaic, unless it forms part of a larger, autonomous Hebrew composition, cited by, or parachuted down into, "the Talmud." Rightly have the Talmudic masters in the Yeshiva-world hypostatized the Talmud in such language as, "the Gemara says...," because the Talmud speaks in a single voice, forms a unitary discourse, beginning, middle, and end, and constitutes one wholly coherent and cogent document, everywhere asking questions drawn from a single determinate and limited repertoire of intellectual initiatives — and always framing those questions, pursuing those inquiries, in Aramaic.

And yet the Talmud also is full of Hebrew. So we must ask where and why framers of this writing utilize the Hebrew language, and when we may expect to find that they speak — rather, "the Talmud speaks" — in Aramaic. Specifically, what signal is given, what purpose is served by the bi- or multi-lingualism of the Talmud what do we know without further ado, when we are given a composition or a component of a composition in Hebrew, and what is the implicit meaning of making a statement in Aramaic? The answer is that the choice of language signals a taxonomic meaning, and language serves as a medium for the classification of discourse, hence, language serves as a medium of taxonomy. In a writing that utilizes two languages, the choice of one over the other conformed to rules of communication and marked what was said as one type of statement rather than another. If we know which language is used, we also know where we stand in the expression of thought, and the very language in which a statement is made therefore forms part of the method of thought and even the message of discourse of the document.

4. THE ROLE OF LANGUAGE ANALYSIS IN THE THEOLOGY AND EXEGESIS OF JUDAISM

In reading Scripture, Judaism brought to bear a particular theory of how language works (Aaron 2005, p. 400). The Rabbinic exegetes of Scripture distinguished their version of Hebrew from that of Scripture; italics signify Aramaic, plain type, Hebrew:

BAVLI HULLIN 137B

V.5 A. *When Issi bar Hini left (to go to the Land of Israel), R. Yohanan found him teaching his son (our Mishnah at L, with a variation in the plural suffix of the word sheep): "Five sheep (masculine plural suffix,* rhylym*)."*

  B. *He (Yohanan) said to him, "It was taught (in the Mishnah differently, namely using the plural feminine suffix): 'Sheep (*rhylwt*).'"*

  C. *He (Issi) said to him, "That is the way it is written in scripture,* 'Two hundred sheep (rhylym) (Gen. 32:15).'"

  D. *He (Yohanan) said to him,* "The Torah has its own language and the sages have their own language. (You should not confuse the two.)"

Their rules of exegesis corresponded with ordinary speech. Thus the argument from analogy (*gezerah shavah*) is a commonplace. Verses that share the same word choice are asked to clarify the meaning of one another. Various particles of speech serve to signal an inclusive meaning of a given concept. Thus, in Aaron's words (Aaron 2005, p. 402), "The rules of common logic that normally govern colloquial discourse are transformed by virtue of the Rabbinic conceptualization of the Torah's language. This transformation results from a distinct theory of word meaning, one that allows for exegetical processes that violate what we would otherwise consider the norms of everyday speech. The upshot is that the text of the Torah bears meanings below its surface. When God revealed his words through Moses his prophet, he provided for layers and layers of meaning.

The traits of the Hebrew language, including its alphabet, yielded theological lessons. "The very letters themselves receive their forms by virtue of divine intent" (Aaron, p. 407).

Genesis Rabbah I:X.

I. A. ("In the beginning God created" (Gen. 1:1):) R. Jonah in the name of R. Levi: "Why was the world created with (a word beginning with the letter) B?

B. "Just as (in Hebrew) the letter B is closed (at the back and sides but) open in front, so you have no right to expound concerning what is above or below, before or afterward."

C. Bar Qappara said, "'For ask now of the days past which were before you, since the day that God created man upon the earth' (Deut. 4:32).

D. "Concerning the day *after* which days were created, you may expound, but you may not make an exposition concerning what lies before them"

E. "And from one end of the heaven to the other" (Deut. 4:32).

F. "(Concerning that space) you may conduct an investigation, but you may not conduct an investigation concerning what lies beyond those points."

Aaron explains, "Midrash relies on a concept of meaning that violates the rules of everyday language usage, even as it relies upon them to convey its meanings…Midrash becomes a vehicle in ordinary language by which to uncover hidden meanings embedded in the extraordinary language of God's revelation" (Aaron, p. 410).

5. Conclusion

Until the beginning of the twentieth century, Hebrew served as the language of synagogue worship and other ritual occasions, study of the Torah or divine revelation, and legal and theological discourse. It was the international language of Judaism, superseding the local languages spoken by Jews. It was comparable in function to Latin in Western Christendom. This ritualization of the language is explained by Aaron in the following language (Aaron 2000a, p. 283):

> During the Rabbinic period, despite relatively low levels of Hebrew literacy among common Jews, Hebrew began serving as Judaism's language in ritual contexts. The success of this ritualization of language wa part o a conceptualization of language that sought to transcend the common level of semantics we normally ascribe to simple utterances…With

ritualization, meaning could be found not only in the semantic values of the words read but also in the act of recitation itself...The whole Rabbinic enterprise is founded upon a meta-semantics of sorts, one that holds that meaning is at once rooted in the words of Torah but not identical to their common connotations."

Hebrew was and is by no means the only language identified with the Jewish group and with Judaism. Yiddish (based on Hebrew and German), Ladino (based on Hebrew and Spanish), Judeo-Arabic, Judeo-Persian, and other local languages have flourished. But when it came to the creation of the Jewish state, the State of Israel, it was Hebrew that was chosen for renewal, and that became the language of the new and renewed culture of the Jewish people.

Bibliography

Aaron, 2000a = Aaron, David, "The Doctrine of Hebrew Language Usage," in J. Neusner and Alan J. Avery-Peck, eds., *The Blackwell Companion to Judaism.* Oxford, 2000, Blackwell, pp. 268-287.

Aaron, 2005 = Aaron, David, "Language and Midrash," *Encyclopaedia of Midrash* (Leiden, 2005) ed. By J. Neusner and others, pp. 400-411.

Aaron, 2000b = Aaron, David, "Readings in the Doctrine of Hebrew Language Usage," in J. Neusner and Alan J. Avery-Peck, eds., *The Blackwell Reader in Judaism,* Oxford, 2000, Blackwell, pp. 202-214.

Hoffman, 2004 = Hoffman, Joel M., *In the Beginning. A Short History of the Hebrew Language.* N.Y., 2004: New York University Press.

Neusner, 1990 = Neusner, Jacob, *Language as Taxonomy. The Rules for Using Hebrew and Aramaic in the Babylonian Talmud.* Atlanta, 1990: Scholars Press for South Florida Studies in the History of Judaism. Now: Lanham, MD: University Press of America.

18

Talmudic Dialectics

DEFINITION OF DIALECTICAL ARGUMENT IN ANCIENT JUDAISM: a moving argument, from point to point; a tool of systematic analysis used in the Bavli or Talmud of Babylonia (ca. 600 C.E.), the authoritative commentary to the Mishnah (200), the compendium of the law of Judaism. With the back-and-forth argument, the Bavli sets forth not so much a record of what was said as a set of notes that permit the engaged reader to reconstruct thought and recapitulate reason and criticism, In the Talmudic framework, then everything is in the moving, or dialectical argument, the give and take of unsparing rationality, which, through their own capacity to reason, later generations are expected to reconstitute the issues, the argument, the prevailing rationality.

A dialectical argument sets forth give and take in which parties to the argument counter one another's arguments in a progression of exchanges, often in what seems like an infinite progress to an indeterminate conclusion. The dialectical argument does not merely address the problem and the single solution alone, but it takes up the problem and the various *ways* by which a solution may be reached. It involves not merely questions and answers or exchanges of opinion, a set-piece of two positions, with an analysis of each, such as formal dialogue exposes with elegance. A dialectical argument thus moves in an unfolding analytical argument, explaining why this, not that, then why not that but rather the other thing; and onward from the other thing to the thing beyond that — a linear argument in constant forward motion.

A dialectical argument is not static and merely expository, but dynamic and always contentious. It is not an endless argument, an argument for the sake of arguing, but a way to cover a variety of cases in testing a principle common to them all.

AN EXAMPLE OF A DIALECTICAL ARGUMENT: The passage that we consider occurs at the Bavli Baba Mesia 5B-6A, which is to say, Bavli to Mishnah Baba Mesia. 1:1-2. The Mishnah is a law code organized by topics, and Baba Mesia — the Middle Gate — concerns civil law, in the present case, torts and damages and contradictory claims. Our interest is in the twists and turns of the argument, on which my comments focus. I give the Mishnah-passage in bold-faced type, which shows the text that is being analyzed. The Bavli is in two languages, Hebrew and Aramaic; I give Aramaic in italics. That is where we find ourselves in the heart of the argument, at the dialectical center of things.

The Bavli deals with a case of two claimants to an object each claims to have found. The Mishnah-passage is as follows:

Mishnah Baba Mesia 1:1

A. **Two lay hold of a cloak —**
B. this one says, "I found it!" —
C. and that one says, "I found it!" —
D. this one says, "It's all mine!" —
E. and that one says, "It's all mine!" —
F. this one takes an oath that he possesses no less a share of it than half,
G. and that one takes an oath that he possesses no less a share of it than half,
H. and they divide it up.

The problem then recalls the two women fighting before Solomon about the disposition of the infant child, but the law of the Mishnah and the decision of Solomon scarcely intersect. The issue now is addressed by the Bavli. What we wish to notice is how the Bavli forms a script that permits us to join in the discussion; if we don't read it out loud, we miss the compelling power of the passage, especially its systematic resort to applied reason and practical logic. And, we must not forget, we want to see precisely how a dialectical argument is written down as a text but provokes us to talk, engage in dialogue, with the text:

Bavli Baba Mesia 5B-6A

[5B] IV.1. A. **This one takes an oath that he possesses no less a share of it than half, [and that one takes an oath that he possesses no less a share of it than half, and they divide it up]:**

The rule of the Mishnah, which is cited at the head of the sustained discussion, concerns the case of two persons who find a garment. We settle their conflicting claim by requiring each to take an oath that he or she owns title to no less than half of the garment, and then we split the garment between them.

Now how does the Bavli undertake its sustained analysis of this matter? Our first question is one of text-criticism: analysis of the Mishnah-paragraph's word choice. We say that the oath concerns the portion that the claimant alleges he possesses. But the oath really affects the portion that he does not have in hand at all:

B. *Is it concerning the portion that he claims he possesses that he takes the oath, or concerning the portion that he does not claim to possess?* [S, Daiches, *Baba Mesia* (London, 1948) ad loc., : "The implication is that the terms of the oath are ambiguous. By swearing that his share in it is not "less than half," the claimant might mean that it is not even a third or a fourth (which is 'less than half'), and the negative way of putting it would justify such an interpretation. He could therefore take this oath even if he knew that he had no share in the garment at all, while he would be swearing falsely if he really had a share in the garment that is less than half, however small that share might be].

C.   *Said R. Huna, "It is that he says,* 'By an oath! I possess in it a portion, and I possess in it a portion that is no more than half a share of it.'" [The claimant swears that his share is at least half (Daiches, *Baba Mesia, ad loc.*)].

Having asked and answered the question, we now find ourselves in an extension of the argument; the principal trait of the dialectical argument is now before us in three key-words:

[1] but!

[2] maybe the contrary is the case, so —

[3] what about?

The argument then is conducting by the setting aside of a proposition in favor of its opposite. Here we come to the definitive trait of the dialectic argument: its insistence on challenging every proposal with the claim, "maybe it's the opposite?" This pestering question forces us back upon our sense of self-evidence; it makes us consider the contrary of each position we propose to set forth. It makes thought happen. True, the Bavli's voice's "but" — the whole of the dialectic in one word! — presents a formidable nuisance. But so does all criticism, and only the mature mind will welcome criticism. Dialectics is not for children, politicians, propagandists, or egoists. Genuine curiosity about the truth shown by rigorous logic forms the counterpart to musical virtuosity. So the objection proceeds:

C.   *Then let him say,* "By an oath! The whole of it is mine!"

Why claim half when the alleged finder may as well demand the whole cloak?

D.   *But are we going to give him the whole of it?* [Obviously not, there is another claimant, also taking an oath.]

The question contradicts the facts of the case: two parties claim the cloak, so the outcome can never be that one will get the whole thing.

E.   *Then let him say,* "By an oath! Half of it is mine!"

Then — by the same reasoning — why claim "no less than half," rather than simply, half.

> F.   *That would damage his own claim* [which was that he owned the
>   whole of the cloak, not only half of it].

The claimant does claim the whole cloak, so the proposed language does not serve to replicate his actual claim. That accounts for the language that is specified.

> G.   *But here too is it not the fact that, in the oath that he is taking, he
>   impairs his own claim?* [After all, he here makes explicit the fact
>   that he owns at least half of it. What happened to the other half?]

The solution merely compounds the problem.

> H.   *[Not at all.] For he has said,* "The whole of it is mine!" [And, he
>   further proceeds,] "And as to your contrary view, By an oath, I do
>   have a share in it, and that share is no less than half!"

We solve the problem by positing a different solution from the one we suggested at the outset. Why not start where we have concluded? Because if we had done so, we should have ignored a variety of intervening considerations and so should have expounded less than the entire range of possibilities. The power of the dialectical argument now is clear: it forces us to address not the problem and the solution alone, but the problem and the various ways by which a solution may be reached; then, when we do come to a final solution to the question at hand, we have reviewed all of the possibilities. We have seen how everything flows together, nothing is left unattended.

What we have here is not a set-piece report of two positions, with an analysis of each, such as formal dialogue exposes with elegance. It is, rather, an unfolding analytical argument, explaining why this, not that, then why not that but rather this; and onward to the other thing and the thing beyond that — a linear argument in constant forward motion. When we speak of a moving argument, this is what we mean: what is not static and merely expository, but what is dynamic and always analytical and by nature contentious. It is not an endless argument, an argument for the sake of arguing, or evidence that important to the Bavli and other writings that use the dialectics as a principal mode of dynamic argument is process but not position. To the contrary, the passage is resolved with a decisive conclusion, not permitted to run on.

But the dialectical composition proceeds — continuous and coherent from point to point, even as it zigs and zags. That is because the key to everything is give and take. We proceed to the second cogent proposition in the analysis of the cited Mishnah-passage, which asks a fresh question: why an oath at all?

What we have accomplished on our wanderings is a survey of opinion on a theme, to be sure, but opinion that intersects at our particular problem as well. The moving argument serves to carry us hither and yon; its power is to demonstrate that all considerations are raised, all challenges met, all possibilities explored. This is not merely a set-piece argument, where we have proposition, evidence, analysis, conclusion; it is a different sort of thinking altogether, purposive and coherent, but also comprehensive and compelling for its admission of possibilities and attention to alternatives. What we shall see, time and again, is that the dialectical argument is the Bavli's medium of generalization from case to principle and extension from principle to new cases.

THE ROLE OF DIALECTICS IN THE BAVLI: The Bavli translates Pentateuchal narratives and laws into a systematic account of its Israel's entire social order. In its topical presentations of thirty-seven of the Mishnah's sixty-three topical tractates, the Bavli portrays not so much how people are supposed to live — this the Mishnah does — as how they ought to think, the right way of analyzing circumstance and tradition alike. The Bavli shows a way of thinking and talking and rationally arguing about reform. When we follow not only what the sages of the Bavli say, but how they express themselves, their modes of critical thought and — above all — their examples of uncompromising, rigorous argument, we encounter a massive, concrete instance of the power of intellect to purify and refine. For the sages of the Bavli, alongside the great masters of Greek philosophy and their Christian and Muslim continuators, exercise the power of rational and systematic inquiry, tenacious criticism, the exchange of not only opinion but reason for opinion, argument and evidence. They provide a model of how intellectuals take up the tasks of social criticism and pursue the disciplines of the mind in the service of the social order. And that, I think, is what has attracted the widespread interest in the Bavli as shown by repeated translations of, and introductions to, that protean document. Not an antiquarian interest in a long-ago society, nor an ethnic concern with heritage and tradition, but a vivid and contemporary search for plausible examples of the rational world order, animate the unprecedented interest of the world of culture in the character (and also the contents) of the Bavli.

The Bavli embodies applied reason and practical logic in quest of the holy society. That model of criticism and reason in the encounter with social reform of which I spoke is unique. The kind of writing that the Bavli represents has serviceable analogues but no known counterpart in the literature of world history and philosophy, theology, religion, and law. That is because the Bavli sets forth not only decisions and other wise and valuable information, but the choices that face reasonable persons and the bases for deciding matters in one way rather than in some other. And the Bavli records the argument, the constant, contentious, uncompromising argument, that endows with vitality the otherwise merely informative corpus of useful insight. "Let logic pierce the mountain" — that is what sages say.

TALMUDIC DIALECTICS AND PHILOSOPHICAL DIALECTICS: In that aspect, the Bavli recalls the great philosophical dialogues of ancient and medieval times. Those familiar with the dialogues of Socrates as set forth by Plato — those wonderful exchanges concerning abstractions such as truth and beauty, goodness and justice — will find familiar the notion of dialectical argument, with its unfolding, on-going give-and take. But Talmudic dialectics differ in two ways. First, the deal with concrete cases and laws, not abstract concepts. Second, the meandering and open-ended character of Talmudic dialectics contrasts with the formal elegance, the perfection of exposition, that characterize Plato's writings. While the Talmud's presentation of contrary positions and exposition of the strengths and weaknesses of each will hardly surprise philosophers, the inclusion of the model of extensive exposition of debate is sometimes puzzling.

What we are given by the Bavli's text of a dialectical argument are notes, which we are expected to know how to use in the reconstruction of the issues under discussion, the arguments under exposition. That means we must make ourselves active partners in the thought-processes that the document. Not only is the argument open-ended, so too the bounds of participation know no limits. Indeed, the Bavli declines to tell us everything we need to know. It exhibits the remarkable confidence of its compilers that generations over time will join in the argument they precipitate, grasp the principles they embody in concrete cases, find compelling the issues they deem urgent. It is that remarkable faith in the human intellect of age succeeding age that lifts the document above time and circumstance and renders it immortal. In transcending circumstance of time and place and condition, the Bavli attains a place in the philosophical, not merely historical, curriculum of culture. That is why the Bavli makes every generation of its heirs and continuators into a partner in the on-going reconstruction of reasoned thought, each generation adding its commentary to the ever-welcoming text.

19

Daniel Boyarin, *Border Lines.*
The Partition of Judaeo-Christianity

Daniel Boyarin, *Border Lines. The Partition of Judaeo-Christianity.*
Philadelphia, 2004: University of Pennsylvania Press. DIVINATIONS REREADING LATE
ANCIENT RELIGION. Edited by Daniel Boyarin, Virginia Burrus, Charlotte Fonrobert,
and Robert Gregg.

From the very beginnings of the Rabbinic system in its preserved writings
border lines distinguished Rabbinic Judaism from all other systemic responses to
the same Scriptures that the ancient Rabbis invoked. Not only so, but those same
main lines of those norms consistently surface in every document of Rabbinic
Judaism. Whether we turn to the Mishnah, ca. 200, or Abot, variously dated as
early in the canonical process and as late, or Song of Songs Rabbah and Lamentations
Rabbah, by consensus situated at an indeterminate point but probably toward the
end of that same continuous process, the outcome is the same. Monotheism has
imposed its logic, which has imparted cogency throughout. The symbolic structure
of Rabbinic Judaism, with its mythic framing of monotheism, pervades, whether in
the invocation of the Torah or in its account of God's participation in Israel's life.
We discern a single cogent construction — the monotheist conception yielded by
Scripture and systematized by the Rabbinic canon — at the foundations of every
document. Then each compilation in sequence takes up its particular burden within
the composition of a complete and cogent statement.

And we have no problem imagining the opposed position, a negotiation
that yields less than the monotheist logic of the Rabbinic system: the rejectionist
and heretical one. That is so even though we can hardly match the Rabbinic system
founded in the bedrock of mythic monotheism with a single contrary system, whether
Christian or pagan, resting on other foundations altogether, e.g., two powers in
heaven against the datum of Pesiqta deRab Kahana. The upshot is, from its earliest
documentary evidence to the latest of late antiquity, a single system of myth and

symbol, law and theology, defined Rabbinic Judaism and distinguished that Judaism from all other religious systems, originating in communities of Judaic, Christian, or pagan venues, whether resting on Scripture or rejecting Scripture altogether. We need hardly ask for the testimony, as to the norms, of articulate sayings, e.g., concerning the unity of God, the justice and mercy of God, the origin with God of the Torah and the origin in the Torah of the critical doctrine of resurrection, judgment, and the restoration of Eden and life eternal. The entire statements of successive composites attest to those same definitive norms of conviction.

Accordingly, Rabbinic Judaism defined itself and designated its opposition. It accomplished the partition of its system from all other, competing ones, whether near at hand or remote, and this it did from its earliest writings to the latest ones of late antiquity. What shifted from the Mishnah to the concluding Midrash-compilations is not the theological norm, the paramount dogma, but only its expression in ever more human terms.

This emergent view of a fully-exposed Judaic religious system, distinct from the very start to the indeterminate finish from all other Judaisms and Christianities and paganisms of late antiquity, bears implications not to be missed. It portrays Rabbinic Judaism as completely realized but for secondary articulation in the Mishnah and present in all subsequent writings. And it yields the presence of both orthodoxy and heresy in the context of formative Rabbinic Judaism. That Judaic system emerges as an inclusionary and exclusionary construction of implicit norms constituting the bedrock of what became normative Judaism. The system says as much in so many words at its critical moment, the declaration of eternal life as the fate of all Israel with few but important exceptions — e.g., those that deny the Torah is from heaven. But we have seen that the system forms the bed rock of the classical writings of that same Judaism. The ancient Rabbis knew who belonged and who did not belong to the Israel that would rise from the grave for eternal life. It goes without saying that Rabbinic Judaism by the canonical writings surveyed here drew border lines between the Torah, which we call in more secular language "Judaism" and the communities of Christianity, with whom it shared some sacred Scriptures.

Daniel Boyarin has set forth a different view of the same matter of the separation of the Torah as Rabbinic Judaism portrayed it from Christianity.[1] Boyarin deals with Christianity and Judaism and argues that the separation of the two into distinct religions represents a process of self-definition. He presents these chapters: Chapter One: Introduction. Part One. Making a Difference: Chapter Two: The Heresiological Beginnings of Christianity and Judaism; Chapter Three: Naturalizing the Border: Apostolic Succession in the Mishnah. Part Two: The Crucifixion of the Logos: How Logos Theology became Christian. Chapter Four: The Intertextual Birth of the Logos: The Prologue to John as a Jewish Midrash. Chapter Five: The Jewish life of the Logos. Logos Theology in Pre- and Pararabbinic Judaism; Chapter Six: The Crucifixion of the Memra: How the Logos Became Christian. Part Three:

Sparks of the Logos: Historicizing Rabbinic Religion. Chapter Seven. The Yavneh Legend of the Stammaim: ON the Invention of the Rabbis in the sixth century. Chapter Eight: "When the Kingdom Turned to *Minut*": The Christian Empire and the Rabbinic Refusal of Religion.

The shank of the several chapters is comprised by extensive *Auseindersetzungen* with scholars who have written on the various topics treated here, whether or not their theses intersect with Boyarin's proposition. These protracted engagements with other scholars are informative but become tedious and make difficult following Boyarin's own view. They furthermore replace and obscure the exposition of the sources for Boyarin's case and substitute a kind of stream-of-consciousness discussion of diverse positions on various issues, not always required for the demonstration of a thesis through exposition, evidence, and argument. Boyarin is an original and interesting scholar, however, and it pays to persevere and to try to follow what he wishes to propose.

A brief account of his thesis will clarify the issues. Boyarin's account of Judaism defines the frame of reference here, even though he deals with Christianity as well: "Even Rabbinic Judaism was struggling to figure out for itself what a 'Judaism' is and who then could be defined as in and out of it" (p. xi). "Authorities on both sides [Judaism, Christianity] tried to establish a border, a line that, when crossed, meant that someone had definitively left one group for another" (p. 2). That line crossed the grave. The Israelite who crossed the line joined the permanently dead. "...Rabbinic texts project a nascent and budding heresiology..." (p. 5). Boyarin stresses the theme of the *minim* (p. 5). Boyarin further redefines the difference between Judaism and Christianity: "the difference between Christianity and Judaism is not so much a difference between two religions as a difference between a religion and an entity that refuses to be one" (p. 8). Quite what is meant here is difficult to say, since Christian orthodox doctrine and Rabbinic orthodox doctrine focus on an agendum of issues common to them both and deriving from the same Scripture; if Christianity conforms to a programmatic model, Judaism responds to the same set of questions. Boyarin states:

> The argument of this book is that ...at the first stage of its existence, at the time of the initial formulation of Rabbinic Judaism, the Rabbis...did seriously attempt to construct Judaism...as an orthodoxy and thus as a 'religion,' the product of disembedding of certain realms of practice, speech, and so on from others and identifying them as of particular circumstance. If you do not believe such and such or practice so and so, you are not a Jew, imply the texts of the period. At a later stage, however,...at the stage of the 'definitive' formulation of Rabbinic Judaism in the Babylonian Talmud, the Rabbis rejected this option, proposing instead the distinct ecclesiological principle that 'an Israelite, even if he...sins, remains an Israelite.' The historical layering of these two ideologies and even self-definitions by the Rabbis themselves of what it is that constitutes an Israel and an Israelite provide for the creative ambivalence in the status of Judaism today...." (p. 10).

The documents of the Rabbinic canon — Mishnah, successive Midrash-compilations such as Sifra and the Rabbah-compilations of late antiquity — contain no judgment upon the status of Israelites that reject principles of practice or belief, except the Mishnah's statement that all Israel has a portion in the world to come except.... That statement comes at the very outset of the Rabbinic canon, in the earliest of its documents beyond Scripture. Then "Israel" is constituted by those destined to enjoy life eternal. Even those that sin are included (with the stated exceptions in mind).

But that is not because of a paramount latitudinarianism adopted by the Talmud of Babylonia. *It is because death atones for sin.* Hence at issue at Mishnah-tractate Sanhedrin 11:1 is only the exceptions to the prevailing norm that death atones for sin and leaves the Israelite sinless in judgment. That is why by the definition of Israel of Rabbinic Judaism — those that live eternally — the sinful Israelite remains an Israelite, that is, will stand in judgment. The matter is explicit at M. Sanhedrin 6:2:

MISHNAH-TRACTATE SANHEDRIN 6:2

A.   [When] he was ten cubits from the place of stoning, they say to him, "Confess," for it is usual for those about to be put to death to confess.

B.   For whoever confesses has a share in the world to come.

C.   For so we find concerning Achan, to whom Joshua said, "My son, I pray you, give glory to the Lord, the God of Israel, and confess to him, [and tell me now what you have done; hide it not from me.] And Achan answered Joshua and said, Truly have I sinned against the Lord, the God of Israel, and thus and thus I have done" (Josh. 7:19). And how do we know that his confession achieved atonement for him? For it is said, "And Joshua said, Why have you troubled us? The Lord will trouble you this day" (Josh. 7:25) — This day you will be troubled, but you will not be troubled in the world to come.

D.   And if he does not know how to confess, they say to him, "Say as follows: 'Let my death be atonement for all of my transgressions.'"

The Bavli understands the passage in exactly the way I have interpreted the Mishnah's statement:

II.1 A.   And how do we know that his confession achieved atonement for him [M. 6:2C]?

B.   *Our rabbis have taught on Tannaite authority:*

C.   And how do we know that his confession achieved atonement for him?

D.   For it is said, "And Joshua said, Why have you troubled us? The Lord will trouble you this day"] (Josh. 7:25).

III.1 A. "This day you are troubled, but you will not be troubled in the world to come" [M. 6:2C].

B. And it is written, "And the sons of Zerah are Zimri, Ethan, Heman, Calcol, Darda, five in all" (1 Chr. 2:6).

C. *What is the sense of* "five in all"?

D. They are five in all destined for the world to come [cf. T. San. 9:5D-F].

E. *Here it is Zimri, but elsewhere Achan [Josh. 7:24].*

F. Rab and Samuel:

G. One said, "His name was Achan, and why was he called Zimri? Because he acted like Zimri."

H. The other said, 'His name was Zimri, and why was he called Achan? Because he [Schachter, Sanhedrin (London, 1948: Soncino Press):] wound the sins of Israel about them like a serpent [Achan = snake in Greek, <u>echidna</u>]."

Death marks the final atonement for sin, which bears its implication for the condition of man at the resurrection. Because one has atoned through sin (accompanied at the hour of death by a statement of repentance, "May my death be atonement for all my sins," in the liturgy in due course), when he is raised from the dead, his atonement for all his sins is complete. He cannot cease to be Israel. The judgment after resurrection becomes for most a formality. That is why "all Israel has a portion in the world to come," with the exception of a few whose sins are not atoned for by death, and that is by their own word. That is the position of Rabbinic Judaism from the Mishnah forward, and the Talmud of Babylonia does not innovate and mark a new and different theology (Boyarin's ideology) at all. We cannot speak as Boyarin does of a "historical layering "…of what constitutes an Israel and an Israelite…." (p. 10).

Boyarin is explicit in his view that "in the end — at least in the end of late antiquity — Rabbinic Judaism refused the option of becoming a religion, another species of the kind that Christianity offered. At the final stage of the development of classical Rabbinism, a reassertion of the 'locative' of identity as given and not as achieved — or lost — came to be emblematic of Judaism" (p. 12). So Boyarin concludes, "Judaism is not and has not been, since early in the Christian era, a 'religion' in the sense of an orthodoxy whereby heterodox views…would make one an outsider… (p. 13). Judaism, Boyarin says, rejected "the option of orthodoxy and heresy as the Jews' mode of self-definition…the refusal…finally to become and be a religion" (p. 13). The Rabbinic documents that fall into Boyarin's classification of the age of orthodoxy (the Mishnah for example), certainly do presuppose theological premises we may categorize as exclusive and normative. But the differentiation of the Talmud's definitions — rejecting the notion of orthodoxy altogether, as Boyarin claims, in favor of indelible ethnicity — from those of the earlier orthodox documents proves dubious.

The Bavli extends the Mishnah's and Tosefta's and other received laws and principles. More to the point, those early documents make provision for sinful Israelites, who remain Israel in the exact sense: those that will rise from the grave. There is no space between the Mishnah's and Tosefta's definition of the status of the sinful Israelite and that prevailing in Lamentations Rabbah, Song of Songs Rabbah, and as a mater of fact the two Talmuds. No other definition of "Israel" surfaces in these later documents, and the shibboleth about the sinful Israelite remaining an Israelite does not for one minute contradict that statement of the Mishnah's and the Tosefta's but confirms it. Rabbinic Judaism sets forth a religious system that, systemically, is not to be distinguished in its basic model and pattern from Christianity: both are religions within the same model and pattern of what is meant by religion. Ethnicity and "Jewishness" in place of religiosity and Judaism would come into play many, many centuries later, in the nineteenth and twentieth centuries to be exact.

How exactly do I propose to demonstrate that Boyarin is wrong in denying normative status to matters of conviction as much as conduct? By "orthodox" here I mean, the normative theological system and its doctrines on particular issues put forth in the Rabbinic canon. By "heresy" I mean, positions contrary to those norms. We know who belongs to the community of correct doctrine by identifying adherents to the implicit norms that animate the canonical writings of Rabbinic Judaism. We know who does not belong by imagining the positions of those that contradict the norms. But of whom do we speak? We do not know the state of public opinion among Jews of various kinds, nor can we assume that what the canon deems normative corresponds with actuality. We do know what the Rabbinic authorities set forth in their canon and can identify the fundamentals on which they formed their consensus. They acknowledge contrary opinion only rarely, and we have no documents produced outside of the Rabbinic circles that set forth contrary systems to the one laid out in the Rabbinic canon. So we deal with the Rabbinic account of matters and extrapolate from that the character of their (imagined) competition and opposition.

One thing is clear. The Rabbinic writings yield a cogent system, and implicitly they construct an equally coherent contrary one. The Rabbinic system rests on the foundation that one God made heaven and earth and governs all things past, present and future. The narrative of Scripture and the laws and traditions set forth by the Rabbinic writings, one by one and all together, systematically explore the implications of the unity of God. Law and narrative present monotheism as a system of culture and a narrative as well: mythic monotheism realized in the Israelite social order. So far as the Rabbinic writings speak of heresy, it is in the context of the orthodoxy framed by monotheism as sustained in the ancient Scriptures. Let us examine the principal parts of that system as these parts form the implicit outcomes of the principal documents.

ONE GOD. GOD'S UNITY EXPRESSED IN THE UNITY OF BEING: NATURE, SOCIETY, HISTORY, COSMOS: all things derive from one thing, and one thing yields all things. The Mishnah forms a concrete demonstration of the abstractions of monotheism. The scriptural account of the cosmos forms the generative categories, which constitute an ordered, hierarchical unity of being. Human events cohere as well, forming a testimony to the governance of history by the one God who made heaven and earth. A single set of principles governs through all time; Israel's history and also the history of the nations embody those principles, so Genesis Rabbah. Nature, history, and Israelite society join together to make a single statement in common, a statement of monotheism realized in the unity of the natural and the social and world order. Torah and the Temple, Torah-study and Temple-sacrifice — all conform to the same pattern, thus Leviticus Rabbah. God is not only benevolent but passionate; God weeps for Israel and shares in Israel's suffering. God mourns when Israel's deeds bring on disaster, Lamentations Rabbah maintains. Song of Songs Rabbah forms the climax of the monotheist exposition. God imposes the obligation to love, and be loved by, God: "You will love the Lord your God with all your heart, with all your soul, and with all your might."

THE TORAH: Sifra takes as premise the claim that the Torah contains God's words in God's own wording and so affords access to God's mind Torah-study in Abot forms the highest calling, because it brings disciples into direct contact with God, his word and his presence. Torah and Torah-learning form the matrix for all other expositions; a trait of the canon as a whole is the constant resort to proof-texts of Scripture.

ISRAEL: Israel is God's special love. That love is shown in a simple way. Israel's present condition of subordination derives from its own deeds. It follows that God cares, so Israel may look forward to redemption on God's part in response to Israel's own regeneration through repentance, so Leviticus Rabbah. So too, nature and supernature, earth and heaven, correlate and make a harmonious statement. The course of Israel on earth embodies the course of the moon and the solar seasons in heaven, and when Israel mends its way, all of astral nature will respond, thus Pesiqta deRab Kahana.

FREE WILL, RESPONSIBILITY, JUDGMENT, AND RESURRECTION: God is just and merciful. Tractate Abot takes for granted that God knows what all persons, endowed with free will and responsible for their exercise thereof, do and judges them, with eternal consequences for resurrection or for perpetual death.

RIGHT ATTITUDE AND EMOTIONS: An Israelite in the teaching of tractate Abot should accommodate his wishes to those of others. He should love God. What is required of Israel is submission to God and conciliation of one's fellow man. Other documents concur, but it is in tractate Abot that the matter is featured.

Monotheism in the Rabbinic context emerges in the initial documents as an abstraction. The Mishnah and tractate Abot Tractate encompass in what is implicit the principles of monotheism. But they contain little of that dense mythic instantiation of God's rule in nature, history, society, and the celestial realm that would emerge in the later Midrash-compilations.

What about heresy emergent from the implicit norms? Abot defines heresy out of its affirmation of resurrection, judgment, and the Torah. These yield in the form of heresies: denial of the Torah, of judgment, and therefore of resurrection as critical to the Torah's construction of human existence. The Mishnah finds heresy in theories of the complexity of being, positing two powers in heaven for example, or distinguishing between and among sources of divine governance. Heretics will not concede the absolute One without distinction and without variety. Sifra will insist that the Torah comes from heaven and is the literal word of God, against the heresy that would attribute the Torah to human fabrication.

The conception that cogent rules do not govern human events but chaos brought on by conflicting actions of diverse gods prevails contradicts the premise of Genesis Rabbah that history reveals the one God's plan for all humanity. Nature follows its own rules, distinct from those that govern history and the social order; the social order does not present the occasion of sanctification, contrary to the position of Leviticus Rabbah and, for the separation of nature from history, Pesiqta deRab Kahana.

God does not respond to the love of the unique People, Israel, contrary to the view of Leviticus Rabbah. The stars in the heavens shape the destiny of humanity on earth, and Israel is governed by the stars just as much as are the gentiles, contrary to Pesiqta deRab Kahana. The God known in the Torah is malevolent and bears no good will for Israel, a Gnostic position that contradicts the point of insistence of Lamentations Rabbah. The malevolence of God for Israel is contradicted by the love of God for Israel instantiated in Song of Songs Rabbah.

All that is required for this characterization of heresy in the setting of Rabbinic Judaism accomplished in stating the opposite of the implicit norms of the canonical writings. A reading of the main points of the normative liturgy in the *Shema* and the Prayer yields a similar exposition of rejected propositions. That liturgy addresses the one God who hears and answers prayer. He creates the world, reveals the Torah, and redeems Israel. Denying the unity of being posited in the liturgy realizes the implicit heresy fabricated by the Rabbinic system. Whether within Israel or beyond its limits such a cogent heresy flourished is for others to determine. It suffices to say that the Rabbinic canon, start to finish, sets forth an exclusive claim to truth and dismisses as null all contrary claims. That system took shape on its own, within its own generative logic, and did not require Christian opposition to precipitate its formation. That is why Boyarin's account of matters is seriously flawed. Two problems seem insurmountable, first, the anachronistic category-formation in play, second, the conflict between his thesis and the Rabbinic documents that bear implicit definitions of orthodoxy and heresy for Rabbinic Judaism.

ENDNOTES

[1] Daniel Boyarin, *Border Lines. The Partition of Judaeo-Christianity* (Philadelphia, 2004: University of Pennsylvania Press).

20

Joel M. Hoffman, *In the Beginning. A Short History of the Hebrew Language*

Joel M. Hoffman, *In the Beginning. A Short History of the Hebrew Language.* New York, 2004: New York University Press.

Hoffman's history of the Hebrew language provides an up-to-date account of some aspects of Hebrew of interest to contemporary linguistic theory. The book is written in a sprightly, inviting prose, and clarifies many complex questions. He begins with theoretical problems of a fundamental order and manages to convey the choices as to principles of learning that face the reader, the theories of language that circulate. Then he turns to antiquity, to which most of the book is devoted. He explains the problem of writing down speech and the choices explored in ancient times: non-alphabetic writing (logographs, syllabic writing, consonantal writing), then identifies Hebrew alphabetic writing as the foundation of Western literacy. Adding vowels to the consonants made all the difference, making literacy possible for a vast population. Then he contributes his own theory of the name of God — Y – H – W – H — stressing that the operative letters are all vowels.

At this point Hoffman turns to an exposition of the Hebrew Scriptures in the form given them by the 9th century scholars of Tiberias, the Masoretes, since their text of Scripture, "the Masoretic text," inclusive of vowels and trope-signs, defines the way in which Judaism receives the Torah. He spells out what they tried to do, what they did, and how we know the upshot of their work. He spells out the problem of pronunciation as well.

This narrative of the history of the Hebrew language thus begins with a beginning and an end-point, the invention of vowels for the consonantal alphabet, and the provision many, many centuries later of a single authoritative version of Scripture. Hoffman doubles back, at this point, and asks, is the Masoretic text a valid representation of the text-tradition? How do we know it is accurate as to beginnings? This requires him to jump from the ninth century C.E. to the Septuagint

— the translation of Scripture into Greek — of the fourth or third century B.C.E., then to Origen, a Church father who represented Hebrew writing in Greek letters, of the third century C.E., then back to the Dead Sea Scrolls of the second and first centuries B.C.E. and what we learn from the Hebrew represented there. What chaos! That is, we are led through problems of orthography and pronunciation of Hebrew texts not in the sequence in which they were written but in a confused and confusing order. The disorder is shown in the titles of the section, "moving on:" the Dead Sea Scrolls, dialects in the Bible ("Late biblical Hebrew"), and post-biblical Hebrew, which covers Aramaic and Greek and Rabbinic Hebrew. Then, at this point skipping the Masoretes of medieval times, we leap to modern Hebrew and the romantic story of Eliezer ben Yehuda and the renaissance of Hebrew as a living language.

The upshot is not history as a sequential narrative but a sequence of topics of linguistic interest, unfolding by a logic private to the field of linguistics: pronunciation, vocabulary, grammar, spelling. History of a language as narrative, history of a language as an account of culture, history of a language as the story of the interplay of power and the social order — the view of language as a dialect with an army, for example — none of these perspectives is asked to shape the presentation. The absence of a cultural program accounts, also, for the fantastic disproportions that prevail. Scripture, including the Masorettes, covers more than half the book, the Dead Sea Scrolls are given an elaborate chapter, which goes over the familiar story of the discoveries and the politics that impeded scholarship. But Rabbinic Hebrew, beginning with Middle or Mishnaic Hebrew, fills scarcely a dozen pages.

This is the history of Hebrew written as though Hebrew belonged to the Karaites. I may say flatly that Hoffman's picture of Middle Hebrew is ignorant and superficial. I looked in vain for appreciation of the work on Middle or Mishnaic Hebrew of a vast range of accomplished scholars, both Israeli and European and American, even the grammars are not listed. He scarcely gets straight the titles and characteristics of some of the Rabbinic canon of the formative age, committing at least a few howlers as to simple facts. He asks no questions such as scholarship has answered, not even explaining the differences between biblical and Rabbinic syntax and semantics such as the Rabbinic sages themselves point to in the difference between *lashon miqra* and lashon *hakhamim,* the language of Scripture and the language of the Rabbinic sages. The bi- or tri-lingualism of the Rabbinic classics, their use of language as a taxonomic indicator of the character of discourse — none of these now-established traits of Rabbinic Hebrew figures. Yet Middle Hebrew defined Rabbinic Hebrew, which wrote the history of the Hebrew language from antiquity to the twentieth century, when Modern Hebrew, inclusive of Israeli Hebrew, came on the scene.

Hoffman's account of the history of the Hebrew language provides a good account of some matters and a slipshod picture of others, and the problem is not length but perspective and proportion and sheer knowledge. Where Hoffman knows the territory, his map serves, where not, not. Pronunciation, vocabulary, grammar, spelling — these issues belong, but so too does cultural history, such as language reveals, which Hoffman ignores. Had he called his book, "issues of linguistics in the Hebrew scriptures and their transmission," we should have had no reason to cavil. But even there, the absence of the Rabbinic sages from the account of the linguistics of Hebrew still registers

One final point: relentlessly, Hoffman passes his opinion on everything, he does not edit himself by asking whether his opinion rests on first-hand encounter with the problems of sources and scholarship on them. This yields the result that his "further reading" is glib. A long list of the names of highly accomplished scholars of the Hebrew language excluded from his bibliography underscores the merely partial success of Hoffman's book.

21

Maren Niehoff,
Philo on Jewish Identity and Culture

Maren Niehoff, *Philo on Jewish Identity and Culture.* Tuebingen, 2001:
Mohr Siebeck. Texts and Studies in Ancient Judaism volume 86, edited by Martin
Hengel and Peter Schaefer. ISBN 3-16-147611-5.

This fully realized work of mature scholarship takes up "the ways in which
Philo constructed Jewish identity and culture in first-century Alexander:" "what
made Philo a Jew in his own eyes? Where did he draw boundaries between 'us and
'them'?" Dr. Maren Niehoff of the Hebrew University recognizes that these questions
derive from contemporary cultural sensibility. She meets the challenge of showing
that her categories — identity, culture — are not anachronistic but illuminate Philo's
own thought. Hence while she invokes issues of our own times, she shows that
"modern scholarship has developed some theoretical categories which do transcend
their particular time and are...useful for a proper understanding of periods other
than modern. They throw new light on Philo and uncover aspects of his writings
hitherto overlooked." So she asks, "What made Philo a Jew in his own eyes.
Where...did he himself decide to draw boundaries between 'us' and 'them'? Who
were for him significant others from whom he distinguished the characteristic
features of being Jewish? What was for him a Jewish cultural discourse? How did
he make sense of the specific customs of his people in a broader context of meaning?"
She describes the work in these terms:

> The first section of the book...on Jewish identity pays particular attention to the
> contemporary Roman discourse as reflected in the Greek East. The impact of Rome on
> political, social and cultural matters has in each instance been considered as an explanation
> for Philo's particular choice of boundaries. The way in which he constructed Jewish descent,
> significant "Others and distinctly Jewish values are interpreted in light of contemporary
> Roman concerns...The second section of the book investigates how Philo's sense of identity
> translates into cultural structures. We examine here which distinctive activities, commitments

and attitudes emerge from Philo's construction of ethnicity. ...the characteristic features of Jewish life are analyzed with a view to the overarching meaning which he attributes too them...he rooted Jewish customs in deeper structures of meaning which were in his view embedded in the overall order of the university.

Niehoff proceeds to treat these topics for Jewish identity: Jewish descent, mothers and mother cities; the Egyptians as ultimate other; Jewish values: religion and self-restraint; Roman benefactors and friends; Greeks and Greek culture. For Jewish culture she presents essays on these themes: transforming new-born children into Jewish adults; the textuality of Jewish culture; parables as translators of culture; inscribing Jewish customs into nature. The recurrent theme is the superiority of the Jews, their identity and culture, over the Egyptians. She concludes that Philo's "overall strategy is to inscribe the Jewish way of life in Nature...observance of Jewish law adjusts to the law and structure of the cosmos and also provides health. Living as a Jew was...not a matter of personal preference but of objective value recommended to any wise person aspiring to an authentic life." The book is lucidly argued throughout, and the absence of a concluding chapter is more than outweighed by the cogency of her exposition. Philo emerges as a proud Jew, who expresses in the idiom of his time and place the excellence of the Judaism he advocates.

The book would have benefited from a close reading by an editor who is a native speaker of English. The publisher, Siebeck, and his editors, Professors Hengel and Schaefer, owe authors at least that much. Niehoff does not know the difference between "which" and "that," for example, and infelicities in word choice and construction sometimes shade over into obscurities. But the book is not much marred, and its merit — a completely fresh, and persuasive reading of Philo — more than compensates. When we compare this book with the author's prior title, *The Figure of Joseph in Post-Biblical Jewish Literature* (1992), we see how an authentic scholar makes the move from collecting and arranging information for a doctoral dissertation to asking important questions and answering them in a major enterprise. She has constructed a cogent argument, amassed evidence that pertains to that argument, and made her case. Not only so, but she has defined a model for inquiry into other statements of ethnicity and culture embodied in writings of antiquity.

22

The Oeuvre of Jonathan Z. Smith

Jonathan Z. Smith, *Relating Religion. Essays in the Study of Religion.* Chicago and London: The University of Chicago Press. 412 pp., ISBN 0-226-76386-2

For the generation of religion-scholars now reaching retirement age Jonathan Z. Smith, University of Chicago, has represented the principal source of critical theory, of positioning the academic study of religion in the setting of the academy and in the context of public intellectual life. No single individual has taken his place as principal theorist of the academic study of religion. And none in his time competed in eminence and influence.

Since in the period now drawing to a close, the academic study of religion reached maturity, the full importance of Smith's work cannot be over-stated. Indeed, for four decades he has been best characterized as academic religion's principal public intellectual. Lesser figures exercise nowhere near an equivalent weight and influence. Here in this newest work we have a collection, compendious and wide-ranging, of his most current, and intellectually experienced, essays, two decades of thought. The work is comprised by a Preface, seventeen essays written from 1983 through 2002, that is, after his *Imagining Religion*, and a list of the author' publications from the first academic one in 1966 to 2003.

But while he has framed a system and structure of thought about the academic study of religion and its results, he has made his contribution in bits and pieces, essays, and not in a coherent statement, not in a book. His books are principally collections of essays, for Smith defines himself as primarily "a writer of essays, which are often reworked versions of lectures. He goes on, "I understand the role of one who identifies himself as a generalist and comparativist to be that of interacting with the agenda and data of others. This has meant that much of my work is situational, designed for particular audiences, often discussing their assigned topics or questions." But if we read his essays all together, a clear program and system emerge — and here and there are articulated, not merely instantiated. A model essay by Smith will begin with a surprising and apparently irrelevant case, focus on a proposition or problem implicit in the case, and with astonishing erudition and breadth of thought set forth a fruitful hypothesis emerging from the facts adduced in evidence and argument. What is implicit always emerges, what is apparently irrelevant always registers in the end. And, as my precis of the seventeen essays in this newest collection is meant to demonstrate, a coherent set of propositions does emerge through the dense and difficult discussion of unfamiliar data. The range of erudition is staggering, the depth of insight into the meaning of the data astonishing and compelling.

His influence reaches circles that scarcely intersect otherwise, specialists in one religious tradition or another, for example, will find illustrations of his generalizations in the specific religious traditions on which they concentrate, respectively. His theses about the character of religion, in the tradition of Mircea Eliade, accordingly illuminate specific religious traditions. The road leads from religion viewed as a coherent phenomenon of society and culture to diverse religions. In Smith's hands the academic study of religion is a generalizing science.

That is why I have found him so useful for the formation of programs in the academic study of the formation of Judaism. Through the decades I have read his writings for stimulation and guidance. My message has been, I have answers, I seek questions. And what I need to frame are the questions that my sources, those of formative Judaism, turn out to answer: focus and purpose for the information supplied by the classical writings. Treating Judaism as a religious system, not as a source of history or a focus of ethnic culture, I found Smith a principal source of stimulation, a source of productive questions, and in these pages, I still do. Since Judaism surfaces in his essays only sporadically and uncommonly, his capacity to illuminate through perspicacious generalizations the traditions of a particular religion truly astonishes.

His editorial leadership in the field is represented *by The HarperCollins Dictionary of Religion* (San Francisco, 1995: Harper), with William Scott Green as managing editor. Green is credited as the source of some of Smith's most engaging aperçus. His books are these: [1] *Map Is Not Territory: Studies in the History of Religions* (Leiden, 1978: Brill. In J. Neusner, ed., STUDIES IN JUDAISM IN LATE ANTIQUITY, VOLUME 23); [2] *Imagining Religion: From Babylon to Jonestown* (Chicago, 1982, University of Chicago Press. In J. Neusner, ed., CHICAGO STUDIES IN THE HISTORY OF JUDAISM); [3] *To Take Place: Toward Theory in Ritual* (Chicago, 1987, University of Chicago Press. In J. Neusner, ed., CHICAGO STUDIES IN THE HISTORY OF JUDAISM); [4] *Drudgery Divine: On the Comparison of Early Christianities and the Religions of Late Antiquity* (London, School of Oriental Lectures in Comparative Religion; and Chicago, 1990: University of Chicago Press: CHICAGO STUDIES IN THE HISTORY OF JUDAISM. The several titles appeared in series edited by me, at Brill and Chicago. And full disclosure requires me to state also that the present one is dedicated to three long-time co-workers and colleagues, of whom I am one.

That brings us to the book at hand. It is unprepossessing but intellectually the most ambitious of the set. After a massive intellectual autobiography in Chapter One, the work is divided into five sections. Chapters Two through Six consist of "critical engagements with figures and scholarly traditions that serve to position" Smith's essays with the work of others. Chapters Seven-Ten take up a long-time interest in taxonomy and classification. Chapters Eleven through Thirteen consist of studies of the construction of difference. Chapters Fourteen and Fifteen "…illustrate the procedures of generalization and redescription that have become key to my understanding of the purpose of the comparative enterprise." Chapters Sixteen through Seventeen represent "the deployment of elements that have become characteristic of my most recent work, especially the notion of translation."

Given the remarkable breadth and depth of the essays, the initial task of the reader is not to criticize the whole but to find the main points of that the chapters make one by one. An effort at accomplishing that task follows. My intent is to show through the systematic survey of the seventeen essays how Smith has produced a system and a structure, not merely observations about this and that, and to specify of what that system and structure consist: his principal results.

1. WHEN THE CHIPS ARE DOWN: "An interest in religion as a generic category, not limited to any particular tradition or canon," characteristic of Smith's *oeuvre,* is the theme of this intellectual autobiography, yielding the question, "how shall we compare?" In his first teaching position, at University of California, Santa Barbara, he settled on "the exemplum and the test case," which "not only served as organizing principle for the courses but came to be stratagems I would deploy in most of my subsequent work." "The world religions course was structured around the notion that each of the major religious traditions should be taken as exemplifying particular structures of religious experience, behavior, and expression as identified by students of religion." Thus: "Hinduism/temple construction and sacrifice; Islam/holy book and pilgrimage; Judaism/holy land and duality, pure impure; Christianity/myth and history and life-cycle rituals." The program involved "understanding the structure by acquiring …a vocabulary, a set of cross-cultural examples that gave some sense of a structure's range and attendant interpretative issues, then to study relevant materials within the particular religious tradition." To this enterprise Smith contributes the analogy of botany: taxonomy seemed a comparative enterprise which sought similarity across obvious individual variations and which asserted significant difference even in the face of apparent resemblances." Here we come to one of the main themes of Smith's essays, both here and in the prior collections. The upshot is clearly stated at the end: "Religion is not best understood as a disclosure that gives rise to a particular mode of experience…religion is the relentlessly human activity of thinking through a 'situation.'" While the essay refers to a vast realm of knowledge in terms so abstract as to lose all but the most erudite, perspicacious readers, the end is clear: "Theory is not life, but I know with perfect surety that it is liveliness." And much depends on how things cash out, what is at stake when the chips are

down. Smith's claim to be a theorist and a generalist rests on the chapters to come. Chapter One is so general and abstract and broad-ranging that no one can follow and respond who has not read these particular books — whether of philosophy or of anthropology or of botany — in this particular way. But Chapter One also is dazzling for its capacity to respond to fields of learning that rarely intersect, and, in religion-study, rarely — and I think, never — outside of Smith's own study. The text fills thirty pages, and the notes the same. The notes constitute the most detailed intellectual autobiography I have ever read. This is the capital essay in the book and shows the thought that animates the prior books as well; it is where Smith registers all together and all at once his principal theses.

2. ACKNOWLEDGMENTS: MORPHOLOGY AND HISTORY IN MIRCEA ELIADE'S PATTERNS IN COMPARATIVE RELIGION (1949-1999). PART I. THE WORK AND ITS CONTEXTS: Smith has one predecessor of major consequence, Mircea Eliade. The context of Eliade's *Patterns* is Goethe's history of biological morphology. "...the morphological and the historical comprise alternative views of the same object...neither view is finally reducible to the other." Eliade "had no interest in the history of biological morphology apart from Goethe. But he did expect his readers to judge *Patterns* in light of the Goethean enterprise. At stake is the evaluation of Eliade's work as ahistorical....the morphological and the historical comprise alternative views of the same object, rather than suggesting that they treat different objects, and to maintain that neither view is finally reducible to the other."

3. ACKNOWLEDGMENTS: MORPHOLOGY AND HISTORY IN MIRCEA ELIADE'S PATTERNS IN COMPARATIVE RELIGION (1949-1999). PART TWO. THE TEXTURE OF THE WORK: The intent was to form "a grand synthesis of morphology and history of religions...a comprehensive view which shall be at once a morphology and a history." Eliade's "most enduring contribution to the study of religion: his all but limitless extension of the boundaries of potential data for the student of religion." The issue "remains for contemporary students of religion to address at the levels of definition, classification, and theory." "What Eliade criticizes is an proposal of explanatory, causal simplicity with respect to religious phenomena in favor of a descriptive, systemic complexity." "Religious facts...form coherent systems." Eliade states, "What I intend is to introduce my reader to the labyrinthine complexity of religious facts, to acquaint him with their basic structures, and with the diversity of culture-circles they bring into relief." Smith's systematic exposition of how Eliade's *Patterns* accomplishes this goal is lucid and accomplishes the task of exposition. To do so, he systematically compares Goethe's "morphological view" with Eliade's ontological view: "For Goethe's morphology, environmental effects may be set aside because they are merely contingently historical, ...because 'they come from without.' For Eliade's ontology, the hierophany is to be supremely valued because it is suprahistorical, because it imposes 'itself on man from without.' In Goethe's morphological view, externality is a mark of disposability; in Eliade's ontological view, it is a mark of indispensability. The difference is one between a focus on the

mundane botanical world in Goethe's *Metamorphosis*, and the supramundane transcendental world in Eliade's *Patterns*."

4. THE TOPOGRAPHY OF THE SACRED: Is 'the sacred best understood as an expression or an experience, as a representation or a presence? I side with the French, in affirming the first member of these two oppositional pairs." "I have tended to think of the sacred/profane distinction as essentially a royal one, the clean/unclean distinction as a cultic one, and the permitted/forbidden as a legal one. Given the reciprocal relations between king/priest, palace/temple/ and law/ cult, it is not, then, surprising that the three systems coexist in texts that are the product of these relations."

5. MANNA, MANNA EVERYWHERE AND /_/_/ : "My interest is the history of religious representations and the history of the academic conceptualizations of religion…In this presentation I should like to examine two instances of evidence that suggest different modes of significance and evaluation…an episode in biblical narrative…an Ocean word/concept that has played a leading role in some anthropological theories of religion." These are Manna and mana. "What has interested me in thinking about the variety of manna texts is not so much a mater of historical confirmation…but rather one of narrative articulation and ratiocination." Mana in the South Pacific went through a century-long drama, "in which a word was transformed into an incarnate power only to be reduced to a word again." "In the case of the biblical manna narratives, too much scholarly energy has been expended on getting 'behind' the word to some natural phenomenon as if that endeavor guaranteed its being of interest…In the case of the argumentative use of the Oceanic mana, too much scholarly energy has been expended on getting 'beneath' the word to either some supernatural 'reality'…or some powerful social 'reality….'"

6. THE DOMESTICATION OF SACRIFICE: In thinking about a "theory of ritual," it would seem more fruitful to focus on the characteristics of those actions that, by one definition or another, we designate as 'rituals,' and to abstain from initial concern for content, which, among other problems, inevitably forces a premature return to myth." "…Ritual activities are an exaggeration of everyday activities, but an exaggeration that reduces, rather than enlarges, that clarifies by miniaturizing in order to achieve sharp focus…Ritual precises [renders precise] ambiguities." "Ritual is no 'big deal.'" "A theory of sacrifice…cannot be found in a quest for origins but can only be found through the detailed examination of elaborations." "Animal sacrifice appears to be, universally, the ritual killing of a domesticated animal by agrarian or pastoralist societies." "Sacrifice is an exaggeration of domestication, a meditation on one cultural process by means of another, …If domestication is a 'focussing' on selected characteristics in the animal, a process of sexual 'experimentation' that strives to achieve a 'perfection' or 'rectification' of the natural animal species…, then sacrifice becomes focus on this focus, an experimentation with this experimentation, a perfecting of this perfection, a rectification of this rectification."

7. A MATTER OF CLASS: TAXONOMIES OF RELIGION: Explaining his plan for the *HarperCollins Dictionary of Religion,* edited by him with William Scott Green as managing editor, Smith states, "A dictionary differs from both an encyclopaedia and a handbook by virtue of its necessary atomism...defining individual words in an arbitrary alphabetical order...An encyclopaedia is essentially topical in orientation...A handbook is an encyclopaedia arranged by some stated principle of order...." "Notably lacking in such definitions are alternative taxonomic strategies, particularly those that do not take some modified form of essential definition as their model. There is no attempt at a polythetic classification which eschews the postulation of a unique differentiation in favor of a large set of characteristics, any one of which would be necessary, but not sufficient, to classify a given entity as an instance of religion." "Nowhere in the taxonomic literature on 'world religions' is there a noticeable sense of the difficulties in defining particular religions." "Scholarly labor is a disciplined exaggeration in the direction of knowledge; taxonomy is a valuable tool in achieving that necessary distortion."

8. RELIGION, RELIGIONS, RELIGIOUS: In the writings of the Catholic missionaries to the New World, these meanings for the word "religion" emerge: "Religion...is [1] a category imposed from the outside on some aspect of native culture...It is the other...who are solely responsible for the content of the term. [2] Even in early formulations there is an implicit universality...a ubiquitous human phenomenon...[3] In constructing the second order, generic category 'religion,' its characteristics are those that appear natural to the other...[4] religion is an anthropological, not a theological category." The usages shifted over time and space, the Catholic emphasis on ritual and the Protestant on faith marking the most important of these shifts. Hume "raises the issue of the adjectival form, 'religious.' What sort of primary human experience or activity does it modify?" "Nineteenth century anthropological approaches focused on increasing the number of 'natural' religious categories, especially for 'primitive' peoples." "It is impossible to escape the suspicion that a world religion is simply a religion like ours, and that it is, above all, a tradition that has achieved sufficient power and numbers to enter our history to form it, interact with it, or thwart it." Smith concludes, Religion "is a second-order, generic concept that plays the same role in establishing a disciplinary horizon that a concept such as 'language' plays in linguistics or 'culture' plays in anthropology. There can be no disciplined study of religion without such a horizon." To this one may add,, language also provides a suggestive metaphor for theology, as I have shown in my *Theological Grammar of the Oral Torah. Vocabulary, Grammar, Syntax* (in three volumes) (1999).

9. BIBLE AND RELIGION: This chapter focuses on the study of the Bible and religion to illustrate the following thesis: the overall project of the study of religion entails definition, classification, comparison, and explanation. Each of these processes have in common that they are varying modes of redescription. From this perspective the end of comparison cannot be the act of comparison itself. I would

distinguish four moments in the comparative enterprise: description, comparison, redescription, and rectification. Description is a double process which comprises the historical or ethnographic dimensions of the work. A first requirement is that we locate a given example within the rich texture of its social, historical, and cultural environments that invest it with its local significance. The second task of description is that of reception-history, a careful account of how our second-order scholarly tradition has intersected with the exemplum, how the datum has come to be accepted as significant for the purpose of argument. Only when such a double contextualization is completed can one move on to the description of a second example undertaken in the same double fashion. With at least two exempla in view, one is prepared to undertake their comparison both in terms of aspects and relations held to e be significant, expressed in the tropes of similarities and differences, and with respect to some category, question, theory or model of interest to the study of religion. The aim of such a comparison is the redescription of the exempla…and a rectification of the academic categories in relation to which they have been imagined." From here the two topics, Bible and religion, are subjected to description, reception-history, comparison, and rectification.

     10. TRADING PLACES: Magic, science, and religion require definition. But substantive definitions of "'magic' have proven empty in concrete instances and worthless when generalized to characterize entire peoples, whole systems of thought, or world views. Such substantive definitions have failed because "in academic discourse 'magic' has almost always been treated as a contrast term, a shadow reality known only by looking at the reflection of its opposite ('religion,' 'science') in a distorting fun-house mirror." "Magic" is "other," thus what I do is religion, what you do is magic. Smith sees "little merit in continuing the use of the substantive term, 'magic' in second-order, theoretical, academic discourse." Better terms exist, with no cognitive loss. Smith then takes up th Preisendanz corpus of Graeco-Egyptian texts and offers "reflections by a generalist for whom the label 'Greek magical papyri' constitutes something of a distraction: "one of the largest collections of functioning ritual texts…from Late Antiquity." "My interest in Late Antique 'magical' texts has stemmed primarily from my long-standing preoccupation with themes related to place, especially the shifting the locus of religious experience and expression from a permanent sacred center, the archaic temple, to a place of temporary sacrality sanctified by a mobile religious specialist (in this case the so-called 'magician')."

     11. DIFFERENTIAL EQUATIONS. ON CONSTRUCTING THE OTHER: "Three basic models of the 'other' have been employed. [1] The 'other' represented metonymically in terms of the presence of absence of one or more cultural traits. [2] The 'other' represented topographically in terms of center and periphery. [3] The 'other' represented linguistically and/or intellectually in terms of intelligibility." The metonymical model most frequently occurs in connection with naming. One group distinguishes itself from another by lifting up some cultural feature, expressed as

the lack of some familiar cultural trait." "Today…the story of religious conflicts and of strong language of alienation is largely intraspecific," focused on the near at hand. "A distance, initially formulated, is relativized…or a proximity initially perceived as too close is distanced." "It is thought about translation across languages, places, and times, between text and reader, speaker and hearer, that energizes the human sciences as disciplines and suggests the intellectual contributions they make."

12. WHAT A DIFFERENCE A DIFFERENCE MAKES: "Otherness is a matter of relative rather than absolute difference. Difference is not a matter of comparison between entities judged to be equivalent, rather difference most frequently entails a hierarchy of prestige and ranking. Such distinctions are found to be drawn most sharply between 'near neighbors,' with respect to what has been termed the 'proximate other.' This is the case because 'otherness' is a relativistic category inasmuch as it is…a term of interaction. A theory of otherness is…essentially political and economic…centers on a relational theory of reciprocity…." "In thinking about the 'other' real progress has been made only when the 'other' ceases to be an ontological category…'otherness' is not some absolute state of being. Something is 'other' only with respect to something 'else.'" So otherness is "a situational category…a transactional matter, an affair of the 'in between.'" "'A theory of the other' requires those complex political and linguistic projects necessary to enable us to think, to situate, and to speak of 'others' in relation to the way in which we think, situate, and speak about ourselves."

13. CLOSE ENCOUNTERS OF DIVERSE KINDS: What the aliens from outer space appear to most want to understand in Abduction Reports is difference. "The fable I want to construct out of the Abduction Reports…is one of singularity and diversity…to lead us to isolate the intellectual moment that made the invention of 'race' necessary — the first, new influential anthropological theory since the classical period, and one that made urgent the emergence of the human sciences." From antiquity to the advent of Columbus, the amalgamation of the Greco-Roman ethnographic tradition and the biblical prevailed. "Differences remained in the realm of accident; similarities in that of essence, I know of no serious challenge to this interpretative system until the post-Colombian debates over the nature of the Americas…a strong language of alterity emerges…the elasticity of the old system finally proved insufficiently flexible." Greco-Roman ethnography produced the solution. "The biblical narrative and, therefore, western ethnologic theory was, up to this point, relentlessly monogenetic…a single focus from which all the intrafamilial diversities of humankind ultimately diffused…such an account could not be sustained if…difference was an affair of essence rather than of accident. Deep within the Greco-Roman theories of migration and diffusion, mixture and borrowing, climate and ecology, as the explanations for cultural similarities and differences, a second, oppositional structure coexisted that emphasized immobility and originality: that of autochthony…a theory of polygenesis." This yielded such concepts as aborigine, indigenous, native: people created in the place they inhabit:

inhabitants found in a place "when we first 'discovered' it." "Monogenesis celebrated similarity; polygenesis, diversity...with the correlation of] biological and cultural characteristics...From the point of view of difference...the intellectual choice wa whether to understand the human 'races' as 'varieties (i.e., accidents) or 'species' (i.e. , essences)."

14. HERE, THERE, AND ANYWHERE: To understand the phenomena of the persistence of antique religions is "to think through the dynamic of religious persistence, reinterpretation, and change; to think through the ways in which a given group at a given time chose this or that mode of interpreting their traditions as they related themselves to their historical past and to their social and political present....To generalize, recognizing that generalization falls between particularity and universality...and is always both partial and corrigible." Smith's exercise takes the form of a topography...in terms of three spatial categories: [1] the here of domestic religion, located primarily in the home and in burial sites; [2] the there of public civic and state religions, largely based in temple constructions; and [3] the anywhere of a rich diversity of religious formations that occupy an interstitial space between these other two loci....While modes of access to and means of protection from imaginations of divine power differ in all three of these loci, I would locate one significant difference between the ancient/classical and Late Antique forms of the Mediterranean religions under review as being the expansion and relative prominent of the third locus in Late antiquity (the religions of anywhere), over against and sometimes at the expense of the persistence and transformations of the first two loci (the religions of here and there)." The central ritual of religions of "here" is commensality among an extended family with ordinary foodstuff. "the central ritual of the religion of 'there' is the sacrifice, a meal among unequals, often coded in complex hierarchies." The third pattern of religion "takes many forms but...is tied to no particular place...religious club, entrepreneurial religious figures, religious practitioners not official recognized by centers of power." In late antiquity these religions of "anywhere" "rise to relative prominence, although the religions of 'here' and 'there' continue, often in revised forms." To account for this change, Smith identifies three elements: a new geography, new cosmography, and new polity. "We may distinguish between religions of 'sanctification,' which elaborate the present, ordered world, having as their goal its maintenance and repair, and religions of 'salvation,' which seek to escape the structures ad strictures of this world through activities having as their goal a constant working toward transcendence."

15. RE: CORINTHIANS: Smith attempts "a redescription of the Corinthian situation in relationship to a set of data from Papua New Guinea" with special reference to the cargo cults and the new religious patterns, spirit healing, and the like. The purpose is defined in this language: "Redescriptions, at the level of data, are in the service of...redescribing the categories employed in the study of religion...the social situation...various mythic formations." The comparable circumstances of Corinth are addressed: "...in a locale such as Corinth, the clear

presence of face-to-face communication networks, and the relative prominent of 'households' suggest the existence of analogous communities within the larger urban landscape that served as the primary sites of earliest Christian experimentations. This suggests the possibility of thinking of Paul...as intrusive on the native religious formations of the Corinthians addressed in 1 Corinthians, analogous...to intrusions on the Atbalmin" of Papua New Guinea. The upshot is this: "This experiment in redescription suggests that a Christ myth, as represented by Paul in the course of his intrusion on the Corinthians, would have been uninteresting to some Corinthians; that a spirit myth... might have been interesting to some Corinthians in that was 'good to think.' The Corinthian situation may well be defined as the efforts at translations between these understandings and misunderstandings." This is the only essay in the present collection that does not fully realize its program; gaps between the two bodies of data, the anthropological out of Papua New Guinea and the literary out of the letter of Paul to the Corinthians, are not successfully bridged; the variables are many.

16. A TWICE-TOLD TALE: THE HISTORY OF THE HISTORY OF RELIGIONS' HISTORY: The history of the history of religions is "not best conceived as a liberation from the hegemony of theology...this way of retelling the tale occludes a more fundamental issue that yet divides us....the debate between an understanding of religion based on *presence* and one based on *representation*." Two major opposing stratagems, the exceptionalist and the assimilationist, seek a place for the study of religion on the map of recognized academic disciplines. "The exceptionalist insists on the distinctive nature of the subject matter of the study of religion; the assimilationist argues for the equivalence of the methods of the study of religion with those of the other human sciences. In either case the mode of representation is genealogical, a narrative of founders and schools that often takes the form of an inverted tree diagram." "Languages and religions became the privileged cultural formations in which controversies of unity and difference were framed" by reason of specific, European, historical causes: "[1] The movement north and west of Greek and Hebrew manuscripts following the capture of Constantinople...A past that was only now accessible through acts of imagination; [2] the European colonial and mission adventures in the Americas as well as in Africa and Asia...shattered the classical biblical and Greco-Roman imagination of the inhabited geosphere as a tripartite world-island, thus giving rise to the first new intellectual confrontation with the problem of human and biological difference as possibly signaling otherness...[3] the schismatic impulses of emergent Protestantisms raised a host of questions as to religious credibility and truth." "Awareness of the plural 'religions'...focused interest in the imagination of a single, generic 'religion.'" The Enlightenment focused on language as "a byproduct of its preeminent concern for thought and thoughtfulness...Th counter-Enlightenment takes the issue of thoughtfulness in a new direction...Language...is not a secondary naming or memorializing, it is not a translation of thought, it is not posterior to experience,

rather, it is the very way in which we think and experience." The emphasis on language study takes over the study of religion. "Philology is the vocation; generalization and theory, the avocation." "Texts are pointed to, paraphrased, or summarized as if their citation is, by itself, sufficient to guarantee significance." "The scholarly imagination of 'religion' as an intellectual category establishes a disciplinary horizon that should play the same sort of role as 'language' in linguistics or 'culture' in anthropology...the generic category supplies the field with a theoretical object of study, different from...their particular subject matters." "The cognitive power of translation, model, map, generalization, or redescription — as...in the imagination of 'religion' — is...a result of its difference from the subject matter in question and not its congruence...a theory, model, conceptual category, generalization cannot be simply the data writ large." I judge this essay the most successful of the set.

17. GOD SAVE THIS HONORABLE COURT: RELIGION AND CIVIC DISCOURSE: Church-state relations in respect to public Christmas celebrations form the occasion for "an exercise in Durkheimian translation." This is "to show that the disciplined study of any subject is...an assault on self-evidence, on matters taken for granted...in the study of religion. The future of our increasingly diverse societies will call on all our skills at critical translation; all our abilities to occupy the contested space between the near and the far; all our capacities for the dual project of making familiar what...seems strange and making strange what we have come to think of as all-too-familiar. Each of these endeavors needs to be practiced and refined in the service of an urgent civic and academic agendum: that difference be negotiated but never overcome."

This precis of the seventeen essays yields a single conclusion, in several parts. This collection, first, marks Smith as the premier theorist of religion of the generation that has now completed its work. He has been, and remains now, the generalist and the essayist best able to explain the entire academic enterprise of studying not only culture and society, history and politics and anthropology but religion. He has, second, shown what is required so as to generalize and so speaks of not only religions but religion. He alone, third, has had the power to validate the academic study of religion in the multiple contexts, e.g., anthropology and philosophy and the history of the West and the world, with which it intersects. An entire field of learning, with its roots deep in Western civilization, yet fresh and new to the secular academy, finds its voice in these remarkable exercises.

23

Amram Tropper, *Wisdom, Politics, and Historiography. Tractate Avot in the Context of the Graeco-Roman Near East*

Amram Tropper, *Wisdom, Politics, and Historiography. Tractate Avot in the Context of the Graeco-Roman Near East* (Oxford and New York, 2004: Oxford University Press).

This Oxford University dissertation by a Jerusalem product covers these topics: "the structure of Avot, Avot, Wisdom, and Artistic prose, the date and the editor of Avot, the cultural horizons of the patriarchate in the early third century, Avot and the Second sophistic, the Graeco-Roman literary context for Avot, Avot in the light of classical Roman jurisprudence, Avot's chain of transmission and early Christian parallels."

Iqqar haser min hassefer! What is omitted is an account of the statement that tractate Abot makes viewed whole, its theological structure and system as a religious writing. Tropper should have set forth at the outset what he conceived the message of the document to be, but after protracted and tedious discussions of tractate Abot in the context of Greek literature and philosophy, he has managed to lose sight of the problem of documentary description, analysis, and interpretation. That is so even though he claims otherwise: "Avot is not the result of a random and haphazard cumulative process but the product of a skilled craftsman." But Tropper does not tell us what that skilled craftsman has to say. So he has compared Avot with Graeco-Roman philosophy and jurisprudence, ancient Near Eastern wisdom writings, Christian succession lists, and on and on, but not defined that which is subject to comparison. If it is like one thing, it cannot be like all the others.

The stated intent of the work, "to interpret Avot as a literary work that was created within a specific historical setting," promises an exercise in the documentary reading of Rabbinic texts, viewing them as distinct pieces of writing. But the document does not emerge as a coherent statement, with a purpose and a program. Nor does his prodigious research help situate the document in a larger cultural context: too many add up to nothing. I state flatly that Tropper does not grasp the documentary approach to the Rabbinic canon and its discipline.

Tropper argues (chapter one) that tractate Abot manifests the work of an editor, not just a compiler. The literary analysis covers much familiar ground and does not materially alter the established account of the document. Tropper finds mnemonic and other obvious patterning in the language. His discussion of literary techniques goes over familiar ground and yields no important and original propositions. I cannot point to a single saying in tractate Abot that has to be understood in a new way because of his literary analysis.

Even though Avot is unique in the Rabbinic canon, Tropper tries in chapter two to set it into its context. He first treats the tractate in the setting of the Israelite and ancient Near Eastern wisdom tradition. A potted survey of that tradition follows, yielding "general thematic continuities with the wisdom tradition," augmented here and there with episodic aperçus and a disjoined discussion of the artistic prose of Abot.

For "the date and the editor of Avot," chapter three, Tropper admits there is no explicit statement on the matter. Nonetheless, he assembles both external and internal evidence, collecting opinions and engaging with them. He holds it was edited in the early decades of the third century, in the time of Judah the Patriarch, "edited in tandem with the Mishnah...to ground and support the Mishnah." This depends on taking at face value the attributions of sayings to named sages, without a word as to why he finds the attributions compelling.

"The cultural horizons of the patriarchate in the early third century" (chapter four), concerns itself with Galilee. Here the evidence once again consists of sayings attributed to third century Galilean rabbis and stories told about them. The footnotes consist of references to unanalyzed texts, e.g., "BT Ketubbot 103b" suffices to provide that when Judah the patriarch died, his body was returned to his home town for burial. "His trip to Syria was made in order to request authority..." bears the embarrassing footnote "Mishnah Eduyyot 7:7"! And this in the twenty-first century!

The retrograde and uncritical utilization of the Rabbinic writings as testimonies to things really said and done when and as and by whom they are alleged to have been said and done makes it unnecessary to dwell on this pathetic chapter. It is completely uncritical, an exercise in total gullibility, and enough said. In his preface Tropper says he represents a new and critical generation of scholarship, operating with a critical program, and that pretense is simply risible in this context.

Avot and the Second Sophistic, chapter five, is the first of the four chapters devoted to the Graeco-Roman context of Avot, the Mishnah, Rabbinic Judaism, you name it. The basic thesis is stated clearly: "In analyzing the broad context for Avot, one discovers that many features of the gentile Near East resemble aspects of the Rabbinic world portrayed in Avot." These are interesting chapters, if not deftly executed, and represent the one genuinely original component of the book. But collecting and arranging "parallels," real or alleged, hardly adds up to astute scholarship. The result is a mass of information not yet mastered and

The account of the philosophical-cultural movement called :the Second Sophistic" is clear and encyclopedic in a good sense, all the facts are lucidly spelled out. Then Tropper compares and contrasts Avot and Philostratus' *Lives of the Sophists.* The parallels are generic and generally formal, e.g., "each author used teacher-pupil transmission to create links between generations...the years of the Second Sophistic roughly coincide with the Tannaite period outlined in Avot:"

> Avot portrays Rabban Johanan ben Zakkai as the bridge between the Pairs of Second Temple times and the Tannaim. Similarly Philostratus marks the beginning of the Second Sophistic with Nicetes of Smyrna, a sophist who was active, like Rabban Johanan ben Zakkai, in the second half of the first century. Thus, both Avot and lives of the Sophists review the history of a movement in the East that thrived from the mid first century until, at least, the early third century. In addition, although the rabbis studied halakhah and the sophists practiced rhetoric, both movements thrived in a scholastic setting.

With inane comments like these comprising the shank of the chapter, one must conclude that too much is being made of very, very little.

Chapter Six proceeds to "the Graeco-Roman literary context for Avot," pursuing the parallels between the chain of transmission and the collection of wisdom sayings attributed to sages, absent in earlier Jewish writings but well known in "a popular Hellenistic anthology genre." The discussion proceeds to the succession list in the Hellenistic period and Avot as a succession list, concluding, "Avot functioned much as a sayings collection would have functioned in a philosophical academy." The comparison is not very exact, since the work Tropper chooses is "not a multiple author sayings collection."

"Avot in the light of classical Roman jurisprudence," chapter seven, gives Tropper the chance to survey Roman law "as the aspect of the ambient Roman setting that seems to offer the most rewarding comparative material for Avot." Since Avot is not a law code, and since Tropper situates it in the Wisdom tradition, that is no easy task, as he himself admits. Nonetheless Tropper uses the occasion for one of his surveys, now of the history of Roman law. Burt he abandons Avot to write on "classical Roman jurisprudence and the Tannaim." Readers must wonder what has happened to Avot in particular in light of such observations as this one: "Just as the Roman jurists wrote profusely, so the Tannaim produced oral collections of Mishnayot which were eventually edited in Rabbi's Mishnah." So, weaving back and forth from the Tannaim, to the Mishnah, to Avot, Tropper compares this and that to these and those, without much order or system. And he seems to find self-evident the consequence of his comparisons and contrasts.

"Avot's chain of transmission and early Christian parallels," chapter eight, concerns itself with "Christian succession lists and Avot." The succession-lists served in both cultures to refute heresies and bolster institutional authority against schismatics. But Christianity gave greater weight to the matter, "a result of the differing social structures of the two movements." That merely-generic judgment could apply to a variety of Rabbinic texts compared with Christian counterparts (if they were counterparts).

The conclusion presents a reprise of the individual chapters: "Whereas the Mishnah is primarily a compilation of Rabbinic law, Avot comes across as a rhetorical treatise especially designed to endorse the knowledge and the representatives of the Rabbinic order.". Then there is a tacked-on discussion, the legitimation of institutions, in dialogue with Berger and Luckmann, *Reality: Treatise on the sociology of Knowledge (1966).*

This summary conveys little of the disorder and tedium of this collection of what this one has said and what that one has said and what the "I" of the dissertation concludes. But if I had to summarize the flaws in the dissertation, I would limit the list to three.

First, Tropper is wrong about the character of tractate Abot, which he does not grasp, the content of which he cannot even summarize accurately. That is because he has not got a conception of Abot as a religious document bearing a theological message. That message may be summarized succinctly. Tractate Abot forms a melancholy meditation on the human condition of the individual Israelite. The problem facing the framer of the document is succinctly stated: "We do not have in hand an explanation either for the prosperity of the wicked or for the suffering of the righteous" (4:15). The resolution of the paradox of palpable injustice — the prosperity of the wicked more than the suffering of the righteous — is in the doctrine of life beyond the grave. Individual existence does not end in death. There is a world to come, which affords eternal life to the righteous but which excludes those who are wicked in this world. In tractate Abot that life is afforded in a juridical procedure, a trial, to individuals in response to their conduct in this life. "This world is like an antechamber before the world to come. Get ready in the antechamber, so you can go into the great hall." How to prepare? "Better is a single moment spent in penitence and good deeds in this world than the whole of the world to come. And better is a single moment of inner peace in the world to come than the whole of a lifetime spent in this world" (4:16-17). The world to come then forms the reward for those that live humbly and righteously. That solution to the problem of evil encompasses three aspects: the fate of the individual in this life and after death, the study of the Torah in response to the human condition, and the nurture of virtue consequent upon Torah-study. Study of the Torah leads to virtue, which defines the righteous life worthy of eternity. The destiny of individuals is to die, with judgment and advent to the age to come for those that merit it. Study of the Torah invokes the presence of God. From Torah study the Israelite learns the lessons of virtue that secures the world to come. Accordingly, a coherent, compelling picture of the human situation emerges. To theology Tropper is oblivious.

Second, as is conventional in Israeli scholarship, Tropper cites whom he will cite, and ignores whom he will ignore, and that leads to huge blunders. I state very flatly that he does not know most of the scholarly literature that pertains to topic after topic, and that his research is superficial. Take the matter of philosophy, for example. He correctly wants to situate tractate Abot in a philosophical framework. But he does not know that that work has been done, for the Mishnah as a whole, in the setting of Aristotle's natural history. So his account of the Second Sophistic provides only a partial answer to the question he raises and seriously misleads. His discussion is all form and no substance.

Third, the book lacks a thesis and a purpose. It treats a subject every which way, but presents no proposition that holds the whole together. This he himself admits: "Each chapter of this study has explored a single, specific dimension of Avot, and accordingly the claims set forth in individual chapters are for the most part independent of one another." Indeed, as we have already noted, if he is right about the context of Abot in one chapter, he has to be wrong about a contrary context in two or three other chapters. He claims, "As a composite whole, the eight chapters have offered a unified portrait of a treatise and its relationship to the literary and historical setting of the ancient Near East and to the local Jewish context." That is just not so, there is nothing unified or coherent in the monograph, which is a typical Jerusalem scholarship, here practiced in Oxford: all footnotes and no text, lots and lots of opinions about this, that, and the other thing — and academic politics everywhere. This is not to suggest that Tropper has written a stupid, moronic book. But it is to say that his erudition outruns his insight; the absence of purpose and proposition exacts a heavy price. He has read what he has read and then produced a research report, not an important book. The essay presented above on Abot sets forth what I conceive a coherent account of the document to comprise.

24

Karin Hedner Zetterholm. *Portrait of a Villain. Laban the Aramean in Rabbinic Literature*

Karin Hedner Zetterholm. *Portrait of a Villain. Laban the Aramean in Rabbinic Literature.* INTERDISCIPLINARY STUDIES IN ANCIENT CULTURE AND RELIGION No. 2. Leuven and Dudley, 2002: Peeters. Pp x+214.

Collecting and arranging references to Laban in the Rabbinic canon, inclusive of Targumim, Karin Hedner Zetterholm, Lund University in Sweden, justifies her work in this language: "As a designation for the authors of the midrashim and Targumim I have generally used the term 'rabbis.' While this may at first seem like an all too harmonizing way of referring to a group of people whose interpretive activity stretches over a time period of roughly a thousand years, I believe that it can be justified on the basis of the common set of assumptions concerning the biblical text that seems to underlie their interpretations, despite the differences of opinion, style, and modes of interpretation which they express" (p. vii). In an elaborate introduction, further, she argues — against the position I have proposed and in favor of that of James Kugel and his school — that traits of the text of Scripture provoke the exegetical work that yields the Rabbinic exegesis, which is Kugel's view, not the particular interests of the documents that present that exegesis, which is my view. As a result, her survey is organized by themes: Laban in the Bible and pre-Rabbinic literature; Laban and Deuteronomy 26:5: A case of intertextuality; Midrashic exegesis of the Jacob-Laban story in Genesis; a narrative analysis of the Jacob-Laban story in Targum Pseudo-Jonathan. These four topics are concluded with a summary.

Readers will immediately observe that while Zetterholm rejects the documentary reading of the Rabbinic compilations, which asks questions of history and theology — context and program — in interpreting Rabbinic writing, she has adopted that documentary approach, without taking advantage of it in interpreting her data. That documentary reading is self-evident in her third and fourth units, exegesis of the story in Genesis focusing on Genesis Rabbah, narrative analysis of the story in Targum Pseudo-Jonathan, respectively. What she rejects at the outset, therefore, she introduces when the work requires it.

But when it comes to what she calls "pre-Rabbinic literature," with special reference to Philo, Josephus, and Jubilees, she surveys bits and pieces of these quite coherent documents without appeal to said documents in explaining the random data. The result is indeterminate and vacuous. Take Jubilees for example:

> According to Jubilees…Laban explains his replacement of Rachel for Leah by referring to 'heavenly tablets' where it is written that one should not give away the younger daughter before the elder and the one who does so will not be righteous 'because this action is evil in the Lord's presence.'…The fact that Laban refers to Jacob's God and continues to lecture Jacob and tell him to order the Israelites not to give the younger before the elder in marriage (28:7) seems to imply that the author of Jubilees wanted to convey this message to his readers and did so by putting it into Laban's mouth. Even though the question remains as to why Laban did not inform Jacob of this state of affairs immediately, this episode rather seems to portray Laban in a favorable light. There is however one instance in which Jubilees gives a negative evaluation of Laban…After Jacob has become rich and Laban and his sons become jealous of him, Jubilees adds, "Laban took back his sheep from him and kept his eye on him for evil purposes" (p. 39).

What this adds up to, so far as I can see, is absolutely nothing, a paraphrase of what is there. There is no systemic inquiry, e.g., into the value-system of Jubilees to which the detail at hand may prove congruent. The deliberate ignoring of context thus exacts its cost: no important questions can be raised. But what of Kugel's approach? It is neglected. Accordingly, how the state of the biblical text generates this comment is simply forgotten.

A still more striking instance involves the system-builder, Philo, who absorbs Laban into his system, just as he processes all data in a single manner. That yields results that illuminate Philo's system and his capacity to absorb into it pretty much anything he wishes. But that is not Zetterholm's view of matters. Here is her contribution:

> The writings of Philo…are the earliest witnesses of a clearly negative understanding of Laban. Philo sees Laban as a contrast to Jacob, who to him represents everything that is good and noble, a polarity that is possibly dependent on his view of the nature of man's soul…Jacob symbolizes the rational part of the soul, the mind and reason…Laban is contrasted with Jacob's virtue, representing passions and above all the senses and corporeal ideas…(pp. 40, 41)

How Philo produces probative evidence of "a common set of assumptions" not particular to himself, assumptions concerning the biblical text, is not specified, but that is because after articulately rejecting the documentary hypothesis, Zetterholm finds herself trapped in the heart of the documentary organization and interpretation of the data. There is no way to read Philo as part of a homogenous "Rabbinic" tradition, without missing all of the signals that Philo gives of processing biblical-exegetical data in his own philosophy, comprised by a coherent system and structure.

When she comes to Josephus, the result is predictably indeterminate. She follows Louis Feldman in her characterization of Josephus's reading of Scripture, then paraphrases the various references to Laban and Jacob, and concludes with the following empty proposition:

> Given Josephus' favorable treatment of Esau...one suspects that perhaps Josephus, like Philo, regarded Laban as a negative contrast to Jacob but felt a need to present him in a more favorable light when writing for a Roman audience... (p. 45)

Once more we find ourselves far from that insistence that justifies her enterprise: a coherent tradition built upon a common approach to the noteworthy traits of the scriptural text itself.

The treatment of Deuteronomy 26:5, "An Aramean destroyed my father" in the language of the Passover Haggadah, occasions a far more systematic, analytical inquiry, with attention to problems of grammar and philology. Now the work is not merely reportorial but informed and critical. Studies of the words and phrases as these occur in various particular venues — Septuagint, Targumim and Midrashim — provide a definitive account of what has been said on the passage. With a measure of economy and wit, Zetterholm might have written an illuminating chapter. But the virtues of economy and wit lack. Rather, to fill up space, Zetterholm accords a hearing to everything and its opposite, collecting and citing opinions that have long since ceased to meet critical standards of contemporary learning. Thus she presents with a perfectly straight face the most outlandish approaches, e.g., Louis Finkelstein's debate with Solomon Zeitlin and S. Stein over a mess of unsubstantiated — and unsubstantiable — *hiddushim,* namely, dating Rabbinic sayings by appeal to their content in a fabricated historical context:

> On the basis of style, content, and above all on his assumption that [the Hebrew phrase] was reinterpreted to mean 'an Aramean destroyed my father' when Palestine was under Egyptian sovereignty, L. Finkelstein dates the midrash to the last half of the third century B.C.E. In his opinion [the Hebrew phrase] can only mean, 'my father was a lost Aramean,' but was distorted into 'the Aramean destroyed my father' in order to placate the Egyptian government by denouncing its rival, Syria. It was particularly im0ortant to do this before telling the story of the exodus, which made reference to unpleasant relations between Israel and Egypt. The fact that LXX which in his opinion was written by Jews under Egyptian rule likewise distorts the meaning of [the Hebrew phrase[is taken by Finkelstein as further evidence of his theory...in Finkelstein's view...the two works were composed under similar circumstances, namely in the third century B.CV.E. under Egyptian control. He also mentions a possibility which he considers less likely, namely that the reinterpretation of [the Hebrew phrase] may have been an expression of Maccabean hostility toward Syria which was identified with Aram. In that case the midrash would date from about 150 B.C.E., but

Finkelstein prefers the first explanation... S. Zeitlin rejected Finkelstein's suggestion on the grounds that he ignored the fact that the Ptolemies, the ruling power in Egypt, were Greek and never considered themselves Egyptians. The Egyptians were a conquered people with no influence...In Zeitlin's view the Haggadah in its present form is from the period after the destruction of the Temple but he believes the basic text to be from the Second Temple period. S. Stein considers the earliest possible date for the midrash to be the middle of the second century C.E., based on the argument that had it existed earlier it would have been mentioned by the Hellenistic Jewish writers (p. 60-1)

Much of Zetterholm's account consists of reports of this kind of unfounded guess-work, a survey of the ruins of scholarship in the aftermath of the advent of critical learning.

The chapter on the exegesis of the Jacob-Laban story in Genesis follows the model of the documentary hypothesis without grasping its purpose of contextualization: "The midrashic collections appear in rough chronological order, and the titles of each subsection refer to a characteristic of Laban specific to that midrashic collection, or to one of his most prominent traits in that collection" (P. 89). She works her way through late antique, medieval, and early modern compilations, at no point proposing to link contents to context, exegesis to hermeneutics. Thus, correctly arranging her data, Zetterholm does not then draw conclusions that her collection yields, at no point proposing to link the details of a document's reading of Laban to its larger polemic. This represents a massive failure to do the most basic analytical work, beginning with the characterization of context.

It makes me wonder whether she has ever analyzed any of the documents that she treats, whether she or her Doctor-Vater has studied them for their indicative traits start to finish. Denying that documentary traits govern, Zetterholm both follows the form of the documentary procedure and pretends there are no consequences. Announcing an explanation for her data, the traits of the biblical text, she ignores through most, though not all, of her exposition. What works works, what doesn't work she covers over in a mountain of pointless information.

The upshot of much industry and erudition then is a mere mass of uninterpreted data, a collection of scholarly opinions registered but not sorted out (Finkelstein/Zeitlin/Stein represent many more). *Portrait of a Villain* yields just one more empty exercise in collecting and arranging information that produces indeterminate results: X says this and Y says that. This kind of aimless, tedious, mind-emptying doctoral dissertation, produced in Jerusalem under Swedish auspices, points to an intellectual crisis in the study of Judaism in the Jerusalem school and its European satellites. The crisis is signaled by the incapacity to cope with mounting piles of uninterpreted data, paralysis in the face of evidence that contradicts the there-prevailing conventions, procedures, and prejudices.

STUDIES IN JUDAISM
TITLES IN THE SERIES
PUBLISHED BY UNIVERSITY PRESS OF AMERICA

Judith Z. Abrams
The Babylonian Talmud: A Topical Guide, 2002.

Roger David Aus
*Matthew 1-2 and the Virginal Conception: In Light of Palestinian
and Hellenistic Judaic Traditions on the Birth of Israel's First
Redeemer, Moses*, 2004.

*My Name Is "Legion": Palestinian Judaic Traditions in Mark 5:1-
20 and Other Gospel Texts*, 2003.

Alan L. Berger, Harry James Cargas, and Susan E. Nowak
*The Continuing Agony: From the Carmelite Convent to the
Crosses at Auschwitz*, 2004.

S. Daniel Breslauer
*Creating a Judaism without Religion: A Postmodern Jewish
Possibility*, 2001.

Bruce Chilton
*Targumic Approaches to the Gospels: Essays in the Mutual
Definition of Judaism and Christianity*, 1986.

David Ellenson
*Tradition in Transition: Orthodoxy, Halakhah, and the Boundaries
of Modern Jewish Identity*, 1989.

Paul V. M. Flesher
*New Perspectives on Ancient Judaism, Volume 5: Society and
Literature in Analysis*, 1990.

Marvin Fox
*Collected Essays on Philosophy and on Judaism, Volume One:
Greek Philosophy, Maimonides*, 2003.

Collected Essays on Philosophy and on Judaism, Volume Two: Some Philosophers, 2003.

Collected Essays on Philosophy and on Judaism, Volume Three: Ethics, Reflections, 2003.

Zev Garber
Methodology in the Academic Teaching of Judaism, 1986.

Zev Garber, Alan L. Berger, and Richard Libowitz
Methodology in the Academic Teaching of the Holocaust, 1988.

Abraham Gross
Spirituality and Law: Courting Martyrdom in Christianity and Judaism, 2005.

Harold S. Himmelfarb and Sergio DellaPergola
Jewish Education Worldwide: Cross-Cultural Perspectives, 1989.

William Kluback
The Idea of Humanity: Hermann Cohen's Legacy to Philosophy and Theology, 1987.

Samuel Morell
Studies in the Judicial Methodology of Rabbi David ibn Abi Zimra, 2004.

Jacob Neusner
Ancient Israel, Judaism, and Christianity in Contemporary Perspective, 2006.

The Aggadic Role in Halakhic Discourses: Volume I, 2001.

The Aggadic Role in Halakhic Discourses: Volume II, 2001.

The Aggadic Role in Halakhic Discourses: Volume III, 2001.

Analysis and Argumentation in Rabbinic Judaism, 2003.

Analytical Templates of the Bavli, 2006.

*Ancient Judaism and Modern Category-Formation: "Judaism,"
"Midrash," "Messianism," and Canon in the Past Quarter
Century*, 1986.

Canon and Connection: Intertextuality in Judaism, 1987.

Chapters in the Formative History of Judaism. 2006

Dual Discourse, Single Judaism, 2001.

*The Emergence of Judaism: Jewish Religion in Response to the
Critical Issues of the First Six Centuries*, 2000.

*First Principles of Systemic Analysis: The Case of Judaism within
the History of Religion*, 1988.

The Halakhah and the Aggadah, 2001.

Halakhic Hermeneutics, 2003.

Halakhic Theology: A Sourcebook, 2006.

The Hermeneutics of Rabbinic Category Formations, 2001.

*How Important Was the Destruction of the Second Temple in the
Formation of Rabbinic Judaism?* 2006.

*How Not to Study Judaism, Examples and Counter-Examples,
Volume One: Parables, Rabbinic Narratives, Rabbis'
Biographies, Rabbis' Disputes*, 2004.

*How Not to Study Judaism, Examples and Counter-Examples,
Volume Two: Ethnicity and Identity versus Culture and
Religion, How Not to Write a Book on Judaism, Point and
Counterpoint*, 2004.

How the Halakhah Unfolds: Moed Qatan in the Mishnah, ToseftaYerushalmi and Bavli, 2006.

The Implicit Norms of Rabbinic Judaism. 2006.

Intellectual Templates of the Law of Judaism, 2006.

Is Scripture the Origin of the Halakhah? 2005.

Israel and Iran in Talmudic Times: A Political History, 1986.

Israel's Politics in Sasanian Iran: Self-Government in Talmudic Times, 1986.

Judaism in Monologue and Dialogue, 2005.

Major Trends in Formative Judaism, Fourth Series, 2002.

Major Trends in Formative Judaism, Fifth Series, 2002.

Messiah in Context: Israel's History and Destiny in Formative Judaism, 1988.

The Native Category - Formations of the Aggadah: The Later Midrash-Compilations - Volume I, 2000.

The Native Category - Formations of the Aggadah: The Earlier Midrash-Compilations - Volume II, 2000.

Paradigms in Passage: Patterns of Change in the Contemporary Study of Judaism, 1988.

Parsing the Torah, 2005.

Praxis and Parable: The Divergent Discourses of Rabbinic Judaism, 2006.

The Religious Study of Judaism: Description, Analysis and Interpretation, Volume 1, 1986.

The Religious Study of Judaism: Description, Analysis, Interpretation, Volume 2, 1986.

The Religious Study of Judaism: Context, Text, Circumstance, Volume 3, 1987.

The Religious Study of Judaism: Description, Analysis, Interpretation, Volume 4: Ideas of History, Ethics, Ontology, and Religion in Formative Judaism, 1988.

Struggle for the Jewish Mind: Debates and Disputes on Judaism Then and Now, 1988.

The Talmud Law, Theology, Narrative: A Sourcebook, 2005.

Talmud Torah: Ways to God's Presence through Learning: An Exercise in Practical Theology, 2002.

Texts Without Boundaries: Protocols of Non-Documentary Writing in the Rabbinic Canon: Volume I: The Mishnah, Tractate Abot, and the Tosefta, 2002.

Texts Without Boundaries: Protocols of Non-Documentary Writing in the Rabbinic Canon: Volume II: Sifra and Sifré to Numbers, 2002.

Texts Without Boundaries: Protocols of Non-Documentary Writing in the Rabbinic Canon: Volume III: Sifré to Deuteronomy and Mekhilta Attributed to Rabbi Ishmael, 2002.

Texts Without Boundaries: Protocols of Non-Documentary Writing in the Rabbinic Canon: Volume IV: Leviticus Rabbah, 2002.

A Theological Commentary to the Midrash - Volume I: Pesiqta deRab Kahana, 2001.

A Theological Commentary to the Midrash - Volume II: Genesis Raba, 2001.

A Theological Commentary to the Midrash - Volume III: Song of Songs Rabbah, 2001.

A Theological Commentary to the Midrash - Volume IV: Leviticus Rabbah, 2001.

A Theological Commentary to the Midrash - Volume V: Lamentations Rabbati, 2001.

A Theological Commentary to the Midrash - Volume VI: Ruth Rabbah and Esther Rabbah, 2001.

A Theological Commentary to the Midrash - Volume VII: Sifra, 2001.

A Theological Commentary to the Midrash - Volume VIII: Sifré to Numbers and Sifré to Deuteronomy, 2001.

A Theological Commentary to the Midrash - Volume IX: Mekhilta Attributed to Rabbi Ishmael, 2001.

Theological Dictionary of Rabbinic Judaism: Part One: Principal Theological Categories, 2005.

Theological Dictionary of Rabbinic Judaism: Part Two: Making Connections and Building Constructions, 2005.

Theological Dictionary of Rabbinic Judaism: Part Three: Models of Analysis, Explanation, and Anticipation, 2005.

Theology of Normative Judaism: A Source Book, 2005.

The Torah and the Halakhah: The Four Relationships, 2003.

The Unity of Rabbinic Discourse: Volume I: Aggadah in the Halakhah, 2001.

The Unity of Rabbinic Discourse: Volume II: Halakhah in the Aggadah, 2001.

The Unity of Rabbinic Discourse: Volume III: Halakhah and Aggadah in Concert, 2001.

The Vitality of Rabbinic Imagination: The Mishnah Against the Bible and Qumran,2005.

Who, Where and What is "Israel?": Zionist Perspectives on Israeli and American Judaism, 1989.
The Wonder-Working Lawyers of Talmudic Babylonia: The Theory and Practice of Judaism in its Formative Age, 1987.

Jacob Neusner and Ernest S. Frerichs
New Perspectives on Ancient Judaism, Volume 2: Judaic and Christian Interpretation of Texts: Contents and Contexts, 1987.

New Perspectives on Ancient Judaism, Volume 3: Judaic and Christian Interpretation of Texts: Contents and Contexts, 1987.

Jacob Neusner and James F. Strange
Religious Texts and Material Contexts, 2001.

David Novak and Norbert M. Samuelson
Creation and the End of Days: Judaism and Scientific Cosmology, 1986.

Proceedings of the Academy for Jewish Philosophy, 1990.

Aaron D. Panken
The Rhetoric of Innovation: Self-Conscious Legal Change in Rabbinic Literature, 2005.

Norbert M. Samuelson
Studies in Jewish Philosophy: Collected Essays of the Academy for Jewish Philosophy, 1980-1985, 1987.

Benjamin Edidin Scolnic
Alcimus, Enemy of the Maccabees, 2004.

If the Egyptians Drowned in the Red Sea Where are Pharaoh's Chariots?: Exploring the Historical Dimension of the Bible, 2005.

Rivka Ulmer
Pesiqta Rabbati: A Synoptic Edition of Pesiqta Rabbati Based upon all Extant Manuscripts and the Editio Princeps, Volume III, 2002.

Manfred H. Vogel
A Quest for a Theology of Judaism: The Divine, the Human and the Ethical Dimensions in the Structure-of-Faith of Judaism Essays in Constructive, 1987.

Anita Weiner
Renewal: Reconnecting Soviet Jewry to the Soviet People: A Decade of American Jewish Joint Distribution Committee (AJJDC) Activities in the Former Soviet Union 1988-1998, 2003.

Eugene Weiner and Anita Weiner
Israel-A Precarious Sanctuary: War, Death and the Jewish People, 1989.

The Martyr's Conviction: A Sociological Analysis, 2002.

Leslie S. Wilson
The Serpent Symbol in the Ancient Near East: Nahash and Asherah: Death, Life, and Healing, 2001.